Early Christian Greek and Latin Literature

A LITERARY HISTORY

Early Christian Greek and Latin Literature

A LITERARY HISTORY

VOLUME ONE

From Paul to the Age of Constantine

Claudio Moreschini AND Enrico Norelli

TRANSLATED BY Matthew J. O'Connell

Translation © 2005 by Hendrickson Publishers, Inc.
P. O. Box 3473
Peabody, Massachusetts 01961-3473

ISBN 1-56563-606-6

From Paul to the Age of Constantine, volume I in *Early Christian Greek and Latin Literature: A Literary History,* by Claudio Moreschini and Enrico Norelli, is a translation of *Da Paolo all'età constantiniana,* volume I in *Storia della letteratura cristiana antica greca e latina;* Brescia: published in Italian by Morcelliana Editrice of Brescia, 1995.

Printed in the United States of America

First Printing — September 2005

Library of Congress Cataloging-in-Publication Data

Moreschini, Claudio.
 [Storia della letteratura cristiana antica greca e latina. English]
 Early Christian Greek and Latin literature : a literary history / Claudio Moreschini and Enrico Norelli ; translated by Matthew J. O'Connell.
  p. cm.
 Includes bibliographical references and index.
 ISBN 1-56563-606-6 (alk. paper)
 1. Christian literature, Early—Greek authors. 2. Christian literature, Early—Latin authors. 3. Greek literature—History and criticism. 4. Latin literature—History and criticism. I. Norelli, Enrico. II. Title.
 BR67.M73 2005
 270.1—dc22

                                        2005019779

TABLE OF CONTENTS

INTRODUCTION

At the present time there is a great enthusiasm for the study of early Christianity, a study that has also profited from the attention being given in recent years to the contemporary pagan culture of late antiquity. What has been lacking, however, is a synthetic presentation devoted to the whole range of Christian literary forms. For the past twenty-five years the work of Manlio Simonetti, *La letteratura cristiana antica greca e latina* (Florence/Milan: Accademia, 1969), has undoubtedly rendered valuable service to nonspecialists desirous of gaining a familiarity with this Christian literature. But, as Quintilian said in justifying his own work, there is no area of research in which others may not hope to take a step forward. So true is this that in his preface to Simonetti's work Lazzati could say in so many words: "Let no one look here [evidently in early Christian Greek and Latin literature] for what is today more commonly understood by 'literature'" (p. 7). (Simonetti cannot, of course, be held responsible for what Lazzati said.) We, too, therefore (*postremissimi omnium*, as Tertullian says), have been bold enough to write a "history of Christian literature."

With the intention of justifying to the reader our approach in this work, let us say immediately that ours is not a history of Christian theology or of the Church or of religion. Our aim has been to write an exclusively *literary* history (although this does not entirely take away our fear of having omitted something that ought to have been said). Now, when dealing with Christianity, a work of this kind is doubtless marked by ambiguity. For as Salvatore Costanza, a scholar who with his school has succeeded in clearly delineating and constantly maintaining the outlines of the Christian literary phenomenon, has remarked in a short but substantial contribution, when we speak of "Christian literature," we are referring, at least verbally, to something of a different kind than "Greek literature" or "Latin literature." In the latter instances (and the same holds for the modern literatures), the identifying factor is the linguistic element. As a result, the areas of research are alike in their methodology, despite the diversity caused by historical events and the political, cultural, and social circumstances of a people, which are reflected in the literature. The aim is always to study the literary products in a particular language.

But when we speak of "Christian literature," we are referring, not to a language as the characterizing element (since there is no Christian language as distinct from Greek or Latin), but to a content. The language, therefore, is a constantly implied instrument, while "Christian" refers to everything expressed by the language, which in each case is that of the people among whom Christians were living. A Christian literature that claimed not to be concerned about the linguistic aspect (understood as the use of an educated or literary language) would thus be a contradiction. In the past, various histories of "Greek Christian Literature" and "Latin Christian Literature" have tried to do what this work does, but the results have been anything but satisfactory.

It is nevertheless not so simple a matter to define concretely the boundaries of Christian literature. Historical research into Christian origins is making it increasingly clear that, at least for many decades, Christianity was one of the religious subsystems within the Judaism of the Second Temple. More accurately, it was one of the movements of revival or renewal that had for their purpose to retrieve what they regarded as the authentic religious tradition of Israel. Even those who, like Paul of Tarsus, struggled to separate Christian identity from the signs which had for centuries defined the Jewish tradition (circumcision, ritual observances), did not doubt that Jesus and his gospel belonged to the history of Israel. They saw it, indeed, as marking a fundamental change, but the change was for the purpose of connecting with something older and "truer" than the Law, namely, the promise made to Abraham. Above all, however, there was no Christianity separate from Judaism until there was a Judaism separate from Christianity. The definition of a Jewish orthodoxy (partly through rejection of Christianity) by the second-century rabbis, after the destruction of Jerusalem, developed pari passu with the definition of an autonomous Christian identity independent of Judaism.

In short, the first examples of Christian literature belong, in fact, to the literature of Hellenistic Judaism. In other words, like this last they are part of the Greek literature of the Hellenistic age. Consequently, only a starting point that a priori separates the Christian phenomenon from the body of other religious phenomena (in other words, a theological prejudgment) can consider it justifiable to include Philo of Alexandria but not Paul of Tarsus in a history of Greek literature. Gradually, of course, and even with some rapidity, Christianity came to understand itself as opposed to Judaism. Since it already knew itself to be different from the Greek and Roman polytheistic tradition, it was faced with the question of its own specific identity in relation to both. It was in response to this question that ideas of a "third race" or a "new people" developed in works from the *Preaching of Peter* down to Eusebius of Caesarea. Rejected as Christians were, sometimes violently, by imperial society and culture, they adopted a variety of attitudes toward the Greek and Latin tradition: from frontal attack to the appropriation for themselves of valid aspects of that tradition. In order to formulate and spread their own positions they had recourse to Hellenistic literary forms.

On the one hand, then, early Christian Greek and Latin literature is one of the literatures of the imperial age that were written in Greek and in Latin. Fully justified, then, from this point of view, are not only those literary histories that discuss this Christian literature at the end of their treatments of "profane" literature, but also those that incorporate Christian literature into the overall picture, as do, for example, Albrecht Dihle's *Die griechische und lateinische Literatur der Kaiserzeit: Von Augustus bis Justinian* (Munich: Beck, 1989), and the two Italian undertakings, *Lo spazio letterario di Roma antica* and *Lo spazio letterario della Grecia antica* (Rome: Salerno).

On the other hand, there is no doubt that Christian literature brought profound changes in comparison with the previous literary tradition. It had a basic and completely new point of reference: faith in Christ. It had for its purpose to proclaim, defend, and spread this faith. It introduced into Greek and Latin literature a new literary tradition, that of the Bible, whose modes of expression were rooted in a specific and different perception of reality, as Erich Auerbach showed in his still memorable analyses. The language and style of the Bible had a major influence on the language and style of Christian writers. In addition, the practice of the community in the area of the sacraments, for example, influenced Christian Greek and Latin both lexically and semantically.

Literary forms and genres were adapted to the needs of the new faith, for, as is always the case, the form is not merely the external garb of the content but is the way in which the content finds expression. Rhetoric was not an embellishment but the instrument by which ideas were formulated and communicated so that they might act on those for whom the texts were intended. Rhetoric was thus closely connected with the content of communication and with the situations in which it took place. All this means that the birth and development of Christianity gave rise to new forms of literary communication that were adapted to the new institutions in relation to which they were to function. In this sense, it is certainly justifiable to make early Christian literature the object of separate study, as we do in the present work.

We have not emphasized in the present work the distinction between *Urliteratur* (primitive literature) and *Literatur* (literature) that has been debated, primarily in the German world, ever since Franz Overbeck and Martin Dibelius propounded their theses. (The discussion of the problems of a literary history of Christian origins is summarized by G. Strecker in his *Literaturgeschichte des Neuen Testaments* [Göttingen: Vandenhoeck und Ruprecht, 1992], 11–48.) When the two are distinguished, *Urliteratur* describes the phase in which Christians used literary forms which they themselves had developed in order to serve the needs of their own religious community (gospels, acts of the apostles, apostolic letters, and so on). *Literatur,* on the other hand, belonged to the phase in which Christians adopted the literary forms of the Greek and Latin tradition, precisely in order to communicate with representatives of that tradition ("literature," properly speaking, would thus have begin with the apologists and, above all, with Clement of Alexandria).

This approach has been, and is, salutary certainly in the area of literary history because it has broken down the barrier between canonical (the New Testament) and noncanonical literature. But the degree of "specificity" and autonomy of the "protochristian" forms is now the subject of debate (affinity of the gospels with ancient biography; of the Acts of the Apostles with ancient historiography and novels; of Christian letters with epistolography, and so on). On the other hand, the special forms of *Urliteratur* continued to be used extensively beyond the temporal bounds assigned to them (we need only think of the apocryphal gospels and acts of apostles).

It goes almost without saying that we ourselves have completely given up the idea of dealing in separate chapters with the New Testament writings, the "Apostolic Fathers," the apocrypha, heretical literature, and so on. These are *corpora* that were established a posteriori and were dictated by theological and not historical or literary considerations. Literary history focuses on the development of literary forms in relation to the development of institutions and ideas, and this is the norm that has guided us.

The present work is a literary history that is devoted exclusively to Christian authors of writings in Latin and Greek; we have not even attempted a treatment of the "eastern" literatures (in Syriac, Armenian, Coptic, or Ethiopic). *Non omnes possumus omnes.* Scientific specialization, which in practice is constantly on the increase, reduces each scholar's field of study; in our case, to the traditional languages of the West. There exist in Italian good outlines of those other literatures that have been prepared by very competent scholars such as P. Bettiolo, T. Orlandi, and S. J. Voicu; it is advisable that we refer readers to them.

Furthermore, certain disciplines, such as the study of hagiography, have long since proved themselves and can boast of a "history" going back to the Renaissance and the controversies of the Reformation period. They have a scientific substance which we can only touch on in our study, even though they have made a fundamental contribution to the history of Christianity.

Finally, we have divided our work according to our individual competencies. Enrico Norelli has written the first sixteen chapters of vol. I, from the letters of Paul and the Pauline tradition down to the early debates about Origen. Claudio Moreschini has written subsequent chapters, on the first Latin translations of the Bible, the Christian literature of Africa, and the literature of the Constantinian age, except for the section on Eusebius of Caesarea—this is from the pen of Lorenzo Perrone, and we thank him for it.

The division of the material in the second volume, which will be followed by an anthology of texts, will be explained in an introductory note to that volume.

Bibliographical references have deliberately been left scanty; in addition to critical editions and translations of texts, they list only fundamental or recent works that will enable readers to carry their own study further.

Periodization is, of course, a further difficulty. It arises not so much within the work, where we have combined and discussed problems according to norms we ourselves have established in each case, as in the question of where to end the work. As everyone knows, history does not end, and each time one sets a cutoff point in light of certain considerations, one can be criticized in light of other considerations. We recognize, of course, that certain periods of transition between late antiquity and the early Latin and Byzantine Middle Ages are difficult to define, and we frankly admit that we have followed criteria which are essentially external.

Finally, we thank the publisher and, in particular, advisor Stefano Minelli, both of whom have always shown their concern and have encouraged us to bring this history to completion in a time when there is little support for studies not destined to quick and abundant success. In this endeavor we have also been supported by the intelligent collaboration and critical skill of our friends, Ilario Bertoletti and Giovanni Menestrina, whom we name with gratitude.

Claudio Moreschini and *Enrico Norelli*

ABBREVIATIONS

General Abbreviations

A.D.	anno Domini
app.	appendix
B.C.	before Christ
c.	century
ca.	circa
ch(s).	chapter(s)
d.	died
diss.	dissertation
ET	English Translation
f(f).	and the following one(s)
frag(s).	fragment(s)
introd.	introduced
IT	Italian Translation
LXX	Septuagint
n.d.	no date
no(s).	number(s)
n.p.	no publisher / no pages
n.t.	no translator
𝔓	Papyrus, manuscript witness of the first order
P.	Papyrus
p(p).	page(s)
par.	parallels
R.	Rabbi
repr.	reprint
rev.	revised
sec(s).	section(s)
theol.	theological
vol(s).	volume(s)

Ancient Sources

Old Testament

Gen	Genesis
Exod	Exodus
Lev	Leviticus
Num	Numbers
Deut	Deuteronomy
Josh	Joshua
Judg	Judges
1–2 Sam	1–2 Samuel
2 Kgs	2 Kings
Ps	Psalms
Prov	Proverbs
Song	Song of Solomon
Isa	Isaiah
Ezek	Ezekiel
Dan	Daniel
Zech	Zechariah

New Testament

Matt	Matthew
Rom	Romans
1–2 Cor	1–2 Corinthians
Gal	Galatians
Eph	Ephesians
Phil	Philippians
Col	Colossians
1–2 Thess	1–2 Thessalonians
1–2 Tim	1–2 Timothy
Phlm	Philemon
Heb	Hebrews
Jas	James
1–2 Pet	1–2 Peter
Rev	Revelation

Apocrypha and Septuagint

1 Kgdms	1 Kingdoms
4 Macc	4 Maccabees
Sir	Sirach/Ecclesiasticus
Wis	Wisdom of Solomon

Old Testament Pseudepigrapha

1 En.	1 Enoch

Ascen. Isa.	*Maryrdom and Ascension of Isaiah 6–11*
Odes Sol.	*Odes of Solomon*

New Testament Apocrypha and Pseudepigrapha

Acts John	*Acts of John*
Acts Pet.	*Acts of Peter*
Acts Phil.	*Acts of Philip*
Ps.-Clem. Hom.	*Pseudo-Clementines Homilies*
Ps.-Clem. Recogn.	*Pseudo-Clementines Recognitions*

Greek and Latin Works

Athanasius
Decr.	*Defense of the Nicene Definition (De decretis)*

Augustine
C. litt. Petil.	*Answer to Letters of Petilian (Contra litteras Petiliani)*
Haer.	*Heresies (De haeresibus)*
Serm.	*Sermons (Sermones)*
Barn.	*Letter of Barnabas*

Clement of Alexandria
1–2 Clem.	*1–2 Clement*
Adumbr.	*Adumbrations (Adumbrationes in epistulas cannonicas)*
Ecl.	*Extracts from the Prophets (Ecologae propheticae)*
Hyp.	*Hypotyposes (Outlines)*
Paed.	*Christ the Educator (Paedagogus)*
Protr.	*Exhortation to the Greeks (Protrepticus pros Hellenas)*
Strom.	*Miscellanies (Stromata)*

Commodian
Carm. apol.	*[Song of] Apology (Carmen Apologeticum)*

Cyprian
Ep.	*Epistles (Epistulae)*
Did.	*Didache*

Dio Cassius
Hist. Rom.	*History of Rome (Romaika historia)*
Diogn.	*Diognetus*

Epiphanius
Pan.	*Refutation of All Heresies (Panarion or Adversus haereses)*

Eusebius
Ecl. proph.	*Extracts from the Prophets (Eclogae propheticae)*
Dem. ev.	*Demonstration of the Gospel (Demonstratio evangelica)*
Hist. eccl.	*Ecclesiastical History (Historia ecclesiastica)*
Mart. Pal.	*The Martyrs of Palestine (De martyribus Palaestinae)*
Praep. ev.	*Preparation for the Gospel (Praeparatio evangelica)*
Theoph.	*Divine Manifestation (Theophania)*
Vit. Const.	*Life of Constantine (Vita Constantini)*

Gregory the Wonderworker

   Orat. paneg.   *Address of Gratitude to Origen (Oratio panegyrica in Origenem)*

Hippolytus of Rome

   Elench.   *Elenchos (Refutation of All Heresies or Refutatio omnium*
                haeresium)

Ignatius

   Eph.   *To the Ephesians*
   Magn.   *To the Magnesians*
   Phld.   *To the Philadelphians*
   Rom.   *To the Romans*
   Pol.   *To Polycarp*
   Smyrn.   *To the Smyrnaeans*
   Trall.   *To the Trallians*

Irenaeus

   Epid.   *Demonstration of the Apostolic Preaching (Epideixis tou apostolikou*
                kerygmatos)

   Haer.   *Against Heresies (Adversus haereses or Elenchos)*

Jerome

   Comm. Eph.   *Commentary on the Letter to the Ephesians (Commentariorum in*
                Epistulam ad Ephesios libri III)

   Comm. Ezech.   *Commentary on Ezekiel (Commentariorum in Ezechielem libri XVI)*

   Comm. Isa.   *Commentary on Isaiah (Commentariorum in Isaiam libri XVIII)*

   Comm. Matt.   *Commentary on Matthew (Commentariorum in Matthaeum libri*
                IV)

   Comm. Mich.   *Commentary on Micah (Commentariorum in Michaeum libri II)*

   Comm. Tit.   *Commentary on the Epistle to Titus (Commentariorum in Epistulam*
                ad Titum liber)

   Epist.   *Epistles (Epistulae)*

   Jo. Hier.   *Against John of Jerusalem (Adversus Joannem Hierosolymitanum*
                liber)

   Jov.   *Against Jovinian (Adversus Jovinianum libri II)*

   Pelag.   *Dialogues against the Pelagians (Adversus Pelagianos dialogi III)*

   Ruf.   *Against Rufinus (Adversus Rufinum libri III)*

   Vir. ill.   *Famous Men (De viris illustribus)*

Justin Martyr

   1 Apol.   *First Apology (Apologia i)*
   2 Apol.   *Second Apology (Apologia ii)*
   Dial.   *Dialogue with Trypho (Dialogus cum Tryphone)*

Lactantius

   Inst.   *The Divine Institutes (Divinarum institutionem libri VII)*

Macarius of Magnesia

   Apocrit.   *Apocritica*

Methodius of Olympus

   Res.   *Resurrection (De resurrectione)*
   Symp.   *Symposium (Convivium decem virginum)*

Origen

   Cels.   *Against Celsus (Contra Celsum)*

Comm. Jo.	*Commentary on the Gospel of John (Commentarii in evangelium Joannis)*
Comm. Matt.	*Commentary on the Gospel of Matthew (Commentarium in evangelium Matthaei)*
Comm. Rom.	*Commentary on Romans (Commentarii in Romanos)*
Fr. Heb.	*Fragment of a Homily on the Epistle to the Hebrews (Fragmenta ex homiliis in epistulam ad Hebraeos)*
Hom. Gen.	*Homilies on Genesis (Homilae in Genesim)*
Hom. Jer.	*Homilies on Jeremiah (Homiliae in Jeremiam)*
Hom. Job	*Homilies on Job (Homilae in Job)*
Hom. Lev.	*Homilies on Leviticus (Homilae in Leviticum)*
Hom. Luc.	*Homilies on Luke (Homiliae in Lucam)*
Hom. Ps.	*Homilies on Psalms (Homilae in Psalmos)*
Or.	*Prayer (De oratione* or *Peri proseuches)*
Princ.	*First Principles (De principiis* or *Peri archon)*

Philo

Praem.	*On Rewards and Punishments (De praemiis et poenis)*

Photius

Lex.	*Lexicon*

Pliny

Ep.	*Epistles (Epistulae)*

Polycarp of Smyrna

Phil.	*To the Philippians*

Pontius

Vit. Cypr.	*Life of Cyprian (Vita Cypriani)*

Prudentius

Perist.	*The Crowns (Peristephanon liber)*

Rufinus

Adult. libr. Orig.	*On the Falsification of Origen's Books (De adulteratione librorum Origenis)*

Shepherd of Hermas

Mand.	*Mandate*
Sim.	*Similitude*
Vis.	*Vision*

Suetonius

Claud.	*Divine Claudius (Divus Claudius)*
Dom.	*Domitianus*

Tacitus

Ann.	*Annals (Annales)*

Tatian

Or. Graec.	*Discourse to the Greeks (Oratio ad Graecos* or *Pros Hellenas)*

Tertullian

An.	*The Soul (De anima)*
Apol.	*Apology (Apologeticus)*
Bapt.	*Baptism (De baptismo)*
Exh. cast.	*Exhortation to Chastity (De exhortatione castitatis)*
Marc.	*Against Marcion (Adversus Marcionem)*

Nat.	To the Heathen (Ad nations)
Or.	Prayer (De oratione)
Paen.	Repentance (De paenitentia)
Praescr.	Prescription against Heretics (De praescriptione haereticorum)
Prax.	Against Praxeas (Adversus Praxean)
Res.	The Resurrection of the Flesh (De resurrectione carnis)
Test.	The Soul's Testimony (De testimonio animae)
Ux.	To His Wife (Ad uxorem)

Theodoret of Cyrrhus

Haer. fab.	Compendium of Heretical Falsehoods (Haereticarum fabularum compendium)

Theophilus

Autol.	To Autolycus (Ad Autolycum)

Dead Sea Scrolls

1QS	Rule of the Community
4Q254	Commentary on Genesis C

Nag Hammadi Codices (NHC)

I,2	Ap. Jas.	Apocryphon of James
I,3	Gos. Truth	Gospel of Truth
I,4	Treat. Res.	Treatise on the Resurrection
I,5	Tri. Trac.	Tripartite Tractate
II,1	Ap. John	Apocryphon of John
II,2	Gos. Thom.	Gospel of Thomas
II,3	Gos. Phil.	Gospel of Philip
II,7	Thom. Cont.	Book of Thomas the Contender
III,1	Ap. John	Apocryphon of John
III,4	Soph. Jes. Chr.	Sophia of Jesus Christ
III,5	Dial. Sav.	Dialogue of the Savior
IV,1	Ap. John	Apocryphon of John
IV,2	Gos. Eg.	Gospel of the Egyptians
V,3	1 Apoc. Jas.	First Apocalypse of James
V,4	2 Apoc. Jas	Second Apocalypse of James
VII,3	Apoc. Pet.	Apocalypse of Peter
VIII,2	Ep. Pet. Phil.	Letter of Peter to Philip
XII,2	Gos. Truth	Gospel of Truth
BG,3	Soph. Jes. Chr.	Sophia of Jesus Christ

Papyri

P.Amh.	Amherst Papyri
P.Berolin.	Berolinensis Papyrus, Berlin Museum
P.Bodm.	Bodmer Papyrus
P.Egerton	Egerton Papyrus
P.Jena	Jena Papyrus

P.Köln	Cologne (Köln) Papyri
P.Laur.	Laurentiana Papyri, Florence
P.Lond.	Greek Papyri, British Museum
P.Lond.Or.	Oriental Manuscript, British Library
P.Mich.	Michigan Papyri
P.Oxy.	Oxyrhynchus Papyri
P.Ryl.	Greek Papyri, John Rylands Library, Manchester
P.Vindob.	Vindobonae Papyrus

Other Manuscripts and Codices

Hierosolym.	Codex Hierosolymitanus, Greek Patriarchate at Jerusalem
Paris gr.	Greek Manuscript, Bibliothèque Nationale, Paris
Paris Suppl. gr.	Greek Supplemental Manuscript, Bibliothèque Nationale, Paris
Vat. Regin. lat.	Latin Codex Reginensis Vatican Library, Rome

Serial Publications and Collections

AB	Anchor Bible
ACW	Ancient Christian Writers
AJBI	*Annual of the Japanese Biblical Institute*
AmUSt.P	American University Studies. Series 5, Philosophy
ANRW	*Aufstieg und Niedergang der romischen Welt*
ASE	*Annali di Storia dell'Esegesi*
AT	*Annales theologici*
Aug	*Augustinianum*
BAB	*Bulletin de l'Académie R. de Belgique*
BAGB	*Bulletin de l'Association G. Budé*
BiToTe	Bible de tous les temps
BLE	*Bulletin de littérature ecclésiastique*
BPat	Bibliotheca Patristica
CBQ	*Catholic Biblical Quarterly*
CClCr	*Civiltà classica e cristiana*
CCSA	Corpus Christianorum, Series Apocryphorum
CCSG	Corpus Christianorum, Series Graeca
CCSL	Corpus Christianorum, Series Latina
CdR	Classici delle religioni
CNT	Commentaire du Nouveau Testament
CP	Corona Patrum
CPG	*Clavis patrum graecorum*
CQ	*Classical Quarterly*
CSANT	Commentario storico ed esegetico all'Antico e al Nuovo Testamento
CSCO	Corpus scriptorum christianorum orientalium
CSEL	Corpus scriptorum ecclesiasticorum latinorum
CSLP	Corpus scriptorum Latinorum Paravianum

CTePa	Collana di testi patristici
DHGE	*Dictionnaire d'histoire et de géographie ecclésiastique*
Div	*Divinitas*
DSp	*Dictionnaire de spiritualité*
EECh	*Encyclopedia of the Early Church*
EKKNT	Evangelisch-katholischer Kommentar zum Neuen Testament
FC	Fathers of the Church
FRLANT	Forschungen zur Religion und Literatur des alten und Neuen Testaments
GCS	Die griechische christliche Schriftsteller der ersten drei Jahrhunderte
HNT	Handbuch zum Neuen Testament
HNT.AV	Handbuch zum Neuen Testament. Die Apostolischen Väter
HTKNT	Herders theologischer Kommentar zum Neuen Testament
HTR	*Harvard Theological Review*
ICC	International Critical Commentary
JAC	*Jahrbuch für Antike und Christentum*
JACErg.B	*Jahrbuch für Antike und Christentum, Ergänzungsband*
JECS	*Journal of Early Christian Studies*
JRitSt	*Journal of Ritual Studies*
JTS	*Journal of Theological Studies*
KAV	Kommentar zu den Apostolischen Vätern (= KEK, Ergänzungsreihe)
KEK	Kritisch-exegetischer Kommentar über das Neue Testament (Meyer-Kommentar)
KIT	Kleine Texte für (theologische und philologische) Vorlesungen und Übungen
LCP	Latinitas Christianorum primaeva
LTJ	*Lutheran Theological Journal*
Mar	*Marianum*
MSLCA	*Miscellanea di studi di letteratura cristiana antica*
NHC	Nag Hammadi Codices (texts of the gnostic Coptic library)
NHS	Nag Hammadi Studies
NovT	*Novum Testamentum*
NovTSup	Novum Testamentum Supplements
NTS	*New Testament Studies*
NV	*Nova et Vetera*
ÖTK	Ökumenischer Taschenbuchkommentar zum Neuen Testament
PG	Patrologia graeca
PL	Patrologia latina
PW	*Paulys Realencyclopädie der classischen Altertumswissenschaft.* New edition, G. Wissowa. 49 vols.
RAC	*Reallexicon für Antike und Christentum*
REA	*Revue des études antiques*
REL	*Revue des études latines*
RevScRel	*Revue des sciences religieuses*
RHE	*Revue d'histoire ecclésiastique*

RivB	*Rivista biblica italiana*
RSLR	*Rivista di storia e letteratura religiosa*
RSR	*Recherches de science religieuse*
RStB	*Richerche storico bibliche*
SC	Sources chrétiennes
SDHI	*Studia et documenta historiae et iuris*
SEAug	Studia ephemeridis Augustinianum
SGLG	Studia Graeca et Latina Gothoburgensia
SHAW.PH	*Sitzungsberichte der Heidelberger Akademie der Wissenschaften. Philosophisch-historische Klasse*
SMSR	*Studi e materiali di storia delle religioni*
SSL	Spicilegium sacrum Lovaniense
StPatr	Studia patristica
TRE	*Theologische Realenzyklopädie*
TU	Texte und Untersuchungen
TUGAL	Texte und Untersuchungen zur Geschichte der altechristlichen Literatur
VC	*Vigiliae christianae*
VCSup	Vigiliae christianae Supplements
VetChr	*Vetera christianorum*
ZKG	*Zeitschrift für Kirchengeschichte*
ZNW	*Zeitschrift für die neutestamentliche Wissenschaft und die Kunde der älteren Kirche*

Chapter 1

THE LETTERS OF PAUL AND OF THE PAULINE TRADITION

Christian literature begins, for us today, with the letters of Paul the Apostle. These letters contain preexisting elements, which scholars describe as "preliterary forms" (P. Vielhauer). These include short professions of faith in the death and resurrection of Jesus (e.g., 1 Thess 4:14) and statements of a comparable kind that were used in the catechesis of new Christians. Such was the tradition regarding the death and resurrection of Jesus, for example, which Paul says he has received and which he passes on in his turn (1 Cor 15:3–5). Other formulas may have been used in a liturgical context, such as certain hymns (which scholars identify in, e.g., Phil 2:6–11 or 1 Tim 3:16). It is difficult to determine the original form of these passages, and in these cases, it is difficult to speak of literary phenomena. Only toward the end of the third century would formulas of belief appear as independent documents and works by individuals; we shall speak of those in connection with their authors. They would appear later still as statements that were in some sense official; these we shall discuss in vol. II.

1. Letter as a Genre

The earliest Christian documents preserved as independent entities are the letters of Paul. At a time when the transmission of the Christian message was primarily oral, letters served as a replacement for oral communication when sender and recipient were separated in space. The first Christian letters were not written for posterity but to meet the needs of the moment. Third John is the only letter from the beginnings of Christianity addressed by one individual to another. The next one is that of Ignatius of Antioch to Polycarp. Of the authentic letters of Paul one is addressed to an individual, Philemon, but it is intended also for the church that gathers in his home. Others are meant for churches or groups of churches; the latter include Colossians, Ephesians, 3 Corinthians, and 2 John, six of the seven letters of Ignatius, and the letter of Polycarp of Smyrna.

The letters to Timothy and Titus claim to be written by one individual (Paul) to another, but that setting is a fiction. *First Clement* is written by one church to another. Other "letters" from early Christianity are rather treatises that have some of the formal elements of a letter and a more or less broad readership. These include Hebrews,

James, 1 and 2 Peter, Jude, and *Barnabas; 2 Clement* is a homily and does not read at all like a letter. The Apocalypse of John contains seven "letters" to communities of Asia Minor (chs. 2–3) but these are in fact prophetic messages. As a whole, the Apocalypse does have an epistolary framework (1:4–6; 22:21), probably due to the author's intention that it be read during the liturgy. Finally, two letters are found within the Acts of the Apostles (15:23–26; 23:26–30).

This variety of forms and functions mirrors the variety of letters in the Hellenistic world. Deissmann distinguished between letters true and proper, which were meant for immediate communication of a private kind and had no literary aspirations, and epistles, in which the letter form was a fiction and served to dress up a treatise intended for a broad public. To the first category he assigned the letters of Paul and 2 and 3 John; to the second, the Pastoral Epistles, Hebrews, James, 1 and 2 Peter, and Jude.

This classification, later modified as a distinction between real letters and artificial letters, had a great influence but is now considered too rigid. Today the scholarly preference is for more flexible classifications that reject two broad categories in favor of a spectrum of possibilities that take into account the ancient treatises on the subject of letter writing. (Hellenistic manuals on the subject distinguished twenty-one types of letters and, later, forty-one.) Thus W. Doty bases his classification on a distinction between "more private" letters (with an immediate relationship between writers and addressees) and "less private" letters (characterized by a formal or distant relationship), and then subdivides the latter into various categories. David Aune distinguishes between the following types of letters: (a) private or documentary letters intended to maintain contact with family or friends, communicate news, or make requests; (b) official letters (written by an authority in the exercise of an office); and (c) literary letters preserved and transmitted through literary channels, as in epistolaries.

Almost any kind of composition could be set within an epistolary framework. The formal elements of letter writing can give the appearance of a letter to writings of various kinds; as we have seen, this was repeatedly the case in early Christianity. Let us look at these elements briefly; they consist of fixed formulas that allow a limited range of variations and occur chiefly at the beginning and the end of a work. A letter begins with a preamble *(praescriptum)* consisting of three elements: the name of the writer or sender *(superscriptio)*, that of the addressee *(adscriptio)*, and a greeting *(salutatio)*, which is usually represented by the infinitive *chairein*, to which might be added a wish for good health *(formula valetudinis)*. An alternative form of preamble was: from sender, to addressee, without a greeting. The three elements may also be expanded, for example, by adding information on the relationship between the two persons, or by adding titles to both names and adverbs to the greeting.

A letter ends with a formula of the kind "Take care of yourself and be well." This is later replaced by a formula in which the greetings of others are added, or the writer asks the addressee to greet their common acquaintances. The final word is often *errōso/errōsthe* ("be well," singular or plural), often followed by the date. The body of the letter is structured by formulas introducing various kinds of communication; for example, "I received your letter"; "you should know that"; "as I write to you"; "I am surprised"; "please . . ." and so on.

Paul, creator of the apostolic letter that served as a model for subsequent early Christian letters, adopts and alters these conventions. The basic form of the *salutatio* becomes "grace and peace be yours," which adds the theologically meaningful *charis* (a reference to the work of Christ) to the traditional Hebrew greeting *shalōm*. The simple form is found in 1 Thess 1:1; in other letters it is expanded to include "from God (our) Father and the Lord Jesus Christ." Paul extends the mention of his own name as sender by adding the title of apostle, which might in turn be expanded by a reference to the origin and meaning of the title (Rom 1:1–6) and possibly by adding the names of collaborators associated with the sending of the letter (1 Cor 1:1: Sosthenes; 2 Cor 1:1: Timothy; 1 Thess 1:1: Silvanus and Timothy). The mention of the addressee can also be expanded (1 Cor 1:2; Rom 1:7).

Next comes the *proem* or introduction; a thanksgiving for the situation of the community being addressed (e.g., Rom 1:8–17; 1 Cor 1:4–9; absent from Galatians, which is a letter of rebuke). It begins with "I thank God," or "blessed be God." At the end, Paul sends greetings (e.g., 1 Thess 5:26; 1 Cor 16:19–20), but he replaces the traditional formula of greeting with a wish, the earliest form of which is "the grace of our Lord Jesus Christ be with you" (1 Thess 5:28). Other features of his greetings are the invitation to exchange a holy kiss (1 Thess 5:26; 1 Cor 16:20; etc.), which alludes to a reading of the letters during the community liturgy, and mention that the greeting is in his own hand (e.g., 1 Cor 16:21; Gal 6:11; Phlm 19). Paul also uses some of these conventional formulas in the body of his letters. He has a special liking, whether in moving from the introduction to the main part of the letter, or in moving to a new subject within the body, for a formula of the type "I want you to know" (Gal 1:11; Phil 1:12) or "I want you not to be ignorant" (2 Cor 1:8; Rom 1:13). He also uses a formula of request, usually with *parakalō* (1 Cor 1:10; 4:16; 16:15).

The letters of Paul are a good deal longer and more complex than most of the private letters that have come down to us on papyri. They expound theological and ethical subjects and make full use of the resources of rhetoric for polemical and apologetic purposes. But the letters are always connected with concrete situations in which the apostle thinks he must intervene from afar, and to which his doctrinal exposés are related. The letter to the Romans is a partial exception: in this letter Paul addresses a community he has not founded, and he gives an organized explanation of the major themes of his gospel. But even this peculiarity is connected with a specific situation: Paul wants to undertake a mission in the west and he needs acceptance and support in Rome. So in this case, too, we have a treatise in letter form, but an authentic letter that abundantly develops a set of issues as required by the real needs of the situation.

BIBLIOGRAPHY

A. Deissmann, *Licht vom Osten: Das Neue Testament und die neuentdeckten Texte der hellenistich-römischen Welt* (4th ed.; Tübingen: Mohr, 1923); ET: *Light from the Ancient East: The New Testament Illustrated by Recently Discovered Texts of the Graeco-Roman World* (trans. Lionel R. M. Strachan, 1927; repr., Peabody, Mass.: Hendrickson, 1995).

W. G. Doty, "The Classification of Epistolary Literature," *CBQ* 31 (1969): 183–99.

J. L. White, "New Testament Epistolary Literature in the Framework of Ancient Epistolography," in *ANRW* II 25.2 (1984): 1730–56.

———, *Light from Ancient Letters* (Philadelphia: Fortress, 1986).

D. E. Aune, *The New Testament in Its Literary Environment* (Philadelphia: Westminster, 1987), 158–225.

S. K. Stowers, *Letter Writing in Greco-Roman Antiquity* (Philadelphia: Westminster, 1989).

2. Chronology of Paul

Thanks to his letters, Paul is for us by far the best-known personage of very early
Christianity; still the chronology of his life is not easily determined. We have at our
disposal two kinds of sources. First, we have the letters, but these are not meant to be
autobiographical and the information they give is therefore shaped by the occasion.
Second, we have the Acts of the Apostles, in which Paul is the principal actor from ch.
13 on; but the author's sources are fragmentary, and the presentation is shaped by a
theological perspective that systematically obscures the conflicts within the Christian
world that manifest themselves so dramatically in Paul's letters. It is nevertheless impossible to do without the testimony of Acts, provided we sift it critically by comparing it with the letters. Among the latter, the principal witness is Galatians 1–2, in
which Paul recalls his activity before and after his vocation. But he is here inspired by
a polemical goal: to show his independence of the authority of the Jerusalem church,
and he therefore mentions only what will serve this purpose.

According to Acts, Paul was born in Tarsus in Cilicia (21:39; 22:3; see 9:11); the
fact is not confirmed by Paul, but Luke can hardly have invented it. Moreover, an origin in Tarsus, a Hellenistic city possessed of a high cultural level, matches the image of
a hellenized Jew that the letter gives. Although he always describes himself as Paul, the
name Saul, which Acts gives him through 13:9, fits in with his origin from the tribe of
Benjamin (Phil 3:5; Rom 11:1). In addition, it was not uncommon in the Middle East
to have a double name: one from the person's original tradition, the other a Greek
name. It is unlikely, however, that Paul received a rabbinical training from the great
Gamaliel in Jerusalem (Acts 5:34; 22:3). In Gal 1:13–14 Paul describes himself in
terms of his calling as a young Pharisee, who was completely won over to the defense
of Israel's religious identity through an intransigent observance of the Law and of the
"traditions of the ancestors." This zeal led to his violent persecution of Christians.
However, the claim that the center of his activity as persecutor was Jerusalem (Acts
9:1–2), so that he was present for the stoning of Stephen (Acts 7:58; 8:1; 22:20), seems
to be contradicted by Gal 1:22, according to which he was personally unknown to the
churches of Judea.

In Gal 1:15–16 Paul describes the experience that turned his life upside down, but
he does so in the language of the calls of the Old Testament prophets, describing the
meaning of the event for him, and not its external circumstances. The threefold description of the event in Acts (9:3–9; 22:6–11; 26:12–18) is Luke's embellishment of it.
Paul did indeed regard it as a vision of Christ (1 Cor 15:8) that was closely connected
to his missionary mandate to the pagans (Gal 1:16). We cannot speak of it, however,
as a conversion in the sense of passing from one religion to another, since Christianity
was still a development within Judaism, and Paul thought of it as completely in
continuity with God's plan for Israel.

Immediately after this event, Paul withdrew to Arabia (probably to the kingdom of the Nabateans, southeast of Damascus). "After three years" (that is, two and a half years according to the method of counting at that time) he went to meet Cephas in Jerusalem and remained fifteen days with him. At this time he also met James, the brother of the Lord (Gal 1:16–18). The setting in Acts, according to which Paul met the apostles in Jerusalem a few days after his conversion (9:19, 26), is therefore not trustworthy: Luke wants to show that Paul received legitimacy from the Church of Jerusalem. Paul then went to Syria and Cilicia (Gal 1:21), surely in order to exercise his mission there.

"Then after fourteen years [thirteen and a half]," he returned to Jerusalem with Barnabas and Titus, evidently as an envoy of the church of Antioch where Barnabas was working, and whither Paul was to be transferred later (Acts 11:25–26). His purpose was to discuss the conditions to be imposed on Christians converted from paganism (Gal 2:1–10). This episode certainly corresponds to the one in Acts 15:1–29. Before the "apostolic council" of Jerusalem, Acts 13–14 places the events that are usually described as Paul's first missionary journey, which supposedly took him, as a missionary of the church of Antioch along with Barnabas and Mark, to Cyprus and southern Asia Minor (Pamphylia, Pisidia, Lycaonia). How this mission can be reconciled with Paul's activity in Syria and Cilicia (Gal 1:21) is not clear. Admittedly, in Galatians Paul's intention is not to describe all of his activity but only to emphasize the time that has passed and his independence of Jerusalem. Some, however, prefer to locate this first missionary journey after the council of Jerusalem.

After the "council," Paul recalls a meeting in Antioch with Cephas and Barnabas about table fellowship with Christians converted from paganism (Gal 2:11–14); this meeting seems to have taken place after Paul had returned from Jerusalem to Antioch. It was probably this, and not the circumstances reported in Acts 15:36, that distanced Paul from Barnabas and even from Antioch, where his position was certainly a difficult one, and sent him off on independent missionary activity. From this point on, Galatians is no longer of any help with Paul's chronology; the account in Acts can be checked against the information in the letters regarding the collection that Paul had pledged to take up on behalf of the Jerusalem community.

Having left Antioch, Paul traveled through Syria and Asia Minor (Cilicia, Lycaonia, Phrygia, the territory of the Galatians), then crossed over into Europe and reached Corinth, where he founded a church and remained for a time. This was the so-called "second missionary journey." The story in Acts 15:40–18:17 is confirmed by the information in 1 Thessalonians, which was composed during this stay in Corinth. On the other hand, there are reasons to doubt the return from Corinth by way of Ephesus and Caesarea to Jerusalem and then to Antioch, with a fresh departure immediately afterward back to Asia Minor and Ephesus, as Luke relates in a few verses (Acts 18:18–23; 19:1: the beginning of the "third missionary journey"). Perhaps Paul simply went from Corinth to Ephesus, where he stayed for three years, during which he supposedly visited the communities of Phrygia and Galatia, carried out a mission in the valley of the Lycus (Colossae, Laodicea, Hierapolis: Acts 19:10), and paid a short visit to Corinth (2 Cor 2:1; 12:21; 13:2).

He then went via Troas and Macedonia to Corinth, and remained there for three months (Acts 20:3) before undertaking the return journey to Jerusalem in order to bring the proceeds of the collection he had pledged to make at the "council." With regard to this journey we have no external confirmation of the account in Acts 20:3–21:17. According to Luke, Paul was arrested in Jerusalem (Acts 21:27–36), then transported to Caesarea (23:21–23), where he remained for two years. He was transferred to Rome as a result of his appeal to the emperor (the journey is narrated in Acts 27:1–28:14), and remained there for two years under house arrest (28:31). *First Clement,* written at the end of the first century, refers to Paul's martyrdom in Rome, which doubtless took place under Nero and, at the latest, during the persecution of Christians in 64 (5.7). A report contained in second century sources of a journey to Spain would presuppose a release in Rome and a second imprisonment. The story was probably based on Paul's plan in Rom 15:28, but it is unlikely that the journey ever took place.

Up to this point the chronology is a relative one; reference points that would turn it into an absolute chronology are few. According to Acts 18:2, when Paul was in Corinth he met Priscilla and Aquila, a husband and wife who had "recently" arrived from Italy as a result of an edict by the emperor Claudius, expelling the Jews. The edict can be dated to 41 or, more probably, to 49. The only fairly solid date is the proconsulate of Gallio in Achaia (Acts 18:2). An inscription at Delphi, discovered in 1905, mentions Gallio as proconsul; this allows us to establish that Gallio's proconsulship lasted from May 51 to May 52 or, less probably, from May 52 to May 53. According to Acts 19:11, Paul remained in Corinth for eighteen months and was accused before Gallio toward the end of his stay, which would therefore have begun at the end of 49 or in 50. With this date as a starting point, it is possible, with some degree of certainty, to situate the events of Paul's life:

- vocation: ca. 32
- first visit to Jerusalem: 34/35
- activity in Syria and Cilicia; move to Antioch and mission on behalf of Antioch: 34/35–48
- second visit to Jerusalem ("council"); dispute with Peter in Antioch: 48/49
- independent missionary journey: 49/50
- stay in Corinth: 50–52
- stay in Ephesus: 52–55
- stay in Corinth (three months): 55/56
- arrival in Jerusalem, arrest: 57/58
- arrival in Rome: 60 (?)

BIBLIOGRAPHY

G. Bornkamm, *Paul* (New York: Harper & Row, 1971).

R. Jewett, *A Chronology of Paul's Life* (Philadelphia: Fortress, 1979).

G. Lüdemann, *Paulus der Heidenapostel* I. *Studien zur Chronologie* (Göttingen: Vandenhoeck & Ruprecht, 1980); ET: *Paul the Apostle to the Gentiles: Studies in Chronology* (Philadelphia: Fortress/London: SCM, 1984).

M. G. Mara, *Paolo di Tarso e il suo epistolario: Ricerche storico-esegetiche* (L'Aquila: Japadre, 1983).

G. Barbaglio, *Paolo di Tarso e le origini cristiane* (Assisi: Citadella, 1985).

J. Becker, *Paulus: Der Apostel der Völker* (Tübingen: Mohr, 1989).

3. Authentic Letters

a. First Letter to the Thessalonians

According to Acts 17, after Paul had founded the church in Thessalonica, capital of the province of Macedonia, he had to flee to Berea, where he left Silas and Timothy behind and went on to Athens. From there he went to Corinth, where his two coworkers joined him (18:1–5). At Corinth he wrote 1 Thessalonians between 50 and 52. In it he mentions his own activity in Thessalonica (1:5–6), then in Macedonia and Achaia (1:7–8), and in Athens (3:1).

The letter can be thought of as having two parts: a lengthy introduction (1:2–3:13) with a parenesis or exhortation (4:1–5:22), followed by a conclusion (5:23–28). The first part is dominated by the theme of the mutual recollections of Paul and the Thessalonians; the apostle recalls, among other things, the superabundant action, in the form of charismatic phenomena and wonders (1:5), of the Spirit who presided over the birth of the community. In 2:1–12 he recalls and defends his apostolic activity at Thessalonica. The apostle probably means to differentiate the impression he gave from that of the other preachers who thronged the "religious marketplace" of the time: itinerant philosophers, mendicant prophets, magicians, and charlatans. The attack on the Jewish opponents of the gospel in 2:13–16 seems odd, since it was at the hands of the pagans that the Thessalonians had suffered. Some exegetes consider these verses to be an interpolation, but this seems unnecessary, since the passage interprets the Thessalonians' difficulties by applying to them both the traditional idea of Jewish opposition to God's messengers, as well as the topoi, or common themes, in pagan attacks on Jews.

First Thessalonians 4:1–12 contains exhortations on the moral life and relationships in the community. The next verse begins an instruction on the lot of deceased Christians, thereby answering concerns of the Christians of Thessalonica (4:13). The latter expect the Lord's return in the very near future, and the death of some brethren has caused them to ask whether the deceased would be excluded from union with Christ at his coming. Paul answers that the dead are not excluded, because they will be raised up at the coming of the Lord and meet him along with the living. The apostle here uses a saying of Jesus that is not transmitted in the gospels; it occurs after 4:16 and makes use of themes traditional in Jewish expectation of the "Day of the Lord." Paul is convinced that he too will be alive at the Lord's coming (4:15), and therefore urges watchfulness for the sake of readiness (5:1–11). He then adds some recommendations for community life (5:12–22) before ending with a prayer and formulas of greeting (5:23–28).

b. First Letter to the Corinthians

Corinth, destroyed in 146 B.C. by the Romans, was founded anew as a Roman colony a century later by Julius Caesar. In Paul's time it was the largest city in Greece. A mixture of peoples and religions set it apart, and its immorality was renowned, though its reputation was doubtless exaggerated. Paul had come there during his "second missionary journey" (Acts 18:1–18) and had founded a community of Christians converted from paganism. He stayed there a year and a half, probably in 50–52. From

Corinth he went to Ephesus, then to Jerusalem and Antioch, whence he left again for Ephesus (Acts 18:19–19:1). We noted earlier that the return to Palestine between the two stays in Ephesus is probably an invention of Luke. In any case, it was from Ephesus that Paul wrote 1 Corinthians, toward the end of his stay there (16:8) and therefore probably in the early months of 55.

The letter is of great help in understanding of the problems that could arise when the good news of Christ was received in a cultural environment that was not Jewish but "pagan." Paul had preached at Corinth in a religious atmosphere in which people did not expect salvation to come by an eschatological divine intervention representing the climax of a lengthy history of relations between a people and their God. They looked for salvation rather from the possibility that individual believers, in an intimacy with the divinity that would break with their individual and collective past, might be seized by the divinity and, through a sharing in this divinity's mythical fate, be immediately freed from demonic forces by the divinity who had overcome them. Characteristics of such an attitude are: enthusiasm, that is, the conviction of the divine spirit dwelling within one; individualism; a tendency in some degree to moral indifference, inasmuch as individuals think of themselves as "beyond good and evil"; and the persuasion that the spirit of the human being is already saved, while the body will never be saved, nor is there any reason why it should be.

The letter does not have a well-defined structure. There are responses to questions raised by the Corinthians (7:1, 25; 8:1; 12:1; 16:1), but also to situations that Paul sees as problems, and first of all to the divisions within the community and the formation of parties.

After the preamble and introduction (1:1–9), Paul confronts the problem of parties (1:10–4:21). He has learned that groups have formed in the community, each of them appealing to a leader: Paul, Apollos, Cephas, Christ (1:12). There has been a great deal of discussion about what distinguished such groups. Paul claims that as evangelizer of the Corinthians he alone is their "father," and he bemoans the fact that some have become puffed up with pride, thinking that he will not return (4:15, 18). He says that it matters little to him if the Corinthians pass judgment on him (4:1–5). He emphasizes the continuity between his own work and the later work of Apollos (3:15–15; see Acts 18:4–26; 19:1).

The basic theme of chs. 1–4 is the contrast between (human) wisdom and foolishness (of the cross). This does not prevent Paul from having another wisdom, which he teaches to adult Christians, but which is unknown to the world and is revealed to believers by the Spirit (2:6–12). He was not able to teach it earlier to the Corinthians because they were babes in the faith. Nor can he teach it now, because their divisions show them to be fleshly, not spiritual (3:1–4), even though they think themselves spiritual (3:18) and base their pride on human beings, i.e., Paul, Apollos, Cephas (3:21–22). These statements of Paul give us a glimpse of two levels in Christian formation: *initiation* could be followed, in a phase which Paul describes as "adult," by *instruction* based on the mysteries of God, which are revealed only by the Spirit (M. Pesce). The reference, it seems, is to a knowledge of the role of Jesus in God's plan, a knowledge perhaps based on an interpretation of the Scriptures and connected with manifestations of the Spirit. We may think that after Paul's departure the Corinthians discovered (possibly from Apollos) elements of this Christian "wisdom," and that some blamed Paul for not having told them of it. They then chose to appeal to other apostles, such as Apollos and Cephas. The latter may never have been in Corinth, but traditions connected with his name were in circulation there.

To interpret this wisdom the Corinthians seem to have used categories supplied by the mystery cults of the day. The spread of these categories in Corinth is attested a few decades later by Apuleius. This perspective allows us to understand the several questions discussed in the letter. The knowledge in question would be reserved to the initiated, whence the importance of baptism, understood as a rite of initiation, and of the names of those who guarantee the tradition. This knowledge would ensure immediate salvation. This belief accounts for the position of the "strong," who extol their freedom in the area of sexual ethics (chs. 5–6) and of flesh sacrificed to idols (chs. 8–10), the spread of enthusiasm and ecstasies (chs. 11–14), and the conviction that they are already risen (ch. 15). In keeping with all this is the importance attached by the Corinthians to knowledge *(gnōsis)*, their slogan, "Everything is permitted" (6:12; 10:23).

Paul responds by identifying the wisdom invoked by the Corinthians as human wisdom, which here has a negative connotation. To this he opposes a "theology of the cross," which is meant to disparage the "strength" that the Corinthians boast of having acquired through their conversion, and by virtue of which they regard themselves as superior to others. In Paul's view, the gospel is the opposite of all that: it is the foolishness and weakness of God, which are manifested in the cross of Christ (1:18–25), in the seemingly weak preaching of Paul (2:15), and in the makeup of the church of Corinth (1:26–29).

In chs. 5–6 Paul discusses some special problems, in particular *porneia,* that is, sexual disorder, rejecting among other things the thought of tolerating in the community a man who lives with his father's (second) wife (5:1–5). In ch. 7 he answers questions on marriage, suggesting that it is better for persons to remain in the state in which they were when they became Christians (i.e., celibacy or marriage), but also making the avoidance of sin the basic norm of behavior.

Chapters 8–10 deal with the eating of flesh sacrificed to idols: May it be eaten? May one share in the meals celebrated in pagan temples? Paul shares the presupposition of the "strong," that Christian liberty permits the eating, because idols do not exist and therefore cannot cause uncleanness. But he also sets down, as the principle that should prevail, the necessity of not scandalizing the "weak" brethren. He rejects participation in the meals because one enters thereby into communion with demons. Chapter 11 settles questions regarding the behavior of men and women during worship and especially during the cultic meal. Here, as throughout the letter, the norm is communion among the faithful and their mutual edification.

Chapters 12–14 have to do with the gifts of the Spirit. Before their conversion the Corinthians had already witnessed or been the subjects of ecstatic phenomena (12:2). Analogous phenomena now appear in the Christian community, with the result that the Corinthians think they have a direct connection with the heavenly world. Paul does not reject the manifestations of the Spirit but, whereas the Corinthians prize chiefly the gift of tongues (an unintelligible language, thought to be produced by the presence of the Spirit), he himself gives first place to prophecy because, being intelligible, it contributes more directly to the welfare of the community. The well-known hymn to love as superior to every other gift occurs in this context (ch. 13).

Some in Corinth claim that there is no resurrection of the dead (15:12). In ch. 15 Paul emphasizes the order followed in the resurrection: first Christ, as the firstfruits, and then, at Christ's return, those who belong to him. Coming as they did from a Greek cultural environment, the Christians of Corinth had difficulty understanding how the body could share in salvation. Paul stresses the spiritual nature of the risen body and incorporates this concept into the scenario for the end of the world that had been developed in Judaism.

Chapter 16 gives practical instructions for the collection for the Church of Jerusalem, news about Paul's travel plans, and, finally, personal greetings.

c. Second Letter to the Corinthians

Other problems were soon added to those faced in 1 Corinthians. These were different in origin but were, like the former, connected with the Hellenistic culture and religious spirit that prevailed in Corinth. Once again, the issue was the model used to envisage the activity of the divinity, that is, the way in which he reveals his power. Now, however, the question is phrased in terms of the model given by the apostle himself as he proclaimed that power and communicated its blessings. But before addressing this point, we must turn to the problems of composition, which are more complex than for any other letter of Paul, and are connected with a time of very sensitive relations with the Corinthian community.

After the preamble (1:1–2) and introduction (1:3–11), Paul explains why he has not returned to Corinth since his last visit (1:12–2:4). He had originally sent Timothy (1 Cor 4:7; 16:10), with the intention of going there himself after traversing Macedonia (1 Cor 16:5–10); subsequently, he decided to go directly to Corinth, then to Macedonia, and then back to Corinth (2 Cor 1:15–16). It would seem that something had spurred him to visit Corinth immediately; Timothy's mission had evidently not been successful. But Paul did not return for the third time, as he had planned, and instead wrote to Corinth "with many tears" (2:4).

In 2:5–13 Paul describes a meeting with someone at Corinth, after which he returned to Ephesus. From here he sent the "tearful letter" and also sent Titus to Corinth. He himself then went to Troas, the port of embarkation for Macedonia. There, contrary to his expectation, he did not find Titus. He then boarded a ship for Macedonia. This subject does not come up again until 7:5, where he speaks of meeting Titus. Instead, 2:14–7:4 is occupied by a lengthy defense of his own apostolic ministry, which is paradoxical in that glory is achieved only through suffering and the scorn of others. Within this section there is a further break: the exhortation to the Corinthians to open their hearts is uttered in 6:13 and has its natural continuation in 7:2, whereas the section 6:14–7:1 seems like an intrusion, since its subject is the exhortation not to be joined with unbelievers. This last passage, which is phrased in a style different from that of the context, is probably a post-Pauline interpolation.

In 7:5–16 the story of the prehistory of the letter continues: Paul met Titus in Macedonia and was delighted by the end of the conflict with the Corinthians. Chapter 8 gives instructions for the collection. Chapter 9 continues the subject, but as if Paul were now only introducing it (9:1), while at the same time he proposes the churches of Achaia as a model for those of Macedonia, whereas in ch. 8 it is the other way around. The atmosphere of these two chapters is one of joy and thanksgiving; but suddenly, beginning in 10:1, Paul's tone hardens, as he defends himself against accusations made in Corinth, especially by one individual, who is surely the one mentioned in 2:5–11. Paul gives a spirited defense of his ministry against those whom he describes as "super-apostles" (11:5; 12:11). He recalls his second visit to Corinth, and announces a third (12:14, 21; 13:1–11). He also urges the Corinthians to be self-critical because, once he comes among them, he will not spare them. The final greeting (13:11–13), however, is unexpectedly quite cordial.

In summary, the letter shows some obvious breaks:

Chapter 2:13 is continued in 7:5. The section in between is not simply a digression by Paul, since it presupposes a different situation: up to 2:13 and then in 7:5–16 Paul views the conflict with the Corinthians as a thing of the past, whereas the defense in 2:13–7:4 seems to suppose that a conflict is imminent, although the tone does not have the same fierceness as in 10:1–13:10.

Chapters 8 and 9 are concerned with the collection, but it is hard to see them as belonging to the same letter.

Chapter 10:1–13:30 reflect a violent controversy and cannot belong to the same letter as 1:1–2:13 and 7:5–16. It is also unlikely that they belong to the same letter as 2:14–7:5, because in the latter section the conflict seems to be still in its beginnings.

Chapter 6:14–7:1 interrupt the argument and are not Pauline in style or content.

It seems therefore that 2 Corinthians is to be regarded as a combination of several letters, or parts of letters, from Paul. This is a phenomenon seen in antiquity in the publication of letters with the same addressee: letters on related subjects were combined by eliminating references to more concrete circumstances. The several letters or parts of letters can be reconstructed as follows:

Second Corinthians 10–13 (except for the greetings) would be "the tearful letter" that Paul wrote from Ephesus (2 Cor 2:4) after the quick visit to Corinth during which he was challenged and offended. This, his second visit, after the visit during which he founded this Church. It took place perhaps in the autumn after 1 Corinthians (possibly 55) or the following spring. As for 2:14–7:4, which is polemical in content, it may be another section of that same letter, but it may also reflect an earlier phase in which the conflict had not yet become serious. In this case, it would have been written after Paul received unsatisfactory information from Timothy and before his second visit to Corinth, which would have been motivated by the letter's lack of success.

When Paul later received good news from Titus in Macedonia, he wrote the Corinthians the letter of reconciliation represented by 2 Cor 1:1–2:13 and 7:5–16. This letter was therefore composed in Macedonia, probably in the year after 1 Corinthians. Chapter 8 on the collection could be part of this letter, while ch. 9 would be a later instruction; but the contrary is also possible, that is, they may be two independent letters.

What caused the crisis, and who were Paul's adversaries? They came from outside with letters of recommendation (3:1; 10:12, 18). This situation was different from that of 1 Corinthians, in which the problems originated within the community. These outsiders, who claimed to be apostles (11:13), Paul derides as "super-apostles" (11:5; 12:11). They took credit for the work of others and boasted of being Hebrews (10:16; 11:22). They challenged Paul's activity, asserting that his letters were forceful but his personal presence was feeble (10:16). Unlike Paul, they asserted their legitimacy with powerful signs, which they claimed should be characteristic of an apostle (12:11–12).

They boasted of their ecstatic experiences, to the point that Paul is forced to remind them that he is not their inferior in this area but chooses not to boast of it (12:1–9). They insisted that they belonged to Christ and were his ministers (10:7; 11:23). In response Paul protests that he does not want to know Christ in a human way (5:16).

It is likely that these outsiders were Christian apostles of Jewish origin who adopted a model of itinerant preacher known to the Hellenistic world: the "divine man," full of the power of the divinity, which enabled him to be in communication with the divine, to work miracles, and to dispense wisdom. They must have preached a Christ who fit that model, drawing from the tradition of his miracles and of his sayings, which took the form of words of wisdom. It is probably this that Paul rejects in 5:16, because for him the Christ who is to be preached is Christ crucified. The Corinthians, who were responsive to the manifestations of the Spirit (as 1 Corinthians had already shown), must have been impressed by these missionaries and allowed themselves to question Paul's apostolic authority.

d. Letter to the Galatians

The date of Galatians, which is not addressed to a single church but to all the communities of Galatia (1:2), depends on the identification of the addressees, giving rise to an age-old controversy. The Galatians, a branch of the Celtic family (the two names are equivalent in Greek) were summoned from the Balkans to Asia Minor in 278 B.C. to serve as mercenaries of King Nicomedes of Bithynia, and later settled in an area of central Asia Minor that then took its name from them. Beginning in 36 B.C., Aminta, an ally first of Antony, then of Octavian, was able to establish a kingdom made up of Galatia, Pisidia, Lycaonia, Pamphylia, and Cilicia. At Aminta's death in 25 B.C., Augustus turned the whole area into the Roman province of Galatia. The question, then, is whether Paul means by "Galatia" the territory of the Galatians as such or the larger Roman province. During his first missionary journey with Barnabas, Paul had already evangelized Pisidia and Lycaonia, which belonged to the province of Galatia (Acts 13–14). If, then, the letter is addressed to the inhabitants of the province, he could have written it shortly after the "council of Jerusalem" in 48/49 (to which reference is made in Gal 2:1–10). On the other hand, he worked in the territory proper of the Galatians only during his "second journey" (Acts 16:6), and returned there during the third (Acts 18:23). Since Gal 4:13 hints that Paul visited Galatia twice, Galatians would have to be dated after 52/53, and therefore would have been written during the two- or three-year stay in Ephesus. Scholars remain divided.

Galatians is a highly polemical letter, elicited by the preaching, after Paul's departure, of Christian missionaries who required pagans converted to Christianity to observe the Jewish law and, in particular, circumcision. They cast doubt on Paul's authority, probably emphasizing the difference between his practice and that of the church of Jerusalem. The issue here was the very identity of Christianity: Were the signs denoting membership in Judaism among the basic things defining Christianity? Such was indeed the view of the missionaries who competed with Paul: in their eyes, the salvation God offers in Christ occurs within the context of the ancient and permanently valid covenant between God and Israel, a covenant ratified by circumcision and the observance of the law. Observance of the law did not mean that the Jews believed that they were saved by their own powers through fulfillment of the law's prescriptions, an unfortunate caricature developed and kept alive down the centuries by Christian anti-Jewish polemics. The point was rather that observance of the law was a sign of membership in the community, which God saves in virtue of the covenant he has made with it.

Paul, on the other hand, following an insight that would be decisive for the success of Christianity, refused to make Christian identity subordinate to Jewish identity, defining it instead solely by faith in Jesus Christ. This presented a difficult problem, because the God of Israel, of Jesus, and of Paul seemed to be in contradiction, since in the Scriptures salvation was always connected to the covenant with Israel and the gift of the law. Paul had therefore to engage in a bold line of thinking in order to set aside the law from the ongoing line of salvation. In this he drew on tendencies already at work in Judaism: he connected salvation instead with the promise, much older than the law, that God had given to Abraham and his posterity. This posterity Paul boldly identified with Jesus and the Christians. In this view, the law represented simply an interlude, a "pedagogue" assigned to Israel until it should become "adult" and capable of receiving the "inheritance." Paul is aware of the delicacy of his position, but he is possessed by the certainty, which also came from his personal experience (and history has justified him), that at this point the whole of Christianity is at stake. He therefore throws himself into the struggle with a passion and a clarity of mind that make Galatians one of the key documents in the history of Christianity. Over the centuries, efforts to rediscover and give radical new expression to Christian identity have repeatedly turned back to this letter.

Already significant are the expansion of the *superscriptio* by a claim of divine origin for Paul's apostolate, and the absence of the introduction, which is replaced (1:6–10) by a rebuke to the Galatians for so easily going astray.

In 1:11–2:14 Paul looks back to his experience as a zealous Pharisee and persecutor of Christians, whom God then called and entrusted with a mission to the pagans. Paul recalls these events in order to show his apostolate as independent of the authority of the church of Jerusalem, and as at the same time acknowledged by that church. He had gone to Jerusalem for the first time more than two years after his call, and for the second time another thirteen years later, in order to meet the leaders of the community there who had acknowledged the divine origin of his ministry to the uncircumcised. Paul had already defended the "truth of the gospel" in a meeting at Antioch with Cephas, who, worried as he was about the Jewish Christians who were observing the law, had abandoned table fellowship with Christian converts from paganism.

Chapter 2:15–21 answers the question raised by the conflict in Antioch and states Paul's position: believers in Christ who seek further justification from the law render void the work of Christ.

Chapters 3:1–5:12 give the line of argument intended to justify Paul's position. This section appeals to the experience of the Spirit, which the Galatians had at the time of their conversion, when there was no question of any law observance. It proves that the divine promise was based on the faith of Abraham (3:6–18) and emphasizes the point that observance of the law ended with the adoption of Christians as the free children of God who must refuse to fall back into slavery (3:19–4:11). After a reference to Paul's founding of the community, an exegesis of the biblical story of Hagar and Sarah contrasts the slavery connected with the Law and the freedom flowing from the promise. An exhortation to remain free then follows.

Chapters 5:13–6:10 contain a parenesis (moral exhortation), a typical element in the second part of Paul's letters: freedom in the Spirit must beget mutual love and service. Chapter 6:11–18 has a final exhortation to guard against those demanding circumcision; it is followed by rather brusque greetings.

Although the adversaries are different, Galatians, like 2 Corinthians is an interesting witness to a fluid Christian mission: the Christian communities gradually came in contact with various missionaries who preached different forms of the gospel. In this case, the missionaries active in Galatia, who, as we saw, made Christian identity continuous with Jewish identity (4:10; 5:2; 6:12–13), called into question the divine origin of Paul's gospel, which moved in the opposite direction. These men appealed to the authorities in Jerusalem against Paul, as can be seen from Paul's efforts to prove that these authorities are in agreement with his gospel, not his adversaries'. But his reference to "false brethren" who had been so bold as to demand the circumcision of Titus in Jerusalem (2:4–5) and his ironical mention of the "pillars" of the mother church (2:6) suggest that, apart from the polemical need to emphasize his agreement with Jerusalem, Paul has no illusions about his reputation among the Judeo-Christians of Palestine.

e. Letter to the Philippians

Philippi, favorably situated on the Via Egnatia that connected Rome and Byzantium, was an economically flourishing city of mixed population and a place of encounter of various religions. Paul founded his first European community there during the "second missionary journey" (around 49). Acts covers his stay in the city at length (ch. 16), but the story has little historical plausibility. However, the persecution he suffered there is confirmed by 1 Thess 2:2.

The introduction of the letter (1:3–11) takes the form of a thanksgiving followed by a prayer. Paul's relations with this community were excellent, and words expressing joy (chairō, chara) characterize the letter. Paul then speaks of his own situation (1:12–26): he is in prison and expects to suffer martyrdom, although he does not exclude the possibility of living on and seeing the Philippians again. In any case, he exhorts them to be constant through the suffering inflicted on them (1:27–30); their situation is apparently one of persecution, although not of an excessively violent kind.

Paul exhorts the Philippians to mutual harmony and submission. They must regard others as better than themselves (2:1–4). This behavior must be based on Jesus Christ: the idea is developed in a christological hymn (2:6–11) expressing the preexistence of Jesus in his divine state and his acceptance of "self-emptying" (kenōsis) by taking on the condition of a slave, that is, human form. Many scholars think that the apostle has here adapted an earlier hymn and added to it in particular the detail "even to death on a cross" (2:8).

In 2:12–18 Paul continues his exhortation. Personal communications follow (2:19–3:1a): he expects to send Titus soon and hopes that he himself can also come in person. Meanwhile, he is sending back to the Philippians Epaphroditus, whom they had put at his disposal, and who has been ill while with Paul.

In 3:2 the tone changes abruptly, as Paul writes a violent attack on "wicked workers," and "mutilators of the flesh." He follows with a defense of his own life, first as a persecuting Pharisee and then as one trusting solely in the righteousness obtained through faith. In his present life he has not yet obtained what he hopes for, but he presses on to the reward God has promised in Christ (3:2–16). Here is one of the key theological points in the letter: when faced with Jewish-Christian missionaries who think themselves "mature" (3:15; see 3:12), probably because of their observance of the law, and perhaps having been attacked personally, Paul does not restrict himself to argument, but throws onto the scale his own life as a Jew who had placed his trust in his own zeal and his blamelessness before the law, but who subsequently threw everything away in order to rely solely on faith in Christ. The Philippians are urged to imitate Paul and not let themselves be led astray by those who "behave as enemies of the cross of Christ" (3:17–4:1).

In 4:2–9 the tone becomes calm once again as Paul urges individuals and exhorts the community to remain in the peace of God. In 4:10–20 Paul thanks the Philippians for the financial help they have given him.

The letter raises problems regarding its integrity. There are two concrete difficulties: First and foremost, the break between 3:1a, which seems to be the beginning of a conclusion of the letter, and 3:2, which picks up the discourse again in an entirely different spirit. Beginning with 4:2 (or 4:4), the tone becomes friendly once again. Many exegetes therefore see in 3:2–4:1 (or 4:3) a later letter elicited by the arrival of Judaizing missionaries in Philippi. The question remains an open one, because tensions within the community also appear in the rest of the letter (1:15; 2:21), but it must be admitted that 3:2 poses a real problem. Second, the thanks for the gift brought by Epaphroditus (4:10–20) seems long delayed, inasmuch as Epaphroditus has been ill for a long time while with Paul, and during this time there has been an exchange of news with Philippi (2:25–30). It has therefore been suggested that 4:10–20 is a thank-you note sent before the main letter. The latter would therefore consist of 1:1–3:1; and 4:2(or 4)–9, 21–23.

The question of the date and place of composition of Philippians depends on the identification of the imprisonment in which Paul is awaiting trial (1:7, 13, 17). We are told at the end of Acts about his imprisonment in Rome. But 2:24–26 supposes frequent contact between Paul and the Philippians, and this does not fit in with the great distance between Rome and Philippi. Similarly, Paul's plan of going immediately to Philippi if he is freed does not harmonize with his plan to go from Rome to Spain as expressed in the letter to the Romans. Because of the distance from Philippi, even Caesarea, where Paul was detained for two years according to Acts 24–26, presents difficulties as the place of composition. For this reason exegetes today prefer Ephesus. We have no direct testimony to an imprisonment of Paul there, but he does allude to the great dangers he experiences there (1 Cor 15:32; 2 Cor 1:8–9). Philippians would therefore belong to the same period as 1 and 2 Corinthians.

f. Letter to Philemon

The letter is addressed not only to Philemon but to the entire church that gathers in his house, with particular mention of Apphia and Archippus. The domestic church or house church was the rule at that time. In the introduction Paul describes himself not as an apostle but as a prisoner (1; see 9, 10, 13, 22–23), so the letter can be taken as composed in Ephesus, at the same period as Philippians. Since Colossians places Onesimus and Archippus in Colossae, it is possible that Philemon likewise lived there.

The occasion of this short letter was a particular incident. Onesimus, a slave of Philemon, had run away and taken refuge with Paul while the latter was in prison. Onesimus has been "useful" to Paul, a play on the meaning of the man's name in Greek, but Paul does not want to detain him. Paul sends him back to Philemon, with the request that the latter treat the slave as a brother, and with the pledge that he, Paul, will make up for possible damages (19). At the same time, Paul reminds Philemon that he owes a debt to Paul. Behind these words and the petition that Philemon would do him a favor (20), there can be glimpsed an unobtrusive request by the apostle that Onesimus be put at his disposal (see 13–14).

Paul does not appeal to Philemon's generosity in urging forgiveness of the slave; Paul does not want the commandment of love to be practiced in a way that would create personal obligations and a need of gratitude. He does not ask for Onesimus' freedom, in keeping with his position in 1 Cor 7:20–24: those who are called while slaves are not to seek their freedom, because the time is short until Christ's return. The change of social relationships did not, in Paul's view, influence the coming of the reign of God.

g. Letter to the Romans

Alone among the letters of Paul, Romans is addressed to a church he did not found. We do not know that church's origins. In Corinth Paul had met Priscilla and Aquila, a couple whom he mentions several times (1 Cor 1:14ff.; 16:19; Rom 16:3–5), who had come there from Rome because of an edict of emperor Claudius (probably in 49 or 41) expelling the Jews. This edict is also mentioned by historian Suetonius, who says the reason for it was that the Jews "were ceaselessly agitating at the instigation of Chrestos" (*Claud.* 25). It is likely that Suetonius, or his source, misunderstood an item of information about conflicts caused within the Jewish community by missionaries preaching Christ. Around the mid-forties, then, there was a Christian community in Rome, the nucleus of which consisted of Jews. On the other hand, when Paul devotes a great deal of attention to the value of the law and the destiny of Israel (Rom 9–11), he is addressing Christians who had come from paganism (1:5–6, 13; 11:13; 15:15–16). There must therefore have been a mixed community of Christians, made up of converts from both Judaism and paganism, but generally tied to the theological tradition, ethics, and modes of expression of Diaspora Judaism. This, at any rate, is the picture that emerges forty years later from the letter of Clement to the Corinthians.

Romans was probably written during Paul's stay of about three months in Corinth (Acts 20:2–3) before leaving for Jerusalem with the collection. Despite all the struggles he has weathered, Paul knows that he is not necessarily well liked by the churches of the East, nor is he sure that the collection he is bringing will be well received in Jerusalem (15:30). He has decided to move his field of activity to the west; in 15:14–33 he makes known his plans, which also explain the writing of Romans. Having proclaimed the gospel from Jerusalem to Illyria, he believes that he has finished his work in the east and is now proposing to go to Spain. For this he needs a base, which can only be Rome. He has therefore decided to violate the principle he has always followed of not going to churches founded by others.

Paul is looking, then, to set up a base in Rome, but he knows that the Roman church, the origin of which, as we saw a moment ago, was closely tied to Judaism, could well have received its information about him from his adversaries. Several times he takes an explicit stand in this letter against the erroneous conclusions that could be, and doubtless were, drawn from his teaching (3:8, 31; 6:1, 15). With the central core of his preaching, namely, justification through faith, as his starting point, Paul seeks to give the Christians of Rome an "authentic" explanation that will unmask the slanders against him and arouse sympathy for him. In particular, he must take a position on the value of the law in relations between God and human beings (chs. 1–8) and on the overall meaning of Israel's religious experience, especially in view of the fact that the Jews are rejecting the very gospel of Christ that should represent the culmination of the history of their relationship with God and give it its full meaning (chs. 9–11). For once, Paul gives in letter form an organized exposition of the essentials of his thought as this has taken shape in the final phase of his activity. This does not mean, however, that the letter to the Romans is less "realistic" and therefore closer to the genre of treatises in letter form. On the contrary, its systematic character is explained precisely by the concrete circumstances in which it was written.

Let us review the content of the letter. After the preamble, which is expanded by a traditional formula of faith (1:1–6), Paul's introduction (1:7–17) states his intention of coming to Rome and introduces his subject: the revelation of God's righteousness in the gospel, through faith and for faith.

Chapters 1:18–3:20 develop the theme negatively: human beings are able to know God from God's works and are therefore without excuse for having alienated themselves from God. For this reason God has abandoned them to immorality. They are sinners and do not escape God's judgment, which falls on Jew and Greek alike, because the words of the law are written in the hearts of all. Circumcision is of no use to Jews if they do not observe the law, which does not bestow any superiority on Jews. The law serves to make sin known, has a negative role, and cannot make anyone just.

Chapter 3:21–31 shows the way of rescue provided by the initiative of God, who has made God's righteousness known in Jesus and has, without human merit, made all sinners just through expiation in the blood of Jesus. Paul insists that he is not stripping the law of its value, which for him is to make sin known. In fact, it is in the light of this manifestation and therefore of the consciousness of being subject to the judgment of God that one appreciates the righteousness of God and the importance of faith.

Justification by faith does not suddenly annul a covenant based on observance of the law. In ch. 4 Paul devotes himself to showing that in the Scriptures justification by faith preceded the law, as is clear from the story of Abraham, who was justified by faith (Gen 15:6). God's promise to him and his posterity applies therefore to all who appeal to the faith of Abraham.

Having been justified by faith, we are at peace with God; our trials indeed continue, but we boast of them because they beget hope, which does not deceive (5:1–12) The second half of ch. 5 goes further into the relations between sin, death, the law, and grace, using the antithesis between Adam, through whose disobedience all have become sinners, and Christ, through whose obedience all have been made just (5:12–21).

In ch. 6 Paul rejects a possible malicious interpretation of his thought: we must not conclude that we should remain in sin so that grace may abound. Christian baptism is a sharing in the death of Christ, in which he removed himself from the control of death; but while Christ is already risen, the believer's sharing in his resurrection has not yet come to pass. This "eschatological reservation" is important for avoiding interpretations of Paul's gospel like the one he fought in Corinth, according to which the resurrection of believers has already taken place.

Chapter 7 argues that this sacramental death is also decisive for the relationship of believers to the law. Just as death breaks the matrimonial bond and allows the surviving spouse to marry again, so the believer's death with Christ frees him from subjection to the law and allows him to belong to Christ. On the other hand, Paul insists, the law simply makes sin known: human beings may delight in the law but they are enslaved to the law of sin, which inevitably drives them to evil. In ch. 8 deliverance comes from the Spirit of God, who gives life in Christ.

Chapters 9–11 contain a meditation on the destiny of Israel: If Israel does not accept Christ, does this mean the word of God has failed of its purpose? No, because Israel is made up not of the fleshly descendants of Abraham but of the children of the promise and therefore of all who share the faith of Abraham. According to Gen 21:12, Abraham's posterity comes through Isaac, the son of the promise. Moreover, God has shown his mercy by justifying the pagans, who were not seeking justice, in order to show the error of the Jews, who wanted to achieve righteousness through works. Behind all this, in Paul's view, there is a "mystery" of divine mercy: the hardening of some in Israel has allowed the pagans access to salvation. When all the pagans have entered in, Israel too will be saved.

Chapter 12 begins the hortatory section: Christians are exhorted to offer themselves as living sacrifices. Chapter 13 contains the important exhortation to submit to the authorities whom God has appointed to ensure respect for what is good and to punish evildoers. Paul here conforms to the ethics of his time.

In 14:1–15:13 Paul takes up the question of the "weak," who observe dietary prescriptions and distinguish between days. The reference seems to be to a form of asceticism, but we cannot judge the extent to which this was a real problem in the Roman community. The principle to be followed is the necessity of not scandalizing the brethren.

In 15:14–33, as was said earlier, Paul explains his plans for evangelizing the west. Before carrying them out, however, he must first go to Jerusalem with the collection from Macedonia and Achaia. We know that during this journey Paul was arrested (Acts 21) and would arrive in Rome only as a prisoner (Acts 28).

Chapter 16 contains a commendation of deaconess Phoebe, quite extensive personal greetings, and a final doxology, or glorification of God (16:25–27). Problems of the letter's integrity arise here. On the one hand, this doxology is found at various points of the letter in the manuscripts and ancient versions: in some, after 16:23 (16:24 is an interpolation); in others between 14:33 and 15:1; in still others twice, after 14:23 and 16:23; between 15:33 and 16:1 in $\mathfrak{P}^{46}$, the oldest manuscript of Paul (ca. 200). In old Latin manuscripts, i.e., of the Latin versions of the Bible preceding Jerome's, the doxology comes after 14:23, and chs. 15–16 are lacking. Marcion (ca. 140) likewise lacks the final two chapters. A unique but comparable situation is to be seen in manuscripts which have the doxology after 14:23, because it is meaningful at this point only if, when placed there, it was at the end of the text. On the other hand, some non-Pauline elements suggest that the doxology is not from Paul, but is a later addition. In any case, the version of Romans that ends with ch. 14 is surely secondary, since 15 continues the argument of 14 and therefore belongs to the letter.

Can the same be said of ch. 16? Here a further problem of integrity emerges from internal criticism. It is surprising that Paul should greet so many people in a community with which he is not familiar. Furthermore, many of the individuals mentioned would be far more at home elsewhere than in Rome. We may accept that Priscilla and Aquila (16:3–5) returned to Rome after the death of Claudius, although 2 Tim 4:19 has them still in Ephesus, but we would have to suppose a move to Rome by Epaenetus, the first convert in Asia (16:5), and by many others who had worked with Paul (16:8–9). In addition, the attack in 16:17–20 on those who cause divisions and have departed from the teaching they have received does not seem attuned to the tone of the rest of the letter. On the other hand, ch. 16 is surely Pauline. It has therefore been suggested that Romans originally ended with 15:33 and that ch. 16 represents either the conclusion of another letter that was added when the letter was published, or an appendix added by Paul himself in a copy of Romans that was sent to Ephesus.

Manuscript $\mathfrak{P}^{46}$ would seem to support this last hypothesis; it has ch. 16 but also has the doxology at the end of 15, thus presupposing a text of Romans that ended with ch. 15. But this solution is likewise not without its problem: Rom 16 has all the characteristics of the endings of Paul's letters and to that extent it is a valid continuation of ch. 15. Furthermore, precisely because Paul was not known personally in Rome, it was in his interest to display friendly relations with many individuals in that community who could recommend him; it is a fact that in no other letter are personal greetings so extensive. Nevertheless, it requires some effort to imagine all the Christians greeted having moved to Rome. This problem remains unsolved.

Bibliography

Texts

The critical edition to be used for all the New Testament writings is *Novum Testamentum Graece*, 27th ed. (ed. B. and K. Aland, J. Karavidopoulos, C. M. Martini, B. M. Metzger; Stuttgart: Deutsche Bibelgesellschaft, 1993). It is cited as Nestle-Aland[27].

Commentaries and Studies

The literature is endless. The major commentary series (HNT, KEK, HTKNT, EKKNT, ÖTK, CSANT, CNT, etc.) contain excellent commentaries on the various letters, as well as huge bibliographies.

Almost all the monographs listed earlier (bibliography, sec. 2) contain expositions of Paul's writings and thought.

I mention here only one commentary in Italian that is useful for a first approach: G. Barbaglio and R. Fabris, *Le lettere di Paolo* (3 vols.; Rome: Borla, 1980).

ANRW II 25.4 (1987) is entirely devoted to the Pauline corpus (problems and state of research).

B. Witherington, *The Paul Quest: The Renewed Search for the Jew of Tarsus* (Downers Grove, Ill.: InterVarsity, 1998).

4. Pseudepigraphical Letters

Scholars today like to speak of a Pauline school that would have arisen during the apostle's lifetime out of his relations with his fellow workers. In the communities that Paul founded and that were the recipients of his letters, and in others that came to know these communities through exchange of the letters, reflection on his message continued and was adapted to new situations and cultural stimuli of various kinds. In the philosophical schools thinkers used to develop the thought of the founder, and it was customary to circulate new works under that founder's name, inasmuch as these were regarded as faithfully continuing and applying his thought. Hans Conzelmann has suggested seeing Ephesus as an important center of Pauline tradition, this being continued by a school in the full sense of the word, one modeled on those in which the sapiential traditions of Judaism were developed. It is undoubtedly to circles that wanted to remain faithful to Paul's message while rethinking it in light of new needs, that we owe a pseudo-Pauline epistolary, much of which entered the canon. Consensus on the pseudepigraphical nature of the letters now to be discussed varies: the authenticity of some of them is still defended, but in practice no serious study of Paul's personal thought would regard itself as authorized to draw on them.

a. Second Letter to the Thessalonians

This was the first to be doubted in the modern era (1801) and remains the one most debated. Let us look first at its content; as in 1 Thessalonians the main subject is instruction about the final days.

Paul takes a position (2:1–12) against those who, on the basis of a letter falsely attributed to him, claim that the Day of the Lord is imminent. Not so, for the signs preceding that Day are not yet visible. From a motif extensively developed in the Jewish apocalyptic tradition the author draws the idea of an expected apostasy, that is, a general state of corruption; this will be climaxed by the manifestation of the "man of lawlessness," who will set himself up in the temple and proclaim himself God. This personage, who will become the antichrist of Christian tradition, is one of the forms taken by the eschatological enemy of God, who has already been actualized numerous times in the Jewish tradition through identification with individuals responsible for terrible actions against the religion of Israel, especially the desecration of the temple—such men as Antiochus IV Epiphanes, Pompey, and Caligula. According to 2 Thessalonians this adversary, a vague figure of the future, does not yet show himself because of "that which" (2:6; "him who," in 2:7) "is holding him back." The addressees of the letter, unlike readers today, had evidently received an instruction on the subject.

Chapter 2:13–17 is a new thanksgiving to God for the Thessalonians and includes an exhortation to hold to the traditions taught by Paul; 3:6 repeats the exhortation to take as a norm the tradition (this time in the singular) received from Paul.

Chapter 3:1–15 is a warning to members of the community who are living disorderly lives and refusing to work, evidently being convinced of the imminent coming of Christ. Chapter 3:16–17 contains the greeting; verse 17 emphasizes the autograph signature, meant to guarantee the authenticity of all of Paul's letters.

As in 1 Thessalonians, the senders of the letters are Paul, Silas (Silvanus), and Timothy. Since Silas disappeared from Paul's circle during the (first) stay in Corinth, 2 Thessalonians would have to be dated before that event and therefore very close in time to 1 Thessalonians. This fact already raises a difficulty: Paul would have sent to the one community, within a short time, two letters with contrary purposes, since in 1 Thess 4:13–5:11 he emphasizes the imminence and suddenness of the Parousia, while in 2 Thessalonians the idea that the Parousia is imminent is called illogical, and the emphasis is on the lack of the warning signs. Moreover, in 2 Thessalonians, section 2:1–12 on the warning signs has no parallel in 1 Thessalonians, although the remainder of the letter shows numerous contacts with the first letter, and the structure is on the whole analogous.

If we add the emphasis on "command" *(parangellō)* (3:4, 6, 10, 12; elsewhere only three times in Paul), on the need to cling to the Pauline "tradition" (2:15; 3:6), and on Paul as a "model" for Christians who work (3:9; Paul's motivation here is quite different from 1 Thess 2:9; 1 Cor 9:15, 18; 2 Cor 12:14!), it is difficult to avoid the conclusion that the author had used the model provided by Paul's eschatological instruction in 1 Thessalonians in order to persuade the churches linked to the apostle's authority to accept a version of Pauline thought that was adapted to the times. In fact, the allusion in 2:15 to a previous letter of Paul to which they must remain faithful is an allusion to 1 Thessalonians, as can be seen from 2:1, which alludes to 1 Thess 4:17. But 2:1 and 2:15 frame a new instruction on the signs of the Parousia!

The setting, then, is one of conflict over the Pauline heritage. Even those whom the author opposes appeal to the authority of the apostle (and have perhaps already written a forged letter of their own: 2:2) and regard themselves as faithful to it precisely by maintaining the expectation of an imminent Parousia. The author of 2 Thessalonians sees the Parousia as delayed, and consequently an orderly community meant to last must be organized. He is worried about the consequences, in the form of social disorder, that the attitude of those individuals might cause. He claims for his position the authority of Paul and presents his own viewpoint as continuous with the tradition passed on by the apostle.

The author and addressees were living, then, in the area covered by the Pauline mission, but the address to the Thessalonians may be a literary fiction resulting from the adoption of 1 Thessalonians as a framework. The period of the composition is likewise uncertain: the mention of Paul's autographed greetings, which are meant to guarantee the authenticity of the letter (3:17), seems to suppose that the originals of Paul's letters no longer existed (they would allow verification of the claim) and suggests the 80s as the time of composition.

b. Letter to the Colossians

Colossae in Phrygia, in the valley of the Lycus, was close to Laodicea and Hierapolis, which in Paul's time had surpassed it in importance. The Christian communities of these three cities had not been founded by Paul (Col 2:1; 4:13) but by his fellow workers, probably by Epaphras (1:7).

Chapter 1 continues the introduction (9–20): Paul prays for the Colossians and exhorts them to thank God, whose intervention is described in language proper to a confession of faith (1:13–14). This leads in turn into a hymn to Christ (1:15–20), which is generally taken to be a citation, with changes, of a preexisting hymn on the role of Christ in creation and redemption. In the original hymn, the body must have been the universe; in Colossians it becomes the church. The Colossians are now reconciled with God thanks to the body of the Son, but they must continue steadfast in the faith and not let themselves be drawn away from the gospel of which Paul is the suffering minister (1:24–2:5).

In 2:6–15 the Colossians are exhorted to continue their journey in Christ without letting themselves be ensnared by philosophy. The meaning of baptism is recalled: believers have died with Christ and have been raised with him. As for the heavenly powers, they have been dragged along in the triumphal procession of the cross. Chapter 2:16–23 is an attack on adversaries who seek to deceive the Colossians. Much of what is said about them consists of commonplaces: they require dietary observances (2:16a) and in particular abstention from certain foods, an ascetic way of life (2:21), and the observance of special days (2:16b). Verse 2:18 alludes to veneration of the heavenly powers and to visions, which were probably received on the occasion of initiations *(embateuō)*. The adversaries probably thought of the world as subject to angelic powers or "basic principles of this world," and of asceticism as needed in order to evade their power. Against them the author argues that Christ is the mediator of creation, even the creation of the powers (1:16), and that by his cross he has reduced their power to nothing (2:10, 15). Through baptism believers have died and risen with Christ and have therefore been removed from the control that the powers exercise through their commands (2:20–21).

Chapters 3 and 4 contain the parenesis. The author exhorts his readers to Christian freedom and fidelity to Christ, while they keep their gaze fixed on heaven (3:1–14). He also gives a catalogue of vices to be avoided and virtues to be "put on" (3:12, 14). Next comes a "domestic code" (3:18–4:1), that is, instructions for the various groups in the community (see Eph 5:22–6:9; 1 Pet 2:18–3:7). Then follow exhortations to prayer and the proper attitude to non-Christians (4:2–6). Chapter 4:7–18 contains personal communications. Many of the names mentioned here are also in Philemon: Onesimus, Aristarchus, Mark, Luke, and Demas.

In this letter Pauline Christology and soteriology take a new direction that was certainly called for by the syncretism of the writer's adversaries, according to whom the cosmic forces retain power over believers. The latter must rescue themselves by an asceticism that leads them to the acquisition of "wisdom" (2:8, 23). Countering this view, the letter emphasizes the cosmic primacy of Christ, mediator of the same creation to which the powers belong, and destroyer of their power through his cross. Thus the Pauline theme of the church (the local community) as body of Christ, of which the head is a member like the others (1 Cor 12:12–27; Rom 12:4–5), is repeated here, but the church is now the universal church, and Christ is its head. He becomes, as it were, the space within which believers are protected, and the vertical dimension (Christ the head in heaven) is emphasized by comparison with the horizontal (relations among Christians) which is dominant in Paul. Thus the reason for hope is sought not in the future but "in heaven" (1:5). Especially important is the modification of the understanding of baptism. The author derives his inspiration from Rom 6:1–11, but whereas in Romans believers have been buried with Christ and will rise (future) with him (6:4–5, 8), according to Colossians they are already risen (2:12–13; 3:1). It is, in addition, this resurrection already accomplished that grounds ethics, allowing believers to "set your hearts on things above" (3:1).

In such a setting, Paul the apostle has a central function, that of making it possible, through suffering and imprisonment, to bring about the mystery of God, that is, Christ, among the pagans (1:23–2:3).

The shift in theological perspective and the emphasis on Paul as exclusive mediator of salvation, along with a style different from that of the authentic letters, lead us to deny Paul the authorship of Colossians (the apostle's situation as a prisoner—4:3, 10, 18—is part of the image of the apostle that the letter is meant to convey). But the themes developed are directly connected with those central to Paul. The author of Colossians is still very close to Paul and was perhaps his immediate disciple. He has chosen as a setting for Colossians the same one that is presupposed in Philemon. The influence of Romans is also considerable. But it is impossible to specify the real place of origin of the letter.

c. Letter to the Ephesians

There is reason to ask to whom this letter was originally addressed. Paul stayed in Ephesus for a long time, and yet Eph 1:5; 3:2 give the impression that he is not known personally to the addressees. Moreover, in the *adscriptio* (1:1) the words "in Ephesus" are missing in the earliest manuscripts. Around 140 Marcion regarded the work as a letter to Laodicea. It has been suggested that Ephesians was a circular letter sent to several communities, with the name of each inscribed on a separate copy, but we know of no comparable procedures in antiquity.

According to 3:1; 4:1, Paul is in prison. There are two introductions, 1:3–14 and 1:15–23. The first is a hymn to God who has chosen believers before the foundation of the world, that they might become his adoptive children in Christ. The second is a prayer that the Ephesians may realize the hope that has been opened to them by the call they have received, and the power that has been exerted for them in Christ. As a matter of fact (2:1–10) believers were formerly subject to the ruler of the powers in the air and were objects of wrath, but God has made them live with Christ through grace and by faith. In 2:11–22, Christ has torn down the barrier that used to separate the two peoples, Jews and pagans. He has made them one and given them free access to God. In 3:1–13, the apostle has received through revelation a knowledge of the mystery that was hidden from eternity and through which the pagans are admitted to the same inheritance as the Jews.

Chapters 4–6 contain the parenesis. Verses 4:1–16 are an exhortation to unity amid the diversity of gifts received, for the sake of building up the body of Christ. Verses 4:17–5:50 exhort the addressees to leave behind the old self and put on the new, which is created in the likeness of God. There follows a "domestic code" (5:21–6:9), comparable to that in Col 3:18–4:1. Exhortations to put on the armor of God for the struggle against the forces of evil (6:10–20) are followed by final greetings (6:21–24).

The extensive contacts between Ephesians and Colossians give rise to a literary problem. Use of the same material does not explain the identical words in the opening (Eph 1:1/Col 1:1) and in the final greetings (Eph 6:21–22/Col 4:7–8). We might think that Paul was writing the two letters at the same time. In some cases, however, the same terminology expresses different ideas. Thus in Colossians 2:10, 19 the body of which Christ is the head is the universe; Ephesians 4:16 uses almost the same words to speak of the body, which is the community. An author would hardly give different meaning to the same words and phrases in two letters close in time. It is therefore likely that Colossians was written earlier, and was later used by the author of Ephesians. This simple hypothesis takes into account the shift from a letter concerned with the concrete problems of a community, as in Colossians, to one such as Ephesians, which does not seem linked to specific circumstances. In this case, and independently of the authenticity of Colossians, Ephesians cannot be regarded as Pauline.

It is precisely when Ephesians uses expressions typical of Paul, such as grace and faith (Eph 2:1–10), that we become aware that the theme of justification has disappeared and has been replaced by salvation and the forgiveness of sins (1:7), an expression unknown to Paul. Ephesians emphasizes salvation already accomplished (6:2). This salvation is made visible in the church, which coincides in its extension with the body of Christ that embraces the universe (1:22–23). In ecclesiology, the hierarchy becomes important: the church is founded not on Christ, as in 1 Cor 13:11, but on the apostles and prophets (2:20). According to 3:5, the latter are the recipients of the revealed mystery, rather than all believers through the mediation of Paul, as in Col 1:25–26. This last thought does appear in Ephesians 3:3–5 but it is restricted precisely by the emphasis put on the apostles and prophets. On the other hand, Ephesians, unlike Colossians, restores the motif of mutual service among believers, the members of Christ's body (4:25; 5:30).

The theology of Ephesians, like that of Colossians, is an extension of Paulinism to problems raised by a view of salvation that was widespread in the Hellenistic world. In this view, the lower realm of the cosmos, where human beings dwell, is controlled by wicked powers of the firmament and the air (2:2; 4:9–10), and salvation consists in escaping this control. The membership of believers in the church incorporates them into a body whose head, Christ, is in heaven; he provides the "armor" that gives protection against the powers (6:10–17). Paul had seen Christ, Adam's opposite, as the second, spiritual man who comes from heaven and is the author of life (1 Cor 15:45–49). In Ephesians this conception is connected with that of the church as the body of Christ (1 Cor 12:12–27) in order to develop the image of the universal church as the body of Christ that unites earth with heaven. An analogous image may be seen in gnostic speculations of the second century, in which the saved belong to a divine figure, the Heavenly Man. This image, however, implies an element essential to gnosticism but lacking in Ephesians: this church/body of the Heavenly Man was originally a part of God that fell into this lower world. The Savior came seeking it out in order to reincorporate it into the divine plenitude, the Pleroma. The word "pleroma" is already a distinguishing mark of Ephesians, where it signifies the divine fullness resident in the church (1:23; 3:9; 4:13). In Col 1:19; 2:9 this fullness resides in Christ, not in the church.

The author suggests a situation in Paul's life that is close to that of the Colossians, but the real historical setting of Ephesians is difficult to identify. We are probably dealing here with the development of the Pauline tradition in western Asia Minor perhaps (Ephesus?). The date may be the end of the first century.

d. Pastoral Letters: 1 and 2 Timothy, Titus

These three letters, which are fairly similar, are the only ones in the Pauline corpus that are addressed to individuals (on Phlm see above, sec. 3f), but Timothy and Titus represent model heads of churches. In writing to them, "Paul" gives instructions for pastors; hence the name "pastoral" usually given to the letters.

On 1 Timothy: Paul has instructed Timothy to remain in Ephesus to carry on the fight against people who teach "alien doctrines" (1:3–20). Paul, foremost of the sinners saved by Christ, is proposed as a model for those who obtain divine mercy. Chapters 2 and 3 contain community regulations on prayer for all human beings and especially those in authority, on modesty in female dress, and on the behavior of bishop and deacons. This section ends with a christological hymn (v. 16). Chapter 4 again takes up the attack on adversaries and exhorts Timothy to be a model for believers, despite his youth. Chapters 5:1–6:2 contain standards of behavior for widows who are in the care of the community, and rules for presbyters and slaves. Verses 6:3–10 attack false teachers and those whom love of money has estranged from the faith. As for Timothy himself, he must "fight the good fight of the faith" (6:11–16). At the end the rich are urged to do good (6:17–19). The final, very short greeting is preceded by an urgent appeal to guard the treasure entrusted to him and avoid contrary ideas of "what is falsely called knowledge."

In the opening of 2 Timothy Paul exhorts Timothy to bear witness to the faith for which Paul is now a prisoner, and to "guard the good deposit" entrusted to him. Timothy is to pass on Paul's teaching, accept suffering after the apostle's example, and not deny Christ (2:1–13). The central part of the letter (2:14–3:13) is taken up with an attack on the authors of empty and wicked discourses. Among the anticipated evils of the last times are enemies who make their way into homes and bewitch silly women. Timothy must instead hold fast to the Scriptures, which are inspired by God and useful for teaching and correcting. He must also proclaim the word in order to offset the tendency of human beings to turn to myths (3:14–4:5). Paul, for his part, is now at the end of his life and drawing near to his reward (4:6–9). Timothy is to come to him as soon as possible, since everyone but Luke has deserted him. But the Lord is at his side (4:9–18).

In Titus, Paul describes himself as an apostle "for the faith of God's elect and the knowledge of the truth that leads to godliness" (1:1–4). He reminds Titus that he left him in Crete in order to complete the organization of the church there. He then sketches a picture of a good presbyter and a good bishop, emphasizing attachment to "the trustworthy message as it has been taught" (1:5–10). At this point an attack is made on adversaries (1:10–16), followed by instructions of the "domestic code" type (2:1–10) to older persons, the young, and slaves. Proper behavior has its basis in the manifestation of God's grace in Christ (2:11–15). Generally speaking, the faithful should be subject to authority, and their relations with one another should be marked by consideration. After all, in the past they had been rebellious and gone astray, but God saved them in his mercy (3:1–8). They must avoid "foolish controversies and genealogies and arguments and quarrels about the law," and have nothing to do with any "divisive person" *(hairetikos;* 3:9–11).

Timothy was a faithful fellow worker of Paul, at least beginning with the "second missionary journey." In Acts 16:1, Timothy is described as a native of Lystra in Galatia, son of a Greek father and a Jewish mother who had converted to Christianity. He was dear to the apostle who had converted him (1 Cor 4:17) and entrusted him with sensitive missions in Thessalonica (1 Thess 3:2–3), Corinth (1 Cor 4:17; 16:10–11), and Philippi (Phil 2:19, 23). He appears as a joint sender of letters in 1 Thessalonians, 2 Corinthians, Philippians, and Philemon (see Rom 16:21). First Timothy claims to belong to one phase of this collaboration, when Paul went from Ephesus to Macedonia and left Timothy behind (1:3). But this does not agree with Acts 19:22, according to which Paul sent Timothy on ahead to Macedonia with the intention of rejoining him later from Ephesus. The circumstances of 1 Timothy do not correspond to what we know of Paul's biography, nor is it clear why Paul needed to give elementary instructions to so seasoned a collaborator as Timothy, especially since he intends to return quickly to Ephesus (3:14).

The situation in 2 Timothy likewise raises questions: Paul is in prison in Rome (1:17) and has left Trophimus in Miletus, but according to Acts 21:19 the latter accompanied Paul as far as Jerusalem. The situation in Titus is no less problematic. Titus, a Christian of pagan origin (Gal 2:3; Acts says nothing of Titus), was one of Paul's most trusted collaborators. He had accompanied Paul to the "apostolic council" (Gal 2:1) and played a decisive part in resolving the crisis mentioned in 2 Corinthians (see above, sec. 3c). According to Titus, Paul left Titus in Crete, but no New Testament source mentions any missionary activity of Paul in Crete or a winter spent in Nicopolis (3:12). It has been suggested that the Pastoral Epistles refer to Paul's activity after being released from the Roman imprisonment at the end of Acts; but in that case he would have returned to the east, contrary to the intentions expressed in Romans and to Acts (20:25; 21:10), according to which Paul would not work in that area again.

To these difficulties is added a vocabulary close to that of Hellenistic theology but pretty much foreign to the authentic letters of Paul: God as *sōtēr* (1 Tim 1:1; 2:3; 4:10; Tit 1:3; 2:10; 3:4; never in Paul); Christ as *sōtēr* (2 Tim 1:10; Tit 1:4; 2:13; 3:6; in Paul only in Phil 3:20, which may be pre-Pauline); God as *despotēs* (2 Tim 2:21; Tit 2:9; never in Paul); God as *dynastēs* (1 Tim 6:15; never in Paul). The Pastoral Epistles set great importance on sound teaching (*hē hygiainousē didaskalia:* 1 Tim 1:10; 2 Tim 4:3; Tit 1:9; 2:1), sound words (1 Tim 6:3; 2 Tim 1:13), sound discourse (Tit 2:8), and being sound in the faith (Tit 1:13; 2:2)—all of this being terminology unknown to Paul. They urge a teaching, *didaskalia,* understood as a body of thought received through Paul (in addition to the four passages cited, see 1 Tim 4:6, 13, 16; 5:17; 6:1, 3; 2 Tim 3:10, 16; Tit 2:7, 10), while Paul uses the word only in Romans (12:7; 15:4), and in a different sense. The attachment to doctrine finds a practical embodiment in "godliness," *eusebeia* (1 Tim 2:2; 3:16; 4:7, 8; 6:3 *hē kat'eusebeian didaskalia;* 6:5, 6, 11; 2 Tim 3:5; Tit 1:1), which is absent in Paul (see 1 Tim 5:4; 2 Tim 3:12; Tit 2:12).

In the letters to Timothy and Titus the law is good, as in Rom 7:12, 16, but in Romans the power of sin prevents the observance of the law. Quite differently in 1 Tim 1:8–11, the law serves precisely to avoid evil and urge to the good, so that it is of no use to those already just. Given this approach, political loyalty is understandable (2 Tim 2:1–8). It comes from the ethics of Hellenistic Judaism and is already found in Rom 13:1–7, but in 1 Timothy the emphasis is on the idea that peace promotes *eusebeia* and the Christian mission. The Pastoral Epistles show a church conscious of its visibility and anxious to gain credibility by reassuring those who think Christians are subversive or immoral (see 1 Tim 3:7). The return of Christ is not on the horizon, and the Christian community is settling down in the world for an indefinite duration.

This outlook also implies a dissociation from Christian tendencies that are potentially contrary to good order within the community and outside it. In the three letters, the attack on false teachers occupies a key place: in the beginning, middle, and end of 1 Timothy; in the middle of 2 Timothy; in the middle and end of Titus. The identification of these adversaries has given rise to endless debates. Some names of individuals appear, but they are unknown to us. They seem to claim a special knowledge of God (1 Tim 6:20; Tit 1:15). They claim to be teachers of the law (1 Tim 1:7), and they defend Jewish myths (Tit 1:14; 1 Tim 1:4; 2 Tim 4:4), legends, and endless genealogies (1 Tim 1:4). These adversaries probably based their teaching on an exegesis of Scripture. First Timothy points to their ascetic outlook, with its rejection of marriage and certain foods (4:3); these tendencies are attacked (1 Tim 2:15; 5:14, 23; Titus 1:15; 2:4). The rejection of marriage may have been connected with an emancipation of women since the teachers were successful among women (2 Tim 3:6).

This doubtless accounts for the massive effort of the Pastoral Epistles to keep women in a condition of subjection. One passage, 1 Tim 2:11–14, orders women to be silent during instruction, in open contradiction to 1 Cor 11:5, which expects women to prophesy during the liturgy. Romans 16 and other passages of Paul show women holding positions of importance in the community; the Pastoral Epistles urge them to return to the silence and submissiveness of family life. This is justified from the Old Testament (1 Tim 2:13–15), probably in order to silence the arguments of the adversaries. Widows, that is, women not subject to the oversight of a father or a husband, seem especially to worry the author (5:3–16). The effort to bring about and show forth an "orderly" Christian community has led to the imposition of a model of family organization that was thought to function properly when hierarchies were respected; 1 Tim 3:5 and 15 make this assimilation perfectly clear. The same line is followed in regulations not only for women but for the elderly and the young (Tit 2:2–8) and for slaves who ought to render their masters even better service if they are Christians (1 Tim 6:1–2; Tit 2:9–10)!

Paul is the model of one who sinned through ignorance but was touched by divine mercy and is held up as an example for the adversaries if they will only repent (1 Tim 1:12–16). This picture of the pre-Christian Paul as a blasphemer and sinner is quite different from the picture the apostle gives of himself in Gal 1:14 and especially in Phil 3:6, where he says that he was faultless in his observance of the law. But Paul serves at the same time as a model of struggle and suffering for the ecclesiastical authorities, represented by Timothy and Titus, who struggle against adversaries. This is a central motif, especially in 2 Timothy, which shows the influence of the "farewell discourse" genre, that is, a testament, uttered as death is imminent, in which the life of the individual becomes a "mirror" for the listeners.

The Pastoral Epistles are located therefore in a line of Pauline tradition that is different from that of Ephesians and Colossians. They are much less concerned with theology and aim above all at managing the apostle's legacy, controlling "destabilizing" tendencies by means of a consolidated ecclesiastical hierarchy based on the bishops (1 Tim 3:1–7; Tit 1:7–9), presbyters (1 Tim 5:17–19; Tit 1:5–6), and deacons (1 Tim 3:8–13) and by holding fast to socially approved hierarchical relationships. Instead of engaging in foolish controversies, the community should accept the tradition of the church, which the bishop is to communicate and safeguard. Hans von Campenhausen has shown how close the language and content of the Pastoral Epistles are to Polycarp of Smyrna; the two must be close to each other chronologically and geographically. The Pastorals can be located in Asia Minor (Ephesus?) in the first decades of the second century.

Bibliography

For individual writings, see the bibliography for sec. 3.

On the Pauline School: H. Conzelmann, "Die Schule des Paulus," in *Theologia crucis—Signum Crucis: Festschrift E. Dinkler* (Tübingen: Mohr, 1979), 85–96.

E. Dassmann, *Der Stachel im Fleisch: Paulus in der frühchristlichen Literatur bis Irenäus* (Münster: Aschendorff, 1979).

K. Kertelge, ed., *Paulus in den neutestamentlichen Spätschriften* (Freiburg: Herder, 1981).

M. Barth, "Traditions in Ephesians," *NTS* 30 (1984), 3–25.

P. Müller, *Anfänge der Paulusschule: Dargestellt am zweiten Thessalonicherbrief und am Kolosserbrief* (Zurich: Theologischer Verlag, 1988).

Y. Redalié, *Paul après Paul* (Geneva: Labor et Fides, 1994).

e. Third Letter to the Corinthians

In several languages and in two versions, of which the longer is certainly secondary, there is a letter of the Corinthians to Paul, in which Stephen (see 1 Cor 6:15) and "the presbyters with him" ask Paul to censure the doctrine preached by two missionaries, Simon and Cleobius, who have come to Corinth. An answer from Paul condemns this preaching. This correspondence, with a short introduction and a narrative passage connecting the two letters, is found together with the *Acts of Paul* in the Coptic version (Heidelberg papyrus); it has also been handed down separately with the connecting passage in Armenian and Latin, as well as in the commentary of Ephraem the Syrian on the letters of Paul. Its presence in Ephraem fact proves that in the fourth century the correspondence was part of the Syrian New Testament canon. The two letters, without any narrative framework, are found in other Latin manuscripts and, more important, in the original language (Greek) and, in what is surely the oldest form, in a papyrus of the Bibliotheca Bodmeriana of Cologny (Geneva). The publication in 1959 of this manuscript, which attests to the circulation of the separate letters in the third century, has undermined the earlier accepted view that the correspondence was composed as an integral part of the *Acts of Paul* near the end of the second century and was only later separated from this document. It now seems rather that the correspondence was originally independent. Therefore, although the letters were never in the canon, they are to be placed among the pseudepigraphical letters of Paul.

According to the letter of the Corinthians, Simon and Cleobius preach that no use is to be made of the prophets, that God is not the Omnipotent One (*pantokratōr:* this probably means that the supreme God is not to be identified with the creator, YHWH Sabaoth, because *pantokratōr* translates Sabaoth in the Septuagint), that there is no resurrection of the flesh, that human beings were not formed by God, that the Lord did not come in the flesh nor was born of Mary, and that the world belongs not to God but to the angels. As W. Rordorf has shown, this doctrine shows close affinities with that of Saturninus (or Saturnilus), one of the first gnostics, who was active in Syria in the first decades of the second century, as described by Irenaeus of Lyons (*Haer.* 1.24.1–2).

The letter is rich, especially at the beginning and the end, in echoes of various Pauline letters, which the author was therefore familiar with. He explains the rule of faith, which he himself had received: Christ was born of Mary in the line of David, "a holy spirit having been sent into her from heaven by the Father" (5), in order to set all flesh free through his own flesh and to raise up the dead in their flesh. Human beings were formed by God. The God of the universe, the Almighty, who made heaven and earth, sent the prophets to the Jews after bestowing on them a share in the spirit of Christ, but the devil, who wanted to pass himself off as God, killed them. Then God "sent down a spirit in the form of fire on Mary in Galilee" (13), namely, Christ, who through his own body saved all flesh. The second part treats (24–32) the resurrection of the flesh, proving it by biblical examples; this development seems to come from the Jewish tradition.

The resurrection of the flesh *(sarx)* is indeed not found in Paul, but it is current in Christian texts beginning in the first decades of the second century. Echoes of Pauline theology appear in the letter. In particular, what is said of the sending of the Son (6) is inspired by Rom 8. But the Pauline elements have lost their unifying center, namely, the themes of justification through faith and of the law, and have been reorganized in the service of a polemic, alien to Paul, against the denial of Christ's human reality and of the value of the material creation.

Many verses of this antidocetist polemic, along with the emphasis on the ecclesiastical hierarchy, headed by the bishop, opposing erroneous teaching, remind one of Ignatius of Antioch and seems to fit well into the same development of "orthodoxy" within which Ignatius retrieves Pauline motifs. As W. Rordorf says, this composition is to be dated to the first half of the second century and to be located in Asia Minor or, as seems preferable, in western Syria, the homeland of Saturninus and Ignatius.

It will be enough to mention here a letter to the Laodiceans, the idea for which came from the mention in Col 4:16 of a letter to the church of Laodicea. The work is a theologically unimportant cento of Pauline phrases. It is perhaps the same document referred to in the *Muratorian Canon,* which regards it as a Marcionite forgery. In that case, the date of the canon, presumably around 200, would be the *terminus ante quem.* The attempt of A. von Harnack and G. Quispel to prove its Marcionite character has not been accepted.

BIBLIOGRAPHY

W. Rordorf, "Hérésie et orthodoxie selon la correspondance apocryphe entre les Corinthiens et l'apôtre Paul," in H.-D. Altendorf et al., *Orthodoxie et hérésie dans l'Eglise ancienne: Perspectives nouvelles* (Cahiers de la Revue de théologie et de philosophie; Lausanne: Cahiers de la Revue de théologie et de philosophie, 1993): 21–63.

———. "Letter to the Laodiceans," *New Testament Apocrypha* II (ed. W. Schneemelcher; Louisville: Westminster John Knox, 1992), 42–46.

Chapter 2

THE GOSPEL TRADITION

In this chapter we shall discuss the transmission or tradition of the sayings and deeds of the man Jesus, while distinguishing this tradition from that of the dialogues of the risen Lord with his disciples (see ch. 8). The units belonging to this tradition—and the longer texts that assemble and develop these units—were formed and passed on after the death of Jesus and after the experience described by his followers as his resurrection. It is essential to note, however, that the risen Lord was seen as in continuity with the earthly Jesus, whose life was now reinterpreted as a manifestation, even if a limited one, of his divine nature. Some gospels restrict themselves to the sayings of Jesus and leave aside the death and resurrection; these, therefore, consider his words decisive for the salvation of believers. This is the case with the "sayings source" and the *Gospel of Thomas*. Others, however, at least from what we know of them, focus on the story of the passion, death, and resurrection; the *Gospel of Peter* is an example. Still others, such as the so-called Jewish-Christian gospels, show a structure similar to that of the canonical gospels.

From this perspective, there is no reason to deal with the canonical gospels separately from the apocryphal gospels; the distinction is one that was made after their composition and not for historical or literary but for dogmatic reasons. From the very beginning of the Christian mission, which the tradition connected directly with the appearances of the risen Lord (Matt 28:19; Mark 16:16; Luke 24:47; Acts 1:8; for Paul, Gal 1:15–16) there existed lines of transmission of the sayings of Jesus and events of his life. These lines quickly diverged, because the units of tradition were chosen and developed as a function of the ways various groups of believers and missionaries understood the meaning of the person of Jesus and the specific identity of his disciples.

Thus the sayings connected with the social marginalization of the Son of Man and his followers were conveyed by itinerant preachers in the rural world of Palestine, men who had cut their familial and institutional ties, and saw in Jesus the Son of Man who was rejected and persecuted but was destined to return as judge. They saw in him the exemplar of their own condition, rejected in the eyes of men but sure of God's promised recompense. But this same patrimony of tradition was rethought and altered where material conditions differed, for example, in urban communities. A study of the gospel literature at the beginnings of Christianity must examine the way the tradition gradually took shape in different texts. In the second half of the second century some of these texts prevailed as the only gospels going back to the "authentic" testimony of the apostles. Yet the papyrus fragments of gospels that have been preserved from that century and the beginning of the third have come in equal measure from books that would later become canonical and from those destined to become apocrypha. Gospel citations and allusions by Christian authors until after the middle of the second century yield a similar finding.

BIBLIOGRAPHY

E. Lohse, *The First Christians: Their Beginnings, Writings, and Beliefs* (Philadelphia: Fortress, 1983).
H. Koester and F. Bovon, *Genèse de l'écriture chrétienne* (Turnhout: Brepols, 1991).

1. The Literary Problem of the Synoptic Gospels: Two-Source Theory

The problem raised by the literary composition of the gospels and therefore also of the materials on which they are based became the subject of scholarly inquiry beginning in the second half of the eighteenth century, emerging from debates over the historical trustworthiness of the canonical gospels and their picture of Jesus. H. Reimarus, an orientalist and naturalist of Hamburg, composed a lengthy critical work, which he left unpublished, on the Old and New Testaments: *Apologie oder Schutzschrift für die vernünftigen Verehrer Gottes*. It was not published in its entirely until 1972, but G. E. Lessing, a philosopher and theologian, had some parts of the manuscript published between 1774 and 1778 as an anonymous, posthumous work. One of these parts, *The Intentions of Jesus and His Disciples* (1778), contrasted the intentions of Jesus to those of his disciples, who, according to Reimarus, gave a completely distorted picture of Jesus in the gospels. In the debate that followed, an effort was made to determine the value of the gospels as a historical source.

The ancient ecclesiastical tradition, for its part, linked the canonical gospels either with immediate disciples of Jesus (Matthew, John) or with followers of the apostles, authors who were thought to have put in writing the testimony of these apostles. Thus at the beginning of the second century Papias of Hierapolis stated that Mark, acting as interpreter of Peter, had published the preaching of Peter on the sayings and deeds of the Lord without following any particular order, but nonetheless correctly and completely. Papias based his remarks on the word of a presbyter, that is, one who carried on apostolic tradition. He also said that Matthew "recorded the sayings in Hebrew, and each individual interpreted them as best he was able" (Eusebius, *Hist. eccl.* 3.39.15–16).

Around 180 Irenaeus of Lyons was familiar with traditions concerning the composition of all four gospels. He summed them up this way:

> Among the Jews, Matthew published a gospel written in their own tongue, while Peter and Paul were preaching the gospel in Rome and founding the church there; after their death, Mark, a disciple and interpreter of Peter, likewise transmitted in writing the content of Peter's preaching. Next, Luke, a companion of Paul, set down in a book the gospel preached by the latter. Then John, the disciple of the Lord, the one who had leaned on his breast, likewise published a gospel while he was living at Ephesus in Asia. (*Haer.* 3.1.1)

When the gospels were thus traced back to four different testimonies concerning the life of Christ, their agreements seemed natural, and their contradictions constituted a limited problem, which was explained in various ways. Augustine, in his *Agreement among the Evangelists* (ca. 400), produced the first outline of a theory of literary dependence among the Synoptic Gospels: he claimed that Mark was an extract from Matthew and that Luke was written after these two.

When, as already noted, early historical critics of the origins of Christianity challenged the idea that the gospel narratives were simply faithful to the deeds and sayings of Jesus, they tried in various ways to explain the Synoptic Problem. This problem arose, on the one hand, from observing that there were close affinities among the Gospels of Matthew, Mark, and Luke, not only in their overall organization but in many details, to the point of verbal identity in the telling of stories. This was something impossible to imagine even on the assumption that the narrators were eyewitnesses, and was explicable only in terms of a literary relationship between the texts. On the other hand, there are differences both in the location of episodes and in their content. G. Lessing (1776) suggested a separate dependence of each of the three evangelists on an original gospel (the *Gospel of the Nazareans* mentioned by Jerome), written in Hebrew or Aramaic. J. Eichhorn (1804) developed this hypothesis by supposing the dependence of the evangelists on three different forms of that gospel, as well as on other sources peculiar to each of them. J. Herder (1896–1897) and J. C. L. Gieseler (1818) suggested instead a dependence on an oral tradition that had already taken solid form. With Luke alone in mind, F. D. E. Schleiermacher (1817) postulated that the evangelists used many short written documents that were circulating independently.

Taking a different tack, others suggested a mutual dependence among the three Synoptics. J. Driesbach (1789–1790) opted for the order Matthew, Luke, and Mark, Mark being an extract from the other two. K. Lachmann (1835), however, noted that where Matthew and Luke both had material in common with Mark, they agreed with one another only to the extent that they agreed with Mark. He therefore inferred a dependence of Matthew and Luke on Mark, as well as the use by Matthew of a collection of sayings of Jesus. This thesis anticipated the theory of the two sources, which was proposed independently in 1838 by C. G. Wilke and C. H. Weisse, and given its classic form by H. J. Holtzmann (1863) and P. Wernle (1899).

The two-source theory says that Mark is the earliest of the Synoptics and that Matthew and Luke used him, but independently of each other. They also used a second source, made up almost exclusively of sayings of Jesus; that source is lost but can be reconstructed from these two gospels. This "sayings source" is currently termed Q (from German *Quelle*, "source").

The arguments for the priority of Mark are as follows: (a) the order of the pericopes (i.e., of the sections into which the gospel texts can be divided): Matthew and Luke never both depart from Mark's order; if one of them differs, the other agrees with Mark. (b) Matthew and Luke improve the language and style of Mark at many points. (c) Almost the whole of Mark is found in at least one of the other two; Luke and Matthew together omit only Mark 2:27; 3:20–21; 4:26–29; 7:31–37; 8:22–26; 9:48–49; 14:51–52; and 15:44. On the other hand, the elimination of this material by both is not easy to explain. To this difficulty two others must be added: first, Luke 9:17 corresponds to Mark 6:44, and Luke 9:18 to Mark 8:27, although in Luke there is no parallel to Mark 6:45–8:26. Second, in the material that Matthew and Luke borrow from Mark they show some minor agreements in contrast to Mark; but this seems to contradict the foundations of the whole theory. For these reasons, scholars sometimes accept that Matthew and Luke did not use the Mark that became canonical but another version, either an early (Proto-Mark) or a more recent one (Deutero-Mark).

The arguments for the existence of Q are these: (a) In the parts that do not come from Mark, Matthew and Luke have many passages in common, mostly sayings of Jesus; these correspondences suggest a literary relationship. It is difficult, however, to believe that one of the two borrowed from the other, because the correspondences occur at different points of the narrative, and the differences that occur are not explicable in terms of the characteristics of the Matthean or the Lukan redaction. (b) Matthew and Luke show a number of doublets, that is passages that appear either twice in one of them or twice in both: one with a parallel in Mark, the other without. Examples: (a) Luke tells of the sending of the disciples (the Twelve) in 9:1ff. parallel to Mark (and Matthew) and in 10:1ff. (the seventy-two) without a parallel but using sayings of Jesus that Matthew uses on the occasion of the other sending, in ch. 10. (b) Matthew 16:24 and Luke 9:23 have Jesus' statement about carrying the cross, in dependence on Mark 8:24; but they have the saying again in Matt 10:38 and Luke 14:27, without any corresponding saying in Mark. This situation can be explained by supposing that Matthew and Luke drew these texts once from Mark and once from another source.

The theory of the two sources is thus not a definitive solution to the Synoptic Problem, but it seems still to be the most satisfactory hypothesis. Other solutions, however, are still being offered. With regard to those who return to Griesbach's hypothesis we may mention, among recent suggestions, the complex hypothesis of P. Benoît and M.-E. Boismard. This postulates four original sources (A, B, C, and Q; B would be a shorter development of A), various combinations of which yield an "intermediate Matthew," an "intermediate Mark," and a "proto-Luke"; these in turn would be the origin of the present three Synoptic Gospels. This theory, simplified in successive presentations by Boismard, tries to take account of all the problems but ends up being excessively complicated.

BIBLIOGRAPHY

W. G. Kümmel, *The New Testament: The History of the Investigation of Its Problems* (trans. S. M. Gilmour and H. C. Kee; Nashville: Abingdon, 1972).
W. Schmithals, *Einleitung in die drei ersten Evangelien* (New York: de Gruyter, 1985).

2. Sayings Source (Q)

Despite uncertainty about a small number of passages, the material belonging to this sayings source can be determined with some accuracy. Since Luke is accepted as having best respected the original order, it is customary to cite Q according to the corresponding verses in Luke. Here is a list of the passages following the order in Luke, with references to Matthew in parentheses.

Q/Luke

3:7–9, 16–17	Preaching of John the Baptist (Matt 3:7–12)
4:1–13	Temptations of Jesus (4:1–11)
6:12, 17, 20a	Introduction to the Sermon on the Mount or Plain (5:1–2)
6:20b–23	Beatitudes (5:3–4, 6, 11–12)
6:27–28	Love of enemies (5:43–44)
6:29	Do not return evil for evil (5:39–41)
6:30	Give freely (5:42)
6:31	"Golden Rule" (7:12)
6:32–35	Act not as sinners do but as children of God (5:45–47)
6:36	Be merciful (5:48)
6:37–38	Do not judge (7:1–2)
6:39	Blind guides (15:14)
6:40	Disciples and teacher (10:24–25)
6:41–42	The mote and the beam (7:3–5)
6:43–44	Good and bad fruits (7:16–20; 12:33–34)
6:45	The heart's treasure (12:35)
6:46	Whoever says "Lord, Lord" (7:21)
6:47–49	Parable of the builders (7:24–27)
7:1–10	The centurion of Capernaum (8:5–10, 13)
7:18–28	John's question and Jesus' answer (11:2–11)
7:31–35	The children in the square and John the Baptist (11:2–11)
9:57–60	Follow Jesus (8:19–22)
10:2	The harvest is great (9:37–38)
10:3	Sheep among wolves (10:16)
10:4–12	Instructions for the missionaries (10:7–15)
10:13–15	Woe to the towns of Galilee (11:20–24)
10:16	The authority of the missionaries (10:40)
10:21–22	Jesus rejoices (11:25–27)
10:23–24	Blessed are the eyes that see (13:16–17)
11:2–4	Our Father (6:9–13)
11:9–13	Prayer (7:7–11)
11:14–23	Accusation of using Beelzebul to cast out demons (12:22–30)
11:24–26	Return of the unclean spirit (12:43–44)
11:29–32	The sign of Jonah (12:38–42)
11:33–36	The lamp and the eye (5:15; 6:22–23)
11:39–44, 46–52	Against the Pharisees (23:4, 6–7, 13, 23, 25–32, 34–36)
12:2–3	Revelation of what is hidden (10:26–27)
12:4–9	Confessing Jesus (10:28–33)
12:10	Blasphemy against the Spirit (12:31–32)
12:11–12	Assistance of the Spirit (10:19–20)
12:22–32	Earthly worries (6:25–33)
12:33–34	Treasure in heaven (6:19–21)
12:39–40	Parable of the householder (24:43–44)
12:42–46	Parable of the faithful servant (24:45–51)
12:51–53	Division on earth (10:34–36)

12:54–56	Signs of the times (16:2–3)
12:57–59	Reconciliation (5:25–26)
13:18–19	Parable of the mustard seed (13:31–32)
13:20–21	Parable of the yeast (13:32–33)
13:24	The narrow gate (7:13–14)
13:25–27	The closed door (7:22–23)
13:28–29	They shall come from the east and the west (8:11–12)
13:30	The first shall be last (20:16)
13:34–35	Lament over Jerusalem (23:37–39)
14:5	Animals rescued on the sabbath (12:11–12)
14:16–24	Parable of the banquet (22:1–10)
14:25–27	Follow Jesus, carry the cross (10:37–38)
14:34–35	Salt (5:13)
15:4–7	The lost sheep (18:12–14)
16:13	Serving two masters (6:24)
16:16	The Law and the prophets until John (11:12–13)
16:17	Permanence of the Law (5:18)
16:18	Divorce (5:32)
17:1–2	Scandal (18:6, 7)
17:34	Forgiveness (18:21–22)
17:5–6	Faith (17:20)
17:23–24, 26–30	Coming of the Son of Man (24:26–27, 37–39)
17:34–35	Two in one bed (24:40–41)
17:37	The corpse and the vultures (24:28)
19:12–27	Parable of the talents (25:14–30)
22:28–30	Promise of thrones at the judgment (19:28)

Also attributed to Q, for various reasons, are some passages found only in Matthew or only in Luke (e.g., Luke 12:13–14, 16–21, 35–38), although the attribution is, of course, less certain; much depends here on the importance assigned to a comparison with the Coptic *Gospel of Thomas* as a witness independent of the canonical gospels.

As the list shows, Q contained essentially sayings of Jesus. The few narratives were the temptation of Jesus (4:1–13), the episode of the centurion of Capernaum (7:1–10), and the question sent by John the Baptist (7:18–23), but even in these cases it is above all the words of Jesus that are common to Matthew and Luke. The fact that Q was a written and not merely an oral source is proved not only by the doublets mentioned but by the number of verbatim correspondences between Matthew and Luke and, in general, by the extent of their agreement in material attributed to Q. Furthermore, the two evangelists knew Q in Greek, as the exactness of their correspondences shows, although the earliest form of the collection must have been Aramaic, the language of Jesus and his disciples. On the other hand, their differences in use of material from Q is not always to be explained by their separate redactional characteristics (e.g., Matt 5:25/Luke 12:57–59). This leads us to suppose that Matthew and Luke used two slightly differing forms of Q. It is hard to believe that Mark knew Q, as some have supposed on the basis of the presence in his gospel of material also transmitted in Q (the doublets). How then can we explain that

Mark left out so much of Q? The coincidences can be explained by the independent use of fragments of the tradition by Mark and Q.

The Sayings Source (Q) did not contain the story of the passion of Jesus nor any prediction of the passion, death, and resurrection. This does not mean that the community in which Q was composed was ignorant of those events, but that the events were not part of its core understanding of Jesus. Q is therefore not a gospel in the proper sense, even if its content can certainly be described as "good news." Recent studies (J. M. Robinson, J. S. Kloppenborg) liken Q to the genre of collections of sapiential sayings that was widely cultivated in the Hellenistic world in various forms (instructions, gnomologies, and chrias; a chria being a discourse or action elicited by a specific situation in the life of an important individual), often for esoteric purposes. In the Jesus tradition, something comparable can be seen in the *Gospel of Thomas*. The order in Q, however, does not seem to be haphazard: there is a chronological principle that runs from the preaching of John the Baptist to the instruction by Jesus on the end of the world, which Mark, too, locates at the end of the preaching of Jesus, just before the account of the passion. The form of Q known to Matthew and Luke was probably the result of editorial development, but attempts to distinguish successive strata of Q have agreed only to a limited extent (D. Lührmann, S. Schulz, J. S. Kloppenborg, H. Koester).

According to some scholars, the original nucleus of Q contained a radical ethic based on the conviction that the kingdom of God was present beginning with the preaching of Jesus, while subsequent expansion shifted the emphasis to expectation of the coming of Jesus in the future. According to other scholars, the threat of apocalyptic judgment appeared in the earliest stratum of Q, and subsequent editing thematized the problem of the delay of Christ's return (Q/Luke 12:49). According to some, the mission to the pagans was due to editing, while according to others it belonged to the initial stratum. In any case Q circulated in communities of Christians who came from paganism. The announcement of judgment against the Jews, and therefore the awareness of an inevitable break with Judaism, would belong to a later redaction. The only title attributed to Jesus in Q is Son of Man, which combines in a paradoxical way the dignity of the future universal judge, which Jewish tradition attributed to this personage on the basis of Daniel 7:13, and the condition of marginalization and persecution, which Jesus foresaw and which was the model for Christian missionaries who brought with them the tradition set down in Q (Q/Luke 10:16; 11:50; etc.).

In addition to Jerusalem, the locations of Jesus' activity mentioned in Q are the towns of Chorazin, Bethsaida, and Capernaum in Galilee at the northern end of the Lake of Genessaret; this may be the area in which the collection originated. Q was therefore an aid to Christian missionaries in their preaching. It was characterized in its earliest form by an ethic of abandonment of family and possessions in order to enter into the present reality of the reign of God which Jesus had begun. It subsequently expressed a less radical perspective, but in all versions strongly emphasizing the community. The composition of Q can be dated between 50 and 70. Its disappearance was certainly connected with the disappearance of the social conditions in which the first mission was carried out, and with its replacement, as a literary document, by Matthew and Luke, especially the former, which brought its content up to date by adapting it to the changed situation of the Christian communities.

BIBLIOGRAPHY

Texts

J. S. Kloppenborg, *Q Parallels: Synopsis, Critical Notes, and Concordance* (Sonoma, Calif.: Polebridge, 1988).

J. M. Robinson, P. Hoffman, and J. S. Kloppenborg, eds., *The Critical Edition of Q* (Hermeneia; Minneapolis: Fortress Press and Leuven, Peeters Publishers, 2000).

Studies

J. M. Robinson, "*LOGOI SOPHON:* On the Gattung of Q," in H. Koester and J. M. Robinson, *Trajectories through Early Christianity* (Philadelphia: Fortress, 1972), 71–113.

J. S. Kloppenborg, *The Formation of Q: Trajectories in Ancient Wisdom Collections* (Philadelphia: Fortress, 1987).

H. Koester, *Ancient Christian Gospels* (Philadelphia: Trinity; London: SCM, 1990), 128–71.

3. Forms of the Earliest Tradition

In its original formulation the two-source theory regarded Mark and Q as documents close in time to the life of Jesus and therefore trustworthy for a reconstruction of that history. It soon became clear, however, that Q was several decades distant from the death of Jesus and that its composition went through several phases. As for the Gospel of Mark, W. Wrede showed in 1901 that the theology of the messianic secret, which guided the presentation of Jesus in that gospel, did not go back to Jesus himself but to the thinking of the Christian communities. This and other studies showing how the very composition of the gospels was dictated by theological reflection, raised the problem of the development of the tradition about Jesus before the composition of Mark and Q. In 1919 K. L. Schmidt showed that the earliest tradition about Jesus was conveyed in pericopes, that is, small units containing narrative scenes or words of Jesus, and that almost all the chronological and topographical information in Mark is "framework" and owes its existence to the narrative plan of the evangelist. According to Schmidt, the individual units of tradition owed their exemplary and ahistorical character to the cultural context in which they were developed and used.

Schmidt was interested primarily in the "framework," but the way was now open to investigate the pre-gospel units. This became a study of "forms," that is, of units of discourse whose composition and transmission obeyed strict stylistic and structural laws. The method, known as "form criticism," was the point of convergence of several lines of study: investigation of the oral traditions in the Old Testament (especially by H. Gunkel); reflection on the forms found in the earliest Christian literature (F. Overbeck); and the interest, with its roots in romanticism, in the simplest forms of popular literature. The term "form criticism" *(Formgeschichte)* was adopted in 1913 by philologist E. Norden in his book *Agnostos Theos,* an investigation into the forms of religious language in antiquity.

Two works endeavored to delimit and classify the material that came together in the Synoptics. Martin Dibelius (1919) proceeded constructively, that is, he defined the forms in light of the situation in which each was used at the beginnings of Christianity *(Sitz im Leben).* He distinguished the narrative material as follows: paradigm (a short narrative culminating in a saying of Jesus: e.g., Mark 3:1–6); novella (a fuller and more detailed narrative focusing on Jesus as miracle worker: e.g., Mark 6:35–44); and legend (a narrative, edifying like the paradigm, but hinging not on a saying of Jesus but on the holiness of the hero and the protection given him by God: e.g., Luke 2:41–51). The account of the passion occupies a special place because its very subject led to the formation of a complex narrative that is quite lengthy and structured.

The tradition of the words of Jesus was assembled and handed on, according to Dibelius, in the service of parenesis (moral exhortation). Dibelius distinguished these materials as follows: sapiential saying or sentence; comparison (e.g., Mark 4:21); parable; prophetic appeal (beatitude, threat, eschatological prediction); short commandment; and longer commandment (using motivation, as in Matt 5:44–48; promise, as in Matt 6:2–4; or threat, as in Matt 5:29–30). A few texts in the pregospel material are to be classified as myths, that is, stories about a divinity (e.g., Mark 9:2–8 among the narratives, Matt 11:25–30 among the saying). Mark in its totality is a book of myth, to say nothing of John, which is completely pervaded by a mythic picture of Jesus.

Rudolph Bultmann (1921), in contrast to Dibelius proceeded analytically, that is, he defined the forms based on an analysis of the texts. He distinguished two categories: miracle stories (e.g., Mark 5:35–42); and stories and legends (e.g., baptism, transfiguration, passion, birth of Jesus). The sayings of Jesus he divided into two large groups. The first, apothegms, are subdivided into dialogues both of controversy and of instruction (e.g., Mark 3:1–6; 10:35–45) and biographical apothegms (e.g., Mark 10:13–16). The apothegms corresponded to the paradigms of Dibelius, but without the preliminary option implied by the latter term, of such stories being used as "examples" in preaching (e.g., 10:17–22; note the inclusion of the apothegms among the sayings, whereas Dibelius includes the paradigms among the narratives). The second large group is the sayings of Jesus, subdivided as follows: logia or sapiential sayings (e.g., Mark 4:22); prophetic and apocalyptic sayings (e.g., the words of Jesus on the destruction of the temple, Mark 13:2; 14:58; and parallels); juridical sayings (e.g., Mark 10:11–12); "I" sayings (in the first person, as in Mark 2:17); and similitudes and parables (similitudes explain both terms of a comparison, as in Luke 17:7–10, while parables contain only a story without an application, as in Mark 4:3–9).

We cannot here trace the intense debate that went on over the subsequent seventy years, but let us mention K. Berger's critical reflection on and attempt to write a form critical treatment of the entire New Testament. Berger emphasizes the distinction between form criticism, which is concerned with the stylistic, syntactic, and structural characteristics of a text, the history of tradition, which studies the transmission of the material, and compositional criticism, which studies the grouping of the materials in the gospels and letters. In Berger's view, attention to form understood as the linguistic configuration of a text must avoid such imprecise classifications as Bultmann's juridical sayings. Berger's division takes its cue from the genres of ancient rhetoric: the symbouleutic or deliberative (e.g., parenesis, beatitudes); the epideictic or panegyric (e.g., hymns, "I" sayings, apocalyptic forms); and the dicanic or judicial (e.g., defenses). He ought, however, to have inserted a section of unique compositions that do not fit precisely into any of the three other groups (e.g., parables and similitudes). Berger devotes attention to the history of each form and its connections to typical situations in the history of Christian origins.

BIBLIOGRAPHY

K. L. Schmidt, *Der Rahmen der Geschichte Jesu: Literarkritische Untersuchungen zur ältesten Jesusüberlieferung* (Berlin: Trowitzsch, 1919).

M. Dibelius, *Die Formgeschichte des Evangeliums* (1919; 6th ed.; Tübingen: Mohr, 1971; ET: *From Tradition to Gospel* (trans. and rev. from 2d ed. by Bertram Lee Woolf; Cambridge: Clarke, 1971).

R. Bultmann, *Die Geschichte der synoptischen Tradition* (1921; 8th ed.; Göttingen: Vandenhoeck & Ruprecht, 1970, with *Ergänzungsheft* by P. Vielhauer and G. Theissen); ET: *The History of the Synoptic Tradition* (trans. J. Marsh; Oxford: Basil Blackwell, 1963).

K. Berger, "Hellenistische Gattungen im Neuen Testament," *ANRW* II 25.2 (1984): 1031–1442 (index: 1821–85).

———, *Formgeschichte des Neuen Testaments* (Heidelberg: Quelle und Meyer, 1984).

———, *Einführung in die Formgeschichte* (Tübingen: Francke, 1987).

G. Strecker, *Literaturgeschichte des Neuen Testaments* (Göttingen: Vandenhoeck & Ruprecht, 1992), 170–205.

4. "Gospel" as Genre

Mark's work begins with the words: "Beginning of the gospel of Jesus Christ." But how is the word "gospel" to be understood? In classical Greek, the word *euangelion* signified a reward for good news. Later, in the imperial age, it meant the good news itself, but not necessarily with the positive connotation: it could mean simply "news." In the Greek of the Septuagint (LXX) the noun means "news" (found only in 2 Kgs 4:10; 18:22, 25). The corresponding verb, *euangelizomai*, has a theological connotation in Deutero-Isaiah (Isa 40:9; 52:7), where it signifies the proclamation of the people's deliverance. *Euangelion* appears in inscriptions of the Augustan age, many of them having to do with the introduction of the Julian calendar; among the best known is the one found in the marketplace of Priene, dating from A.D. 9, and reading (lines 40–41): "[The birthday] of the god [= of Augustus] was for the world the beginning of the good news *(euangelion)* that is owing to him." Thus, shortly before the word was adopted by Christian circles, the imperial propaganda of Augustus had given it a deeper sense: it marked the beginning of a new era due to the peace established by Augustus.

Paul uses *euangelion* as an already current technical term, probably following the usage of Hellenistic Christian communities, and he does so beginning in his earliest letter: "our gospel," that is, the one he preached (1 Thess 1:5); "the gospel of God," that is, coming from God (2:2, 8, 9). He also speaks of "the gospel of Christ" (objective genitive: 1 Cor 9:12, etc.). In 1 Corinthians the gospel proclaimed by Paul is identified with a formula, which he received and had passed on in turn, on the passion, death, and resurrection of Jesus, that is, on the core of the Christian kerygma (15:1–5). Somewhat similarly, the gospel is identified in Romans with the saving event accomplished by Jesus and foretold in the Scriptures (1:1–4). It is probable, then, that Paul inherited from Hellenistic Jewish Christianity an understanding of "gospel" that was connected with formulas for confessing faith in Jesus. In the Deutero-Pauline tradition, in Acts (15:1; 20:24), and in Ignatius of Antioch, *euangelion* continues to signify the message of salvation having to do with Jesus and not a particular written work.

Mark's innovation consists of using "gospel of Jesus Christ" (1:1) as a subjective genitive to mean the proclamation of the reign of God in the preaching of Jesus. This is confirmed by 1:14–15, the beginning of the preaching of Jesus. In 1:1 Mark makes it known that the preaching of the Baptist (1:2–8) is already the beginning of the gospel proclaimed by Jesus (Koester). In Mark 1:1 *euangelion* is therefore not the title of the book. There is disagreement over whether the references to the gospel in the *Didache* are to a written text or to the oral tradition of the sayings of Jesus (*Did.* 8.2; 11.3; 15.3–4).

The determining factor in the shift to "gospel" as a particular written text was probably the activity of Marcion (see below, ch. 9, sec. 3). Around 140, in an effort to recover the proclamation by and about Jesus in a pure form free of Judaizing falsifications, Marcion identified the "my/our gospel" of which Paul speaks with the work of Luke. According to later testimonies Marcion gave the name "gospel" to his revised version of Luke (Tertullian, *Marc.* 4.2; Epiphanius, *Pan.* 42.10; etc.). Around 155, Justin Martyr, who wrote against Marcion, used the word "gospel" three times, always of a written work: *1 Apol.* 66.3; *Dial.* 10.2; 100.1. In the first passage, the word is plural and is expressly identified with the "memoirs (*apomnēmoneumata*) of the apostles." Justin probably presupposes an antimarcionite use of the word, one that emphasizes the reliability of the gospels as authentic testimonies to the salvation-historical significance of the Jesus event, a significance corresponding to the Old Testament prophecies. The connection between the written work of Mark (which is not called "gospel" in the fragments left us) and the terminology of remembering (*[apo]mnēmoneuō*) in reference to the testimony of the disciples of Jesus was already present in Papias of Hierapolis (Eusebius, *Hist. eccl.* 3.39.15).

From the end of the second century on, *euangelion* regularly signifies a literary genre (Irenaeus, *Haer.* 5.26.6; Clement of Alexandria, *Strom.* 1.136.1; *Diog.* 11.6). Around 190 Serapion of Antioch mentions a community in his diocese that read "the gospel going under the name of Peter" (Eusebius, *Hist. eccl.* 6.12.3). The titles "Gospel according to . . . ," which the canonical gospels carry in the manuscripts, are the work of later scribes; the suggestion of M. Hengel, that the titles of the Synoptics go back to the first century, has met with a great deal of resistance.

Debate continues on the definition of the genre of "gospel" and on its derivation from ancient literary genres. Among the many suggestions the following may be noted.

1. The gospels cannot be traced back to any ancient literary genre but are an original creation of Christianity, and their form was built up starting with the kerygmatic formulations of the Christian faith. But the kerygmatic formulations that include ref-

erences to the ministry of Jesus are found primarily in Luke (especially Acts 10:34–43; 13:23–31) and are not ancient but are due to Lukan redaction.

2. The gospels were composed as cycles of liturgical readings, which replaced the cycles of readings in the synagogues. But there is no proof that the synagogue cycles already existed when the gospels were composed. Moreover, it is difficult to accept that the gospels were originally intended to function as sacred Scriptures in worship.

3. There has recently been a new investigation of the affinities between the gospels and ancient biography, with an emphasis on the many variants within the latter genre and its various levels of language and style. Hellenistic biography was concerned not with the individual psychology of the personage but with his correspondence to a type, as well as with his role or function. As a result, it assembled his sayings and deeds and placed them between his birth (or investiture) and death, some of these sayings and deeds being transferred from one individual to another in virtue of their conformity to a type, which took precedence over historical fact. These were arranged in a more or less artificial order. A variant of this approach links the gospels not to Hellenistic biography but to the "biography of a prophet (or, more broadly, a just man)" in Judaism. Such biographies were rarely independent but were mostly parts of larger texts. At the present time, this assimilation of the gospels to biographies is enjoying a great deal of favor among scholars.

BIBLIOGRAPHY

P. Stuhlmacher, *Vorgeschichte* (vol. I of *Das paulinische Evangelium;* Göttingen: Vandenhoeck & Ruprecht, 1968).

D. Dormeyer and H. Frankemölle, "Evangelium als literarische Gattung und als theologischer Begriff: Tendenzen and Aufgaben der Evangelienforschung im 20. Jahrhundert, mit einer Untersuchung des Markusevangeliums in seinem Verhältnis zur antiken Biographie," *ANRW* II 25.2 (1984): 1543–1704.

M. Hengel, *Die Evangelienüberschriften* (*SHAW.PH* 3; Heidelberg: Winter, 1984).

D. E. Aune, *The New Testament in Its Literary Environment* (bibliog., I, 1; Philadelphia: Westminster, 1987), 17–76.

H. Koester, "From the Kerygma-Gospel to Written Gospels," *NTS* 35 (1989): 361–81.

G. Strecker, *Literaturgeschichte des Neuen Testaments* (bibliog., II, 3; Göttingen: Vandenhoeck & Ruprecht, 1992), 123–48.

G. Segalla, *Evangelio e vangeli: Quattro evangelisti, quattro vangeli, quattro destinatari* (Bologna: Dehoniane, 1993).

B. Chilton and C. A. Evans, *Authenticating the Words of Jesus* (Boston: Brill, 1999).

5. Mark

If we accept the two-source theory then, Mark is the earliest gospel that has been preserved, and its author "invented" the gospel form, in parallel with John. The only unit of some length which we can say with great probability that Mark used is the story of the passion. For the earlier part of his book Mark had at his disposal other materials from a tradition that was probably partly oral, partly set down in writing. It is difficult, however, to say to what extent he had available collections of the deeds and sayings of Jesus. As for the deeds, Mark describes two parallel series of events (6:34–56 and 8:1–30), which are found in the same order in John 6; it has therefore been thought that this assemblage was already in existence, and that Mark used it twice, following two different versions. As for the sayings, Mark must have used materials that already combined the parables of ch. 4 and the sayings of ch. 9. The eschatological discourse of 13:5–27 must have been an independent apocalypse which Mark puts on the lips of Jesus. As stated earlier, it is unlikely that Mark was familiar with Q.

Mark organized this material into a narrative that runs from "the beginning of the gospel of Jesus Christ" (1:1), that is, from the preaching of John the Baptist and the baptism of Jesus, to the proclamation of his resurrection. The story of the passion (which began as in 14:1) is preceded, beginning in 11:1, with the entrance into Jerusalem and the driving of the traders from the temple, followed (still in the temple) by debates with adversaries, teachings, and, finally, the eschatological discourse, which, with its exhortation to keep watch in expectation of the Lord's coming (13:33–36), concludes the teaching of Jesus.

The earlier part of the gospel describes an itinerant ministry of Jesus, centered in Galilee and continuing through the return to Capernaum, the site of 9:33–50; in 10:1 the journey to Jerusalem begins. Within chs. 1–10 the declaration of Peter at Caesarea Philippi represents a turning point (8:27–30), as he recognizes the Messiah but is told to keep silent. There follows immediately the first of the three predictions of the passion (8:31–33; 9:31; 10:32–34). These give structure to this section in which Jesus leaves Caesarea and re-enters Galilee (9:30) by way of the mountain of transfiguration, finally reaching Capernaum, whence he will leave for Jerusalem.

It is thus possible to distinguish three main sections in Mark's gospel:

1. Mark 1:1–8:26. In a series of journeys with Galilee as their center, various aspects of the person and activity of Jesus are brought to light: the baptism in which he is adopted as Son of God; the proclamation of the kingdom of God (beginning in 1:14–15); the call of the disciples (1:16–20; 2:14); the teaching with authority (from 1:21–22 on); the conflict with the forces of evil that imprison human beings (healings from 1:23 on, followed by a series of them in 4:35–5:43, and up to the cure of the blind man in 8:22–26, a paradigmatic episode that concludes this first part and immediately precedes Peter's declaration at Caesarea); the teaching given at various levels to the disciples and the people (especially 3:7–4:34); the rejection of Jesus in his native place (6:1–6); the sending of the disciples (6:7–13, 30–31; the sending and the return are separated by the novelistic account of the death of John the Baptist).

2. Mark 8:27–10:52. The recognition of Jesus as Messiah marks the beginning of a revelation of what kind of Messiah he is, within a field of strong tensions, which the disciples do not understand until after the resurrection: the transfiguration (9:2–10) reveals to Peter, James, and John the glory of Jesus, who is proclaimed Son of God, but they are forbidden to speak of it until the resurrection. There follow announcements of the fate (necessary in the divine plan, 8:31) of the Son of Man and expositions of the reversal of values and the radical conditions required for discipleship (9:33–50; 10:17–31, 35–45).

3. Mark 11:1–16:20. Mark organizes events here according to a temporal scheme. First day (11:1–11): entry into Jerusalem (from Jericho, 10:46–52) and removal to Bethany; second day (11:12–19): from Bethany to Jerusalem (cursing of the fig tree),

expulsion of the traders, departure from the city; third day (11:20–14:37): from Bethany to Jerusalem (the dried-up fig tree), entrance into the temple, teaching and controversies, eschatological discourse. In 14:1 Mark gives a fixed point of reference: two days before Passover, that is, the vigil (13 Nisan). This date must go back to the pre-Markan account of the passion, whereas 14:12, "the first day of the unleavened bread, the day on which the passover lamb was sacrificed," gives information that is incorrect from the Jewish viewpoint (the first day of unleavened bread began only at sundown of the day the passover lambs were slaughtered—therefore the following day, according to the Jewish way of counting). That must be an addition of Mark for the purpose of turning the last supper of Jesus into a Passover meal. In the earliest tradition, as in the Gospel of John, the supper must have been dated on the evening of 13 Nisan. In Mark's redaction 14:1–11 represents 13 Nisan, and 14:12–72, represents 14 Nisan. The latter section contains the preparations for the meal, the announcement of Judas' betrayal, the institution of the sacrament, Gethsemane, the arrest of Jesus, the interrogation before the Sanhedrin, and the denial of Peter. Mark 15:1–47 gives the events of 15 Nisan (Friday): trial before Pilate, mistreatment, crucifixion, death, and burial of Jesus. The events between 15:47 and 16:1 are set on 16 Nisan (Saturday). Mark 16:1–8 tells of the women's discovery of the empty tomb and the angel's announcement of appearances in Galilee. The depiction of further appearances of Jesus and of the ascension (16:9–20) is a later addition.

In this final section, then, Mark carefully distributes events over the course of a week. In the first ten chapters, however, after the information that the activity of Jesus began after the arrest of John (1:14), Mark's chronological indications are vague. He mentions only one Passover, giving the impression that the ministry of Jesus lasted less than a year. John speaks of three Passovers, but none of the depictions carry any guarantee of historicity, although the duration in Mark is a priori more probable. Geographical indicators are likewise vague: Jesus moves about in Galilee and on the non-Galilean side of Lake Genessaret, but with regard to the latter, the mention of the "country of the Gerasenes" (5:1) is vague, since Gerasa was located about sixty kilometers from the lake, and its territory did not extend that far.

The intention of Mark's chronological and geographical ambiguity is theological: Jesus is active in the Decapolis (5:20), outside of Galilee proper, thus preparing the reader for meetings with non-Jews (7:24–37: Tyre, Sidon, Decapolis). As already noted, Mark's geography highlights the contrast between Galilee (and surrounding territories) and Jerusalem, the city that finally rejects and condemns Jesus. This is the point of the murderous vineyard workers, 12:1–11, which occupies a central place in the teaching in Jerusalem. Mark sets within this framework the various materials he had at his disposal, often linking the pieces together in elementary ways: with the general indications of time and place already noted, but also with the simple conjunction "and" *(kai)* or "again" *(palin)* or, his favorite, "and immediately" *(kai euthys;* forty-one times: 1:12, 23; etc.). Another device for both transition and continuity is the summary, a short passage intended to show that the episodes told in greater detail are only examples of a much fuller activity of Jesus (1:14–15, 32–34, 39; 3:7–12; 6:6b, 34, 53–56; 10:1). In these summaries the emphasis is placed primarily on cures, but also on the preaching of Jesus and the reception of his message. This device is characteristic of ancient biography.

A unifying element at the editorial level is the so-called theology of the messianic secret, which was first presented by W. Wrede (1901): Jesus orders that his supernatural power, evidenced in the healings, not be made known until after his resurrection (9:9). Mark incorporates into the messianic secret, which does not correspond to historical fact, the imposition of silence that is found in preexisting episodes (1:25, 44). He then reinterprets and extends it to a number of other cases (1:34; 3:12; 5:43; 7:36; 8:26, 30; 9:9). The disciples, on the other hand, do not understand the person of Jesus, his teaching, and his predictions of his fate (4:13, 40; 6:49–51; 8:17–18; 9:32); this is true even of the four to whom Jesus grants a special revelation, namely, Simon and Andrew, James and John (5:37; 9:2; 13:3; 14:33). As the point in time (the resurrection) that is set down in 9:9 shows, the theology of the secret expresses the awareness that a true understanding of Jesus is possible only through faith in the resurrection, but that this faith, refers us back to the whole of Jesus' life, culminating in the passion, and sheds light on it as the time in which his dignity already made itself visible.

Mark's writing style is very close to the spoken language; this can be seen in his predilection for diminutives as well as in military, administrative, and numismatic Latinisms (5:9, 15; 6:27, 37; 12:14–17, 42; 15:15, 16, 39). He translates Aramaic words (5:41; 7:11, 24; 15:34) except for words that had entered Christian liturgical use (*amēn,* thirteen times; *rabbi,* three times; *rabbouni,* once; *ōsanna,* 11:9–10). In imitating Semitic expressions in Greek (8:12) Mark comes close to the Septuagint. He frequently uses double negatives, as well as circumlocutions (especially in the imperfect tense) combining the verb "to be" and a participle of another verb. He uses the historical present 150 times lending an air of immediacy to the narrative.

The ending of the gospel poses a problem of literary integrity: in the most important manuscripts (Sinaiticus, Vaticanus) and in the Syro-Sinaitic version, the text ends with the words *ephobounto gar* in 16:8, and therefore without an account of the appearances of the risen Jesus. Other manuscripts have either an even shorter ending (only manuscript k of the *Vetus Latina*) or a long one (vv. 9–20). The great majority of scholars today accept the secondary character (2d c.) of both endings, which were probably added at first independently to a conclusion, that seemed too abrupt (16:8). There is less agreement whether 16:8 is the original conclusion of the gospel, although this seems to be the case.

Ancient testimonies make Mark the author of this gospel. The first we know of is that of Papias in Eusebius's *Ecclesiastical History* 3.39.15, on which Irenaeus, *Haer.* 3.1.1, depends, as does Clement of Alexandria in the sixth book of his *Hypotyposes* (Eusebius, *Hist. eccl.* 2.15.1–2; 6.14.5–7; *Adumbr.* on 1 Pet 5:13). All of these writers link Mark to Peter. Such a connection appears in 1 Pet 5:13. On the other hand, in antiquity the author of the gospel was never identified with John Mark, nephew of Barnabas (Acts 12:12; 13:5, 13; 15:37, 39) nor with the Mark in Paul's circle (Phlm 24; also Col 4:10; 2 Tim 4:11). Justin cites a passage of Mark as coming from the "memoirs of Peter" (*Dial.* 106, 3). The connection of this gospel with Peter is meant, as Papias suggests, to legitimize a gospel not ascribed to an eyewitness of the life of Jesus. The connection to Rome appears for the first time in Clement, where it comes from the connection between Mark and Peter. According to Irenaeus (*Haer.* 2.11.7), the Carpocratians favored this gospel; according to a passage from Clement of Alexandria, the authenticity of which is not established, that group possessed a "secret gospel of Mark" (see below, sec. 10), that was in circulation in Alexandria about 170. Otherwise, a connection between Mark and Alexandria is not attested before the end of the third century.

The name "Mark" may be that of the real author, but the latter does not appeal to any testimony, direct or indirect, regarding the life of Jesus. The destruction of the temple in Jerusalem, which is regarded as imminent or as having already occurred, constitutes the background of the gospel (12:9; 13:14–19), thus locating Mark before or a little after 70. The lack of specificity in geographical indications that do not come from his sources argues against his having been a Palestinian. Mark writes for Greek readers, but is still fairly close to the Palestinian Jesus tradition, which suggests a locale not far removed from Palestine, perhaps Syria; but it is not possible to be more accurate.

BIBLIOGRAPHY

Commentaries

R. Pesch, *Il Vangelo di Marco* (2 vols.; HTKNT 2; 4th–5th ed.; 1984); IT (Brescia: Paideia, 1980–1982).

J. Gnilka, *Das Evangelium nach Markus* (2 vols.; EKKNT 2; 2d ed.; Zurich: Benziger Neukirchen-Vluyn: Neukirchener Verlag, 1986).

D. Lührmann, *Das Markusevangelium* (HNT 3; Tübingen: Mohr, 1987).

M. D. Hooker, *The Gospel according to Saint Mark* (Peabody, Mass.: Hendrickson, 1991).

B. Witherington, *The Gospel of Mark: A Socio-Rhetorical Commentary* (Grand Rapids, Mich.: Eerdmans, 2001).

J. R. Donohue and D. J. Harrington, *The Gospel of Mark* (Collegeville, Minn.: Liturgical, 2002).

Studies

W. Marxsen, *Der Evangelist Markus* (2d ed.; Göttingen: Vandenhoeck & Ruprecht, 1959); ET: *Mark the Evangelist* (trans. J. Boyce et al.; Nashville: Abingdon, 1969).

R. Pesch, ed., *Das Markusevangelium* (Darmstadt: Wissenschaftliche Buchgesellschaft, 1979).

G. Rau, "Das Markusevangelium: Komposition und Intention der ersten Darstellung christlicher Mission," *ANRW* II 25.3 (1985): 2036–2257.

6. Matthew

Matthew made use of Mark and Q. Beginning in his ch. 12, Matthew follows the order of Mark (2:23ff.). In chs. 1–11, however, he assembles, according to theme, passages found at various points in Mark: Matt 8–9 narrates ten miracles, using passages from Mark 1, 4, and 5; Matt 10 combines the selection of the disciples and their instruction for mission, which are found respectively in Mark 3:13–19; 6:6–13; 13:9–13 (and in Q). Moreover, he has brought together a good many of the sayings of Jesus and arranged them in five major discourses: "Sermon on the Mount" (5:1–7:27);

missionary discourse (10:1–42); 13:1–52 (parables); relationships within the community (18:1–35); eschatological discourse (24:1–25:46). The author calls attention to this structure by following each discourse with the words "And it happened, when Jesus had finished these words" or, after the final discourse, " . . . *all* these words" (26:1), which marks the transition to the account of the passion.

The formation of these discourses did not, however, force Matthew to change the Markan framework. Rather, he introduced them either into situations already present in Mark or into new situations, but ones that fit nicely into Mark's structure (this is the case with the Sermon on the Mount, which is introduced between Mark 1:21 and 1:22). As for the material proper to Matthew *(Sondergut)*, which consists largely of legends, he has placed it at the beginning (chs. 1–2, which have no parallels in Mark) and at the end (appearances of the risen Lord, which have no parallels in Mark). But Matthew also makes additions to the passion story (27:3–10, 19, 24–25, 51b–53, 62–66; 28:2, 4, 11–15) and he leaves out the division of the Jerusalem activity into days. Into the body of the narrative he introduces only 14:28–31 (Peter on the water) and 17:24–27 (the coin in the mouth of the fish).

Peter's confession at Caesarea, though expanded by a revelation formula and the conferral of authority (16:17–19), does not signal so clear a turning point as in Mark; in Matt 14:33 the disciples have already recognized Jesus as the Son of God. But the section in which this confession is found (16:13–20:28) retains its special character as an esoteric instruction, quite different from the activity in Galilee that occupies the corresponding section of Mark (8:27–10:45). Nor is it accidental that the discourse of Jesus introduced here (of which 18:10–35 is not from Mark) contains instructions for the internal life of the community. The geographical framework remains essentially that of Mark, the activity taking place first in Galilee and its environs, then in Jerusalem, which is reached via the country east of the river Jordan and then via Jericho.

Matthew has thus been able to combine respect for Mark's chronological and geographical framework with a systematic concern that finds expression chiefly in chs. 5–13 and that probably contributed to his work's great popularity in early Christianity. The ministry of Jesus begins in 4:12–25, where the call of the disciples introduces the ecclesiological dimension of the story of Jesus. This is followed by his great programmatic discourse (chs. 5–7), then by a series of miracles (chs. 8–9). These first two sections are framed by 4:23 and 9:35 and thus form a unit presenting the words and actions of Jesus. Next come the discourse to the disciples being sent out into the world (ch. 10), a series of controversies (ch. 12); and finally the parables (ch. 13). Starting as he does, no longer only with separate units or short collections but with two works that had already organized the materials (Mark and Q), Matthew is able to make a more systematic distribution of the material in the interest of his own picture of Jesus.

The content of the gospel may therefore be summarized as follows.

Chapters 1–2: genealogy and stories about the birth; chs. 3–4, introduction to the ministry of Jesus: preaching of John the Baptist, baptism of Jesus, temptations, call of the first four disciples.

Chapters 5–20, ministry in Galilee: 5–7, Sermon on the Mount; 8–9, ten miracles, but also two apothegms on requirements for following Jesus (8:18–22); call of Matthew (9:9); table fellowship with sinners and controversy with the Pharisees over fasting (9:11–17). At the end, a saying on the need of workers for the harvest (9:36–30) effects the transition to the next section. Chapter 10: list of the Twelve and missionary discourse. Chapters 11–12: Jesus on himself and on John the Baptist (11:2–15); debates with adversaries; the true family of Jesus (12:46–50). Matthew 13:1–52: seven parables on the kingdom of heaven. Matthew 13:53–17:27, activity of Jesus in Galilee and its environs, toward a definition of his identity: Herod thinks he is John restored to life (14:2); the first multiplication of loaves and the walking on the water cause the disciples to proclaim him Son of God (14:33); the signs of the times and the prediction of the sign of Jonah (16:1–4); Peter's profession of faith at Caesarea, proclaiming Jesus to be the Christ, the Son of God, followed by the order to remain silent and by a first prediction of the passion (16:13–23), then by the conditions for the following of Jesus (16:24–26); transfiguration and statement about John the Baptist as Elijah (17:1–13); second passion prediction (17:22–23). Chapter 18: discourse on discipleship and relations within the community. Chapters 19–20, on the way to Judea: teachings of Jesus on conditions for discipleship and on the disciples' prospects; third passion prediction (20:17–19).

Chapters 20 to 28 relate activity in Jerusalem and the passion and resurrection. Chapters 21–23: entrance into Jerusalem, expulsion of the traders from the temple, teachings and controversies of Jesus, especially regarding his rejection by Israel. Included are parables of the two sons, the murderous vineyard workers, the banquet (21:28–22:14); lament over Jerusalem and prophecy concerning it (23:37–39). Chapters 24–25: eschatological discourse, with clear reference to the destruction of Jerusalem; exhortations to watchfulness (24:37–25:13); in conclusion, the final judgment and the identification of Jesus with "his least brethren" (25:31–46). Chapters 26–27: passion and burial. Chapter 28: the empty tomb, appearance to the women at the tomb, final appearance in Galilee, and universal missionary mandate.

Matthew's additions at the beginning and end of the book are important. The additional structured story of the origins of Jesus (chs. 1–2) is an innovation of Matthew (as it is also, but independently, of Luke) by comparison with Mark. Pre-existing materials of various origins (their original extent is much debated) are brought together here, but Matthew has extensively reworked them in the interests of his own Christology. The genealogy (1:1–17) is meant to show that, as a descendant of David and Abraham, Jesus has a legal claim to messiahship, being rooted as he is in the people of Israel. The virginal conception (1:18–25) traces the status of Jesus as Son of God back to the moment of his human origin. The adoration of the magi (2:1–12) connects his birth with the acknowledgment of his messiahship by the pagans whom Matthew and his readers saw now in the church. The descent into Egypt and the return (2:13–21) show that the life of Jesus reproduces the journeying of the people of Israel. Persecution by Herod anticipates the opposition from Jerusalem and the Jews, which will ultimately bring Jesus to his death and which will be prolonged in Jewish hostility toward the first Christians.

While the fabulous events surrounding the birth will seem to be negated by the ministry of Jesus, it is true that in telling the story of this ministry Matthew highlights much more than Mark the dignity of Jesus, whom his disciples call not "rabbi" but *kyrios.* His Jesus is also frequently the recipient of adoration (*proskyneō:* 2:2, 8, 11; 8:2; 9:18; 14:33; 15:25; 20:20; 28:9, 17; only once in Mark). Matthew's editorial insertions in the story of the passion serve to emphasize Jesus' foreknowledge and control of events (26:18, 50, 52–54, 61, 64; 28:16–20); thus turning the account of the passion into a christological revelation (Dibelius).

The ecclesiological dimension of this gospel is fundamental, framed as it is (U. Luz reminds us) between the interpretation of the name of Jesus, "Emmanuel," as "God with us" (1:23) and the promise "I am with you all days until the end of the world" (28:20), between the call of the disciples at the beginning of Jesus' ministry (4:18–22) and the sending of them on the mission of making disciples of all people (28:18–20). Only Matthew's gospel among the Synoptics mentions the *ekklēsia* (16:18; 18:17) in connection with the bestowal of authority to bind and loose. Chapter 18 is an instruction on the life of the community. But the church is not identified with the kingdom, for in it the good and the bad live together until the final judgment, which is God's, a point emphasized in the parables of the weeds and of the fish (13:24–30, 37–43, 47–50).

Of special interest is Matthew's development of the relation between the history of Jesus and the history of Israel. As we saw above, Jesus is the awaited Davidic Messiah. Typical are the formulaic citations, so-called because they are introduced by the formula "[this happened] in order to fulfill what the Lord said through the prophet" (1:22–23; 2:15, 17–18, 23; 4:14–16; 8:17; 12:18–21; 13:35; 21:4–5; 27:9). This introductory formula seems to be Matthew's work, whereas the form of the citations is not that of the Septuagint (which the evangelist cites elsewhere) and suggests the intervention, visible in other passages, of Christian scribes (see 13:52; 23:34) in the author's community, who reflected on the relationship between Jesus and the Scriptures of Israel. In any case, these citations serve to show that the Scriptures are fulfilled in Jesus, not simply in the sense that his story marks the fulfillment of the divine prophecies to Israel, but in the sense, too, that the individual events of his history have been foretold. Matthew wants to defend the Christian use of the Scriptures against their interpretation in Judaism. In general, the observance of the law is essential in his eyes (5:17–20, with the emphasis on justice, a key term in Matthew, as the fulfillment of the law), but the law has no meaning except by reference to Jesus.

In light of this Jewish-Christian character of Matthew and of the tensions visible in the gospel, U. Luz has offered a convincing hypothesis on the location of the work in space and time. The fundamental step taken in this gospel, namely, the introduction of Q into Mark, takes place in a way that suggests that Q contained the traditions proper to Matthew's community, which would therefore have had its origins in the itinerant preachers and prophets who transmitted the sayings of Jesus. Matthew's Jewish-Christian community was faced with a choice: the catastrophe that struck Jerusalem in 70 was interpreted as a divine judgment and led to a decision to bring the gospel to the pagans. Matthew defends this choice, which was evidently challenged in the community, and this explains the only rupture depicted in his account: the contradiction between the limitation of Jesus' message to Israel during his lifetime (10:5–6) and the order of the risen Jesus to evangelize all nations (28:19–20). The similar rupture in the history of Matthew's community is anticipated by the Jesus who brings the message of the kingdom to Israel but is rejected and killed, and who in response gives the order for a universal mission. However, the mission to the pagans has not (yet) led, as in Paul, to a rejection of observance of the law; in this sense Matthew is not far removed from Paul's adversaries in the letter to the Galatians.

The language and style of Matthew have been described as "Synagogal Greek": in syntax he often improves on Mark, his source, and uses a vocabulary that is more precise and elevated. He is also more concise and seeks, for didactic purposes, to give only the essentials of his stories. His style is consciously influenced by the language of the Septuagint.

Papias of Hierapolis knew of a tradition according to which "Matthew composed the sayings in Hebrew, then each person interpreted them as he was able" (Eusebius, *Hist. eccl.* 3.39.17). But the Matthew we have is not a translation from a Semitic language but depends on Greek texts such as Mark and Q, he uses the Septuagint as his biblical text, and his style is Greek and contains Greek word plays (24:30 *kopsontai/opsontai*). The other ancient writers depend on Papias; Irenaeus adds that Matthew was the first to write a gospel, at the time when Peter and Paul were preaching in Rome (*Haer.* 3.1.2). But these are legends. Matthew certainly wrote after the destruction of Jerusalem in 70 (22:7; 23:38); if this event was still felt as a painful historical rupture, as Luz suggests, the composition of the gospel could be dated to the early eighties. As for the place of composition, the most persuasive of the many hypotheses is a Greek-speaking city of Syria, probably Antioch, where there were several Christian communities of divergent tendencies, and where this gospel was (probably) used by Ignatius around 110. However, on the basis of Matt 19:1, which locates Judea beyond the Jordan River, G. Thiessen suggests a community located east of the Jordan.

BIBLIOGRAPHY

Commentaries

U. Luz, *Das Evangelium nach Matthäus* (EKKNT 1; 2d ed.; Zurich: Benziger Verlag Neukirchen-Vluyn: Neukirchener Verlag, 1989–). Two of three volumes have appeared.

W. D. Davies and D. C. Allison, *A Critical and Exegetical Commentary on the Gospel according to Saint Matthew* (3 vols.; ICC; Edinburgh: T&T Clark, 1988, 1991, 1997).

Studies

G. Bornkamm, G. Barth, and H. J. Held, *Überlieferung und Auslegung im Matthäusevangelium* (5th ed.; Neukirchen-Vluyn: Neukirchener Verlag, 1968); ET: *Tradition and Interpretation in Matthew* (1963).

E. Schweizer, *The Good News according to Matthew* (trans. D. E. Green; London: SCM, Atlanta: John Knox, 1975).

G. Stanton, "The Origin and Purpose of Matthew's Gospel," *ANRW* II 25.3 (1985): 1890–1951.

7. Luke

a. Gospel

Like Matthew, Luke uses Mark and Q in addition to traditions peculiar to him. His intention, however, is quite different from Matthew's. First and foremost, he is writing a work in two parts: the period of Jesus is followed by that of the preaching of the word of God by the apostles and by Paul, as far as Rome, the center of the empire. He therefore takes over the gospel genre, but broadens it to fit a larger and more ambitious framework. The prologue (1:1–4) consciously follows the conventions of Hellenistic historical works: his references to predecessors and their limitations, his claim for the accuracy of his investigations and for the organization and carefulness of his compositions, are commonplaces of the genre. It is clear that Luke has ambitions as a historian. Let us look first at the part on the life of Jesus, or the "gospel."

Luke alternates blocks of material from Mark with others from Q and his own *Sondergut*. From 3:1 to 6:19 he follows Mark; in 6:20–8:3 he uses other material; in 8:4 to 9:50 he follows Mark but omits Mark 6:45–8:26; in 9:51–18:14 he uses other sources; from 18:15 on he follows Mark, while perhaps also using a second story of the passion. The *Sondergut* of Luke displays specific traits that suggest a certain homogeneity and cohesion before it was taken into the gospel. Namely, it contains a series of narratives that are meant to serve as examples, such as the Good Samaritan, Lazarus and the rich man, the Pharisee and the tax collector. It also contains scenes of special intimacy, such as that of Martha and Mary (10:38–42).

Let us make our way through the contents of the gospel. Chapters 1–2 contain a cycle of stories on the birth of John the Baptist, along with another on the birth of Jesus. These end with the episode of the twelve-year-old Jesus teaching in the temple. Verse 3:1 with its chronological points of reference marks a new beginning and opens the section 3:1–9:50 on the activity of Jesus in Galilee. Following the line established by Mark, the narrative includes the preaching of John, the baptism of Jesus, the genealogy (not in Mark), the temptations (from Q), the inaugural discourse of Jesus in the synagogue of Nazareth (Matt and Mark: of his native place) and his rejection by his fellow townsmen, the cures worked at Capernaum (4:31–43). Next there are the call of the first disciples (5:1–11), the healing of a leper and a paralytic, the call of Levi (5:27–28), disputes with the Pharisees and scribes, the list of the twelve apostles. The "discourse on the plain" (6:20–49), the raisings from the dead in Capernaum and at Nain, the dialogue with the messengers from the Baptist and Jesus' statements about John—all these depend on material other than Mark. The forgiveness of the sinful woman in the house of Simon the Pharisee (7:36–50) anticipates here (and therefore shifts to Galilee) the anointing which Mark 14:3–9 (and Matthew, following him) places in Bethany on the threshold of the passion, as does John 12:1–8. Chapter 9 contains, among other things, the sending of the Twelve and their return, the multiplication of the loaves and fishes, the confession of Peter, followed by the prediction of the passion and the sayings on the following of Jesus; finally there is the transfiguration and a second prediction of the passion.

The material in 9:51–19:27, which for practical purposes is parallel to Mark (10:13–52) only in 18:15–43, is organized into a lengthy journey of Jesus and the disciples from Galilee to Jerusalem. This is characteristic of Luke, whereas the same journey in Mark occupies only ch. 10. In addition to controversies and other teachings, this section contains the great parables of the Lukan *Sondergut*: the Good Samaritan (10:29–37), the importunate friend (11:5–8), the foolish rich man (12:16–21), the prodigal son (15:11–32), the dishonest steward (16:1–9), the rich man and Lazarus (16:19–31), the judge and the widow (18:1–8), and the Pharisee and the tax collector (18:9–14). It also contains the episode of Zacchaeus (19:1–10), which takes place in Jericho, "near Jerusalem" (19:11).

In 19:28 Jesus goes up to Jerusalem; here the triumphal entrance and the expulsion of the traders from the temple inaugurates an activity in Jerusalem that is not distributed over a week's time as in Mark, but which Luke does suggest is of some duration (19:47; 21:37). Chapters 20–21 contain controversies with adversaries and the eschatological discourse. In 22:1 (parallel to Mark 14:1) the account of the passion begins. For this story Luke seems to have had at his disposal not only Mark, but also units of tradition such as the account of the supper (22:14–18), a prophecy of the betrayal and flight of the disciples (22:21, 31–32), and an account of Peter's denial and of the trial before the Sanhedrin (22:54–71). However, it is not certain that he had a second complete account of the passion. Among the appearances of the risen Jesus, the one to the disciples at Emmaus (24:13–35) is peculiar to Luke. He also has a record of an earlier appearance to Simon (24:34), which is found in the tradition cited by Paul (1 Cor 15:5). Luke locates the appearance to the disciples in Jerusalem, not in Galilee (24:36–53).

In 4:44 and 7:17, the theater of Jesus' activity is said to be not Galilee but Judea in the broad sense of the area occupied by Jews. Still, Jesus does not venture outside this territory. Only the missionary mandate in Acts 1:8, after the resurrection, will broaden the scope of the mission to Samaria and the ends of the earth. But the point of departure, even here, remains Jerusalem, which is central in the work of Luke, who, as just noted, places the first appearances of the risen Jesus here. Moreover, in Acts the Jerusalem community is the constant point of reference for the entire expansion of Christianity. The distinction between the activity of Jesus and that of his disciples after the resurrection also has a chronological significance. The history of salvation forms a triptych: the time of Israel, the time of Jesus, and the time of the church (Conzelmann). The activity of Jesus, in its turn, is signposted by two appearances of Satan: after the temptations the devil departs from him until the appointed time (4:13), and Satan enters into Judas, thus beginning the passion (22:3). In the period between these two points, the activity of Jesus is not hampered by the demon.

Luke's language is Koiné, but with some claim to a literary style, as is apparent in, among other things, the careful use of the tenses and moods of verbs, especially the optative, of which there are twenty-eight instances, in the present and aorist tenses. Paul uses only the aorist, and there are very few instances in the rest of the New Testament. Luke also seeks to improve on Mark's style by reducing the number of Semitisms, using a more careful and graceful terminology and phraseology, and making extensive use of hypotaxis in place of the parataxis favored by Mark.

According to Irenaeus (possibly dependent on Papias), Luke, companion of Paul (Phlm 24; see Col 4:14; 2 Tim 4:11), "edited in a book the gospel preached by Paul" (*Haer.* 3.1.1). The *Muratorian Canon* places this gospel third in order of composition; it identifies Luke as the companion whom Paul took with him, and describes him as a physician and a literary man. But the author of Luke-Acts does not seem to be close to Paul either chronologically or theologically. The composition certainly dates from after 70, because the destruction of Jerusalem is presupposed (21:20–24); some scholars place it as late as around 125, but 80–90 seems more likely (in Acts the letters of Paul seem to be unknown, and this can hardly have been the case in 125).

BIBLIOGRAPHY

Commentaries

J. A. Fitzmyer, *The Gospel according to Luke* (2 vols.; AB 28–28A; New York: Doubleday, 1981–1985).

F. Bovon, *L'Evangile selon Saint Luc* (CNT 2d series, 3a; Geneva: Labor et Fides, 1991–). One of three volumes published.

Studies

H. Conzelmann, *Die Mitte der Zeit: Studien zur Theologie des Lukas* (3d ed.; Tübingen: Mohr, 1960); ET: *The Theology of Luke* (trans. G. Buswell; New York: Harper, 1961).

F. Neirynck, ed., *L'Evangile de Luc: Problèmes littéraires et théologiques. Mémorial L. Cerfaux* (Gembloux: Duculot, 1978).

L. E. Keck and J. L. Martin, eds., *Studies in Luke-Acts* (2d ed.; Philadelphia: Fortress, 1980).

F. Bovon, *L'oeuvre de Luc: Etudes d'exégèse et de théologie* (Paris: Cerf, 1987).

b. Acts of the Apostles

At its beginning, Acts, like Luke's gospel, addresses Theophilus. It refers explicitly to the "first book," which told of the actions and teachings of Jesus until his ascension into heaven. The new narrative starts with that last episode, which is now located forty days after the resurrection, unlike Luke 24. The final words of Jesus (1:8) set out the program of the book: the disciples are to be his witnesses in Jerusalem, throughout Judea, in Samaria, and to the ends of the earth. As a result, Acts 1–7 tell of the community in Jerusalem; chs. 8–12 tell of the mission in Judea and Samaria, Jerusalem being both the point of departure and of arrival; chs. 13–28 tell of the mission to the pagans, as far as the preaching of Paul in Rome, starting from Antioch. Each of the first two sections creates the premise for the next. Thus in ch. 2 Jews of every nation hear Peter preach on Pentecost and are converted. Chapter 6 tells of the formation of the group of Hellenists who will carry on the mission outside of Jerusalem. In ch. 10 Peter receives a revelation that allows him to start receiving pagans into the Christian community.

In greater detail, the contents are as follows: ch. 1: the ascension; establishment of the first community consisting of the Twelve; replacement of Judas; ch. 2: Pentecost; chs. 3–5: Peter cures a cripple; arrest of Peter and John and interrogation before the Sanhedrin; Ananias and Sapphira; new arrest and release of the apostles; ch. 6: formation of the group of Hellenists; martyrdom of Stephen.

Chapter 8: preaching of the Hellenists; Philip in Samaria (Simon Magus) and in the south; ch. 9: conversion of Paul; chs. 10–11: conversion of centurion Cornelius at Caesarea; beginning of the preaching to the pagans; the church of Antioch; ch. 12: martyrdom of James; arrest and liberation of Peter.

Chapters 13–14: "first missionary journey" of Paul, along with Barnabas, as emissaries of the church of Antioch, to Cyprus, Pamphilia, Antioch of Pisidia, Iconium, Lycaonia, and back to Antioch. In the various mission sites, initial success in the synagogue provokes a reaction from the Jews that impels Paul and Barnabas to preach to the pagans, who receive the word with joy; this pattern is conveyed in exemplary fashion at Antioch in Pisidia (13:14–49). The result is to raise the crucial problem of the mission to the pagans and the demands to be made of them; this is faced in ch. 15 at the so-called "council of Jerusalem" or "of the apostles."

The "second journey" of Paul, this time by himself, begins in 15:40; after Paul passes through Asia Minor, a revelation causes him to take ship for Europe (16:9–10). He preaches in Philippi, Thessalonica, Berea, and Athens. In this last place he delivers the well-known discourse on the Areopagus (17:22–31), a creation of Luke that draws upon the motifs of Jewish apologetics. Paul's success here is scanty. He establishes the church in Corinth; then, continually persecuted by the Jews, he returns to Antioch by way of Jerusalem (18:22).

Luke goes on immediately to the "third journey" (18:23). After the departure of Apollos, a Jewish-Christian missionary, from Ephesus, Paul goes to that city and remains there for two years. A riot caused by the makers of souvenirs of the temple of Artemis forces him to leave. He continues his work on the coast at Troas and then Miletus, where he summons the elders of Ephesus and delivers a farewell discourse to them (20:17–38). Chapter 21: return of Paul to Jerusalem, where the Jews of Asia stir up the people against him; intervention of the Roman guard and arrest of Paul.

Chapter 22: in an address to the Jews of Jerusalem Paul tells his own story and the charge he received of preaching to the pagans. Chapter 23: on learning that Paul is a Roman citizen, the tribune has him appear before the Sanhedrin to respond to the accusations. Since the Jews are plotting to kill Paul, the tribune has him transferred to Caesarea, residence of Felix the governor. Chapter 24: trial of Paul before Felix, who decides to keep him in prison for two years. Chapters 25–26: before Porcius Festus, successor to Felix, Paul appeals to Caesar; on occasion of a visit of King Agrippa and his wife Berenice Paul delivers an autobiographical address, at the end of which Festus and Agrippa agree that he is innocent. Chapter 27: embarkation of Paul for Rome, storm and shipwreck; the castaways manage to reach Malta. Chapter 28: after three months in Malta, departure for Rome. The Christians of Rome welcome Paul; while under house arrest, Paul meets with the leaders of the Jewish community, whom he does not persuade. His last words reassert the hardening of Jewish hearts and the sending of salvation to the pagans. A final note adds that for two years Paul continued to receive people and proclaim Christ to them.

This seemingly abrupt conclusion of Acts, which does not follow Paul as far as his martyrdom (probably in Rome under Nero), is not to be explained by supposing that the book was written before the martyrdom, for the discourse in ch. 20 shows that Luke knew of Paul's death. Nor should we suppose that Paul was freed and then traveled to Spain before being imprisoned again in Rome. The reasons for the abrupt ending are probably that (a) Luke is not writing a biography of Paul but a history of the spread of the word of God from Jerusalem to Rome, the center of the empire, and (b) a report of the execution of Paul by the Roman authorities would not fit in with the author's apologetical approach. He wishes to show in fact that the civil authorities have no reason to fear and persecute Christianity. While the Jews are unremittingly hostile to Paul, the Roman authorities, even if they sometimes yield to Jewish pressure, are capable of recognizing his rights, as in the case of the tribune in Jerusalem (22:25–30) and governor Porcius Festus, and also of Agrippa and Berenice (ch. 25). In

Paphos, proconsul Sergius Paulus, "an intelligent man," is ready to listen to the word, but a wicked Jewish magician tries to prevent his hearing it (13:6–12). It is therefore not accidental that Acts should end by emphasizing the freedom with which Paul is able to teach in Rome.

While stressing the opposition of the Jews to Christianity, which he sees as opposition to the will of God, Luke is open to the Hellenistic cultural tradition, as can be seen from the address on the Areopagus. Here Greek religious thought, in its highest form, is seen as leading to acceptance of the Christian message. Still, Paul's failure in Athens, especially when it comes to the subject of the resurrection, shows that Luke does not gloss over the differences.

The discourses in Acts are thus important for a study of the author's thought. The historiographical conventions of antiquity allowed authors to place in the mouths of historical figures discourses which they did not actually deliver, but which served to illustrate the meaning of a situation. In addition to Paul's discourses as a prisoner with their political apologetic and the discourse at Athens with its religious apologetic, the discourse to the elders of Ephesus is also important (ch. 20). This is a kind of testament containing instructions that are valid more for Luke's own time than for Paul's, and that have to do with the behavior of authorities in the church, especially watchfulness in regard to heresy. Paul offers himself as a model; Luke wants to establish continuity, through presbyterial succession, between the church of his time and the church of the founders.

In contrast, the discourses addressed to the Jews by Peter (chs. 2, 3, 4) and Paul (ch. 13) follow a kerygmatic outline, based on the relation between the Scriptures and the fate of Jesus, and culminating in a call to conversion. This was for Luke the model followed in the apostolic preaching. Finally, the discourse of Stephen in ch. 7 contains a harsh criticism of the constant disobedience that Israel showed to God throughout its history, and is a prelude to the preaching to the pagans. The discourse is Luke's work, but may preserve theological elements proper to the tradition of the Hellenistic Christians, of whom Stephen was the leader.

But if the discourses are Luke's creations in the service of his theological vision, what historical value does his book have for the reconstruction of Christian origins? This is the problem of Luke's sources, which requires different answers for chs. 1–12 and for chs. 13–28. In the first part, it is generally agreed that Luke used written sources containing particular episodes and having various degrees of historical value. More specifically, scholars think of an Antiochene source for the sections on Antioch, including Paul's first journey and the "council," and of another source, connected rather with Jerusalem and Caesarea, that had an interest in Philip the Hellenist. But Luke has incorporated these preexisting materials into a framework controlled by some leading ideas. In addition to the discourses, the summaries, which are also typical of the historiographical method of that age, are of redactional importance.

Among Luke's leading ideas is the central place of Jerusalem as point of departure for missions, as the place where the risen Jesus appeared, and as the residence of the twelve apostles. The identification of the Twelve and the apostles is especially marked in Luke, who does not grant this title to his hero Paul, although as is clear from Paul's letters it was the focal point of his self-awareness. Jerusalem is also the center of control over the other communities, to the point that independent missionary undertakings had to be approved by Jerusalem (9:14–17). The Jerusalem community is greatly idealized, especially in the summaries, as a result of a historico-theological framework that gives a privileged place to the golden age of beginnings, with its sharing of possessions and its absence of people in need (1:14; 2:42–47; 4:32–35; etc.). Luke tends to minimize conflicts, as in the account of the appointment of the Hellenists (6:6) and the council of Jerusalem (ch. 15). Paul's letters reveal situations that are far more diverse and marked by tensions.

In the second part of Acts, the main problem with sources is the sections in which a first-person narrator appears, the so-called "we sections." These have to do with journeys: from Troas to Philippi (16:10–17), from Philippi to Troas (20:5–15), from Miletus to Jerusalem (21:1–18), and from Caesarea to Rome (27:1–28:16). It has been suggested that these passages show either a real participation of Luke in these journeys of Paul, or the use of the diary of someone who accompanied the apostle. In either case, they would be known in Troas. But these sections contain elements that are probably not historical, such as Paul and Silas's imprisonment in Philippi, and the shipwreck story, which is a common motif in the ancient novel. The "we" seems rather to be a literary device for giving an impression of realism and immediacy. Moreover, this second part, as it stands, is strongly marked by motifs that are apologetical and belong to anti-Jewish polemics; these reveal Luke's theological purpose.

Richard Pervo has endeavored to show that Acts is intended not as a historical work but as a historical novel; its purpose is to edify while delighting, like some Hellenistic novels. But D. E. Aune has rightly objected that what must be defined is this bipartite work as a whole. Aune shows that Pervo's model does not fit the combination of Luke-Acts, which instead has that affinity with Hellenistic historiography.

Finally, an interesting problem arises with regard to the text of Acts. In the manuscript tradition, the witnesses to the "western" text-type ($\mathfrak{P}^{38}$, $\mathfrak{P}^{48}$, codex D from the 5th/6th century, the early Latin versions, the marginal notes in the Syriac version produced by Thomas of Harkel in 616) differ from the other texts in a much more marked manner than for the other books of the New Testament. It has been suggested that Luke composed two successive versions, but this view cannot be sustained, because between the two texts there are real contradictions (e.g., 15:20 and 29 in the Jerusalem decree). Nor can the western text be earlier, since it shows clear signs of stylistic improvements and of explanatory and edifying expansions. This text appears to be secondary, and it cannot be evaluated separately from the western text of Luke's gospel: both writings have been harmonized with the other gospels and, in general, improved stylistically by the elimination of the most marked Lukan characteristics.

BIBLIOGRAPHY

Commentaries

E. Haenchen, *Die Apostelgeschichte* (KEK 3; 16th ed.; Göttingen: Vandenhoeck & Ruprecht, 1967).

H. Conzelmann, *Die Apostelgeschichte* (HNT 7; 2d ed.; Tübingen: Mohr, 1972).

R. Pesch, *Atti degli Apostoli* (EKKNT 5,1–2; 1986); IT (Assisi: Cittadella, 1993).

C. K. Barrett, *A Critical and Exegetical Commentary on the Acts of the Apostles* (Edinburgh: T&T Clark, 1998).

Studies

M. Dibelius, *Aufsätze zur Apostelgeschichte* (4th ed.; Göttingen: Vandenhoeck & Ruprecht, 1961).

J. Dupont, *Etudes sur les Actes des Apôtres* (Lectio divina 45; Paris: Cerf, 1957).

————, *Nouvelles études sur les Actes des Apôtres* (Lectio divina 118; Paris: Cerf, 1984).

E. Plümacher, *Lukas als hellenistischer Schriftsteller: Studien zur Apostelgeschichte* (Göttingen: Vandenhoeck & Ruprecht, 1972).

M. Hengel, *La storiografia protocristiana* (1979; Brescia: Paideia, 1985).

P. Van Linden, *The Gospel of Luke and Acts* (Wilmington, Del.: Glazier, 1986).

D. E. Aune, *The New Testament in Its Literary Environment* (Philadelphia: Westminster, 1987), 77–157.

R. I. Pervo, *Profit with Delight: The Literary Genre of the Acts of the Apostles* (Philadelphia: Fortress, 1987).

8. Jewish-Christian Gospels

This name is usually given to some gospels that did not become canonical but were used in communities of Jewish origin; of these only fragments have been preserved in indirect tradition. It is difficult to describe or define them because the citations through which we know them are often only vaguely attributed to one or another of them. Their very number is uncertain; the only one given a title by the early writers is the *Gospel of the Hebrews*. But the thesis that there was only one Jewish-Christian gospel, possibly in two versions, has been abandoned today. Either two gospels (of the Hebrews or Nazareans and of the Ebionites or the Twelve Apostles) or three (of the Hebrews, the Nazareans, and the Ebionites or Twelve Apostles) have been identified. The latter solution seems preferable for the following reasons (for further discussion see Vielhauer-Strecker.

Clement of Alexandria attests to the existence in Egypt of a *Gospel according to the Hebrews,* from which he cites (*Strom.* 1.9.25) a logion given more completely (without naming the source) in *Strom.* 5.14.96. The same logion occurs in P. Oxyrhynchus 654 and in the Nag Hammadi *Gospel of Thomas,* where it is given in the second place. From the same *Gospel of the Hebrews,* Origen cites a saying of Jesus, who says that he was taken by his mother, the Holy Spirit, and carried to a high mountain, Tabor; the context must have been a reworking of the story of the temptations (*Comm. Jo.* 2.12.87; same citation in *Hom. Jer.* 15.4 without naming the source). The idea that the Holy Spirit (a feminine noun in the Semitic languages) is Jesus' mother seems to exclude his being the son of Joseph; this was asserted by the Jewish-Christian sect of the Ebionites.

Eusebius of Caesarea mentions, among the books whose canonicity is debated, the *Gospel of the Hebrews* (*Hist. eccl.* 3.25.2). A little further on, Eusebius asserts that all of the Ebionites reject the preexistence of Christ, while some of them do not reject the virginal birth. They use only the *Gospel of the Hebrews* (*Hist. eccl.* 3.27.3–4). But since two fragments of the *Gospel of the Hebrews* presuppose the preexistence of Christ, it is doubtful that the Ebionites really made use of the work. Eusebius also says that Papias of Hierapolis told the story of a woman accused of many sins before the Lord, a story which (according to Eusebius, not Papias) was contained in the *Gospel of the Hebrews* (*Hist. eccl.* 3.39.17). Finally, the last mention of this gospel in Eusebius is in a reference to Hegesippus, who "gives some citations from the *Gospel according to the Hebrews* and from the *Syriac Gospel,* and especially in Hebrew" (4.22.8). Eusebius thus distinguishes the *Gospel of the Hebrews* from a gospel in Aramaic ("Syriac"), from which, evidently, the citations by Hegesippus in "Hebrew" come.

In his *Divine Manifestation* Eusebius cites two fragments of gospels, attributing the first (4.22) to the "gospel that has come down to us written in Hebrew letters," and the second (in a part of the *Divine Manifestation* that has been preserved only in Syriac) to the "gospel in Hebrew that [circulates] among the Jews." This Aramaic gospel, which Eusebius contrasts in both cases to canonical Matthew, is probably to be identified with the one cited by Hegesippus, and is certainly to be distinguished from that according to the Hebrews. Eusebius had a direct knowledge of the Aramaic gospel; it is not certain that he had direct knowledge of the *Gospel of the Hebrews.*

Epiphanius of Salamis speaks of the Nazareans (Jewish Christians of Coelesyria) in ch. 29 of his *Refutation of All Heresies (Panarion).* He says that "they possess the gospel according to Matthew, in its entirety and in Hebrew; it still exists among them in Hebrew letters, just as it was originally written" (29.9.4). But the context shows that Epiphanius did not see this gospel, for he does not know whether it contained the genealogy of Jesus.

On the other hand, he does know the gospel used by the Ebionites: "they too accept the gospel according to Matthew; like the followers of Cerinthus and Merintus, they too use only this gospel. They call it, however, 'according to the Hebrews,' and the reason is that Matthew alone in the New Testament presents and proclaims the good news in Hebrew with Hebrew letters" (*Pan.* 30.3.7). A little further on Epiphanius explains that they have distorted and mutilated this gospel of Matthew, which they call the "Hebrew" gospel (30.13.2). In this setting he cites seven fragments of it; he is therefore quite familiar with it, as he is not with that of the Nazareans. He knows, among other things, that it lacks the genealogy and begins with the preaching of John the Baptist in the time of Herod (the *incipit* is cited twice: 30.13.6; 30.14.3).

The information given by Epiphanius agrees with that of Irenaeus of Lyons, according to whom the Ebionites used only the gospel of Matthew (*Haer.* 1.26.2; 3.11.7) but removed the part about the birth of Christ (3.21.1; 5.1.3). The fragments cited by Epiphanius show that this gospel is not in fact an Aramaic original of canonical Matthew (which was written in Greek) but a Greek reworking of the latter. The identification with Matthew by both authors must have depended on the idea, circulated by Papias, that Matthew was composed originally in Aramaic: Epiphanius mentions this in 29.9.4.

It follows that the gospels of the Nazareans and the Ebionites were different works. However, even if Epiphanius seems to know the latter as "according to the Hebrews" or "in Hebrew," it must not be identified with the *Gospel according to the Hebrews* that was known to Clement and Origen, for the latter work accepted the preexistence of Jesus and the role of the Holy Spirit in his birth. Epiphanius's identification of the two is probably influenced by what Eusebius says about the use of the *Gospel of the Hebrews* by a branch of the Ebionites (see above).

Jerome provides numerous citations, but the terms he uses to describe their sources are muddled: gospel according to the Hebrews, of the Hebrews, Hebrew, Hebrew according to Matthew, and, once, gospel according to the apostles. He says (*Vir. ill.*) that in his time the library at Caesarea had a copy, but he adds that he had seen and copied it when he was with the Nazareans of Berea in Coelesyria. The placement of it in Caesarea (although Jerome did stay there) may therefore be an inference based on the identification of the gospel known to him with that used by Eusebius. An example of the way in which Jerome writes is this citation: "The gospel used by the Nazareans and the Ebionites, which I recently translated from Aramaic into Greek and which many call 'Hebrew Matthew' " (*Comm. Matt.* 12.3). We have seen that the gospels of the Nazareans and the Ebionites were different. A little earlier (*Vir. ill.* 2–3) Jerome speaks of his translation of this gospel into Latin, but in later writings he does not speak of any such translation, and it is likely that he never made it. The identification of it with Hebrew Matthew is attributed to others.

There is a tendency today to be quite distrustful of what Jerome says. He certainly believed in the existence of only one Jewish-Christian gospel and attached to it all the information he found in the works of other writers. It is probable, moreover, that he used only fragments, and it is difficult to say how they came to his attention; perhaps he took some passages of the *Gospel of the Hebrews* from earlier authors (Origen, certainly) and himself transcribed some passages from the *Gospel of the Nazareans.*

Three manuscripts of the gospels (566, 9th c.; 899, 11th c.; 1424, 9th/10th c.) contain some marginal variants taken from a gospel described as *tōn Ioudaikōn*, which is mentioned in the *subscriptiones* of 36 manuscripts that refer to a copy preserved on the "holy mountain," that is, Mount Zion in Jerusalem. A. Schmidke (1911) showed that this exemplar must have been an edition of the gospels made between 370 and 500 and preserved in the basilica on Mount Zion. It was probably a text in Aramaic, related if not identical to the *Gospel of the Nazareans.* A fragment (probably spurious) of Cyril of Jerusalem that has come down to us in a Coptic translation cites, as from the *Gospel of the Hebrews,* a passage on the birth of Jesus according to which Mary was the incarnation of a heavenly power named Michael. On the other hand, a fragment of the *Gospel of the Hebrews* preserved by Origen and Jerome (see above) says that the Holy Spirit was the mother of Jesus. It is doubtful, then, that the fragment cited by Cyril belonged to the same work.

There are, finally, some medieval citations. Haymo of Auxerre (ca. 850) attributes to the *Gospel of the Nazareans* a passage on the conversion of many Jews at the death of Jesus. A thirteenth-century manuscript of the *Aurora,* a versification of the Bible by Peter of Riga in the twelfth century, has in a margin a citation from "the books of the gospels used by the Nazareans." A Celtic catechesis contains a citation from the *Gospel of the Hebrews* on the day of judgment, which will occur during the Easter season (Vat. Regin. lat. 49; 9th c.). In addition, B. Bischoff has published, with a study, a fragment on the adoration of the Magi that is cited in a commentary on Matthew by Sedulius Scotus as coming from the *Gospel of the Hebrews;* an instruction attributed to the *Gospel of the Hebrews* in an Irish commentary on Luke; extracanonical information drawn from this Irish commentary and from a commentary on Matthew, which Bischoff would assign to the same gospel; and seven fragments ascribed to the *Gospel of the Nazareans* in a *History of the Lord's Passion* contained in a fourteenth-century manuscript, one fragment of which corresponds to a point made twice by Jerome.

These fragments seem not to have come from the original works, but to have been passed on to the medieval authors, especially the Irish, in florilegia and catenas; the writings of Jerome seem to have played an important part in that transmission.

It seems legitimate, therefore, to distinguish three gospels, which we shall now characterize.

The following fragments are to be assigned to the *Gospel of the Nazareans,* so titled only in the medieval testimonies.

1. Pseudo-Origen, *Comm. Matt.* 15.14 (on Matt 19:16–30: a variant of the episode of the rich man).
2. Eusebius, *Theoph.* 4.22 (variant of the parable of the talents, Matt 25:14–30).
3. Eusebius, *Theoph.* (Syriac) 4.12 (on the division within families; see Matt 10:34–36).
4. Jerome, perhaps *Famous Men* 3 (the two citations "From Egypt I have called my son" and "Therefore he will be call a Nazirite," taken from the Hebrew biblical text and not from the Septuagint; but in the context it is possible that Jerome is referring here simply to Matt 2:15, 23).
5. Jerome, *Comm. Matt.* 6:11 and *Treatise on Psalm 135* (in place of the *epiousion* of Matt 6:11 this gospel has *mahar,* "of tomorrow").
6. Jerome, *Comm. Matt.* 12:13 (a novelistic expansion of the episode of the man with the withered hand, Matt 12:9–12).
7. Jerome, *Comm. Matt.* 23:35 (instead of "Zechariah the son of Berekiah" as is Matt 23:35, this letter has "the son of Jehoiada").
8. Jerome, *Comm. Matt.* 27:16 (Barabbas explained as "son of [their] teacher").
9. Jerome, *Comm. Matt.* 27:51, and *Letter* 120 to Edibia; same theme as in the anonymous *History of the Lord's Passion* (collapse of the architrave of the temple at the death of Jesus, different from Matt 27:51).
10. Jerome, *Pelag.* 3.2 (despite his cousin's protests, Jesus is baptized by John).
11. Jerome, *Pelag.* 3.2; a parallel in the *Ioudaikon* to Matt 18:22 (forgive seventy times seven times, because even the prophets sinned; see Matt 18:21–22).
12. Variants of the *Ioudaikon* at Matt 4:5
13. Matt 5:22
14. Matt 7:5 (rather: 7:21–23)
15. Matt 10:16
16. Matt 11:12
17. Matt 11:25
18. Matt 12:40
19. Matt 15:5
20. Matt 16:2–3
21. Matt 16:17
22. Matt 26:74
23. Matt 27:65 (see also item 11 above)

Probably to be ascribed to this gospel (see item 9 above), entirely or in part, are also the medieval testimonies listed earlier; but among these the gospel is expressly mentioned only by Haymo, the manuscript of the *Aurora,* and the *History of the Lord's Passion.*

Item 5 above shows that this gospel was written in Aramaic; *mahar,* however, cannot be the Semitic original of the very rare *epiousios* but must rather be an interpretation of it. The gospel must therefore have been an Aramaic version of Greek Matthew and contained secondary alterations and amplifications. Novelistic amplifications are seen in items 1 and 6, in both cases with the addition of a social interest. In item 9 there is a novelistic motif, but also a clearer allusion than in Matthew to the destruction of the Jerusalem temple and the end of the old covenant. If item 4 refers to this gospel, then it contained the story of the birth of Jesus; the fragment in Sedulius Scotus also refers to this gospel, even though Sedulius attributes it to the *Gospel of the Hebrews.* In the *Gospel of the Nazareans* the words, too, of Jesus show secondary expansions, as is evident in item 2. Item 4 connects with Matt 7:21–23 a noncanonical saying that is preserved in *2 Clem.* 4.5. Since this gospel is probably the "Syriac" gospel used by Hegesippus (according to Eusebius; see above), its composition is to be located between that of Matthew and the work of Hegesippus (ca. 180), probably in Berea in Coelesyria, in the same Jewish-Christian circles in which it was being used in the time of Epiphanius and Jerome.

The seven citations in Epiphanius, *Panarion* 30, are to be assigned to the *Gospel of the Ebionites.*

1. 13.2–3 ("a certain man, Jesus by name, aged about thirty" brings to mind the calling of the disciples).
2. 13.4 (activity of John the Baptist; he feeds on honeycakes, not on grasshoppers as in the Synoptics).
3. 13.6 (beginning of the gospel: baptism of John, son of Zechariah and Elizabeth, in the time of Herod and Caiaphas).
4. 13.7–8 (baptism of Jesus).
5. 14.5 (those who are the mothers and the brothers and sisters of Jesus; see Matt 12:47–50).
6. 16.5 (Jesus came to do away with sacrifices).
7. 22.4 (Jesus refuses to eat meat at the Passover meal).

According to Epiphanius, the Ebionites called their gospel "The Gospel according to Matthew," which agrees with the information in Irenaeus. Item 6 has a parallel only in Matthew. In any case, Epiphanius' identification of the work with the *Gospel of the Hebrews* is in error. The language was Greek, as is shown by the play on the words *akris* (grasshopper) and *egkris* (honeycake) in item 2. The accounts of the birth were missing, while the gospel did contain the Last Supper and doubtless the passion as well. Item 1 is spoken by one of the disciples who uses "we"; perhaps the speaker is Matthew, who is given a position of prominence at the end of Jesus' list ("and you, Matthew, who sat at the moneychanger's table"). Was the entire gospel thus narrated? The identification of this gospel with the *Gospel of the Twelve* mentioned by Origen and Jerome is uncertain. D. A. Bertrand has shown that this gospel is a gospel harmony, that is, one that summarizes and reconciles what is said in Matthew, Mark, and Luke (though not also John, as in Tatian's *Diatessaron*).

Typically Ebionite theological traits are evident even in these few fragmentary passages. The absence of the stories of the birth is in keeping with the Ebionite rejection of the virginal conception; the same holds for the stress on Jesus as "man" in item 1; Jesus becomes the Son of God when the Spirit enters into him at his baptism (item 4). Jesus came to do away with the sacrificial worship of the temple, which the Ebionites fiercely opposed (item 6). John eats honeycakes, not grasshoppers (item 2), and Jesus refuses to eat meat (item 7); both of these reflect Ebionite vegetarianism. The apostles bear witness to Israel (item 1), which is fitting in a Jewish Christian gospel. G. Howard has suggested, however, that the "heretical" readings in this gospel were not created *ad hoc* by the sect but were derived from a repertory of variants that were originally theologically neutral and from which every gospel author could choose. The date of composition was between the beginning of the second century, when the three Synoptics were widespread and accepted, and Irenaeus. They probably originated in the country east of the Jordan, where Epiphanius and other writers situate the activity of the Ebionites.

To the *Gospel of the Hebrews* are to be ascribed, first and foremost, the fragments passed on by Clement of Alexandria and Origen. The former has:

1. The saying "He who is astonished will reign, and having reigned he will rest" (*Strom.* 2.9.45.5), and cites it again in *Strom.* 5.14.96.3 without naming the source but in a more complete form that corresponds to logion 2 in the Coptic *Gospel of Thomas* (NHC II,2 80.14–15) and in P. Oxyrhynchus 654.
2. Origen, *Comm. Jo.* 2.12, repeated in *Hom. Jer.* 14.4; also in Jerome, *Comm. Mich.* 7.6; *Comm. Isa.* 4.9; *Comm. Ezech.* 16.13 ("a little while ago my mother, the Holy Spirit, took me by one of my hairs and transported me to the high mountain Tabor").
3. Didymus of Alexandria, *Commentary on the Psalms* in the Tura Papyrus (the disciple Levi is to be identified not with Matthew but with Matthias in Acts 1:23.
4. (Pseudo-?) Cyril of Jerusalem, *Discourse on Mary Theotokos,* Coptic translation (Christ was carried for six months by a celestial power named Michael, who descended to earth in the form of Mary).

Fragments transmitted by Jerome (in addition to item 2):

5. *Comm. Eph.* 5.4 ("You shall never be happy except when you have looked upon your brother with love").
6. *Famous Men* 2 (the risen Lord goes to James, celebrates the Eucharist with him, and urges him to cancel the vow he had made at the Last Supper of not eating food until he should see Jesus risen).
7. *Comm. Isa.* 4, on Isa 11:2 (when Jesus comes up from the water of baptism, "the entire fountain of the Holy Spirit" comes down and rests on him, saying that he, the Spirit, had been waiting for him in all the prophets).
8. *Comm. Ezech.* 18.7 (one of the most serious sins is to sadden the spirit of one's brother).
9. Eusebius of Caesarea, *Hist. eccl.* 3.39.7, attributes to the *Gospel according to the Hebrews* the story told by Papias of Hierapolis of "a woman accused of many sins before the Lord," a story not necessarily to be identified with that in John 7:58–8:11, because different stories were in circulation of the encounters of Jesus with sinful women. The *Gospel of the Hebrews* could well have contained a version of such a story, but we do not know where Eusebius, who seems not to know this gospel, could have learned of it.

The title *Gospel according to the Hebrews* is used earlier by Clement and Origen; it is therefore original, which is not true of the titles of the other two gospels. According to the *Stichometry* of Nicephorus, the text contained two thousand verses, three hundred fewer than Matthew, so that the surviving fragments constitute a very small part of it. That item 4 belongs to it is not really certain, since this text expresses a pronounced docetism that is not confirmed in the other testimonies. We are not certain, therefore, that it contained the birth of Jesus, but if it did, the story was heavily mythologized. It did, however, tell of the baptism (item 7), and the temptation (item 2), although with obvious differences from the Synoptic version. Also quite different was the story of the passion, in which there was a strong emphasis on James, who has an important place at the supper and receives the first appearance of the risen Jesus (after the priest's servant). The pre-Pauline tradition in 1 Cor 15:7 tells of an appearance to James, but Paul does not regard it as the first. For this gospel, then, James is the principal authority; this attests to the Jewish-Christian character of the work but also constitutes another link, in addition to (item 1), with the Coptic *Gospel of Thomas* (logion 12).

Item 7 belongs to a line of thought that is rooted in the sapiential thinking of the Old Testament: the Wisdom of God makes its way from generation to generation by way of the souls of the prophets and friends of God (Wis 7:27); it sought a resting place in all peoples before finding it in Israel (Sir 24:7). According to the *Pseudo-Clementines* the "true" preexisting "prophet" manifested himself in a series of individuals down through the history of the world until he found his definitive repose in Jesus (*Ps.-Clem. Hom.* 3.20.1; see *Ps.-Clem. Recog.* 2.22.4). In this fragment and in item 2, Jesus is seen as the son of the Holy Spirit, as in the Nag Hammadi *Apocryphon of James.* The understanding of the Spirit as Mother of Jesus is due to the feminine gender of "spirit" in the Semitic languages, although this does not mean that the *Gospel of the Hebrews* was written in a Semitic language.

"Rest" is also a key term in item 1, where it refers to eschatological rest, the point of arrival of Christian development, a process that also includes astonishment. The same climate of thought is found in Hellenistic mysticism and in Christian gnosis. Apparently lacking these implications are the two sayings of Jesus (items 5 and 8), which some ascribe to the *Gospel of the Nazareans* (Jerome's statements are muddled); in any case, the theme of "saddening the spirit" has a "technical" Jewish-Christian background (see the Shepherd of Hermas, *Mand.* 10). Concern for brotherly love may suggest that this gospel was used in a rather limited community with strong internal ties and a degree of separation from the world, a community practicing a Christianity with mystical traits; its aim was interior progress and "rest."

The *Gospel of the Hebrews* was written in Greek, for it uses the Septuagint. It certainly owed its name to its use in a community of Christians of Jewish origin. All the witnesses point toward Egypt (Jerome certainly depends on Origen). Knowledge of it by Hegesippus fixes 180 as the *terminus ante quem.* Unlike the other two gospels we have been discussing, this one seems to depend on its own traditions, not on the canonical gospels. Therefore it is not possible to establish a *terminus post quem.*

BIBLIOGRAPHY

Texts

E. Klostermann, *Apocrypha II: Evangelien* (KIT 8; 3d ed.; Berlin: de Gruyter, 1929).
K. Aland, *Synopsis quattuor evangeliorum* (13th ed.; Stuttgart: Deutsche Bibel-gesellschaft, 1985); ET: K. Aland, *Synopsis of the Four Gospels: Greek-English Edition* (3d corr. ed.; United Bible Societies, 1979).
W. Schneemelcher, ed., *New Testament Apocrypha* (2 vols.; Louisville: Westminster John Knox, 1991).

Studies

P. Viclhauer and G. Strecker, "Jewish-Christian Gospels," in vol. I of *New Testament Apocrypha* (ed. W. Schneemelcher; Louisville: Westminster John Knox, 1991): 134–78 (with translation of the fragments).
A. F. J. Klijn, "Das Hebräer- und das Nazoräerevangelium," *ANRW* II 25.5 (1988): 3997–4033.
G. Howard, "The Gospel of the Ebionites," ibid., 4034–58.
L. Cirillo, "I vangeli giudeo-cristiani," in *Da Gesù a Origene* (ed. E. Norelli; vol. I of *La Bibbia nell'antichità cristiana;* Bologna: Dehoniane, 1993): 275–318 (with translation of the fragments).
H. J. Schoeps, *Jewish Christianity: Factional Disputes in the Early Church* (Philadelphia: Fortress, 1969).

9. Gospel of the Egyptians

In his *Homily on Luke* 1, speaking of the attempts to tell the story of Jesus, Origen mentions the heretical gospels, among them a *Gospel of the Egyptians.* Clement of Alexandria cites some passages of this gospel in his *Miscellanies:*
- 3.9.63 (a saying of the Lord to Salome: "I have come to destroy the works of the female");
- 3.9.64 (another saying of the Lord to Salome, against carnal generation, which perpetuates the power of death);
- 3.9.66 (another exchange between Salome and Jesus, on the same subject);
- 3.13.92 (a reply of the Lord to Salome: such things [which things?] will be known "when you have trodden on the garment of shame and when the two shall become one and the male with the female, neither male nor female"; the same saying is cited and interpreted in *2 Clem.* 12.2 and 4–5, as a reply to the question: When will the kingdom come? Other forms of the same saying are in the *Gos. Thom.* 22 and 37).

In addition, Hippolytus, *Elench.* 5.7.8, says that the views of the Naassenes on the soul were taken from the *Gospel of the Egyptians;* Epiphanius, *Pan.* 62.2 maintains that the Sabellians got their doctrines from the apocrypha and in particular from the *Gospel of the Egyptians.*

From the little that the fragments in Clement enable us to discover, this gospel contained a dialogue of Jesus with Salome. The dialogue was a genre dear to the Gnostics, who also gave a privileged place to women as partners in dialogue with Jesus; for this reason we are not sure that the work does not belong rather to the literary genre of dialogues of the risen Jesus. The tone is clearly encratite, with its elimination of the difference between male and female (see logion 114 of *Gos. Thom.*) and its abolition of marriage and generation. According to Clement, *Strom.* 3.13.93 is cited by John Cassian, an encratite. Contrary to W. Bauer, who identified the work as the first gospel of the Christians of Egypt, other scholars have rightly maintained that it must have been the gospel of a group of Egyptian encratites. It can be dated to the second century. As Hippolytus and Epiphanius make clear, this was the preferred gospel of "heretical" groups. In the time of Origen it had already been rejected as apocryphal in Egypt.

BIBLIOGRAPHY

Texts

E. Klostermann, *Apocrypha II: Evangelien* (KIT 8; 3d ed.; Berlin: de Gruyter, 1929): 15–126.
W. Schneemelcher, ed., *New Testament Apocrypha* (Louisville: Westminster John Knox, 1991).

Studies

M. Hornschuh, "Erwägungen zum 'Evangelium der Ägypter,' insbesondere zur Bedeutung seines Titels," *VC* 18 (1964): 6–13
W. Schneemelcher, "The Gospel of the Egyptians," in vol. I of *New Testament Apocrypha* (2 vols.; ed. W. Schneemelcher; trans. R. McL. Wilson; Louisville: Westminster John Knox, 1991–1992), 209–15 (study and translation of the fragments).

10. Fragmentary Gospels

Fragments of written gospels have been preserved primarily in papyri; their sources are hardly ever possible to identify.

The first to be found (1885) and published (1887) was a third-century fragment (P.Vindob. G 2325), which came from Fayum and is therefore often called the Fayum Fragment. Its complete form is uncertain, but it contains Jesus' citation of Zech 13:7 and the prediction of Peter's denial. It shows elements of the two canonical parallels, Mark 14:27, 29–30 and Matt 26:31, 33–34. The passage may be simply a free citation of canonical texts; it appears, in any case, to be secondary to the Synoptics.

Papyrus Oxyrhynchus 840 (4th/5th c.), a page from a very small format codex, contains the end of a discourse of Jesus that is undoubtedly addressed to the disciples, whom he warns against unjust behavior. The discourse is followed by an entrance into the temple, into the Court of the Israelites, and a very angry dispute between Jesus and a "Pharisee, a high priest named Levi," who accuses Jesus of having entered without performing the required ablutions. The situation, a controversy over the precepts of ritual purity, recalls Mark 7:1–23 (parallel: Matt 15:1–20), although in the latter case it does not take place in Jerusalem, while the attack of Jesus on the Pharisees who are outwardly clean but inwardly full of uncleanness suggests the attack in Matt 23:27–28 (in Jerusalem). The fragment has been at various times attributed to all the gospels of which fragments are known, but in fact nothing certain can be said of it.

Papyrus Egerton 2 (P.Lond. I) consists of two sheets and the remainder of a third, to which has been added another fragment from the same papyrus, identified in P. Köln 255 and containing five additional lines. The handwriting seems to date the fragments to around 200. Their state does not allow us to establish with certainty the order of the episodes, except that those numbered 1 and 2 below must follow this order. It is quite possible, as the first editors supposed, that the order should be 4, 3, 1, 2.

1. Lines 1–31 = the verso (to be completed from P.Köln) and beginning of the recto of a sheet: the end of words of Jesus attacking the lawyers, then a dispute of Jesus with the leaders of the people about Moses as one who pointed ahead to Jesus; there are clear contacts with John (in this order: 5:39, 45; 9:29–30a; 5:46; 10:31; 7:30; 10:39).
2. Lines 32–41 = recto of the first sheet (to be completed from P.Köln): cure of a leper, corresponding to Mark 1:40–44 and parallels; Luke 7:14.
3. Lines 43–59 = recto of the second sheet: a question about the legitimacy of paying tribute to the king, a question put to Jesus in order to test him, and a harsh response from the latter; the contacts with the canonical gospels are, in order, John 3:2; 10:25; Mark 12:14–15 par.; Mark 1:43; Luke 6:46; Mark 7:6–7.
4. Lines 60–75 = verso of the second sheet: this is much less legible and contains a miracle of Jesus without parallel in the known texts: it seems that he casts seed into the river Jordan and it bears fruit; probably a reference to the resurrection.
5. Verso of the third fragment: little groups of letters.
6. Recto of the same fragment: groups of letters that perhaps refer to a decision to kill Jesus and a reply of Jesus (perhaps a connection with John 10:30–31).

This papyrus thus combines elements of John and the Synoptics. Scholars still argue for one or other of two theses: according to some (e.g., Mayeda, Koester, Crossan), this is a text from the beginning of the second century, independent of the canonical gospels, and even anterior to John; for others (e.g., Jeremias, Schneemelcher, Vielhauer, Neirynck), it is dependent on the four canonical gospels, which the writer cites from memory. The arguments in favor of the first thesis seem to us less convincing. Even from the viewpoint of the transmission of forms it shows a more advanced stage than the corresponding passages of the canonical gospels (e.g., the novelistic development in the second section, where the leper tells how he contracted his sickness).

Papyrus Oxyrhynchus 1224 (beginning of the 4th c.) consists of some pages of a codex that are legible only on one small part. One of the columns contains a series of sayings of Jesus that correspond roughly to Matt 5:44 and Luke 9:50; there follows a saying without any parallels ("He who is distant today will be close to you tomorrow"); finally, there is perhaps a connection with the Matt 5:25 parallel. Another column contains an apothegm of Jesus that is parallel to Mark 2:5–17 and Luke 5:27–32 (Jesus at table with sinners). The words of Jesus are inspired by love of all human beings, especially those who are enemies or estranged. D. Lührmann cautiously suggests attributing this material to the *Gospel of the Hebrews*.

Papyrus Oxyrhynchus 4009 (2d c.) recently published by Lührmann, contains, on the recto side, a saying parallel to Matt 10:16b, the exhortation to be like serpents and doves, but here addressed to a single person. It is followed by the prediction: "You will be like lambs in the midst of wolves," which recalls Matt 10:16a, but in a form closer to the dialogue between Jesus and Peter in *2 Clem.* 5.2–4. The papyrus goes on to give the rest of the same dialogue, but narrated by Peter in the first person. Lührmann has therefore suggested that the fragment is from the *Gospel of Peter*. Since this suggestion is plausible but not certain, we place it here instead of below with the sure fragments of that gospel. The verso side is difficult to piece out, given the absence of known parallels: mentioned perhaps are Galilee, the sending, and the sequel. It is difficult to say whether this dialogue precedes the passion (as in the Synoptic parallels) or follows it (as a dialogue of the risen Jesus with the disciples, comparable to John 21); the second option seems preferable.

Papyrus 10735 of Cairo (6th/7th c.) contains on its verso words of the angel (possibly Gabriel) to Mary that expand upon Luke 1:36, and, on its recto, words of the angel to Joseph, parallel to Matt 2:13. It is uncertain whether this is really a gospel and not rather a homily. Coptic Papyrus Strasbourg (two sheets from the 5th/6th c.) contains a prayer of Jesus to the Father and, on the verso, a farewell discourse to the disciples (with a "we" narrator), probably on the occasion of the Last Supper. On the other sheet, the disciples appear as witnesses to the glory of Jesus and receive "strength for the apostolate"; the context may be the ascension. Matthew and John are used. Papyrus Berlin 11710 (6th c.) contains some remarks from a dialogue between Jesus and Nathanael that develop John 1:49.

In 1973 M. Smith published an extract from a letter of Clement of Alexandria, which Smith discovered in 1958 in the monastery of Mar Saba near Jerusalem. The extract, which breaks off suddenly, was written on the last three blank pages of the edition of the letters of Ignatius of Antioch, which I. Voss had published in 1646. Addressing a certain Theodore (according to the copyist's note at the beginning), Clement warns against the teachings of the Carpocratians, a gnostic sect, and in particular against a *Secret Gospel of Mark* that was in use among them. According to Clement, that gospel was a falsified version, done by Carpocrates, of a "more spiritual gospel," which Mark had supposedly written in addition to his public gospel and had given to the church of Alexandria, which still had it in Clement's time. The church allowed it to be read "only by those initiated into the great mysteries." Clement then cites a passage which would have its place between 10:34 and 10:35 of canonical Mark, then another phrase (after Mark 10:46) of the gospel preserved in Alexandria: here it is said that a young man raised from the dead by Jesus "looked at him, started to love him, and began to beg that he might stay with him." Six days later, the young man went to Jesus, "clad in a sheet over his naked body [see Mark 14:51], and stayed with him that night; Jesus taught him the mystery of the kingdom of God." Among the false additions that the Carpocratians supposedly made to this passage, Clement mentions only "naked with naked."

This thesis raised problems at various levels. Is the letter of Clement authentic? No one but Smith has been able to view the manuscript. Smith cites a large number of lexical and stylistic points in favor of the letter's authenticity, but the content does not always correspond to what we find in the writings of Clement; he never says a word about Alexandrian archives containing secret writings, and the esoteric tradition of the church is, for him, an oral tradition. But even if the letter is authentic and Clement indeed cites a different recension of the gospel of Mark, what is the relationship between it and canonical Mark? The discussion goes on. According to some, the *Secret Gospel* is secondary in relation to the canonical gospels, from which it takes and combines elements. According to others, the canonical Mark is derived from the *Secret Gospel*. In this case, Matthew and Luke would be based on a more ancient version of Mark, while canonical Mark would have to be dated to the second century. This hypothesis would explain among other things, the "minor agreements" of Matthew and Luke against Mark, but the first hypothesis seems to us more likely.

Agrapha are sayings of Jesus not included in the earliest redaction of the canonical gospels. In this sense they include sayings found in the Jewish-Christian gospels and the papyrus fragments already discussed here, as well as in the apocryphal gospels, acts of the apostles, and letters which we shall see further on. We prescind here from the question of whether some of these may go back historically to Jesus. For more complete information the reader may refer to the works cited in the bibliography below; here we shall limit ourselves to recalling:

- Sayings contained in the New Testament, but outside the gospels: Acts 1:4, 7–8; 20:35; 1 Thess 4:15–17.
- Variants found in some manuscripts of the gospels. Relevant here is the so-called Freer Logion, a dialogue between the risen Jesus and the disciples on the end of Satan's power; it is inserted in Mark 16:14 in Codex W of the gospels (5th c.), which is preserved in the Freer Gallery of Art, Washington, D.C. Another noteworthy variant is in manuscript D (5th c.) at Luke 6:5, where Jesus says to a man working on the sabbath: "Man, if you know what you are doing, you are blessed; but if you do not know, you are accursed and a transgressor of the law."
- Sayings cited by ecclesiastical authors: a list is given by J. Jeremias (see bibliography below).
- One *agraphon* in rabbinic literature: Babylonian Talmud, ʿ*Abodah Zarah* 17a (a saying of Jesus spoken to R. Eliezer ben Hyrkanos by a Christian, James of Cephar-Sekhanja, in the characteristic genre of rabbinical opinions, as an answer to the question: Is it permitted to build a study for the high priest with the money of a prostitute, which cannot be carried into the temple?).
- Numerous *agrapha* attributed to Jesus in Muslim literature, beginning with the Quran, and especially in Al-Ghazali (1059–1111).

BIBLIOGRAPHY

Papyrus Fragments Texts

E. Klostermann, *Apocrypha II: Evangelien* (3d ed.; Berlin: de Gruyter, 1929).
G. Bonaccorsi, *Vangeli apocryphi I* (Florence: Libreria Editrice Fiorentina, 1948): 2–57.

K. Aland, *Synopsis quattuor Evangeliorum* (13th ed.; Stuttgart: Deutsche Bibel-
gesellschaft, 1985).

W. Schneemelcher, ed., *New Testament Apocrypha* (Louisville: Westminster John
Knox, 1991).

Studies

D. F. Wright, "Apocryphal Gospels: The 'Unknown Gospel' (P. Egerton 2) and
the Gospel of Peter," in *The Jesus Tradition Outside the Gospels* (*Gospel Perspectives 5;* ed. D. Wenham; Sheffield: JSOT Press, 1985), 207–32.

J. Jeremias and W. Scheemelcher, "Fragments of Unknown Gospels," in vol. I of
New Testament Apocrypha (ed. W. Schneemelcher; Louisville: Westminster
John Knox Press, 1991), 91–109.

H. Koester, *Ancient Christian Gospels: Their History and Development* (London:
SCM/Philadelphia: Trinity, 1990), 205–16. P. Egerton 2.

D. Lührmann, "POx 4009: Ein neues Fragment des Petrusevangeliums?" *NovT* 35
(1993): 390–410.

Secret Gospel of Mark

M. Smith, *Clement of Alexandria and a Secret Gospel of Mark* (Cambridge, Mass.:
Harvard University Press, 1973); with an edition of the text.

S. Levin, "The Early History of Christianity, in Light of the 'Secret Gospel' of
Mark," *ANRW* II 25.6 (1988): 4270–92.

Agrapha

A. Resch, *Agrapha: Ausserkanonische Schriftfragmente* (TU 30; 3,4; 2d ed.; Leipzig:
Hinrichs, 1906).

J. Jeremias, *Gli agrapha di Gesù* (4th ed.; 1965); IT (2d ed.; Brescia: Paideia, 1976).

M. Erbetta, *Apocrifi del NT* I/1 (Casale Monferrato: Marietti, 1975), 83–96.

S. Leanza, *I detti extracanonici di Gesù* (Messina: n.p., 1977).

O. Hofius, "Isolated Sayings of the Lord," in W. Schneemelcher, ed., *New Testament Apocrypha* I, 88–91.

11. Gospel of Thomas

The *Refutation of All Heresies*, which is attributed to Hippolytus (5.7.20), Origen
(*Hom. Luc.* 1, year 233), Eusebius of Caesarea (*Hist. eccl.* 3.25.6), and other authors,
mentions a *Gospel of Thomas*, of which the *Refutation* cites a saying that is to be linked
to saying 4 of this *Gospel*. This gospel was usually regarded as heretical. Beginning in
the fourth century, it was thought (by Cyril of Jerusalem, and others), to be used or
even composed by the Manichees. A work of this title, in a Coptic translation, was
identified in 1958 as the second text of Nag Hammadi Codex IV.

The work consists of a series of sayings *(logia)* or parables of Jesus. The numbering
of the sayings differs from scholar to scholar; we shall follow here the numbering of the
critical edition: 114 logia. They are introduced by the phrase "Jesus said," and in some
cases by a question from the disciples (e.g., 6; 12; 18; 20; 21; 24; and 37) or by a loose
narrative frame in an apothegmatic manner (22; 60; 72; 79; 100). Sometimes there is a

real dialogue (13; 60; 61). Some of the logia are in fact series of originally independent sayings (21). Some papyrus fragments from Oxyrhynchus that contain sayings of Jesus and were published between 1897 and 1904 actually came from manuscripts of the *Gospel of Thomas* in its original Greek form (P.Oxy. 1 = logia 26–33 + 77a; P.Oxy. 654 = prologue + logia 1–7; P.Oxy. 655 = logia 24 + 36–39). Papyri 1 and 655 can be dated to the beginning of the third century, which indicates that the *Gospel of Thomas* was widely circulated in the second century. The Greek witnesses, however, show differences in the order of the logia as compared to the Coptic version.

The following prologue precedes the sayings: "These are the secret sayings which Jesus uttered while alive and which Didymus Judas Thomas wrote down." Thomas is one of the Twelve (Mark 3:18 par.; Acts 1:13), and he seems to be a favorite of the gospel of John (11:16; 14:5; 20:24–28; 22:1; except in ch. 14 he is always "Thomas, called Didymus"). The names Didymus and Thomas have the same meaning, "twin," in Greek and Aramaic respectively (in P.Oxy. 654, which is mutilated at this point, there is only the name Thomas, with no room for either Judas or Didymus; usually the former is preferred). Judas and Thomas appear as two different apostles in Luke 6:16; Acts 1:13, while a brother of Jesus named Judas appears in Mark 6:3; Matt 13:55, and the pseudepigraphical letter of Jude is presented as his work.

The identification of Judas with Thomas and his description as twin of Jesus seem peculiar to Syrian Christianity. Moreover, it was in western Syria that Judas, the twin of Jesus, became important in the tradition. The *Acts of Thomas* (3d c.) come from Syria, while tradition concerning the evangelization of Edessa, at the beginning of the fourth century (Eusebius, *Hist. eccl.* 1.13.11), claims that Addai had been sent for this purpose by Thomas. This was probably in opposition to an earlier tradition, dear to the local gnostics, which assigned the evangelization directly to Thomas. In the *Book of Thomas the Contender* found at Nag Hammadi, this personage is again described as the twin of Jesus. Thomas appears in the *Gospel of Thomas* as the depository of a knowledge granted him through revelation. According to logion 13, he, unlike Simon Peter and Matthew, is the only one to have grasped the true identity of Jesus. H.-C. Puech and G. Quispel have shown the extent to which this description of Thomas is typical of the *Acts of Thomas* and how Thomas is regarded in this tradition as the twin of Jesus not only in a fleshly sense but in the sense of being a mystical twin, an alter ego, and an initiate into knowledge of him.

The literary genre of the text is the collection of sayings, more accurately of sapiential sayings that focus on the relationship between God and human beings and between the latter and the world, with special attention to the nature and destiny of the human being. Sayings of this type are found on the lips of Jesus in the canonical gospels, and in fact seventy-nine sayings in the *Gospel of Thomas* have Synoptic parallels, forty-six of them in Q.

Ever since the text was published, there has been a lively discussion of whether Thomas depends on the canonical gospels, taking from them sayings of Jesus and reinterpreting them on gnostic lines. The contrary view seems preferable. The order of the sayings in Thomas does not match the order in any of the canonical gospels. Moreover, many sayings in Thomas have a more archaic form than in the canonical gospels. Thus in the parable of the sower (logion 9) the redactional elements in Mark 4:3–9 are lacking; the same holds for the three parables told successively in Matt 13:44–50 as compared with logia 109, 76, and 8 of the *Gospel of Thomas*. In addition, the parallels to Q lack the characteristics that critics assign to a later redaction of that source, especially the return of Jesus as Son of Man for the final judgment. Thus, Thomas and the canonical gospels have in common only a much earlier stage in the tradition of the sayings of Jesus (see Koester).

The first logion says: "And he said: Anyone who finds the interpretation of these sayings will not taste death." A salvific efficacy is thus attributed to the correct understanding of the sayings of Jesus, and in this sense the text means to be taken as "good news" or gospel, even if, literally, it has nothing in common with the "gospel form" inaugurated by Mark. There is no interest here in the historical dimension of the man Jesus; salvation comes not from his death and resurrection but from the appropriation of the wisdom contained in the sayings of "the living Jesus" (who is not to be identified with the risen Jesus: 22; 60; 100), for these enable a human being to find the true self and rescue it from the grip of the world.

The discovery of the *Gospel of Thomas* has confirmed the existence of the literary genre presupposed by Q: the collection of sayings of Jesus without any biographical framework and without the passion story. It is not possible to discern a general principle governing the order of the sayings of Jesus in this gospel; there are short series linked by the presence of a key term (e.g., "rule/kingdom" [2–3]; "few/many"[73–75]; or a series of parables introduced by "the kingdom of the Father is like . . . " [96–98; 107; 109]. Every saying, however, has a meaning independent of the others. Because of the heterogeneous provenance of the sayings, and because they were probably composed over several phases, it is impossible to reduce the thought of the whole to a single, close-knit theological idea. Still, some lines of thought are clear.

As already noted, the *Gospel of Thomas* presents a conception of the kingdom that differs greatly from that of the Synoptic tradition; in Thomas the kingdom is a present, not a future reality, and it is heavily spiritualized (113). It consists in the knowledge of ourselves precisely as children of the living Father; it is both within believers and outside of them, because the knowledge they have of themselves is identical with God's knowledge of them, that is, with the divine wisdom (3). The elect, that is, solitaries, can reach this knowledge (49); they know whence they come, that is, from the light, to which they shall also return (49; 50). The Greek word *monachos* (49; 16; 75) here means the "solitary," who has recovered the original unity (4; 11; 22; 23; 106) that precedes the separation of the sexes (22; 114: "Every woman who makes herself a male will enter the kingdom of heaven").

The text here displays an emphatic sexual asceticism that is consistent with the negative view both of the world, which is described as a corpse (56; see 80) from which one must keep one's distance (110), and of interpersonal relations, in favor of an extremely individualistic outlook (55). Human beings in the world are "drunk" and blind (28). Jesus is the revealer sent in order that they may drink from his mouth and become identical to him (108); but he is not to be confused with the prophets or the Messiah of the Jews (52). The kingdom seems to be conceived as a return to the paradisal state at the beginning (18: a summons to seek not the end—an expectation of the future reign of God—but the beginning, because there the end also shall be). Logion 37 refers clearly to transcending the situation in Gen 3:10: "When you unclothe yourselves without shame and take your clothes and put them beneath your feet, as children do, and trample on them, then you shall see the Son of the Living One and you shall not be afraid."

The importance of the *Gospel of Thomas,* the affinity with the *Acts of Thomas,* and the encratite tendency suggest that the work was written in eastern Syria, possibly Edessa, toward the middle of the second century. The traditions that are used certainly go back to the first century but a very early composition of the gospel does not seem demonstrable.

Despite its having been found in a gnostic library and having some obvious characteristics of gnostic interpretation, the *Gospel of Thomas* is not really a gnostic text in that it does not presuppose the basic myths of gnosticism. It develops the tradition of the logia of Jesus in the setting of a strong antiworldly and encratite tendency. It pushes to extremes certain possibilities of the sapiential tradition, which move in the direction of seeking a salvation that lies in the recovery of the individual's interior unity, this last being also seen as an original oneness with the divine. In this perspective, the death of Jesus is of no account; he is simply a heavenly messenger who is to rescue human beings from intoxication (the gnostics refer to a sleep) that is caused by an interior disunity, and to bring them back to their origin. This synthesis would fail to hold its own amid the polarization of orthodoxy and gnosticism in the second half of the second century. During that process the *Gospel of Thomas* was taken over by gnosticism and rejected by the "great church," as we saw at the beginning of this section. But as the existing papyri show, in the second century its manuscript tradition was not quantitatively inferior to that of the subsequently canonized gospels.

BIBLIOGRAPHY

Edition

Nag Hammadi Codex II, 2–7: Together with XIII, 2*, Brit. Lib. Or. 4926(1), and P.OXY. 1, 654, 655 (vol. 1; ed. B. Layton; NHS 20–21; *The Coptic Gnostic Library;* New York: Brill, 1989), 37–128.

Studies

The bibliography is immense; one may start with F. F. Fallon and R. Cameron, "The Gospel of Thomas: A Forschungsbericht and Analysis," *ANRW* II 25.6 (1988): 4195–4251.

G. Quispel, *Gnostic Studies II* (Istanbul: Nederlands Historisch-Archaeologisch Institut, 1975).

H.-C. Puech, S*ur l'Evangile selon Thomas: Esquisse d'une interprétation systématique* (vol. II of *En quête de la Gnose;* Paris: Gallimard, 1978).

H. Koester, *Ancient Christian Gospels: Their History and Development* (London: SCM/Philadelphia: Trinity, 1990): 75–128.

E. H. Pagels, *Beyond Belief: The Secret Gospel of Thomas* (New York: Random House, 2003).

12. Gospel of Peter

A parchment manuscript of the eighth-ninth century discovered in the winter of 1886–1887 in the tomb of a monk at Akhmin in upper Egypt contains a lengthy fragment of the story of the passion of Jesus, a Greek recension of the *Apocalypse of Peter,* and the Greek abridgment of *1 Enoch*. The first text begins directly after Pilate's washing of his hands (see Matt 27:24) and ends mid-sentence at the beginning of the scene of fishing in Galilee, during which the risen Jesus appears to some disciples. The story is told in the first person by Simon Peter (v. 60; see 26–27, 59).

The fragment was immediately identified as the *Gospel of Peter*, which had been mentioned in some ancient testimonies. Conspicuous among the latter is a letter of Bishop Serapion of Antioch (ca. 200) from which Eusebius cites two passages (*Hist. eccl.* 6.12.3–6). According to these, a community in Rhossus, near Antioch, had asked the bishop for permission to continue reading the *Gospel of Peter*, and he had initially consented. Later, disturbed by heterodox views in the community, he learned that the gospel had been brought in by "docetists." On reading it, Bishop Serapion found that for the most part it reflected true teaching, while adding "extra precepts." As E. Junod has shown, Serapion makes his judgment on the gospel secondary to his judgment on the orthodoxy of its readers; Eusebius tendentiously cites this testimony in order to make the *Gospel of Peter* appear in a bad light. After Serapion, Origen mentions this gospel (*Comm. Matt.* 10.17) but does not seem to have personal knowledge of it. Eusebius limits himself to listing it among the non-"catholic" books because it is not acknowledged by ecclesiastic writers (*Hist. eccl.* 3.3.2; 3.25.6); Jerome and the *Decretum Gelasianum* rely on Eusebius.

Two short fragments of the *Gospel of Peter* were discovered in P. Oxyrhynchus 2949 (ca. 200). One contains some mutilated phrases that correspond to the passage in Eusebius (6.12.3–5), while the other is so hard to read that its setting cannot be determined. Still, they help to show (a) the degree to which this gospel circulated in second-century Egypt and (b) that the form of the work in the Akhmin fragment is to some extent a revision of an earlier work, since numerous variants occur in the very small section that can be compared.

As noted, the *Gospel* (using von Harnack's division into sixty verses) begins with the refusal of the Jews to wash their hands, as has evidently just been done by Pilate, who at this point leaves the place of the trial. It is therefore Herod with "his judges" who condemns Jesus (1–2). Next comes the request of Joseph of Arimathea for the body of Jesus (3–5; in the canonical gospels this takes place after the death of Jesus, Mark 15:43–45 par.), the insults to Jesus (6–9), the crucifixion between two criminals, the darkness over the land, and the last cry of Jesus, followed by his "exaltation" and the tearing of the veil in the temple (10–20). The removal from the cross causes an earthquake, and then the light returns. On receiving the body from the Jews, Joseph buries it in his own tomb, while the Jews, realizing the evil they have done, begin to feel the coming of judgment and the end of Jerusalem. Peter and his companions, who are being hunted, are terrified and remain hidden (21–27).

The scribes, Pharisees, and elders obtain from Pilate a centurion and some soldiers to guard the tomb and prevent the theft of the body. The tomb is closed and sealed, as is observed by a crowd that comes on the morning of the sabbath (28–34). The following night before dawn, the soldiers hear a voice from heaven and see the descent of two men clad in light. The stone rolls away by itself, and the two enter the tomb and emerge holding the hands of a third personage; the three are of immense stature, especially the one in the middle. They are followed by the cross, which answers "yes" to a question from heaven: "Have you preached to those asleep?" Another angel comes down from heaven and enters the tomb (35–44). The soldiers report to

Pilate, who refuses to share the responsibility of the Jews but does agree to impose silence on the soldiers (45–49).

In the morning, Mary Magdalene and her women friends come to the tomb to weep for Jesus. They find it open and see seated within it a young man clothed in light, who tells them that the crucified one is risen and "has gone whence he had been sent." The women flee (50–57). When the Feast of Unleavened Bread has ended, the Twelve return, grief-stricken, to their homes; Peter and Andrew, accompanied by Levi, go toward the sea (of Galilee) in order to fish (58–60). Here the text breaks off. It was evidently followed by a first appearance of the risen Jesus in Galilee, as promised in Mark 16:7, although in the *Gospel of Peter* this is not announced by the angel.

Léon Vaganay has rebutted attempts to link the *Gospel of Peter* to episodes in the life of Jesus outside the story of the passion. There are no indications that this gospel contained anything but the unit made up of the passion, resurrection, and appearances. Even if the new fragment in P. Oxyrhynchus 4009 belonged to it, according to the suggestion of D. Lührmann (see above, sec. 10), it seems to be part of the story of an appearance of the risen Jesus.

Immediately after the fragment's discovery, a lively debate took place on the relationship of the *Gospel of Peter* to the canonical gospels. Vaganay seemed to put an end to the discussion by establishing the dependence of the former on the latter, but the question has recently been reopened. J. Denker, H. Koester, and J. D. Crossan, among others, have expressed the view (with variations) that contacts with the canonical gospels are due to a common tradition. These scholars have emphasized the importance of the exegesis of Old Testament passages, read as prophecies of the passion of Jesus, in shaping the story in the *Gospel of Peter*. R. E. Brown maintains the dependence of the *Gospel* on the canonical gospels, but by way of an oral tradition based on them. In our opinion, the *Gospel of Peter* shows some knowledge of the gospels later canonized, but it does not seem to be bound by them, and relies equally upon other written or oral traditions, some of them predating the redaction of the gospels. This is true, e.g., of the description of the resurrection of Jesus, which seems to have been known also to Matthew. These traditions, however, do not contain historically reliable elements but were developed in a Hellenistic Christian milieu (note, e.g., the ignorance of the Palestinian situation and institutions) in light of theological and apologetic needs and thorough exegetical work on the biblical *testimonia* (esp. Denker and Crossan, independent of the latter's weak thesis of an original "Gospel of the Cross").

The attack on the Jews is obvious: it is Herod and the Jews, not Pilate, who condemn Jesus (1–2). They and not the Roman soldiers mistreat him, crucify him, divide his garments among them, take him down from the cross, and dispose of his body (6–23; in 4, Pilate has to ask Herod for the body!). The Roman soldiers reappear only as guards at the tomb (31). This development occurs much later than the canonical gospels, during a process tending increasingly to place responsibility for the passion and death of Jesus on the Jews. Contacts have been noted between the *Gospel* and the anti-Judaism of the Easter homily of Melito of Sardis. This development has nothing to do with historical fact and reflects a strongly polemical relationship between Christians and Jews. This supposes in turn a clear awareness of reciprocal separation and opposition, which dates material after the end of the first century. The role of the Roman soldiers is likewise apologetic: they are neutral witnesses to the resurrection, the truth of which therefore does not depend solely on Christian claims. The description of the resurrection, too, is secondary from the viewpoint of the history of the tradition, but there are good reasons for considering it to be older than Matthew, who retained the guards at the tomb while inconsistently eliminating the vision that justified their presence.

Another debated point is the presumed docetism, that is, the refusal to acknowledge the human dimension of Jesus. The connection between this gospel and the "docetists" of Serapion's letters, of whom we know nothing, does not authorize us to draw conclusions about the theology of the text. Factors such as the seeming absence of suffering in the crucified Jesus (10) or the use of *anēlēphthē* for his death (19: the verb means "was taken up," but can also signify a completely normal death) have been used to that end, but are not convincing. We think that the *Gospel of Peter* belongs to a theological tradition connected with Jewish-Christian Hellenistic circles in Antioch, which appealed to the memory of Peter, were very much concerned with the divine identity of Christ, and tended to minimize his human dimension. Some gnostic developments of the second century could well have come from such circles. In our view this material expresses not so much a fully conscious docetism as a docetist tendency springing from a soteriology based on the supernatural aspect of Jesus.

Thus the *Gospel of Peter* seems to have arisen where it was first attested, in the area of Antioch, even if fragments bear witness to its rapid spread in Egypt; Mara's choice of Asia Minor does not seem persuasive. The letter of Serapion establishes the *terminus ante quem*: because of the *Gospel*'s freedom in relation to traditions that subsequently became canonical, we would date it no earlier than the middle of the second century.

BIBLIOGRAPHY

L. Vaganay *L'Evangile de Pierre* (2d ed.; Paris: Gabalda, 1930); the edition, translation, introduction, and commentary are still essential.

M. G. Mara, *Evangile de Pierre* (SC 201; Paris: Cerf, 1973); edition, translation, introduction, and commentary.

J. Denker, *Die theologiegeschichtliche Stellung des Petrusevangeliums: Ein Beitrag zur Frühgeschichte des Doketismus* (Bern-Frankfurt/M. Lang, 1975).

D. Lührmann, "POx 2949: EvPt 3–5 in einer Handschrift des 2ten/3ten Jahrhunderts," *ZNW* 72 (1981): 216–26.

J. W. McCant, "The Gospel of Peter: Docetism Reconsidered," *NTS* 30 (1984): 258–73.

R. E. Brown, "The Gospel of Peter and Canonical Gospel Priority," *NTS* 33 (1987): 321–43.

J. D. Crossan, *The Cross That Spoke: The Origins of the Passion Narrative* (San Francisco: Harper & Row, 1988).

E. Junod, "Eusèbe de Césarée, Sérapion d'Antioche et l'*Evangile de Pierre:* D'un évangile à un pseudépigraphe," *RSLR* 24 (1988): 3–16.

Chapter 3

THE JOHANNINE TRADITION

The term "Johannine corpus" is customarily used for a group of New Testament writings which ancient tradition attributed to John, son of Zebedee and disciple of Jesus: a gospel, three letters, and the Apocalypse. The gospel and the letters do not carry an author's name; the second and third letters are signed "the presbyter," while the gospel appeals to the testimony of a disciple who was especially close to Jesus: "the disciple whom Jesus loved." The gospel and letters surely belong to the same tradition. The Apocalypse, on the other hand, names its author, John, who since the second century has been identified as the son of Zebedee. The language and thought-world of the Apocalypse show notable differences from the gospel and the letters, as well as some notable similarities. There is disagreement over whether the grouping of the Apocalypse with the gospel and letters is due simply to a secondary attribution of the entire complex to the apostle John or whether there is indeed a historical connection among them. In this chapter, we shall deal with the gospel and the letters, which, though belonging to different genres, cannot be historically separated. We shall study the Apocalypse in the following chapter on the first Christian apocalypses; there we shall also call attention to some aspects of the discussion of its connection with the "Johannine world."

1. Gospel of John

Hypotheses on the structure of the gospel of John are many and varied. Let us review the contents and indicate some points of reference. A major division occurs between Chapters 12 and 13, with the latter beginning the story of the passion.

Chapters 1–12 do not unfold in linear fashion. A prologue in the form of a hymn opens the book and identifies Jesus with the preexistent Logos (1:1–18). This being was the subject of reflection in Hellenistic Judaism. The Logos is the very mind of God, but it is hypostatized: it has become an independent person alongside God, a person whose purpose is, among other things, to complete the work of creation in accordance with the divine plan.

The narrative then begins with a first testimony of John the Baptist to Jesus (1:19–34); this corresponds to the Synoptic account of the baptism and is followed by the assent of the first disciples to the call of Jesus (1:35–51). The first miracle of Jesus, at the wedding feast in Cana, is followed by a visit to Capernaum (2:1–12); then there is a first Passover in Jerusalem, with the expulsion of the traders from the temple

(2:13–25), an incident which in the Synoptics directly precedes the passion. After the conversation at night with Nicodemus, a Pharisee, in which Jesus speaks of being sent by God (3:1–21), Jesus baptizes in Judea, and there is a second testimony of John concerning him (3:22–36). Moving then from Judea to Galilee, Jesus passes through Samaria, where the conversation with the Samaritan woman takes place (4:1–42).

At Cana in Galilee, Jesus cures the son of a royal official of Capernaum (4:43–54). On returning to Jerusalem for "a feast of the Jews," Jesus cures a paralytic at the pool of Beth-zatha (5:1–17) and follows with an apologetical discourse on his own activity (5:19–47). The scene then shifts to a mountain near the Lake of Tiberias at Passover time: Jesus multiplies the loaves and fishes (6:1–15), then walks on the water (6:16–25) and discourses on the Eucharist to the crowd that has followed him (6:29–59). Some of the disciples are scandalized by his language; Jesus predicts his betrayal by one of them (6:60–70). At the time of the Feast of Booths, Jesus goes from Galilee to Jerusalem where he engages in controversy with "the Jews" regarding his person and mission (7:1–52; 8:12–59). These discussions are interrupted in many manuscripts by the episode of the adulterous woman (7:53–8:11), which was not originally part of the gospel.

In Jerusalem on the Sabbath Jesus heals the man born blind, whom the Pharisees expel from the synagogue (9:1–41). This episode is prolonged into the discourse of Jesus on the Good Shepherd (10:1–22). Still in Jerusalem, on the Feast of the Dedication, Jesus continues the flock metaphor in a dispute with the Jews, who seek to stone him. He returns across the Jordan at the place where John had baptized (10:22–42). Jesus is called to Bethany where he raises Lazarus (11:1–44). The Sanhedrin takes counsel against him, and Caiaphas, the high priest, urges his removal. Jesus stays a while in Ephraim, on the edge of the wilderness, as Passover draws near (11:45–47). Returning to Bethany, he dines in the house of Lazarus, where Mary anoints his feet with perfume (12:1–11). He then enters Jerusalem in triumph (12:12–19) and there foretells his death, which will also be his glorification (12:20–50).

Chapters 13–20 tell of the passion, but are clearly subdivided into two parts. Chapters 13–17: after the supper Jesus washes the feet of the disciples; this scene takes the place of the institution of the Eucharist in the Synoptics. He then delivers a lengthy farewell address, a "testament," in which he announces the sending of the Spirit, urges the disciples to mutual love after his own example, and prays to the Father to protect them. Chapters 18–19 give an account of the passion and death. Chapter 20: on the morning after the Sabbath, Mary Magdalene, who is alone, discovers the empty tomb and is granted the first appearance of the risen Jesus. On the evening of the same day Jesus appears to the disciples while Thomas is absent. Eight days later he shows himself to them again in order to overcome the unbelief of Thomas. Chapter 20:30–31 is a conclusion; ch. 21 is a later addition that describes an appearance of the risen Jesus to the disciples in Galilee and Peter's mandate to "feed the flock."

A comparison with the Synoptics brings out certain characteristics of John.

1. The geographical and chronological framework. In the Synoptics there is a single Passover and a single journey of Jesus to Jerusalem, the one preceding the passion; in John's account, Jesus moves several times between Galilee and Judea and travels four times to Jerusalem (2:13; 5:10; 7:10; 12:12), three times for Passover and once for the Feast of Booths (7:2, 10). Another Passover is mentioned in 6:4 in the context

of the multiplication of loaves; in 10:22 there is the Feast of the Dedication. The feasts thus have an important place in the chronology of the gospel; the activity of Jesus seems to extend over several years.

2. The teaching of Jesus. In the Synoptics this is expressed in parables and individual sayings, which are set within a narrative framework or assembled into "discourses." The parables are missing from John; instead Jesus delivers extensive discourses on his own identity, his heavenly origin, and his sending by the Father. Some sayings of Jesus correspond to Synoptic sayings but are set in different contexts: thus John 13:16 (= 15:20) corresponds to Matt 10:24; John 13:20 to Matt 10:40; John 15:7 to Matt 7:7, but all are incorporated into Jesus' great farewell discourse and thereby reinterpreted, being made to refer to the relationship between the community of disciples and Jesus.

3. The miracles of Jesus. The exorcisms are missing from John, and he has in common with Mark or Q only the following: the cure of the son of the royal functionary of Capernaum (John 4:46–54; Q/Luke 7:1–10; in Luke and Matthew it is the centurion's servant who is cured); the multiplication of the loaves and the walking on the water (John 6:1–21; Mark 6:30–52; and the miraculous catch (21:1–14; Luke 5:1–11). John tells of eight miracles in all, of which the first two, both performed at Cana, are explicitly narrated as the first and second miracles of Jesus (2:11; 4:54).

4. The special link between miracles and discourses. The two miracles at Cana—the transformation of water into wine and the healing, at a distance, of the son of the official of Capernaum—frame the conversations of Jesus with Nicodemus and the Samaritan woman (as well as the expulsion of the traders from the temple) and demonstrate the power of Jesus. In ch. 5 the cure of the paralytic leads into a discourse on Jesus as giver of life; in ch. 6 the multiplication of the loaves introduces the discourse on the Eucharist. Jesus says: "I am the bread of life." Similarly, the discourse beginning with "I am the light of the world" (8:12) is followed by the cure of the man born blind, while the statement "I am the resurrection" (11:25) is a prelude to the raising of Lazarus. The miracles are thus "signs" whose symbolism is explained in the discourses. The content of the discourse is first and foremost the self-revelation of Jesus.

5. The beginning of the gospel. While the overall outline of the gospel corresponds to that of the Synoptics (activity of Jesus in word and deed, in Palestine, followed by the passion, death, and resurrection), the beginning of John is special. Mark begins with the preaching of the Baptist, and Matthew and Luke with the birth of Jesus, but John goes further back, to the eternal preexistence of Jesus as the Logos with God, in a "beginning" that goes further back even than the beginning of the Bible.

In John's gospel Jesus is the preexistent revealer who has "come down" from "heaven" as the one sent by God (3:17, 34; 5:36, 38; 6:29, 57; 7:29; 8:42; etc.) into this world of "darkness" (1:5, 8, 12; 12:35, 46) in order to bring it the "light" (1:4, 5, 7, 8, 9; 3:19; etc.), which he himself is. Revealer and revelation are one: by making himself known, Jesus makes the Father known (14:7–11), and after his return to God he will be present to his followers as Paraclete, the Spirit who ensures complete knowledge (14:16–20, 26; 16:13–14). Those who accept him in this world are the ones God has given to him; like Jesus, they are not of the world (ch. 17). Others think they know Jesus, but they deceive themselves, because they see only his human origin (7:27, 35–36); they belong to "this world" (8:23).

The dialogues of Jesus are grounded in irony: understanding of their real meaning, beyond appearances, requires an initiation. Clearly the outlook of the author is reflected here: only those belonging to the community can understand the nature of Jesus and the meaning of his revelation. This perspective approximates that of the gnostic groups for which salvation springs from the knowledge transmitted by the heavenly revealer, and the real humanity of the latter is unimportant, This "docetist" tendency in John's gospel has been noted by scholars (E. Käsemann, L. Schottroff), but it is balanced in the gospel by an emphasis on the flesh of Jesus (1:14). The death of Jesus is real and not merely apparent, as in the gnostics, even though the Jesus of John controls the events of his passion from beginning to end (18:4, 11; 19:11, 28, 30). The ethic of the gospel is summed up in the commandment of mutual love, which is modeled on the love of Jesus who gave his life for his friends (15:12–13). But this is love for one's friends, that is, those belonging to the same group; the Johannine community seems to be rather turned in upon itself.

Some questions of literary criticism need to be raised. The author's knowledge of the Synoptics has been and still is energetically debated, but it is probably to be ruled out: John would therefore have "invented" the gospel genre, parallel to Mark but not dependent on him. On the other hand, John and the Synoptics have a similar structure, even while being profoundly different in character. The contacts go back to common traditions and are quite limited both for the narrative tradition and for the sayings tradition. For the story of the passion, however, it must be acknowledged that John uses a basic story comparable to that used by Mark, and perhaps a tradition comparable to that which Luke had available in addition to Mark. In any case, John has developed even the story of the passion, and in particular the dialogue with Pilate (18:29–38a; 19:1–15), in accordance with his own perspective.

As for the sources of the first part of John's gospel: the prologue (1:1–18) probably reworks a hymn used in the Johannine community. In addition to the source for the passion story, R. Bultmann identifies two principal sources in John: (a) A collection of the miracles of Jesus, in which the wonders were numbered. The two miracles at Cana are represented as the first and second (2:11; 4:54), which seems inconsistent with the mention of other miracles in 2:23 and 3:2, before the "second" miracle has been reported. Bultmann has shown that the style and language of these narratives differ from the typical style and language of John. John seems to have taken the miracle stories from several sources rather than from a single one. (b) A collection of pre-Christian revelatory discourses of a gnostic kind, which John would then have reworked. This thesis has probably been revised even more radically than the previous one: the Johannine tradition seems rather to have developed the discourses and dialogues of Jesus as interpretations of the traditional sayings, following specific hermeneutical principles, just as the gnostic dialogues have done in which Jesus acts as revealer (H. Koester).

There are some inconsistencies in the present text of the gospel. At the end of ch. 4 Jesus has returned from Judea to Galilee, but in the next verse (5:1) he has returned to Jerusalem, while in 6:1, immediately after the discourse in Jerusalem, we see him crossing the Sea of Tiberias in Galilee. It has therefore been suggested that the order of chs. 5 and 6 has been reversed. In 14:31 Jesus ends his discourse before the passion by urging the disciples to go forth, but in 15:1 he continues as if nothing has happened, and the disciples leave the room only in 18:1. Here again it has been suggested that the order of 13–17 has been disrupted. At present, scholars prefer to explain these inconsistencies by the thesis of successive stages in the composition of the gospel, these being characterized by theological positions that were gradually modified and made more specific due to the evolution of the Johannine community. In any case, ch. 21, as noted above, is an addition to an already finished gospel; what remains problematic is the degree to which it can be regarded, within the gospel as a whole, as a development connected with the final intervention attested by this chapter.

This final chapter mentions three times "the disciple whom Jesus loved" (21:7, 20, 24). Verse 24 adds: "This is the disciple who is testifying to these things and has written them." The Johannine community thus appeals to an immediate disciple of Jesus as guarantor of the content of the gospel and even as its material author. The same disciple appears three times in the body of the work: in 13:23–25 he is seen as especially close to Jesus during the supper; in 19:26–27 he is at the foot of the cross, and Jesus entrusts his mother to him; in 20:2 he is a witness, along with Peter, to the empty tomb. In addition, the mention of an eyewitness of an incident connected with the death of Jesus in 19:35 certainly alludes to him. Although this personage has sometimes been taken as a symbol (of the ideal disciple, of Hellenistic Christianity, of the community in which the gospel took form), this is unlikely; 21:23 seems to have been written under the impact of this person's death, which must have seemed to contradict a tradition according to which Jesus had assured him he would not die.

The tradition on which the gospel depends appealed therefore to an eyewitness to the life of Jesus, and in particular to his passion, but this does not mean that, with this testimony at its core, the redaction of the gospel was not a lengthy and complex process. The fact that the gospel draws on written sources and presents a well developed theological reworking of the sayings of Jesus does not favor the idea that the gospel's author was in direct proximity to the events.

Early tradition, beginning in the second half of the second century, identified the author of the gospel as John the apostle, son of Zebedee. According to Irenaeus (*Haer.* 3.1.2 [see 3.3.4]), John published his gospel in Ephesus, after the other three evangelists. The so-called anti-Marcionite prologue to John says that it was Papias of Hierapolis, a disciple of John, who wrote the gospel under dictation from the apostle. The *Muratorian Canon* likewise attributes the gospel to the apostle John, who is, however, presented here in a legendary setting as editor of the memoirs of all the disciples of Jesus. Around 190, Polycrates of Ephesus identifies John, who was buried in Ephesus, as the one who reclined on the Lord's breast (Eusebius, *Hist. eccl.* 3.31.; see Clement of Alexandria in *Hyp.*, Eusebius, *Hist. eccl.* 6.14.7). All these testimonies, however, contain legendary traits and concerns proper to a period when attention was on the problem of the canonization of the gospels.

Many scholars accept the connection of the gospel to the apostle John, but the beloved disciple does not seem to belong among the Twelve, nor does the evangelist seem to say he does. The very hypothesis seems to be contradicted by 21:2, where the sons of Zebedee, including John, appear with Peter, Thomas, Nicodemus, and two other disciples, one of whom must have been the beloved disciple, who speaks in v. 7.

Rather than seek to identify the disciple as a known person (which seems contrary to the author's intentions), it is more profitable to observe that the gospel shows signs of a lengthy development within a Christian community that originated in Judaism but was expelled from the synagogue (an experience reflected in 9:22; 16:2), and

against the background of the reconstruction and consolidation of Palestinian Judaism in the nineties. This explains why Jesus and his disciples are portrayed in opposition to "the Jews"; such opposition would have been meaningless in Jesus' time, but
reflects the time in which the gospel was edited: the Christian community was by now
clearly separated from the Jewish community. Since the gospel is attested by $\mathfrak{P}^{52}$,
which can be dated to around 125, its redaction can be dated to around 100. The area
of origin is still debated; if we accept the path followed by John the disciple, we look to
Asia Minor, with which he is connected by the early tradition. Others look rather to
the indisputable importance of theological elements originating in Judaism (though
there is no agreement about which elements, in the variegated Judaism of the 1st c.)
and to contacts with themes from gnosticism, and so opt for Syria. Still others suggest
the Transjordan area. Scholars are far from a consensus.

BIBLIOGRAPHY

Commentaries

R. E. Brown, *The Gospel of John* (2 vols.; AB 29, 29A; Garden City, N.Y.:
   Doubleday, 1966, 1970).
R. Schnackenburg, *The Gospel according to St. John* (3 vols.; New York: Crossroad,
   1968–1982).
F. J. Moloney, *Belief in the Word: Reading the Fourth Gospel, John 1–4* (Minneapo-
   lis: Fortress, 1993).
———, *Signs and Shadows: Reading the Fourth Gospel, John 5–12* (Minneapolis:
   Fortress, 1996).
———, *Glory not Dishonor: Reading the Fourth Gospel, John 13–21* (Minneapolis:
   Fortress, 1998).

Studies (including those on the gospel-letters combination)

O. Cullmann, *Origine e ambiente dell'evangelo secondo Giovanni* (1975; Casale
   Monferrato, 1976).
R. E. Brown, *The Community of the Beloved Disciple* (New York: Paulist, 1979).
J.-D. Kaestli, J.-M. Poffet, and J. Zumstein, eds., *La communauté johannique et son
   histoire: La trajectoire de l'évangile de Jean aux deux premiers siècles* (Geneva:
   Labor et Fides, 1990).
G. Segalla, *Evangelo e vangeli: Quattro evangelisti, quattro vangeli, quattro destina-
   tari* (Bologna: Dehoniane, 1993), 271–381.
M. Hengel, *Die johannische Frage: ein Lösungsversuch,* with an essay on the Apoca-
   lypse by J. Frey (Tübingen: Mohr, 1993).

2. Letters of John

Throughout the three letters the writer is a "we"; the author of the second and
third letters describes himself as an "elder," never as an apostle. First John, although
always described by the tradition as a letter, has neither an epistolary introduction nor

final greetings. Still, the message comes from a "we" and is addressed to a "you" (e.g., 2:1, 12, 14), to persons who are called "my little children" and "beloved." As the reference of the message to a real situation shows (see below), the addressees must have been a real community or group of communities. The work can be described as a theological manifesto composed for well defined purposes, rather than as a letter.

The manifesto begins with a prologue in which the direct testimony of the writer is the basis of communion between writer and addressees, and between both and God (1:1–4). The message is that God is light, and in order to be in communion with him one must walk in the light, admitting and confessing one's own sins in the awareness that Christ is our defender (Paraclete) before God (1:5–2:2). Proof that one knows God is the observance of his commandments; the commandment that has been given since the beginning is that of love for the brethren (2:3–11).

Next come several warnings: one must not love the world, which is passing away (2:12–17), and one must guard oneself against the antichrist, who is identified with persons coming from outside the community and denying that Jesus is the Christ (2:18–26). Thanks to the Father's love, believers are children of God; they must remain faithful to their state by avoiding sin, practicing justice, and loving one another according to the commandment of Jesus (2:27–3:24). There follows another warning to guard against false prophets, who do not confess that Jesus Christ came in the flesh (4:1–6), and another exhortation to mutual love as a consequence of God's love for us and in the belief that Jesus is the Son of God and came through water and blood (4:7–5:13). After an exhortation to prayer for the brother who sins (but not one whose sins lead to death), the work ends by summing up the self-consciousness of the community, which is based on the awareness of being from God, whereas the world belongs to the Evil One (5:14–21).

The language and ideas show clear affinities with those of John's gospel, and this raises the question of the author's identity. The answer is given by the fact that the same vocabulary serves to convey different ideas in the two writings. The term *arché* in the gospel signifies the beginning of all things (1:1–2); in the letter (1:1; 2:7, 24; 3:11) it signifies the beginning of the church in the life of Jesus. So too the *pneuma* is certainly divine in John's gospel, whereas in 1 John it may be the spirit of either truth or error and must be tested (4:1–6). It is therefore probable that 1 John comes from the school of the evangelist under the influence of events later than the writing of the gospel; these events have led to the tailoring of certain themes along specific lines. F. Vouga distinguishes the role of the author in each work: in John the author ("we") is present (1:14, 16; 3:11; 9:4; 21:24), but in the background, guaranteeing the christological confession and the testimony of the beloved disciple; in 1 John the writer ("we") is in the foreground: the school that originated in the beloved disciple takes on the role of a witness representing the authoritative tradition.

The event that arose between the composition of the two works is signaled in 1 John 2:18–27: some members of the community (perhaps a majority: 4:5–6) have separated from the author's group. The author wants to show that this separation proves they had never belonged to the group: in them is fulfilled the traditional preaching on the antichrist. Chapter 4:1–3 suggests that these others are claiming to be spiritual persons. According to the author, their Christology is in error: they deny that Jesus Christ came in the flesh (4:2–3) and their ideas are therefore docetist. They deny that Jesus is the Christ, they deny the Son of God (2:22–23), perhaps by separating the heavenly Son of God from the man Jesus. On the basis of 5:6, where the author repeats that Jesus Christ came not only in water but in water and blood, it appears that those who left believed that the Son of God was united to the man Jesus at the baptism, but separated from him again before the passion. They claim to know God (2:4; 4:8) and to be without sin (1:8–10); this claim seems to have been an interpretation of the idea in the gospel that believers are removed from sin (John 3:9; 8:31, 34). The author rebukes them for not loving the brethren; perhaps they had an individualistic religious spirit and ethic.

These adversaries form a branch of the Johannine tradition that had pushed to the extreme certain aspects of the tradition that took shape in the gospel. It seems they insist on the preexistence of Jesus, on the glory of God that is made visible through his humanity (1:14), and the control he had over the events of the passion. All this brings the danger of minimizing the humanity of Jesus and eventually considering it irrelevant to salvation. The charismatic claims of the adversaries (4:1–3) seem to go along with an interest in the knowledge of heavenly things that can be glimpsed in the community of the fourth gospel.

First John seeks to respond to this development of the Johannine tradition by offering a different interpretation of it, one that retrieves elements of the Christian tradition that were marginal in the gospel but could counterbalance the tendency of the adversaries. Thus not only does the tradition establish the criterion of true faith (the adversaries could have agreed on this point), but the man Jesus is identical with the preexistent Christ, the Son of God. The absence of sin is possible only through acknowledgment and confession of one's sins. Moreover, an interest in future eschatology is present in John but not central, because in the evangelist's thinking the judgment happens in the present, by way of the reception or rejection of the faith (John 3:18–26); the tension toward the future is now recovered in 1 John (2:28; 3:2; 4:17).

First John thus has its place at a point of crisis in the Johannine tradition. With this historical perspective, the other two, much shorter letters become intelligible. Unlike 1 John, they are true letters, written by a *presbyteros,* a title that may signify a member of the circle of itinerant preachers (this is certainly the world of 2 and 3 John; see below) who were guarantors of the apostolic tradition to which Papias of Hierapolis, Irenaeus, and Clement of Alexandria trace back their own tradition. Papias mentions a presbyter John but in our letters the presbyter does not give his name.

Second John is addressed "to the elect lady and her children," which is probably the designation of a community belonging to the Johannine tradition. It repeats the commandment of love, censures the "many deceivers who have gone out into the world, those who do not confess that Jesus Christ has come in the flesh," and urges that no one be welcomed who does not abide in the teaching of Christ, if such a person should turn up. The letter is therefore a warning against itinerant teachers representing the tendency already resisted in 1 John.

In 3 John the presbyter addresses "beloved Gaius," whom he praises for his receptivity to the "brothers," who are certainly itinerant preachers belonging to the author's group. On the other hand, he censures the conduct of Diotrephes, who is *philoproteuōn* in the church, that is, eager to occupy the first place; he refuses to welcome the brothers and has not allowed others to do so. Finally, the writer praises a certain Demetrius.

The canonical order of the letters probably reflects their chronological order. The first Letter of John seems to be a discourse within a divided community. The author's group is perhaps already a minority, but the debate is still going on. The author must define his own circle and strengthen its identity. The second Letter is addressed to a different community; the author's community must by now have been rent beyond repair, and the presbyter tries to keep the evil known to him from spreading to others. In 3 John the presbyter cannot even address a community, but only a private individual. The leader of that community, Diotrephes, rejects missionaries who are in communion with the presbyter. In the view of the church led by Diotrephes, the author of 3 John is probably a heretic.

Georg Strecker has recently revived a different thesis, according to which the presbyter-author of 2 and 3 John was at the origin of the Johannine school. The two letters would therefore dated around A.D. 100, because of Papias' testimony. First John and the gospel would be later works, produced perhaps by two different branches of the school. In the gospel, the presbyter would have become the beloved disciple, a personage who was part of Jesus' history, for the purpose of guaranteeing the content of the gospel. But 2 and 3 John make use, without explanation, of terms and concepts intelligible in the light of the gospel and 1 John; moreover, it is in light of the thought world of the gospel that the twofold development in the letters and their adversaries can be explained. Finally, as mentioned, the situation with regard to communication in the letters seems to be a further development of the situation presupposed by the gospel.

The letters of John seem, therefore, to have their location in the first decades of the second century, perhaps in Asia Minor, the area of activity of the presbyters mentioned by Papias. That location is all the more likely if the gospel is from that same area, but this is not certain (see above). In all probability 2 and 3 John come from the same author, but this is less sure for 1 John.

According to Eusebius (*Hist. eccl.* 3.36.1–2), Papias of Hierapolis used testimonies taken from 1 John. Polycarp of Smyrna (*Phil.* 7.1), may allude to 1 John 4:2–3 and 2 John 7, but this is not certain. Clearly, Irenaeus of Lyons was familiar with 1 and 2 John, for he cites passages from them as being by "John, the disciple of the Lord." But he does not seem to regard them as two separate letters (*Haer.* 1.16.3; 3.16.5; 8). The *Muratorian Canon* tells of a legend about the composition of the gospel of John, "one of the disciples," then mentions "his letters," citing 1 John 1:1. A little further on, in a passage difficult to interpret, it remarks: *epistola sane Iude et superscrictio* [= *suprascripti?*] *Iohannis duas* [= *duae*] *in catholica habentur* (lines 68–69). Its author knows, then, of two letters of John (*in catholica* = in the catholic church?).

Clement of Alexandria cites 1 John several times, calling it "the longer letter" (*Strom.* 2.15.66); therefore he knows of at least one other. His *Hypotyposes* contained a commentary on 2 John. For 3 John we must wait until Origen, who, according to Eusebius (*Hist. eccl.* 6.25.10), knew 2 and 3 John, but also knew that not everyone regarded them as authentic. In the works that have come down to us, however, Origen cites only 1 John. Eusebius places 1 John among the books that are accepted without reservation (*homologoumena*), but 2 and 3 John among the ones debated (*antilegomena*), along with James, Jude, and 2 Peter (*Hist. eccl.* 3.24.17; 3.25.2–3). In the second half of the fourth century acceptance of 2 and 3 John spreads throughout Greek and Latin Christendom, while in Syria it does not come until the sixth century.

BIBLIOGRAPHY

Commentaries

R. E. Brown, *The Epistles of John* (AB 30; Garden City, N.Y.: Doubleday, 1982).
G. Strecker, *Die Johannesbriefe* (KEK 14; Göttingen: Vandenhoeck & Ruprecht, 1989).
F. Vouga, *Die Johannesbriefe* (HNT 15,3; Tübingen: Mohr, 1990).

We assume, therefore, that the Johannine community or school went through a complex evolution. Starting with testimony still close to the historical Jesus, a body of thought developed which increasingly highlighted, behind the man Jesus, the preexisting heavenly Savior and his divine power, which was the condition for and instrument of salvation. When faced with its rejection and marginalization by the Jewish world in which it originated, the Johannine group distanced itself from "the Jews" (while projecting the same attitude back into the history of Jesus) and claimed a superior knowledge of God's plan that had been brought to fulfillment in Jesus, the heavenly messenger. This teaching perhaps developed in the framework of an understanding of revelation that yielded a knowledge of heavenly mysteries (John 3:11–13).

The situation prompted the community of the saved to withdraw into itself. This community saw itself set against a hostile world immersed in darkness. It claimed to have belonged to Christ from the very beginning by a divine election. At the same time, the situation fostered a soteriology in which salvation and condemnation were linked to the present choice for or against Jesus, while the expectation of a future judgment became secondary, although it would be retrieved probably in a relatively late phase in the redaction of the gospel (see, e.g., John 5:28–29 which seems to be a corrective of 5:24–27). This complex of ideas quickly gave rise to strong internal tensions, as it could easily lead to a minimalization of the humanity of Jesus and to an ethic based on a salvation already acquired. The turning in of the Johannine communities on themselves (love is directed to within the community) must have intensified their isolation. The final chapter of the gospel perhaps bears witness to a later effort at consolidation by way of a bridge thrown over to other groups that were under the authority of Peter, who is here heralded by the risen Lord, while the problem of the relationship between Peter and the beloved disciple is raised.

The internal tensions led, however, to a rupture between one party which soon became the majority and developed a docetist attitude, and another that reinterpreted the gospel and emphasized the humanity of Jesus, ethical demands, and a futurist eschatology. First John, which is a discourse for use within a community, shows this dramatic situation as full-blown, but the two tendencies are held in balance. Second and Third John, however, document the progressive withdrawal of the second community. This latter community probably was absorbed in the second century by more solidly established "Petrine" groups (John 21) or some others (think of the meeting of Johannine and Pauline influences in Ignatius of Antioch), in the process of forming a Christian orthodoxy. The adversaries, for their part, would become part of gnostic groups, bringing with them the gospel as they interpreted it. In fact, the gospel of John was to be especially dear to the gnostics (Heracleon), but the great church was able to retrieve it precisely through the reading of the Johannine letters.

Chapter 4

THE EARLIEST CHRISTIAN APOCALYPSES

1. Apocalypse as Genre

Modern scholars at the beginning of the nineteenth century first spoke of apocalypse as a literary genre. They did so when they realized that in order to understand the canonical Apocalypse they had to take account of a vast Jewish literature. The writings that make up this literature present themselves as records of revelations of God's plan for world history and, in particular, of an imminent divine intervention (if necessary by way of a messenger, the messiah) that will destroy evil and establish the reign of God. These revelations are recorded by a seer who writes of them in the first person and is their beneficiary. Since the Apocalypse of John begins precisely with the word *apokalypsis* (revelation), this literature is described as apocalyptic, although the word is not meant as the title of the book (much less of its genre) but refers rather to God's revelation of mysteries.

The earliest mention of the Apocalypse, by Justin Martyr around A.D. 155–160 (*Dial.* 81.4), uses the word not as a title but as meaning "a revelation he [John] had," while some decades later Irenacus and Tertullian regard it as the title of the book. The use of "Apocalypse of John" as a title for the book in the manuscripts and in the *Muratorian Canon* likewise goes back to the second century. Around A.D. 140, *apokalypsis* appears as the title of a section (*Vis.* 5) in the Shepherd of Hermas that contains a revelation. Beginning in the second century, the title "Apocalypse" is also given to writings containing a revelation but not corresponding to the concept of apocalypse developed by modern scholars; for example, dialogues of the risen Jesus with his disciples, such as the *Apocalypse of James,* found at Nag Hammadi.

The contemporary discussion of apocalyptic as a genre is far from yielding a consensus. For many decades, descriptions of the genre generally listed the elements to be found in all, or almost all, apocalypses: pseudonymity, visions as means of revelation, the symbolism of the images shown to the seer, the explanation of these, the organization of phenomena by means of chiefly numerical patterns, interest in the course of history and especially in the future; descriptions of the other world, visions of God's throne-room, and so on. The problem is that not only does this description combine elements of both form and content, but every work classified as an apocalypse contains only some of them, so that it is not possible to determine which elements are really decisive. In recent years, an effort has been made to define a "paradigm," that is, a model established by interrelated traits having to do with form, content, and function. Here is the paradigm proposed by the group under the leadership of J. J. Collins; it seems to us to be the most matured statement:

> Apocalypse is a genre of revelatory literature with a narrative framework, in which a reve-lation is mediated by an otherworldly being to a human recipient, disclosing a transcen-dent reality which is both temporal, insofar as it envisages eschatological salvation, and spatial insofar as it involves another, supernatural world. . . . [Its purpose is] to interpret present circumstances on earth in the light of the supernatural world and of the future and to influence both the understanding and the behavior of the public by divine author-ity. (*Semeia* 36, 2 and 7)

The basic component is therefore the representation of two levels of reality: one accessible to human experience, and the other proper to spiritual beings and know-able only to the extent to which it is revealed. This second level exerts a decisive influ-ence on events in our world "here below," for these events are often only the visible face of conflicts going on in the "other world." Knowledge of these conflicts is there-fore essential for a correct understanding of the meaning of history and for correct behavior. This knowledge is granted to privileged individuals either by allowing them access to that other world or through a vision or a communication from a messenger.

The demand for such knowledge grows historically out of situations perceived as disordered, in which it is difficult to think that there is any communication with the divine world; the revelations and their message are therefore attributed to great per-sonages of the past. As a result, pseudepigraphy is frequent, as is the command to keep the revelation hidden until the last times, which are, as a rule, those of the true author. In fact, it becomes necessary to explain why a revelation supposedly received so long ago should become known only now. These conventions, as we shall see in connection with the Apocalypse of John, would change at the beginning of the Christian era, when believers held that they were living in an age in which the Spirit of God is poured out on the community.

The paradigm (rather than definition) that has been described must, however, be distinguished from an understanding of apocalyptic that is much more closely tied to content; for this the term "apocalyptic eschatology" has been suggested. It must also be distinguished from an understanding that is closely tied to the social behavior con-nected with that content; for this the preferred term is "millenarianism." As a matter of fact, elements of both form and content that are characteristic of apocalypses are found in protest movements that arise during times of crisis and loss of identity. Apocalypses often function as a means of consolidating a collective identity that is en-dangered, and of consoling and encouraging in critical situations, but such is not always the case.

For example, it is certainly true of the book of Daniel which has long been re-garded as the earliest Jewish apocalypse (ca. 165 B.C.). But it does not seem to be the case in the oldest parts of the *Book of Enoch* (*Book of the Watchers* = *En.* 6–36; *Book of Heavenly Luminaries* = *En.* 72–82), which go back to the third century B.C. Among the first Christian apocalypses, it seems once again to be the case in the Apocalypse of John and in that of Peter, but not in the older—and more properly "apocalyptic"—part of the *Ascension of Isaiah*. It seems questionable, therefore, to define the role of apocalypses in a way broader than the already fairly broadly defined paradigm given above.

Apocalyptic is to be found not only in Judaism and Christianity, but throughout the ancient world and in successive periods. In structure, therefore, it is interreligious and intercultural, which makes it difficult to trace direct influences of any text on another. It is not possible to set down constant conditions for the production of apocalypses or to identify an "apocalyptic movement," even just within Judaism. Since the distinction mentioned above between apocalypse as a genre and apocalyptic eschatology is not always observed and, for that matter, does not seem satisfactory, we think it expedient to renounce the ambiguous term "apocalyptic" and to speak instead of individual apocalypses as representatives of a genre.

We ought to start, however, not with the genre as a category for defining the "apocalypticity" of an individual text, but with an analysis of the way each text that matches the paradigm of apocalypses (our hypothetical starting point) is situated in relation to the tradition to which it appeals or which it even creates. In other words, we ought to ask how the individual apocalypse is related to the body of texts from which it takes elements as meaningful units that can be reorganized to express its own special message. This approach seems suitable for giving an account of the historical development in which the outward appearance, the conditions for production, and the functions of apocalypses may vary, but the various texts produced are still described as apocalypses both by their authors and by subsequent reception.

We shall discuss here the three oldest Christian apocalypses, while leaving later ones to the second volume of this work.

BIBLIOGRAPHY

Early Christian Apocalypticism: Genre and Setting (Semeia 36; 1986).

D. Hellholm, ed., *Apocalypticism in the Mediterranean World and the Near East: Proceedings of the International Colloquium on Apocalypticism, Uppsala, August 12–17, 1979* (2d ed.; Tübingen: Mohr, 1989).

J. J. Collins and J. H. Charlesworth, eds., *Mysteries and Revelations: Apocalyptic Studies since the Uppsala Colloquium* (Sheffield: JSOT Press, 1991).

Apocalittica e origini cristiane (*Ricerche storico bibliche* 2; Bologna: Dehoniane, 1995).

2. Apocalypse of John

The Apocalypse shows a very complex structure. To begin with, there are undoubtedly three parts. The first, consisting of ch. 1, contains a vision of the Son of man, who orders the narrator to see and write down. Chapters 2 and 3 contain the letters that Christ dictates to seven churches of Asia Minor. Chapters 4–22 contain a vision of the divine throne and heavenly worship; in this vision the narrator is shown a book sealed with seven seals, which no one can open except the slaughtered Lamb, that is, Christ crucified. The book contains the mystery of the divine plan for history, and the breaking of the seven seals inaugurates a series of events that culminate in the defeat of the forces of evil, the final judgment, and the disappearance of the present world, which is replaced by the city of God, the Jerusalem that comes down from heaven. The visions in chs. 4–22 do not follow a single advancing line but involve a series of intervals, anticipations, and returns, the justification of which, within the work as a whole, is difficult and largely conjectural.

The seven letters have no independent existence as real letters, but are closely connected with the message of the Apocalypse as can be seen from their parallel structure and thematic links to the rest of the work. However, the work as a whole has an epistolary framework: there is an introduction (1:4–6) and a final greeting (22:21). Still, the Apocalypse is not primarily a letter, as is already clear from the fact that the introduction is preceded by a title that describes the text as revelation and prophecy. The formal elements of a letter probably reflect the intention that the text be read during the liturgy in the communities addressed (1:3), as was regularly the case with letters. By and large, there is a close connection between the Apocalypse and the liturgy. Not only is the heavenly liturgy the setting of the visions in chs. 4–22, but the overall vision takes place on a Sunday, the day of worship, and liturgical elements are introduced after the *praescriptum* (1:4–7) and at the end (22:15).

Here is an outline of the contents.

Chapter 1:1–3 serves as a kind of title. God has given his revelation to Jesus Christ, who has given it by way of his angel to John, who in turn must pass it on to the servants of Christ, that is, the community, which is viewed as a collection of prophets. Chapter 1:4–5 is the prescript, and 1:7–8 a prophetic utterance. Chapter 1:9–20 contains the vision of the glorified Christ, who orders John to write to the seven churches; this vision introduces not only the seven letters but the entire Apocalypse. The two sections that follow seem to be referred to in v. 19, which orders the writing of what is (chs. 2–3) and what is to take place after this (4:1, introducing chs. 4–22).

Each of the letters which Christ dictates to the churches of Ephesus, Smyrna, Pergamum, Thyatira, Sardis, Philadelphia, and Laodicea follows the same pattern: "These are the words" (an Old Testament prophetic formula), followed by a self-description that contains one of the elements in the vision of ch. 1. A commendation is followed by a rebuke (but the letters to Smyrna and Philadelphia, which are placed symmetrically in the second and sixth places, do not contain a rebuke). Finally, there is an exhortation to hear the message of the Spirit, followed by a promise. The letter to Thyatira lacks the exhortation; the exhortation and the promise are in inverse order in the last three letters, which confirms that the symmetry is intentional. The series of seven churches is the first of four septenaries that play a structuring role in the Apocalypse—there are other groups of seven and, in general, the work is attentive to the symbolism of numbers. The number seven symbolizes totality; the letters refer to particular situations but at the same time have in mind the universal church, to which the following section (chs. 4–22) is certainly addressed. In each letter, Christ announces his proximate coming; this motif also has its corresponding motif in chs. 4–22, which has to do with the proximate intervention of God in the history of the world.

Chapter 4 introduces a new vision: the seer, caught up in an ecstasy, enters the throne room of God. In it are twenty-four elders (whose meaning is still debated), seven lit lamps (symbolizing the Spirit of God), and four living beings in the form of lion, calf, man, and eagle. These various elements are taken from the Bible, Zechariah, Isaiah, and Ezekiel in particular. All of these beings celebrate the liturgy as they sing the praises of God the creator. In ch. 5 he who sits on the throne holds in his right hand a book (scroll) that is sealed with seven seals. No one is worthy to open the book except the Lamb who has been slaughtered, that is, the once dead but now glorified

Christ, who appears and accepts the book. In other words, Christ is the key to the interpretation of God's plan for history, a plan symbolized by the book, and he is at the same time the Lord of this history.

In 6:1–7 the Lamb opens the first of the seals, each of which unlooses a scourge on the earth, except for the fifth, which brings a vision of the martyrs, who are shielded beneath the altar of God. They ask in a loud voice how long God will wait to do justice, and how long they are to wait for the completion of their predestined numbers. Chapter 7 is a kind of interlude that symbolically specifies the number of those predestined for salvation and describes their blessedness, but as something future: this blessedness is only anticipated, not yet attained.

The opening of the seventh seal (8:1) gives rise to a silence which the prophets announced would mark the beginning of God's final interventions. The opening of this seal does not unloose a scourge, but it does "open the way" to a new septenary, that of the trumpets which the angels sound. The first six trumpets unloose new scourges; yet even these do not exhaust the wrath of God (chs. 8–9). After the sixth trumpet there is once again an interlude (10:1–11:14): an angel announces that at the seventh trumpet the mystery of God will be fulfilled. The seer is given a little book to eat, that is, borrowing a motif from Ezek 3:1–3, he is to prophesy further calamities. He must also measure the temple in Jerusalem, which will be placed in the power of the pagans. The latter period will see the ministry of the two witnesses/prophets, who will preach repentance. These mysterious figures will be slain by the beast from the abyss, who will appear again only in ch. 13. But they will be called back to life and received into heaven. These figures are inspired by the eschatological traditions of Judaism and probably represent the community of believers, which in the last times will be crushed by the forces of evil but will be protected by God.

The sound of the seventh trumpet (11:15) gives rise to a hymn of praise by the twenty-four elders, because God is inaugurating his reign; at the same time, however, new scourges begin that will take the form of a final septenary, that of the bowls. But first there is a new delaying factor: in a series of symbols, chs. 12–14 connect the eschatological prophecies with the present experiences of believers. As a woman prepares to give birth, a dragon (the devil) is cast down from heaven to earth, where he intends to devour the woman's child. But as soon as the child is born he is taken into heaven, and the dragon turns against the rest of her children. The woman is the preexisting heavenly church. The devil, driven from heaven according to Hebrew traditions, is unloosed against Christ, but Christ ascends into heaven. Then the dragon's anger is turned against Christians.

Chapter 13 describes the manner of the dragon's attack: by means of a beast risen from the sea, who replaces God (the Roman empire), and a beast risen from the earth, who uses marvelous signs to compel the inhabitants of the earth to worship the statue of the first beast (the priests of the cult of the emperor). All those who do not obey are excluded from civil society. Chapters 12–13 thus reveal that the persecutions inflicted on Christians by the empire are the visible face of an invisible and radical conflict between God and the devil. But 14:1–4 describes the Lamb standing on Mount Zion with the saved, the proclamation of the fall of Babylon (Rome), and the declaration that God's wrath will strike those who worship the beast; the hour of the "harvest" has come. Chapter 15:1 announces the *final* seven scourges that make up the final septenary, that of the bowls, which are handed to seven angels (15:7). Chapter 16 describes the scourges in the seven bowls; at the seventh (16:17–21) a voice proclaims: "It is done!" and the wrath of God falls upon Babylon.

Chapters 17–18 describe the "judgment of the great whore" (17:1), that is, of Rome. Like 12–14, these chapters connect earthly events with the drama already played out at the divine level. The symbolism is explained, characteristically, in terms permeated with mystery: the prostitute/Babylon is Rome, drunk with the blood of Christians; the beast on which the prostitute is seated, the same beast that rose from the abyss in 13:1, is the imperial power in its diabolical aspect, which will immediately be concentrated in the antichrist figure of Nero brought back to life (the eighth king, who is one of the seven: 17:11). In an act of remarkable insight, the author foretells the dismemberment of the empire by the peoples subject to Rome (17:15–17). The power of the kings born of the dismemberment will likewise be diabolical. Chapter 18 contains the proclamation of divine judgment on Babylon/Rome and a lament by the kings of the earth and the merchants who have done business with them. The lament is touching in its evocation not only of the political and economic power of Rome but also of all the aspects of its civilization and even of its daily life, aspects destined to be swept away because of their antidivine basis. Chapter 19:1–10 ends this section with a chorus of praise of God who has avenged the blood of his servants, and with an announcement of the imminent marriage of the Lamb.

The transition to this marriage is a series of events for which the author draws on eschatological traditions current in Judaism. Chapter 19:11–21 describes the coming of the Messiah and the final struggle against the beast and its false prophet, both of whom are thrown into the lake of burning sulfur. There follows (20:1–6) the imprisonment of Satan and a reign of Christ, with his martyrs, for a thousand years; this is the reward for the patience required of them in 6:10–11. After the thousand years, Satan will be set free and, using the earthly nations Gog and Magog (semimythical figures derived from Ezek 38–39), will make war on the saints, but he will be defeated by fire from heaven and be thrown forever into the lake of sulfur and fire; then the final judgment will take place (20:7–15).

In chs. 21:1–22:5, heaven, earth, and sea disappear, to be replaced by a new heaven and a new earth. From heaven comes the heavenly Jerusalem, the city of God, the bride of the Lamb, the place where the saints will dwell, with God and the Lamb as their temple and their light. Chapter 22:6–21 is an epilogue containing the repeated announcement of the Lord's coming; the angelic assurance that everything written is true; an exhortation to the seer not to keep the book secret (contrary to the tradition of the pseudepigraphical apocalypses; see above, sec. 1), but to broadcast it, because God's intervention is near at hand; and finally, a threat against anyone who changes the text of the prophecy. The Apocalypse is thus the only New Testament writing that claims to be divinely inspired.

The tensions and doublets in the book have prompted proposals that it is a redaction on the basis of short texts of varied provenance, the combination of two or more preexisting writings, or the reworking of a base text. Today there is a tendency to emphasize the compositional coherence of the Apocalypse, while not denying the author's use of various traditions and perhaps even of preexisting textual units. The fact that the book is shot through with allusions to Old Testament writings without ever giving a true citation is enough to show that the author has made free use of traditional themes and motifs and reworked them into a whole of noteworthy complexity and expressive power. It is therefore difficult to interpret both the meaning of each symbol and the overall meaning of the Apocalypse.

The disagreements about interpretation began in antiquity. The first attestations to the book (Justin, Irenaeus, Hippolytus) interpret it as a prophecy of the last times, which are still in the future. But a reading of the Apocalypse as a survey of sacred history during the Old Testament and Christian eras soon became dominant in the church (Tyconius, Augustine). On the other hand, marginal prophetic movements of protest read the Apocalypse as a prophecy of an end time that had already begun; they did their best to calculate times and to see in present events the fulfillment of the various prophecies.

Today scholars still take sides in interpreting the Apocalypse either as a retrospective reading of the history of salvation (e.g., E. Corsini) or as an announcement of future events in which God will intervene to change a present situation characterized by oppression by the forces of evil. We ourselves opt for the second interpretation, which in no way detracts from the central place of Christ: the conviction that he by his death has already won the victory over evil is what makes it possible to tell believers that, despite the seemingly dominant power of antidivine institutions, they are under the protection of God whose hand does not cease to control history. It is impossible to understand the Apocalypse as a cento of Jewish apocalyptic motifs. Christology is the key to the book, for it is in function of Christology that all the traditional elements are reorganized.

The language of the Apocalypse is unusual; the writer often violates Greek norms of grammar and syntax. His language is Greek, but he thinks in Hebrew; as a result, we seem to be dealing with the Hebrew of the Bible rather than with a Semitic language actually used by the writer. He uses both the Septuagint and the Hebrew Bible, and it is often difficult to decide from which he draws.

The author of the Apocalypse calls himself John (1:1, 9; 22:8). Justin Martyr, referring to Rev 20:4–6, says that the passage is from the revelation given to John, one of Christ's apostles (*Dial.* 81.4), thus depending on a tradition that identified the author with the son of Zebedee. Irenaeus of Lyons takes the same tack and identifies this John with the author of the Fourth Gospel (*Haer.* 5.21.11; 5.26.12); he also dates the Apocalypse toward the end of the reign of Diocletian (81–96). Around A.D. 200, Gaius, a Roman priest, and the mysterious "Alogi" attributed the book to Cerinthus, a heretic; this represented a reaction against the Johannine writings because of their use by the Montanists.

Around the middle of the second century, Bishop Dionysius of Alexandria, an opponent of millenarianism, used criteria of style and content to reject the attribution of the Apocalypse to John the apostle, whom he regarded as author of the gospel and 1 John. He proposed, instead, an attribution to a John of Asia and remarked that there were two tombs of John in Ephesus. Eusebius of Caesarea (*Hist. eccl.* 3.39.7) adopted Dionysius' suggestion and identified the second John with the "presbyter John" mentioned by Papias of Hierapolis as someone different from the apostle (in Eusebius, 3.39.4). Eusebius was also aware that some regarded the Apocalypse as canonical, others as "spurious," that is, apocryphal (3.25.2 and 4). Indeed, it was only during the fourth century that the book was accepted in the east.

In the ecclesiastical tradition the attribution to John the apostle has won out, despite the fact that for the author of the work the twelve apostles are a thing of the past

(21:14). The attribution to "presbyter John" has reappeared several times, even in our day, but it, too, is problematic, because the John of the Apocalypse never gives himself this title, although, according to Papias, it was part of the self-description of the presbyter whom he mentions. Moreover, the John of the Apocalypse never seems to claim any authority other than that of the message entrusted to him. Because pseudepigraphy is considered a characteristic of apocalypses, scholars sometimes maintain that the Apocalypse is a pseudepigraphon. This view begs the question; moreover, the very reasons already given against the authorship of the son of Zebedee and presbyter John contradict the notion that the author wanted to suggest composition by one of those two.

The best solution, and the one widely accepted, is that the author was a charismatic figure named John, an authority in the group of communities in Asia Minor to which the letters are addressed. Even though he does not expressly call himself a prophet, it is probable that he understands himself to be one (see 22:9), and he does expressly call his work a prophecy (1:3; 22:7, 10, 18). As for the date, the end of the first century, according to a tradition already known to Irenaeus, seems the most probable. It is true that the sources do not justify the claim that a broad persecution was unleashed by Domitian, but we know that he gave new life to emperor worship, and that the situation supposed by the book is precisely one of local persecution, or threats of persecution, due to a refusal to accept such emperor worship.

Scholars also disagree on the relationship of the Apocalypse to the gospel and letters of John. Some repeatedly emphasize lexical contacts, which would suggest a community, if not precisely a "school," as the setting. Such contacts do exist, but the study of them always turns up noteworthy differences. For example, in the New Testament writings, Logos as a christological title occurs only a few times (John 1:1, 14; 1 John 1:1; Rev 19:13). In the first two writings the title is used absolutely; it refers to preexistence, and it is connected with the Jewish sapiential tradition. In the Apocalypse, however, it takes of the form of "Logos (Word) of God," and is one of the four titles given to Christ who comes for judgment; it is connected with other occurrences of "word/words of God" which in the same book (see 21:5; 22:6) express the fidelity of God who fulfills the prophetic words spoken in the Apocalypse, and it does not imply preexistence.

So too in both gospel and Apocalypse Jesus is described as the "lamb," but the word occurs twenty-eight times in the Apocalypse and only twice in John. The Greek words are different: in John Jesus is "the Lamb of God," but in the Apocalypse he is the "Lamb" without qualification; in the Apocalypse, unlike the gospel, the blood of the lamb has no expiatory value. The best explanation (in agreement with E. Schüssler Fiorenza) seems to be that the two works independently come to an interpretation of Jesus as Passover lamb (see 1 Pet 1:19).

The eschatology is very different in the two works: the Apocalypse reaches out to the future, while the gospel hinges on a present eschatology. There is a retrieval of future eschatology in a later phase of the gospel (and then in 1 John), but there is nothing close to the world of ideas found in the Apocalypse. In general, the little that the Apocalypse and the gospel of John have in common can be explained by contacts between the Johannine "school" and the prophetic "school" to which the author of the Apocalypse belongs. The latter work also shows contacts with the Pauline tradition.

BIBLIOGRAPHY

Commentaries

E. Lohse, *Die Offenbarung des Johannes* (3d ed.; Göttingen: Vandenhoeck & Ruprecht, 1971); IT: *L'Apocalisse di Giovanni* (Brescia: Paideia, 1975).

E. Corsini, *Apocalisse prima e dopo* (2d ed.; Turin: Società Editrice Internazionale, 1993).

P. Prigent, *L'Apocalisse di Giovanni* (1981; 2d ed.; Geneva: Labor et Fides, 1988); IT (Rome: Borla, 1985).

U. B. Müller, *Die Offenbarung des Johannes* (Gütersloh: Mohn, 1984).

B. J. Malina and J. J. Pilch, *Social Science Commentary on the Book of Revelation* (Minneapolis: Fortress, 2000).

Studies

E. Schüssler Fiorenza, "The Quest for the Johannine School: The Apocalypse and the Fourth Gospel," *NTS* 23 (1977): 402–27.

U. Vanni, *La struttura letteraria dell'Apocalisse* (2d ed.; Brescia: Morcelliana, 1980).

———, *L'Apocalisse: Ermeneutica, esegesi, teologia* (Bologna: Dehoniane, 1988).

3. Ascension of Isaiah

The *Lives of the Prophets,* a collection of Jewish origin but preserved in various recensions that have all been christianized, tell us that the prophet Isaiah "died under Manasseh, King of Judah, by being sawn in two." This legend circulated in the first century of our era and is alluded to in the Letter to the Hebrews (11:37). From the second century on, the motif became a common one in works by Christian authors. By reason of an ambiguity in translation from a Semitic language which turned "saw for wood" into "saw of wood," these authors found in Isaiah, slain by means of wood, a figure of Christ who died on the wood of the cross. The *Ascension of Isaiah* is an early and complex Christian development of this traditional motif.

Of the original Greek *Ascension* only a lengthy fragment (2.4–4.2) remains in a papyrus from the sixth or seventh century A.D. (P.Amh. I). The complete text has come down in a translation into Ge'ez (classical Ethiopic) that was introduced into the Ge'ez translation of the Old Testament. There are also two fragments of an early Latin translation used by the Arians (2.14–3.13; 7.1–19); fragments of two Coptic versions; an Old Slavic version and a Latin version, both based on a revision of the second part (chs. 6–11) that was probably done in the early Middle Ages. A Byzantine abridgement, though extensively revised, allows us to retrieve some elements of the original Greek.

The story is in two parts, corresponding to the present chs. 1–5 and 6–11. The first episode takes place in the royal palace in Jerusalem in the twenty-sixth year of the reign of Hezekiah, who summons his son Manasseh to the presence of the prophet Isaiah, in order that Manasseh may be informed of a vision which the prophet has had

of the future coming of Christ into the world. But Isaiah tells Hezekiah that when
Manasseh becomes king, he will lead the people into idolatry and will put Isaiah himself to death (ch. 1). This indeed takes place after the death of Hezekiah: Isaiah opposes the religious depravity of Manasseh, who at the urging of the Samaritan false
prophet Belkira, has the prophet arrested and sawn in two. It is Beliar, the devil, who
drives Belkira and Manasseh: he is furious with Isaiah because the prophet has, by
means of his vision, revealed Beliar's deceitful action as he tries to get human beings
to worship him instead of God.

The vision, which will be described in the second part of the work, is briefly
evoked here, between the arrest and the martyrdom of Isaiah, and prolonged in a development that does not belong in the first part. It tells of the flowering of the church
after the ascension of Christ and the later corruption during the last times. This corruption leads to the activity of the antichrist, the Lord's return, and the end of the
present world.

The second part is an account of the vision to which the first part has repeatedly
alluded and which takes place in the twentieth year of Hezekiah's reign. After coming
to Jerusalem and Hezekiah's palace, Isaiah conducts a liturgy together with forty
prophets. As he is prophesying, Isaiah falls into an ecstasy and his spirit, accompanied
by an angel, traverses the heavens to the seventh, which is God's dwelling place. Here
Isaiah gazes upon the preexistent Christ and the Holy Spirit, who are leading the
heavenly liturgy. He is then given a vision of the future descent of Christ into the
world. Christ descends through the heavens, adopting in turn, lest he be recognized,
the form of the angels who dwell in the five lower heavens and of the demons who occupy the firmament. On earth he takes a human form, pretending to be born of Mary
and Joseph in Bethlehem. The devil, who does not suspect his divine identity, has him
killed by the Jews. Descending into the lower world, Christ reveals his glory, destroys
the power of the angel of death, and takes from him those of his prisoners who are
just. He then ascends in glory through the heavens. The demons of the firmament are
compelled to worship him as their Lord, as are the angels of the other heavens, until
he sits at the right hand of God. Isaiah is sent back to earth, where he tells the vision
and the order not to spread it until the coming of Christ.

The second part is properly an apocalypse, since here, through a revelation and
under the guidance of an interpreting angel, Isaiah is given knowledge of divine mysteries. The knowledge has to do with the last days, which are identified with the
earthly life of Christ (9.13). The salvation of humanity does not depend on Christ's
incarnation (his human form, like that of the angel, is only an appearance) but on his
victory over the powers in the firmament, which have rebelled against God; this victory is the real judgment (7.12; 10.12). In relation to the time when the writer lived
and to the real addressees of the work, who are Christians, salvation seems to be located in the past, at the ascension of Christ, and there seems to be no interest in a
return of Christ at the end of the world.

On the other hand, the first part of the *Ascension* is a kind of midrash: it follows
the narrative model of the biblical stories about kings and prophets and makes use of
haggadic traditions developed within Judaism. It makes use especially of a pattern repeated throughout the history of Israel, namely, conflict between true prophets and
false prophets allied with wicked and idolatrous kings. The eschatological prophecy
that is included in this first part (3.13–4.22) can be described as an apocalypse only in

the sense that it is meant to seem to be a part of Isaiah's vision. The prophecy is connected with the vision by the following device: into the history of persecution suffered by Isaiah there is introduced a summary of the content of the vision that will be told in the second part. This summary imperceptibly changes into a prophecy of the future (3.13) within which Isaiah appears unexpectedly as the speaker (3.31; 4.1, 13, 20) and which then suddenly shifts once again into a third-person account of the prophet's martyrdom (5.1).

In this first part, the present world is controlled until the end by the devil, who persecutes and kills the prophets. Salvation comes as a result of the return of Christ for the universal judgment. The difference between this and the ideas of chs. 6–11 is obvious. The decline of the church which Isaiah predicts for the last times is seen as consisting essentially in a decline of prophecy (3.26–27; the prophetic charism is an essential mark of a prosperous church, 3.19) and in a rejection, by presbyters and pastors of the communities, of prophecies and in particular of the visions of Isaiah (3.31).

The organization of the work is unusual: the chronological order of the two parts is inverted. The second part, which has a separate textual tradition in Slavic and Latin, has its own title. The first part contains a prophecy of Isaiah that interrupts the narrative and is given as part of the vision to be told in chs. 6–11. This has led some to regard the *Ascension* as a composite work. According to R. H. Charles (1900), it was formed by combining three originally independent texts: a Christian *Vision of Isaiah* (chs. 6–11), a Jewish *Martyrdom of Isaiah* (1.1–3, 13a; 5.1–16, except for small additions by the final editor), and a Christian eschatological vision, which Charles thought had been originally attributed to Hezekiah (3.13b–4.18 or 22). A different hypothesis, but one also assuming a combination of preexisting documents, is that of A. Acerbi (1989).

The structure of the *Ascension* may be explained as the result of two successive phases of composition within the history of a group of prophetic Christians. The present second part was the first to be written and circulated; the Slavic and Latin versions derive from a revision of it. In it, traditions about the birth of Jesus from the Virgin were reinterpreted (11.2–18) in the interests of a Christology that viewed the man Jesus as a manifestation in human form of a preexisting heavenly being described as the Beloved and the Lord. Jesus, Christ, and Son were considered to be names belonging exclusively to an "earthly" knowledge of him. The revelation of the heavenly identity of Jesus and therefore of the real meaning of these traditions constitutes the purpose of the prophet's ascension. Behind this story is a group of Christian prophets who receive revelations enabling them to give a christological interpretation of Old Testament prophecies, and in particular those of Isaiah (*Ascen. Isa.* 6–11 is woven of allusions to his texts), as well as of Christian traditions. The ability to give such an interpretation is doubtless the basis of the claim to authority.

This claim is finally challenged by "presbyters and pastors," that is, authorities who are not necessarily charismatic and who gradually consolidate their position as leaders of the Christian communities. These men deny validity to the manifesto of the prophetic group, namely, the *Vision of Isaiah*. The prophets then propose the *Vision* once again, but preface it with the first part; here they expand the traditional basic story of Isaiah's martyrdom into a narrative in which the martyrdom becomes part of a pattern of persecution of the prophets by false prophets and by rulers who are urged on by the false prophets and ultimately by the devil. The implication is that the present lot of the prophets, who are being opposed by the ecclesiastical authorities, is proof that they are really on the right side in God's eyes, just as the earlier persecuted and slain prophets were. To this vision of Isaiah is now added a prophecy (3.13b–4.18) on the eschatological decline of the church as seen in the almost complete loss of the presence of the Spirit and of prophecy and in the rejection of the *Vision* by the ecclesiastical authorities.

The properly apocalyptic part of the *Ascension* (chs. 6–11) has for its purpose, then, not to communicate revelations about the imminent end of the world (a function usually thought to be a strict part of an apocalypse), but to support a Christology that by its nature requires a revealed knowledge of heavenly mysteries. An interest in the eschatological crisis was added later and was dictated by the historical crisis of the group that now seeks to interpret and justify its own position by means of a "reading grid" imposed on history past, present, and future. According to this grid, revelation has to do with spiritual forces that clash beneath the surface of human conflicts. The framework for this revelation was already provided by the existing *Vision*, but the addition must have been made independently of the latter, since it was already in circulation as an autonomous document.

The *Ascension* shows a dependence not on writings that were to become part of the New Testament, but on traditions that were also taken over by the evangelists, especially Matthew (birth and resurrection of Jesus). There is also an affinity with traditions represented by Ignatius of Antioch and the *Odes of Solomon*. The struggle of the ecclesiastical authorities to impose control within the communities on charismatic groups that purveyed a docetist Christology is also attested by Ignatius of Antioch. Some themes of the *Ascension* can be found in writings connected with Petrine traditions, probably spreading from Antioch. A consideration of all the factors suggests placing the composition of the *Ascension* in Syria, possibly Antioch, at the beginning of the second century, in two phases not far apart in time.

BIBLIOGRAPHY

Editions

R. H. Charles, *The Ascension of Isaiah, Translated from the Ethiopic Version, Which, Together with the New Greek Fragment, the Latin Versions and the Latin Translation of the Slavonic, Is Here Published in Full* (London: Black, 1900).

P. Bettiolo, A. Kossova, C. Leonardi, E. Norelli, and L. Perrone, eds., *Ascensio Isaiae* (2 vols.; CCSA 7–8; Brepols: Turnhout, 1995); critical edition of all the texts, translation, summary, commentary.

Studies

M. Pesce, ed., *Isaia, il Diletto e la Chiesa: Visione ed esegesi profetica cristiano-primitiva nell'Ascensione di Isaia* (Atti del Convegno di Roma, 9–10 Aprile 1981; Brescia: Paideia, 1983).

A. Acerbi, *L'Ascensione di Isaia: Cristologia e profetismo in Siria nei primi decenni del II secolo* (Milan: Vita e Pensiero, 1989).

E. Norelli, *L'Ascensione di Isaia: Studi su un apocrifo al crocevia dei cristianesimi* (Bologna: Dehoniane, 1994).

J. Knight, *Disciples of the Beloved One: The Christology, Social Setting, and Theological Context of the Ascension of Isaiah* (Sheffield: Sheffield, 1996).

4. Apocalypse of Peter

The manuscript of the eighth-ninth century that was found at Akhmim in the winter of 1886–1887 and that contained the *Gospel of Peter,* also contained a Greek text that was identified as the *Apocalypse of Peter* on the basis of its agreement with a citation in Clement of Alexandria. According to the *Muratorian Canon,* this work was accepted by the church on a par with the Apocalypse of John, though not everyone allowed its reading in the liturgy. Until this discovery there existed only a few fragments cited by Clement of Alexandria, who regarded it as an inspired writing and, according to Eusebius (*Hist. eccl.* 6.14.1), had commented on it in his *Hypotyposes.* Methodius of Olympus cited a passage from it (without giving it a name) as taken from "writings inspired by God" (*Symp.* 2.6). Eusebius lists it among books that Catholic writers had never used (*Hist. eccl.* 3.3.2), while elsewhere (3.25.4) he places it among the *nothoi* ("bastard, spurious"), which, though not recognized, were not to be regarded as heretical. Two more fragments are preserved by Macarius of Magnesia (ca. 400: *Apocrit.* 4.6.16; 4.7).

Between 1907 and 1910, S. Grébaut published two Ethiopic treatises attributed to Clement of Rome, from manuscript 51 of the D'Abbadie collection (probably from the 16th c.). The second of these treatises, titled *The Second Coming of Christ and the Resurrection of the Dead,* contained a translation of the *Apocalypse of Peter.* A second Ethiopic manuscript, probably from the 18th century, was found in 1968 on the island of Kebran in Lake Tana. Both manuscripts are full of errors. Then there are two fragments in Greek that come from the same manuscript, probably of the fourth century. One of these (10.6–7) is in the Bodmer Collection of Oxford and was published in 1911; the other (14.15) is in the Rainer Collection in Vienna and was published in 1924 (and identified in 1931).

The differences between the Ethiopic manuscript and the Greek manuscript of Akhmim raised the question of which text is older. For an understanding of the problem we must summarize the contents of the two manuscripts, beginning with the Ethiopic. We follow D. D. Buchholz in the numbering of the sections.

In 1.1–2.13, as narrated by Peter in the first person, Jesus sits on the Mount of Olives, and his disciples ask him to tell them the signs of his coming and of the end of the world. Since this conversation will end with the ascension of Jesus, it belongs among the dialogues of the risen Lord with his disciples. He warns them against false messiahs and gives an explanation of the two parables of the fig tree, the tree that bears fruit (Matt 24:32) and the tree that is barren (Luke 13:6–9), applying both to Israel. During the last days, when the tree's branches produce precious stones, an impostor will appear who, when rejected, will cause many martyrdoms. Enoch and Elijah will be sent to unmask him.

In 3.1–13.4, Christ makes known to Peter the final destiny of the just and of sinners. Peter timidly objects on the grounds of God's mercy. Jesus rebukes Peter and, to make known to him the actions of sinners, describes how the judgment will take place and, in great detail, the punishments for the various categories of sinners.

The destiny of the just is described much more briefly (13.1; 14.1–2): they will receive baptism and salvation "in the lake of Acherusia, in the field of Elysium" (14.1). Christ therefore orders Peter to go to the city of the west (Rome) and there announce Jesus' martyrdom "at the hands of the son of him who is in Hades, in order that his destruction may be begun" (14.4–5 according to the Rainer fragment, which is more accurate than the Ethiopic).

In 15.1–17.7 Christ invites the disciples to follow him to the "holy mountain," where they see, unexpectedly, two men resplendent in light. Jesus tells them that the two are Moses and Elijah. Peter asks where, then, are the patriarchs and the other fathers, and he is granted a vision of them in a splendid garden. Peter suggests building three tents, as in the gospel story of the transfiguration (Matt 17:4), but the Lord accuses him of having his mind darkened by Satan, and urges him to understand that there is but a single tent, made not by human beings but by the heavenly Father and intended for Christ and his elect. A voice from heaven proclaims Jesus to be the beloved Son (see Matt 17:5); a cloud carries Jesus, Moses, and Elijah aloft; the heavens open and the disciples see human beings with fleshly bodies who join Jesus and ascend with him to the second heaven amid angelic acclamations. The heavens are shut, and the disciples come down from the mountain praising God.

The Greek text from Akhmim shows one large-scale difference: it inverts the vision of the two resplendent individuals and that of the punishments in hell. It begins with the end of a discourse of Jesus on the corruption in the last times and on the coming of God to rescue his oppressed faithful (chs. 1–3). Jesus then invites the disciples to climb the mountain, where the two individuals appear. The two are not, however, Moses and Elijah, but "your just brothers." Peter's question is about the place not of the patriarchs but of all the just. The garden shown him is clearly paradise (chs. 4–20). Peter then sees hell, too, and its torments are described in a way that parallels chs. 7–10 of the Ethiopic text (chs. 21–34). The Akhmim fragment ends at this point. The punishments of hell are not the content of an eschatological prophecy from Jesus, prior to the vision on the mountain, but part of the vision itself. The vision does not represent a rereading of the account of the transfiguration but makes known, in two parallel scenes, the fates of the just and the damned. In the Ethiopic version, the garden is the earthly paradise, where the great just individuals of the Old Testament remain until they ascend to heaven with Christ; in the Greek text, it is the final dwelling place of all the just.

There is agreement today that the text represented by the Ethiopic translation is earlier. In describing the punishments of hell the Oxford fragment and the ancient citations have the verbs in the future tense, which indicates that there was originally a prophecy and not a vision told of as past, as in the Akhmim fragment. The vision of the two persons on the mountain was originally a rereading of the (Matthean) story of the transfiguration. It placed the emphasis on two points. The first point: We have not yet reached the Parousia. Peter has wrongly interpreted the presence of Moses and Elijah as signaling the immediate coming of the reign of God, and for this reason he asks about the coming of the other patriarchs, in keeping with current Jewish expectations.

At present, these persons are in the earthly paradise, a place of provisional happiness, but they will ascend to heaven with Jesus. The second point: The kingdom of heaven manifests itself not as an earthly kingdom but as a heavenly; this is the meaning of Jesus' angry reply about the tent not made by human hands.

These two points or motifs were relevant to the situation in which the text was composed, as we shall see in a moment, but they were no longer relevant at a later period, when a different situation prompted an interest in the destiny of human beings after death (a theme of later Christian apocalypses: e.g., *Vision of Paul*). Our text was reworked along the latter lines, in the form attested by the Akhmim fragment.

The interpretation of the parable of the fig tree as referring to the coming, in the last times, of a false messiah whom the Jews will follow and who will produce many martyrs among the Christians who reject him (2.7–13) is an allusion to the anti-Roman revolt of a Jew, Simon Bar Kochba, in A.D. 132–135 and to his persecution of the Christians who did not follow him. The author of the *Apocalypse of Peter* does not know of Bar Kochba's end; it is therefore to be dated before A.D. 135. This hypothesis (R. Bauckham) explains well the organization of the text. The eschatological discourse of Jesus is intended to console the Christians persecuted by Bar Kochba, by showing that the latter is the antichrist, that these Christians are therefore martyrs, and that Christ will come soon to destroy him.

As for the punishments in hell, studies based on the discovery of the Akhmim fragment have shown a dependence, on the one hand, on Orphic-Pythagorean traditions and, on the other, on the Jewish apocalypses. To the traditional lists of sins, however, the author has added the sins of those who have blasphemed the way of justice (7.2), those who have persecuted and betrayed upright Christians (9.2), and those who use lies to put the martyrs to death (9.4).

Clearly, the martyrs are Christians who did not join the revolt against Rome. The discourse ends with the sending of Peter to Rome and the prediction of his death under Nero, who is described as son of the devil. This death will mark the beginning of the destruction of the devil himself, that is, it begins the age of diabolical rage that precedes the intervention of the Lord. The tradition about Peter's death in Rome, of which our text is one of the earliest witnesses, is thus taken as a sign to convince persecuted Christians that the last times are running their course and deliverance is at hand. Peter's martyrdom will make him worthy of the promise (14.5). After the final judgment Jesus will lead his chosen ones into the everlasting kingdom, where they will rejoice with the patriarchs at the fulfillment of the promises (14.3). The subsequent account of the ascension of Jesus ensures the fulfillment of the promise, because the apostles can see that the pre-Christian just are indeed rising to heaven. If the transfiguration is incorporated into this account (in the canonical gospels it has a quite different place, before the death of Jesus), the reason is that it too plays a part in the author's message: believers are put on guard against the claims of Bar Kochba that the reign of the messiah has come and that his kingdom is an earthly one.

The author emphasizes the bodily resurrection as connected with the judgment (4.4–12), saying that those who ascend with the Lord are in their bodies (17.3). The reward of the just, however, is not in a kingdom of this world, but in a space outside the world. Characteristically, the latter is described by linking the Hellenistic tradition (Lake Acheron in the Elysian fields, 14.1) with the Jewish-Christian tradition (note the influence of the exegesis of Genesis 2 on the description of the earthly paradise in ch. 16). In a similar way, as we have already seen, the description of hell arises from the convergence of two cultural traditions. The heart of the work is the final judgment. As Buchholz has shown, the *Apocalypse* gives no importance to the "earthly" Jesus, who is here only a human being, or to his resurrection. He becomes the Son of God only when the heavenly voice proclaims him such, immediately before the ascension. He is thus appointed universal judge, and the judgment will be based on human actions, with the martyrs having, of course, a privileged status. This entire scenario is in the service of the author's purpose: to encourage Christians to resist the attractions and threats of Bar Kochba. The area in which the *Apocalypse of Peter* originated must have been Palestine or western Syria.

BIBLIOGRAPHY

D. D. Buchholz, *Your Eyes Will Be Opened: A Study of the Greek (Ethiopic) Apocalypse of Peter* (Atlanta: Scholars Press, 1988); introduction, text, translation, and commentary.

R. J. Bauckham, "The Apocalypse of Peter: An Account of Research," *ANRW* II 25.6 (1988): 4712–50.

Chapter 5

NON-PAULINE LETTERS

S ome letters proper, that is, works elicited by particular circumstances and addressed to specific communities or individuals, would not become part of the
New Testament canon, even though they were more or less contemporary with the
later writings in the canon and were highly regarded. It was precisely their lack of
pseudonymity that made it possible to distinguish them from the apostolic writings.
We are still dealing with works intended for the internal use of the Christian communities, but like the Pastoral Letters, composed around the same period they seem to
share concerns that look to the boundaries of the community at least as much as to
its center.

1. Letter of Clement of Rome to the Corinthians

Clement of Rome enjoyed great success in early Christianity. Hegesippus, who had
been in Rome in the time of Bishop Anicetus (155–166), mentions a letter Clement
wrote to the Corinthians during the persecution of Domitian (ca. 96; Eusebius, *Hist.
eccl.* 3.16; 4.22.1). Around 170, Bishop Dionysius of Corinth attests to the reading of
that letter during the liturgy (Eusebius, *Hist. eccl.* 4.23.11). Irenaeus of Lyons cites a list
of Roman bishops that names, after "the apostles," Linus, Anacletus, and Clement, the
last of whom supposedly had a direct knowledge of the apostles. In his time, the church
of Rome wrote to the church of Corinth in order to restore peace there after an internal
rebellion (*Haer.* 3.3.3). Clement of Alexandria often cites the letter in his *Miscellanies*,
attributing it at times to Clement, and at times to the church of Rome.

Origen, followed by Eusebius, identifies Clement with Paul's fellow worker of
that name (Phil 4:3). Tertullian says that Clement was ordained bishop of Rome by
Peter (*Praescr.* 32). In the fourth century Epiphanius tries to reconcile this statement
with that of Irenaeus, by saying that Peter had ordained Clement but the latter had
yielded his place to Linus (*Pan.* 27.6). As early as the third century there was in circulation a kind of autobiographical novel, Jewish-Christian in origin and antipauline in
character, in which Clement told of his noble pagan origin, his conversion to Christianity, and his journeys in the east along with Peter, who was involved in controversies with Simon Magus. Two versions of this work survive from the fourth century,
the so-called *Pseudo-Clementines* (see vol. II of this history). A tradition not attested
before the beginning of the fifth century tells of the martyrdom of Clement; the claim
is based on the unlikely identification of Clement with the consul Flavius Clemens, a

cousin of Domitian whom, according to Suetonius and Dio Cassius, the emperor had beheaded around 95–96 for "atheism and a fondness for Jewish customs."

Clement, ennobled as he was by his supposed direct connections with Peter and the apostles, was gradually assigned an entire literature. But the only text that can be connected with him historically is the one known as *1 Clement,* in which his name is not mentioned; the link with Clement comes from the second-century tradition already mentioned.

The fifth-century manuscript A of the New Testament contains, after the Apocalypse of John, two letters in Greek that are attributed to Clement of Rome, the second being a homily that has nothing to do with him (see below, ch. 7, sec. 2a). A second manuscript (codex 54 of the Greek Patriarchate in Jerusalem, from the year 1056) enables us to fill in the lengthy gaps found in the two letters in A. Of the first letter there also exist a very early Latin translation (probably of the second century), another in Syriac, and two in Coptic.

Chapters 1–3 recall the "wicked and sacrilegious" rebellion stirred up in Corinth by "a few rash and presumptuous individuals" (1.1) and speak of "jealousy and envy, discord and rebellion, persecution and disorder, war and imprisonment" (3.2). The root of the troubles in Corinth is said to be jealousy; after the manner of a synagogal homily, a series of examples is then given of the disastrous effects of jealousy, these being taken from the Scriptures but also from the recent history of the Christian community. Peter and Paul are regarded as victims of jealousy, as is a "great throng of the elect" (6.1) who have recently suffered. The "suffering" is usually regarded as an allusion to the persecution of Domitian. God calls for repentance, obedience, faith, humility, meekness, peace and concord, and fear of God. All these virtues are abundantly illustrated by biblical examples (chs. 7–21). God will fulfill his promises, and first of all the promise of resurrection, to those who fear him. The need, then, is to draw close in purity to the one who from the beginning of the world has justified human beings through faith (chs. 22–32). This does not mean that they are to neglect works; even God worked in creating. We must submit to God's will, as the angels do, and struggle to obtain the promised blessings; the way by which we can attain them is Jesus Christ (chs. 33–36).

The author then turns to the subject of the letter. Examples taken from military life and from the role of members in a body exhort the readers to mutual submission and service. Just as God ordained the priestly hierarchy in Israel, so God has sent Christ, who commanded the apostles, who in their turn instituted bishops and deacons. The apostles also arranged for an orderly succession in these offices, but this succession has now been upset in Corinth, where bishops and presbyters are deposed (chs. 37–44). This is a real persecution of the just, a wounding of the members of Christ, comparable to that censured by Paul in his first letter to the Corinthians. Love must therefore be restored to its place. The instigators of the rebellion must ask forgiveness, allow the common good to take priority over their personal advantage, submit to the presbyters, and accept correction (chs. 45–58). The church of Rome, for its part, prays that God will preserve throughout the world the limited number of the elect. This prayer, inspired broadly by the Roman liturgy, is valuable to us for our knowledge of Roman theology at that period (chs. 59–61). Finally, the letter again exhorts to peace, names the carriers of the message, and ends with a blessing (chs. 62–65).

Despite its length, this is a true letter. It comes from a church, not from an individual, even if the personality of the author emerges clearly. As a true letter, it was elicited by concrete circumstances, with a prescript and final communications according to the norms of the epistolary style. The document is self-described as an *enteuxis* (63.2), a term which in juridical language meant a petition addressed to a king with the purpose of urging him to give judgment in a case. If it be accepted that this technical term is deliberately used, then the letter will be seen as an exhortation to the community to pass judgment on the "rebellion" for the sake of "peace" (Lindemann). Within the letter there appear various other forms, too: similarities to the synagogal homily, especially in chs. 4–38 with its examples of the virtues and vices (and see chs. 45; 55); similarities to the Cynic-Stoic diatribe (examples from military life, from the human body, chs. 37–38); moralizing exegesis (e.g., chs. 13–16; 56); parenesis; and liturgical prayer (59.3–61.3). The author, although not a Jewish Christian, gives evidence of a Christianity that is deeply rooted in the theological and exegetical tradition of Diaspora Judaism. He makes use of the rhetoric and popular philosophy of Hellenism but in such a way that these could very well have come to him through the Hellenistic synagogue.

The occasion for the letter is the deposition of presbyters/episcopi in Corinth (44.3; 47.6). Though the men have not been accused of any particular fault (44.3–6), and the author tries to minimize the number of guilty participants ("one or two individuals," 47.6; see 1.1), it would seem that the majority of the community agreed with what was done. The reasons for the action are not clear; the constant references in the text to jealousy and envy do not, of course, reflect anything but the polemical strategy of the author.

Doctrinal reasons have been suggested (W. Bauer): a party with gnostic tendencies, heir to the groups combated by Paul in the 50s, may have rebelled against the leadership of presbyters who were promoting an "orthodoxy" that sprang from the union of the parties of Cephas and Paul (1 Cor 1:12), an orthodoxy welcomed in Rome but always weaker in the face of tough local opponents. Evidence has been seen in the emphasis on expectation of the future resurrection (chs. 24–26) and on the tradition that links God and Christ with the ecclesiastical authorities in office at any given time (ch. 42). When the gnostics became sufficiently strong to take power, Rome (according to Bauer) intervened to support the party that was theologically close and politically loyal to it.

However, even if we accept that Rome would adopt the political strategy that best suited it rather than a strategy more in keeping with the real situation, the arguments for this hypothesis are weak, because no doctrinal polemic is perceptible in the letter. Moreover, 54.1–4 exhorts the guilty parties to leave Corinth, thereby winning great glory in Christ, acting as true citizens of God, and deserving to be welcomed everywhere; this does not suggest that the author is dealing with "heretics." It is of interest that Rome sees no other way of settling the matter except the emigration of the leaders. Finally, it is not said that the rebels aspired to be presbyters or took the places of those expelled.

Andreas Lindemann prefers the idea that the rebellion was aimed at eliminating the presbyterate, this being an office not attested at Corinth in Paul's time and one that was clearly felt to be a novelty. This is quite possible, but if this be so, it will have to be admitted that Rome's intervention was not due to a simple desire to protect the good name of Christians and, in general, the order willed by God (as Lindemann thinks), since these could be safeguarded independently of the presbyterate, but rather to support the office of the presbyters as such, which must have been regarded by Rome as guarantor of a philoroman sentiment. Nor does the letter prove that Rome arrogated to itself the authority to interfere in the affairs of other churches. In fact, the language and extent of the argumentation show precisely that Rome could not appeal to any right. Instead, the text is undoubtedly an evidence of the will and ability of the Roman community to intervene in other churches in order to create or preserve conditions in keeping with its own interests.

The letter makes extensive use of Scripture, but essentially for purposes of example and exhortation: the citation of Isa 53:1–12 in ch. 16 serves only to offer the humility of Christ as a model. The value of the law does not create any problem. The relationship between faith and works in 32.4–33.1 corresponds to Paul's perspective; it is God's intention to justify the human beings whom he has called in Christ because of their faith, which must, however, be followed by works. Justification by faith starts not with Christ but with the beginning of the world, and Abraham is cited as an example not of faith but of justice and truth that are practiced because of faith (31.2). Justice does not have the same meaning here as in the Pauline approach.

There is an isolated instance of typological exegesis (12.7, on Josh 2:18), which comes to the author from tradition. Otherwise, the letter uses no allegories and supposes that between Israel and the church there is complete continuity, which allows the takeover of the ethical heritage of Judaism while questions of ritual norms are ignored. The author is familiar with at least 1 Corinthians (47.1; see 37.5; 38.1) and Romans (32.4–33.1; 35.5–6). This understanding of Paul, which places him in continuity with Judaism, is of great interest for an understanding of how disturbing Marcion's reading of Paul some decades later must have been in Roman theological circles. Our author uses the gospel tradition (13.2; 46.8), but not necessarily on the basis of the gospels known to us. It is highly probable that 36.2–5 depends on Heb 1:3–13.

With regard to authorship: as already noted, Clement is never named in the letter. It appears as the work of the Roman community. possibly of some of the Christian communities of Rome, even though the style and unity of thought presuppose an authorial personality. This could have been Clement, an authoritative member of the church. In any case, he was not the "pope," because at this period there was no monarchical episcopate in Rome but rather a collegial leadership of presbyters/episcopi. The lists of successive bishops known to Hegesippus and Irenaeus are creations of the second century. The traditional date, the last years of the first century (end of the persecution of Domitian or immediately after, under Nerva), has been upheld especially by A. von Harnack; arguments for a later date are not convincing. The Christian victims of persecution described in chs. 5–6 reach back to Nero. "The unexpected and repeated calamities and disasters that have befallen us" (1.1) and delayed the sending of the letter may well refer to the persecution of Domitian, as the entire early tradition maintained.

BIBLIOGRAPHY

A. Lindemann and H. Paulsen, *Die Apostolischen Väter: Neu übrsetzt und herausgegeben* (Tübingen: Mohr, 1992), 77–151.

A. Jaubert, *Clément de Rome: Epître aux Corinthiens* (SC 167; Paris: Cerf, 1971); text, translation, introduction, and notes.

A. Lindemann, *Die Clemensbriefe* (HNT 17; Tübingen: Mohr, 1992); commentary.

O. B. Knoch. "Im Namen des Petrus und Paulus: Der Brief des Clemens Romanus und die Eigenart des römischen Christentums," *ANRW* II 27.1 (1993): 3–54.

J. B. Lightfoot and J. R. Harmer, *The Apostolic Fathers: Greek Texts and English Translations of Their Writings* (2d ed.; trans. and ed. M. W. Holmes; Grand Rapids, Mich.: Baker, 1992).

B. E. Bowe, *A Church in Crisis: Ecclesiology and Paraenesis in Clement of Rome* (Minneapolis: Fortress, 1988).

D. A. Hagner, *The Use of the Old and New Testaments in Clement of Rome* (Leiden: Brill, 1973).

2. Ignatius of Antioch

In dealing with the period of Trajan (98–117), Eusebius of Caesarea mentions Ignatius, second successor of Peter as bishop of Antioch, and reports what he knows about him (*Hist. eccl.* 3.36.5–11). Ignatius was taken as a prisoner from Syria to Rome, there to suffer martyrdom. As he crossed Asia Minor, he met representatives of the churches of that region and exhorted them to beware of the heresies that were beginning to spread, and to hold fast to the tradition of the apostles. Eusebius then lists seven letters written by Ignatius during his journey: he is said to have written from Smyrna to Ephesus, Magnesia, Tralles, and Rome; from Troas to Philadelphia and Smyrna; then, separately, to Polycarp, bishop of Smyrna. Eusebius derives his knowledge from the letters themselves, of which he cites some passages. Without naming Ignatius, Irenaeus had already cited a passage from the letter to the Romans (4.1; *Haer.* 5.28.4). Later, acts of the martyrdom of Ignatius without historical value would circulate in two versions and various rewritings.

The formation of a collection of Ignatius' letters is attested by one of his correspondents, Bishop Polycarp of Smyrna (*Phil.* 13.2). Until the seventeenth century, a collection of letters of Ignatius, in Greek and Latin, was known, that included not only the seven mentioned by Eusebius but another six as well. In 1646 in Amsterdam, Isaac Voss published an edition of six of the letters listed by Eusebius (a Latin translation had already been published in 1644), for which an eleventh-century Greek codex, and some copies of it, are known. The seventh, that to the Romans, is found instead as part of the *Martyrium Colbertinum* of Ignatius and was published in 1689. In addition to a papyrus fragment of the letter to the Smyrneans and many citations by ecclesiastical writers, translations of this recension into Latin, Syriac, Armenian, Arabic, and Coptic are known. Finally, there is a shortened Syriac translation of the letters to Polycarp, the Ephesians, and the Romans, which was published in 1845.

While everyone regarded the long recension as secondary, doubts were also expressed for a long time about the intermediate recension, until critical studies, especially those of T. Zahn (1873) and J. B. Lightfoot (1885; 2d ed., 1889), established its authenticity. In recent years, doubt has again been cast on its authenticity, which had been accepted by the great majority of scholars. R. Weijenborg (1969) has attempted to show the priority of the long version, but has not found agreement. J. Rius-Camps (1979) thinks that while in Smyrna Ignatius, who lived between 80 and 100, composed only the letters to the Romans, Magnesians, Trallians, and Ephesians. In his view the other three were later forgeries that used passages from the authentic letters and composed new sections, especially in the letter to Polycarp. According to Rius-Camps, along with the authentic passages, new material was introduced on the authority of bishops, this in the interest of the bishop of Philadelphia who sponsored the work. A simpler and more radical suggestion was made by R. Joly (1979), who regards the intermediate recension as a forgery from the years 160–170, as shown by a number of anachronisms and unlikely features; the reference to Ignatius' correspondence in the letter to Polycarp is an interpolation.

We side with the majority of scholars in rejecting this suggestion: nothing is sufficiently convincing to warrant our regarding the intermediate recension of Ignatius' letters as a forgery, in whole or in part (see Munier, in the bibliography).

Attention has long been called to the occasional and spontaneous character of the letters. W. R. Schoedel, however, has rightly stressed the "planned" nature both of the contacts between Ignatius and the churches of Asia (the delegations from these communities devoted considerable time and resources to the undertaking) and of the interpretation Ignatius gives of his own fate. He connects his martyrdom with the problems he had met in Antioch, which were already affecting the communities of Asia: he had to struggle against groups of Christians whose views, in his opinion, threaten the salvific nature of the passion and death of Christ. After Ignatius's arrest, "peace" returned; that is, his views won out (*Phld.* 10; *Smyrn.* 10–11). Against the background of the claims of aberrant groups and of conflicts within the church at Antioch, Ignatius's martyrdom was to prove beyond doubt the justice of his cause. It is probably for this reason that he also rejects any effort of the Roman church to save him (*Rom.* 4–8).

To the groups he opposes, Ignatius attributes both a denial of the reality of Christ's flesh and therefore of his death and resurrection (especially in *To the Trallians* and *To the Smyrnaeans*) and a Judaizing mentality (especially in *Magn.* 8–10 and *Phld.* 6–9). There has been endless discussion of whether Ignatius combats one tendency, which combines docetism and Jewish practices, or two. On the one hand, it is difficult to find any group known to fit this framework; on the other hand, antidocetist polemics are found in passages on Judaism (see *Magn.* 9.1; 11; *Phld.* 6.1). The hypothesis that Ignatius is also fighting a third group, namely, itinerant preachers who challenge the episcopal ministry (C. Trevett), seems superfluous inasmuch as the description of the itinerant preachers fits the docetists exactly (cf. *Smyrn.* 4.1 with *Eph.* 7.1; see also *Eph.* 9.1).

The docetist tendency is very clearly described. Ignatius does not use the term, but he says that according to those people Jesus suffered *to dokein*, "in appearance" (*Trall.* 10.11; *Smyrn.* 2.2; 4.2). The docetist opponents deny that Christ was of the line of David according to the flesh (*Smyrn.* 1.1; *Trall.* 9.1), that he was prosecuted under Pontius Pilate, was crucified, and died (*Smyrn.* 1.2; 2; *Trall.* 9.1), and that he truly rose (*Smyrn.* 2; *Trall.* 9.2).

Their attitude to the church is consistent: they abstain from the Eucharist and the liturgy, because they deny that the Eucharist is the flesh of Christ (*Smyrn.* 7.1); they have no regard for love (*Smyrn.* 6.2). They reject the authority of the bishop; they challenge the presbyters; they do not respect the deacons (*Smyrn.* 8.1; *Trall.* 2–3); and they are swollen with pride (*Trall.* 7.1), which is based on their rank (*Smyrn.* 6.1). Since they are neither presbyters nor deacons, what rank can this be? It seems from

Trall. 5.1–2 and *Smyrn.* 6.1 that they boast of knowing heavenly secrets, the angelic hierarchies, and the throngs of celestial powers, presumably on the basis of ecstatic experiences. The reference here must be to charismatics who claim a special authority because of their ability to receive and communicate revelations, especially during the liturgy, while probably belittling the bishop, who "remains silent" (*Eph.* 6.1; *Phld.* 1.1) because he does not have charismatic gifts.

According to *Smyrn.* 5.1, these people are dissuaded neither by prophecies nor by the law of Moses, that is, they do not accept that the Old Testament foretells the reality of the incarnation, passion, and death of Jesus. This attitude seems similar to that described in *Phld.* 8.2, where Ignatius recalls a debate he had with them. They said: "If I do not find it in the records [i.e., the Scriptures], I do not believe [it] in the gospel." To the objection of Ignatius, "But it is written," they replied: "That is precisely what has to be shown." The subject of contention here is certainly the christological interpretation of the Scriptures; the adversaries claim that any statement about Christ must be proved by exegesis. Ignatius accepts the principle, but does not succeed in imposing his interpretation. He prefers to say: "For me, the records are Jesus Christ," thus giving priority to the christological profession of faith as an exegetical norm. In general, he makes very little use of Scripture in his letters, perhaps also for the reason that his adversaries were better trained in exegesis.

The attack on those who want "to live according to Judaism [variant: the law]," while professing "heterodox views and useless old wives' tales" (*Magn.* 8.1), is much fuzzier. The "Judaizing" (*Magn.* 10.2) seems reducible to an attachment to the Hebrew Scriptures, especially the prophets (*Magn.* 8.2; 9.2) and is comparable, therefore, to the attitude in *Phld.* 8.2, which, as we saw, reflects the position attacked in the antidocetist polemics. The attack on Sabbath observance in *Magn.* 9.1 seems to be introduced by Ignatius to emphasize the contrast between "ancient customs" and the "new hope," and does not necessarily imply that the adversaries observed the Sabbath; on the other hand, in the same sentence Ignatius makes a polemical point against the docetists. In *Phld.* 6–9, too, the accusations of Judaizing seem to presuppose only an attachment to the Hebrew Scriptures.

On the whole, the evidence seems insufficient to maintain that there is a separate Judaizing tendency which Ignatius attacks in parallel to the docetist tendency. We agree with Schoedel's conclusion: "We can conclude that someone has told Ignatius of (relatively slight) Judaizing tendencies in Magnesia, that he interprets this as a more serious threat than it actually was, and that he tries to deal with it by signaling a connection between these tendencies and the more dangerous threat of docetism" (p. 125 of his commentary).

The conflicts that have arisen in Antioch and, according to Ignatius, either actually or inchoatively in the communities of Asia Minor, lead him to emphasize unity. The vocabulary of unity is fundamental in his writings, and he describes himself as "a man devoted to unity" (*Phld.* 8.1). His main concern is unity within the church around the bishop, whose primacy he founds on a theological pattern: As there is but one God, so there is but one bishop, who is an image of the Father (*Trall.* 3.1) and is in the place of God (*Magn.* 6.1). The bishop must be regarded as Jesus Christ and receive the submission due to Jesus Christ (*Eph.* 6.1; *Trall.* 2.1). The bishop is in the place of God, the presbyters in the place of the apostles, and the deacons are engaged in the service of Jesus Christ (*Magn.* 6.1; *Trall.* 3.1). This does not mean that the bishop has the same authority as God the Father, but rather that we must obey the bishop as Christ obeyed the Father. Still, this is undoubtedly an important passage in the consolidation of the monarchical episcopate.

At the same time, Ignatius' passionate polemic makes it clear that this position has not thus far prevailed. The church is in the midst of a process whereby a bishop managed to gain control over an entire community and over Christian groups that had hitherto been pretty much independent each of the others, as must have been the case in Antioch. The process naturally meant the exclusion of groups that did not agree with the prevailing ecclesiological and theological model.

Ignatius's theology, too, is to be read in light of this effort at unity and at a definition and consolidation of boundaries. The heart of this theology seems to be a Christology centered on the unity of the truly divine and the truly human in Jesus (*Eph.* 7.2; *Pol.* 3.2) and therefore dominated by the idea of an incarnation that involves the uniqueness of the birth of Jesus as ensured by the virginity of Mary (*Eph.* 18–19). Only this set of circumstances can guarantee to human beings a salvation that is understood as a resurrection in union with the resurrection of Christ (*Trall.* 9) and that presupposes participation in the Eucharist, that is, in the flesh of Christ which God has raised up (*Smyrn.* 7.1).

An important aspect of Ignatius is his mystical spirituality; this is not to be understood, however, as a union with God in a quasi-gnostic framework. Contacts between Ignatius and gnosis have been emphasized especially by H. Schlier (1929) and, more cautiously, by H.-W. Bartsch (1940). The comparison with gnosis is important for understanding Ignatius, especially given the extent to which he and the gnostics were drawing conclusions from common premises but in different ways. These premises were probably developed largely in Antiochene circles. In the crucial passage in *Eph.* 19, Ignatius does not seem to presuppose the idea of a hidden descent of a heavenly savior, though Schlier based his thesis to a large extent on this interpretation. Central to Ignatius's mysticism is the role of martyrdom, through which he expects to "gain God" (*Rom.* 4.1) and Christ (*Rom.* 5.3). This is the theme of the letter to the Romans, which is permeated by a throbbing desire to be united with Christ by martyrdom (*Rom.* 6.1, 3).

Ignatius cites the Old Testament only three times (*Eph.* 5.3; *Magn.* 12; *Trall.* 8.2; the first two times with "it is written"). In contrast, there are many contacts with the gospel materials, especially Matthew (see *Eph.* 14.2; 19.2; *Smyrn.* 1.1; 6.1; *Pol.* 1.3; 2.2), although these contacts can be explained by the dependence of both on oral tradition. Noteworthy, too, are contacts with Johannine theology (*Rom.* 2.7; 7.3; *Phld.* 7.1; 9.1), but these do not seem to depend directly on the gospel. Ignatius knows various letters of Paul (*Eph.* 12.2); a direct use of 1 Corinthians is certain (at least in *Eph.* 16.1; 18.1; *Rom.* 5.1; 9.2; *Phld.* 3.3), while the use of other letters, especially Ephesians and Galatians, is possible.

Ignatius's style is very personal, impassioned, impetuous, and rich in syntactically difficult constructions, as well as in anacoloutha, metaphors, and similes. He uses the devices of the Asianist rhetoric practiced in his day, as O. Perler has shown (1949) by a comparison of Ignatius with 4 Maccabees: antithetical parallelism, symmetry, rhyme, paronomasia, parecheses, anaphora, oxymoron, climax. It remains true, however, that the letters of Ignatius are true letters—they respect the epistolary form with its elaborate *praescriptum* and final greetings. They are animated by a powerful personality, even though at the same time they express theological and ecclesial thought and planning that is broader in range and more close knit than, for example, the vision emerging from the letters of Paul.

BIBLIOGRAPHY

Editions

J. B. Lightfoot, *S. Ignatius, S. Polycarp,* vol. II of *The Apostolic Fathers* (3 vols.; 2d ed.; London: Macmillan, 1889; repr., Hildesheim-New York: Olms, 1973); still unsurpassed as a collection of materials.

J. B. Lightfoot and J. R. Harmer, *The Apostolic Fathers: Greek Texts and English Translations of Their Writings* (2d ed.; trans. and ed. M. W. Holmes; Grand Rapids, Mich.: Baker, 1992).

A. Lindemann and H. Paulsen, *Die Apostolischen Väter: Neu übersetzt und herausgegeben* (Tübingen: Mohr, 1992), 176–241.

Commentaries

W. R. Schoedel, *Ignatius of Antioch* (Hermeneia; Philadelphia: Fortress, 1985).

H. Paulsen, *Die Briefe des Ignatius von Antioch und der Brief von Polycarp von Smyrna: Zweite, neubearb. Auflage der Auslegung von W. Bauer* (HNT 18; Tübingen: Mohr, 1985).

Studies

W. R. Schoedel, "Polycarp of Smyrna and Ignatius of Antioch," *ANRW* II 27.1 (1993): 272–358.

C. Munier, "Où en est la question d'Ignace d'Antioche? Bilan d'un siècle de recherches 1870–1988," *ANRW* II 27.1 (1993): 359–484.

3. Polycarp of Smyrna

One of the letters of Ignatius is addressed to Polycarp, bishop of Smyrna. Irenaeus of Lyons tells of Polycarp in a letter he wrote to Roman presbyter Florinus around 190 (text in Eusebius, *Hist. eccl.* 5.20.6–7), in which he recalled his childhood spent with Florinus in Asia Minor at the school of Polycarp, who had known John and other disciples of the Lord. In *Haer.* 3.3.4, Irenaeus says that Polycarp was made bishop of Smyrna by the apostles, and he adds that Polycarp underwent martyrdom at a very advanced age. The same Irenaeus tells of Polycarp going to Rome in the time of Anicetus (154/55 to 166/67) to discuss the Easter question, but without in reaching agreement, though he remained in communion with the Roman bishop (Eusebius, *Hist. eccl.* 4.14.1; 5.24.16). The Christians of Asia Minor celebrated Easter on 14 Nisan, in keeping with Jewish custom and the custom of the earliest Christian communities; Rome wanted to impose its own practice of celebrating it on a Sunday and thus on a varying date; this practice won out at the end of the second century. The account of Polycarp's martyrdom, which took place in 155, 166, or 167, was written less than a year after the event and is one of the more reliable accounts of the acts of the martyrs (see below, ch. 11, sec. 2).

Eight or nine manuscripts preserve a letter of Polycarp to the church of Philippi. In all of the manuscripts, the letter is followed by the *Letter of Barnabas,* and all have a gap between Polycarp, *Phil.* 9. 2 and the middle of *Barn.* 5.7, showing that they descend from a single original. The gap can be partially filled from Eusebius of Caesarea, who cites chs. 9 and 13, except for the final sentence (*Hist. eccl.* 3.36.13–15); the rest can be retrieved only with the help of a rather free early Latin translation.

Polycarp begins by congratulating the church of Smyrna for having recently welcomed and escorted Ignatius and the other prisoners on their journey to Rome (ch. 1), and he exhorts the church to abide in the truth and in faith in the risen Christ (ch. 2). Polycarp writes because his addressees have urged him to do so, but he is certainly not of the caliber of Paul, who in his day wrote a letter (or letters) to the Philippians that enabled them to make progress in the faith (ch. 3). There follows a "domestic code" against greed and on the duties of wives, widows, deacons, the young, and presbyters (4.1–6.1). He then exhorts the Philippians to fear God and to ask forgiveness of one another with a view to the judgment at Christ's tribunal (6.2–3). A plea to avoid false brethren serves as a transition to an attack on those who do not confess that Jesus Christ has come in the flesh and to an exhortation to remain devoted to the tradition and to Christ (7.1–8.2). To this end, it is necessary to persevere in patience, of which the martyrs Ignatius, Zosimus, and Rufus, as well as Paul and the other apostles, offer an example (ch. 9).

After exhortations to mutual love and to behavior that is blameless in the sight of the pagans (ch. 10), Polycarp takes up the case of Valens, who had been a presbyter in Philippi but had gone astray, probably out of greed (ch. 11). The plea not to be harsh toward him and his wife gives way to an exhortation to patience and forbearance, as well as prayer, especially for the authorities who persecute Christians (ch. 12). Ignatius had asked Polycarp to send someone to Antioch to congratulate them on the restoration of peace (Ignatius, *Pol.* 7.2; 8.1; see *Smyrn.* 11.2), and the Philippians had evidently asked that the messenger also carry a letter from them. Polycarp promises that this will be done, and meanwhile sends to Philippi, along with his own letter, such letters of Ignatius as he has been able to gather. At the same time, he asks for information about the fate of Ignatius and his companions (ch. 13). Finally, Polycarp commends to the Philippians both Crescens, who brings this letter, and his sister (ch. 14).

There is no reason to deny the authenticity of this letter, though it is often challenged chiefly in connection with doubts about of the authenticity of Ignatius's letters. The letter shows how early Ignatius's letters were collected, except for the letter to the Romans, which has come down to us separately. There is, however, a literary problem: in 9.2 Ignatius and companions appear to be already dead, but in 13.2 they seem to be still alive *(de ipso Ignatio et de his qui cum eo sunt),* and Polycarp asks the Philippians for more detailed news of them. P. N. Harrison (1936) proposed an explanation: chs. 13–14 constitute a brief letter that was written shortly after Ignatius' departure from Smyrna, and was intended to accompany his letters to Philippi; chs. 1–12 form a different letter, written some years later (around 135), and inspired by an antimarcionite controversy (as shown by ch. 7). Other scholars have preferred to separate only ch. 13, while combining ch. 14 with the letter made up of chs. 1–12; moreover, the antimarcionite character of ch. 7 is doubtful.

Harrison's suggestion has been widely accepted and is certainly an ingenious solution to the problem; it is not certain, however, that the solution is really needed. Unfortunately, the key words in ch. 13 have come down only in Latin; in any case, *qui cum eo sunt* could translate a Greek *hoi syn autōi,* which would eliminate the problem raised by the use of the present tense. In addition, the request for information about Ignatius and his companions could refer to the circumstances of their martyrdom.

If we accept Harrison's suggestion, the note made up of ch. 12 (or chs. 13–14) must have been written soon after Ignatius' departure from Smyrna, during the time required for Ignatius to pass through Philippi and for Polycarp then to receive a letter from that church. The second letter could be dated at least to 135 in order to support the hypothesis of an antimarcionite controversy. However, if we hold fast to the unity of the letter, then it must have been written after Polycarp had received news of Ignatius's martyrdom, and therefore at least several months after Ignatius's stay in Smyrna, but not much later.

BIBLIOGRAPHY

Editions

A. Lindemann and H. Paulsen, *Die Apostolischen Väter: Neu übersetzt und herausgegeben* (Tübingen: Mohr, 1992), 242–57.
J. A. Fischer, *Die apostolischen Väter* (Darmstadt: Wissenschaftliche Buchgesellschaft, 1956), 227–65; introduction, edition, translation, and notes.
J. B. Lightfoot and J. R. Harmer, *The Apostolic Fathers: Greek Texts and English Translations of Their Writings* (2d ed.; trans. and ed. M. W. Holmes; Grand Rapids, Mich.: Baker, 1992).

Commentaries

H. Paulsen, *Die Briefe des Ignatius von Antioch und der Brief von Polycarp von Smyrna: Zweite, neubearb. Auflage der Auslegung von W. Bauer* (HNT 18; Tübingen: Mohr, 1985), 111–26.

Studies

P. N. Harrison, *Polycarp's Two Epistles to the Philippians* (Cambridge: Cambridge University Press, 1936).
P. Meinhold, "Polykarpos," PW 21 (1952): 1662–93.

Chapter 6

TREATISES IN LETTER FORM

1. Letter to the Hebrews

This letter has always been handed down with the letters of Paul. However, it is a special kind of letter: although there are greetings at the end (13:18–25) it lacks the opening formulary (preamble, introduction). It has the typical rhetorical structure of a discourse, with a series of elements that establish a structure: 6:1–2 announces the coming subject matter and what will be passed over; 8:1 introduces "the main point *(kephalaion)* in what we are saying"; in 9:2 the author says that this is not the time for explaining in detail certain points he has mentioned. In 13:22 the work is described as a *logos tēs paraklēseōs*, a "word [or discourse] of exhortation," and in fact Hebrews should be regarded as a discourse (though too long to have been really delivered).

In a systematic way Hebrews develops a central theme, that of the priesthood of Christ. To this, it adds exhortation, which is not limited to the second part but comes up repeatedly, thus showing how important its function is. In this perspective, a section such as 5:11–6:20, which speaks of how slowly the addressees are making progress in the faith, but which nevertheless gives them some of the solid food reserved for the perfect, is not addressed toward a real situation. Rather it has a rhetorical function: it marks the transition to instruction on a higher level. The element of discourse is thus dominant, while the epistolary formalities at the end are secondary and seem to have been added when the discourse was sent to someone.

There have been many suggestions as to how Hebrews is structured. We call attention to A. Vanhoye, who, on the basis of such formal criteria as key words, announcements of subjects, inclusions, and so on, distinguishes five sections, four of them arranged chiastically around the central discussion of sacrifice (5:11–10:39). We shall here sketch the arrangement of the contents.

Chapter 1: In these last days (that is, today) God has spoken to humanity through the Son, on whom he has bestowed this name and whom he has raised above the angels; proof from Scripture follows. Chapter 2:5–18: It is not to the angels that God has subjected the world to come, but to Jesus, whom he has humbled to the point of enduring death, in order that through suffering he might become perfect. Having become like human beings, he has been able to become a high priest for them in their relations with God. At this point, the discussion of Christ as high priest begins (3:1–6): He is superior to Moses, who was head of God's house, but as a servant, not as a son. Chapters 3:7–4:13 contain a commentary of a midrashic kind on Psalm

95:7–11. Chapters 4:14–5:10: Having learned obedience from his sufferings, Christ has become the source of salvation for all who obey him.

Chapters 5:11–6:20: As was said above, this section begins the main discussion of the priesthood of Christ. Chapter 7:1–28: Melchizedek (Gen 14:7–20) received tithes from Abraham and thereby, in a way, from Levi, Abraham's descendant; Melchizedek's priesthood was therefore superior to the Levitical priesthood. The application of Psalm 110:4: "You are a priest forever, according to the order of Melchizedek," shows Christ's superiority over the sacrificial order of the law, which is thus abrogated in favor of a new intercession. Chapter 8: Christ exercises his priestly function in a new setting, because he sits at the right hand of the divine Majesty in the heavenly sanctuary, of which the earthly sanctuary is only a shadow. He is the minister of a new covenant, foretold in Jer 31:31–34.

Chapter 9: The old covenant was based on a cultic ritual, with its first tent into which all the priests used to enter, and a second into which the high priest alone entered, once a year. As long as the first tent existed, giving access only to another tent and not to the true sanctuary, the way of entering the true sanctuary was not yet made known, and worship was based only on human rites. But Christ has effected a definitive liberation by means of his blood, and has entered the sanctuary once for all. Chapter 10:1–18: The law cannot bring about the perfection of those who offer sacrifices; Christ, however, thanks to the single offering of his own body, sits at the right hand of God and has perfected those whom he sanctifies.

Chapter 10:19–39 deals with the consequences of this soteriology in the lives of believers. Access to the sanctuary, guaranteed by the blood of Jesus, is the basis of our hope, but we must avoid sin in the future, since there is no longer any other sacrifice for sin. It is necessary to persevere in faith. Chapter 11:1–40 gives a series of biblical examples of faith. Chapter 12:1–29: Following this "cloud of witnesses" and, above all, Jesus, the pioneer of our faith, we must persevere through suffering, continuing to fear God's judgment and not separating ourselves from the grace of God. Chapter 13:1–17 has further exhortations for the life of the community and regarding obedience to leaders.

The work uses literary forms from Jewish tradition. One example is the treatment of faith in ch. 11: the statement of the theme is followed by a list of exemplary persons. This was a type of discourse widely used in Hellenistic synagogues, as can be seen from, for example, from 4 Maccabees (ca. A.D. 100), ch. 10 of Wisdom, and some treatises of Philo (e.g., *Praem.* 7–14). A Christian example is *1 Clem.* 4.39.

Hebrews uses an exegesis of Scripture in which personages and institutions of Israel symbolize other realities. In thus proceeding allegorically, the work shows particular affinities in method and content with the exegesis of Philo of Alexandria. But whereas for the latter things found in the Bible point to moral or heavenly realities, in Hebrews they refer instead to things future, having to do with Christ and the Christian era. More specifically, Hebrews uses typology, which in the view of the ancients was a form of allegory. It is with the aid of this kind of exegesis that Hebrews bases its Christology and soteriology on the Bible and at the same time asserts a movement beyond the religious institutions of the Bible and, in particular, its sacrificial system. The replacement of Israelite worship by the one sacrifice of Christ is a central theme.

Hebrews does not claim to be a work of Paul. The mention of Timothy in 13:23 seems too casual to support a pseudepigraphical claim; the real author and his addressees probably knew Timothy personally. On the other hand, the work certainly owed its inclusion in the canon to its attribution to Paul. The earliest manuscript of the Pauline corpus, $\mathfrak{P}^{46}$ (Egypt, ca. 200), has Hebrews in second place after Romans. Still in Egypt and around the same time, Clement of Alexandria attributed the work to Paul on the authority of a presbyter (*Hyp.*, in Eusebius, *Hist. eccl.* 2.14.2–4). However, realizing that the Greek was not that of Paul, Clement believed that Luke had translated into Greek a letter Paul had written in Hebrew. Origen attributed the substance but not the form to Paul, while for the form he mentioned two suggested attributions, Luke and Clement of Rome (*Fr. Heb.*, cited by Eusebius, *Hist. eccl.* 6.25.12–14). In the East the attribution to Paul and therefore the letter's canonicity were immediately accepted, while in the West this acceptance came only at the end of the fourth century, due to the authority of Jerome and Augustine.

Nowadays almost no one maintains Paul's authorship. Not only is the Greek style very different from Paul (the author joins Luke in writing the best Greek in the New Testament) but the theology differs as well: cultic categories are much more important in Hebrews than in Paul, whereas the fundamental themes of the latter are lacking. The treatments of faith are quite different in the two. Despite many hypotheses both ancient and modern, the author remains unknown. He must have been a well-educated person with a good theological training and seems to know Paul's theology (but not by way of the latter's letters). He probably has some connections with Alexandrian culture. He is a Christian of the second generation (2:3); present tense references to the ritual of sacrifice (see 10:1–3) do not suffice to locate the composition before the destruction of the temple in 70, because the author is not referring to the Jerusalem temple but to the tent containing the ark as described in the Pentateuch. Still, a composition before 70 cannot be excluded. If, as seems probable, *1 Clement* 36.2–6 cites Heb 1:4–13, then the end of the first century becomes a *terminus post quem;* the mention of Timothy as still alive (13:23) suggests the same.

As for the place of composition, the final greeting by "those from Italy" might indicate composition in Italy, but could also indicate a colony of Italian origin in the place of composition. Theological and liturgical affinities with *1 Clement* beyond the probable citation already mentioned might suggest a Roman origin, but for the same reason the addressees might be Roman, as scholars prefer to think today. All the historical coordinates of the letter remain puzzling. The title "To the Hebrews" is of later origin, and the text itself does not name them as addressees. The extensive use of Jewish exegetical procedures and the attack on Jewish worship have since antiquity produced the conviction that the work is addressed to Jewish Christians and intended to keep them from returning to Judaism. But, as the ongoing discussion shows, it is not even possible to say whether the addressees came from Judaism or paganism or both.

BIBLIOGRAPHY

Commentaries

H. Braun, *An die Hebräer* (HNT 14; Tübingen: Mohr, 1984).
H. W. Attridge, *The Epistle to the Hebrews: A Commentary on the Epistle to the Hebrews* (Hermeneia; ed. H. Koester; Philadelphia: Fortress, 1989).

Studies

G. Theissen, *Untersuchungen zum Hebräerbrief* (Gütersloh: Mohn, 1969).
A. Vanhoye, *La structure littéraire de l'épître aux Hébreux* (2d ed.; Paris: Desclée de Brouwer, 1976).
H. Feld, "Der Hebräerbrief: Literarische Form, religionsgeschichtlicher Hintergrund, theologische Fragen," *ANRW* II 25.4 (1987): 3522–3601.
A. Vanhoye, *Structure and Message of the Epistle to the Hebrews* (Rome: Editrice Pontificio Istituto Biblico, 1989).

2. Letter of James

In contrast to the letter to the Hebrews, the letter of James has an addressee and an initial greeting (1:1) but no final greeting. Some points in the letter refer to such specific situations as trials and relations between rich and poor, but the naming of the addressees, "the twelve tribes in the Dispersion," indicates that this is a treatise or discourse in which the epistolary dress is superficial. Still, it is not easy to distinguish a precise outline.

In 1:2–18 the theme of trial and perseverance seems to dominate. The author seems to speak of interior temptations rather than trials imposed from outside (see 1:13–15). In such a situation we must trustingly ask God for wisdom (1:5–8). Also tackled here is a recurring subject of the work: the relationship between rich and poor in the community (1:9–11).

Chapter 1:19–27 speaks of the readiness to put the heard word into practice. The reference to good works in 1:27 serves as a transition to the next section (2:1–13), which attacks the preferential treatment of the rich. The statement about the need to practice mercy in order to obtain mercy at the judgment (2:13) effects a transition to an attack on faith without works (2:14–26).

Chapter 3:1–12 begins with an exhortation that not everyone should try to be a teacher, for teachers will be judged more severely. All of us make mistakes; those who do not err in speaking are perfect, able to control their entire bodies. It is, however, the tongue above all that needs to be restrained, for it can be the source of great evil. Chapters 3:13–4:12: The wise demonstrate this control by the gentleness and wisdom of their works. There is an earthly wisdom that shows itself in evil deeds, and a wisdom from on high that is peaceable, lenient, and free of partiality and hypocrisy. Conflicts within the community come from attachment to the world; we ought not to judge one another, for there is but one judge.

A rather abrupt passage introduces the denunciation of businessmen who plan for their profits as though they were the masters of their own lives, and of the rich who have amassed possessions by exploiting others (4:13–5:6). Chapter 5:7–20 contains various exhortations, beginning with one to be patient until the coming of the Lord, without grumbling against one another. There is also an exhortation to engage in private or communal liturgical actions: prayer, songs, anointing of the sick, confession of sins to one another, and rescue of sinners.

There is a noteworthy similarity here to the themes and genres of Jewish sapiential ethics. Furthermore, the name of Jesus appears only in 1:1 and 2:1, the latter being a passage of such poor syntax that it may be a secondary addition. Although the letter is clearly a Christian work, the role of Jesus does not determine its thought. In 1930 A. Meyer even suggested the letter was a slightly christianized summary of a Jewish work in the genre of the testaments of patriarchs: James would originally have been the patriarch Jacob, and the subjects raised successively in the letter would allude to symbolic meanings given in Hellenistic Judaism to the names of his twelve sons, the leaders of the tribes of Israel. This would account for the description of the addressees in 1:1. His thesis, however, has not prevailed.

The letter is thus a work of Christian parenesis, constructed partly in the form of collections of sentences about a theme (e.g., 3:13–5:6), and partly in the form of discussions of topics (e.g., 2:1–3, 12, where three topics can be distinguished: against the rich, against faith without works, and against misuse of the tongue). The author employs the model of the diatribe, which at that time was widely used in popular moral philosophy and consisted of expounding the material in the form of a fictitious dialogue.

The most familiar of these diatribes is that on faith and works (2:14–26). The target is Pauline teaching on justification by faith, as is demonstrated by the antithesis of faith-works and the connected exegetical discussion of Abraham, two topics not found linked prior to Paul (see Rom 3:27–4:24). The author even seems to refer directly to Paul: compare Rom 3:30 ("God is one,") with Jas 2:19 ("You believe that God is one; you do well. Even the demons believe—and shudder").

At the same time, James seems to speak of something different from Paul. According to Paul, the faith that saves is an attachment to Christ as the one who justifies sinners, and works flow naturally from faith. James mentions faith in Christ (2:1), but this faith is absent from the controversy on works, in which the faith in question is the conviction that there is but one God; Paul would never have attributed a saving power to such a faith. Finally, in James's discussion of works there is lacking an element fundamental for Paul: the law. Paul's statements are meaningless outside the context of the dramatic debate over the necessity of the law for salvation. James's choice is not between faith in Christ and the works of the law but between an intellectual faith in God and a faith that produces works. James thus belongs in a historical context in which the problem of the role of the Jewish law in salvation is not put in the same terms as in Paul. He seems to attack developments within Paulinism in which he sees a departure from the demands of ethics. Perhaps his attack on earthly wisdom (3:13–18) is aimed at groups that claim to possess a wisdom that transcends morality.

Who, then, is the author? This James is not the son of Zebedee, who had been martyred in 44 (Acts 12:2), but the brother of Jesus, who is mentioned by Paul in 1 Corinthians and Galatians, in Mark 6:3 (and parallels), and several times in Acts. He was put to death in Jerusalem in 62, a date too early for so broad a post-Pauline debate as this. Furthermore, the early testimonies (which are not untendentious, but are certainly not completely false) describe James as a scrupulous observer of the law, whereas the letter says nothing of questions of ritual law. As the address to the twelve tribes in the Dispersion shows, the addressees, while being Jewish Christians, like the author himself, belong to the Greek world. Although still defended, the authorship of this James does not seem sustainable. It was debated even in antiquity, as Eusebius of Caesarea attests for the fourth century (*Hist. eccl.* 3.25.3). The work is mentioned by Origen as belonging to the Scriptures, but is missing from the *Muratorian Canon*. The first sure citation is from the third century and does not help in dating the letter.

Those who consider the letter authentic place its composition in Jerusalem and date it to the mid-forties. Those who (rightly in our opinion) believe it to be pseudepigraphical date it near the end of the first century, but it is not possible to determine where it was composed.

BIBLIOGRAPHY

Commentaries

M. Dibelius and H. Greeven, *Der Brief des Jakobus* (KEK 15; 11th ed.; Göttingen: Vandenhoeck & Ruprecht, 1964); ET: M. Dibelius, *James: A Commentary on the Epistle of James* (rev. H. Greeven; Philadelphia: Fortress, 1976).

F. Vouga, *L'Epître de Saint Jacques* (CNT 13a; Geneva: Labor et Fides, 1984).

H. Frankemölle. *Der Brief des Jakobus* (ÖTK 17; Gütersloh: Mohn, 1994–).

Studies

P. H. Davids, "The Epistle of James in Modern Discussion," *ANRW* II 25.5 (1988): 3621–45.

E. Baasland, "Literarische Form, Thematik und geschichtliche Einordnung des Jakobusbriefes," ibid.: 3646–84.

3. First Letter of Peter

Let us review the contents. The preamble (1:1–2), with its address to the faithful of Pontus, Galatia, Cappadocia, Asia, and Bithynia (therefore, Asia Minor), is followed by an introduction in the form of a blessing (1:3–12) that refers to trials presently being endured by the addressees.

Chapters 1:13–2:10 give a description of the proper state of Christians, which is one of holiness and fraternal love. At the same time, these passages exhort believers to live in that way and become part of the community as a result of the mercy they have received from God.

Chapters 2:11–3:12 contain exhortations in the form of a "domestic code": behavior toward authorities (2:13–17), duties of slaves to masters (2:18–25), of wives and husbands (3:1–7), and of community life (3:8–12). The exhortation continues in 3:13–4:11: believers are called to follow the example of the suffering Christ and endure persecution, but also to break with sin and live a life of mutual service in the community, while awaiting the end of all things, which is close at hand. The same exhortations are repeated in 4:12–5:11, with the addition of others (5:1–5) for the elderly and the young. Chapter 5:12–14 contains the conclusion and greetings.

Because of the allusions to baptism, especially in 1:3–2:10, it has been suggested that the first part of the letter, down to 4:11, where there is a kind of liturgical conclusion, be understood as a sermon to catechumens. At the time when the sermon was delivered, persecution was to be feared. Later, when persecution actually broke out, the same author would have added the remainder of the letter, which makes the exhortations more concrete and extends them to categories of people, such as the

elderly, who were obviously not in mind in the original baptismal sermon. This hypothesis is still debated. In any case, the letter seems to be addressed to a community
in which there are many converts, and the author seeks to compensate them for the
loss of the social status they had as non-Christians, a loss they feel especially in their
experience of persecution. The author makes his point by emphasizing the lofty dignity of believers in the eyes of God, as well as the example of Christ, who after suffering now sits at the right hand of God, having subjected the powers to himself (3:22).

In a letter issued under the name of Peter, it is striking to see so many Pauline elements. The addressees listed in 1:1 live in parts of Paul's mission field. Silvanus, the
scribe who wrote down the letter (5:12), is a fellow worker of Paul (1 Thess 1:1; 2 Cor
1:19). The preamble is close in form to those of Paul's letters. In 2:24 and 3:18 we find
the idea that the death of Christ on the cross had made us dead to sin and alive for
righteousness (see Rom 6:2, 11). This teaching is rare in early Christian writings apart
from the letters of Paul. Also close to Paul are the conception of the freedom made
possible by Christ (2:16) and, throughout the letter, the grounding of the ethical im-
perative in the indicative of salvation. However, the problem of the law is of no importance in this letter, and this points to a period later than the life of Paul.

This last fact militates against the composition of the letter by the apostle Peter.
Other reasons are the high quality of the Greek, the use of the Septuagint as the biblical text, and the wide-ranging persecution presupposed in Asia Minor. The letter
claims to be written from Babylon, that is, Rome. The name "Babylon" (see the
Apocalypse of John) was used for Rome in Judaism after the destruction of Jerusalem
in 70, in order to liken this destruction to that of the city's destruction in 586 B.C. This
point, too, militates against authenticity. The absence of traces of 1 Peter in *1 Clement*,
which was written in Rome at the end of the first century, and in the *Muratorian
Canon* (if this is indeed a Roman text from the end of the second century), does not
favor a connection of 1 Peter with Rome. The "Roman" element may be part of the
pseudepigraphical character of the work (the death of Peter in Rome is implicit in
1 Clement and in the *Ascension of Isaiah,* and explicit in the *Apocalypse of Peter*).

Meanwhile, 1 Peter was used in Asia Minor by Papias of Hierapolis (Eusebius, *Hist.
eccl.* 3.39.17) and by Polycarp of Smyrna (*Phil.* 1.3; 8.1; 10.2). The letter may, therefore,
have been composed in Asia Minor at the end of the first century. Its pseudepigraphical
character might be explained by its composition during a period when there was no
central Christian authority, and when relations between churches were established as
needed. Therefore, a writer living in the area of Pauline missionary activity might seek
to foster a bond between the communities of Asia and Rome, under the authority of the
latter. This would explain why Peter, who represented the church of Rome, is given as
the apostolic authority, and Paul is not mentioned, but only Silvanus, his fellow worker.
Perhaps the situation of persecution led the unknown author to try to place the
churches of his area under the authority and protection of Rome.

BIBLIOGRAPHY

Commentaries

L. Goppelt, *Der erste Petrusbrief* (KEK 12, 1; Göttingen: Vandenhoeck & Ru-
    precht, 1978).

N. Brox, *Der erste Petrusbrief* (EKKNT 21; 3d ed.; Zurich: Benziger/Neukirchen-Vluyn: Neukirchener Verlag, 1989).

Studies

J. H. Elliott, *A Hope for the Homeless: A Sociological Exegesis of 1 Peter, Its Situation and Strategy* (Philadelphia: Fortress, 1981).
C. H. Talbert, ed., *Perspectives of First Peter* (Macon: Mercer University Press, 1986).
E. Cothenet, "La Première Epître de Pierre: bilan de 35 ans de recherches," *ANRW* II 25.5 (1988): 3685–3712.

4. Letter of Jude

This short document has a rather simple plan. Verses 1–2 form the preamble; vv. 3–19 contain an attack on adversaries; vv. 20–23 are an exhortation to remain in the love of God and to try to persuade the adversaries or else abhor them; and vv. 24–25 are a doxology. There is no final greeting as in other letters.

The addressees are not clearly identified. The adversaries in mind, however, are very real. The letter attacks them at length but does not explain their teaching, although some aspects of it may be glimpsed. The adversaries are perhaps itinerant preachers who have "infiltrated" the community (v. 4). They live in the community, share in the love-feasts (v. 12), cause divisions (v. 19), and manage to persuade some (vv. 22–23). It appears that they have ecstatic experiences (the author describes them as "dreamers" *enhypniazomenoi*) and they think themselves better than the angels (vv. 8, 10). They seem to consider themselves not bound by current morality, for the author accuses them of homosexuality, like the people of Sodom and Gomorrah (vv. 7, 8). We ought to take into account, however, that the author is certainly trying to disqualify them by accusing them of immorality (see also vv. 10, 16, and 23), a device also used against Christians, and then taken over by the "great church" against "heretics." On the other hand, these accusations when not overemphasized, may fit the historical picture: the adversaries seem to claim a higher knowledge obtained through contacts with the heavenly world and to devalue matter and the body, and as a result to regard sexual ethics as unimportant for salvation. Traits of this kind are found in the second-century gnostics, but these adversaries cannot be identified with groups otherwise known.

In contrast, the author defends "the faith that was once for all entrusted to the saints" (v. 3). The content of faith, like the "deposit" of the Pastoral Letters, is given and unchangeable, and believers receive it through tradition, which dates from a time of beginnings that is already past. The adversaries are described as a phenomenon of the last times; this allows them to be seen as a manifestation of the forces of evil, whose activity, according to current expectations, was to reach its climax before the end of the world. As such, they were foretold by the apostles (vv. 17–19); the judgment on them was even foretold by Enoch. The author cites here a passage from the *Book of Enoch* (1.9), which, though not accepted into the rabbinical canon, enjoyed great authority in certain Jewish circles and in first-century Christianity, where it is repeatedly cited as Scripture. Our

author also alludes to it at least in vv. 6 and 13. In v. 9 he makes use of an incident narrated in another Jewish pseudepigraphon, the *Testament of Moses*. Our writer is thus
close to the contemporary writers and readers of apocalypses.

In describing himself as brother of James, the author means to be accepted as the
brother of Jesus who is mentioned in Mark 6:3 and Matt 13:55. According to
Hegesippus (in Eusebius, *Hist. eccl.* 3.20.1–2), two of that brother's grandsons were
questioned by Domitian as possible messianic claimants because they were descended
from David. But the author dates the apostles in the past (v. 17), and speaks of the
faith as being received through tradition (v. 3); he must therefore be regarded as a
pseudepigrapher. The writer's description of himself as a servant of Jesus Christ and a
brother of James seems to echo Jas 1:1. Jude would therefore be later than James, but
this does not help much for the dating. The place of composition is likewise unknown. The letter is used in 2 Peter (see below) and mentioned as canonical in the
Muratorian Canon, in Tertullian, and in Clement of Alexandria.

BIBLIOGRAPHY

Commentaries

R. J. Bauckham, *Jude, 2 Peter* (Waco: Word Books, 1983).

Studies

R. J. Bauckham, "The Letter of Jude: An Account of Research," *ANRW* II 25.5
      (1988): 3791–3826.
————, *Jude and the Relatives of Jesus in the Early Church* (Edinburgh: T&T
      Clark, 1990).

5. Second Letter of Peter

In the preamble of this letter (1:1–2) the writer introduces himself as Simon
Peter, and addresses believers generally. He then reminds them of the gifts they have
received from God that have made them sharers in the divine nature, and he exhorts
them to accompany faith with all the virtues, so that they may enter the kingdom of
Christ (1:3–11). Peter knows as a result of a revelation from the Lord that he is at the
end of his life. He wishes to remind his readers that his preaching on the power and
coming of Christ is based on eyewitness testimony: he saw the majesty of Christ at the
transfiguration (1:12–18). It is therefore necessary to hold tenaciously to the message
of the prophets, which is not a matter for private interpretation, because prophecy
does not depend on the will of a human being (1:19–21). Chapter 2: Just as there were
false prophets in Israel, so there will be false teachers among Christians. A strong attack on these follows. Chapter 3:1–13: In the last days, some will jeer at the idea of a
return of Christ; against them the author asserts once again the coming of the day of
the Lord, which he describes in apocalyptic language. Chapter 3:14–18 is an exhortation to become blameless, as "our beloved brother Paul" preached in all his letters.
These indeed have their obscure points, the meaning of which is distorted by some.

It is not only the preamble that introduces Peter as the author; in 1:14 the writer says that Jesus told him in advance about his death, a tradition regarding Peter that is found, in varying forms, in the gospel of John (21:18–19) and in the *Apocalypse of Peter* (14.1). In 1:16 the author recalls his presence at the transfiguration of Jesus. In 3:1 he speaks of this letter as his second, which is certainly a reference to 1 Peter. In 3:15 he mentions "our beloved brother Paul." More specifically, 1:13–14 (on death as near) defines the letter as a testament of Peter.

The intention of the letter is to strengthen expectation of the Parousia of Christ, despite the delay that has caused many to lose confidence or even to scoff at this expectation. Expressions similar to those in 3:4 are found in *1 Clem.* 23.3–4, which cites them from an unknown work and refutes them. The same citation appears again in *2 Clem.* 11.2–4, where it is introduced as a "prophetic discourse." This indicates that at the end of the first century there was in circulation a polemical work against the loss of confidence due to the delay of the Parousia; our author probably made use of that work. He defends the expectation by observing that for God a thousand years are as a day (see Ps 90:4), that the delay is due to God's patience, and that by means of a holy life and prayer it is possible to hasten that event (3:8–13).

In attacking his adversaries, the author makes extensive use of the letter of Jude: his second chapter depends on Jude 4–13, and other points of contact are to be found in the rest of the letter. For this reason it is not possible to derive from ch. 2 the real traits of those who deny the Lord's return. The dependence of 2 Peter on Jude is illustrated by, among other things, the reordered chronology of the succession in 2:4–7 (fall of the angels, flood, Sodom and Gomorrah), as compared with Jude 5–7 (Israel in the wilderness, fall of the angels, Sodom and Gomorrah); by the fact that 2 Pet 2:11 is a generalization that can be understood only in the light of Jude 9; and by the omission of the citation of noncanonical *Enoch* (Jude 14–15). In all probability, 2 Peter takes its cue from the reference in Jude 17–18 to the preaching of the "apostles" about the "scoffers" of the last times and aims to be taken precisely as one of those apostolic prophecies.

There is general agreement that Peter cannot be the author of the letter. This is proven by, among other things: the dependence on Jude; the controversies over the delay of the Parousia, which, as we saw, are typical of the end of the first century; the high level of the Greek, with its use of terminology from Hellenistic theology (e.g., "participants of the divine nature" in 1:4; and *epoptai*, "eyewitnesses," a term from the language of the mysteries, in 1:16). Finally, 3:16 mentions a normative collection of Paul's letters, which are regarded as "Scriptures," and the controversies over their interpretation—both of which were unthinkable during Peter's lifetime and demand a date well into the second century, although it remains uncertain whether the date presupposes the use of the writings of Paul by Marcion and the gnostics. Second Peter is probably the last work accepted into the New Testament.

BIBLIOGRAPHY

Commentary

R. J. Bauckham, *Jude, 2 Peter* (Waco: Word Books, 1983).

Study

R. J. Bauckham, "2 Peter: An Account of Research," *ANRW* II 25.5 (1988): 3713–52.

6. Letter of Barnabas

The letter contains an epistolary greeting at the beginning (but without mention of the sender, 1.1) and at the end (21.9). Chapter 1 refers to earlier personal relations between sender and addressees (1.2–5), but the work is not inspired by a particular situation: it is a treatise, and the meager epistolary framework is artificial. The name Barnabas is not found in the text, but the work is attributed to this missionary companion of Paul in the first citations known to us, those of Clement of Alexandria (*Strom.* 2.31.2; 2.35.5; etc.) and then of Origen (*Cels.* 1.63). The attribution to Barnabas is also found in the colophon of Sinaiticus (4th c.), which for the first time gave us the integral Greek text. In this important Greek manuscript of the Bible, the letter of Barnabas appears at the end of the New Testament and thus on the periphery of the canon. On one occasion, Eusebius of Caesarea places it among the books whose canonicity is debated (*Hist. eccl.* 4.13.6) and on another among the spurious books (3.25.4; see 6.14.1); Jerome places it among the apocrypha, but regards it as useful for edification (*Vir. ill.* 6).

Until the discovery of the Sinai manuscript (1863), the text was known from various Greek codices, all of them lacking 1.1–5.7, and from an second–third century free Latin translation that lacked chs. 18–21. The complete Greek text is also in Codex Hierosolymitanus 54 of the Greek Patriarchate of Jerusalem; it is dated to 1056 and was discovered in 1873.

In 1.1–2.3, which is a kind of introduction, the author declares his intention of conveying "perfect knowledge": if we understand the prophecies and see their fulfillment, we can make progress in fear of the Lord. He then begins to cite and comment on prophetic texts in order to show that the Jews never understood God's message. He quotes and comments on prophetic passages against sacrifices (2.4–10) and fasting (3.1–6). It is in the present, therefore, that we must seek that which can save us, especially since the end is near (4.1–4), not trusting blindly in the covenant, as the Jews did (4.6–8), but not trusting either in our call to become Christians (4.9–14). The Lord suffered in the flesh to win forgiveness of sins and to fulfill the promises given to the fathers, in order that human beings might be saved by looking to him, but also in order to bring to a climax the sins of Israel, which had already persecuted and killed the prophets (5.1–14). There follow several series of prophetic passages to illustrate these points: first, prophecies about Christ as stone, on his suffering, and on the forgiveness of sin, which was symbolized by the entry into the promised land (6.1–19). Then prophecies of the passion are found in the Old Testament regulations about the day of fasting, the scapegoat, and the sacrifice of a red heifer for purification from sin (7.1–8.1).

The Scriptures foretold that the Jews would not grasp their true meaning and would not listen to the Lord's voice. God asked not for the circumcision of the body but for that of the heart, for the circumcision of Abraham was really a christological prophecy (9.1–9). The same was true of the dietary regulations set down by Moses, for they have a moral meaning (10.1–12). The Scriptures also contain prophecies of the water of baptism and the wood of the cross; Jesus is prefigured by Joshua (11.1–12.11). The writer then turns to the subject of the covenant, proving from the Scriptures that Israel had rendered itself unworthy of the Covenant by worshiping the golden calf, and that the covenant therefore passed from Moses to Christians (13.1–14.9). The author then turns once again to worship: the true sabbath that is to be made holy is that of the new world that God will create at the end of time (15.1–9); similarly, the temple in which God dwells is not that of Jerusalem, it is the believer, who is a spiritual temple (16.1–10).

After a short conclusion (ch. 17), the discourse begins again with a transition to "another knowledge and teaching" (18.1). This marks the beginning of a version of the treatise on the "two ways," other forms of which are found in the first part of the *Didache* (1.1–6.1) and in a Latin *Teaching of the Apostles* that is known in two manuscripts. These are probably independent revivals of a lost treatise on Jewish ethics that had affinities with the Qumran teaching on the two spirits, of truth and perversity, which God has set over the world. To the way of light, which is governed by the angels of God, belongs a lengthy series of commandments (19.1–12); the way of darkness, or of the "Dark One," on which are posted the angels of Satan, is characterized by a series of negative attitudes (20.1–2). The conclusion (ch. 21) contains urgent exhortations to "superiors" to behave properly, to let God be their teacher, and to be mindful of the author.

The letter of Barnabas is undoubtedly the work of a single author, but one who uses sources, the most obvious of which is the treatise on the two ways (chs. 18–20). Also used are collections of *testimonia*, biblical passages that are interpreted as prophecies of Christ and the Christian era. Such texts were selected and grouped by theme, often around a key word (e.g., "stone" or "wood") and interpreted, following a technique already used in Judaism, by extending an interpretation developed for one of them to others that contain the same word. These groups, initially short, tended to increase in size and sometimes introduced citations from noncanonical texts or even passages invented as *testimonia*. The conviction that, thanks to the Spirit, Christians possessed the correct understanding of the Scriptures often led to alteration of the citations and to combinations of them forming new texts, always for the purpose of bringing out the "true" meaning.

An example is the series of *testimonia* on Christ as a stone (*Barn.* 6.2–4): Isa 28:16ab (a cornerstone placed on the foundations of Zion); Isa 28:16c (faith in this stone shows that it is not a material stone and authorizes an allegorical interpretation), in which, however, the original sentence, "Whoever believes in it will not be confounded," becomes "whoever believes in it will live forever," thus adding part of Gen 3:22, which is likewise interpreted as referring to Christ; Isa 50:7 ("he has made me like a solid stone"), which is connected a few lines earlier with the passion; and finally, Ps 118:22 ("the stone rejected by the builders has become the cornerstone"), which is given a christological interpretation thanks to v. 24 of the same Psalm, cited immediately afterwards as a prophecy. In introducing the first text, Barnabas says that Christ is established as a hard stone "for grinding." This is an allusion to Isa 8:14–15, a *testimonium* on the "stumbling stone," that is cited, along with Isa 28:16, in Rom 9:33 and in 1 Pet 2:6, 8.

Thus Barnabas too is familiar with a collection of *testimonia* that combined these two passages of Isaiah, although he does not explicitly cite the first of them.

A basic theme of the letter is that the Jews did not show themselves worthy of the law they received from Moses, which has passed on, via the passion of Christ, to Christians, who have become the people of the inheritance (4.7–8; 14.4). The Jews never understood the law, which Barnabas denies was ever meant to be taken literally; its meaning has always been spiritual, allegorical (but Barnabas uses *typos* and not *allēgoria*). The anti-Jewish attitude is harsh. Barnabas not only claims for Christians the only correct understanding of the Scriptures, but he also takes over from Judaism exegetical methods, eschatological traditions (the 6000 years since creation: 15.3–4), and ethical motifs, and puts all of them in the service of his Christian theology. This is a striking example of the "expropriation" of Jewish religious identity by Christians.

Since it is difficult to think that such arguments could have persuaded any Jew, such attacks on Judaism served primarily to strengthen Christian identity by distancing Christians from their mother religion, depreciating it in order to heighten the value of their own. Thus viewed, Barnabas represents a stage in the process of distancing Christianity from Judaism and contrasting the one with the other. The distance is not seen here simply as a fact; it is a conscious development of an ideology by systematically invalidating the presuppositions of the opposing ideology.

It has recently been suggested (P. F. Beatrice, 1989) that we see in Barnabas primarily an attack, by an orthodoxy in process of development, on Christian groups of enthusiasts and encratites whose background was the Jewish-Hellenistic sapiential tradition. The key text would be 4.10–14, with its warning against the temptation to withdrawal into oneself "as though God had already pronounced you holy" and against reliance on one's call, independent of observance of the commandments. This suggestion seems to require a more detailed examination, but it does have the merit of focusing attention on the intra-Christian values in the author's discourse.

Despite the emphasis on the passion and resurrection of Jesus (chs. 5–6; 12) and the allusion to some aspects of his life (5.8–9), it is not certain that the author makes use of the Gospels. In 4.14 there is a saying, cited as Scripture, that is placed on the lips of Jesus in Matt 22:14, but our text does not enable us to say with certainty that Barnabas regards it as a saying of Jesus.

The author seems to be a Christian teacher (see 1.8; 4.9) but does not claim to be Barnabas; nor do we know why the work was attributed to him. In any case, the author is not Paul's companion on missions: the work postdates the destruction of Jerusalem in 70 (16.3–4). In order to determine the date more closely, use has been made of the statement that those who destroyed the temple of Jerusalem are now setting about restoring it (16.3–4), which is interpreted as a reference to Jewish hopes of rebuilding the temple with Roman help in the early years of Hadrian (118–120), or to the building of the temple of Jupiter Capitolinus by the same Hadrian after the Jewish rebellion of 135. But it is possible that Barnabas or his source (an apocryphal *testimonium*) may be thinking of the building of a spiritual temple. In 4.4–5 there is an allusion to ten kings (Roman emperors) that is based on Dan 7:7–24, but it is of no use in determining the time of the writing. The fact that the themes are foreign to the gnostic debate suggests that we cannot date it beyond 140.

As for the place of origin, scholars have long thought of Alexandria, where the first attestations of the work occur and where there was a tradition of allegorical exegesis (Philo). Today scholars are increasingly inclined to believe it was composed in Asia Minor or western Syria. This second hypothesis seems to us preferable in view of the contacts with other writings from that area, such as Matthew, the *Ascension of Isaiah,* the *Odes of Solomon,* and the *Gospel of Peter.* Then, too, the collections of *testimonia* that are used seem to be largely of Syro-Palestinian origin.

BIBLIOGRAPHY

Editions and Commentaries

P. Prigent and R. A. Kraft, *Epître de Barnabé* (SC 172; Paris: Cerf, 1971).
F. Scorza Barcellona, *Epistola di Barnaba* (CP 1; Rurin: Società Editrice Internazionale, 1975).
J. B. Lightfoot and J. R. Harmer, *The Apostolic Fathers: Greek Texts and English Translations of Their Writings* (2d ed.; trans. and ed. M. W. Holmes; Grand Rapids, Mich.: Baker, 1992).

Studies

F. Prigent, *Les Testimonia dans le christianisme primitif: L'Epître de Barnabé I–XVI et ses sources* (Paris: Gabalda, 1961).
K. Wengst, *Tradition und Theologie des Barnabasbriefes* (New York: de Gruyter, 1971).
L. W. Barnard, "The 'Epistle of Barnabas' and Its Contemporary Setting," *ANRW* II 27.1 (1993): 159–207.
K. Derry, "One Stone on Another: Towards an Understanding of Symbolism in the Epistle of Barnabas," *JECS* 4 (1996): 515–28.
R. Hvalvik, *Struggle for Scripture and Covenant: The Purpose of the Epistle of Barnabas and Jewish-Christian Competition in the Second Century* (Tübingen: Mohr-Siebeck, 1996).

Chapter 7

ECCLESIASTICAL DISCIPLINE AND HOMILIES

1. Ecclesiastical Discipline

a. Didache

Until the last century, the title *Didache* was known from ancient lists of books not included in the New Testament, the first such being that of Eusebius of Caesarea in his *Eccl. hist.* 3.25.4, and from the *Festal Letter* 39 of Athanasius (A.D. 367). Christian writers had cited the work perhaps as early as Clement of Alexandria (*Strom.* 1.100.4), but since the citations were implicit, they were not recognizable as such. In particular, the seventh book of the *Apostolic Constitutions* (end of the fourth century) contains a paraphrase of the *Didache*. But the text of the latter work was discovered only in 1873, in an eleventh-century manuscript that was initially in Constantinople but later passed into the possession of the Greek Patriarchate of Jerusalem (Hierosolym. 54), and which also contains *Barnabas, 1* and *2 Clement*, and the long recension of the letters of Ignatius of Antioch.

The collection represented by this manuscript goes back perhaps to the fifth century; its purpose was to bring together writings which at that time had been definitively excluded from the New Testament canon. Two parchment fragments from a fourth-century codex (P.Oxy. 1782) preserve *Did.* 1.3c–4a and 2.7–3.2. There is also a rather free Coptic translation of 10.3b–12.2 in a papyrus of the fourth or fifth century (P.Lond.Or. 9271). Extracts from the *Didache* were introduced into the Ethiopic recension of the *Ecclesiastical Canons of the Apostles,* which go back to a compilation not older than the fourth century.

In the Jerusalem manuscript, the work has two titles: "Teaching *(Didache)* of the Twelve Apostles," and "Teaching of the Lord through the Twelve Apostles to the Nations." The second is an expansion of the first. Nothing in the first text suggests the twelve apostles as its authors, so we will not assume primary authorship.

The *Didache* is a composite work, a kind of handbook for Christian communities, bringing together texts of various origins and various kinds.

Chapters 1.1–6.3 reproduce a treatise on the "two ways." The way of life is based on the love of God and neighbor (1.2), a series of commandments both negative (2.1–3, 6) and positive (humility and meekness: 3.7–10), the proper attitude toward the brothers and sisters of the community (4.1–4), almsgiving (4.5–8), and a prudent management of household and family (4.9–11). Into this part has been inserted a series of *logoi* (sayings) that correspond to sayings of Jesus in the Gospels (especially Matthew) but are not presented as such. The way of death is then described in 5.1–2, in the form of a list of vices to be avoided. Chapter 6 concludes the section on the two ways and forms a transition to the next part.

Other recensions of the *Two Ways* are to be found in *Barnabas* 18–20; in a treatise, the *Teaching of the Twelve Apostles,* that has come down to us in two Latin manuscripts; and in a form that allots the precepts to the twelve apostles, in the *Constitution* (or *Ecclesiastical Canons*) *of the Apostles* (canons 4–14), which dates from the third century. At the base of such writings was a Jewish treatise on ethics, now lost, that was influenced by the dualist tradition of Qumran (see 1QS 3.13–4.26). The dualism can still be perceived in the versions of the two ways in *Barnabas* and the *Teaching of the Apostles* (where the two ways are connected with two angels), and to a much lesser degree in the *Didache*.

Chapters 7–10 contain instructions for worship: baptism (7.1–4); fasting (8.1); prayer (8.2, with a form of the Our Father that is close but not identical to that in Matt 6:9–13, and is probably derived not from that gospel but from the liturgical tradition); Eucharist (9.1–5); and thanksgiving after the Eucharist (10.1–6). A sentence in 7.1 explains that the earlier instruction on the two ways was to be used in pre-baptismal catechesis.

Chapters 11–15 are given over to questions of discipline. Here again, an introductory formula refers to what has preceded, describing it as teaching that must be accepted. These passages reflect an archaic situation in which itinerant Christian preachers stay for a time in the communities. The communities are faced with the problem of evaluating the teaching of these men, and norms are given here for evaluating the itinerant apostles (11.3–6) and prophets (11.7–12) on the basis of their behavior. The *Didache* then adds rules for itinerants who intend to settle down in the communities (ch. 12: they must work), on the wages of prophets and teachers (ch. 13), on the Sunday celebration (ch. 14), the local hierarchy of bishops and deacons (15.1–2), and fraternal correction (15.3–4). Chapter 16 breaks off suddenly, surely because the model, the Jerusalem manuscript, was incomplete; it takes up the signs of the last times and of the Lord's return.

A Christian author thus adapted the treatise on the two ways, making it Christian especially by the addition of 2.1–3.6 (taken from the tradition of the sayings of Jesus). He added chs. 7–10, in which he collected liturgical material that was very early and close to the Jewish blessings at meals. He then added chs. 11–16. Within this section on discipline, however, it seems necessary to distinguish various strata that correspond to different phases in the evolution of ministries. The situation presupposed in ch. 11 seems to be the earliest: the only ministers are the itinerant apostles and prophets. The settled communities of Christians must soon have found it necessary to distinguish, among those who came to them, between "genuine" prophets and missionaries and those who wanted only to be supported by the communities. To reject a genuine prophet was regarded as a serious fault against the action of the Spirit. Since the assumption was that prophecy was free and not bound to stable ministries, it was urgently necessary to establish criteria to recognize fraud without thereby subjecting the manifestations of the Spirit to human judgment

(Matt 10:40–42 reflects the same situation). We may, therefore, with K. Niederwimmer, see in 11.4–12 a very early instruction.

Chapters 12–15, however, tackle a different problem, that posed by itinerants who come intending to settle down in the community. The reference is both to individuals generally (12.3–5) and to prophets (no longer to apostles), to whom are added teachers, mentioned in 13.2 (elsewhere only in 11.1–2; 15.1–2). Chapter 15.1–2 suddenly urges the election, from within the community, of bishops and deacons who "carry out the [primarily liturgical] functions of the prophets and teachers." Here we are in a phase in which stable ministries, not marked primarily by charismatic gifts, are replacing the triad of apostles, prophets, and teachers, which is attested as early as the first half of the first century in the Pauline communities (1 Cor 12:29, then Eph 4:11) and was probably modeled on the Hellenistic community of Antioch (see Acts 13:1). There is disagreement over whether we should see here the result of a second redaction of the *Didache* (thus Rordorf-Tuilier), or whether the passage is from the editor of the preceding chapters, who now addresses those communities in which prophets had not settled down and which must therefore provide leaders from within (thus Niederwimmer). Chapter 16 contains a teaching on the last times that shows affinities with the material proper to Matthew in his version of the eschatological discourse of Jesus (Matt 24:10–12, 30).

It is accepted today that the *Didache* does not depend on any of the writings that came together to form the New Testament. There are numerous points of contact with the Gospel of Matthew, but an examination of each of them shows that the likely explanation is dependence on a common tradition. This is true especially of: the precepts in 1.3b–2.1, many of which have a form that seems more archaic than that in Matthew; other sentences that appear in Matthew as sayings of Jesus (e.g., *Did.* 9.5 [see Matt 7:6]; 11.7 [see Matt 12:31]; 13.1–2 [see Matt 10:10]; the Our Father (8.2), which was probably taken from liturgical usage; and the eschatological pronouncements in ch. 16, as already noted. The word "gospel" in 8.2 and 11.3 refers, in all likelihood, to oral traditions. In 15.3 and 4, which speak of precepts in the gospel, it seems to refer to a written source; still, there is no evidence that the source is our canonical Gospels.

The exhortation to choose bishops and deacons in ch. 15, and the care taken to indicate that these replace prophets and teachers, show that the position of bishops and deacons in the communities was still being established. This situation takes us back to the end of the first century or the beginning of the second. The redaction of chs. 1–13 must therefore be earlier, a dating that corresponds to the archaic character of the liturgy and, as already noted, to the situation of the ministries. The entire work would have acquired its present form by the beginning of the second century at the latest. This claim is in harmony with the recourse to the gospel tradition as found outside texts destined to become canonical. As for the place of origin, while Egypt has been suggested on the basis of the ancient testimonies, we should think rather of western Syria, because it is from there that we have testimonies about itinerant charismatic ministries and about problems of their acceptance by the communities, problems analogous in form to those in the *Didache*. See also in 7.2 the reference to a lack of running water, which does not seem to fit well with Egypt. Matthew, too, whose special traditions are close to those of the *Didache*, must have come from that region.

BIBLIOGRAPHY

Editions (with commentary)

W. Rordorf and A. Tuilier, *La Doctrine des douze Apôtres Didaché* (SC 248; Paris: Cerf, 1978).
K. Wengst, *Didache (Apostellehre), Barnabasbrief, Zweiter Klemensbrief, Schrift an Diognet* (Darmstadt: Wissenschaftliche Buchgesellschaft, 1984).
J. B. Lightfoot and J. R. Harmer, *The Apostolic Fathers: Greek Texts and English Translations of Their Writings* (2d ed.; trans. and by M. W. Holmes; Grand Rapids, Mich.: Baker, 1992).

Commentaries

K. Niederwimmer, *Die Didache* (KAV 1; Göttingen: Vandenhoeck & Ruprecht, 1989).
K. Niederwimmer and H. W. Attridge, *The Didache: A Commentary* (Hermeneia; Minneapolis: Fortress, 1998).

Study

C. N. Jefford, ed., *The Didache in Context: Essays on Its Text, History, and Transmission* (NovTSup 77; New York: Brill, 1995).

b. Apostolic Tradition

The need to regulate the life and liturgy of the churches in ways progressively adapted to new situations and at the same time faithful to the tradition led to the compilation of canonico-liturgical collections into which earlier documents were incorporated and changed in the process. Such was the case with the *Didache,* which, as we saw, was incorporated into the seventh book of the *Apostolic Constitutions.* But while that document was also recovered in its own textual tradition, such is not the case with the *Apostolic Tradition,* which has had to be reconstructed on the basis of later collections. In addition, its identification as a work of Hippolytus remains conjectural, and for this reason we deal with it outside the chapter on that author.

The canonical collection of the church of Alexandria, the *Alexandrian Synodos,* has not come down to us in its original Greek but in Coptic (in two versions: Sahidic and Bohairic), Arabic, and Ethiopic, all dependent on an original Sahidic version, which is lost. The work contains canonical texts known in other ways: extracts from the eighth book of the *Apostolic Constitutions* (end of 4th c.) and the so-called *Ecclesiastical Constitution of the Apostles* (also called *Apostolic Ordinance* and *Apostolic Canons;* 5th–6th c.). The part that remains after these texts have been put aside, and to which scholars initially gave the name *Constitution of the Egyptian Church,* shows affinities with other known canonical collections: an *Epitome* of the eighth book of the *Apostolic Constitutions,* with the subtitle *Constitutions of Hippolytus;* a fourth-century Arabic collection titled *Canons of Hippolytus;* and the fifth-century *Testament of the Lord,* which is preserved in Syriac, Arabic, and Ethiopic, and in Latin fragments.

A comparison between the text taken from the *Alexandrian Synodos* and the parallels (which are in fact revisions) in the other collections has made it possible to identify in the former a version of a text that has been identified with the work *Apostolic Tradition,* which is mentioned in a list of works inscribed on a statue and currently attributed to Hippolytus of Rome (on this complicated question see ch. 13, sec. 2). Part of a Latin version of the same work, but independent of the *Alexandrian Synodos,* was identified in a palimpsest from the end of the fifth century that is in the Capitular Library of Verona. This manuscript contains three collections, the *Didascalia apostolorum,* the *Ecclesiastical Constitutions of the Apostles* (see above), and the *Apostolic Tradition* (which must originally have comprised twenty-six pages, of which fourteen remain; these are often called the "Hauler Fragments" after their first editor). This is the earliest canonical compilation known to us; its archetype goes back to the end of the fourth century.

The beginning of the text preserved in Latin and in Ethiopic states that the explanation of the charisms is now complete; now begins the explanation of "the essentials of the tradition proper to the churches." This fact, along with the attribution to Hippolytus of two of the rewritings mentioned above, has been a decisive argument for the attribution to Hippolytus, in view of the title in the list on the statue: *Apostolic Tradition.* This title suggests either a work in two parts or two successive works, the first on the charisms, and the second on apostolic tradition.

But this attribution rests on foundations less solid than is commonly thought. Apart from the problems of the statue and its link to Hippolytus, there is also the fact that a Greek fragment of this work, published in 1963, does not attribute it to Hippolytus, nor does it call itself *Apostolic Tradition* but rather "*Diataxeis* [Regulations] of the Holy Apostles." Moreover, this work has no parallel in the literary production of Hippolytus. According to P. Nautin, the work is a fusion of two works, one mentioned on the statue, and the other showing similarities to the works of the "eastern" Hippolytus (see ch. 13, sec. 2). The question is still open; it ought not to be forgotten that all studies are based on conjectural reconstructions of the original Greek text (the most widely used is that of Botte), alongside which one should always have the synopsis of the various versions that have been preserved (Hanssens, 1970). Let us briefly indicate the contents of the work.

After the introduction already mentioned, the first part (chs. 1–14) has to do with the election of a bishop and the ceremonies of his consecration: he is to be elected by the people and consecrated by other bishops, after which he celebrates the Eucharist with the presbyterium. Next come instructions on presbyters, deacons, confessors (those who have borne witness to the faith before the authorities, giving them a dignity equivalent to that of priests), widows, lectors, virgins, subdeacons, and those who have the gift of healing. The second part (chs. 15–21), which has its own conclusion, deals with all the stages of Christian initiation: from the first interrogation of those who present themselves to embrace the faith, through the rules about a change of manner of life for those in certain trades, the duration of prebaptismal catechesis, the laying on of hands, the preliminary testing before baptism, and finally the baptismal ceremony with the ensuing Eucharist, which is described in detail. The third part (chs. 22–42) is less homogeneous and contains various regulations on Sunday communion, fasting, the sick, the rite of lamplighting (bringing in a lamp that represents the light of Christ) and the ritual common meal (the *agape*) that follows, on burial places, the times of prayer, and the sign of the cross. Chapter 42 is a short conclusion.

Also to be mentioned among the canonical documents is the *Didascalia of the Apostles,* written by a bishop of northern Syria in the first decades of the third century. The Greek original of the work is lost except for some fragments (it is revised in the first six books of the *Apostolic Constitutions*), but the work is preserved in a Syriac translation. There are also 18 Latin fragments. Of special interest is the quite moderate teaching on penance, which allows for the forgiveness of all sins (except the sin against the Holy Spirit), including apostasy.

BIBLIOGRAPHY

B. Botte, *La Tradition apostolique de saint Hippolyte: Essai de reconstitution* (5th ed.; Münster: Aschendorff, 1989).

———, *Hippolyte de Rome: La Tradition apostolique d'après les anciennes versions* (SC 11; 2d ed.; Paris: Cerf, 1968).

J. Magne, *Tradition apostolique sur les charismes et Diataxeis des saints apôtres: Identification des documents et analyse du rituel des ordinations* (Paris: from the author, 1975).

R. Tateo, *Ippolito di Roma: La tradizione apostolica* (2d ed.; Rome: Paoline, 1979).

Studies

J. M. Hanssens, *La liturgie d'Hippolyte: Ses documents, son titulaire, ses origines et son caractère* (Rome: Pontifical Oriental Institute, 1959).

———, *La liturgie d'Hippolyte: Documents et études* (Rome: Gregorian, 1970).

A. Faivre, "La documentation canonico-liturgique de l'Eglise ancienne," *RSR* 54 (1980): 204–19, 273–97.

G. Dix, ed., *The Treatise on the Apostolic Tradition of St. Hippolytus of Rome, Bishop and Martyr* (London: SPCK, 1968).

T. M. Finn, "Ritual Process and the Survival of Early Christianity: A Study of the Apostolic Tradition of Hippolytus," *JRitSt* 3 (1969): 69–89.

Didascalia apostolorum

A. Vööbus, *The Didascalia Apostolorum in Syriac,* vol. I–II (4 vols.: CSCO 401, 402, 407, 408; Louvain: Peeters, 1978).

2. Homilies

a. Second Letter of Clement of Rome

This work is preserved with *1 Clement* in two Greek manuscripts: the Alexandrian (A) of the fifth century, and Hierosolymitanus 54 from 1056. It is also found, again with *1 Clement,* in a Syriac manuscript of 1170, where it is placed among the New Testament letters. Possible allusions to it are found in Origen and Hippolytus, but the first sure mention is by Eusebius (*Hist. eccl.* 3.38.4).

Although the work shows some characteristics of a "news letter" (e.g., "you ought to know": 5.5; 9.2; 16.3), it is not a letter but a sermon. E. Baasland, who has studied its rhetoric, describes it as "a symbouleutic discourse [one containing advice; used especially in politics] of a very particular kind. . . . It is an urgent address *(enteuxis)* for internal use, with protreptic elements, and intended to strengthen the self-understanding of the community" (1993, 107–8). The structure is difficult to determine.

Chapter 1.1–8 is an introduction that urges the hearers to regard Jesus Christ as God and not to have a low regard for our salvation. The fundamental theme is stated: In light of the greatness of what we have received, what can we give in exchange? Chapter 2.1–7 explains the scope of our salvation by commenting on Isaiah 54 and Matt 9:13b: Christ called us when we were lost and made of us a people, a church. Chapters 3–6: our response must be to praise him by obeying his commandments; to this end we must detach ourselves from this world, regarding its good things as alien to us, and devote ourselves to holy and just works. Chapter 7.1–16: like those who go down into the arena, we must fight with perseverance in order to receive the crown.

Chapter 8.1–3: we must therefore do penance as long as we live in time. Chapters 8.4–9.5: we must keep our flesh chaste, for it is in the flesh that we are called, and the flesh will be raised up and judged. Chapters 9.6–10.5: as long as time for healing is left to us, let us entrust ourselves to God the physician and, in return, let us give God our sincere repentance. As the Lord bids us (Matt 12:50), we must do the Father's will. Those who prefer the pleasures of this world and persuade others to do the same will be condemned. Chapters 11.1–12.6: citation and commentary on a "prophetic saying" (of unknown origin; it also appears in *1 Clem.* 23.3–4; see 2 Pet 3:4) that threatens those whose souls are divided and who have lost hope of winning the reward. Conversely, we must expect the reign of God at every moment. A saying of Jesus found in the *Gospel of the Egyptians* (see Clement, *Strom.* 3.13.92) is interpreted to mean that the kingdom will come when truth, good works, and chastity reign in the community. Chapter 13.1–4: a new exhortation to penance and to good works so that the name (of God) will not be blasphemed by pagans. Chapter 14.1–5: When we do God's will, we belong to the spiritual church that was created before the sun and the moon and has become visible in the flesh of Christ; since the flesh is a copy *(antitypos)* of the spirit, whatever defiles the flesh/church cannot participate in the Spirit/Christ.

Chapter 15.1–5 is transitional. The advice given thus far on continence is important, for this is the recompense we can give to God, and which we can preach and hear with faith and love. Chapters 16–17: let us hasten, therefore, to do penance in view of the judgment that is near. Almsgiving is especially recommended, as is mutual help and constant heeding of the Lord's commandments. At the final judgment, the just will give glory to God; let us try to live justly so that we will be of their number.

Chapters 19.1–20.5: the speaker suddenly speaks of himself as reader of the address that follows on the reading of the word of God. The reward he asks for the contribution he thereby makes to the salvation of the hearers is that these hearers will repent and act justly, without worrying whether at the present time the just suffer and the wicked prosper. If God were immediately to reward the just, we would not be practicing religion but bartering.

Chapters 19–20 raise a question of the work's integrity. On the one hand, these chapters show affinities with the preceding at the levels of vocabulary and content, e.g., 20.4, the recompense of the just: compare 9.5 and 11.5; in 19.2, the pair "admonish and convert": compare 17.2–3. On the other hand, there are differences, e.g., in 19.1; 20.2, "brothers and sisters," as compared with "brothers" in the preceding part; in 19.1 and 4; 20.4, the emphasis on words with the roots *euseb-* and *theoseb-*, which are missing in 1–18.

It has therefore been suggested that chs. 19–20 are a later addition. Since 19.1 seems to mark a transition from the reading of the biblical text to preaching, it has also been supposed (Lindemann) that chs. 19–20 were written by a reader as an introduction to the sermon of another author (chs. 1–18), and were transferred to the end when the sermon was united with *1 Clement* as a "second letter of Clement." This second hypothesis seems improbable, since chs. 19–20 as a whole do not have the appearance of an introduction to a homily and the transition from 20.4 to 1.1 would be extremely abrupt. In addition, the eschatological themes fit better with a conclusion. In separating chs. 19–20 from what precedes, one might better see in these two chapters a complete short address on a liturgical reading, perhaps by the same author (the supposed contradictions between the content of the two parts do not seem compelling). But many scholars accept the unity of the work, among them, recently, Baasland, who sees in these chapters the concluding *peroratio* of the entire discourse.

Of special interest in *2 Clement* are the citations of sayings of Jesus. Some of these correspond to sayings in the canonical gospels, but the differences suggest that our author got them from the oral tradition. This is the case, for example, with 3.2 (see Matt 10:32; Luke 12:18); 4.2 (see Matt 7:21); 15.4 (see Matt 7:7; Acts 20:35). Others do not correspond to the canonical sayings: 4.5; 5.2–4; 12.2. Because one citation is introduced by "the Lord says in the gospel" (8.5), it has been thought that all were derived from a lost gospel. For 5.2–4 we have a parallel in what is probably a fragment from the *Gospel of Peter;* for 12.2, a parallel in the *Gospel of the Egyptians;* therefore, in two different works. But our author probably draws on collections of the sayings of Jesus, for the interpretation he gives of the saying in 12.2 is quite different from the interpretation in the *Gospel of the Egyptians.* We have, therefore, two reinterpretations of sayings drawn from a common tradition. Chapter 11.2–4 cites a "prophetic saying," which is cited as Scripture in *1 Clem.* 23.3–4 and presupposed in 2 Pet 3:4; it is probably an apocryphal *testimonium,* fabricated to answer complaints about the delay of the Parousia. In 11.2 there is a passage that is cited as Scripture by Paul in 1 Cor 2:9, but the statement is often found in other apocalyptic texts and does not prove dependence on the letters of Paul.

Various hypotheses have been offered on the target of the author's attacks. A widely held thesis maintains that Valentinian gnostics were active in the community and that in order to unmask them the author emphasizes the flesh of Christ and of human beings, the resurrection, the final judgment, and ethics. But the work lacks a specific attack and, in particular, a singling out of a group of "adversaries" against whom the community is urged to be on guard; the exhortation to penance and good works applies to everyone. Nor has it been shown that the exhortation to have a high regard for the salvation won by Christ is aimed as a depreciation of the human dimension of Jesus, such as was found among the Valentinians. Such concepts as the *anapausis* (6.7) and the preexistent spiritual church (ch. 14) were not necessarily gnostic.

On the other hand, the author must have lived in a theological environment nourished by ideas and traditions (e.g., of the sayings of Jesus) that were also used in the gnostic systems. Yet he does not seem to see an urgent need to distance himself from such ideas, and he can even cite, while interpreting them in a way proper to his own theology, texts otherwise known to have been dear to the gnostics. What he seems to oppose is the conviction that salvation is already here, an attitude that leads to ethical indifferentism. In response *2 Clement* strongly emphasizes the future judgment. As already noted, the author's own leading idea seems to be that the salvation accomplished by God through Jesus Christ is an immense gift to which the saved must respond with a "repayment" (*antimisthia:* 1.3 and 5; 9.7) which consists in repentance. Repentance is understood as obedience to the commandments, chiefly chastity, and as the practice of good works in the Christian community. It is incorrect to accuse him, as has been done rather frequently, of legalism, or justification through works, because according to the author good works are the human response to the utterly unmerited initiative taken by God in kindness.

In particular, the author seems to make an effort to dissuade his readers from attachment to riches (4.3; 5.6–7; 6.4); in fact, he gives almsgiving first place among good works (16.4). He seems therefore to live in an environment in which social and economic asceticism is possible and sought, and to be addressing a well-to-do readership. He urges them not to renounce their wealth, but rather to use part of it for good purposes. He addresses a readership accustomed to the language of exchange, of gift and recompense; if the final two chapters belong with the rest of the work, then the warning against bartering with God in 20.4 also has its place in this setting.

He wants to persuade these readers, who are ready to accept that a benefaction calls for a repayment, that the repayment due to God is honor, not with the lips alone, but with obedience to God's commandments, that is, by doing good to the neighbor. Such action will in turn win a repayment, the acknowledgment by the Son at the judgment (3.2–4.3), and, here and now, the respect and regard of non-Christians, something that obviously means social gratification (13.1–4). In this perspective, the emphasis on the *sarx* as place of salvation received and of final recompense (9.1–5) has a validity that is not only theological but also, and above all, ethical and social: salvation does not have to do solely with the spiritual dimension of the person; it also vitally affects interpersonal relationships and the use of possessions. The circumstances of *2 Clement* are probably comparable to those presupposed in the letter of James, with its attacks on the rich and on merchants who plan their profits as if these had nothing to with their relationship with God.

But these reflections do not allow us to locate or date the work precisely. Proposed places of composition have included Rome, Corinth, Syria, and Egypt, but no decisive arguments have been adduced. The dating depends in part on the letter's purpose; those who see a decidedly antivalentinian polemic date *2 Clement* after the middle of the second century, while those who discern rather an incipient gnosticism take it back to the beginning of that century. The free use of the sayings of Jesus suggests a not very late date; the work is perhaps to be dated between 120 and 150.

Bibliography

Edition

K. Wengst, *Didache (Apostellehre), Barnabasbrief, Zweiter Klemensbrief, Schrift an Diognet* (Darmstadt: Wissenschaftliche Buchgesellschaft, 1984).

J. B. Lightfoot and J. R. Harmer, *The Apostolic Fathers: Greek Texts and English Translations of Their Writings* (2d ed.; trans. and by M. W. Holmes; Grand Rapids, Mich.: Baker, 1992).

Commentary

A. Lindemann, *Die Clemensbriefe* (HNT.AV 1; Tübingen: Mohr, 1982), 183–261.

Studies

K. P. Donfried, *The Setting of Second Clement in Early Christianity* (Leiden: Brill, 1974).

R. Warns, *Untersuchungen zum 2. Clemens-Brief* (theol. diss., Marburg, 1985).

E. Baasland, "Der 2. Klemensbrief und frühchristliche Rhetorik: 'Die erste christliche Predigt' im Lichte der neueren Forschung," *ANRW* II 27.1 (1993): 78–157.

b. Melito of Sardis

We discuss Melito in this chapter and not with the apologists because we have from him a complete Easter homily, whereas only a few fragments of his *Apologia* have survived. Most of our information about it comes from citations in Eusebius of Caesarea.

Following what must have been the practice of the first Christians of Palestine, the Christian communities of Asia Minor used to celebrate Easter on the same day as the Jewish Passover, namely, 14 Nisan, whence the name "Quartodecimans" given to these Christians. In other words, they celebrated Easter on a fixed date and a variable day of the week. In the other churches, Easter was always celebrated on a Sunday, the day of Jesus' resurrection. This divergence led to tensions between Rome and Asia Minor as early as 160, when Polycarp, Bishop of Smyrna, came to Rome to confer with Anicetus (155–166) on the subject. The two men did not reach agreement but went their separate ways within the one communion (Eusebius, *Hist. eccl.* 4.14.1).

The question became critical when Pope Victor (189–199), in the early years of his pontificate, tried to impose the Sunday observance on the churches of Asia. Polycrates of Ephesus, the most authoritative of the bishops of Asia, defended the quartodeciman observance in a letter to Victor, of which Eusebius has preserved extracts (*Hist. eccl.* 5.24.2–8). Polycrates cited the "great luminaries" buried in Asia who had followed the quartodeciman usage. The last cited, and therefore probably the most recent, was "the eunuch [i.e., celibate, ascetic] Melito, who always lived in the Holy Spirit and who lies in Sardis awaiting the visitation from heaven at which he shall rise from the dead" (5.24.5). Melito therefore was buried at Sardis, and had been a prophet, a point confirmed by a Montanist work of Tertullian that is cited by Jerome (*Vir. ill.* 24). According to Eusebius, he was bishop of Sardis (4.26.1), but the claim cannot be verified.

Eusebius gives a list of Melito's works (*Hist. eccl.* 4.26.2):
- *Easter,* two books
- *The Prophets and the Way of Life (politeia)*
- *The Church*

- *The Lord's Day*
- *The Faith of Man*
- *Creation*
- *The Obedience of Faith of the Senses* [according to Jerome and to Rufinus, translator of Eusebius, there were two works, *The Obedience of Faith* and *The Senses*]
- *Soul and Body, or On Unity* [the second title is a conjectural correction of an unintelligible word in Eusebius' text; other hypotheses: *On Union; On the Intellect*]
- *Baptism, Truth, Faith, and the Origin of Christ* [possibly several titles];
- a discourse on prophecy [?]
- *The Soul and the Body* [probably an erroneous repetition of a preceding title]
- *Hospitality*
- *The Key*
- *The Devil and the Apocalypse of John* [preceded by the plural article, possibly indicating several books]
- *God in the Body*
- *Petition to Antoninus*

Eusebius also cites a fragment from the *Extracts,* in six books, in which Melito tells of having traveled in the East "in order to learn the exact list of Old Testament books" (4.26.13–14). Since the *Apologia* of Melito was dedicated to Marcus Aurelius, it must have been composed when the latter was emperor, between 169 and 177.

Apart from the works on this list, only fragments of Melito were known until 1936, when C. Bonner identified a homily in a fourth-century papyrus codex as Melito's work. The pages of the codex are in the Chester Beatty collection in Dublin and at the University of Michigan. The papyrus names Melito but does not give the title of the work, and Bonner, who was able to identify fragments of the homily in Greek, Coptic, and Syriac, published it as *Homily on the Passion,* on the basis of what is said by Anastasius the Sinaite, who cites a fragment of it. In 1960 M. Testuz published the complete text of the homily as found in P. Bodmer 8 (which lacks the first page, that is, sections 1–5), which bore the accurate title: "Of Melito, on Easter." Other witnesses to the text are a Coptic papyrus, possibly from the sixth century, containing sections 48–105; Georgian versions of 1–45 and 46–105, the two circulating separately under the names respectively of "Bishop Meletius" and John Chrysostom; and a Latin epitome handed down under the names of Leo the Great and Augustine.

What is the connection between the homily and the books on *Easter* mentioned by Eusebius? The difficulty in identifying the two lies not only in the number of books; it is due also to the fact that Eusebius cites a passage from the beginning of the work to which he refers (*Hist. eccl.* 4.26.3), showing it to have been composed on the occasion of a controversy over Easter that broke out in the time of Servilius Paulus, Proconsul of Asia, and the martyr Sagaris, of whom we know nothing. A Servilius Paulus, Proconsul of Asia, is unknown, but Rufinus' Latin translation of Eusebius has "Sergius Paulus" at this point. This last may be simply an assimilation of the personage to the well known proconsul in Acts 13:7; on the other hand, we do know of a Sergius Paulus, a consul, who could have been Proconsul of Asia before 162 or in the years 166–177. Also suggested is a correction of the name in Eusebius to "Servilius Pudens," since there was a consul of that name in 166. The problem, however, is whether the work cited by Eusebius can be identified with our homily.

Another difficulty is created by Eusebius's statement that Clement of Alexandria wrote his own work *Easter* "because" *(ex aitias)* of Melito's (*Hist. eccl.* 4.26.4); Eusebius later gives references to Clement's work (6.13.9). All this might suggest that the work of Melito known to Clement was a defense of the quartodeciman Easter.

Various solutions have been proposed: there may be two different works of Melito; the homily may constitute the first or second book of a work in two books; or the two books of which Eusebius speaks may correspond to two different parts of the homily (see the double doxology at the end of 45 and 105, and the transmission in two distinct parts in the Georgian textual tradition). According to still others the homily is not by Melito (thus P. Nautin). Whatever the connection between the work known to Eusebius and our homily, the style and content of the latter are similar to those of the fragments of Melito, and it seems justifiable, therefore, to accept the attribution given in the manuscripts.

The opening sentence shows that the homily followed upon the reading of Exodus 12, which gives the regulations for the slaying and eating of the Passover lamb. There follows, down to section 10, a statement of the contents: the hearers must understand the mystery of Easter, that is, the fulfillment of the law in Christ. The remainder of the work is clearly divided into two parts, and the division is marked by the doxology at the end of 45 and the transition at the beginning of 46. In 11–45 the author describes the night of the first Passover and of the death of the first-born in Egypt. He says that those events merely prefigure the event that is Christ and the church; they were like a model made by an artist, which loses its value once the work of art is produced.

The second part (46–105) has to do with the fulfillment that comes in the Christian Passover. By means of a false etymology, the name *pascha* is connected with the Greek verb *paschō*, "suffer," that is, with the passion of Christ, which was the focal point of the quartodeciman Easter. In order to render intelligible the origins of Christ's suffering, Melito first recalls "the preparation for the mystery" (46), that is, the history that led to it: original sin and its consequences (48–56) and the prediction of the suffering of Jesus by the prophets (57–65). Melito points to Christ, who has come from heaven to earth, as "the Passover of our salvation," the lamb slain as our savior (66–71). There follows a strong attack on Israel, which slew him who had done good to it, failed to recognize the Lord who had protected it, and repaid him with ingratitude. The bitter herbs prescribed for Passover are a sign of the bitterness that comes to Israel from the sufferings it inflicted on Jesus (72–93). Israel has been destroyed because of that terrible crime (94–99). The final section describes the resurrection and exaltation of the Lord, who has conquered death and brought the forgiveness of sins (100–105).

The homily is a carefully composed rhetorical production in the style of second-century Asianism, which was connected with the so-called "Second Sophistic," a style represented especially by such contemporaries of Melito as Maximus of Tyre (ca. 125–185), Lucian of Samosata (ca. 120–200), and others. It shows a great liking for such formal devices as exclamation, question, anaphora, antithesis, isocolon (succession of short phrases with the same structure; see 1), oxymoron (combination of opposites; see 2), and homoioteleuton ("rhyming" phrases; see 2–3). This type of oratory was practiced in the "sacred discourses" at pagan sanctuaries, where rhetorical devices were used to help in the memorization of religious formulas. Melito places it at the service of the Christian liturgy.

Easter is here the unconditional center of the history of salvation. The celebration calls to mind not only the deliverance of the Hebrews from Egypt and the resurrection of Jesus, but the entire "history of salvation" from the sin of Adam, by way of the prophetic preparation, to the birth, passion, death, resurrection, and ascension of Jesus. We have also noted the importance of the passion for the quartodeciman Easter.

A seeming antithesis marks the work. On the one hand, there is the strikingly violent antijudaism: the Jewish Passover, which in any case never had value except as prefiguration, no longer has any meaning after the coming of Christ (35–45). In addition, Israel is accused at length of ingratitude to its benefactor, of an "unparalleled crime" (73), and even of deicide (68: "God is murdered," a sentence used later on by the "Theopaschites," according to whom God himself underwent suffering and death). The destruction of Jerusalem is viewed (as in an entire line of Christian tradition) as punishment for the crucifixion of Jesus (99). This work is thus a stage in the disastrous history of Christian antijudaism and anti-Semitism. The influence of Melito is also evident in the *improperia*, the reproaches of Israel as slayer of Christ that were until recently part of the Catholic Good Friday liturgy.

On the other hand, we see alongside this anti-judaism a strong influence of the Passover haggadah, that is, the Jewish way of celebrating the Passover, which was codified a few years after Melito in the tractate *Pesachim* of the Mishnah, but was doubtless already in use in his time (S. G. Hall). Consider, for example, the story of enslavement and deliverance (see Deut 26:5–9) and the misfortune-glory sequence, which is seen by the Mishnah as part of the Passover story, or the explanation (different, of course, from that of the Jews) of the meaning of the unleavened bread and bitter herbs (93).

Only in appearance, however, are the anti-judaism and continuity with the Jewish Passover tradition contradictory. What we see here is an important episode in the "expropriation" of the Scriptures and the religious tradition of Judaism that was carried on by Christians, especially in the second century, as they claimed for Christianity the authentic understanding of the Bible and continuity with the "true Israel." In this perspective, polemical violence against the Jews came naturally in the effort to prove that the Jews had no right to appeal to the revelation that the Christians had inherited from them, but of which the Christians now claim to be the sole possessors. We see this process in Justin in the area of biblical interpretation; in Melito it is applied to the very core of Jewish identity as represented by the celebration of Passover.

Among the fragments of Melito (the most complete collection is in S. G. Hall's edition, the numbering of which we follow), special importance belongs to those of the *Apologia*, which he addressed to Emperor Marcus Aurelius. Three of these are reproduced by Eusebius (*Hist. eccl.* 4.26.5–11: frag. 1), and a shorter one is found in the *Chronicon Paschale* (frag. 2). In the first two fragments in Eusebius, Melito deplores the selfish denunciations and spoliations of Christians in Asia as a result of new edicts. According to some, these represent a hardening against Christians following the rebellion of Avidius Cassius against the emperor in 175; the *Apologia* would then date from ca. 176.

The third fragment is of special interest: in it Melito stresses the contemporaneity of the birth of Christianity ("our philosophy") and the birth of the Roman empire, and suggests a link between the spread of the former and the prosperity of the latter. Only Nero and Domitian, men urged on by malicious people, leveled accusations against Christianity, but the predecessors of the reigning emperor have taken measures against the lamentable custom of anonymous denunciation and have written to the governors to censure them. Melito thus takes the bold ideological step of trying to make the emperor accept Christianity as the official "philosophy" that will protect the empire. This approach would not to have any immediate effect, but would become a reality with Constantine. A defense in Syriac under Melito's name is spurious.

Of special interest also is a fragment which Eusebius cites (*Hist. eccl.* 4.26.12–14: frag. 3) from the introduction to the *Extracts (Eklogai)*, which are testimonies about Jesus taken from the Scriptures, arranged in six books, and dedicated to a Christian named Onesimus. Melito shows himself aware of the problem arising from the differences between the Hebrew canon of the Bible and the Septuagint, and he says that he went to the East to find out the number and exact titles of the books of the Old Testament, of which he gives a list. For his *testimonia*, then, he limits himself to the books of the Hebrew canon.

A christological fragment cited in *The Guide* by Anastasius Sinaita (7th–8th c.) as being from the third book of Melito's *Incarnation of Christ* (frag. 6), defends the real nature of Christ's humanity, both body and soul. However, the language is characteristic of a later period (possibly 4th c.), fueling doubts about its authenticity. Other fragments, found in catenas, have to do with the baptism of Christ (frag. 8b: from a work titled *Baptism*) and the types of Christ found in the sacrifice of Isaac, where Christ is prefigured both by Isaac and by the ram that substitutes for him and thus rescues him from his sentence (frag. 9–12).

Bibliography

Editions

S. G. Hall, *Melito of Sardis: On Pascha and Fragments* (Oxford: Oxford University Press, 1979).

O. Perler, *Méliton de Sardes: Sur la Pâque et fragments* (SC 123; Paris: Cerf, 1966); important especially for the commentary.

Commentary

R. Cantalamessa, *I piu antichi testi pasquali della Chiess: Le omelie di Melitone di Sardi e dell'Anonimo Quartodecimano e altri testi del II secolo* (Rome: Edizioni liturgiche, 1972).

c. Anonymous Homily

We discuss here another Easter homily that seems to come from Quartodeciman circles. It is preserved in eight manuscripts (the oldest from the 11th c.), plus one now lost, as part of a group of seven Easter homilies under the name of John Chrysostom. It is also partially preserved (1.1–6 and 22; 9.19–17.38) in a palimpsest of Grottaferrata (8th–9th c.) under the name of Hippolytus of Rome, to whom other passages of the homily are also attributed in the Syriac *Florilegium Edessenum anonymum* (before 562) and in another florilegium that was attached to the acts of the Lateran Council of 649.

The overall structure of the homily corresponds to that of Melito's homily. After a hymn to Christ the Light, a statement of the contrast between Old Testament figures and Christian reality and an exhortation to participate in the cosmic dimension of the feast (1–12) are followed by the text of Exodus 12, an Easter reading, and by an outline of the explanation to follow (13–25). As in Melito, the explanation has two parts: a typological exegesis of the biblical text (26–72) and an explanation of the "economy," that is, of God's saving action, which begins with the coming of Christ, through which he brings freedom, adoption as his children, the forgiveness of sins, and true life (73–116). This part dwells successively on the incarnation, the passion (with an emphasis on the etymological connection between *pascha* and suffering, and on the cosmic scope of the cross, the tree of salvation that makes up for the sin committed by means of a tree), and the glorification (defeat of death, descent to the world of death, resurrection, and ascension). The text ends with a hymn to Christ, the divine Passover (117–121).

While the attribution to Chrysostom is evidently mistaken, the attribution to Hippolytus, especially in the Grottaferrata manuscript, seemed to confirm the hypothesis to this effect by C. Martin in 1926, before the discovery of the palimpsest, who identified it with the work *On Easter* that was attributed to Hippolytus in antiquity (see below, ch. 13, sec. 2c). But in 1950, P. Nautin dated the Christology of the homily to the second half of the fourth century, while maintaining that the work was directly inspired by the *Easter* of Hippolytus. In an extensive study in 1967, R. Cantalamessa recognized in the homily a Quartodeciman work composed in Asia Minor between 164–166 (the date of the Easter controversy in Laodicea) and the end of the second century. Finally, G. Visonà has stressed the point that when looked at as an Easter liturgy rather than simply as a homily, the work does not reflect ecclesiastical tradition after the end of the third century, that the connection with the collections of *testimonia* reflects a use of Scripture that is documented for the second century and the first half of the third, and that its binitarianism (limitation of the divine life to the relationship of Father-Son), which is connected with pneumatic Christology (the Pneuma or divine Spirit constitutes the divine element in Christ), would hardly have been plausible after Origen. But Visonà also points out that the obvious rhetoric of the work could have led, even in a later age, to an inaccurate use of terms and theological themes and thereby given an erroneous impression of something archaic. He remains undecided, therefore, between an undoubted impression of doctrinal archaism and the impossibility of excluding a later date of composition (4th–5th c.).

BIBLIOGRAPHY

G. Visonà, *Pseudo Ippolito. In Sanctum Pascha: Studio edizione commento* (Milan: Vita e Pensiero, 1988).

R. Cantalamessa, *L'omelia "In s. Pascha" dello Pseudo-Ippolito di Roma: Ricerche sulla teologia dell'Asia minore nella seconda metà del II secolo* (Milan: Vita e Pensiero, 1967).

W. J. McCarthy, "Christ, the Arbor Mundi," *NV* (1998): 53–69.

Chapter 8

DEVELOPMENTS OF THE GOSPEL TRADITION

1. Dialogues of the Risen Lord

In the canonical Gospels, and doubtless in the Jewish-Christian gospels as well, the sayings of Jesus are given as uttered by him during his earthly life; only a few are attributed to the risen Christ. But critical exegesis shows that some sayings placed in the mouth of the "earthly" Jesus were originally sayings of the risen Jesus, possibly uttered through the mouths of Christian prophets. Moreover, the glorified Lord was a figure especially suited to communicating to his disciples clear revelations that would differ from the teaching in parables that he had given before his death. Thus, while in Mark there is no appearance of the risen Christ at all, and while Matthew only attributes to the risen Christ a short message to the women (28:9–10) and the missionary command to the disciples (28:16–20), Luke has Jesus explain the christological meaning of the Scriptures to the disciples traveling to Emmaus (24:25–27) and then to the apostles (20:36–49). John further increases the number of appearances (20:14–21:23). Still, these stories do not contain any special revelations.

In Acts, Luke says that Jesus appeared to the apostles for forty days, teaching them about the reign of God (1:3). This period seems chosen precisely to counteract the tendency (already known to Luke) to lengthen the stay of the risen Lord on earth and multiply new revelations. Along the same line, at the moment of the ascension Jesus refuses to reveal to the disciples the times appointed by the Father (1:6–8). The tendency to attribute further revelations to the risen Lord has left traces even in the textual tradition of the canonical Gospels, in the form of the "Freer Logion" that is inserted in Codex W at Mark 16:14 (see above, ch. 2, sec. 10).

The inclination to lengthen the stay of the risen Lord on earth soon manifested itself: at the beginning of the second century, the *Ascen. Isa.* 11.16 speaks of 545 days, that is, eighteen months, a figure that was to enjoy great success among the gnostics but did not originate with them. The gnostics adopted it in order to have time for the secret revelations of Jesus to which they liked to appeal (Irenaeus, *Haer.* 1.3.2; 1.30.14; see below, sec. 4). In only a few cases do such revelatory dialogues take place during the earthly life of Jesus (e.g., the gnostic *Apocalypse of Peter* = NHC VII,3). These revelations take the form of dialogues between the risen Lord and his disciples or, more accurately, questions of the disciples and replies of Jesus.

In the second century these works constituted a true and proper literary genre, the origins of which are debated. In very summary form, the two main positions are these. On the one side (K. Rudolph), the dialogues of the redeemer are regarded as a revival in gnostic circles of the literary genres used in Greek philosophical instruction; i.e., the dialogue and the question-and-answer method *(erotapokrisis)*, for the purpose of expounding. The gnostics used them to communicate their teaching in a clear and organized form. On the other (H. Koester), the dialogues are viewed as a development of a form found in the gospel tradition, the collection of the Lord's sayings, interpreted by means of an exegetical amplification in the form of a dialogue. Koester sees this process at work in such writings as *Dialogue of the Savior* and *Apocryphon of James* from Nag Hammadi, but also in the discourses of Jesus in the Gospel of John.

These two solutions are not mutually exclusive, but potentially complementary. The genre known as dialogues of the redeemer was also used by the "orthodox," as demonstrated by the *Letter of the Apostles,* which uses it against the gnostics. Clement of Alexandria, for his part, appealed to an esoteric tradition of revelations given by the risen Lord to James the Just, John, and Peter, by these three to the apostles and then to the seventy, and so on (see below, ch. 14, sec. 2d). The idea of such dialogues did not take hold in the church, which in the course of the antignostic controversies of the century chose to renounce special traditions entirely, developing instead the orthodox model of a public tradition that went back to the apostles who had been with Jesus before his death and was then passed on to the bishops whom they appointed. This model was guaranteed by episcopal succession in the churches.

In addition, the predilection of the gnostics for revelations from the risen Lord was another example of their depreciation of the earthly Jesus in favor of the glorified Jesus. The "great church," for its part, held fast to the unity of the two and to the importance of the incarnation, thereby giving christological and soteriological priority to the earthly Jesus. Let us look briefly at some of the oldest dialogues.

a. Gnostic Dialogues

The *Apocryphon of James* (NHC I,2 1.1–16, 30) has an epistolary preamble, being addressed by James, brother of the Lord, to a personage of whose name only the ending is preserved *"-thos".* Scholars have thought of Cerinthus, an obscure individual who is opposed, along with Simon Magus, in the *Letter of the Apostles,* and contrasted by the tradition with the apostle John (Irenaeus, *Haer.* 3.3.4). He is variously described as a gnostic (*Haer.* 1.26.1; Hippolytus of Rome, *Elench.* 7.33.1–2) and as a millenarian (Gaius wanted to make him author of the Apocalypse of John; see above, ch. 4, sec. 2). James writes in order to satisfy the request of his addressee, who wanted to have the secret book given by the Lord to James and Peter. James has written it out in the Hebrew alphabet and sends it along with the request that it not be given to anyone else.

After a gap in the text, the narrative framework of the revelation begins: The Lord appeared to the Twelve 550 days after his resurrection and took James and Peter aside in order to "fill them" (with the Spirit). When the two disciples ask to be delivered from temptation, Jesus answers that they will be tempted and persecuted by Satan, but on that account the Father will love them. Like Jesus they must face martyrdom, because the kingdom belongs to those who believe in the cross. Some scholars judge this section to be a later addition. Further teachings follow, after which Jesus ascends to heaven and the two disciples return to the others.

It has been possible to show (as R. Cameron and H. Koester have done) that many of the utterances of Jesus in this dialogue are expansions of sayings found in the *Gospel of Thomas*, in John, and in the Synoptics. In addition, the text refers to well-known gospel parables such as the seed, the building, the torches of the virgins, the wage of the laborers, and so on. It has therefore been suggested that we see as the basis of the work a dialogue between the disciples and the earthly Jesus that would then have been placed in two settings: a narrative one connecting it with the post-resurrection situation, and an epistolary one. The statement in the narrative setting that at the moment of Jesus' appearance the Twelve were recalling what the Savior had said to each of them and writing it down in books, might provide the hermeneutical key to the work, for to "recall" the words of Jesus is often a technical term for "interpreting" them, and here the interpretation is connected with the writing. The work's content and form mark it as a kind of farewell discourse of Jesus, similar to those in John 15–17. In the present state of the text it is difficult to establish its date; it may go back to the second century.

In Codex V from Nag Hammadi there are, in succession, two writings that are both titled *Apocalypse of James*. In the work just discussed we saw James as recipient, along with Peter, of a special revelation; in these two works James is alone. This tradition of Jewish-Christian origin assigns great importance to James, the brother of the Lord (although the first of the two apocalypses hastens to say that he is brother only in a spiritual sense, that is, closely akin to Jesus). Traces of this tradition are found in the *Gospel of Peter*, in which the first appearance of the risen Lord is to James (see above, ch. 2, sec. 8c); in the passage of the *Hypotyposes* of Clement cited above; in logion 12 of the *Gospel of Thomas;* and in the *Gospel of the Egyptians,* in which "James the Great" is listed among the heavenly powers (NHC IV,2 64.13).

The *First Apocalypse of James* (NHC V,3 24.10–44.10) is composed of two dialogues between James and Jesus. The first takes place before the passion: Jesus instructs James on the powers of the Hebdomads (here subdivided into 72 heavens), which seek to prevent a passage between heaven and earth. He tells James of his own suffering and of the future martyrdom of James, who is anxious as to how he can escape the powers. Jesus assures him that after ascending to heaven he will reveal to James the latter's salvation. After the passion (30.12–31.1), Jesus appears again to James, comments on his passion, attributing it to the heavenly archons, and explains in detail how James can answer the heavenly "customs officers" who will attempt to restrain his spirit after death.

The end of the work, which is in a rather ruinous state, perhaps told of James' martyrdom. The work also explains the chain of tradition to which it appeals: James is to communicate the revelation to Addai, the apostle of Edessa in Syria (see Eusebius, *Hist. eccl.* 1.13, and the apocryphal *Teaching of Addai*). Thus there seems to be some contact between *1 Apocalypse* and Syria. Addai will put it in writing after the destruction of Jerusalem. It will then pass to a woman (the text is full of gaps here) and to her two sons, the younger of whom will preach perfect gnosis (36.13–38.10). Here, perhaps, is a connection to a notice in the *Elenchos* of Hippolytus of Rome (5.7.1; 10.9.3), according to which the Naassenes considered themselves trustees of a secret teaching of the Lord, which James had communicated to Mariamne. The work is Valentinian,

for it alludes to the myth of Sophia Achamoth. The influence of Jewish-Christian traditions is very strong and may be seen in, among other things, the connection of the
destruction of Jerusalem in 70 with both the death of Jesus and the martyrdom of
James the Just. For this latter connection see Hegesippus in Eusebius, *Hist. eccl.*
2.23.18, who also stresses the nickname "Just," which is central in both apocalypses.

The presence of the Jewish-Christian tradition with its pivot in James the Just is
even stronger in the *Second Apocalypse of James* (NHC V,4 44.11–63.32). The revelatory dialogue with the Savior is here only the central part of a discourse by James the
Just to the Sanhedrin prior to his execution; the discourse was supposedly written
down by one of the priests. It offers rather a vision of the glorified Lord than a true
and proper dialogue with the risen Jesus. In line with the general gnostic assessment
of him, James describes himself as equal to Jesus: "I [am the] first [son] who was begotten. . . . I am the beloved. I am the righteous one. I am the son of [the Father]"
(49.5–10; Robinson, 271). He is the foster brother of Jesus (50.11–23). In his discourse Jesus appoints James as his successor and gives him a central place in the history of salvation. After James's discourse, a detailed description of his martyrdom
shows numerous contacts with the account given by Hegesippus (Eusebius, *Hist. eccl.*
2.23). The fact that James utters his discourse standing on the fifth flight of the temple
steps (45.23–25) raises the question of its relationship to *The Steps of James (Ana-
bathmoi Iakōbou)*, an Ebionite work mentioned by Epiphanius (*Pan.* 30.16.7) and the
source of the account of James's death in the Pseudo-Clementine *Recognitions*
(1.66ff.; on this last work see vol. II of this history). This *Second Apocalypse* comes
from gnostics with strong roots in Jewish Christianity and probably goes back to the
second century.

The *Book of Thomas the Contender* (*Athlētēs* to be more accurate; the epithet belongs to the subtitle: *Book of Thomas: The Contender Writes to the Perfect*) takes us into
the area of western Syrian traditions. The work is probably to be dated to the beginning of the third century (NHC II,7 138.1–145.19). It takes the form of a dialogue between Jesus and Judas Thomas (the "twin" of Jesus; see above, ch. 2, sec. 11), which
took place between the resurrection and the ascension and was written down by
Mathaias (Matthew). In structure it consists of twelve statements of Jesus, of differing
length, interspersed with eleven questions from Thomas. The basic themes are self-
knowledge, hidden truth (in contrast to the visible body which is destined to perish),
and above all, fire: the fire of passion and the hellfire reserved for those who have
let themselves be "made drunk" by the fire of passion. Here we find an ascetical Platonism that urges the gnostic to leave the world of ignorance, which is described as a
prison and a cave.

It has been suggested (H.-M. Schenke) that the basis of the work is a Jewish-
Hellenistic sapiential treatise. The author describes himself as the "contender," a
name given to James in the Jewish tradition. This treatise was reworked by a gnostic in
the form of a dialogue between Thomas and Jesus, hence the twofold title. According
to others (e.g., J. D. Turner), the work arises rather from the combination of two
parts: a dialogue between Thomas and Jesus (down to 142.21) and a collection of sayings of the Lord in the form of a homiletic discourse that was edited by Mathaias,
hence the twofold opening attribution, which would be the work of the editor who
combined the two parts.

The *Gospel of Mary,* from the second century, has been partially preserved by two witnesses. There is a Coptic version that is the first work in P. Berolinensis 8502, in which it occupies the first eighteen pages and the beginning of the nineteenth, but it now lacks pages 1–6 and 11–14. The last part is preserved in the original Greek in P.Ryl. 3.463 (beginning of 3d c.). Another Greek fragment has recently been published from P. Oxyrhynchus 3525. The work is divided into two parts: the first is a dialogue between Jesus and the disciples before his departure (ascension). In the part preserved, Jesus answers a question of Peter about sin and explains that procreation perpetuates the wrongful mingling of spirit and matter. He then says farewell to the disciples and sends them to preach. After his departure they are fearful, and Mary strengthens them. Peter then asks her to share the words which the Savior spoke to her in private. She tells of a conversation she had with the Savior in a vision in which he described the journey of the soul through the heavens and the way in which it eludes the grasp of the celestial powers.

Andrew and Peter attack Mary, refusing to believe that she has received private and higher revelations, but Levi rebuts Peter's charge by saying that the Lord knows her well and evidently loves her more than them. This ending probably reflects tensions between the gnostic groups that produced the text and Christian circles that appealed to Peter and refused to accept other revelations. In general, Mary Magdalene was dear to the gnostics who made her equal or even superior to the Twelve, as well as the recipient of special revelations; in some texts she plays a role equivalent to that of the beloved disciple in John's Gospel.

From among the many other gnostic texts that fall into the genre of dialogues with the risen Lord it will suffice to mention: *Sophia of Jesus Christ* (NHC III,4 = BG,3); *Dialogue of the Savior* (NHC III,5); *Letter of Peter to Philip* (NHC VIII,2); the two *Books of Jeu* in the Codex Brucianus; and the *Pistis Sophia* (see below, ch. 9, sec. 4).

BIBLIOGRAPHY

K. Rudolph, "Der gnostische 'Dialog' als literarischer Genus" in *Probleme der koptischen Literatur* (ed. P. Nagel; Halle: Martin-Luther Universität Halle-Wittenberg, 1968), 85–107.

H. Koester, *Ancient Christian Gospels* (Philadelphia: Trinity/London: SCM, 1990) 173–200.

P. Perkins, *The Gnostic Dialogue: The Early Church and the Crisis of Gnosticism* (New York: Paulist, 1980).

H. Koester, "Gnostic Writings as Witnesses for the Development of the Sayings Tradition," in *Rediscovery of Gnosticism,* vol. 1 (ed. B. Layton; Leiden: Brill, 1980), 238–56.

b. Letter of the Apostles

The *Letter of the Apostles,* written in Greek, is preserved in its entirety only in an Ethiopic translation based on an Arabic version, as an appendix to the *Book of the Agreement (Mazchafa kidân).* It is preceded by an apocalyptic discourse of Jesus to the disciples in Galilee after the resurrection. This explains the frequent double numbering of the chapters of the *Letter,* which was introduced by Schmidt and depends on whether or not one takes into consideration the eleven chapters into which the preceding discourse is divided; here we shall list only the chapters of the *Letter* proper. This Ethiopic translation was first published in 1913 on the basis of five manuscripts; today we know of fourteen. A papyrus from the fourth-fifth century, discovered in 1895 but published only in 1919, contains parts of an Akhmimic Coptic translation which lacks in whole or in part, chs. 1–6, 21–22, 31–38, 49–51. In addition, some fragments of a Latin translation are contained in a palimpsest page in Vienna (5th–6th c.).

The work takes the form of a letter of the eleven apostles. Peter and Cephas appear as different persons in the list. The letter, which contains a revelation received from Jesus after his resurrection is addressed to all the churches and directed against the preaching of the false apostles Simon and Cerinthus (chs. 1–2). The presentation begins with a profession of faith in Jesus Christ that refers to the work of creation, then the incarnation and various episodes of his earthly life, including an extra-canonical story of the child Jesus and a schoolmaster that is found in the *Childhood of the Lord Jesus* and among the Marcosian gnostics. Emphasis is placed on the miracles: cures, miraculous catch of fish, multiplication of loaves (chs. 3–6).

After saying again that the occasion for the letter is the teaching of Simon and Cerinthus, which the apostles oppose with their own testimony (chs. 7–8), they describe the setting of the dialogue: on Easter morning, Mary and the other women, who were not believed by the apostles when they told them of the Lord's resurrection, return to complain of this to the risen Jesus. He accompanies them home, where he shows himself to the disciples and proves to them the reality of his body (chs. 9–12). At this point, the new revelation begins. This has to do first of all with the incarnation: Christ descended through the heavens in the form of the angels so that he would not be recognized. This motif is characteristic of other texts as well, especially the *Ascension of Isaiah*. Taking the form of the angel Gabriel, Jesus announces to Mary the birth of a son and he entered into her (chs. 13–14). He then exhorts the disciples to celebrate the Passover (ch. 15) and links with this the deliverance from prison of one of the disciples (Peter; see Acts 12:3ff.). Revelations follow that have to do with the Parousia, the mission of the disciples, the resurrection of the flesh along with soul and spirit (chs. 16–26), the descent of Christ to the lower world in order to preach to the just and the prophets and to baptize them (ch. 27), and the destiny of the just and with the judgment (chs. 28–30).

After predicting the call and apostolate of Paul (chs. 31–33), Jesus moves on to the evils of the last times and the manner in which the final judgment will take place (chs. 34–40). Next come instructions for the guidance of the community: the apostles must become fathers to those to whom they bring the revelation, servants insofar as they bring deliverance from sin through baptism, and teachers because they are to instruct and correct the faithful (chs. 41–46). An interpretation of the parable of the ten virgins (Matt 25:1ff.) is also applied to the life of the community; here the five who remain asleep are explained as the weakening of knowledge, understanding, obedience, patience, and mercy in an individual believer. Subsequent chapters deal with fraternal correction (chs. 47–49) and the reaction of those who are unwilling to hear correction and who preach alien doctrines and persecute those who admonish them (ch. 50). The work ends with a description of the Lord's ascension.

The work seems to have originated in a time of tension within the Christian community. The writer speaks out against those who not only preach false doctrines but are in a strong enough position to persecute true believers who criticize them. This idea is repeated at key points: at the end (chs. 49–50), and in chs. 37–38, where it is placed within the apocalyptic scenario of the evils of the last times and of the judgment. This setting generally serves in apocalypses as a criterion for evaluating a present situation. It was traditionally accepted that at the end of time the just would be few, so persecuted, minority, and marginalized groups fell back on an eschatological understanding of the present in order to ensure that they would be among the just. At the same time it offers, from the doctrinal viewpoint, a clear defense of the reality of Christ's incarnation (chs. 3; 13–14; 19; 39) and of his resurrection and that of believers, against a spiritualizing outlook that denied the resurrection of the body (chs. 11–12; 20–26). Also clear is the position taken in favor of free will and human responsibility (ch. 39).

In the persons of Simon and Cerinthus the author is, then, opposing adversaries with gnostic tendencies (see below, ch. 11) who had powerful influence in his environment. It is in this perspective that the literary form of a gospel (tradition about the life of Jesus) is combined with that of an apocalypse (a revelation of heavenly mysteries and, in particular, of events of the last times). Of interest is Paul's claim to the line represented by the apostles and, more specifically, his subordination to them ("I . . . will speak to him through you," ch. 33), also how he describes himself as apostle to the Gentiles, as in the Acts of the Apostles (chs. 31–33). The *Letter of the Apostles* uses the form of dialogue with the risen Lord, so dear to the gnostics, in order to combat them, opposing revelation to revelation. This tactic was not without risk. It would have no future in the "great church," once the latter had selected its canonical Gospels and had connected them with witnesses authorized by Christ. But this, of course, was not the situation in which the *Letter* was meant to play a part.

This work combines the literary forms of dialogue and apocalypse with that of the letter, by means of an opening which reveals specific polemical purposes: the revelation is not given privately to individual apostles but to the entire college, and is meant for everyone. On the other hand, the author's polemical situation leads him to sketch out, on the basis of the traditions available to him, the characteristics that define the community's identity: baptism and the confession of faith, preaching and teaching, mutual service, and the observance of the commandments. (J. Hills has a good study of these themes.)

The author knows the four Gospels and Acts but does not yet regard them as canonical, and he sees no difficulty in making free use of materials that would remain limited to the apocrypha, regarding the descent of the Savior into the world, the childhood of Jesus, the *descensus ad inferos*, and the resurrection of Christ. The place of composition of the *Letter* is disputed: generally speaking, scholars suggest Egypt or Asia Minor, less often Syria. Internal arguments seem to favor a date around 150.

BIBLIOGRAPHY

C. Schmidt, *Gespräche Jesu mit seinen Jüngern nach der Auferstehung: Ein katholisches-apostolisches Sendschreiben des 2. Jahrhunderts* (trans. from Ethiopic by I. Wajnberg; TU 43; Leipzig: Hinrichs, 1919); edition of the other texts, extensive study.

M. Hornschuh, *Studien zur Epistula Apostolorum* (Berlin: de Gruyter, 1965).

J. Hills, *Tradition and Composition in the Epistula Apostolorum* (Minneapolis: Fortress, 1990).

R. Cameron, "The Apocryphal Jesus and Christian Origins," *Semeia* 49 (1990): 1–176.

2. Childhood of Jesus

The Gospels of Mark and John show no interest in the birth and childhood of Jesus. Matthew and Luke, on the other hand, use various traditions about the circumstances of his birth. On the basis of a small set of shared information (names of the parents, Bethlehem as place of birth, virginity of the mother, annunciation by an angel), the two have independently developed stories that do not seem to mirror historical circumstances but are rather linked to theological reflection on the Messiah Savior, a descendant of David and messenger from God. The "infancy stories" in the canonical Gospels are organized into a more or less fragmentary narrative, Luke's being the more complex and structured. These short narrative units were not necessarily connected before, when they had circulated independently. The units often take shape as a result of meditation on Old Testament passages that were regarded as prophecies of the Christ, such as the so-called "formulaic citations" in the gospel of Matthew, which, not by chance, are plentiful in the first two chapters (see above, ch. 2, sec. 6).

The motif of Mary's virginity, despite its enormous popularity in later Christianity, has but a very limited place in the canonical Gospels; it is found only in Matt 1:18–25 and Luke 12:26–28, and there not without some tension with the context. Nevertheless, by the time these gospels were written, it was already a subject of interest in certain Christian circles. These had collected more or less authentic biblical *testimonia* on the subject, so as to emphasize the extraordinary character of the birth of Jesus, sometimes minimizing his humanity to the advantage of his divine identity. These *testimonia* sometimes then produced the story of their fulfillment; that is, accounts of the birth of Jesus were composed that corresponded to these passages regarded as prophetic.

In the Gospels of Matthew and Luke the stories of the birth and infancy were not independent of the narratives that follow, either theologically, for they expressed christological ideas in narrative form, or literarily, for they would have been meaningless apart from the gospels to which they belonged. But from the second century on, there appeared a tendency to compose works based either on the circumstances of the birth of Jesus and those that preceded it or on the period of his childhood, which the Gospels of Matthew and Luke passed over completely, except for the incident of the twelve-year-old Jesus in the temple with the teachers (Luke 2:41–50).

These later writings were a new kind of literary production, namely, "gospels" in which only those early phases of the life of Jesus were narrated. The tendency was to emphasize the miraculous element, which showed the divine plan at work not only in the ministry of Jesus but from his birth on and even before. These writings could still freely use the stories of Matthew and Luke, since the latter were only in course of becoming canonical. They joined these to the narrative elements of which we spoke above, making extensive use of biblical episodes that served as models, and showing that in the story of Jesus' origins the same structures were operative which had manifested the divine presence in the course of sacred history. All of this was brought together and developed by an imagination left free to create. This imagination was given ever freer rein in the successive rewritings to which these compositions were subjected without interruption right into the Middle Ages, since their texts were not protected and were even barred from canonization. We shall limit the discussion here to the two earliest writings in this genre, writings quite different from each other.

a. Birth of Mary

The author of the story tells us at the end (25:1) that he is James, stepbrother of Jesus. When the work was printed for the first time, in a Latin translation at Basel in 1552, by Guillaume Postel, the publisher gave it the title *Protevangelion* in order to emphasize the claim that the work was of very great antiquity, older even than the canonical gospels. Origen already knew the work as being by James (*Comm. Matt.* 10:17). It is in fact a pseudepigraphon whose author displays a considerable ignorance of Palestine and its customs. The title of the earliest manuscript is *Gennēsis Marias: Apokalypsis Iakōbou (Birth of Mary: Revelation of James)*. There are at least 140 manuscripts of the Greek texts, but Tischendorf used only eighteen for his edition. Among subsequent discoveries are some very old fragments, in particular the Turin Papyrus from the fourth century (containing 13.1–23.3) and, above all, P. Bodmer V, from the fourth century, which contains almost the complete text, but in a form that already shows secondary features.

There are, in addition to some Greek paraphrases, fragments of Latin versions, among them a ninth-century manuscript containing 8.1–25.2 (with gaps); a Syriac translation done in the fifth century and a witness to an early state of the text; translations into Georgian, Old Irish (translated from Latin), Armenian, Arabic, Ethiopic, Sahidic Coptic (two frags.); and an early Slavic version of which 169 manuscripts are known. The work thus had considerable success; when rewritten in Latin *(Gospel of Pseudo-Matthew: The Birth of Mary)* it exerted a strong influence on medieval piety, liturgy, and art in the West.

The birth of Jesus is the point of the story, but the subject indicated by the title *Birth of Mary* occupies the first part. A rich and devout Israelite, Joachim, has no children and finds himself prevented from offering his gift in the temple. Dismayed, he withdraws into the wilderness, while his wife Anna is in despair because of her barrenness. But the prayers of both are heard: an angel tells them of the coming birth of a child, which Anna promises to consecrate to the Lord.

Mary is born and is raised in a room that has been turned into a sanctuary, in order that she may not come in contact with anything profane. When she is three, her parents take her to the temple, where she remains to be reared by the priests and fed by an angel. When she is twelve, the onset of her puberty threatens to pollute the temple. The high priest Zacharias, in response to an angelic vision, calls together all the widowers in Israel and orders each of them to bring a staff. A miracle in the form of a dove, which comes forth from the staff, singles out Joseph, an elderly carpenter, to take Mary into his charge and safeguard her purity. When Joseph is absent on a job, Mary receives the angelic announcement and then goes to visit Elizabeth. After three months she comes home, where the returning Joseph finds her pregnant; he is miserable until an angel appears to him in a dream and reassures him, telling him of the birth of Jesus. Joseph is accused before the priests of having violated Mary's chastity. When both deny it, they are subjected to the test of drinking bitter water, from which both emerge vindicated.

When the order regarding the census comes, Joseph sets out with Mary. On the journey she feels birth to be imminent, and Joseph has her take refuge in a cave while he goes to find a midwife. During his search, he experiences an extraordinary cessation of movement throughout the universe, which (though he does not know it) signals the moment of the Savior's birth. Returning with the midwife, they find the cave, enveloped in a cloud. When this disperses, they discover the child already born and being nursed by his mother. As the midwife leaves the cave, she comes upon an acquaintance, Salome, to whom she says that a virgin has given birth. In her disbelief Salome wants to see for herself, but in punishment her hand is paralyzed; she repents, and it is made whole again. All this is followed by the episodes of the wise men and the slaughter of the innocents. Mary hides the child in a manger, and Elizabeth flees with her son John to a mountain, which miraculously opens up to conceal them. In revenge Herod's soldiers kill John's father, the high priest Zacharias. James, a son from Joseph's first marriage, takes refuge in the wilderness and writes down this story.

This summary is enough to show that the author has combined the stories in Matthew and Luke, while using some devices, such as the absence of Joseph, that help to harmonize the annunciation and Mary's visit to Elizabeth (Luke) with the consternation of Joseph on discovering Mary's pregnancy (Matthew). But the author has access to other current traditions and apparently feels authorized to make free use of them. For example, the tradition of the birth of Jesus in a cave (attested by Justin, *Dial.* 78, and later by Origen and others), obliges him to find a reason (the search being made by Herod's soldiers) for changing the scene to a manger in accordance with Luke (2:7, 12, 16). The blanking out of the other stars by the star of the wise men corresponds to an interpretation (known to Ignatius of Antioch, *Eph.* 19.2) of the cosmic importance of the birth of Jesus (victory over the forces of fate).

The story of the woman who doubts Mary's virginity is a narrative interpretation of a *testimonium* (Isa 7:13–14) that was widely applied to the birth of Jesus in a form in which the prophecy "a virgin shall conceive and give birth" was made the object of a debate proposed by God to human beings. The motif of the midwife who arrives too late is likewise a narrative development of another *testimonium* (this one apocryphal) that is attested elsewhere, according to which the birth of Jesus took place without pain and without a midwife. We referred earlier to biblical narrative structures: the opening story of the barren mother whose prayers are heard reflects Old Testament models, especially 1 Samuel 1, where Hannah, the mother of Samuel, is in a similar situation. The use of this model is therefore already meaningful in itself, since it signals the birth of a messenger from God to his people.

There is also a motif that explains the genesis of the entire work. This motif insists in an obsessive way on the absolute purity of Mary from her birth and her virginity even after childbirth, a feature foreign to the canonical Gospels. As early as 177–180, the pagan Celsus, in his critique of Christianity, took over a Jewish interpretation of the birth of Jesus: his mother was a poor weaver who was seduced by a Roman soldier and repudiated by her husband, and who then fled to Egypt (Origen, *Cels.* 1.28; 1.32, 39). The Jewish charge that Jesus was a bastard returns in the apocryphal *Acts of Pilate* (2.3), in the Talmud, and in later Jewish anti-christian polemics. In the present work, the purity of Mary is protected by the Jewish priests until her twelfth year; it is again ascertained by them after the test of the bitter water and it is confirmed by the Jewish midwife whom Joseph brings in, which explains the unusual emphasis on his search for a *Jewish* midwife (18.1, 19.1). These testimonies from authoritative Jews were probably intended to counter Jewish accusations of Jesus' illegitimacy, which evidently made the rounds in the author's world.

This intention accounts for the author's concern to explain that the brothers of Jesus named in the gospel tradition are his stepbrothers, the children of a first marriage of Joseph, and to make Joseph a man of venerable age, something that is completely alien to the canonical gospels but would subsequently play a major part in the stories of Jesus' infancy. This apologetic intention explains why the account becomes a glorification of Mary as it shifts the center of gravity in the stories of Jesus' birth to her, with important consequences for the history of Christian spirituality, and thereby introduces Mariology alongside Christology.

After a lengthy period in which the tendency of critics was to treat the work as a compilation from various sources, the trend today is to look upon it as a unified whole. It was certainly composed before the end of the second century, perhaps in Syria (as shown by contacts with such Syriac works as the *Ascension of Isaiah,* Ignatius of Antioch, and the *Odes of Solomon*) or, according to others, in Egypt.

b. Childhood of the Lord Jesus

The title is *Ta paidika tou Kyriou Iēsou* (*The Childhood of the Lord Jesus*). It is attributed to Thomas, who in some manuscripts is identified as a Jewish philosopher, in others as an apostle; but the first chapter, where this attribution occurs, is a late addition. The work is not to be confused with the *Gospel of Thomas* found at Nag Hammadi (see above, ch. 2, sec. 6). Although the work in question was combined with the *Protevangelium of James* in later apocryphal infancy gospels, it is completely different from the latter. It consists of disparate episodes from the childhood of Jesus between the ages of five and twelve. Such a structure evidently encouraged changes and, above all, additions. Furthermore, curiosity about a period in the life of Jesus that was left mostly in obscurity by the canonical Gospels, and the tendency, already noted above, to see his divine nature manifested in his childhood years likewise led to a gradual amplification of the work and an increasingly wider circulation.

It is understandable, then, that the work has a rich and extremely complicated textual tradition. Constantin von Tischendorf, editor of Greek and Latin texts in the last century, distinguished two Greek recensions, Greek probably being the original language, though some prefer Syriac. He published the first recension (A) on the basis of two manuscripts, those of Dresden and Bologna, and the second (B) and shorter from a Sinai manuscript. Since Tischendorf's day other manuscripts have been identified that are close to recension A, yet not simply attributable to it. In addition, we know now of a series of early translations, made between the fifth and seventh centuries, into Latin (frags. in a 5th-c. Vienna palimpsest), Syriac, Georgian, and Ethiopic. To a later period belong a second Latin translation (ed. Tischendorf) and an Old Slavic one. Later infancy gospels in Syriac, Armenian, Arabic, Old French, English, and Irish, which have used this work, likewise serve as witnesses in its reconstruction.

A comparison of the translations and recensions shows that Greek A, the best known form due to Tischendorf's publication, is one of the latest and most interpolated. Studies in recent decades are opening the way for a new critical edition.

It can be shown that some episodes circulated independently. For example, with a remark on *alpha* and *beta*, Jesus confounds the schoolmaster who wants to teach him the alphabet (twice in Greek text A: 6.3–4; 14.1–2). This episode already appears in the *Letter of the Apostles* 3. Irenaeus (*Haer.* 1.20.1) says that it was used by the Marcosian gnostics. The *Gospel of Truth* (NHC I,3 19.19–25) and the *Acts of Thomas* (79) also refer to it. In addition, it was a widespread fairy-tale motif. Other episodes, too, have analogies in Jewish and Christian texts.

There has been an emphasis, probably excessive, on the gnostic scope of many episodes. The preexistent Jesus has come to teach a hidden wisdom (6.2; 7.2–3). Those with whom he converses are "foreigners" (6.2), a typical gnostic term. Do the sparrows made of clay, which Jesus causes to rise out of matter and soar on high (2.2–4), symbolize the gnostics delivered by the redeemer? As we saw in such an episode used by the Marcosians, gnostics certainly employed the story. But as a result of the rewritings, these episodes, taken in their most obvious meaning, have fed the devotion and imagination of the people down to our own time.

Then, too, there is the Jesus who causes the death of the boy who bumped into him; who raises to life a friend who has fallen from the roof; who carries water in his cloak; who sows a single corn of wheat and reaps a tremendous harvest; who heals James when the latter is bitten by a poisonous snake; who rides a ray from the sun. In this gospel Joseph has an important role, whereas Mary barely puts in an appearance. The earliest form of the work goes back probably to the third century, but it is not possible to pinpoint the place of origin.

BIBLIOGRAPHY

E. de Strycker, *La forme la plus ancienne du Protévangile de Jacques* (Brussels: Société des Bollandistes, 1961).

For a critical edition of the *Childhood of the Lord Jesus* in Greek and Latin, one must still fall back on C. von Tischendorf, *Evangelia apocrypha* (2d ed.; Leipzig: Mendelssohn, 1986; repr., Hildesheim: Olms, 1987), although it is unsatisfactory as compared with the present state of our knowledge; ET: *New Testament Apocrypha* (ed. W. Schneemelcher; Louisville: Westminster John Knox, 1991), 1:439–51.

On the childhood of Jesus in the apocrypha, see W. Bauer, *Das Leben Jesu im Zeitalter der neutestamentlichen Apokryphen* (Tübingen: Mohr, 1909; repr., Darmstadt: Wissenschaftliche Buchgesellschaft, 1971).

H. R. Smid, *Protoevangelium Jacobi: A Commentary* (Assen: Van Gorcum, 1965).

E. Cothenet, "Le Protévangile de Jacques: origine, genre et signification du premier midrash chrétien sur la Nativité de Marie," *ANRW* II 25.6 (1988): 4252–69.

S. Gero, "The Infancy Gospel of Thomas: A Study of the Textual and Literary Problems," *NovT* 13 (1971): 48–80.

M. F. Foskett, *A Virgin Conceived: Mary and the Classical Representation of Virginity* (Bloomington, Ind.: Indiana University Press, 2002).

R. F. Hock, *The Life of Mary and Birth of Jesus: The Ancient Infancy Gospel of James* (Berkeley, Calif.: Ulysses Press, 1997).

3. Apocryphal Acts of the Apostles

Traditions about individual apostles and missionaries (e.g., Peter, Paul, Philip) circulated in the Christian communities even during their lifetimes, and were later used by Luke in composing the Acts of the Apostles. The literary form Luke gave to these traditions was determined by their placement in the second part of a work that ran from the birth of Jesus to the coming of the gospel to Rome, and by the fact that this second part had a bipartite structure in which a section about the Twelve in Jerusalem (chs. 1–12) was followed by another in which the protagonist was Paul (chs. 13–28). Despite the large amount of attention given to Paul, the intention of Acts was not to describe all of Paul's activity (it lacks, in particular, his martyrdom, of which Luke knew), but to chronicle the spread of the word of God to the center of the empire.

The writing of apocryphal *Acts* began during the period when the Acts of the Apostles was in process of entering the canon. The canonical Acts are understood as the acts of all the apostles (thus the *Muratorian Canon*), while the apocryphal take as their subjects the lives of individual apostles. The apocryphal *Acts* do not begin with the birth of their subject, but with his being sent on a mission to a particular territory. The *Acts of Thomas* begin by describing a tradition, later also cited by Origen (in Eusebius, *Hist. eccl.* 3.1.1–3), according to which mission territories were distributed to the apostles by lots. It is not known how other *Acts* began, for the beginnings of the very early ones have been lost, except for Thomas. They must have provided other ways of assigning missionary areas, while ensuring that no mission field was assigned to two apostles. The martyrdom of the particular apostle usually formed the conclusion of the work (the *Acts of John* excepted).

Between the assignment and the martyrdom come various episodes, which are united by the more or less emphasized motif of a journey. Consequently some *Acts* come closer to the literary genre of *praxeis* ("acts"), which is based on the sequence of a hero's actions (thus the *Acts of Peter,* in which a journey from Jerusalem to Rome served only to link the apostle's activities in the two cities), while other *Acts* are closer to the genre of *periodoi*, in which the movements of the hero from place to place have a decisive function (thus the *Acts of Paul* and of the *Acts of Andrew*). Since each apostle is identified by the mission entrusted to him, it is easy to understand why the journey motif must have become important. Still, even when the motif is emphasized, it serves mostly to link together the *praxeis.* In ancient rhetoric from Aristotle on, these *praxeis* had a quite special place in the *enkōmion* (discourse) celebrating a famous person.

In the Hellenistic period writers produced series of the marvelous actions by which specific divinities manifested their presence and beneficent power among human beings. Modern scholars have given the name "aretology" to this genre, and have recently called upon it to help explain the gospels. Indeed, the divinity often manifested itself through the deeds and sayings of some extraordinary personage. This was the genre used in the stories of philosophers and "holy men" in late antiquity, such as the

Life of Apollonius of Tyana by Philostratus, the *Lives of the Philosophers* by Diogenes Laertius, and the *Life of Plotinus* by Porphyry.

The apocryphal *Acts* share many traits with the aretologies, but they do not begin with the marvelous events that attended the birth of the individual and presaged his exceptional destiny; this describes rather the tendency of the tradition about Jesus. The aretologies in the *Acts* could begin only at the point when the activities of these men replaced that of the Master. From this point of view, the apocryphal *Acts* diverge from the *Lives* inasmuch as their content is the divine plan that continues its fulfillment in the midst of humanity through the apostles. In this setting, martyrdom represents the supreme *praxis* in which the divine power shows itself most clearly at work in the hero, who remains his own master until the very end.

Paradoxically, the apostle as pictured in the apocryphal *Acts* corresponds to the person who, as far as we can still discern, is censured in the New Testament as a "false prophet," especially in Paul's controversies with competing Christian missionaries at Corinth and elsewhere. Such a one represents a Christian preaching based on the efficacy of the *theios anēr,* who thereby attests to the power of his God, and not, as Paul would have it, on the testimony of the weak and suffering apostle through whom God nevertheless manifests all his power, as he did in the cross of Christ. But in an atmosphere such as we see in the first Christian centuries, which were characterized by free competition among the emissaries of various religions and divinities, it was natural to assimilate the apostle of Christ to the model generally used in spreading the worship of this or that divinity.

It has been observed (F. Bovon) that of the literary forms found in the gospels, the one especially developed in the apocryphal *Acts* is the one to which M. Dibelius gave the name of novella: an episode revealing the thaumaturgic power of the individual (Jesus in the gospels, the apostle in the apocryphal *Acts*). Unlike the gospels, however, these *Acts* do not consist for the most part of traditional material that has undergone a lengthy development. These *Acts* do indeed use preexisting elements in varying degrees, but literary inventiveness seems to be dominant, although this, as we shall explain further, does not exclude a theological intention.

In the narrative material, miracle stories generally treat the wonder as an end in itself, as in the stories of the dog who speaks, the broken statue that is restored, and the kipper that is brought back to life (*Acts Pet.* 9; 11; 13). Some episodes are downright comical, like the incident in which John finds his bed in a rundown inn to be infested with bedbugs; he speaks to the bugs and sends them away from his bed for the night (*Acts John* 60–61); but the story might have had an ascetical overtone because of the possible play on words between "bedbugs" *(korides)* and "girls" *(korai).* There is a rather notable presence of animals who participate in the redemption brought by the apostle, as when an ass gives a divine message to the apostle in the *Acts of Thomas* 39–41 (the allusion to Balaam's ass in Num 21 is explicit in the text). In the same work (69–74) some wild asses collaborate with the apostle in a marvelous way. In the later *Acts of Philip* a leopard and a kid are converted, follow the apostle, receive the Eucharist, and are buried in a church. This derives from Isa 65:25; the present time is identified with the eschatological era.

The spoken material contains prayers, hymns, missionary discourses, sermons, and dialogues. Narrative and speech go together in the conversion stories that typify this literature. The authors introduce into these stories novelistic plots very similar to those of the Hellenistic novel, as in the story of Drusiana, Andronicus, and Calli-machus in the *Acts of John* (63–86). The kinship between the apocryphal *Acts* and the secular Hellenistic novel has long been studied; even, and especially, the themes of the love story are extensively used. The apocryphal *Acts* are undoubtedly an instance of the adoption of existing literary genres by early Christianity, although, as noted ear-lier, this did not occur without a reorientation of the genre as dictated by the religious message to be communicated. The renewal of this literary tradition enabled the au-thors of the *Acts* to produce works that were sure of success and would contribute greatly to the spread of Christianity.

But what kind of Christianity? In the past, many scholars shared the conviction that the apocryphal *Acts* were products of gnosticism (R. A. Lipsius). In doing so, they were in fact reviving the viewpoint of the early "orthodox" tradition. However, the various works must be judged separately, and we need to keep in mind not only that they do not show a consistent doctrinal system, but also that their production and cir-culation took place in a setting in which people often did not see a clear difference be-tween orthodoxy and gnosticism.

Furthermore, some elements of the apocryphal *Acts* could attract gnostic groups and lead both to their adoption of these writings and to doctrinal changes and addi-tions. An exemplary case is the *Acts of John,* which contain in a discourse of Jesus a passage of obviously gnostic origin on suffering and the cross of light (94–102). On the other hand, the docetist expressions in the work (93) and what is said there of the many forms of the Lord (87–90) are not necessarily gnostic. In the *Acts of Peter,* the apostle, who is later crucified head downwards, speaks of the symbolic meaning of the cross in relation to the remedy brought by Christ for Adam's sin; this is certainly inspired by an esoteric tradition that repeats and interprets, among other things, a saying attributed to Jesus in the *Gospel of the Egyptians* (it will also influence *Acts Phil.* 140) but which in our view is not necessarily gnostic. It is difficult to assess the *Acts of Andrew* in this perspective, for they have come to us in a rather fragmentary state.

The gnostic element seems more accentuated in the *Acts of Thomas,* in keeping with the characteristics of Syrian Christianity. Thomas as twin of Jesus is a motif dear to the gnostic. In these *Acts,* too, there is included the "Song of the Pearl" (108–113), a splendid and doubtless preexistent short poem that features the myth of the divine element that has fallen into the world, where it is reawakened by the Savior, repre-sented by the heavenly letter, and brought back to its original dignity.

On the whole, and probably not by chance, the most "orthodox" of these works seem to be the *Acts of Peter* and the *Acts of Paul,* the two apostles to whom the "great church" chiefly appealed during the years when these first apocryphal *Acts* were being written.

Many of the apparently gnostic features of these works seem due to a reappraisal of the earthly dimension of life in favor of a striving for the life of heaven. Consistent with this tendency is the value put on asceticism and especially on sexual encratism, which is common to all these works. At the beginning of the *Acts of Thomas,* the apostle reaches India just in time to prevent, with the Lord's help, the consummation of the marriage of the king's daughter. A later text, the *Letter of Pseudo-Titus,* says that similar stories were to be found in the lost parts of the *Acts of John* and the *Acts of An-drew.* Furthermore, in the *Acts of Thomas* and those of Peter, Andrew, and perhaps of John, a woman acceptance of the given apostle's preaching leads her to abandon the marriage bed. This brings the husband's anger on the head of the man of God and is often the cause, direct or indirect, of the hero's martyrdom (Peter, Andrew). In the *Acts of Paul,* Paul's convert Thecla abandons her fiancé, who has Paul arrested. Paul is subsequently set free and Thecla escapes execution to follow the apostle as his collaborator.

Some scholars suggest that the apocryphal *Acts* originated in female circles for which the maintenance of sexual continence was a means of emancipation and of equality between the sexes at a time when the patriarchal model, as codified in the Pastoral Letters, was gaining a firm hold in the "great church."

The five earliest *Acts,* of differing origins, were composed in the second and third centuries. The *Acts of John* were probably composed in Egypt (or in Asia Minor, according to others) in the second half of the second century; about two-thirds of the text has survived. The *Acts of Peter* were composed in Greek, perhaps in Syria (or in Rome, according to others) toward the end of the second century. A papyrus fragment and the martyrdom have survived in Greek, but the largest part, except for the beginning, has come down in a Latin translation, probably of the third–fourth century in a single manuscript of the Capitular Library of Vercelli. An episode in a Coptic translation (but not in the Latin) is preserved in P. Berolinensis 8502 from Nag Hammadi (see below, ch. 9, sec. 4).

The *Acts of Andrew* were composed in the second century, perhaps in Achaia, and large sections have come down in Greek; there is a Coptic fragment, an Armenian translation of the martyrdom, and some rewritings in Greek and Latin. The *Acts of Paul,* mentioned by Tertullian in his work *On Baptism,* were composed before 200, probably in Asia Minor. Surviving in Greek is the section known as the *Acts of Paul and Thecla,* Paul's correspondence with the Corinthians (see above, ch. 1, sec. 4e), and the martyrdom. A Greek papyrus in Hamburg (ca. 300) and a Coptic papyrus in Heidelberg (6th c.), which contain parts of the three sections just mentioned, prove that these were originally parts of the same work. Another episode in a Coptic translation, on papyrus, is still unpublished; only the translation has been made known. There are also translations into Latin and various Oriental languages. The *Acts of Thomas* were composed in Syriac in eastern Syria at the beginning of the third century and preserved in a Greek translation and a Syriac rewriting.

In the fourth century these five *Acts* were brought together in a collection that was already known to Augustine. The collection was probably the work of Manichaeans and in any case was highly regarded by them. According to Photius (9th c.), the author of the five *Acts* was a certain Lucius Carinus; the name comes from the two individuals raised from the dead according to the Latin *Gospel of Nicodemus.* The last section of each of these *Acts,* which described the apostle's martyrdom, is preserved in the original language in many manuscripts, because it had been set aside as a liturgical reading for their feast days. The *Acts* as such, however, were repeatedly condemned by synods because of their doctrinal content, which was gnostic or otherwise inadequate or suspect according to the orthodoxy that had taken hold after their composition, and even more so because they had been adopted by heretical movements, the Manichees in the East and the Priscillianists in the West. However, the works continued to find readers, especially in monasteries. They were also expurgated and summarized, either because some passages were embarrassing from a doctrinal viewpoint or because of their length. In the West, a compilation in Latin known as Pseudo-Abdias enjoyed great success. In the East, summaries and extracts were preserved in menologies, that is, the collections of readings for the feasts of the saints.

Only the *Acts of Thomas* survives complete, while of the other original texts only more or less extensive sections, which are often difficult to link together, have survived. But the recent discovery by F. Bovon and B. Bouvier of a large part of the Greek original of the *Acts of Philip* in a monastery on Athos shows that we ought not give up hope of recovering some of what has been lost.

BIBLIOGRAPHY

R. A. Lipsius and M. Bonnet, *Acta apostolorum apocrypha* (3 vols.; Leipzig: Mendelssohn, 1891–1903; reprint: Hildesheim-New York: Olms, 1972; critical ed. of the Greek and Latin texts).

New critical editions, with translation and commentary, are appearing in Corpus Christianorum, Series Apocryphorum (Turnhout: Brepols). E. Junod and J.-D. Kaestli, *Acta Iohannis* (CCSA 1–2; 1983).

J.-M. Prieur, *Acta Andreae* (CCSA 5–6; 1989).

D. R. MacDonald, *The Acts of Andrew and the Acts of Andrew and Matthias in the City of the Cannibals* (Atlanta: Scholars Press, 1990).

There are English translations in *New Testament Apocrypha*, ed. W. Schneemelcher, vol. 2.

Studies

R. A. Lipsius, *Die apokryphen Apostelgeschichten and Apostellegenden* (4 vols.; Braunschweig: Schwetschke, 1883–1890; reprint in 2 vols.: Amsterdam: Philo Press, 1976).

F. Bovon, A. G. Brock, and C. R. Matthews, eds., *Les Actes apocryphes des apôtres: Christianisme et monde païen* (Geneva: Labor et Fides, 1981); ET: *The Apocryphal Acts of the Apostles* (Harvard Divinity School Studies; Cambridge, Mass.: Harvard University Center for the Study of World Religions, 1999).

Chapter 9

PROBLEMS OF TRADITION AND AUTHORITY: GNOSTICS AND MONTANISTS

1. Papias of Hierapolis

For this author we have a few scattered bits of information that are not entirely impartial. In one fragment (frag. 16, following the numbering of J. Kürzinger) Papias refers to the reign of Hadrian; he must therefore have written sometime during this emperor's time (117–138). Irenaeus of Lyons (*Haer.* 5.33.3–4 = frag. 1 of Papias) cites a saying of Jesus about the extraordinary fruitfulness of the soil in the kingdom, this last being depicted in very materialist colors; the passage has exact parallels in Jewish apocalyptic texts such as *1 En.* 10.19 and *2 Bar.* 29.5. According to Irenaeus, this was a tradition passed on to the presbyters by John, the disciple of Jesus, and put in writing by Papias, "who had heard John, was a companion of Polycarp, and an old man," in the fourth of the five books he composed.

Eusebius speaks of this work of Papias and dates the author to the time of Trajan, making him a contemporary of Polycarp and Ignatius (*Hist. eccl.* 3.36.2 = frag. 2). He lists him among the successors of the apostles (3.37.4 = frag. 3) and devotes a long chapter to him, to which we owe some of the most important fragments (3.39 = frag. 4). Eusebius transcribes the words of Irenaeus cited above and tells us that Papias's work was titled *Explanation of the Lord's Sayings.* Against Irenaeus, Eusebius asserts in his preface that Papias described himself as a disciple or direct hearer, not of the apostles, but of those (the presbyters) who had heard the apostles. To confirm this, Eusebius cites a passage from the preface in which Papias says that on every occasion he eagerly inquired of those who had been with the presbyters, what the presbyters had said: what Andrew, Peter, Philip, Thomas, James, John, Matthew and any other disciple of the Lord had said, as well as what Aristion and presbyter John, disciples of the Lord, had said. Papias speaks of his persuasion that what was written in books could not help as much as "what a living and abiding voice has said" (*Hist. eccl.* 3.39.4). Eusebius points out that Aristion and John the Presbyter had drawn extensively on the sources given in Papias' work.

This work came into existence at the point of transition between a living oral tradition of the sayings and actions of Jesus, and their being written down. That logia here includes both sayings and actions is clear from a further citation in which Papias explains the word as meaning "the Lord's sayings and doings," 3.39.15. Although Papias says that he prefers what is heard, considering this to be more lasting than writing, he nevertheless composes a truly literary work, as is shown by the careful wording of the preface, in order to establish the tradition about Jesus. Of course, Papias does not claim canonical status for his work or that it is the only authoritative testimony to the tradition. The passage preceding what he says about the presbyters reveals polemical intentions; he contrasts "those who have much to say" with "those who teach the truth"; he contrasts "those who call to mind alien commandments" with "those who call to mind the commandments which the Lord entrusted to faith and which come from Truth itself."

Here we can see that Papias's undertaking is inspired by a need to define the "true" tradition amid a swarm of traditions about Jesus. The standard he adopts is the verifiability of the chain of transmission—Jesus to the apostles to the presbyters to Papias—so that he can "guarantee its truth" (ibid.). The presbyters are to be understood, as later in Clement of Alexandria, not as ministers of the church but as itinerant apostles who are the carriers of tradition as links in a presumably unbroken chain since Jesus and the apostles. Unlike the writings of Clement, however, the fragments of Papias do not suggest anything esoteric about the tradition or parts of it. The historical trustworthiness of the traditions which Papias has gathered in this way is shown by the passage already cited from Irenaeus, which cannot go back to Jesus. The important thing is to see here an essential stage in the motives and decisions that led to the fixing of the Jesus tradition in writing.

Papias certainly did not inaugurate this practice; in his time various gospels had already been composed, among them the four that became canonical. In his work he passes on traditions about the composition of the gospels of Mark and Matthew (*Hist. eccl.* 3.39.15–16) that we discussed earlier (see above, ch. 2, secs. 5–6). In regard to Mark, Papias's concern is to ensure its authority as a written form of the sermons of Peter the apostle, and to defend it against charges of a lack of order in its composition (*akribōs . . . ou mentoi taxei,* "carefully, although not in order"). As for Matthew, he explains the connection between Matthew's original composition in Hebrew and the forms of it that were circulating in Greek.

Important though Papias's testimonies are because of their antiquity, we must not forget that they are inspired by an apologetic intention like that which led him to compose his own work: to discover where the chain of tradition going back to the apostles makes it possible to track down the authentic tradition about Jesus. Some later testimonies have placed Papias at a quite early point in that chain, making him the one who wrote the Fourth Gospel at the dictation of John the apostle (frags. 20 and 21). One of these fragments (21) links him, in a confused way and without historical warrant, with Marcion, who was supposedly unmasked as a heretic by Papias and chased away by John.

Other citations show that Papias reported not only sayings and actions of Jesus but also traditions, often anecdotal, about the apostles and other important individuals at the beginnings of Christianity. These include: the apostle Philip and his two prophetess daughters (not the Philip who was one of the twelve, but the deacon [Acts 8; 21:8–9]; similar confusion exists in Polycrates of Ephesus, cited in Eusebius [*Hist. Eccl.* 3.31.3]; their burial at Hierapolis could be a link with Papias); Justus Barsabbas, a candidate, along with Matthias, to replace Judas according to Acts 1:23–24 (frag. 4); a version of the death of Judas (frag. 5); the raising to life of the mother of Manaen (?); and the survival till the end of Hadrian's reign of some persons who had been raised to life by Jesus (frag. 16).

In his second book Papias supposedly narrated the deaths of James and John at the hands of the Jews (frags. 16 and 17). Papias supposedly applied himself also to the exegesis of the creation story: according to the *Commentary on the Apocalypse* of Andrew of Caesarea, Papias told the story of the fall of the angels to whom God had entrusted the government of the world (frags. 13 and 23). According to Anastasius the Sinaite he interpreted Genesis 1 as referring to Christ and the church (frag. 14), and the story of Paradise (Gen 2–3) as referring to the church of Christ (frag. 15). We do not know whether Papias did all this in the same work discussed above.

Finally, Eusebius (*Hist. eccl.* 3.39.12–13), Jerome (frag. 7; he depends on Eusebius), John of Scythopolis (frag. 11), Stephen Gobarus in Photius (frag. 18), and Photius himself (frag. 19) all say that Papias was a millenarian, that is, he believed that at the return of Christ the just would be resurrected first and would reign with him for a thousand years on an earth restored (as we saw) to a paradisal state. Eusebius, a strong antimillenarian, condemns Papias for this, describing him as a man of limited mind and accusing him of distorting what the apostles had said (*Hist. eccl.* 3.39.12–13). Indeed, Papias wanted to be the faithful conservator of traditions from the "presbyters," but these traditions sprang from a milieu such as that of Asia Minor, characterized by strong and concrete eschatological expectations. The same was true later of Irenaeus, who depended on the work of Papias and would put millenarianism at the service of his antignostic polemics.

BIBLIOGRAPHY

U. H. J. Körtner, *Papias von Hierapolis: Ein Beitrag zur Geschichte des frühen Christentums* (Göttingen: Vandenhoeck & Ruprecht, 1983).

J. Kürzinger, *Papias von Hierapolis und die Evangelien des Neuen Testaments* (Regensburg: Pustet, 1983); both works give text and translation of the fragments and an extensive bibliography.

J. B. Lightfoot and J. R. Harmer, *The Apostolic Fathers: Greek Texts and English Translations of Their Writings* (2d ed.; trans. and ed. M. W. Holmes; Grand Rapids, Mich.: Baker, 1992).

C. M. Nielson, "Papias: Polemicist against Whom?" *JTS* 35 (1974): 529–35.

2. The Shepherd of Hermas

This work was known from citations going back to the second century, but it was recovered only in 1885 in an Athos manuscript (15th c.), which lacks the final section (from *Sim.* 9.30.2 onward). The work is also in the famous Codex Sinaiticus (4th c.), which C. Tischendorf discovered between 1844 and 1859; here the Greek Bible is followed by the *Letter of Barnabas* and the Shepherd of Hermas, which, however, is preserved only down to *Mand.* 4.3.6. Fragments of the work have been recovered from numerous papyri (the latest thus far published is P.Bodm. 38), among which the most important is P.Mich. 129 (3d c.), which contains many sections of *Similitude* 2–9. Translations are also important: two in Latin, the first, known as the Vulgata, being very old (ca. 200) and very literal; the second, the Palatina (4th–5th c.), in a more correct Latin; one in Ethiopic; fragments of two Coptic versions, one in Sahidic, the other in Akhmimic; and one in Georgian, found recently and in course of publication. Currently, knowledge of the last part of the work depends on the translations, except for some Greek fragments.

In its present state the work has three parts: five *Visions* (Greek: *horaseis*), twelve *Mandates* (Greek: *entolai;* Latin: *mandata*), and ten *Similitudes* (Greek: *parabolai*), all of which correspond to revelations received and written down by the main figure, Hermas. The "Shepherd" who gives the work its title is Hermas's guardian angel, sent to him as a mediator and interpreter of the revelations. This personage, however, is introduced only after the fifth vision "in order to show you once again all that you have already seen," while in the first four visions the personage who plays that part is an old woman, who represents the church that exists before the creation of the world. Along with this difference there is another: the divergent titles of the fifth vision in the manuscript tradition: *apokalypsis* instead of *horasis* in the Sinaiticus, "fifth vision, beginning of the Shepherd" in the Vulgate, "the twelve mandates of the Shepherd" in the Palatine. Furthermore, the fifth vision has no content of its own, but contains only the announcement of the mandates and similitudes, along with an order to write them down.

Visions 1–4, therefore, were originally an independent work; they contain no reference to what follows, while *Vis.* 5.5 evidently refers to them. To these visions were added, in a second stage, the mandates and similitudes, which are mentioned together as a unified piece (*Vis.* 5.5–6; *Sim.* 9.1). This unity is reinforced when in *Sim.* 7.7 the similitudes as a body are called mandates, and when in *Mand.* 10.1.3 the mandates are described as parables. On the other hand, *Sim.* 9.1 clearly marks a new beginning after Hermas has written down the mandates and similitudes; something similar occurs in *Sim.* 10.1.1. *Similitude* 9, which alone is as long as the first eight together, develops at great length the parable of the tower from *Vis.* 3. *Similitude* 10 introduces the appearance of the supreme angel, the Son of God. These two similitudes seem to be later additions, with the second probably intended to serve as a conclusion.

The Shepherd of Hermas is thus made up of two parts: to the first, which consisted of visions 1–4 and circulated separately, was added the book of the mandates and the similitudes, with the fifth vision as an introduction. The whole was given two further additions, the last two similitudes. This theory, which N. Brox has taken over in his recent commentary, seems to us to explain the situation best, but we also agree with those who admit only one author and refuse to get into complicated hypotheses that multiply authors (as many as six). Any lack of internal cohesion is better explained by the juxtaposition of the elements of varying provenance than as indicators of disparate documents or authors.

Let us briefly outline the contents. The first vision begins with some unusual "autobiographical" information: in Rome Hermas sees his former mistress (he had therefore been a slave) as she is bathing in the Tiber, and he, though married, desires her. Some days later, while on the road to Cumae, he is carried by the Spirit to a solitary place, where the same woman appears to him from heaven, explains to him that his mere thoughts have made him guilty, and urges him to pray for the healing of sins, his own and those of all. While he remains there in confusion, a chair appears to him and an old woman comes and sits on it. She rebukes Hermas in a kindly way for not having properly educated his children, but at the same time tells him that God is merciful to him and his family. She then reads to him from a book containing revelations impossible to remember.

In the second vision, which takes place a year later in similar circumstances, the woman reappears and gives him the heavenly book, which Hermas copies without understanding it, after which the book disappears. After fourteen days of fasting and prayer Hermas is able to grasp the meaning of the book: it contains an order that Hermas henceforth practice sexual abstinence and, more important, that he let the church's authorities know that God is granting believers a second and final chance to repent and wipe away sins (*Sim.* 9.26.6), the first opportunity having come in baptism, which in early Christianity was widely regarded as the final chance (see Heb 6:4–8; 10:26–31; 12:16–17; 1 John 3:6). Also revealed to Hermas is that the woman is the church, old because she existed before the foundation of the world, according to an idea that goes back to a very early Jewish-Christian theology.

In the third vision Hermas is shown six young men in the act of building, on water, a tower of shining stones that are carried in by countless other people. Some of the stones, brought up from the depths of the water, fit well into the structure; some of those brought from the land are thrown away or even broken up. The vision is explained to him: the tower is the church, built by six angels who were created first (the seven angels created first likewise belong to Jewish and Jewish-Christian tradition; in the Shepherd the seventh is the Son of God, represented as an angel). The tower is built on water because salvation comes from the water of baptism. The stones correspond to the various types of believers: those that fit perfectly are apostles, bishops, teachers, and deacons who have lived holy lives; those drawn from the depths of the abyss are the martyrs; those thrown not far from the tower are those who have sinned but are disposed to repent and who can be used as long as the tower is being built; those broken and thrown far away are sinners beyond retrieval; and so on. Further visions, among them one of seven young girls representing the seven virtues, and a vision of the church that gradually grows young, are also explained allegorically.

In the fourth vision Hermas sees a huge marine monster, a symbol of coming tribulation, and a girl with white hair, in whom he recognizes the rejuvenated church.

In the fifth vision appears the Shepherd, who is to remain always with Hermas and who tells him to write down mandates and parables. The twelve mandates have to do with faith in God, fear, and continence; simplicity and blamelessness in relations with the neighbor; love of truth; chastity, and relations with a spouse guilty of adultery; second marriages after the death of a spouse (not prohibited); patience and anger; the way of justice and the way of wickedness, and the two angels associated with them; fear of God and not of the devil; vices to be avoided and good works to be done; praying without discouragement; the sadness that drives away the Holy Spirit, and joy; true and false prophets in the community, and the ways of recognizing them (by their behavior in the liturgical assembly); and evil and good desires.

The first parable or similitude has to do with the situation of Christians as strangers on earth and bound to obey the laws of their true city, which is in heaven. The second presents the elm and the vine as symbols of the rich and the poor who must support one another, the former helping the latter with their possessions, and the latter helping the former with their prayers. The third and fourth similitudes use a group of dry winter trees to signify the undifferentiated condition of the just and the sinners in the present world, and a group of trees of which some are blooming, some withered, to symbolize the difference between the just and the sinners on the day of the Lord. The fifth similitude shows a faithful slave who, because he has taken good care of his master's vine during the latter's absence, is set free and made co-heir with the master's son; the reference is to the man Jesus, in whom the Holy Spirit dwelt as a divine principle and was so well served that the flesh obtained its reward. We have here an archaic "pneumatic" Christology in which Christ is seen as a human being indwelt by the Holy Spirit. Thus there is not always a distinction between the preexistent Son and the Spirit; Hermas is not entirely clear on this point.

The sixth parable, which is connected with the theme of the two ways, shows two shepherds, namely, the angel of pleasure and error and the angel of punishment. This theme is continued in the seventh parable, which has to do with tribulations inflicted on Hermas as a punishment. In the eighth there appears a large willow tree that covers plains and mountains; this is the law of God that is given to the world and is identical to the proclamation of his Son throughout the world. The details of the vision are given a meticulous allegorical interpretation as referring to the members of the church. The ninth similitude, as was said earlier, is a full repetition of the vision of the tower, with many new details and modifications (e.g., the stones taken from the water are now not the martyrs but the baptized, *Sim.* 9.16). In the tenth, the Son of God appears and exhorts Hermas regarding his future life.

The central point in the message of the Shepherd of Hermas is the announcement of a second repentance, offered to Christians after baptism; this motif returns repeatedly throughout the different parts of the work. The conviction that there was no further forgiveness of sins after baptism had been linked to the expectation of Christ's imminent return; as this expectation gradually weakened and Christianity spread, it became less and less realistic to maintain this position. Hermas wants a community that retains a strong moral code (whence his discussions of the mutual behavior of Christians and of the virtues and vices), but without rigorism; he looks for a way to satisfy these two requirements in the possibility of one, and only one, repentance that will wipe out sins. The allegory of the tower is meant to make it clear that the time for repentance is not unlimited. The work ends with the tension between the announcement that work on the tower is being suspended in order to allow for repentance, and the exhortation to make haste because the tower is almost finished (*Sim.* 10.4.4). In *Vis.* 3.8.9 this tension is connected with a refusal to say how close the end is.

The Shepherd as a whole takes the form of an apocalypse inasmuch as a heavenly mediator brings a human being a revelation of divine mysteries, with the help in particular of visions and allegories. Motifs such as a heavenly book or letter are also typical of apocalypses, as is the parenetic element. Lacking here, however, is any description of the history of the world, and especially of the end events as the visible face of a struggle between spiritual forces. Hermas chooses the apocalypse form in an effort to give his message the highest authority by linking it directly to God. Hermas's intention is to propose a decisive change in the prevailing rigorist view. He acknowledges the authority of the church's presbyters, but wants his message to take precedence over that authority. This accounts for the vivid picture in *Vis.* 3.1.8, in which

Hermas is invited to sit beside the Lady but says: "lady, let the presbyters take the first places." But she makes him sit down at once, though not at her right hand, which is reserved for the confessors and martyrs.

In this context, we certainly think that Hermas writes under his real name. In this respect, too, his book differs from the Jewish apocalypses and most of the Christian ones as well, but not from the canonical Apocalypse, which in all probability is not pseudepigraphical.

It is difficult to identify exact sources for the work. In it there are echoes of the Old Testament and points of contact with writings destined to become part of the New Testament, especially with Ephesians and James. The only source that Hermas explicitly cites (*Vis.* 2.3.4) is a lost apocryphal work, *The Book of Eldad and Medad* (which was inspired by Num 11:26). There are also influences from revelatory literature and from Jewish and pagan pareneses. Attention has been called especially, among pagan texts, to the *Poimandres,* a treatise in the *Corpus Hermeticum,* and to the so-called *Table of Cebes.* But these are matters of resemblances and allusions, not of specific references and citations.

Hermas provides a great deal of information about himself and his family. A former slave, he goes into business, but misfortune brings the loss of all his profits. He is married, but he does not have an easy life with his wife, and his children lead disordered lives. Not all of this, indeed, is strict truth, and many details are meant to be symbolic, but there is probably a solid basis for it, especially since, as everything suggests, Hermas writes under his real name, so that what he writes must be, at least to some extent, verifiable by his readers.

The *Muratorian Canon* (lines 73–80) allows private but not liturgical reading of the Shepherd, because "Hermas wrote it quite recently, in our time, in the city of Rome, when his brother Pius was occupying the [episcopal] chair of the city of Rome." This entry is tendentious inasmuch as it seeks to make the date of the Shepherd recent in order to exclude it from the canon. Still, the information seems quite reliable, because it is possible to regard Hermas as the brother of Bishop Pius (140–55) and to locate the composition of the work during those years and in Rome.

A dating to the first half of the second century is confirmed by the fragment in P.Mich. 130, from the second century (even, according to some, from the first half of the second century), and by citations and references beginning with Irenaeus (*Haer.* 4.20.2; etc.). Clement of Alexandria had the highest regard for the work; in one instance (*Strom.* 6.131.2–4) he gives an allegorical interpretation of a passage from Hermas alongside another of a passage from Isaiah. As is attested not only by these citations but also by the presence of the work at the end of Codex Sinaiticus, a manuscript of the Bible, and by the precise information in the *Muratorian Canon,* the Shepherd, despite its artlessness and even its clumsiness, for a long time enjoyed almost a canonical authority in both East and West, not just because of its antiquity but also because of its serious moral teaching.

Bibliography

M. Whittaker, *Der Hirt des Hermas* (vol. I of *Die Apostolischen Väter;* GCS 48; 2d ed.; Berlin: Akademie Verlag, 1967); critical edition.

R. Joly, *Hermas. Le Pasteur* (SC 53; 2d ed.; Paris: Cerf, 1968); edition, translation, introduction, and notes.

N. Brox, *Der Hirt des Hermas* (KAV 7; Göttingen: Vandenhoeck & Ruprecht, 1991); extensive commentary with a vast bibliography.

C. Osiek and H. Koester, *Shepherd of Hermas: A Commentary* (Hermeneia; Minneapolis: Fortress, 1999).

M. B. Cunningham and P. Allen, eds., *Preacher and Audience: Studies in Early Christian and Byzantine Homiletics* (Leiden: Brill, 1998).

K. P. Donfried and P. Richardson, *Judaism and Christianity in First-Century Rome* (Grand Rapids, Mich.: Eerdmans, 1998).

3. Marcion, the Marcionites, and the Earliest Refutations

In the Roman church during these same years, but dealing with an entirely different set of problems in an entirely different spirit testifying to the variety of settings, we come face to face with Marcion. His place in the history of literature is small, given the loss of his writings, but he is very important in the history of theology. The surviving sources of information about him are the writings of his adversaries. These include: a few lines by his contemporary, Justin Martyr (*1 Apol.* 26.5; 58.1–2), who must have dealt with him in much greater detail in his *Syntagma against Heresies,* so much so that this work could be cited as *Against Marcion* (Irenaeus, *Haer.* 4.6.2; Eusebius, *Hist. eccl.* 4.11.8); a short notice in Irenaeus (*Haer.* 1.27.2–4; see also 3.12.12; 4.33.2; Irenaeus also refers to him in a polemical way, with or without naming him, in many passages of his work); and numerous lost refutations (see below).

The fundamental source, however, is the *Against Marcion* of Tertullian, the third and only surviving edition of which dates from 207 to 212. Tertullian not only attacks the principles of Marcion's theology, but also discusses in detail his canon of sacred Scripture and many passages of his *Antitheses,* which can be partially reconstructed, although with many uncertainties (the work of A. von Harnack is indispensable here). Attacks on Marcion in other works of Tertullian have much less documentary value. Other important sources are: Clement of Alexandria in various passages of his *Miscellanies,* especially on Marcion's anticosmicism and encratism; Hippolytus of Rome, *Elench.* 7.29–31; Epiphanius, *Panarion* 42 (he too cites some passages from Marcion's text of the Bible); Adamantius, *Dialogue on the Orthodox Faith;* Ephraem the Syrian, *Prose Refutations of Bardesanes, Mani, and Marcion* and *Hymns;* Eznik of Kolb, *On God.* These last three authors in particular have in view later developments of Marcion's teachings.

Marcion, born perhaps ca. 85, was a native of Sinope in Pontus, on the Black Sea, and was a wealthy shipowner. According to the lost *Syntagma* of Hippolytus, he was the son of a bishop and was thrown out by his father for having seduced a virgin; but this detail was evidently a later invention, meant to symbolize a heretic who corrupted the virgin church. Other bits of information that connect Marcion with Papias and even with John the apostle in Asia are legendary. Nor should any greater credence be given to a meeting with Polycarp (in Asia? on occasion of Polycarp's visit to Rome?) during which the bishop spurned Marcion as "firstborn of Satan."

Marcion emerges from the world of legend only with his coming to Rome (ca. 139), where he gave the community a gift of two hundred thousand sesterces. According to Irenaeus, Tertullian (*Marc.* 1.2.3), and the later heresiologists, in Rome Marcion was a disciple of Cerdon, a personage of whom we know almost nothing, for statements about his thought seem in large measure to project Marcion's teachings onto him. Cerdon seems to have wavered for a long time between heterodoxy and a profession of faith within the church. Marcion, however, made a clean break with the Roman church when, in a disagreement with its leaders in 144, he was unable to get them to accept his doctrine of two gods and his interpretation of Paul. Marcion left for the East where he proselytized with great success and where he died. When Justin wrote his first *Apologia,* Marcion was still alive, which places his death at probably around 160 or a little later.

A collection of Paul's letters was in circulation in Rome. This church, which was of Jewish-Christian origin (see our discussion of Paul's Rom, and *1 Clem.*), did not, however, make the most of the more radical aspects of the apostle's theology with its opposition between law and grace. Paul was respected there as an apostle and martyr and not as a theologian. Marcion knew the writings of Paul and some gospels; in addition to the gospel of Luke, the only one he accepted, he certainly knew at least the gospel of Matthew. From his reading and meditation on Paul and the gospels and his comparison of them with the Hebrew Bible that Christians had taken over as their own, Marcion concluded that the revelation contained in the Hebrew Bible was incompatible with the revelation brought by Jesus.

Jesus proclaimed a God different from the God revealed to the Hebrews as creator of the world and human beings. The very revelation of this creator-God showed his imperfection: he created a world for himself that he might exercise power over it. On the humanity he had created, especially the people of Israel, he arbitrarily imposed a law on the basis of which he judges and rewards or punishes. His nature, then, is strictly retributive justice; nor does he even respect the rules of fair play, since he takes satisfaction in leading human beings into temptation. He did not even manage to anticipate the sin of Adam. His rages, his changes of plans, and his capriciousness show how like he is to this lowly world and how distant from the idea any educated person can conjure up of the supreme divinity. Limited as he is, this God is ignorant of the existence of another God who is far superior to him and who is well aware of this inferior God and his creation.

When this supreme God, whose nature is goodness, saw human beings crushed by their creator, he was moved to pity and sent his own Son to ransom them, by his own death on the cross, from the God who legally owned them by virtue of having created them. The Son of the supreme God also told them that they could remove themselves from that just God and reach happiness in the kingdom of the father of Jesus. They had, however, through faith in Jesus and his gospel, to accept the grace offered to them.

Marcion's lever was the Pauline opposition between the law and the gospel, which he saw as an opposition between two different gods. However, he could not fail to see also that Jesus in the gospels and Paul often appeal to the God of the Law. From this fact and also from Paul's attacks, especially in Galatians, on false brethren who clung to the practices of the law and, in defense of the "truth of the gospel," even on Peter (Gal 2:11–14), Marcion drew a conclusion: even the first disciples of Jesus had not correctly understood his preaching, and "Christians" who were attached to Judaism and the law had increasingly preached Jesus as Son of the Creator and had taught obedience to the law. This, according to Marcion, kept them from being saved, because they were subordinating salvation to obedience to the creator, an obedience from which Jesus had come to deliver human beings.

According to Marcion, Christ had returned to heaven and had communicated his authentic gospel to Paul at the moment of the latter's conversion. But the writings of Paul were interpolated anew by Judaizers after his death, so that the entire church was now at the mercy of error. Marcion felt called to remedy the situation by bringing the authentic gospel to light. In his view, this authentic gospel was to be found in the letters of Paul, of which Marcion uses ten, without the Pastorals and Hebrews. Furthermore, Marcion identified Luke as the gospel to which Paul often refers as "my gospel." He needed, of course, to purify these writings of what he regarded as Judaizing interpolations. He maintained that the end result of his work was the only place in which the true gospel of Jesus could be found.

Marcion was thus the first to establish a canon of the Christian Scriptures. This was extremely restricted as compared to the canon that would become the Bible of the church, because Marcion rejected the entire Old Testament as the revelation of a different God, and the entire remainder of Christian tradition as being contaminated by Judaism. Many scholars, in particular H. von Campenhausen in his classic 1968 work on the formation of the Christian Bible, regard Marcion as the inventor of the very idea of a Christian Scripture, and they see the canon of the "great church" as a response to that of Marcion. But a more nuanced approach seems advisable, placing Marcion and his opponents within the framework of a larger process, in which Christians faced the question of the authentic revelation concerning Jesus and his work, and of the criteria for identifying this tradition. As we have seen and will see again, different answers were given these questions by Papias, the gnostics, Irenaeus, and Clement, to name but a few examples. A similar process was going on in Judaism during the same decades, as the third part of the Hebrew Bible, the Writings, was solidly established and the Mishnaic traditions were codified.

To this document or tool *(Instrumentum)* containing the Scriptures Marcion prefixed another work, the *Antitheses*, in which he justified his theological theses by showing how the two revelations were irreconcilable. In it he also grounded his negative judgment on the theology of the church, which appealed to the tradition of the Twelve. At the beginning of the work he gave his interpretation of the already-mentioned meeting of Peter and Paul in Antioch (Gal 2:11–14); this allowed him to place Peter and the other apostles in opposition to the "truth of the gospel" as represented by Paul. Because of its implications, which were both theological and ecclesiological, Galatians was Marcion's main document, and he placed it at the beginning of the Pauline letters in his *Instrumentum*. The *Antitheses* must also have included exegeses of the texts that Marcion accepted, as is shown by the knowledge Tertullian and others had of those interpretations; today, however, it is impossible to form an accurate idea of the work. Tertullian also mentions a letter of Marcion, now lost, but this was perhaps a work of second-century Marcionites.

A probably original Marcionite document, but not from Marcion himself, is preserved in seven short Latin prologues to the letters of Paul, which are given in Marcion's order: Galatians, Romans, Thessalonians, Laodiceans (prologue not preserved, but an idea of it can be gotten from the next prologue; "Laodiceans" was Marcion's name for our Ephesians), Colossians, and Philippians. These prologues can easily be distinguished from a larger body containing prologues to the other letters of the corpus (except for Hebrews); the latter are found as introductions to the Pauline letters in the majority of manuscripts of the Vulgate, but they were already present in the early Latin translation. The prologues in question consider the letters to be so many witnesses to Paul's struggle in defense of the faith, the truth, and the gospel against false apostles who were pleading on behalf of the law and circumcision. The Marcionite character of the prologues was shown at the beginning of this century and, despite recent energetic efforts to deny it, must be reaffirmed because their content matches very specific traits of Marcionite teaching. The prologues can be dated to the end of the second century and the beginning of the third.

Marcion's excellent organizational abilities and the attractiveness of his teaching won him great success, short-lived in the West but lasting in the East, where the Marcionites were still strong in the fifth century. They succumbed at last to persecution by emperors who wanted the empire to be unified religiously.

In the second half of the second century Marcion was seen as the adversary par excellence, and many writers combated him in works that are now largely lost. We earlier mentioned Justin, on whom later heresiologists often depended. Irenaeus of Lyons (*Haer.* 4.27–32; see below, ch. 13, sec. 1b) has preserved the antimarcionite treatise of an anonymous presbyter of Asia Minor who had heard Marcion around 170 at the latest; the treatise refuted interpretations of the Pentateuch which were certainly to be found, at least in part, in the *Antitheses* and by means of which the Marcionites showed up the imperfect character of the Creator. Eusebius (*Hist. eccl.* 4.23) mentions seven "catholic" letters written by Bishop Dionysius of Corinth (in the time of Marcus Aurelius) to as many churches, plus one to an individual, a Christian woman named Christophora. In one of these letters, addressed to Nicomedia, the bishop combated Marcion. In another, addressed to the Romans and their bishop Soter, he praised their zeal in comparison with the other churches. We know nothing of the antimarcionite writings of Philip of Gortyna and Modestus (Eusebius, *Hist. eccl.* 4.25). Also lost are those of Melito of Sardis (mentioned by Anastasius the Sinaite, but not by Eusebius) and Theophilus of Antioch, whose work may have been used by Irenaeus (S. F. Loofs).

Finally, Eusebius provides valuable citations (*Hist. eccl.* 5.13) from an antimarcionite work by a certain Rhodon, who came to Rome from Asia Minor and was a disciple of Tatian. Rhodon emphasized the splintering of the Marcionites and gave information on the teaching of Apelles, a Marcionite and older contemporary of Rhodon, who had developed Marcion's teaching along gnostic lines: he professed a single principle, while others, like Marcion before them, allowed for two of them. We know that Apelles wrote 38 books of *Syllogisms,* fragments of which Ambrose has preserved in his *On Paradise;* Apelles also wrote some *Revelations.* Other fragments of his works are preserved by Tertullian, Hippolytus, Filastrius, Epiphanius, and others.

BIBLIOGRAPHY

A. von Harnack, *Marcion: Das Evangelium vom fremden Gott. Eine Monographie zur Geschichte der Grundlegung der katholischen Kirche* (TU 45; 2d ed.; Leipzig: Hinrichs, 1924; repr., Darmstadt: Wissenschaftliche Buchgesellschaft, 1960, 1985); still essential.

E. Norelli, "La funzione di Paolo nel pensiero di Marcione," *RivB* 34 (1986): 543–97.

B. Aland, "Markion/Markioniten," *TRE* 22 (1991): 89–101.

K. Tsutsui, "Das Evangelium Marcions: Ein neuer Versuch der Textrekonstruktion," *AJBI* 18 (1992): 67–132.

L. M. McDonald and J. A. Sanders, *The Canon Debate: On the Origins and Formation of the Bible* (Peabody, Mass.: Hendrickson, 2002).

On the Prologues

E. Norelli, "La tradizione ecclesiastica negli antichi prologhi latini alle epistole paoline," in *La tradizione: forme e modi. XVIII incontro di studiosi dell'antichità cristiana, Rome, 7–9, Maggio 1989* (Rome: Augustinianum, 1990), 301–24.

The fragments of Apelles are published in A. von Harnack's *Marcion: Das Evangelium von fremden Gott* (TUGAL 45; Leipzig: Hinrichs, 1921), 404–420; ET: *Marcion: The Gospel of the Alien God* (trans. J. E. Steely and L. D. Bierma; Durham, N.C.: Labyrinth, 1990).

E. Junod, "Les attitudes d'Apelles, disciple de Marcion, à l'égard de l'Ancien Testament," *Aug* 22 (1982): 113–33.

On Dionysius of Corinth, see P. Nautin, *Lettres et écrivains chrétiens des IIe et IIIe siècles* (Paris: Cerf, 1961), 13–32.

4. Gnostics

We shall discuss the gnostics here in the context of problems of tradition and authority, because their teachings had important implications in the Christian churches, and because we think it appropriate (see below) to situate gnosticism historically in the vast process by which Christianity defined itself. But gnosticism is a very complicated phenomenon, and scholars continue to debate its definition and historical placement. Far from dealing exhaustively with this problem, we restrict ourselves here to some points that will be useful in situating the remaining gnostic texts.

The very name "gnosticism" is already problematic, since the ancient heresiologists who combated it applied to an extensive set of groups, only a minority of which applied the name "gnostics" to themselves. The early ecclesiastical writers saw gnosticism as a heresy, that is, a recent departure from the tradition of true teaching that came from Christ and the apostles. According to the heresiologists, it was a movement within Christianity that was inspired by the devil (Justin already uses this language), broken up into divergent groups and sects, all desirous of innovating instead of preserving sound doctrine unchanged. The ecclesiastical writers described these groups as interdependent in a kind of genealogy of error that had its origin in Simon Magus, a contemporary of the first Christian missionaries, and soon grew like a multiheaded hydra.

The heresiologists knew, however, that gnostic groups also appealed to a tradition received from Christ and, more particularly, to a secret teaching given by the risen Lord to certain disciples and passed on in an esoteric fashion. Thus Valentinus claimed to be a disciple of Theudas, who had been a follower of Paul (Clement of Alexandria, *Strom.* 7.106.4); Basilides appealed to Glaucia, a disciple of Peter (ibid.) or, according to others, to the apostle Matthias (Hippolytus of Rome, *Elench.* 20.7.1). In that manner the gnostics claimed a place in the coexisting and competing throng of traditions, linked with the disciples of Jesus and passed on orally, that formed the soil in which the earliest Christian doctrines developed. We referred to this above in connection with Papias, and Clement of Alexandria later would find this situation to his liking.

All this, however, is only the formal side of the situation. Gnosticism took primitive Christian thought and incorporated it into a systematic intellectual structure, the fundamental lines of which came largely from earlier intellectual and religious traditions that were alien to Christianity. In Greek "gnosis" means "knowledge"; gnosticism asserted that human salvation was made to depend on a knowledge reserved to a few elect. This knowledge, obtained through revelation, pertained to the true nature of the self, which comes to recognize itself as part of the divinity, as a divine spark which, by a process not depicted uniformly, became separated from its source and was debased and imprisoned in the material world. This world was the creation of lesser divinities and the self could not be liberated from it by its own powers; indeed, human beings do not even remember their true origin.

God therefore sends a savior who acts essentially as a revealer: through his preaching he brings those who possess the spark to consciousness of their true origin and thus of their true nature, which is incomparably superior to the matter in which it is sunk. They are thus given the knowledge *(gnōsis)* that assures them salvation in the form of a deliverance, which remains potential in the present life and becomes actual after death. Then they will escape the heavenly powers that govern this world according to the iron law of fate, and be joined again to the divine substance from which they came.

The separation of substances is characteristic of gnostic thought. Matter cannot be given life by the divine spirit but remains opposed to it. The soul *(psychē)*, which differentiates living creatures, has an origin and an end that are distinct both from matter and from the divine spirit. This ontological difference is expressed as a difference in the origins and destinies of incompatible "substances," within a stratified universe in which the coexistence of the various levels is perceived as a disorder to be eliminated. In other words, the world of God and the Spirit is original and forms a self-sufficient totality *(plērōma* = fullness). But the outpouring of God's internal life, which finds expression in an overwhelming generation of spiritual beings that are at an increasingly greater distance from the "center," leads at last to a point of crisis. At this turning point, a being is produced; it is often conceived as feminine to indicate its relative "weakness" but also its fruitfulness. This being breaks away and remains enclosed in a matter that has been produced outside the series of spiritual beings and contrary to the orderly unfolding of the divine being.

Between the divine and material substances there is an intermediate substance, which is thought of as angelic or "psychic," and is responsible for creation, or at least for the organization of matter. This being is the god who created and now governs the present world.

Typical of this outlook is a depreciation of the logos, which corresponds to fallacious reason as seen in this world, and a fostering of myth, which alone can in some degree express realities of a completely different world. Although the language is more or less mythical, depending on the various schools and currents of thought, some fundamental attitudes can be identified. Gnostic thought springs from the sense of alienation that persons have when they feel "thrown" into the world but also feel infinitely superior to the limitations that this world imposes. They suffer from their condition and long to be delivered from it, but this deliverance cannot come from within this world. Because they understand themselves to be aliens in the world, they assume that there exists within them a dimension that is radically different from the world; they identify this dimension with their true selves and conceive of this consciousness as a revelation. This in turn sets them free, as they now know that whatever may befall them in this world, their origin lies elsewhere, in a blessed sphere to which they are destined to return.

A further element in this conception of reality was the sense of anxiety that was widespread in the Hellenistic world, in which individuals increasingly perceived themselves as less the masters of their own destiny and more the subjects of forces that they identified with the astral powers. They believed these powers governed the world through the regular, eternal, and inescapable movement of the celestial spheres. But the people of the Hellenistic world also sought to escape the grasp of fate through membership in a religion which offered them "salvation" through participation in a divine reality that was superior to the powers of this world. The roots of this outlook were much older than Hellenism and went back to Orphism.

Essential to gnostic thought, then, was the conviction that our world, including the celestial spheres, was governed by a divinity different from and incomparably inferior to the supreme God, in whom gnostics had their origin. On this point gnosticism represented a divergence both from Hebrew thought, which identified the creator with the supreme God, and from the Platonic tradition, which maintained a devolution of the divine and the existence of a second God who was mediator of creation; Platonism did not admit a break in the chain of being nor an opposition between the first and second Gods. Indeed, the gnostic systems turned Hebrew thought upside down, because they degraded the God of biblical (Old Testament) revelation to the rank of an inferior God, who was at best limited and ignorant, but more often (and in the earliest systems), a rebel against the supreme God. Gnosticism was to a great extent the heir of Judaism, but only by inverting it. So true was this that gnosticism is thought by some scholars to have been a violent reaction of groups within Judaism after the disappointment of the Jewish War, which had shown that their God was unable to protect his people. This explanation may have an element of truth, but it does not adequately account for the entire phenomenon of gnosticism.

The origin of gnosticism is much debated. At the beginning of our century, the "history of religions school" *(religionsgeschichtliche Schule)*, especially in the persons of R. Reitzenstein and W. Bousset, saw gnosticism as originating in a myth that supposedly developed in the Iranian world in the pre-Christian period. According to the myth, the primordial Heavenly Man was cast down from the divine world, dismembered by hostile powers, and his parts imprisoned in matter. God sent a redeemer to make these parts remember their divine nature. Because the redeemer and the primordial man possess the same nature, the myth was called the myth of the "redeemed redeemer."

But more recent studies (C. Colpe) have shown that this myth does not go back to the pre-Christian period but is found in its complete form only in third-century Manichaeism. Even today the tendency to regard gnosticism as a pre-Christian phenomenon dominates the field: gnosticism supposedly arose through a synthesis of oriental, Greek, and Jewish elements, and then made its way into Christianity, where it provided a framework within which to locate the redemptive work of Jesus and various elements of Christian theology and soteriology. The representatives of this tendency strongly emphasize the gnostic element in the *Corpus Hermeticum,* a collection of pagan revelatory writings in which the revealer is identified with Hermes Trismegistus. They also emphasize the presence of non-Christian gnostic writings in the Nag Hammadi library (see below, sec. 6).

Today, however, there is a growing current of thought that takes more seriously the ancient testimonies not only of Christians (who, as we noted, regarded gnosticism as a Christian heresy) but also of pagans (especially Plotinus), who knew only Christian gnostics. Thus M. Simonetti has recently drawn attention to the teachings which the early heresiologists regarded as the foundation of gnosticism, those of Simon Magus; it matters little whether the teaching goes back to that individual or to his followers. According to the heresiologists, these teachings posit the redemption of a feminine component of the divine that had fallen into the world (a typical element in gnosticism), but not the creation of the world by an inferior divinity (also a typical gnostic idea). This teaching can be well explained as pagan, without any need of recourse to Judaism or Christianity; the fall of divine particles into the world comes from Orphism.

Christians of pagan origin and strong anti-Jewish sentiments, persons active in Syria at the beginning of the second century (where the heresiologists locate Saturnilus, author of the first clearly outlined gnostic system) might well have supplemented their own line of thought by adding this conception of a split in the androgynous divinity and a fall of its feminine component into the lower world which has its own proper tendencies. In this perspective, the gnostic synthesis with its two fundamental features (consubstantiality of the divine element that fell into the world with the supreme divinity, and creation of the world by an inferior divinity who is identified with the God of the Old Testament) would have been of Christian origin, and the gnostic writings that are seemingly non-Christian (but in which traces of Christianity can be identified on close examination) would more likely be "de-christianized" than pre-Christian.

This thesis will, of course, be debated, but it seems to us to be the one that best accounts for the data in the sources, where gnosticism in the strict sense is always connected with Christian theology. Readers ought also bear in mind that during the late first and early second century, the period of gnosticism's origins, Christianity did not constitute a separate intellectual universe but a body of thought that was in process of development out of something peculiar to it, namely, faith in Jesus as Savior. Christian thinkers were endeavoring to express the significance of Jesus in relation to the religious and intellectual tradition into which he had been born (the very complex and largely Hellenized Judaism of the 1st c. A.D.) and to the tradition in which he was being rapidly received (a no less variegated Hellenism with its cults and its philosophical syncretisms). In other words, gnosticism seems readily understandable as one of the possible ways of maintaining the specific nature of Christian salvation over against preexisting religious traditions especially Jewish, from which it needed urgently to differentiate itself.

It is perhaps not by chance that a work such as the letter of Barnabas, which is not gnostic in the proper sense, but which energetically seeks to disparage the Jewish understanding of revelation as compared with the Christian understanding, should lay so much emphasis on knowledge *(gnōsis)*. The knowledge of God and his saving will, made possible by Jesus the Redeemer/Revealer, seems to play a key role in replacing Judaism with Christianity. In Barnabas, indeed, what is challenged is the understanding the Jewish tradition had of its own revelation, not that revelation itself or the God who is its author. But even the denigration of Israel's revelation and Israel's God could very well be employed for the purpose of establishing Christianity as Judaism's replacement in that one might maintain that Christianity had no longer any need of the foundations established by the revelation to Israel.

In this regard, a comparison with Marcion is appropriate, for we are dealing with two assertions of the Christian specificity and identity that see in Christianity a radical transcending of Jewish religious identity. Nevertheless, even if the ancients and moderns alike have preferred to regard Marcion as a gnostic, we are still dealing with two different options, because Marcion lacks one of the two key elements of gnosticism, namely, the consubstantiality of the saved with the supreme divinity; in Marcionism the saved belong entirely to the creator, and possess nothing that comes from the Father of Jesus.

By and large, gnosticism was an elite phenomenon. According to the heresiologists, the gnostics distinguished several classes of people, depending on whether or not they had the divine spark within them; only these, of course, could be saved. The awakening of awareness of one's divine nature, that is, the acceptance of gnosis, was proof of belonging to the privileged category. This acceptance was followed, in the sphere of ethics, by one of two choices: asceticism with its radical separation from the material world, or indifferentism, because salvation was "natural" for these people, whatever their moral behavior.

Scholars today are cautious of automatically attributing to gnostics the idea of a "natural" salvation. But this idea must have existed, especially in certain Valentinian groups, which nevertheless distinguished three categories of persons: those who were spiritual, being endowed with the divine seed; those who were material (or hylic), being composed of the present world's matter and destined for ultimate destruction along with the world; and in between, those who were psychic or shared the nature of the god of the present world. This third class could receive an inferior kind of salvation, provided they obeyed the law of the creator. The Valentinians identified nongnostic Christians as psychics because they held to the Old Testament and the creator god. But many texts, even Valentinian ones, express the idea that salvation comes rather from divine grace (perhaps there is, speaking generally, an interpretation of Paul on these lines, with emphases like those in Marcion's reading of him) and that even gnostics are in danger of losing it. In other words the divine "nature" of the gnostic is closely connected with the gift of grace.

These texts are important because they show how the problems faced by the gnostics were close to those faced by the church, and how in solving them the gnostics were led by the effort to define Christian identity, to which we referred above, and did not stick stubbornly to a doctrine of a mechanical "natural" salvation, although this doctrine certainly did have its adherents.

Gnostic exegesis of the Scriptures was no less complex. Marcion, for his part, had based his criticism of the creator on a literal interpretation of the Old Testament and had rejected the Old Testament in its entirety as being completely alien to the gospel of Jesus. But the gnostics, if we may generalize somewhat, used allegorical interpretation to distinguish various levels of revelation in the Old Testament in keeping with their conception of the coexistence of various levels in Christology and anthropology. Alongside the laws and the prophecies, which were dictated by the creator, there are texts having to do with the history of the divine seed in the world. These passages are secretly inspired by the divine being from whom the gnostics themselves come forth.

In this view it was possible to give a positive meaning to the enemies of Yahweh and, first of all, to the serpent of Genesis; the Ophites and Naassenes, whose names derive from the respective Greek and Hebrew words for "serpent," saw in the serpent a saving figure who wanted to help the first human beings to acquire the knowledge (gnōsis) which the creator wanted to withhold from them. Similarly, the flood could be interpreted as an attempt by the creator to destroy the spiritual seed, while Noah escaped destruction thanks to the help of messengers from the divine world; and so on, in a reading that turned the entire history of Israel upside down. The story of creation and the fall (Gen 1–3) was naturally of special importance to the gnostics, because in it they saw the circumstances of the fall of the divine particles and the formation of the material world in order to receive the particles. By means of allegorical interpretation, the Gnostics also found in the sayings of Jesus a series of allusions to the gnostic drama of fall and redemption. This method of exegesis was in itself less distant than it might seem from the methods used at the same time in the "great church," which used allegorical interpretation to bring the Old Testament into line with the new demands created by faith in Jesus.

It remains to say, finally, that many factors contributed to keep gnosticism marginalized: its elitist character, the complexity of its teachings, its lack of concern for organization and its fragmentation into many groups and sects, as is clear not only from the attacks of their adversaries but also from the gnostic texts themselves. The contrast is striking between gnosticism and the strong organizational abilities of the Marcionites and the universal accessibility of their teachings.

The last remaining gnostic conventicles were eliminated by persecution by Christian emperors in the fourth and fifth centuries. Gnosticism, however, has cropped up again under various names and in various forms down to our day, testifying to the difficulty of the problems it proposed to resolve and the attraction exerted by a response that emphasized the election of the believer and his affinity with God.

Until the eighteenth century our sources of information on early gnosticism were limited to the works of Christian heresiologists who summarized the teachings of the various schools and cited fragments or even entire works. In using these sources, we are, of course, dependent on the choices made by the heresiologists, on their understanding of the sources, and on their polemical tendencies, such as their genealogical interlinking of doctrines, which often involves a degree of arbitrary assimilation of some doctrines to others. Now lost is Justin's rather influential *Syntagma,* or Treatise, *Against Marcion and All the Heresies.* The earliest work preserved is the *Unmasking and Refutation of Gnosis Falsely So Called* by Irenaeus of Lyons, who regards as especially important the Valentinian teachings of the school of Ptolemy but also describes other systems.

Next comes the *Elenchos* or *Refutation of All Heresies* by a Roman writer who has been identified, problematically, with Hippolytus and whose aim is to trace Christian heresies back to currents of Greek philosophy. Although he is often less detailed than Irenaeus, he reproduces the actual sources to a greater extent than does Irenaeus. In third place there is the *Panarion* ("Medicine Chest") of Epiphanius of Salamis, who wrote near the end of the fourth century, describing and refuting eighty heresies. His understanding of these is limited, but his work is valuable for its extended citations of sources. In addition to other antiheretical compendia (Pseudo-Tertullian, Filastrius of Brescia) there are valuable works which are not specifically antiheretical but do preserve fragments of gnostic writings. First among these writers is Clement of Alexandria, who cites, among others, Valentinus, Basilides, Isidore, and Carpocrates. Origen, in his *Commentary on John,* cites passages from the Valentinian commentary of Heracleon on the same gospel.

Original gnostic works, but translated from Greek into Coptic, were recovered in Egypt in the eighteenth century, especially in two codices, named after their owners. One is the Askewianus (London, British Library Add. 5114, mid-4th c.), containing a four-part work that is made up of dialogues between Jesus, Magdalene, and the other disciples and bears the name *Pistis Sophia.* The other is Brucianus 96 (Oxford, Bodleian Library; 4th c.), containing the two *Books of Jeu* and an untitled work that is also described as *The Book of the Great Initiatory Treatise* and *Heavenly Topography.* But these are late works. More important is the Berlin Codex (P.Berolin. 8502; 4th–5th c.), acquired by the Berlin Museum in 1896 but published only in 1955 and containing four works that go back to the second–third century: *The Gospel of Mary, The Apocryphon of John, The Wisdom of Jesus Christ,* and *The Act of Peter.*

Of exceptional importance was the discovery in 1946, at Nag Hammadi in Upper Egypt, of thirteen papyrus codices. These contained fifty-three writings translated from Greek into Coptic, most of them gnostic and some in several recensions (there were also Hermetic treatises, Hellenistic sapiential writings, and a passage from Plato's *Republic*). In all, there were forty-one previously unknown works that have made an indispensable contribution to our knowledge of gnosticism. The publication of the works has unfortunately been dragged out, so that while translations of individual writings have gradually been published, and a first American translation of all the texts became available in 1977, the facsimile edition was completed only in 1984. At present, various efforts to produce a critical edition and a commentary on the entire corpus are in the works.

There are serious problems of interpretation, due to the poor preservation of some codices and the poor quality of the Coptic translations, but these problems take nothing away from the importance of the discovery. The literary genres represented in the collection are quite varied: prayer, apocalypse, dialogues of the risen Lord with the disciples, collection of sayings of Jesus *(Gospel of Thomas),* and theological treatise. Of the texts that can be assigned to the second or third century, some have already been discussed here (see above, ch. 2, sec. 11 and ch. 8, sec. 1a). Of some others that are especially important, we shall give a description further on, referring the reader for complete information on the editions to *CPG* 1175–1222 and to the editions cited in the bibliography here.

BIBLIOGRAPHY

Editions

For editions of the early heresiologists see the chapters on them in the present work.

M. Simonetti, *Testi gnostici in lingua greca e latina* (Milan: Fondazione Valla-Mondadori, 1993); gives the Greek and Latin texts on the gnostics, with an introduction, translation, and commentary.

Indispensable for the history of the word "gnostic," the tools of scholarship, and Codices Askewianus, Brucianus, and Berolinensis is M. Tardieu and J.-D. Dubois, *Introduction à la littérature gnostique* I (Paris: Cerf, 1986); a further volume is in preparation.

For the Berlin Codex: M. Tardieu, *Ecrits gnostiques: Codex de Berlin* (Paris: Cerf, 1984); introduction, translation, and commentary.

Facsimile edition of the Nag Hammadi texts: *The Facsimile Edition of the Nag Hammadi Codices* (11 vols.; Leiden: Brill, 1972–1984).

Critical edition with commentary: *The Coptic Gnostic Library: A Complete Edition of the Nag Hammadi Codices* (5 vols.; Boston: Brill, 2000).

Bibliothèque Copte de Nag Hammadi, Section "Textes" (Quebec: University of Laval, 1977–).

ET of all the texts, with short introductions but without any apparatus: J. M. Robinson, ed., *The Nag Hammadi Library in English* (3d ed.; Leiden: Brill, 1988).

ET of the Greek and Coptic texts, with introduction and notes: B. Layton, *The Gnostic Scriptures* (Garden City, N.Y.: Doubleday, 1987).

Bibliography

Bibliography on the Nag Hammadi texts: D. M. Scholer, *Nag Hammadi Bibliography 1948–1969* (Leiden: Brill, 1971); continued annually by Scholer in "Bibliographia gnostica: Supplementum," in *NovT* since 1971.

Studies

From the vast bibliography on gnosticism we shall mention here only a few recent comprehensive works that can serve as starting points.

H. Jonas, *Gnosis und spätantiker Geist;* FRLANT 33, 45; Göttingen: Vandenhoeck & Ruprecht, 1934); ET: *The Gnostic Religion: The Message of the Alien God and the Beginnings of Christianity* (n.t.; 3d ed.; Boston: Beacon, 2001).

U. Bianchi, ed., *Le origini dello gnosticismo: Colloquio di Messina* (Leiden: Brill, 1967).

A. Orbe, *Cristología gnóstica* (2 vols.; Madrid: Editorial Católica, 1976).

K. Rudolph, *Die Gnosis: Wesen und Geschichte einer spätantiken Religion* (3d ed.; Göttingen: Vandenhoek & Ruprecht, 1990).

B. Layton, ed., *The Rediscovery of Gnosticism* (2 vols.; Leiden: Brill, 1980–1981).

G. Filoramo, *L'attesa della fine: Storia della gnosi* (Bari: Laterza, 1983).

————, *Il risveglio della gnosi ovvero diventare Dio* (Rome-Bari: Laterza, 1990).

M. Simonetti, "Alcune riflessioni sul rapporto tra gnosticismo e cristianesimo," *VC* 28 (1991): 337–74.

G. C. Benelli, *La gnosi: Il volto oscuro della storia* (Milan: Mondadori, 1991).

S. Pétrement, *A Separate God: The Christian Origins of Gnosticism* (trans. C. Harrison; San Francisco: Harper, 1990).

K. King, *What is Gnosticism?* (Cambridge, Mass.: Harvard University Press, 2003).

5. Indirect Transmission of the Second- and Third-Century Gnostic Writers

As we have already said, the heresiologists agree in seeing as the origin of all heresies Simon Magus, a man described in the Acts of the Apostles (8:9–11) as a magician active in Samaria, who called himself the "Great Power." According to Irenaeus (*Haer.* 1.23.1–3; earlier, Justin, *1 Apol.* 26.1–3), Simon described himself as the supreme Power who by means of his first Thought had created angels and archangels. These in turn, after creating the world here below, imprisoned therein their Mother (that is, the divine Thought; the noun is feminine in Greek) and subjected her to every kind of insult. She gradually incarnated herself in various human individuals, among them Helen of Troy and a prostitute named Helen whom Simon had bought in a brothel in Tyre and took around with him. He claimed that the divine Power had come down from heaven, unknown to the angels and archangels, in order to save his Thought and all human beings from the tyranny of the celestial powers. This Power appeared in Judea in the form of Jesus and in Samaria in the form of Simon.

As was noted earlier, this synthesis, which certainly represents the thinking of later Simonians rather than of the founder (there were Simonians in Rome in the second century), is not truly gnostic, inasmuch as the creation of the world is not ascribed to another God. The genealogy of error that was drawn up by the heresiologists has Simon followed by Menander and the latter by Saturninus of Antioch, who is of interest because with him appears for the first time a clearly gnostic system in which the God of the Hebrews is identified with one of the angels who created the world. But because we do not have their writings, these several personages cannot contribute to a history of literature.

Hippolytus of Rome attributes to Simon a *Megalē apophasis* (great revelation), which he connects with the philosophy of Heraclitus and which he reproduces in part (*Elench.* 6.9.3–18.7); this was in fact a later work of the Simonians and dealt with theology and cosmology. It posits a single principle, which is identified with fire and possesses hidden (potential) and manifest (actual) aspects that contain within themselves the intelligible and sensible universes respectively. The world that is generated has its origin in the development of six pairs of powers, the first of which is either

Intellect and Thought or Heaven and Earth, while a seventh power is the very image of the infinite Power. This cosmology could thus claim to be based on an exegesis of the biblical story of the six days of creation, plus the seventh, the day of God's rest. The text is characterized by a syncretic mixture of biblical themes (Gen, first of all, but also other texts, among them the prophets and the gospels) and Greek themes (Empedocles, Homer). Again, this work does not attribute the origin of the world to an inferior divinity and is therefore not gnostic in the strict sense.

We referred above to the Ophites (or Naassenes) and their use of the serpent. Irenaeus summarizes an Ophite system that seems to have influenced the Valentinians (*Haer.* 1.29). Hippolytus (*Elench.* 5.7–9) cites extensively, and in part summarizes, a Naassene work (possibly third century) according to which Adam was created by inferior powers in the image of the primordial man, Adamas. Because Adam lay on the ground lifeless, the Son of the primordial Man came down to give him life, but was imprisoned in Adam's body by the powers. Through natural generation, this Son was scattered among countless human beings, and only the gnosis acquired by these human beings would make his deliverance possible.

The interesting point here is the great number of references not only to the biblical tradition but to the mythologies of the most varied peoples, in order to show that all of them speak of the primordial Man. What is clear is not only the syncretist character of the gnostic systems, but their intention of presenting each system as a universal religion that organizes and explains the information obscurely contained in the most varied religions and cultures. Contrary to what scholars thought in the past, it is impossible to remove Jewish and Christian references from the text and be left with an original pagan myth of the primordial man.

Hippolytus also cites (*Elench.* 5.24.2–3; 5.26–27) the *Book of Baruch* by Justin, who posits three principles at the origin of things. Two of them are masculine, namely, Good, which is endowed with foresight, and the Father, or Elohim, who lacks foresight. The third principle is feminine, known as Eden (Earth) and Israel, lacking in foresight, and characterized by anger. Elohim wedded Eden and with her begot twenty-four angels, who make up paradise, and man, who is the symbol of their love. To man Eden gave the soul and Elohim the spirit. But then Elohim with his twelve angels returned to heaven, where Good detained him. Eden, now abandoned, ordered her angels to torment the spirit of Elohim in human beings by means of evils (adulteries, divorces, illnesses).

Elohim then sent his angel Baruch to help human beings; Baruch in turn sent various liberators, such as Moses, the prophets, and Hercules. All of them, however, were corrupted by Naas, one of Eden's angels, via the soul that was in them; here then the serpent has a negative function. Finally, Baruch went to look for Jesus, a twelve-year old boy who was pasturing the flock, and sent him. Jesus alone resisted Naas, and Naas had him crucified out of revenge. But Jesus was able to give the spirit back to the Father (Luke 23:46) and ascend to the Good. The *Book of Baruch* is unusual among gnostic texts, in that it is not the descent of the divine principle but rather its abandonment of creation that is regarded as evil. Creation is therefore initially good, and evil is not intrinsic to its nature.

According to Clement (*Strom.* 7.106.4), Basilides of Alexandria was active in the time of Hadrian and Antoninus Pius (117–161). Basilides appealed to the secret tradition stemming from Glaucias, a disciple of Peter (ibid.) or to another from the apostle

Matthias (*Elench.* 7.20.1). Irenaeus has Basilides, like Saturninus, depending on Menander; but his review of Basilides is an unconvincing summary that seems to make the teaching of Basilides the same as that of Saturninus (1.24.3–7).

The *Elenchos* gives a better review of Basilides and his son Isidore (7.20–27), for it shows a specific philosophical commitment at work in the emphasis on the absolute transcendence of God, which makes it impossible to affirm anything of God, even his being. By his will, not by an emanation, God produces a seed of the world that comprises three "filialities": the first two return on high, the second with the help of the Holy Spirit, who then continues to act as a firmament separating the divine realm from the world; the third remains below "to give and receive benefits," and from it spiritual persons are derived. The latter are destined to return on high, but first they must assist the psychic, intermediate element, which is governed by the great Archon, who dwells in the ogdoad (8th heaven, starting from the bottom), and by his son, who is established in the Hebdomad (the other seven heavens) and who is the God of the Old Testament. From the gospel that is sent from on high, the Archon learns of his own creaturely condition and of the existence of a supreme divinity. Then, gripped by a salutary fear and rescued from ignorance, he too collaborates in the salvation of the spiritual seed.

This gnosis, which is more optimistic about the created world, is close in various respects to that of the Valentinians, but we do not know the extent to which it reflects the original thinking of Basilides. Only a few fragments remain to help us to grasp his thought.

According to a passage from Agrippa Castor (cited in Eusebius, *Hist. eccl.* 4.7.6–7), a quasi-contemporary opponent of Basilides, the latter composed twenty-four books on the gospel, which are certainly the ones cited by Clement of Alexandria as *Exegetika (Explanations)*. According to Origen, Basilides composed a gospel of his own (*Hom. Luc.* 1), as well as *Odes* (*Hom. Job* 21.11). The *Acts of Archelaus* by Hegemonius (67.4–17) cite a fragment from the thirteenth of the twenty-four books; it has to do with dualistic cosmogonies. Some passages of the twenty-third book, cited by Clement (*Strom.* 4.81–83), meditate on martyrdom and suffering. Basilides says he cannot believe that there is not a divine providence and that God cannot prevent other powers from causing human beings to suffer. He explains the suffering of the innocent and of children as due to a natural disposition to sin which each person has, even if for lack of an occasion it may never be actuated. His is a pessimistic and tragic vision of the human condition, and it is accompanied, according to Origen (*Comm. Rom.* 5.1), by a belief in the transmigration of souls and, according to Clement (*Strom.* 4.86), by an ethics of asceticism and compassion.

Isidore, son of Basilides, was thought to have composed a treatise *On the Adventitious Soul*, in which he traced sin back to "appendages" (*prosartēmata*) that are attached to the soul and incite it to sin; however, he refused to justify sin with this excuse (Clement, *Strom.* 2.113–14). Isidore also wrote *Explanations of the Prophet Parchor* in at least two books in which he claimed that the Greek philosophers had drawn on the prophets (*Strom.* 6.53.2–5). In another work, the *Ethics (Questions on Morality)*, Isidore urged his readers to calm their passions by taking an impetuous lover or even marrying, so that they might be able to pray with a good conscience. On the other hand, he rebuked ascetics who believed they could not sin. Overall, the fragments of Basilides and Isidore do not suggest a gnostic outlook, so it is difficult to establish a connection between them and the heresiologist's descriptions of their doctrines.

Irenaeus (*Haer.* 1.256, reproduced in Hippolytus, *Elench.* 7.32) speaks of the teachings of the followers of Carpocrates, which were broadcast in Rome by a certain Marcellina in the time of Anicetus (ca. 155 to ca. 166). According to these, the world was created by the angels; the soul of Christ, remembering what he had previously seen when with God, scorned the angels, and by doing the same the souls of his followers can be saved. The Carpocratians practiced magic and an ethical libertinism, and believed in the transmigration of souls. Clement of Alexandria (*Strom.* 3.5–9) has preserved some passages of a treatise, *On Justice,* by the son of Carpocrates, Epiphanes, who died on Cephalonia at the age of seventeen and was worshiped there as a god. Some scholars have suggested that Epiphanes was a lunar deity of the Cephalonians, and Carpocrates was the god Horus, who was known outside Egypt as Harpocrates. In any case, the passages transcribed by Clement define the justice of God as "community with equality" and assert that human law has violated the natural God-given arrangement, by opposing the sharing of possessions and women. Nothing in all this seems truly gnostic; the creator God is evidently the only God.

Valentinian gnosticism was undoubtedly the most developed intellectually; it is also the best known to us. Very little, however, is known of Valentinus himself. He came from Alexandria to Rome in the time of Bishop Hyginus, around 140 (Irenaeus, *Haer.* 3.4.3), and opened a school there; he was also supposedly a candidate for the episcopacy. He remained in Rome until the reign of Anicetus (ca. 155–66), then moved to Cyprus, and finally back to Rome. He wrote homilies, letters, and poetic compositions, of which only a few fragments remain, but these are of high poetic quality.

One of them (Clement, *Strom.* 2.36.2–4) describes the dismay of the angels when the human being they had just created uttered words beyond his creaturely condition, due to the "seed of the higher substance" which had been invisibly given to him. In fear of the preexistent man now present in Adam, the angels "hid" their work. The meaning of the verb *ēphanisan* is not certain; perhaps they reacted by imprisoning the human being in a material body. This passage can be read against a gnostic background, but need not be. It smacks of the view, attested in Alexandrian Judaism, that the angels created the lower elements of the human being, while God infused the spirit. It is not said that the angels created the human being in opposition to God, but that they reacted negatively to the revelation of the higher nature that had been introduced into him.

Another fragment (*Strom.* 2.114) is akin to that of Isidore regarding the appendages (see above) and has to do with the impure human heart, which is the prey of demons and is set free by the graces of God, who alone is good. This is one of the texts that seems difficult to reconcile with a strict doctrine of salvation by nature. Also of interest are a passage on the nature of Christ's body (*Strom.* 3.59) and another, drawn from a homily, on the condition of the saved, who destroy death and the world (*Strom.* 4.89). Still another, taken from a homily *On Friends* (*Strom.* 6.52), sets up an opposition between the law written in the heart in the church of God, which produces love as a consequence of love received from the Beloved (Christ), and the "public books," which are surely the Scriptures. The *Elenchos* (6.37.6–8) preserves a poem of Valentinus titled *Harvest (Theros),* which has to do with the chain of being that reaches from the matter of this world to the interior of God. In this case, too, the connection between the literary fragments and the teaching that the heresiologists attribute to Valentinus (especially Irenaeus, *Haer.* 1.11.1) is obscure. The teacher seems to have been quite a poet and mystic, heavily influenced by (Middle) Platonism.

According to the *Elenchos* (6.35.6–7), Valentinian's school broke up into two branches, an eastern and a western. The latter is better known in the persons of its two principal representatives, Ptolemy and Heracleon. Epiphanius (*Pan.* 33.3–8) has preserved in its entirety Ptolemy's *Letter to Flora,* a Christian woman who asked what Christians should think of the law of Moses, a serious problem for Christians of the second century (see above, ch. 6, sec. 6).

In Ptolemy's view, the law promulgated by Moses could not have come from God the Father, because it is secondary, imperfect, and in need of completion by Christ. Neither is it from the devil, because it is opposed to injustice. The criterion for assessing the law is the words of Jesus, which show that the law did not come from a single author but had three parts, which went back respectively to God, Moses, and the elders of the people. The part coming from God is in turn divided into three parts: the pure law, unmixed with evil, which the Savior came not to abolish but to fulfill, since it was not alien to his nature (more accurately, to his psychic part); the part mingled with evil and injustice, which the Savior abolished because it was not consonant with his nature; and the typical and symbolic part, which the Savior's coming shifted from the sensible realm to the spiritual. This last part is in harmony with the allegorical interpretation generally practiced in Christianity. The first of the three parts is the Decalogue; the second is essentially the law of talion or retaliation, which, by insisting that one injustice be remedied by another, shows its origin in a god who is not perfect. The law must, then, go back to a personage intermediate between the perfect God, who is good by nature, and the devil, whose mark is injustice; this intermediate personage is the demiurge, the creator, who is characterized by justice.

This work was intended not for the use of gnostic circles but for propaganda. It lays some foundations, which, if accepted, will be completed, as the end of the letter promises, by a more thoroughgoing instruction on how a single principle that is simple, incorruptible, and good can be the source even of natures not consubstantial with it, that is, psychic and material substances. The letter, which is elegantly written and carefully structured, is a further witness to the connection between gnostic treatises and the need to define the specific nature and the superiority of Christianity as compared with Judaism. The kind of solution given here to the problem of the Old Testament in the church is analogous, to some extent, to the distinction between true and forged pericopes that is proposed in the *Pseudo-Clementines* (see vol. II of this history). This kind of solution, based on a distinction between true and forged parts of Scripture, was too complicated and risky to win acceptance, and the "great church" preferred to accept the Old Testament in its entirety and to use allegorical exegesis (from Pseudo-Barnabas to Clement and Origin) as a way of overcoming difficulties.

From Ptolemy comes also an exegesis of the prologue of John's Gospel (Irenaeus, *Haer.* 1.8.5–6) in which the gnostic author sees mentioned the first eight aeons of the Pleroma, which are the fundamental spiritual realities: Father, Thought (*ennoia*), Only Begotten, Truth, Son, Logos, Man, and church. This is an example of sophisticated biblical exegesis that made it possible to give an apparently abstruse doctrinal system a basis in the biblical text. In fact, when the inner logic of the system is studied, it manifestly represents an effort to systematize the data of revelation. Thus viewed, the gnostics were the first Christian theologians. On the orthodox side, neither Irenaeus nor Clement achieved this level of organized thought; this task fell to Origen.

At the beginning of *Against Heresies* (1.1–9), Irenaeus explains at length a gnostic system that F. Sagnard has shown corresponds to that of the school of Ptolemy. It starts with the unknown God, the Abyss *(bythos)*, who through his Thought *(ennoia)* gives rise to the Intelligence, which alone is capable of knowing him and revealing him to others. There then emerge, through successive emanations, pairs of "aeons," which are a kind of universes that express the divine perfections, the whole divine world, the Pleroma (fullness). But the thirtieth and last aeon, Sophia (Wisdom), is overcome by a desire to know the incomprehensible Father before he is revealed to her, and thus falls victim to a passion that excludes her from the Pleroma. It is possible for Sophia to be strengthened and reincorporated into the Pleroma thanks to an intervention of divine providence, but her sinful tendency, which is separate from her and indestructible, remains outside her.

This tendency bears the name Achamoth, from the Hebrew *hokhmah*, "wisdom," but his is a "wisdom of this world." In the course of Sophia's effort to reascend to the Pleroma, elements of her "passion" take concrete form: sadness, fear, anxiety, ignorance. By a complicated process these elements, which are material inasmuch as they are passions, give rise to the world here below, the organization of which Achamoth entrusts to the Demiurge, a being which he has formed of the psychic substance that has sprung from his turning to the Pleroma. This Demiurge is the God of the Hebrews, who, being of an inferior substance, is ignorant of realities superior to him. Even in the world he governs there is, unknown to him, something superior to him, for Achamoth has introduced into it the spiritual seed he had produced when the Savior, sent from the Pleroma, had come to save it (the seed) from the passions; the seed is therefore the "mother" of spiritual persons. This spiritual seed, introduced into some human beings, is meant to grow in the world, which is established for this purpose, so that it may finally reascend to the Pleroma.

After this return the world will be destroyed along with those human beings who are composed solely of matter, which corresponds to the passions. Those possessing psyches, which are of the same substance as the Demiurge, will be able to attain to a salvation of a lower level, provided they have obeyed the law of the Demiurge, that is, the law of the Old Testament. Evidently the Valentinians reached out in this way to the members of the "great church."

Turning to Heracleon: Origen, in his *Commentary on John*, transmits a good many (48) fragments of a commentary by Heracleon on the same gospel. Fragments are cited down to John 8:50, in the twentieth book of Origen's work. When the part of Origen's commentary that has been preserved begins again with book 29, Heracleon is no longer cited, probably because his commentary had broken off before that point. Heracleon discovered that the elements of the Valentinian system were also in the gospel; if necessary, he adapted the meaning of the gospel to his purpose. For example, in commenting on John 1:3, according to which all things were made through the Logos, he interprets "all" as meaning the lower or inferior world, since according to the Valentinians the Pleroma was not made through the Logos, the latter being only an intermediate aeon (frag. 1).

In the preserved fragments Heracleon does not explain the gnostic myth as such; he emphasizes rather the distinction of natures. By a broad application of allegorical exegesis he sees John the Baptist as a symbol of the Demiurge, who admits his own inferiority of nature as compared to Christ (frag. 5–8). In the "going down" of Jesus to Capernaum (John 2:12), Heracleon sees the descent of the Savior into the material world (frag. 11); conversely, the "going up" to Jerusalem represents the ascent from the material realm to the psychic (frag. 13). The Samaritan woman in John symbolizes the spiritual element that is imprisoned in the material world (Samaria) but is open to receive the Savior (frag. 17–39). The royal *(basilikos)* official in Capernaum, who gives orders to those under him (John 4:46ff.), symbolizes the Demiurge, while his sick son represents ignorance and the sins that weigh down the psychic substance; the latter, however, is capable of salvation (frag. 40). The psychic person, who is not by nature the devil's child, can become such by his will or his demerits (frag. 46).

On the basis especially of certain passages asserting that human beings become children of the devil by doing his works, some scholars (H. Langerbeck, E. Pagels, and others) attribute to Heracleon the idea that salvation does not depend on the essence of the human being, and that psychics, too, can reach the Pleroma (an idea that appears in the *Tripartite Tractate* of Nag Hammadi). The question remains open.

Heracleon's commentary is important because it is the first systematic Christian commentary to survive at least in part, and because of its influence on Origen, who sometimes agrees with Heracleon (e.g., frag. 8 on John the Baptist). Clement (*Strom.* 4.71; *Ecl.* 25.1) and Photius (*Lex.* 134) have preserved other fragments of Heracleon; notably, the second of these the author gives priority to a confession in the form of faith and life over a confession made orally.

To the eastern Valentinian school the *Elenchos* assigns Assionicus and Ardesianes, both unknown to us, unless the name Ardesianes is a corruption of Bardesanes. But the manuscript Laurentiana 5.3 has transmitted among the works of Clement of Alexandria one titled *Extracts from the Works of Theodotus and the So-Called "Eastern" School in the Time of Valentinus*. We do not know who Theodotus was, and in any case, the extracts surely do not all come from a single author. Theodotus is mentioned five times; six times the words "it is said" are used; seventeen times "they say," and ten times "the Valentinians." The work consists of notes taken on readings from Valentinian texts, intermingled with remarks by Clement, which cannot always be easily distinguished from the citations of his sources (on this point see below, ch. 14, sec. 2g).

Following F. Sagnard, we may divide the work into four sections. The first (1–28) has to do with the spiritual seed emitted by Sophia, deposited in the soul of Adam by the Logos, awakened by the Savior at his coming, and entrusted to the Father by Jesus during his passion (Luke 23:46). This first section deals also with the baptism of Jesus, the structure of the Savior, and the first aeons of the Pleroma. The second section (29–42) has to do with the first pair in the Pleroma (Abyss and Silence), and then with the myth of Sophia, and with the entities emitted by inferior Wisdom, in particular the church of the spirituals and its destiny.

The third section (45–65) is parallel to the "great notice" of Irenaeus and ranges from the sending of the Savior by the Pleroma to deliver inferior Wisdom from its passions, through cosmogony and the formation of the three categories of human beings, to Christology (the sending of the Savior into this world) and eschatology. That this section belongs to the western Valentinian school, contrary to what is announced by the title of the extracts, is confirmed by the fact that the body of Christ is defined as psychic (59.3), whereas the *Elenchos* of Hippolytus of Rome asserts that the eastern Valentinians regarded it as pneumatic. The fourth section (66–86) deals with the female seed, that is, the spirituals, with astrology (the birth of the Savior breaks the control of fate), and with baptism and its efficacy.

All four sections of the *Extracts* are marked by an interest in the earthly life of Christ (annunciation, conception, birth, adolescence, baptism, temptation, passion, and resurrection). Also noteworthy is the extensive use of Scripture, especially the Gospels and the Letters of Paul. The distinction between the three human natures (material, psychic, and spiritual) and the conditions that influence their destinies are clearly brought out (especially 54–57).

Finally, we note what Irenaeus says (*Haer.* 1.13–21) about Mark the Magician and his disciples. These were Valentinians active in the area of Lyons, where they seduced women by means of conjuring tricks and under the pretext of initiating them into the gnostic mystery of the zyzygy (couple or pair). We have already seen the importance of the androgyny in the pairs of aeons that make up the Valentinian Pleroma, and in the final union of the spirituals, who are described as female, with their angels, who are described as male. Mark had developed a complicated grammatology and numerology that symbolized the entities of the Valentinian system. He also taught formulas that the souls were to recite after death in order to evade the guardians of the heavenly gates, who sought to prevent them from reaching their heavenly goal; this practice is well known in Hellenistic cults and in Judaism.

BIBLIOGRAPHY

The Greek and Latin texts are given with translation and commentary in M. Simonetti, *Testi gnostici in lingua greca e latina* (Milan: Fondazione Valla-Mondadori, 1993); see there the bibliography on the various groups.

On the Simonians

K. Beyschlag, *Simon Magus und die christliche Gnosis* (Tübingen: Mohr, 1974).
S. Haar, "Lens or Mirror: The Image of Simon and Magic in Early Christian Literature," *LTJ* 27 (1993): 113–21.

On Valentinus

C. Markschies, *Valentinus Gnosticus? Untersuchungen zur valentinianischen Gnosis mit einem Kommentar zu den Fragmenten Valentins* (Tübingen: Mohr, 1992).

On the Extracts from Theodotus

F. Sagnard, *Clément d'Alexandrie. Extraits de Théodote* (SC 23; 2d ed.; Paris: Cerf, 1970).
E. H. Pagels, "Conflicting Versions of Valentian Eschatology: Irenaeus' Treatise vs. the Excerpts from Theodotus," *HTR* 67 (1974): 35–53.

6. Gnostic Writings of the Second and Third Centuries in Direct Transmission

It is impossible in the present work to discuss all the gnostic texts discovered at Nag Hammadi; we shall touch briefly on some of the earliest and most important.

The *Apocryphon of John* has reached us in four versions, two longer, contained in codices II,1 (1.1–32.9) and IV,1 (1.1–49.28) from Nag Hammadi, and two abridged, in codex III,1 (1.1–40.11) from Nag Hammadi and in P. Berolinensis 8502 (19.6–77.7).

As John is going up to the temple after the resurrection of Jesus, he is rebuked by a Pharisee for letting himself be deceived by the Nazarene. Saddened, he goes off to a lonely mountain where he asks himself questions about the Lord, about the Father who sent him, and about the eternity toward which he is traveling. Jesus appears to him in three forms: a child, an old man, then a child again; the same motif is found in the *Acts of John*. He reveals to John that he is the Father, the Mother, and the Son. This assertion is then explained in a revelation about the Father, who is an invisible spirit and transcends any possible utterance about him; about the Mother, Barbelo, who has emerged from contemplation of herself; and about the self-generated Son, who receives the anointing of the Spirit and develops into twelve aeons.

The story is then told of the sin of Sophia, who wanted to communicate her own self-understanding without waiting for the assent of the Spirit; of the production of the Demiurge as the miscarriage of Sophia; of the Demiurge's creation of the heavens and angels. The heavenly powers create the psychic human being as a mirror image of the primordial Man, who is glimpsed in the waters below. By way of the Demiurge, but without his knowledge, the spirit of the Mother (Sophia) is introduced into the psychic Adam. But when the powers see his light, they are jealous and hurl Adam down into the lower realms of matter. Here begins the story of salvation, which involves a rereading of the account of paradise and original sin, the latter being a trick of the Mother to allow Adam and Eve to acquire gnosis. The story continues to the birth of Seth, who is the ancestor of those who are spiritual (Gen 4:25–26). After some questions about fate and retribution, there follows an exegesis of the next part of Genesis, the story of the flood (Gen 5–6). The attempt by the demiurge to destroy the human race is frustrated by divine providence, which saves Noah and his family. The treatise ends with a hymn to providence.

Here we have a systematic and carefully planned exposition of the foundations of the gnostic myth. The work has been given various labels, among them "Valentinian" and "Sethian," but it must first be examined in itself. There are many specialists who want to see the work as a coherent gnostic system based on the texts that give a high place to Seth, the son of Adam, as the carrier of the spiritual seed and therefore ancestor of the gnostics; but the idea is debated. The work is a midrash on Scripture that answers the objection raised by the Pharisees against John and often raised against Christians: that they have abandoned Jewish tradition to follow Jesus.

The answer is to interpret the Jesus tradition and the biblical story in such a way as to prove that the God of the Jews, the creator of the world, is inferior to the Father of Jesus; it is therefore necessary to cast aside the first and follow the second. The demiurge has power only over this lower universe, including the human body; he has turned both this universe and the human body into a hellish machine that imprisons the divine seed, as the author shows by drawing liberally on the astrology of the "Chaldeans." The organized use of Johannine themes has suggested to some that the author is a dissident follower of John who wants a radical separation between faith in Christ and the Jewish tradition (M. Tardieu). If we take into account the use of the Gospel of John and probable successive redactional additions to the original form of the *Apocryphon,* the completion of the work can be dated to shortly after 150, perhaps in Asia Minor where the Johannine tradition was strong.

The fifth and final treatise in the first codex from Nag Hammadi (NHC I,5 51.1–138.27) is a lengthy Valentinian work. It lacks a title, but scholars have given it the name *Tripartite Tractate,* because in the manuscript it seems to be divided by means of scribal decoration into three parts that correspond to three phases: the development and crisis of the divinity and the formation of things external to it; the origin and fall of the human being; and eschatology and reintegration of the divinity. The general framework is that of the Valentinian myth, but the treatise has several distinctive characteristics.

The Father, who is the source of everything and who can be described only by the *via negationis,* is one, and has no female partner. Through a process of self-knowledge, he generates the Son and the church. The idea of the church as a preexistent entity, which was widespread among the Valentinians, came from Jewish Christianity. The triad of Father, Son, and church constitutes the Pleroma, which is therefore extremely simplified here as compared with other Valentinian texts. On the other hand, while the church is one, it is made up of countless aeons.

After a lengthy description of activity within the Pleroma, the *Tractate* moves to the key motif of the fall. Once again it differs from other sources in which the fall is due to the error of a feminine aeon. Instead the responsible party is a masculine aeon, the Logos, and his action stems from excessive love for the Father. The event is thus given a positive interpretation: the Logos does not act against the will of the Father but, on the contrary, his initiative is in keeping with an "economy," that is, a plan of salvation that the Father has established. Like the other aeons produced along with him, the Logos acts out of free will. This esteem of free will corresponds, as we shall see, to the importance assigned to the salvation of the psychics. On being expelled from the Pleroma, the Logos divides into two: his better part returns to the Pleroma and, with the other aeons, produces the Savior, who is entrusted with the revelation to beings outside the Pleroma. The latter are organized into a universe in which the Logos inhabits the upper, spiritual region, and the two lower regions, the psychic and the material, are subject to the Archon (the demiurge).

The second part (104.4–108.12) has to do with the creation of the human being, sin, the expulsion from paradise, and the reign of death; the section is a rereading of Gen 1–3. As in other Valentinian texts, the demiurge provides Adam with a psychic soul and material substance, while the Logos provides the spiritual soul. In this mingling of substances, the psychic substance is "open": it understands higher things but inclines toward evil. The co-existence of "right" and "left," which flows from evil in the world (see the beginning of the third part: 108.13–138.27), has produced the varying opinions held by humans. The threefold substance present in Adam then produced in his descendants three types of human beings, who reveal what they are by their attitude to the Savior: the spirituals immediately accept him and join him, the psychics delay in acknowledging him and need to the guided, and the hylics or material persons distance themselves from him as darkness does from light. The treatise pays special attention to the fate of the psychics: those who are good and humble will be saved, and those who are proud will be lost (an appropriation of the Jewish Christian theme of the "two ways"). Unlike other Valentinian systems, in the *Tractate* the psychics who are saved are admitted into the Pleroma.

Such details as these show a desire to reach out to the "great church," which the Valentinians identified with the psychics. The positive attitude displayed toward the psychics and the demiurge has led some scholars to attribute the *Tripartite Tractate* to Heracleon, but as we saw above, Heracleon's view of the psychics is not clear. In any case, this work seems to represent a revision of Valentinianism on important points, perhaps in order to reply to criticisms from the "orthodox." If so, the work can be dated to the beginning of the third century.

The *Gospel of Truth* (two copies: NHC I,3 16.31–43.24; and, in fragmentary form, XII,2 53.19–60.30) takes its name from its opening words. Irenaeus cites a Valentinian *Gospel of Truth,* but does not report its contents. If the two works are the same, then it is to be dated before 180; similarities to other fragments have led some critics to attribute it to Valentinus, but this is not supportable. The *Gospel of Truth* does not belong to the literary genre of the gospel; the word here retains its original meaning of good news, referring to the preaching of Christ. The work is rather a kind of homily that extols the salvation bestowed by God often in lyrical language. It is not a systematic treatment of doctrinal foundations, as the two previous works are, but an outpouring of religious feeling in which gnostic themes are suggested rather than explained.

It is difficult to outline the contents; H. W. Attridge and G. W. MacRae distinguish three sections. The first describes in mythical form the reign of error, which is characterized by forgetfulness, anxiety, and lies. It contrasts with this the gospel brought by Christ, which won for him persecution and crucifixion by error. The second part dwells on the effects of truth, which leads to unity with the Father and "awakens" (a typical gnostic metaphor) the person from the sleep and nightmares that mark the state of ignorance. The third part deals with the return to the Father: spiritual persons are like a fragrance that rises sweetly to him, so that they may find rest in the Father. This section contains a disquisition on the Son as Name of the Father. That is, in him alone does the Father become knowable; this expands on a Jewish Christian motif.

The *Treatise on the Resurrection* (NHC I,4 43.25–50.18) is a letter addressed to a certain Rheginos that explains the idea of resurrection with the aid of the Neoplatonic categories on which Valentinian gnosticism is based. The work briefly touches on the fundamental mythological themes of Valentinianism: the Pleroma, the crisis on its periphery, and the reintegration. The author asserts the reality of the resurrection of believers because of his faith in the resurrection of Christ; the certainty of resurrection is based not on philosophical reasoning but on the experience of election. The resurrection will not take place at the end of time and with the creation of a new body; rather, at the death of the individual, the interior body, the "living members," will be set free of the visible members, which cannot receive salvation. In this sense, the resurrection is a passage from illusion, represented by the present world, to incorruptible reality: "it is the revelation of what is, and the transformation of things, and a transition into newness" (48.34–38; Robinson, 56). Believers possess the resurrection even now, in virtue of their participation in the death and resurrection of the Savior; the writer relies here on a free citation of Paul (Rom 8:17; Eph 5:2–6). The resurrection is a spiritual one, as opposed to a psychic and a material one.

This realized eschatology agrees with what we know from Tertullian and Irenaeus about Valentinian ideas of the resurrection, but the attribution of the *Treatise* to Valentinus himself, which was proposed in the past, cannot be maintained. The tendency is rather to date the work in the second half of the second century, both because of the advanced knowledge of a New Testament canon (as seen in the distinction between Gospel and Apostle), and because of an affinity with the debate on the resurrection that was emerging in Christianity during those decades.

The *Gospel of Philip* (NHC II,3 51.29–86.19) is likewise not a gospel in the proper sense, but seems to be a collection of extracts from a Valentinian catechesis on the sacraments. It is of great interest for the information it provides on the sacraments of gnostic initiation, which perhaps followed the order given in 67.27–30 (Robinson, 150): "The Lord [did] everything in a mystery, a baptism and a chrism and a eucharist and a redemption and a bridal chamber," where, moreover, the "bridal chamber" signifies the entire initiation. Connected with this initiation is the importance of Christian identity, of the name "Christian," and of the formula "I am a Christian," which was uttered on emerging from the baptismal immersion.

The root of evil, according to the author, was the separation of Eve from Adam, which brought death as its result. Death will be destroyed only by the reconstitution of the original androgynous unity (68.22–26), and this is the work accomplished by Christ (70.9–22). The reunion is effected in the sacrament of the bridal chamber. Excluded from it are animals, slaves, and women who are polluted, whereas free males, sons, and virgins are Christians. The freedom of the Christian begets love, which is expressed in the beautiful words: "He who is really free through knowledge is a slave because of love for those who have not yet been able to attain to the freedom of knowledge. . . . Love [never calls] something its own. . . . It never [says 'This is yours'] or 'This is mine,' but ['All these] are yours' " (76.26–35; Robinson, 155).

It is impossible, however, to give a comprehensive idea of this quite unfocused work, freighted as it is with symbolic language. It cites and interprets seventeen sayings of Jesus, eight of which are unknown elsewhere. It also contains narratives about Jesus, among them the story of the boy Jesus mixing seventy-two colors in the workshop of Levi the dyer and producing white (63.25–30), and another about Joseph making the cross on which Jesus would be crucified (73.8–15). The original Greek text is dated to the second half of the second century.

BIBLIOGRAPHY

For editions and translations, see the bibliography of sec. 4 above.

7. Montanism and the Anti-Montanist Writers

Very little has come down to us from either the Montanist prophets (Tertullian, of course, is a different story; see below, ch. 18, sec. 2e) or their first opponents. Our information comes substantially from Eusebius (especially *Hist. eccl.* 5.14–19), Hip-

polytus of Rome (*Elench.* 8.19), and Epiphanius (*Pan.* 48–49). The Montanist movement sprang up in Phrygia around 155–160 (the date is debated; others, who follow
Eusebius, place it a little after 170), when Montanus and two women, Prisca (or
Priscilla) and Maximilla, began to prophesy in ecstasy, claiming that God was speaking in them, putting himself in place of their consciences, and using them as instruments. Montanus declared: "I am the Father, the Son, and the Holy Spirit [the
Paraclete]" (oracles 1, 2 Aland; see nos. 3, 4), and the voice of the Lord asserted
through him: "See, a human being is like a lyre, and I glide over him like a plectrum;
he sleeps and I keep watch" (no. 5). This was not the kind of prophesying that had
marked Christianity since its origins, for that had a specific institutional setting and
took the data of revelation (Scripture) as its point of departure.

The Montanist prophecy dealt rather in new revelation. The movement originally
called itself "New Prophecy"; only in the fourth century was it called Montanism. It
did not challenge the authority of the existing Scriptures, but did claim that revelation
was still, or once again, open, because the Paraclete whom Christ had promised to
send (John 14:26; 16:7) was revealing himself in Montanus and his followers. There
was, in fact, a trend opposed to the closing of a Christian canon of Scripture; the
Montanist prophets claimed an authority that was independent of the Scriptures and,
much more, of ecclesiastical authorities. The point, then, was not so much a defense
of an existing and primordial preeminence of prophets in the church as it was a revival of the primitive eschatological enthusiasm that reacted to the delay of the
Parousia not by asserting its imminence once again but by showing the factual presence of the Lord and the Spirit. This presence was a prelude to the end of the world,
which Maximilla believed would occur immediately after her death (Aland, no. 13).

The descent of the heavenly Jerusalem was feverishly awaited; it was to take place
in Pepuza or Tymion, a city of Phrygia. During the wait martyrdom was encouraged,
and a quite rigorous morality was preached (fasting, prohibition of marriage, almsgiving). After 200, the movement's center of gravity shifted from prophetic activity
(which ceased after Montanus, Prisca, and Maximilla) to ethical rigorism. The movement did not profess heretical doctrines, so that synods convoked to examine it in
Asia Minor did not see clearly whether or not to condemn it. However, its aforementioned tendency to resist processes that were in other respects irreversible, such as the
definition of the canon and the consolidation of ecclesiastical authority, eventually
brought about the condemnation of Montanism.

Montanus, Prisca, and Maximilla (or only the last two, in support of the first)
composed many books, of which nothing has survived except for a few oracles. Kurt
Aland lists sixteen authentic ones; we have already referred to some of these. A throng
of controversialists arose to refute the works. Eusebius (*Hist. eccl.* 4.27; 5.16.1) mentions some writings of Apollinaris of Hierapolis, who was active under Marcus
Aurelius (161–180), but he does not cite from any of them. The same writings were
also mentioned in a letter of Serapion of Antioch (*Hist. eccl.* 5.19.1–2).

On the other hand, Eusebius cites rather extensively (*Hist. eccl.* 5.16.2–22) a three-
volume treatise *Against the Cataphrygians* (supporters of the heresy *kata Phyrgas*). The
anonymous author, who lived in Asia Minor and had personal knowledge of the
churches troubled by Montanism, says that he had hesitated to write lest he seem desirous of adding something "to the words of the new covenant of the gospel," referring to a
central theme in the controversy over Montanism. He then recalls the origins of the

movement in the ecstatic raptures of Montanus and the two women. He refers to the Montanist leaders' understanding of themselves as persecuted prophets and to the legends about the deaths of Montanus and Maximilla and of Theodotus, one of their directors. He notes that at the time of his writing, thirteen years have passed since the death of Maximilla (in 179). In his third book he criticizes the Montanist quest of martyrdom and endeavors to disqualify the Montanist martyrs by citing cases in which some "orthodox" martyrs had dissociated themselves from their Montanist companions. According to Eusebius (*Hist. eccl.* 4.3.4), it was in connection with similar disagreements that the martyrs of Lyons wrote in conciliatory language to the churches of Asia and Phrygia and to Eleutherus, bishop of Rome.

Eusebius then cites another antimontanist treatise, this one by Apollonius, composed forty years after Montanus began to prophesy (*Hist. eccl.* 5.18.1–2). This treatise was devoted rather to personal attacks on the moral behavior of the founders of the movement: Montanus supposedly organized a system for collecting and managing money offerings; Prisca supposedly abandoned her husband. Alexander is denounced as a false martyr. Themiso, who bought his release from prison and composed a "general letter" in defense of Montanism, is also attacked. In Rome, Montanism was in process of being accepted, but it was finally rejected due to the efforts of the mysterious Praxeas, whom Tertullian attacks. Later, under Zephyrinus (199–217), a Roman priest named Gaius composed a work (*zētēsis*, search) against Proclus, a Montanist. Eusebius has passed on to us some fragments of Gaius's writings: one that refers to the monuments of Peter and Paul in Rome (*Hist. eccl.* 2.25.6–7); one on the grave of the prophetess daughters of Philip at Hierapolis in Asia Minor (3.31.4); and one against Cerinthus (3.28.2). To Cerinthus, Gaius attributed the Apocalypse of John, because of this work's millenarianism, which the Montanists could exploit. We know of this from the fragments of the *Chapters against Gaius* of Hippolytus, which have been preserved by Dionysius bar Salibi (see below, ch. 13, sec. 5).

BIBLIOGRAPHY

Texts

P. de Labriolle, *Les sources de l'histoire du montanisme* (Paris: Leroux, 1913).
R. E. Heine, *The Montanist Oracles and Testimonia* (Macon: Mercer University Press, 1989).

Studies

We shall mention only the classic work of P. de Labriolle, *La crise montaniste* (Paris: Leroux, 1913).
K. Aland, "Bemerkungen zum Montanismus and zur frühchristlichen Eschatologie," in idem, *Kirchengeschichtliche Entwürfe* (Gütersloh: Mohn, 1960) 105–47; includes an edition of the oracles.
G. Visonà, "Il fenomeno profetico del montanisme," *RStB* 5 (1993): 149–64; establishes the state of the question and provides an extensive, up-to-date bibliography.
A. Stewart-Sykes, "The Asian Context of the New Prophecy and of Epistula Apostolorum," *VC* 51 (1997): 416–38.

8. Hegesippus

According to Eusebius, Hegesippus belonged "among the first heirs of the apostles" (*Hist. eccl.* 2.23.3). He drew upon the *Gospel of the Hebrews,* the *Syriac Gospel,* and Jewish oral tradition, thereby showing that he was a convert from Judaism (*Hist. eccl.* 4.22.8). He traveled to Rome (4.22.1) and composed five books of *Hypomnēmata.* The citations in Eusebius, plus two in Philip of Side and in Stephen Gobarus (in Photius), are all that remain of his work. While the other information given by Eusebius cannot be verified, the journey to Rome by way of Corinth is confirmed by a fragment of Hegesippus himself (*Hist. eccl.* 4.22.2–3) in which the latter speaks of having established, while in Rome, the succession of bishops down to Anicetus (155–166). He then mentions Anicetus's successors, Soter and Eleutherus; the journey can therefore be dated to the time of Anicetus and the composition of the work to that of Eleutherus (174–189).

Hegesippus must have had literary ambitions for his work, as its title suggests, for it means "records" and was used for writings that varied in genre and content, the common denominator being a literary aim. The work was not, however, a history of the church, as was maintained for a long time due to confusion with another genre, a*pomnēmoneumata* ("memorable events"). On the one hand, Eusebius claims that he himself had no predecessor in the writing of church history (*Hist. eccl.* 1.1.3); on the other, he describes Hegesippus's work as "a very complete record of his own ideas" (4.22.1) and as containing "the tradition, without error, of the apostolic preaching." Nor was the work an apology, as has also been suggested because of the mention of the apotheosis of Antinous, a slave of Hadrian (*Hist. eccl.* 4.8.2), a fact recorded also by Justin in *1 Apology* (29.4).

Hegesippus's main concern can be seen in the passage mentioned above, in which he told of having been able to verify the orthodoxy of the church in Corinth, and of having drawn up a list of episcopal succession in Rome. He thus showed that "in every succession [of bishops] and in every city there is agreement with the preaching of the Law, the prophets, and the Lord" (*Hist. eccl.* 4.22.2–3).

In another fragment Hegesippus deals with the origin of heresies. Until the death of James the Just and the accession of his successor, Simon, son of Clopas, as bishop of Jerusalem, the church was described as a virgin because it had not yet been tainted by foolish doctrines. It was Thebuthis, a man disappointed at not having been elected bishop, who disseminated the theories of Jewish sects among believers, and so gave rise to Christian heresies (*Hist. eccl.* 4.22.4–6). In the same context, Hegesippus told of the martyrdom of Simon, which resulted from denunciations by heretics. He added information about the descendants of the family of Jesus, mentioning in particular that Simon must have seen the Lord (*Hist. eccl.* 3.32.2–6). What follows in Eusebius must also have depended on Hegesippus: as long as the apostles were alive, the church remained a virgin, but after their deaths the heretics began to spread "knowledge wrongly so called" (see 1 Tim 6:20). Hegesippus's main concern, then, must have been to oppose the single, uncorrupted tradition of the church to the multiplicity of heretical teachings.

This tradition, however, is now to be found not in the sequence of presbyters, as in the view of Papias of Hierapolis, but in the succession of bishops in the churches (or rather in certain churches). And the content of the tradition is no longer the say-ings of Jesus but, as Eusebius writes, the errorless transmission of the apostolic preaching. It is certainly with this in mind that the traditions about the relatives of Jesus are given, for they are meant to show that heresy is a recent growth (beginning of the 2d c.) and a foreign body (of Jewish origin) and therefore doubly lacking in au-thority to claim continuity with the preaching of the apostles and of those who saw Jesus. It is significant, however, that in his own time Hegesippus no longer looks to Je-rusalem for correct teaching, but to the "orthodox" churches of his day and first of all to Corinth and Rome. The latter were closely connected in the second century; see the surviving fragments of the correspondence between Dionysius of Corinth and Soter of Rome (Eusebius, *Hist. eccl.* 4.23). The historical situation of Hegesippus is closer to that of Irenaeus than to that of Papias.

BIBLIOGRAPHY

Edition

E. Preuschen, *Antilegomena: Die Reste der ausserkanonischen Evangeliun und urchristlichen Überlieferungen* (2d ed.; Giessen: Ricker, 1905), 107–13.

Studies

P. Vielhauer, *Geschichte der urchristlichen Literatur* (New York: de Gruyter, 1975), 765–74.

T. Halton, "Hegesippus in Eusebius," StPatr 117, 2 (1982): 688–93.

Chapter 10

THE GREEK APOLOGISTS

In the first decades of its existence, the Christian church seemed to outsiders to be a Jewish sect and therefore a permitted religion. Christians, for the most part, beginning with Paul in Romans 13:1, urged obedience to authority. But Christian propaganda in Jewish communities sometimes elicited reactions and conflicts of a kind that drew the attention of authorities. Luke describes such incidents several times in the Acts of the Apostles, always putting the synagogue leaders in a bad light (e.g., 17:1–8 [Thessalonica] and 18:12–17 [Corinth]). But decades before the composition of that work, conflicts caused by Christian propaganda in the Jewish community of Rome had resulted in the Jews being driven from Rome by Emperor Claudius in 41 or 49, if we are thus to interpret what Suetonius says (*Claud.* 25.4) about Chrestus, an agitator who supposedly stirred up riots. Clearly, the Roman authorities of that period drew no distinction between Christians and Jews.

The situation changed after July 64, when a terrible fire devastated Rome. Nero blamed it on the Christians, who were then hunted down and put to death; popular hatred of Christians helped in this scapegoating. The secrecy of their worship made them disliked, and the most atrocious slanders were circulated about them, so that even the historian Tacitus, although convinced they were not responsible for the fire, maintained that Christians were guilty of "hatred of the human race" and deserved their punishment (*Ann.* 15.44.4–5). Tertullian (*Nat.* 1.7.9) mentions an *institutum Neronianum* as the basis for criminal proceedings against Christians, but most scholars do not think that there was a true and proper juridical provision aimed at punishing the Christian *nomen* as a crime in itself. The procedure followed was that of a *coercitio* (thus Suetonius), that is, an act of referral to the police by a local magistrate. But while condemnation could be based on the obstinacy of the accused Christian, the acceptance of a denunciation must have had a different basis. This basis is not clear, but is probably to be seen in the position of Christianity as a *religio illicita*.

According to Eusebius of Caesarea, a second persecution took place under Domitian (see Suetonius, *Dom.* 15; Dio Cassius, *Hist. Rom.* 67.14.1–5), but the testimonies are vague. The one fundamental document is the letter of Pliny the Younger to Trajan and the latter's reply in 111–112 (Pliny, *Ep.* 10.96, 97). Pliny, as *legatus pro praetore* of the province of Bithynia, had received denunciations of Christians and wrote for guidelines. The emperor answered that Christians were not to be sought out; they were, however, to be punished if they were denounced openly (not anonymously), convicted of being Christians, and refused to sacrifice to the spirit (*genius*) of the emperor. These arrangements, which showed, among other things, the lack of any specific existing legislation, were confirmed by Hadrian and Antoninus Pius. Also obscure are the limits of the persecution by Septimius Severus in 202–203, all the more so because the tendency today is no longer to believe that there was an imperial edict for the purpose. Emperor Maximinus (235–238), who was obsessively concerned with the defense of the empire, a defense in which the Christians did not take part, ordered the persecution of the leaders of the churches, but the order does not seem to have had any great effect.

The first really general persecution was that of Decius who, in his concern to secure unity even in the area of religion, gave the order in 249 that all citizens should offer sacrifice to the divinities of the empire. This action unleashed a short but violent persecution during which many Christians gave in (the *lapsi*). Their apostasy led to a lively debate and even a schism when many of them later asked for readmission to the church. Another general persecution took place under Valerian (257–258). The final persecutions were political weapons in the hands of the tetrarchs during their struggles for power, which lasted from 303 to 324. Diocletian, Galerius, and Maximinus Daia all persecuted Christians in the East (Galerius: 303–311; Maximinus: 303–313). Licinius, successor to Galerius, began to persecute Christians once again, in contrast to his western rival, Constantine. When the latter defeated and killed Licinius in 324, he definitively espoused the Christian cause, betting on Christianity as the means of ensuring the religious unity of the empire. The historical debate over Constantine's own "conversion" remains quite complicated.

It was in this historical setting that the literary activity of the Christian apologists developed in the second century. These writers had for their purpose, on the one hand, to show the baselessness of accusations brought against Christians, whether by popular hatred, by educated circles, or by the tribunals of the state, and on the other, to criticize polytheism by showing the superiority and truth of the Christian religion. In this second area, they used to their advantage an apologetic tradition already extensively developed within Judaism. They did not have the same resource in the first area, however, because Judaism was not persecuted as such.

The authors of the apologies often addressed them to the emperors or the Roman senate as the authorities who could and should put an end to the unjust persecutions. The apologists argued that Christians could contribute more than anyone else to the common good of society, which it was the duty of these authorities to protect. The authors sometimes addressed pagan intellectuals as the representatives of a cultural tradition characterized by polytheism. Some writers adopted a conciliatory attitude, as did the author of *To Diognetus;* others, like Tatian and Hermias, were openly hostile.

The accusations brought by the educated pagan classes against the Christian religion are summarized in the *True Discourse* of Celsus (177–180), which is preserved in large measure in Origen's refutation of it (see below, ch. 15, sec. 4b). In Celsus's work, scorn for the multitude of ignorant and presumptuous Christian wretches alternates with indignation at the abandonment of the traditions on which the identity and strength of the political community depended, and at the lack of attachment to the social and political order, the guarantors of civilization itself, at a time when the empire was beginning to feel the disturbing pressure of the barbarians.

Against accusations of disloyalty to the state and sabotage of the common interest, the apologists protested their loyalty. Only on one point did they remain unyielding: their refusal to worship the emperor or his *genius.* Against accusations of superstition, ignorance, and of novelty (newness being in itself cause for suspicion in the ancient world), the apologists boldly accepted comparison with a venerable cultural tradition. They even dared to assert that their religion supported, in plenary form, the values which, in their view, only the highest minds in the pagan tradition had been able to glimpse. This line of thought was based on a theology of the Logos. Appropriating categories developed by Alexandrian Judaism, the apologists carried further the identification of Christ with the Logos, the divine Reason that was the mediator of creation; biblical revelation, culminating in the preaching of Jesus, the incarnate Logos, made available the ultimate and universal truth which the pagan philosophers had sought amid uncertainties and deviations, reaching it at best only in a very partial manner.

The contribution made by the apologists was imperfect from the theological point of view, and their writings were to lose their relevance once the stature of Christianity within the empire changed. This change helps to explain the meagerness of the manuscript tradition of their works. Still, what they accomplished represented an indispensable stage in the formation of a Christian self-awareness and of the energy that enabled the new religion to assert itself in unfavorable conditions.

BIBLIOGRAPHY

Comprehensive Edition

E. J. Goodspeed, *Die ältesten Apologeten* (Göttingen: Vandenhoeck & Ruprecht, 1914; repr., 1984); Theophilus is not included.

General Studies

M. Pellegrino, *Gli apologeti greci del II secolo: Saggio sui rapporti tra il cristianesimo primitivo e la cultura classica* (Rome: Anonima Veritas, 1947).
R. M. Grant, *Greek Apologists of the Second Century* (Philadelphia: Westminster, 1988).

1. Preaching of Peter

Apologetics and mission were already connected in the *Acts* of the various apostles. The same is true, as far as we can tell, in the *Preaching of Peter (Kerygma Petrou)*, of which only a few fragments remain, almost all of them preserved by Clement of Alexandria in the sixth book of his *Miscellanies*. There is another elsewhere in that work and in the *Extracts from the Prophets*. The *Preaching of Peter* was also cited by Heracleon, according to Origen (*Comm. Jo.* 13.7); it must go back to the year 100–120, and have been composed in Egypt.

The work took the form of a missionary discourse, in the first part of which Peter, speaking in the name of the Twelve, recalls their missionary mandate. The risen Lord had ordered them to preach to Israel for twelve years before making their way through the world (frag. 3, Klostermann). In another group of fragments (frag. 2, Klostermann), Peter exhorts his hearers to acknowledge a single God who created the universe through his Logos, and to venerate him, but not as the Greeks, who worship material objects, nor as the Jews, who worship the angels. Christians are a new race who worship God in a new way, through Christ, in whom a new covenant has been established. It seems, then, that this work accepts as a positive value the "novelty" that pagans regarded as reprehensible; a similar attitude is clearly manifested in the *Letter to Diognetus.*

Other fragments (frag. 4) deal with the christological interpretation of the prophetic Scriptures, which speak of Jesus, sometimes in parables, sometimes mysteriously, and sometimes clearly. This early apology already contains the themes that will be typical of apologetics: explanation of the one God and his transcendence, a theme inherited from Hellenistic Judaism; creation as carried out through the Son/Logos (or "law and logos," according to another fragment); attack on idolatry and on Judaism. It seems, however, from the surviving fragments, that the work was addressed not to pagans but to believers, perhaps to catechumens (frag. 2d: vocabulary typical of catechesis). The text thus had for its purpose to form and strengthen the identity of the community, partly by differentiating its religion from that of the pagans and that of the Jews. The consciousness of mission was an indispensable element in that identity.

Bibliography

E. Klostermann, *Reste des Petrusevangeliums, der Petrusapokalypse and des Kerygma Petri* (vol. I of *Apocrypha;* KIT 3; 3d ed.; Bonn: Marcus und Weber, 1933), 13–16; critical edition.

M. G. Mara, "Il Kergyma Petrou," *SMSR* 38 (1969): 314–42; text, translation, and commentary.

H. Paulsen, "Das Kerygma Petrou und die urchristliche Apologetik," *ZKG* 88 (1977): 1–37.

J. K. Elliott, ed., *The Apocryphal New Testament: A Collection of Apocryphal Christian Literature in an English Translation* (rev. and trans. M. R. James; Oxford: Clarendon/New York: Oxford University Press, 1993).

2. Quadratus and Aristides of Athens

Eusebius of Caesarea cites a passage that he claims comes from an apologia that Quadratus, an Athenian, delivered to Emperor Hadrian (*Hist. eccl.* 4.3.1–2). According to the *Chronicle* of the same Eusebius, Aristides and Quadratus delivered their apologies to Hadrian at the same time, on the occasion of his visit to Athens in 124 or 125; the manuscripts disagree on the date. In this apology, perhaps in a comparison with pagan miracles, Quadratus said that it was possible to prove the reality of the healings and raisings from the dead effected by Jesus because some of the beneficiaries were still alive in the writer's time. P. Andriessen has suggested that the *Apology* of Quadratus is actually the *Letter To Diognetus;* he hypothesizes that the passage cited by Eusebius belonged in one of the lacunae in the latter work; but the suggestion has not been accepted.

Immediately after mentioning Quadratus, Eusebius goes on to speak of the *Apology* of Aristides, which was also addressed to Hadrian (*Hist. eccl.* 4.3.3). A Syriac version of the work was discovered in 1878, and there was agreement at that time that the *Apology,* with omissions and alterations, had been included in ch. 37 of *Barlaam and Joasaph,* a novel from the Byzantine period. There are also two fragments of the original on papyrus, and a rather free Armenian translation of the first two chapters. None of these witnesses corresponds fully to the original, because the Syriac version has been enlarged; on the whole, however, they make possible a fairly good grasp of the work. The Armenian translation, like Eusebius, names Hadrian (117–138) as the addressee. The Syriac has a title that includes the name of Hadrian, but is followed by a dedication to Antoninus Pius (138–161). Perhaps Aristides wrote for Hadrian but produced a new edition under Antoninus (thus R. M. Grant).

According to Aristides, the order of the world requires a universal mover, namely, God (ch. 1). The four peoples who populate the earth have sought him, each in its own way: barbarians, Greeks, Jews, and Christians (thus the Syriac and Armenian versions; the Greek version lists polytheists [subdivided into barbarians, Greeks, and Egyptians], Jews, and Christians, but this distribution seems to be secondary). Each group goes back to a founder: the Christians go back to Jesus (ch. 2). There follows a critique of the several religions; the barbarians (chs. 3–7) and the Greeks (chs. 8–13, with a digression on the Egyptians in ch. 12) are condemned unconditionally. The Jews are discussed more briefly: because of their monotheism they have come close to the truth, and they rightly practice love of neighbor in imitation of God, but their worship of the angels and following of the astral calendar have distanced them from true knowledge (ch. 14). This kind of criticism was already to be seen in the *Preaching of Peter.* Alone among human beings, Christians truly know God and observe his commandments (chs. 15–16). People ought therefore to cease slandering them and should instead join their religion, lest they be condemned at the judgment (ch. 17).

The *Apology* develops fully the idea of Christians as a people like other peoples, with Jesus as the founding ancestor. The ancients used the idea of a founding ancestor to express awareness of a people's unity and special character. Here, however, unlike in the *Preaching of Peter,* it does not positively connote the newness of Christians, although this newness is acknowledged (2.7). It is notable that the motif of revelation plays an insignificant role; Judaism and Christianity are presented as ways of seeking God, just as are the religions of the barbarians and the Greeks. If the latter have gone astray, it is not because they did not have revelation or had it only imperfectly or because they allowed themselves to sin; they went astray out of foolishness, because they erred *(planē).* Christians alone, therefore, meet the requirements of reason by correctly knowing not only God but also the world as the one God's work; proper moral behavior is a result of this knowledge. In addition, Aristides suggests that Christians contribute to social order and stability by practicing a solidarity that eliminates need and the tensions that can spring from it.

BIBLIOGRAPHY

Aristide di Atene, *Apologia* (ed. C. Alpigiano; Florence: Nardini, 1988). Greek text, with IT of the Syriac and Armenian, introduction, and commentary.

D. W. Palmer, "Atheism, Apologetic, and Negative Theology in the Greek Apologists of the Second Century," *VC* 37 (1983): 234–59.

3. Justin Martyr

Justin was born in Flavia Neapolis, formerly Shechem, in Samaria, of a non-Jewish family, and received a Greek education. In the early chapters of the *Dialogue with Trypho* (chs. 1–8) he describes his youthful journey through the various philosophies: Stoicism, Aristoteleanism, Pythagoreanism, and Platonism, and how he finally came to Christianity, in which he found the only sure and useful philosophy. Stylized and stereotypical though this story is, it does, on the one hand, express Justin's real criticism of the several philosophies, and on the other, preserves the traces of a quest that led him to Middle Platonism (see *2 Apol.* 12.1), the philosophy that, in his view, made it possible to rise above material things and attain the vision of God. In Christianity alone, however, did he find the original, genuine philosophy that had subsequently degenerated into the multiplicity of philosophical schools. This conception of the history of philosophy came from Numenius of Apamea, a Middle Platonist.

The courage of the martyrs drew Justin to the Christian community, and it was certainly there that he first came upon the Scriptures. Justin spent two periods in Rome, where he opened a Christian school of philosophy, wrote some of his works, and around 165 suffered martyrdom, the acts of which have survived (see below, ch. 11, sec. 2). Hatred by his corrupt rival, the Cynic philosopher Crescens, is thought to have played some part in the martyrdom (*2 Apol.* 8; Tatian, *Or. Graec.* 19; Eusebius, *Hist. eccl.* 4.16).

Eusebius (*Hist. eccl.* 4.18) mentions the works of Justin that were known to him: the first is an *Apology* addressed to Antoninus Pius, his sons Marcus Aurelius and Lucius Verus, and the Roman senate; the second is another *Apology* addressed to Marcus Aurelius. Greek codex 450 of the Bibliothèque Nationale of Paris (dated 1364) has preserved two apologies of Justin, one addressed to Antoninus Pius, Marcus Aurelius, and Lucius Verus, and the other, according to the title, to the Roman senate. However, the ending of the latter work shows that it is addressed rather to an emperor, and in the text there is an allusion (2.16) to Antoninus Pius, Lucius Verus, and, if we accept a probable correction, Marcus Aurelius. The strange thing is that Eusebius cites passages from both of these apologies, claims to cite only the first. As a result, scholars debate whether the shorter apology is an appendix or a second part of the first, or an independent work connected with a particular circumstance of which the writer speaks at the beginning (see below). The question remains unsettled, but for practical purposes we shall speak here of the first and second apologies.

First Apology (29.2–3) mentions Felix, prefect of Egypt; this was probably Gaius Munatius Felix, who held the office from 148 to 154, although it is not clear whether the work was written under him or under his successor. In any case, the probable date of composition ranges from 153 to 157. A first part (chs. 1–12) is devoted to rebutting the accusations leveled against Christians. Justin asserts that demons, that is, angels fallen from heaven, gave rise to polytheism by managing to have themselves worshiped as divinities. Moreover, they have always secured the death of those human beings who unmasked them. Now they are doing the same to Christians, but they had already done so among the Greeks in the case of Socrates.

The divine Logos made it possible, even within Greek culture, to denounce the demons. He was uttered by the Father before every other creature; Justin tends to subordinate the Son to the Father, a constant feature of the early theology of the Logos (*Dial.* 61.1–3). The Logos manifested himself to human beings in the Old Testament theophanies, since God cannot make himself visible. The Logos has also manifested himself to all human beings, although in a less continual and complete way. It is precisely this partial communication of the seed of the Logos diffused throughout the world *(logos spermatikos)* that produced the disagreements among the Greeks. Christians, however, have received the seed in its completeness, and therefore the demons have attacked them all the more fiercely by unleashing persecutions.

This motif of the *logos spermatikos,* which is Stoic in origin, is also explained at length in *2 Apology.* It is basic for Justin; it gives expression to the quest for a dialogue with the Hellenic cultural tradition and the effort to retrieve that tradition for the expression of the Christian faith. This implies that the Greek philosophers had expropriated such truths as they found, because they were simply fragments of the revelation that is the property of Christians, coming as they did from the Logos (e.g., *2 Apol.* 13).

The work of Justin that has been preserved for us takes the form of a systematic program for reclaiming for Christians both the truths possessed by the Greeks and barbarians, that is, the true philosophy (*1–2 Apology, Dial.* 1–8), and the truths possessed by the Jews, that is, the Scriptures *(Dialogue* and *1 Apology).* It was a highly ambitious project for which Justin did not have adequate tools; it would be taken up again with much greater vigor by Clement. The same program has its analogue, to some extent, in gnostic documents, sought to reduce the various religious revelations to a common denominator which, probably at a time not far distant from Justin (for example, the sermon of the Naassenes; see above, ch. 9, sec. 5). The difference is that Justin does not develop a religious syncretism, but totally rejects pagan religion; he allows for no revelation outside the Jewish-Christian Scriptures.

In his *1 Apology,* Justin is also concerned to answer the accusation of subversion by stressing the point that Christians do not await an earthly kingdom. They do not even try to escape death, because they hope through death to obtain a share in the true kingdom. On the contrary, by preaching the judgment of God Christianity induces people to lead a virtuous life, something that is of great value in any civil society.

A second and much longer part (chs. 13–67) explains Christian teaching and practice. Justin notes among other things that there is no reason to deride the stories about Jesus, since pagan mythology contains comparable stories, although these are full of immorality. In order to explain the similarities, Justin develops three points. The first is that just as before the coming of Jesus the demons fostered the birth of myths, so after his ascension they have raised up the heretics to lead believers astray. Here Justin briefly mentions Simon Magus, Menander, and Marcion, whom he discussed at length in his *Syntagma* against heresies.

The second point is that the fulfillment of the prophecies shows that Jesus, unlike the heretics, is not a human being who tried to pass himself off as God. We have here a real treatise on prophecy (chs. 30–53, a third of the work), which was for Justin the main rational argument in favor of Christianity. The third point is that the fables of mythology are demoniacal imitations of the biblical prophecies. Here Justin takes up a motif dear to Jewish apologetics and soon to be frequently used in Christianity (by Tatian, Theophilus of Alexandria, Clement, and so on): whatever is good in Greek philosophy was taken from the much earlier books of Moses. The last part of

1 Apology has to do with Christian life and provides valuable information about baptism and the liturgy. In an appendix, Justin copies a rescript of Hadrian to Minucius Fundanus, proconsul of Asia (probably in 124), in which he requires that accusations against Christians be proved.

Second Apology, which is in large measure devoted to the subject of the *logos spermatikos,* makes reference to events in Rome under Prefect Marcus Lollius Urbicus, who held office probably from 146 to 160. A Roman matron who had lived a dissolute life was converted to Christianity and changed her ways; she then tried to convince her husband as well. When her efforts failed, she decided to divorce him, but her people (her family or the Christian community) persuaded her to wait. When her husband went to Alexandria, his behavior degenerated there, so she sent him a bill of divorce. He in revenge denounced her as a Christian. The husband was angry because in a divorce in which he was at fault, he would have to return his wife's dowry, whereas if she were found guilty, he could retain at least a part of it. The woman then turned to the emperor and asked him to separate the two matters: first, the question of her patrimony; second, the accusation of being a Christian. The emperor agreed, and the husband, seeing his efforts to be in vain, avenged himself on the woman's Christian teacher, one Ptolemy, whom some have wished to identify with the gnostic teacher of that name. The husband had Urbicus arrest Ptolemy and condemn him to death. Justin protests against the condemnation of Ptolemy because it was based solely on his being a Christian.

The incident is an example of the social impact that conversion to Christianity could have, especially among the well-to-do, which the woman evidently was.

Of the other works listed by Eusebius, only the *Dialogue with Trypho the Jew,* composed around 160, has survived. One dialogue depicting a controversy between a Jew and a Christian had already been written: the *Dialogue of Jason and Papiscus.* According to Maximus the Confessor (7th c.), this work, now lost, was composed by Ariston of Pella (mentioned in Eusebius, *Hist. eccl.* 4.6.3). Celsus knew the *Dialogue* and mocked it; Origen replied that while the work was not for persons of advanced understanding, there was nothing ridiculous or blameworthy about it (*Cels.* 4.52). At a later date, a vast literature of this kind appeared, including the *Dialogue of Athanasius and Zacchaeus* and the *Dialogue of Simon and Aquila.*

There has been much speculation as to the real addressees of such works: some scholars regard the works as Christian propaganda aimed at pagans; and others see them as tools for the internal use of Christian communities or possibly for use against heretics. In any case, it seems to us that in Justin's period this literature could serve in real controversies, while at the same time its addressees could be of the various kinds just indicated. This is confirmed for Justin's *Dialogue* by the fact that it begins with the already mentioned philosophical journey of Justin; its placement here serves to present Christianity as the true philosophy. The same is shown by the scriptural proof, which indicates the specific purpose of the *Dialogue,* namely, to show the continuity between the Old Testament and Christianity, thereby excluding contemporary Judaism. We have already signaled the importance of the scriptural proof in *1 Apology,* which is addressed to pagans. Justin undoubtedly thinks of his works as forming a unity within a plan for defending Christianity against pagans though it is not clear how conscious this was. He also expects them to strengthen the identity of the community and distinguish it from the "heresies" that were attacking the Old Testament and its God.

The *Dialogue,* which is certainly fictitious, is set in Ephesus during the Second Jewish War. As Justin walks in the portico of the gymnasium, he is approached by a group of Palestinian Jews who are refugees because of the war. Their leader is Trypho, who recognizes Justin to be a philosopher from his dress and asks him about his philosophy, meaning his conception of God. Justin tells of his philosophical search down to his finding of Christianity, which has convinced him because of the fulfillment of the prophecies contained in its Scriptures. This story leads to a discussion of the interpretation of the Scriptures, in which Justin defends christological exegesis: the Jews, he says, do not understand the Scriptures because, not believing in Christ, they do not have the key; as a result, the Scriptures no longer belong to them but to the Christians.

As can be seen from some references in the second part to subjects dealt with the day before (e.g., 78.6), the dialogue went on for two days. The end of the first and the beginning of the second would have been marked gap between 74.3 and 74.4, in which a considerable part of the text must have been lost (the *Dialogue,* like the *Apologies,* has been transmitted in a single manuscript). It has been suggested that a fragment of Justin published in 1941 should be inserted into the gap. Despite the often harsh language with which Justin addresses his interlocutors, they depart in a friendly manner, and Trypho acknowledges the pertinence of what Justin has said. Readers have observed that the Jew in this dialogue is overly accommodating and precisely engineered to bring out the truth professed by the Christian. This is in keeping with the aforementioned multiple functions of the work.

The *Dialogue* is full of digressions, with the result that it is difficult to determine a specific plan. However, scholars agree in distinguishing, after the introduction (1–9), a first part (10 to 29 or 30; for some, even to 47), which is devoted to an assessment of the Jewish law. Unlike Pseudo-Barnabas, Justin thinks that the prescriptions of the law, such as circumcision, the sabbath, and so on, were valid at one time, but that since the coming of Christ they must be transferred to a spiritual level. A second part (to 108) seeks to demonstrate that Jesus is the Christ on the basis both of the *typoi,* that is, events in which the figurative sense overlies the literal, and of the *logoi,* that is, prophecies which, though formulated with reference to the present or even the past, have an exclusively christological meaning. When Trypho objects that the promised Messiah is a glorious Messiah, Justin falls back on the thesis of the two comings of Christ, the first in lowliness, the second in glory, both of which are foretold in the Scriptures.

The third part (109–141) proves that the church is the new Israel; it therefore inherits, along with the Scriptures, all the privileges and promises that Israel has lost because it has not believed in Christ. We should also point out that Justin, along with the Asian tradition, is a millenarian, and that he appeals for justification to the Apocalypse of John (80).

Justin is not a profound or systematic thinker. As we pointed out, he is inclined to digress, although his works do show an underlying plan. His style is often wearying and convoluted. He is nevertheless inspired by the quest for and communication of the truth, and is ready to acknowledge the fragmentary presence of this truth in the Greek tradition. His effort to formulate the relationship between Christianity and the philosophical tradition is admittedly a naive one when compared with what Clement of Alexandria later accomplishes. But among Clement's predecessors Justin is probably the one who most clearly formulated the question and attempted to answer it.

Justin's other works are lost. He refers to a *Syntagma against All the Heresies,* which he wrote prior to *1 Apology* (28.6); this was probably the same as the work against Marcion to which Irenaeus refers (*Haer.* 4.6.2, which cites a bit of it, on the condemnation of the devil) as does Eusebius (*Hist. eccl.* 4.11.8; 4.18.9). Eusebius refers only to the testimony of *1 Apology* and to Irenaeus; it is therefore doubtful that he had a direct knowledge of the work. It has been shown that the *Syntagma* was used by later heresiologists; it contained a genealogy of heretics that began with Simon Magus (to whom a sect active in Rome in Justin's time appealed), Menander, and Saturninus. The work must have been chiefly an antimarcionite work; Marcion had been active in Rome a few years before Justin and was propagandizing with great success while Justin was writing his books.

Eusebius (*Hist. eccl.* 4.18) lists other works of Justin that have been lost: a *Discourse to the Greeks,* in which he dealt with "many questions debated between us and the Greek philosophers" and with the nature of demons (4.18.3); a *Refutation (Elenchos),* which was likewise addressed to the Greeks; a treatise on *The Monarchy of God,* which is demonstrated both from the Scriptures and from the writings of the Greeks; a *Psalter (Psaltēs);* and a work in the form of *scholia,* that is, short remarks, *On the Soul,* in which the author explained the opinions of the Greek philosophers while promising to refute them and to explain his own views in a subsequent work.

The *Sacra Parallela* of John of Damascus has preserved three lengthy passages from a treatise *On the Resurrection,* which he attributes to Justin. This work rebuts the opinions of those who deny the resurrection of the flesh because they consider it impossible, or because they consider it unworthy of God to restore something so contemptible as the flesh, or because the Scriptures do not promise resurrection to the flesh ("flesh" understood here as the material body, not as the sinful condition of the human being, as in Paul).

The reply to the first objection is based in part on philosophical arguments, which are intended to show that the restoration of matter is possible even according to pagans; and even more so to those who believe in God's omnipotence. The reply to the second objection is based on the creation story. Unlike the Alexandrians and the gnostics, the writer does not distinguish two creations in Gen 1:26 and 2:7, but finds in both passages the creation of the fleshly human being. On this point and the next, the author expounds an anthropology which identifies the human being not as body alone or soul alone but as the union of the two. The resurrections worked by Jesus anticipate and prove the reality of the resurrection of the flesh. This resurrection will restore the human being in its integrity, the soul dwelling in the body and the spirit dwelling in the soul.

This treatise fits perfectly into the debates at the end of the second century as these are attested by the works of Tertullian and possibly Athenagoras on the resurrection and by the fifth book of Irenaeus *Against Heresies.* Justin's authorship, however, is much debated.

Numerous works have come down under Justin's name that are surely not his; even the *Letter to Diognetus* is attributed to him in the manuscript. We shall mention three that certainly go back to the third century, while the others are surely later. The author of the *Discourse to the Greeks,* which is a concise and well written work, seeks to explain to the Greeks why he has distanced himself from their customs: in them he found nothing holy or pleasing to God. The author is therefore a convert to Christianity, who criticizes in detail the immorality and ridiculous nature of the myths and urges the Greeks to make the choice he has made and to let the divine Logos be their teacher.

This work, sometimes attributed to Tatian, also exists in a significantly longer version that has survived in a Syriac translation, the *Exhortation (Logos parainetikos) to the Greeks*. It urges the Greeks not to fear abandoning the tradition of the ancients if this proves to be in error (a typical motif of protreptic writings) and embracing the true religion. It criticizes what the poets and the philosophers say about the divinity, and emphasizes the contradictions therein; it asserts that there is no truth to be found in the Greek traditions. The truth is found in the books of Moses, who, as even pagan writers admit, was much earlier than the poets and philosophers. It was from Moses that these latter got the little bit of truth they convey. Christ has restored to humanity the religion of the first parents, which their descendants had abandoned due to the malicious teaching of the devil. The Greeks are exhorted to listen to the Sibyl, for she too foretells Christ. The assessment of Greek culture in this work is far different from that of Justin.

Finally, the work on *The Monarchy of God* (that is, on the government of the one God) is little more than a cento of verses from the Greek poets on God, accompanied by an exhortation to return to the original monotheism that has been obscured during human history. According to Eusebius, Justin's work of the same title must also have contained proofs taken from Scripture but that is not the case with the present work.

BIBLIOGRAPHY

Editions

Saint Justin, *Apologies* (trans. and ed. A. Wartelle; Paris: Etudes Augustiniennes, 1987); translation, introduction, and commentary.

———, *Dialogue*, in *Die ältesten Apologeten* (ed. and trans. E. J. Goodspeed; Göttingen: Vandenhoeck & Ruprecht, 1914; repr., 1984), 90–265.

———, *Dialogue avec Tryphon* (trans. and ed. G. Archambault; 2 vols.; Paris: Picard, 1909); translation, introduction, and notes.

Writings of Pseudo-Justin

Pseudo-Iustinus, *Cohortatio ad Graecos; De monarchia; Oratio ad Graecos* (ed. M. Marcovich; New York: de Gruyter, 1990).

Studies

L. W. Barnard, *Justin Martyr: His Life and Thought* (Cambridge: Cambridge University Press, 1967).

G. Otranto, *Esegesi biblica e storia in Giustino* (*Dial.* 63–84) (Bari: Istituto di letteratura cristiana antica, 1979).

R. Joly, *Christianisme et Philosophie: Etudes sur St. Justin et les apologistes grecs du deuxième siècle* (Brussels: Editions de l'Université de Bruxelles, 1973).

D. Bourgeois, *La sagesse des anciens dans le mystère du Verbe: Evangile et philosophie chez saint Justin* (Paris: Téqui, 1981).

H. Chadwick, *Early Christian Thought and the Classical Tradition: Studies in Justin, Clement, and Origen* (New York: Oxford University Press, 1966).

4. Tatian

Tatian was from Assyria (probably Syria), where he received an education in Greek culture (*Or. Graec.* 42; Clement, *Strom.* 3.81.1). He says that he had traveled a great deal before his conversion (*Or. Graec.* 35) and had been initiated into the mysteries (*Or. Graec.* 29). He went to Rome, perhaps as a teacher of philosophy or rhetoric. He probably became a Christian and composed his *Discourse to the Greeks* in that city, although others think he wrote the *Discourse* in Athens. He became a student of Justin, and after the latter's martyrdom must have remained in Rome for a time, since he had Rhodo, the antimarcionite writer, as a pupil (Eusebius, *Hist. eccl.* 5.13.1 and 8).

His moral rigorism led him subsequently to distance himself from the Roman church; Irenaeus (*Haer.* 1.28.1; 3.23.8) already regards him as a heretic, a founder of the encratites who were vehemently opposed to marriage; Eusebius in his *Chronicle* dates that event to the year 172. Tatian returned to his homeland and, according to Epiphanius of Salamis (*Pan.* 48.1), opened a school in Mesopotamia. According to Irenaeus, Tatian became a gnostic, excogitated aeons after the fashion of Valentinus (see *Or. Graec.* 20 on the aeons), and denied that Adam had been saved. According to a passage handed on by Clement of Alexandria (*Ecl.* 38.11; see Origen, *Or.* 24), Tatian interpreted the words "Let there be light" in Gen 1:3 as a prayer of the creator to a higher God; this is certainly a gnostic concept. According to Clement (*Strom.* 3.82.2), Tatian attributed the law to a God different from the God of the gospel.

Tatian's *Discourse to the Greeks* has survived in its entirety and in its original language. According to R. M. Grant, the work may have been written as a reaction to the episode of the martyrs of Lyons (see below, ch. 11, sec. 2). Rather than a defense of Christianity, the work is a violent attack on the Hellenic cultural tradition. Unlike Justin, Tatian does not see in that tradition any participation in the divine Logos. Furthermore, he would have it that every element in it came from the barbarians whom that tradition so despised (ch. 1). The philosophers, ancient (ch. 2) and contemporary (ch. 19), are ridiculed; Socrates alone is one of the few just men of Greek history (ch. 3). Of interest is Tatian's effort to break down the Greek identity by emphasizing pluralism as its capital sin, in its dialects (ch. 1) as in its government (ch. 14) and legislation (ch. 28); the end result of this pluralism is that we do not know what "Greek" means. Tatian points, in contrast, to the unity of Christians, who form a people united by the possession of the true revelation and by a moral code that accords with God's will.

Over against a culture supported by polytheism Tatian sets the Christian idea of God, the relationship of the Father to the Logos, the creation of the world and human beings, the resurrection, and the judgment (chs. 4–6). Like Justin and others, Tatian sees polytheistic religion as originating in the rebellion of the angels, but he emphasizes as the chief result of that rebellion, astrology and the subjection of human beings to fate, from which Christ has delivered them (chs. 7–11). He then goes on to interpret original sin as the separation of the human soul from the divine Spirit, who was the "wings" of the soul; as a result, the soul fell into the depths and must recover the Spirit (ch. 20).

Tatian goes on to attack all aspects of Greek culture: its mythology, the theater and other spectacles, the philosophers and grammarians (chs. 21–26), and the sculpture that glorified the most immoral personages (chs. 33–34). The last part of the work is devoted to the traditional arguments for the priority of Moses over the Greek poets and philosophers (chs. 35–41). Unpolished though it is, Tatian's attack is an energetic one and expresses the particular Christian spirit, found especially in the tradition of the apologists, that clashed head on with Greek culture, and attributed to demonic influence all aspects of that culture, not simply its religion. In style, Tatian practices the Asianism of his time.

The multiplicity of the gospels was to some extent a problem for the early church. Toward the end of the second century Irenaeus had to fall back on more or less persuasive arguments to show that the church could not accept either more or less than four gospels (*Haer.* 3.11.8–9). Another solution was to make up a single text (a "gospel harmony") on the basis of all the gospels; this was probably the intention of the *Gospel of the Ebionites* (see above, ch. 2, sec. 8b). But the attempt that met with real success was the *Diatessaron* (a term from music) which Tatian composed probably around 170. He certainly used the four gospels that by this time were canonical, and perhaps apocryphal materials as well; the links with specific texts, especially the *Gospel of Thomas,* are debated. Also in dispute is whether the *Diatessaron* was composed in Greek and then translated into Syriac, or the other way around. In any case, it no longer exists in complete form in those languages.

Only a fragment of the Greek text remains; it was found in 1934 during the excavation of Dura Europos, a Roman outpost on the Euphrates that was destroyed by the Persians in 256–257 (the fragment is therefore older than that date). The passage in the fragment (Matt 27:56–57 and parallels) makes it possible within limits to show the skillful interweaving, word by word, of the text of the four gospels.

The *Diatessaron* became the official gospel of the Syrian church. However, when "orthodoxy" was definitively established in Syria in the fifth century, bishops devoted themselves to destroying all copies of the *Diatessaron,* the prestige of which had been damaged by Tatian's reputation as a heretic. Theodoret of Cyrrhus says that he had destroyed about two hundred copies (*Haer. fab.* 1.20). But we still have the citations of the *Diatessaron* by Syrian authors who used it, in particular the *Commentary on the Diatessaron* by Ephraem of Nisibis (d. 373); it survives in part in the Syriac original and in whole in an Armenian translation. In addition, numerous revisions were made down to the Middle Ages, which offer glimpses of it original structure and of individual passages.

A distinction is usually made between an eastern tradition, consisting of the aforementioned Syriac and Armenian texts, as well as translations into Arabic and Persian, and a western tradition, consisting of translations into Latin, Dutch, Italian, English, and German.

Only scattered fragments remain of Tatian's other works. He himself mentions a treatise *On Animals* (*Or. Graec.* 15). Clement of Alexandria cites a passage from a work *On Perfection according to the Savior* (*Strom.* 3.81.1). In Eusebius, Rhodo attributes to Tatian a work *On Problems,* in which he interpreted obscure passages of the Scriptures (*Hist. eccl.* 5.13.8).

BIBLIOGRAPHY

Tatian, *'Oratio ad Graecos' and Fragments* (ed. and trans. M. Whittaker; Oxford: Clarendon Press, 1982); edition, translation, introduction, and notes.
M. Elze, *Tatian und seine Theologie* (Göttingen: Vandenhoeck & Ruprecht, 1960).
On the complicated transmission of the *Diatessaron,* see the abundant information in *CPG* 1106 and, above all, W. L. Petersen, *Tatian's Diatessaron: Creation, Dissemination, Significance, and History in Scholarship* (Leiden: Brill, 1994).

5. Athenagoras of Athens

The manuscript copied by Bishop Aretas in 914, which is important for the textual transmission of the Greek apologists, contains a *Supplication of Athenagoras, a Christian Philosopher of Athens, Concerning Christians.* Apart from what the title says of him, we know almost nothing about the author. He is mentioned once by Methodius of Olympus in a reference to *Supplication* 24 (*Res.* 1.36.6–37.1) and by Philip of Side (5th c.) in an enigmatic remark that identifies Athenagoras as the first head of the catechetical school of Alexandria.

The *Supplication* is addressed to Marcus Aurelius and his son Commodus; the titles given to them refer to the prevailing peace and date the work to 177. Athenagoras seeks to prove that the persecution of Christians is unjust, and he sets about refuting the accusations against them. The first is the charge of atheism, which takes up the greater part of the work (chs. 4–30). Christians are monotheists, not atheists, as were also the best of the Greeks. Christians do not sacrifice to the gods because, as one ought to realize, God needs nothing. The traditional critique of idols takes account of three objections: idols are only images of the gods; the gods are allegorical representations of the elements of the world; certain idols really act and must therefore be moved by a divinity. In regard to this last point, Athenagoras says those who make idols act are demons, that is, fallen angels and the souls of their sons, the giants (*1 En.* 6–11 is used here). Athenagoras also makes use of the views of the euhemerists, who saw in the gods great men of the past who were later divinized. He replies more briefly to the charges of incest (chs. 32–34) and of ritual infanticide and cannibalism (chs. 35–36), and emphasizes instead the superiority of Christian morality.

While influenced by Stoicism and Middle Platonism, Athenagoras depends on Justin in several ways. With the latter he believes that demons inspired imitations of biblical themes in pagan literature (24.6) and that the persecutions endured by Pythagoras, Heraclitus, Democritus, and Socrates anticipated those inflicted on Christians (31.1–2). He allows that the Greeks sought the truth, but claims they did not find it because they preferred to rely on their own conjecture rather than learn the truth from God (ch. 72). His respectful attitude toward the emperors is significant; while he rebukes them for permitting attacks on Christians, who as citizens ought to be protected, he professes a devotion to their rule, although without yielding on the matter of their divinity (1.3–4). He also sets forth an analogy between the universal empire that is subject to the emperors, father and son, and the government of the universe by God and his Son, the Logos (18.3).

As is consistent with that outlook, in his conclusion Athenagoras puts in a good word for Christians by pointing out that they pray for the government of the emperors and for an orderly succession of father by son, even in the interests of Christians themselves. Here we already have the idea that thanks to Christianity's conformity to the will of God, who grants emperors their power, it is the only religion capable of ensuring the peace and order of the state.

At the end of the *Supplication* (ch. 37), Athenagoras postpones to another occasion what he has to say about the resurrection. In the manuscript, the *Supplication* is followed by another work titled *Of the Same Author, On the Resurrection of the Dead.* This work contains nothing specifically Christian, but is an attempt to use the categories of Greek philosophy (Aristotle, in particular) to defend the resurrection of the dead, a concept which that philosophy found unacceptable. The first part of the work answers the usual objections (see above, sec. 3, what was said of the work *On the Resurrection,* attributed to Justin), according to which God cannot raise bodies, or is unwilling to do so because this action is unworthy of him (chs. 1–10). On the first point, he answers, among others, the following challenge to the resurrection: Since many unburied human beings have become the food of animals, so that their substance has become an integral part of the animals' substance, how can they be raised to life? In replying, the author appeals not only to the omnipotence of God but also to medical ideas, more specifically, to the distinction between natural foods, which are assimilated, and nonnatural foods (such as human flesh) that are eliminated and therefore do not enter into the composition of other beings.

The second part of the work (chs. 11–25) establishes that the resurrection follows logically from the purpose for which human beings are created (the unending contemplation of God); from the nature of the human being as a composite of body and soul and not simply as a soul; and from the justice of God, inasmuch as body and soul are co-responsible for human behavior and ought therefore alike to receive rewards and punishments.

Examination of the condition of the text of the two works has led to the hypothesis that they were combined at a late date; as for doubts about the attribution to Athenagoras (R. M. Grant and others), the question is still open.

BIBLIOGRAPHY

Athenagoras, *Supplique au sujet des chrétiens; et Sur la résurrection des morts* (ed. and trans. B. Pouderon; SC 379; Paris: Cerf, 1992).

———, *Legatio and De Resurrectione* (ed. and trans. W. R. Schoedel; Oxford Early Christian Texts; Oxford: Clarendon Press, 1972).

B. Ponderon, *Athénagore d'Athènes: Philosophe chrétien* (Paris: Beauchesne, 1989).

6. Theophilus of Antioch and Hermias

Eusebius (*Hist. eccl.* 4.20) says that Theophilus, a pagan convert to Christianity (*Autol.* 1.14) was bishop of Antioch. Of the works listed by Eusebius (*Hist. eccl.* 4.24) only *To Autolycus,* in three books, survives; in the third (3.27) Theophilus speaks of the death of Marcus Aurelius, which occurred on March 17, 180.

Autolycus, a pagan, has asked the author to explain his God to him. Theophilus offers him a negative theology: nothing can be said directly about God (1.3–4); if one is disposed to believe, one will know him from his works and his providence. Faith is also necessary when it comes to the resurrection, which pagans like Autolycus reject, even while believing in ridiculous divinities that have the names of dead human beings (1.9; like Athenagoras, Theophilus falls back on euhemerism for tactical reasons, even though he elsewhere describe Euhemerus as "an utter atheist," 3.7). Christians honor the emperor but it is not permissible for them to worship him (1.11).

In the second book, the writer contrasts the Greek poets and philosophers and their contradictions with the prophets, who were instructed by God (2.4–9). The prophets teach creation from nothing, which God has accomplished through his Logos, who is first of all immanent *(endiathetos),* and then generated, literally "disgorged" *(eructavit,* according to Ps 44:2), with a view to creating. Theophilus here uses the distinction between *logos endiathetos* and *logos prophorikos,* which Philo of Alexandria had used in describing the relationship between thought and speech, and which the Valentinian gnostics, whom Irenaeus opposes, were using in Christology.

Theophilus comments at length on the biblical story from creation to the time after the flood, and in particular on Genesis 1–3, which played a crucial role throughout the theology of the second and third centuries, because these chapters were made the basis of teaching on God, Christology, anthropology, and evil. Theophilus's exegesis is predominantly literal, with few allegorical and moral reflections. In many ways it reflects ancient Jewish exegesis, with which the writer was clearly in close contact. As for Justin, so for Theophilus the Old Testament theophanies are manifestations of the Logos. Theophilus contrasts the true story in the Scriptures with the uncertain information of the Greeks, who lived long after Moses and the prophets. The Sibyl and other poets, however, did have an idea of divine justice and of the final destiny of human beings. (Theophilus cites parts of the Jewish Sibylline books; see below, ch. 12, sec. 2).

The third book attacks the philosophical and literary works of the Greeks, in which can be found the crimes of those who wrongly accuse Christians (3.1–8). By contrast, the Law, the Prophets, and the Gospels display a far different consistency and are on a much higher ethical level (3.9–15). The entire second part of this book is a detailed chronology largely dependent on the *Against Apion,* a defense of Judaism by Flavius Josephus. It attempts to prove that the Jewish tradition, which Theophilus evidently claims for Christians, is far older than the Greek, and that biblical history is far more trustworthy.

Without realizing it, Theophilus follows a completely Christian logic, so that his work would have had a hard time convincing any kind of pagan. While citing the gospel, he never speaks of Jesus by name; his problem is to show that through the biblical tradition Christian ideas of God, human beings, and salvation are far more compelling than those of the Greeks. But the continuity between Judaism and Christianity, that is, the idea that the Jewish tradition belongs to Christians, is so evident to him that he feels no need to prove it, although it would not have been so clear to a non-Christian. This conviction permits him so serenely to appropriate the Jewish-Hellenistic doctrine of the Logos and Jewish exegesis, ethics, and apologetics.

We must admit that our knowledge of Theophilus's thought, restricted as it is to the *To Autolycus,* is quite limited. For example, in his *Against Marcion,* which influenced such important writers as Irenaeus of Lyons, he must have discussed specifically the question of the continuity between Judaism and Christianity, and it is likely that in his apologetics he regarded the question as already settled. At the same time, however, he does not succeed in grasping the viewpoint of pagans, who would probably not have been impressed by the lengthy exegesis of Genesis and would have needed an explanation of the term "gospel." (3.12).

According to Eusebius (*Hist. eccl.* 4.24), Theophilus also composed a work *Against the Heresy of Hermogenes,* who maintained that God created the world from matter that was co-eternal with him. This work, in which he used the Apocalypse of John, is now lost; it was used by Tertullian in his *Against Hermogenes.* Finally, Eusebius mentions catechetical writings of Theophilus, but does not describe them. Jerome (*Vir. ill.* 25) speaks of commentaries of Theophilus on the Gospel and on the Proverbs of Solomon. In *To Autolycus* (2.13; 2.30; 3.19), Theophilus himself speaks of his work *On History,* in several books.

It will be enough to make brief mention of the short *Satire on the Pagan Philosophers* that has come down in various manuscripts under the name of Hermias, who is not to be identified with known individuals having more or less the same name. The work is devoted entirely to mocking the views of the pagan philosophers who, according to the author, began to replace the one original and true wisdom with teachings by the fallen angels (Gen 6:1 and *1 En.*). This reading of the biblical episode has better parallels in the second and third century, a point that provides one of the few arguments for the date of the text (which varies among the critics between 200 and 600). Hermias ends with a profession of skepticism toward all philosophies (ch. 19). These seem to be the only ideas in the work. The only Christian trait is an opening reference to the first letter of Paul to the Corinthians; the erroneous geographical placement of Corinth suggests that the author did not live near that city.

BIBLIOGRAPHY

Theophilus of Antioch, *Ad Autolycum* (ed. and trans. R. M. Grant; Oxford: Clarendon, 1970).

Hermias, *Satire des philosophes païens* (trans. D. Joussot; ed. R. P. C. Hanson et al.; SC 388; Paris: Cerf, 1993).

7. Letter to Diognetus

The *Letter to Diognetus* (henceforth: *Diognetus*) was never cited in ancient or medieval literature and was accidentally discovered in Constantinople around 1436 in a manuscript, probably of the fourteenth century, which a fishmonger apparently had used to wrap his wares. After being placed in the City Library of Strasbourg, it was

destroyed by a bomb in 1870, during the Franco-Prussian War. The establishment of
the text must therefore rely on copies, collations, and editions made between those
two dates. In the manuscript, the work followed four others that were erroneously attributed to Justin and are known from other manuscripts, among them the work on
the divine monarchy and the two *Discourses* to the Greeks (see above, sec. 3). The
Diognetus, too, was mistakenly attributed to Justin. Attempts to assign it to known
writers have not been persuasive.

Among the places of origin suggested, Alexandria was long preferred, but this is
difficult to maintain nowadays; today scholars think of Asia Minor and Rome as possibilities. The reference to persecutions seems to ensure a date before Constantine; the
tendency is to date it between the middle of the second century and the early part of
the third. This dating is based on the degree of development of its apologetic themes.
The message of the work seems to fit well into the period of the last Antonines or the
Severi. Especially striking is the high level of the Greek, which is a sign of a real literary
education; it is certainly the best Greek to be found in the writings of the apologists.

The work is probably not an apologia in the strict sense and still less a letter, as it
was called in the first edition of 1592 and as it is still usually described. It is more nearly
a protreptic work, that is, an invitation to accept the Christian faith (on the protreptic
genre see below, ch. 14, sec. 2b). The author addresses an educated pagan named
Diognetus, who may be real or fictitious, and who has asked the writer about God and
the kind of worship that allows Christians to regard themselves as superior to the world,
to scorn death, and to reject the religions of the Greeks and the Jews (ch. 1).

The reply begins with a critique of polytheism as a mere human illusion, and of
Judaism, which has canceled out its insight into the one God with its superstitions and
ritual practices (chs. 3–4). Christianity, in contrast, is a mystery, the instruction of
which cannot come from human beings. It is also a paradox to outsiders: Christians
do not form a people apart but live in cities both Greek and barbarian as resident foreigners. They practice superior ethics, but this virtue gains them only hatred and persecution (ch. 5). Their condition is like that of the soul, which acts for the good of the
body but is held prisoner and resisted by the same body. Yet just as the soul perse-
veres, so Christians do not fail in the task assigned them by God, which is to hold
together the very world that lodges them as in a prison (ch. 6).

Chapters 5 and 6 have become very well known for this description of the Christian condition, but if they are to be understood, they must not be taken out of the
context of the argument as a whole. Here is the real explanation of the paradox: the
religion of Christians is the only one that is not a human invention but comes from
the supreme God and has been handed down by his Logos, the same who created the
universe. This religion is therefore the only one conformed to God's will. The courage
of the martyrs is the proof of its more than human character (ch. 7). Here the writer
accepts, in its most radical form, the novelty of Christianity, which the other apologists try to play down with the argument of the priority of the biblical prophets over
the Greek poets and philosophers. According to *Diognetus*, no one ever knew God before he sent his Son, who, beyond all expectation, has made him known and has made
it possible to share in his blessings (ch. 8).

This is an extremely bold position because it seems to deny a divine revelation to
the Jews; it explains the importance of describing the Jews in this perspective in chs. 3
and 4. Before the coming of the Son there was only error: God was waiting for human

beings to see clearly their inability to gain life for themselves. Then, at a predetermined moment, he sent the Son, who took on himself the sins of the wicked in order to reveal the extraordinary goodness of God and to allow human beings to enjoy it (ch. 9). If Diognetus will accept this, he too can attain to the knowledge of God. By doing good to others who are less fortunate, he will become an imitator of the God who does good to human beings; he will then understand the behavior of the martyrs and the full meaning of Christianity's apparent paradox, because he too will be a citizen of heaven (ch. 10).

At this point the manuscript indicated a gap in its exemplar (another is indicated within ch. 7). After it the text resumes with a passage (chs. 11–12) in which the speaker says that his explanation came from the apostles, who in their turn were instructed by the Logos, who was sent into the world to reveal divine mysteries. This same Logos is still being born today in the hearts of the faithful through the mediation of the church, providing them with an understanding of the divine mysteries. It is precisely because the Logos continues to manifest himself through the members of the church that the author has set down the teaching in chs. 1–10. But knowledge must be linked to a way of life; the basis of this unity is the Logos, who is life and at the same time bestows understanding.

The final part is clearly the end of a more extensive discourse, as the concluding doxology also shows. But is this discourse part of *Diognetus?* There are very noticeable differences: the "you" (plural) of the community to which an instruction is addressed now replaces the "you" (singular) of the pagan to whom an appeal is being made. In addition, these final chapters presuppose knowledge of a Christian vocabulary: apostles, church, gospels, Passover of the Lord, and so on. The argument here is based on an exegesis of Genesis 2–3, whereas in chs. 1–10, as we have seen, the writer seeks to convince the addressee that there has been no revelation to the Jews, nor does he refer to the Old Testament. The Christology, too, is different, as are other matters. Chapter 10 has the marks of a conclusion to a proptreptic discourse, so that we must assume that little has been lost in the lacuna.

Therefore, despite the current strong trend to the contrary, we join those who hold that chs. 11 and 12 were not originally part of *Diognetus.* They seem to form the conclusion of an exegetical treatise; affinities with Hippolytus, the exegete, have been pointed out. It is difficult to say why they were added to *Diognetus.*

The author of *Diognetus* thus relies on the absolute newness of Christianity, a feature that, as we have seen, was brought out in the *Preaching of Peter,* at the beginnings of apologetics. In Christianity, God has directly shown himself for the first time; human beings must embrace Christianity if they are to be attuned to God's plan for the world. This radical approach, as well as the kind of reading of Paul and John that underlies the text, have at times caused scholars to suggest Marcion or Valentinus as the author of the work. Their authorship, however, is excluded because the writer deliberately identifies the supreme God with the Creator of the world. He is not at all willing to separate being a Christian from being faithful to the world. So despite the apparent loss of status, even to the point of martyrdom, that Christians have experienced, the author proposes Christianity to his educated and well-to-do addressee, that is, the Roman ruling class, as an enhancement of status: by imitating God, the addressee becomes a god to those he benefits. The author of *Diognetus* hopes that this prospect of a reward that is even social will prove attractive to the recipient.

While Melito of Sardis (see above, ch. 7, sec. 2b) and, to some extent, Athenagoras had promoted Christianity to the emperors as the best means of stabilizing the empire, the author of *Diognetus* understands that Christianity as the basis of a healthy social order must be made acceptable to the ruling class, and he intends to do what he can to support this class. For this reason, the tone of the brief critique of polytheism is not that of a head-on collision, nor of a demonstration; it is the tone of one who knows that his addressee can only agree with him, and who wants simply to remind him of it. *Diognetus* does not seem to have had any important influence on later Christianity, or even to have had its desired effect. Nevertheless, it represents perhaps the boldest and most self-aware undertaking in second-century Christian apologetics.

BIBLIOGRAPHY

A Diognète (ed. and trans. H.-I. Marrou; SC 33; 2d ed.; Paris: Cerf, 1965).
A Diogneto (ed. and trans. E. Norelli; Milan: Paoline, 1991).
J. B. Lightfoot and J. R. Harmer, *The Apostolic Fathers: Greek Texts and English Translations of Their Writings* (2d ed.; trans. and ed. M. W. Holmes; Grand Rapids, Mich.: Baker, 1992).

Chapter 11

THE EARLIEST LITERATURE
ON THE MARTYRS

1. General Points

"Acts," "passions," "martyrdoms," and "legends" are the names given to accounts of the arrest, trial, and execution of early Christians by the authorities. The last name, "legends," designates narrative works of late or at least post-Constantinian origin that use every type of secondary development to extol the deeds of the martyrs; they are connected with the cult paid to the martyrs in the many basilicas dedicated to them after "the peace of the church." Our concern here is with the first three types. The names do not, strictly speaking, correspond to specific literary forms. The "acts" are not necessarily the records of a trial, although in some instances such records may have been used; the term *acta* is used here of the entire heroic behavior of the martyrs. The same holds for the term *passiones,* which emphasizes the sufferings endured in the confession of faith, and also for the term *martyria,* which originally stressed the idea of testimony given before persecutors. Still, the three names have been used to distinguish, correctly, the various forms found in this literature.

The following tripartite division is rather commonly accepted. (a) Accounts of interrogations before a magistrate. In some cases, the accounts are based on the official acts, which were stored in the archives and which Christians were able to consult; in these instances, the structure is essentially one of question and answer, and the culmination is the confession of faith. We should not overlook the part played by the Christian editors, who show a tendency to stylize the behavior of both the magistrates and the martyrs, and who sometimes place in the magistrates' mouths questions designed to elicit edifying answers from the Christians. The name "acts" is often reserved for this type of document. (b) Narratives that include the arrest (and sometimes the preceding circumstances), imprisonment, torture, and execution of Christians. The sources here are eyewitnesses, and the editors have a freer and more personal part to play than in the acts and may be more open to the inclusion of legendary elements. The name "passions" is generally reserved to this genre. (c) Legends, written long after the events, using stereotyped elements, and aimed primarily at the exaltation of the martyrs.

But even documents based on the official acts and having little further development were composed not for purposes of historical knowledge but for celebration (veneration at the tomb of a martyr on the anniversary of death), edification, and propaganda. The process of determining the actual events is therefore very complicated. Historical criticism began in the seventeenth century with the Maurists (a group of Benedictines: *Acta primorum martyrum* by J. Ruinart, 1689) and the Bollandists (a group of Jesuits: *Acta Sanctorum* by J. Bolland, beginning in 1643), in response to Protestant attacks on the reliability of the acts; the work has continued to the present century. In particular, Hippolyte Delehaye, a Bollandist, wrote numerous, still fundamental works in which he undertook to set down criteria for recognizing acts that have historical value. It remains true, however, that every text must be studied and evaluated individually, and that scholars often remain unsure of the judgment to be passed.

The question of the origin of literature on the martyrs is much debated. In any case, an adequate explanation is not to be found in the so-called "acts of the pagan martyrs," that is, narratives, recovered on papyri, of trials before the emperor against Alexandrians responsible for anti-Roman and anti-Semitic actions in the second and third centuries A.D. Nor is it to be found in the literature of the *exitus virorum illustrium,* that is, the deaths of aristocrats who fell victim to the despotism of the emperors. Both of these genres had too many political overtones to be of interest to Christians, who never refer to them.

Various factors play a part in the Christian acts of the martyrs, but all are essentially linked to the Jewish-Christian religious tradition. Judaism had developed a theology of martyrdom in two ways: (a) through the application to individual cases of the theological claim that Israel had always persecuted and killed the prophets (see, for example, the compilation known as the *Lives of the Prophets,* which is probably from the first century A.D. and is concerned chiefly with their deaths); (b) through the celebration of the Maccabean martyrs, especially the elderly Eleazar and the seven brothers with their mother, as reported in 2 Maccabees and expanded in 4 Maccabees with touches of Stoicism.

These models were doubtless in mind in even the earliest Christian documents: the *Martyrdom of Polycarp* and, explicitly, in the letter of the Christians of Lyons and Vienna. On the other hand, the passion of Christ was the primary model for narrating the martyrdoms of Christians, beginning with that of Stephen (Acts 6–7). Thus not only did the fate of the martyrs connect them with the lot of divine emissaries throughout the history of salvation, it placed them in an especially close union with their Lord; think of the mysticism of martyrdom in the work of Ignatius of Antioch, especially in his letter to the Romans.

This special closeness to Christ and God explains the cult celebrated at the tomb of a martyr. In this setting the narrative of the martyr's passion was often read along with the Scriptures, at least in earlier times. Beginning with the arrest and even before the execution (the key element in a martyrdom was the confession made before the authorities, so that it was even possible to be a martyr several times if the person were released), the martyr became a kind of focal point in the life of the community, which enveloped him in its veneration, regarding him as already in contact with God and able to prophesy and to speak with special authority even on ecclesiastical questions. The *Apostolic Tradition* unquestioningly attributes priestly rank to those who have confessed the faith.

All this can be seen in the acts of the martyrs, the exhortations to martyrdom, and other sources. Once the martyr's testimony was completed by his death, the memory of the martyr became a permanent point of reference for the local church, but not for it alone. At the spatial level people gathered at the tomb or went on pilgrimage to it. On the temporal level the year was signposted by the *dies natales* of the martyrs; the *Depositio martyrum* that is attached to the early Christian calendar known as the *Calendar of 354*, gives the date of death and place of burial for each martyr. In this perspective we can see why the first acts of the martyrs appeared almost contemporaneously at various places in Christendom, in various forms, and with different ancestries and ideological characteristics. The literary genre as such was established gradually through the development of the texts and the reciprocal relations among them.

The churches made collections of the acts of the martyrs. Eusebius of Caesarea (*Hist. eccl.* 5. pref. 2, and elsewhere) tells us that he made a *Collection of the Early Martyrs (synagōgétōn archaiōn martyrōn)* that contained not only the historical record but also a doctrinal treatment. He made extensive use of the collection in his *Ecclesiastical History.* He also composed the *Martyrs of Palestine,* which has come down in two recensions. It deals with the persecutions in Caesarea between 303 and 311.

We shall briefly review the earliest Greek acts of the martyrs; the Latin acts will be left to a later chapter (see below, ch. 18, sec. 1 and ch. 19, secs. 5–6).

BIBLIOGRAPHY

Texts

H. Musurillo, *The Acts of the Christian Martyrs* (Oxford: Clarendon, 1972); useful introduction and bibliography.

A. A. R. Bastiaensen et al., *Atti e Passioni dei martiri* (Milan: Fondazione Valla-Mondadori, 1987); useful introduction and bibliography.

H. Delehaye, *Les passions des martyrs et les genres littéraires* (2d ed.; Brussels: Société des Bollandistes, n.d.).

G. Lazzati, *Gli sviluppi della letteratura sui marturi nei primi quattro secoli, con appendice di testi* (Turin: Società Editrice Internazionale, 1956).

G. Lanata, *Gli atti dei martiri come documenti processuali* (Milan: Giuffré, 1973).

T. Baumeister, *Die Anfänge der Theologie des Martyriums* (Münster: Aschendorff, 1980).

2. Individual Acts and Passions

The *Martyrdom of Polycarp,* bishop of Smyrna, has come down in seven manuscripts; much also appears with slight differences, in Eusebius (*Hist. eccl.* 4.15.3–45). It is narrated in a letter from the church of Smyrna to the church of Philadelphia. Since it speaks in the future tense of celebrating the anniversary of the martyrdom, it was written less than a year after the fact. The date of the event is debated: on the basis of what the text says about the day of the death, and Eusebius's statement that it took place under Marcus Aurelius, scholars choose February 23, 167. However, other factors, such as the name of the consul, point to 156; 177 has also been suggested.

In a simple style, the account tells of the arrest of the eighty-seven-year-old bishop during a persecution, his trial in a stadium before a rabidly anti-Christian crowd, his refusal to yield to prayers and threats, his condemnation, the heartfelt prayer of the martyr, and his execution at the stake. There are some obvious tendentious elements: the persecutions are the devil's work (3.1; 17.1–2), and the Jews are his eager collaborators (12.2; 13.1; 17.2; 18.1). There is an argument against seeking martyrdom: Polycarp agrees to hide, thereby teaching others to put the good of the neighbor before one's own (i.e., before martyrdom). Above all, the behavior of a certain Quintus is censured as contrary to the gospel: a recent arrival from Phrygia, Quintus had turned himself in and had persuaded others to follow his example, but then had sacrificed to the gods out of fear (ch. 4). Polycarp is described as possessing the prophetic spirit (16.2), especially when his martyrdom is imminent (5.2).

The death is marked by miraculous, symbolic incidents: the flames form a niche around the body, so that the martyr resembles bread being baked in an oven (perhaps an allusion to the Eucharist), and a sweet fragrance emanates from it (15.2). More specifically, many points in the narrative liken the passion of Polycarp to that of Christ: he is betrayed, the eirenarch who arrests him is named Herod, and so on. Attention is explicitly called to these coincidences. As a result, it has been argued (H. von Campenhausen) that the *Martyrdom* that has come down to us, unlike the one known to Eusebius, has been worked on by an "evangelical editor," who gave the work this stamp. This thesis is not widely accepted.

Another martyrdom account in letter form is the letter of the Christians of Lyons and Vienna to those of Asia and Phrygia reporting the ferocious anti-Christian pogrom that broke out in Lyons under Marcus Aurelius in 177. It has been preserved almost in its entirety by Eusebius (*Hist. eccl.* 5.1.3–4, 8). Its author may have been Irenaeus, who was bishop of Vienna and then of Lyons (see below, ch. 13, sec. 1d). It is very likely that the martyrdom was due to the initiative of the people of Lyons, who dragged the Christians before the city authorities and had them imprisoned until the arrival of the governor. The latter finally yielded to the pressure of the mob and ordered that Christians be hunted and arrested, among them Bishop Pothinus, who was over ninety and died in prison. All this was contrary to regulations going back to Trajan.

Unlike the *Martyrdom of Polycarp,* which focuses on the person of the bishop, the Lyons letter sounds like a chorus. In addition, luminous figures rise up out of the crowd: Deacon Sanctus; Attalus, who is subjected to the worst torments even though he is a Roman citizen; fifteen-year-old Ponticus; and above all, Blandina, a slender young slave-girl who encourages and comforts her companions and dies last, after heroically enduring frightful torments. Although the substance of the story is undoubtedly authentic, some details may stem from a third-century revision.

The *Martyrdom of Saints Justin, Chariton, Charites, Euelpistus, Hierax, Paeon, Liberianus, and Their Community* exists in three versions: the shortest (A), which, as attested by a Paris manuscript, is terse and contains only the examination of the group before Quintus Junius Rusticus, Prefect of Rome (in office between 163 and 167); a mid-length version (B); and a long and clearly secondary one (C). While B had long been regarded as the oldest version, G. Lazzati has shown that priority belongs to version A. Justin (see above, ch. 10, sec. 3) had opened "a school of (Christian) philosophy" in Rome and remarks in one of his works (*2 Apol.* 3) that he expects to be denounced by Crescens, a Cynic philosopher and rival; that is probably what occurred. Some details are of interest: When the prefect wants to know where Christians meet, Justin avoids the question and gives only his own address, while noting that he used to explain the words of the truth to anyone who wanted to find it. His companions, when directly asked, avoid saying that it was Justin who converted and instructed them. Recensions B and C mention that the community saw to the burial of the martyrs.

Eusebius (*Hist. eccl.* 4.15.48) says that the *Martyrdom of Carpus, Papylus, and Agathonice* took place in Pergamum in the time of Marcus Aurelius. Some scholars, however, relying on the imperial order to offer sacrifice that is found in the Greek acts, prefer to date the event during the persecution of Decius. The latter date is explicitly given in the Latin version, but does not seem to be original, nor do some other details in this version, for example, the identification of Carpus as a bishop and of Papylus (here: Pamphilus) as a deacon. The story has two parts: the examination, the tortures. This *Martyrdom* has come down in a Latin version and a Greek, which differ on a few points. The most important of these has to do with the death of Agathonice. In the Greek version, she is in the crowd that is watching Carpus's death at the stake, and she voluntarily joins him. In the Latin version, she is tried and condemned after the other two. The Latin perhaps represents a revision aimed at eliminating an attitude of self-denunciation that was not approved in the church (see above on the martyrdom of Polycarp).

Eusebius (*Hist. eccl.* 5.21) records the trial and execution of Apollonius, a Roman aristocrat, which took place in Rome in the time of Commodus (180–192). When interrogated before the senate, Apollonius offered a defense of the Christian faith, which Eusebius included along with the minutes of the examination in his collection of early martyrs. The Perennius who interrogates Apollonius seems to have been the pretorian prefect in office from 180 to 185. Two different versions of the *Martyrdom of Apollonius,* Greek and Armenian, have come down, but both are later expansions that make Apollonius an Alexandrian and Perennius the proconsul of Asia. It is not possible to say to what extent the two addresses attributed to Apollonius and containing motifs widespread in Christian apologetic and protreptic writings, reflect the defense of which Eusebius speaks.

According to the exact date given at the end of their acts, the *Martyrdom of Pionius* describes events that must have taken place on March 12, 250, and therefore during the Decian persecution which is mentioned in ch. 2. Eusebius, however, dates it to the time of Marcus Aurelius (*Hist. eccl.* 4.15.47). In any case, the long document has been extensively enlarged by two discourses of Pionius, one to the judges, the other to his companions in prison. These works are rich in rhetoric, biblical references, and anti-Jewish animosity. The narrative emphasizes the hostility of the populace toward Christians. According to Eusebius and the acts, one of the martyrs, Metrodorus, was a Marcionite.

Chapter 12

THE BEGINNINGS OF CHRISTIAN POETRY

Pliny's letter to Trajan regarding Christians (10.96) says that in Bithynia Christians used to meet in order to "sing a hymn to Christ as to a god." Even earlier, Paul (1 Cor 14:26) attests to the fact that during liturgical assemblies hymns were improvised under divine inspiration; Col 3:16, Eph 5:19, and Acts 16:25 confirm this for the post-Pauline period.

While there may have been some cases of improvisations, some hymns had already achieved a set form and were used in the liturgy. Relying on observations of both form and content, scholars think it possible, with varying degrees of accuracy, to identify parts of such hymns in the earliest Christian writings, especially Phil 2:6–11, 1 Tim 3:16, and Col 1:15–20, all christological in content.

In his "infancy gospel" Luke has apparently taken over and christianized two hymns from devout Jewish groups inspired by eschatological expectations: the *Magnificat* (Luke 1:46–55), and the *Benedictus* (1:68–79). The prologue of John's gospel may be an adaptation of a hymn used in Baptist circles. Poetry, however, could also serve for instruction and theological propaganda, a practice that would be destined for a long history in Christianity. The author of the *Refutation of All Heresies* (Hippolytus of Rome?) cites a psalm of the Naassene gnostics on the soul (5.10.2) and a poem of Valentinus titled *Harvest* (6.37.6–8), while the *Muratorian Canon* contains an obscure note on a "a new book of Solomon," written by Marcion of Arsinoe, Valentinus, and Milziades (lines 81–84). The *Acts of John* contain a scene, obviously of gnostic inspiration, in which Jesus and his disciples dance in a circle while singing a hymn (94–95). The *Acts of Thomas* include two hymns: an allegory of wisdom sung at a wedding feast (6–7), and the *Song of the Pearl* (108–113), a splendid allegory of the gnostic myth of fall and salvation.

1. Odes of Solomon

The *Odes of Solomon* is a collection of 42 poetic pieces, only the title of which was known before the twentieth century. The title is contained in two lists of texts of disputed canonicity *(antilegomena)* that are found in the *Stichometry* of Nicephorus (difficult to date) and in the pseudo-Athanasian *Synopsis sacrae scripture* (6th c.). A short citation in Latin from *Ode* 19 is in the *Divine Institutes* of Lactantius (4.12.3). Five odes (1, 5, 6, 22, and 25) were included in the gnostic *Pistis Sophia* that survives in Coptic. In 1909 a Syriac manuscript was discovered that contains *Odes* 3 (without its opening) to 42; in 1912 a second manuscript was found that contains from 17.7 to the end. In 1959, *Ode* 11, in Greek, was published from P. Bodmer 11 (3rd c.); in addition to confirming the title given in the indirect transmission, this papyrus contains some lines of the Syriac version, showing that the text underwent revisions. Of the entire work, then, only *Ode* 2 is missing.

Still discussed is whether the original language was Syriac or Greek; Aramaic or Hebrew seem less convincing possibilities to the experts. Scholars lean toward Syria as the place of composition and toward the middle of the second century as the date. The material is not in meters but, after the Oriental manner, in a rhythmic prose that is based on parallel elements and on repetition and variation.

In the poems it is sometimes "I" that speaks, sometimes "we." While the "we" is the voice of the community (as in *Odes Sol.* 13), the "I" is sometimes the believer, as in *Ode* 3, a love song of a believer who unites himself to his Lord as a lover to his beloved, and sometimes the Savior, as in *Ode* 42. The *Odes* are permeated by a mysticism in which the saved are one with the Savior. The latter has become a human being in order that human beings may receive him and put him on (7.4), and the Spirit of the Lord speaks in the members of the faithful as the hand makes the harp sing (6.1–2). Thus the singer may begin by speaking of himself and suddenly don the person of the Savior, as in *Ode* 17, where the believer, having been crowned by God, justified, and delivered from vanities, travels the same path followed by the Lord in his descent into the lower world. Like the Lord, he frees the prisoners and bestows his knowledge generously on them. A similar process, again connected with the descent to the lower world, is found in *Ode* 22. Almost all the odes extol the deliverance gained by the Savior's action.

Emphasis has often been placed on the gnosticism of the *Odes of Solomon*, implying a connection to the gnostic myth of the heavenly redeemer's descent and ascent. But the evidence is not sufficient to warrant describing the collection as gnostic, for, while the poems stress the heavenly identity of the Savior and the fact that he is a "stranger" to this world (17.6; 28.10; 41.8), they do not presuppose any ontological dualism. They presuppose only the mythical scenario of the heavenly redeemer's descent into the world in order to snatch human beings from the control of the adverse powers; this scenario is not specifically gnostic. Nor is the believer regarded as divine in nature from his very origin; it is the saving activity of the redeemer that makes it possible for the believer to become like him. Such phrases as "May we also be saved with you" (42.18) do not express the myth of the "saved Savior," but are a prayer for participation in the power by which the Savior was able to leave the lower world.

In the perspective adopted by the *Odes* the reality of the incarnation and death of Christ is minimized, but this was usual in this kind of soteriology, which resembles that of the *Martyrdom and Ascension of Isaiah* 6–11, it does not suggest a strictly gnostic structure of thought, despite the importance given in the *Odes* to "knowledge" as a means of redemption. The knowledge is not of the person's own divine nature but of salvation won.

The collection is undoubtedly Christian. The Redeemer is obviously Jesus, even though the name "Jesus" never occurs, and there are many allusions to his life, especially the crucifixion. Two passages that seem to presuppose Old Testament *testimonia* on the extending of the hands as prefiguring the cross (27.21; 42.1–2). The virgin birth, which is given an allegorical interpretation in *Ode* 19, is also prominent. Here, too, are used *testimonia* which are elsewhere attested as referring to the virgin birth.

BIBLIOGRAPHY

Editions

M. Lattke, *Die Oden Salomos in ihrer Bedeutung für Neues Testament und Gnosis* (3 vols. in 4; Fribourg, Switz.: Editions Universitaires/Göttingen: Vandenhoeck & Ruprecht, 1979–1986).
Les Odes de Salomon (ed. and trans. M.-J. Pierre; Turnhout: Brepols, 1995).
Odes of Solomon (trans. J. H. Charlesworth; in vol. 2 of *The Old Testament Pseudepigrapha;* ed. J. H. Charlesworth [New York: Doubleday, 1985]), 725–71; with introduction and notes.

2. Christian Sibylline Oracles

In antiquity, a Sibyl was a woman who, it was believed, became possessed by a divinity, fell into an ecstasy, and uttered oracles, often of disasters. The gradually growing collections of these utterances came to be attributed to a mythological Sibyl who was assigned to various places (Eritrea, Delphi, Cumae, Tibur, and many other locations), with the result that there were a number of collections. In Rome, the Sibylline books were kept in the temple of Jupiter on the Campidoglio, and their obscure prophecies were consulted and interpreted when a disaster struck. In 83 B.C. the books burned up in a temple fire, but other oracles were collected. Augustus had them moved to the temple of Apollo and saw to it that the ones thought to be forgeries were destroyed.

The Jews of the Diaspora exploited the authority of the Sibylline oracles for their own propaganda; to the pagan oracles they added compositions which, in the same manner, presented past events, usually catastrophes, as predictions of the future. Very little remains of the pagan oracles, mostly in Jewish collections. For similar propaganda purposes, Christians then added oracles in a spirit similar to that of the Jewish oracles, making them prophecies of divine vengeance on the oppressor, represented by Rome. But the Christians also added prophecies concerning Christ, which fit nicely into the tradition of the Cumean Sibyl, who had inspired Virgil to write in his fourth *Eclogue* of the coming of an eschatological renewal of the world in connection with the birth of a divine child.

In its present form, the collection contains twelve books of Greek hexameters; they are unpolished in form and quite obscure in meaning. The books are numbered 1–8 and 11–14. Books 9 and 10 do not exist. Book 14 results from a later division of book 8 into three parts. Book 3 is a Jewish production of the second century A.D., as are books 4 and 5, which take over pagan material and show some Christian revision; books 11–14 are also Jewish. Books 1 and 2 graft a good deal of Christian material onto a Jewish nucleus that was composed about the middle of the second century. These books include "prophecies" of the life of Christ and the destruction of Jerusalem, the end of the world, the resurrection, and the judgment. Books 6–8 are entirely

Christian and were composed in the second century. The sixth, which is very short, is a hymn to Christ; the seventh contains eschatological oracles. The eighth book, which includes scraps from the pagan Sibyl, voices Christian feelings of revenge toward Rome. It calls to mind the emperors from Hadrian to Marcus Aurelius; the reign of the latter is the setting for the end of the world, which was to be set in motion by the return of Nero. The idea of Nero as enemy of God in the last times is a theme dear to Jewish and Christian apocalyptic literature. The power of Rome will be destroyed, and God will inaugurate his reign with the elect. The second part of the eighth book is focused on Christ in his role as universal judge but also in his human life; it also contains precepts for Christian life.

BIBLIOGRAPHY

A. Ezach, *Oracula Sibyllina* (Vienna-Prague: Tempsky, 1891); critical edition.
J. Geffcken, *Die Oracula Sibyllina* (GCS; Leipzig: Hinrichs, 1902; repr., 1967).
Sibylline Oracles (trans. J. J. Collins; in vol. 1 of *The Old Testament Pseudepigrapha*, ed. J. H. Charlesworth; New York: Doubleday, 1983), 317–472.

3. Inscriptions of Abercius and Pectorius

The *Life of Bishop Abercius of Hierapolis,* a late work (end of 4th c.), tells of an inscription, in twenty-two Greek hexameters, on the tomb of its subject; this was actually found in Hieropolis (not the same as Hierapolis) in Phrygia in 1883. Since another Christian inscription from the same region is dated 216 and depends on the inscription of Abercius, the latter must have been composed before that date. Abercius himself dictated the inscription when he was seventy-two years old; in it he speaks in the first person and recalls incidents of his life. He says that he is a "disciple of a pure shepherd who pastures flocks on mountains and plains." Abercius was instructed by him and sent to Rome "in order to contemplate a kingdom and see a queen in golden robes and golden shoes." But he also traveled in the East, traversing Syria as far as Nisibis, a frontier city, "having Paul with him in the carriage; it was Faith above all that urged me on, and it prepared for me, above all else, a food, a fish from the fountain, very large, pure, and caught by a pure virgin; she always gave her friends food to eat: possessing a good wine, she gave (the fish) as diluted wine, with bread."

The enigmatic and allusive language has given rise to lengthy debates: according to some, all the images refer to the cult of Attis; most today agree the symbols are Christian. Thus the shepherd is, of course, Christ, who has a community of saints in heaven (the mountains) and on earth (the plains); the kingdom and the queen would refer to Rome and/or the church. "Paul" refers to a collection of Paul's letters. The succeeding verses allude to the Eucharist: the fish is Christ, the fountain is baptism. This unique epitaph, which has no great poetic value, is interesting as evidence of the way one could speak of Christianity in almost completely ambiguous language and even in terms suitable for the mysteries. It probably represents a Christian lifestyle that resembled the way in which initiates into the mysteries lived their faith.

Mention may be made here of the inscription of Pectorius, which was found near Autun in 1830 and probably goes back to the fourth century. It consists of three elegiac distichs and five hexameters, and the first five verses form the acrostic "fish," a symbol of Christ. The fish is mentioned several times, with an allusion in particular to the Eucharist. The first part addresses the reader, describing him as "divine progeny of the heavenly Fish," recalling his baptism, and urging him to the Eucharist. The second part is a prayer that the Lord may grant the author's mother to rest in peace, and a plea to his dead parents and siblings that in their state of peace they would be mindful of Pectorius.

BIBLIOGRAPHY

W. Wischmeyer, "Die Aberkiosinschrift als Grabepigramm," *JAC* 23 (1980): 22–47.

J. Quasten, *The Beginnings of Greek Patristic Literature* (vol. 1 of *Patrology*; ed. J. Quasten; Westminster, Md.: Newman, 1950); translation and commentary.

Chapter 13

IRENAEUS AND HIPPOLYTUS

1. Irenaeus of Lyons

a. Life

Knowledge of the life of Irenaeus comes to us chiefly from his own writings, from which even Eusebius drew his information (*Hist. eccl.* 5.3–8). Irenaeus was born in Asia Minor and educated in his early youth in Smyrna, where he was able to listen to Polycarp, bishop of that city and a disciple of the apostles (*Haer.* 3.3.4); in a letter to Florinus, he recalls their shared discipleship under Polycarp (in Eusebius, *Hist. eccl.* 5.20.5–6). Before going to Vienna and Lyons, where we find him later on, Irenaeus probably stayed in Rome for studies, perhaps during the pontificate of Anicetus (155–166), since he knows that Polycarp visited Rome during that period (3.3.4; letter to Victor in Eusebius, *Hist. eccl.* 5.24.16–17).

Shortly after the violent persecution that broke out in Lyons around 177, Irenaeus was in that city. The community of Lyons, or perhaps Irenaeus himself (see below) composed an account of the persecution for the churches of Asia and Phrygia; extracts of it are given by Eusebius (*Hist. eccl.* 5.1–3; see above, ch. 11, sec. 2). This account was accompanied by a letter from the martyrs, i.e., those who had borne witness to the faith but had survived. A copy of the letter was sent to Eleutherus, Bishop of Rome. The one who carried it was Irenaeus, on whose behalf the martyrs wrote a short note of recommendation to Eleutherus (reproduced in Eusebius, *Hist. eccl.* 5.4.2). It is probable, according to P. Nautin, that the term "presbyter" used of Irenaeus in the letter means that he was a bishop; perhaps he had already been Bishop of Vienna (which is mentioned for the first time in the account) and then became Bishop of Lyons after Bishop Pothinus died in the persecution.

Later, Victor (189–199), successor of Eleutherus, adopted an intransigent position on the date for the celebration of Easter, and threatened to break off communion with the churches of Asia. These churches followed the so-called quartodeciman practice, and celebrated Easter on the fourteenth of Nisan, in keeping with Jewish custom, whereas elsewhere Easter was always celebrated on a Sunday. Victor's threat elicited a harsh response from Bishop Polycrates of Ephesus. The controversy is described by Eusebius (*Hist. eccl.* 5.23–25). Many other bishops likewise disassociated themselves from Victor's hard line; among them was Irenaeus, who wrote to the bishop of Rome expressing his compliance with celebrating Easter on Sunday, but also urging Victor not to break communion with churches that were preserving an ancient practice. According to the extracts given by Eusebius (*Hist. eccl.* 4.24.12–17), Irenaeus reminded Victor that preceding Roman bishops had never broken communion with Asia for such a reason, and that in the time of Anicetus (ca. 154) Polycarp had gone to Rome to discuss the matter. Although the two bishops had not come to an agreement, they had departed in peace and communion.

We have no information about the remainder of Irenaeus's life. Later sources telling of his martyrdom cannot be checked.

BIBLIOGRAPHY

A. Benoît, *Saint Irénée: Introduction à l'étude de sa théologie* (Paris: Presses Universitaires de France, 1960).

A. Orbe, *Antropología de San Ireneo* (Madrid: Editorial Católica, 1969).

————, *Teología de San Ireneo: Comentario al libro V del "Adversus haereses"* (3 vols.; Madrid/Toledo: Editorial Católica, 1985–1988).

L. Doutreleau and L. Regnault, "Irénée de Lyon (saint)," *DSp* 7,2 (1971): 1923–69.

R. M. Grant, *Irenaeus of Lyons* (*The Early Church Fathers*; London/New York: Routledge, 1997).

b. Unmasking and Refutation of Falsely Named Gnosis

Irenaeus's most important work contained five books; the third was written during the pontificate of Eleutherus (174–189). The work is addressed to a friend of whom we know nothing; Irenaeus sent him the first two books and then, gradually, the others (see the prefaces to the individual books). The writing of it became necessary (1. pref. 2) because the disciples of Valentinus were spreading gnostic doctrines through the region of Lyons and, in particular, because of the activity of Mark the Magician, who on the pretext of instructing rich women in gnosticism was seducing them (1.13).

The complete title of the work, *Elenchos kai anatropē tēs pseudonymou gnōseōs*, is given by Eusebius (*Hist. eccl.* 5.7.1) and is undoubtedly original, inasmuch as Irenaeus's own text alludes to it repeatedly (1. pref.; 4. pref. 1; 4.41.4). Irenaeus's intention is first to bring into the open *(elenchos)* the teachings that the gnostics were conveying secretly in order to persuade believers, and second to refute them *(anatropē)*. The expression "knowledge falsely so-called," that is, "pretended," is from 1 Tim 6:20, where it is used of adversarial teachings that claimed a special level of knowledge geared to salvation. In keeping with the plan of the work, the first book contains an exposition of the gnostic systems that Irenaeus has managed to learn about, and the other four contain a refutation that probably grew gradually. The work is usually cited by the shorter title *Against Heresies (Haer.)*.

The first book begins with an extensive exposition of the system taught by the disciples of Ptolemy (see above, ch. 9, sec. 5). The explanation moves from the internal structure of the divinity, through the tragedy of the breaking of the divine unity and the origin of the world, to the final salvation of the divine particles imprisoned in the world, that is, the salvation of the gnostics themselves (1.1–8.4). There follows an exegesis, from the same school, of the prologue of John's gospel (8.5). Irenaeus is here following two written documents. After a critique of gnostic exegetical method (1.9) and a passage on the unity of the faith of the church, which everywhere passes on the same tradition (1.10), Irenaeus contrasts with this unity the variations in the Valentinian systems (1.11–22), beginning with Valentinus himself and with special attention to the magical ceremonies and kabalistic doctrines of Mark the Magician. A third part of this book (1.23–31) gives a genealogy of gnosticism, beginning with Simon Magus, Menander, Saturninus, and Basilides, and including Marcion, the encratites, and Tatian; in 1.29 there is a summary of a version of the *Apocryphon of John* (see above, ch. 9, sec. 6).

The purpose of the second book is to offer rational arguments against the teachings previously set forth. Since Irenaeus has devoted the greater part of the first book to the Valentinians, he does the same in the second, while saying that the refutation of the Valentinians can be applied to all the others. In the first section (2.1–30) he therefore refutes the doctrine of the Pleroma, that is, of the divine world (by showing that it can neither be external to creation nor contain creation), the doctrine of the aeons or divine hypostases, numerology, and gnostic exegesis and eschatology. This is followed by a much shorter refutation of particular aspects of other gnostic doctrines: the magical practices of Carpocrates and Simon, metempsychosis, and the teaching of Basilides on the 365 heavens.

In the third book Irenaeus sets out to refute the gnostics on the basis of the Scriptures. He begins with a discussion of the authority and truth of the Christian Scriptures, which faithfully contain the teaching of the apostles and of the ecclesiastical tradition; this tradition is ensured in the various churches by episcopal succession, which prolongs the ministry of the apostles. To the ecclesiastical tradition the gnostics oppose their own misleading tradition, which is not linked to Christ but only to the recent heads of their schools (3.1–5). Irenaeus then demonstrates the oneness of God (3.6–15) on the basis of the words of the prophets, Paul, and the Lord himself, of the four Gospels, and of the Acts of the Apostles, which contain other apostolic testimonies. After the section on the Gospels there is inserted a justification for having four Gospels, and after the section on Acts there is an attack both on those who accept only Paul's testimony and reject that of Luke (the gnostics), and on those who reject Paul and deny him the dignity of an apostle (Judaizing Christians).

The second part of the book (chs. 16–23) has to do with the person of Christ. It rejects, among other things, the idea that the heavenly Christ descended on the man Jesus at his baptism, and the idea that Christ was a mere man (the Ebionites). Irenaeus also develops the idea of recapitulation, that is, the saving summation, in the humanity of Christ, of the humanity that was formed by God and conquered by sin. The book ends (chs. 24–25) with a rebuke of the heretics who, by leaving the church, separate themselves from the truth in order to cling to a God who is useless and indifferent to the world.

The fourth book claims to be a refutation of the heretics based on the words of Christ, but in fact is largely devoted to the unity and progress of the history of salvation. On the basis of the Gospels, Irenaeus shows that Jesus acknowledges the Creator, author of the law, as his Father; that Jesus himself observed the law; that the relationship between law and gospel is one not of opposition, but of growth, and can be expressed in terms of figure and reality, prophecy and fulfillment, promise and presence, so that the God from which both come is one (4.1–11). The gospel is the completion of the law, which was imposed on the Jews not because God needed their services, but in order to educate and rein in a people always inclined to idolatry and disobedience (4.12–16). In the new covenant the Eucharist replaces the offerings and sacrifices of the old covenant, which were figures of things spiritual (4.17–19).

At this point the author begins an extensive discussion of prophecy (4.20–35). God, who cannot be known in himself, has shown himself to creatures through his Logos and his Spirit. These made known to Moses and the other prophets certain "economies" (aspects of the saving plan of God), as well as mysteries by which human beings would some day be able to see God (first in the person of Jesus and then in God's kingdom). The actions of the patriarchs and prophets likewise prefigured the salvation sent by God, while the actions of Jesus were figures of it. As a result, those who read the Scriptures in this perspective will find in them both Christ and the new call that comes through him; provided, that is, that they understand them as read by the presbyters of the church, for these, as successors of the apostles, have received the sure charism of truth. At this point, therefore, Irenaeus turns to a presbyter to whom he has listened on other occasions, and cites his exegesis of Old Testament passages on the sins of Israel, the exodus of Israel from Egypt, and the story of Lot (4.27–32). These were favorite passages of the Marcionites in their effort to prove the inferiority of the God of the Old Testament, but the presbyter shows that they reflect the one God. A spiritual disciple will correctly interpret the Scriptures and pass judgment on the erroneous exegesis of the heretics. In the last part of the book (4.36–41), the one-ness of God is proved from the parables of Jesus.

The fifth book is presented as a completion of the refutation of heretics, this time on the basis of other sayings of the Lord and the letters of Paul. However, it is devoted to specific subjects, the first of them (5.1–14) being the salvation of the flesh, which the gnostics and Marcion reject. Irenaeus emphasizes the connection between the in-carnation of Christ and the resurrection of the flesh, a phenomenon that attests to the power of God: the God of the gnostics and Marcionites is weak, for he cannot restore life to the flesh. Irenaeus advances his discussion by means of an exegesis of Pauline passages on the resurrection, especially 1 Cor 15:50 ("flesh and blood cannot inherit the kingdom of God"), to which the heretics appeal to deny the salvation of the body. Irenaeus explains that the flesh is dead unless the Spirit of God is inserted into it, for God alone can give it life. Thus the flesh does not inherit the kingdom, but instead is possessed as an inheritance; the works of the flesh that are opposed to the kingdom are those done in the absence of the Spirit. The healings and raisings from the dead accomplished by Jesus point to the life and incorruptibility that God intends to give to the work of his hands, that is, the human body.

A second part of the book (5.15–24) proves the identity of the Creator with the Father of Jesus from three episodes in the life of Christ: the cure of the man born blind (John 9) repeats and reveals the original creative action of the divine Logos, who is "the hand of God" which formed the human being at the creation; the crucifixion of Jesus is a remedy, effected through the wood of the cross, for the disobedience Adam committed through the wood of the tree of knowledge; Christ's victory over the devil through obedience to the law at the temptation in the desert reverses the effect of Adam's defeat by the devil, when he was tempted.

Finally, the oneness of the Creator with the Father of Jesus is proved by exegesis of the Scriptures having to do with events at the end of the world (5.25–36). The fu-ture coming of the antichrist shows that the devil wants to be worshiped as God. The resurrection of the just marks the beginning of a beatitude that is reached in stages: first, in the reign of the just with Christ in the present creation that will have been restored to its original splendor; and then, still without any renunciation of the body, in a renewed universe in which the blessed will have their place on a new earth (to which the heavenly Jerusalem will have descended), in paradise, and in heaven, while they continue to know God in new ways.

The complexity of the work, as well as some evident internal tensions, have raised the problem of the sources used by Irenaeus. On the one hand, we have seen that he draws upon original gnostic sources; to those already listed we may add the *Gospel of Truth,* which he mentions in 3.11.9 (see above, ch. 9, sec. 6). He certainly also used Justin's *Syntagma against Heresies,* which he cites as *Against Marcion* (4.6.2) and which already offered a genealogy of the gnostic sects. Although Irenaeus's understanding and criticism of gnostic theology are not always penetrating, and although the reconstruction of the genealogy of gnostic errors (taken from Justin) is quite unreliable, his work is nevertheless valuable as a sourcebook on Christian gnosticism, and many points in it have been confirmed by recently discovered texts.

He also cites *1 Clement* (3.3.3) and the Shepherd of Hermas (*Haer.* 4.20.2; see *Epid.* 4). But other sources besides Justin play a more important part in this discussion. Some are explicitly cited: thus the presbyter's antimarcionite treatise on the subject of prophecy (4.27.1–32.1). Irenaeus several times cites a person who is "better than I," an "elder" (1. pref. 2; 1.13.3; 1.15.6; 3.17.4; etc.), who may be the same as the preceding and/or Polycarp of Smyrna; on other occasions he cites the presbyters who were disciples of the apostles and, in particular, those belonging to the circle of John, a disciple of the Lord in Asia (2.22.5; 5.5.1; 5.30.1; 5.33.3; 5.36.1, 2; *Epid.* 3 and 61). These presbyters must be the same as the "transmitters of apostolic tradition" to whom Papias of Hierapolis and Clement of Alexandria appeal, but Irenaeus doubtless got their utterances from Papias's *Explanation of the Lord's Sayings,* which he cites in connection with one of the sayings (5.33.4). It has also been shown (W. Bousset) that Irenaeus must have used an already existing work on free will (4.37–39) and two treatises (or perhaps just one) on the antichrist and the thousand-year reign (5.25–36).

The scholar who has searched for Irenaeus's sources most extensively is F. Loofs (1930). According to him, the trinitarian teaching on God–Logos–Wisdom that is found in some passages of Irenaeus depends on the lost work *Against Marcion* of Theophilus of Antioch (source IQT). Irenaeus's Christology likewise reveals the influence of an Antiochene source (IQU), which Loofs finally identifies with the preceding. The texts going back to the presbyter are traced back to a source IQP, which is characterized by a "pneumatic" Christology *(Geistchristologie)* and maintains that the Holy Spirit is the divine element in Jesus; the same type of teaching is to be found in an Asian source that influenced the treatise *On the Resurrection,* which is attributed to Justin and which Loofs regards as authentic. Finally, from source IQE, that is, Papias, Irenaeus derived the sayings of the presbyters, as noted above. Loofs's conclusion is this: since the thinking of Irenaeus is to be found in what remains after these sources have been set aside, he was a rather unpretentious theologian.

Despite the merits of this research, the rigidity and complexity of its results, as well as some methodological deficiencies, led to a reaction. As a result, while the presence of sources in Irenaeus is acknowledged, the laudable tendency today is to take the

Against Heresies as a unified work, and its theology as an original and deliberately worked out achievement.

All of Irenaeus's theological thought is conditioned by his opposition to the gnostics and Marcionites, but especially to the Valentinians, on the problem of salvation. The latter admit the salvation only of the spiritual element (although in Marcion this element is not of the same nature as the supreme God) and deny it to the body, which is therefore not, properly speaking, an integral part of the human being made in the image and likeness of God. Irenaeus, on the other hand, regards the salvation of the flesh as inalienable, because the human being *is* the material body that was formed by God (so that the body itself bears the image and likeness), animated by the psyche, and given life by the divine Spirit. There can, therefore, be no other God besides the Creator. The gnostics, by contrast, considering matter to be the result of decay, see it as organized and controlled by an inferior, limited god, who is the author of the Old Testament law.

According to the gnostics, then, there is a break between the Old Testament and the gospel. If the Old Testament contains elements of a revelation of the true God, these have been introduced into it by someone other than the creator and his prophets. The gnostics create a system of simultaneously present but not intercommunicating levels that corresponds structurally to the constitution of the human being and to that of the person of the Savior. For Irenaeus, on the contrary, the two Testaments come from the same God, even though there is progress in revelation, inasmuch as the Old Testament is only the preparation, not the fullness; the necessity of a typological exegesis of the Old Testament is therefore inherent in his system. This typology, however, does not mean a simple juxtaposition of the two Testaments but rather an inclusion of both in a progressive movement that is signposted by economies, that is, salvific interventions organically introduced into the plan of God.

According to Irenaeus, this plan was put to work immediately after original sin, which subjected human beings to death, and it included even the expulsion from the earthly paradise. It continued in the form of Old Testament revelation, which was the work of the divine Logos. This idea of a progressive working out, which is already to be seen in Justin, includes the entire activity of the Logos, which began with participation in the formation of the human being from the mud (Logos and Spirit are the two "hands" God used) and was destined to continue, in the form of a progressive education, through the revelation of God in the person of Jesus. Jesus "recapitulates" Adam, in the sense that in Jesus the human being, in his physical nature as shaped by God, a nature which is the same as that of Adam, makes his way back along the path taken by Adam toward sin. In Christ, humanity "rises up," reversing the movement of the fall and by his obedience makes up for the original disobedience. In this way he restores to the *plasma*, that is, the human creature, the divine life communicated by the Holy Spirit.

The action of the Logos, like that of the Spirit, continues in the church, leading to the growth which the saved will continue to experience with the risen Christ in the millennial reign of the just on a renewed earth. The entire creation shares in this salvation of the human being, whose dignity as one formed by the very hands of God raises him above even the angels.

God is therefore not an unknown God who, like the God of the gnostics, reveals himself only in Jesus and whose revelation has implications solely for the spiritual dimension of the human person. He is, on the contrary, a God who has made himself known to humanity since the beginning and has continued to reveal himself in a patient and wise pedagogical process throughout the history of Israel. He must be a just God as well—an attribute rejected by Marcion and the gnostics because they made goodness and justice contradictory. Indeed, in Irenaeus's view, as later in the antimarcionite writings of Tertullian, a God who does not reward or punish the actions of human beings is a God who has no concern for the world and does not accept his own responsibilities.

This theological approach does, of course, exact a price. Irenaeus is forced to emphasize the continuity between the Old Testament and the New instead of the newness brought by Christ. The defense of the just God shifts the emphasis to the exercise of his power, in contrast to a Pauline theology of the seeming weakness shown by God in the cross of Christ. The assertion of the value of the material world in relation to the history of salvation supports a marked optimism over against the earthly powers, that is, first of all, the activity of the Roman empire. As a result, the author's retrieval at the end of his work of the essential themes of Jewish apocalyptic amounts to a kind of "de-apocalypticization," to the extent that the activity of the antichrist, like that of the devil throughout world history, has nothing to do with the activity of the earthly powers. In this Irenaeus differs from the apocalypses and from Hippolytus, as well as from millenarian enthusiasts.

Unlike the Marcionites, the gnostics based their teaching and their exegesis of the Scriptures on revelations given by the Savior to privileged disciples and passed on by secret tradition, oral or written. These can often be described as apocryphal, in the positive sense of what is hidden and reserved to a circle of initiates. We shall see that Clement of Alexandria accepted the idea of an esoteric tradition and connected it with the chain of transmission formed by the presbyters; this tradition was, of course, not opposed to ecclesiastical teaching. As we have seen, Irenaeus, too, appeals to the tradition of the presbyters (of Asia Minor) but, it is important to note, joins it to the episcopal succession in the churches: "For this reason, we must listen to the presbyters in the church: they are the successors of the apostles, as I have shown, and with their episcopal succession have received the sure charism of truth with the approval of the Father" (4.26.2).

As the context of this passage already makes clear, the reason for this admonition is the need to have a "place" where the truth can be identified reliably, in contrast to the many, often mutually contradictory streams of tradition and revelatory writings of the gnostics. Irenaeus's solution to this problem is recourse, first, to the apostolic succession that is found in the episcopate of the churches, In practice he limits himself to giving the episcopal list of the church of Rome (2.3.3). Second, he resorts to the rule of faith received from the apostles and publicly handed on by the successive bishops (1.10.1; the rule of faith is also the starting point of the *Epideixis*). The problem and the solution were not new, as we can see from Hegesippus. In Irenaeus, however, we see a full and explicit development (especially in 3.1–5) of the "historical" model that the solution supposes, namely, the passing on of the true teaching of Christ to the apostles, the installation of the first bishops in new churches by the apostles, the giving to them of the true teaching, and the conviction that opinions not in accord with this teaching are later deviations prompted by the devil.

Irenaeus is an important witness to the process, even then drawing to a close, of defining the body of Christian Scriptures and especially of the Gospels. With regard to the Pauline corpus the disagreement with the gnostics was about interpretation rather than extension. The process is attested in the *excursus* intended to show, with quite unpersuasive arguments, that there must be four gospels, no more or less (3.11.7–9); the first error is gnostic, the second Ebionite and Marcionite. Valentinian writings such as the *Gospel of Truth* are condemned because they are "not at all in agreement with the gospels of the apostles" (3.11.9). The process that began with Papias of Hierapolis is now complete: legitimating the four, now "canonical" Gospels by connecting them, directly or indirectly, to the apostles. The problem of clearly determining the texts from which to derive the authentic teaching of Jesus had been posed first by Marcion, but he resolved it by taking as his touchstone a doctrinal criterion. Irenaeus, however, while not ignoring the question of content, assigns primary importance to a formal criterion: the guarantee given to the four Gospels by the ecclesiastical tradition.

Against Heresies has not come down to us in its original Greek, except for two papyrus fragments. One (P.Oxy. 405, 3d c.) contains a few lines of 3.9.3. The other (P.Jena, end of 3d, beginning of 4th c.) comprise 5.3.2–13.3. But citations from books 3–5 are found in catenas and florilegia and, above all, extensive extracts from book 1 appear in works by later heresiologists, who preserve about seventy-four percent of the Greek text. Most of these extracts are found in the *Medicine Chest* of Epiphanius of Salamis and in the *Elenchos (Refutation)* of Hippolytus of Rome. The complete text has been preserved only in a Latin version that is attested by nine manuscripts and was made before 420, the year in which Augustine cites it in *Against Julian*. An Armenian translation of books 4 and 5, which goes back to the sixth century, was discovered in 1904 and published in 1910; it is valuable for establishing the text of that section. In addition, there are some fragments in Armenian preserved in florilegia, and some fragments in Syriac.

BIBLIOGRAPHY

Irénée de Lyon, *Contre les hérésies: Livre I* (ed. A. Rousseau and L. Doutreleau; 2 vols.; SC 263–264; Paris: Cerf, 1979); critical edition, with translation and notes, but not a real commentary.

———, *Livre II* (ed. A. Rousseau and L. Doutreleau; 2 vols.; SC 293–94; Paris: Cerf, 1982).

———, *Livre III* (ed. A. Rousseau and L. Doutreleau; 2 vols.; SC 210–11; Paris: Cerf, 1974).

———, *Livre IV* (ed. A. Rousseau, B. Hemmerdinger, L. Doutreleau, and C. Mercier; 2 vols.; SC 100–100; Paris: Cerf, 1965).

The extensive commentary on the fifth book of A. Orbe, *Teología de San Ireneo: Comentario al libro V del "Adversus haereses"* (3 vols.; Madrid/Toledo: Editorial Católica, 1985–1988), goes into all aspects of Irenaeus's thought.

Ireneus, *St. Irenaeus of Lyons against the Heresies* (ACW 55; trans. D. J. Unger; New York: Paulist, 1992).

c. Demonstration of the Apostolic Preaching

This work is mentioned by Eusebius (*Hist. eccl.* 5.26). The original Greek is lost, but an Armenian translation is found in the same manuscript that contained the Armenian translation of *Against Heresies* 4–5; it was published in 1907. A few other

Armenian fragments have also survived. The *Demonstration* is later than Irenaeus's major work, to which it refers (ch. 99), and very different in character. This short treatise, addressed to a Christian named Marcianus, is a compendium of the main points of the faith, and was written in order that the addressee might have in hand the proofs of things divine (ch. 1). In a sense, then, it is a catechism, but not for catechumens, since it is intended for baptized persons (ch. 3). In addition, it contains not only a section of exposition (chs. 30–42a), but also a section of demonstrations (chs. 42b–97), which is followed by a conclusion (chs. 98–100).

Irenaeus first cites and comments on two formulas of faith (chs. 3–7). He then discusses God, the Logos, and the Holy Spirit, the universe, and the creation of the human being (chs. 8–11). This is followed by a biblical history down to Moses. The writer then moves quickly, via a mention of the prophets, to the incarnation of the Logos (chs. 12–30). He sketches the saving activity of the incarnate Logos in the framework of his own theology of recapitulation and the salvation of the flesh. To the recapitulation of Adam in Christ he links the recapitulation of Eve (disobedient virgin) in Mary (obedient virgin). He also contrasts the wood of disobedience (the tree of Paradise) with the wood of obedience (the cross) (chs. 31–34). The promises made to Abraham and David are fulfilled in the work accomplished by Christ (chs. 35–37).

However, it is possible to receive salvation from Christ only if one believes that he was really born of a virgin and that he really died and rose (chs. 38–39). The Son who is mediator of creation, the Logos who was revealed to Moses, is Jesus, who guarantees us communion with God and immortality. John the Baptist prepared the people of Israel to receive him, and his apostles have proclaimed him among the pagans, showing them the way to life. The Holy Spirit who dwells in believers accompanies them on the way into the kingdom (chs. 40–42a). The Spirit has made all things known beforehand through the prophets.

The remainder of the work (chs. 42b–97) is a true and proper "demonstration" that the prophecies did indeed refer to Christ. This section gives an exegesis of a series of Old Testament passages that are applied to the preexistence of Christ (chs. 43–51), to his incarnation (chs. 53–85), and to the missionary activity of the apostles and the calling of the pagans (chs. 86–97). The conclusion (chs. 98–100) contains an appeal to defend the preaching of the truth against heretics; here Irenaeus refers to his earlier work on heresy.

The *Demonstration* adds nothing substantial to the theology of *Against Heresies;* this is natural, given its character as an exposition of the fundamentals of the faith. The work does, however, take some motifs a step further, for example, by connecting the theme of the divine economies with the concrete history of the Jews, or by adding to the recapitulation of Adam in Christ that of Eve in Mary. The attention given to elements of theology that are close to the Jewish tradition is of interest, in relation to the more important work: the angelic cosmology of the seven heavens, which is linked to the seven gifts of the Holy Spirit (Isa 11:2) and to the typology of the seven-branched candelabrum (ch. 9); or the interpretation of the cherubim and seraphim in Isaiah 6 as referring to the Logos and the Holy Spirit (ch. 10). The second part gives insight into the use of collections of christological *testimonia* in early Christianity; Irenaeus undoubtedly uses already-existing collections of biblical passages that were applied to Christ.

BIBLIOGRAPHY

Irénée de Lyon, *Démonstration de la prédication apostolique* (ed. and trans. L. M. Froidevaux; SC 62; Paris: Cerf, 1959).

Ireneo di Lione, *Epideixis: Antico catchismo degli adulti* (ed. and trans. E. Peretto; Rome: Borla, 1981).

Irenaeus, *On the Apostolic Preaching* (trans. J. Behr; Crestwood, N.Y.: St. Vladimir's Seminary Press, 1997).

d. Letters and Fragments

It has often been thought that the letter of the Christians of Lyons to those of Asia and Phrygia, containing the account of persecution and martyrdoms (Eusebius, *Hist. eccl.* 5.1–3) is the work of Irenaeus. P. Nautin and others have pointed out important affinities with Irenaeus's works, and the attribution is all the more possible if, as Nautin thinks, Irenaeus was acting as bishop of Lyons after the death of Pothinus during the persecution. But there is no certainty in this matter.

Mention was made earlier (see above, sec. 1a) of Irenaeus's letter to Pope Victor, in which he urged him to adopt a moderate attitude to the churches of Asia on the question of Easter.

Eusebius (*Hist. eccl.* 5.20.1) mentions several letters of Irenaeus, among them one *To Florinus on the (Divine) Monarchy, or That God Is Not the Author of Evil,* of which he cites a passage. In it Irenaeus recalls the teaching of Polycarp, whom both (Florinus and Irenaeus) had heard as boys in Smyrna, when he told of his conversations with those who had seen the Lord (*Hist. eccl.* 5.20.4–8). Eusebius had also read a treatise of Irenaeus *On the Ogdoad,* in which he again opposes Florinus after the latter had succumbed to the heresy of Valentinus. Florinus was a Roman priest whose gnosticism is also noted by Agapius. A Syriac fragment preserves part of a letter of Irenaeus to Pope Victor in which the writer asks that steps be taken against Florinus, because his writings are circulating in Gaul and harming the faith.

Eusebius mentions also a letter *To Blastus, On Schism,* of which we know nothing (*Hist. eccl.* 5.20.1). A bit of another letter, to someone named Alexander, has come down in Greek, Arabic, and Ethiopic. Finally, there are numerous Greek fragments, almost all of them of doubtful authenticity.

BIBLIOGRAPHY

P. Nautin, *Lettres et écrivains chrétiens des IIe et IIIe siècles* (Paris: Cerf, 1961): 33–104.

2. The Body of Writings Attributed to Hippolytus

A large number of writings, and a very large number of fragments, have come down to us under the name of Hippolytus. Eusebius notes that he "had presided over a church, somewhere or other" (*Hist. eccl.* 6.20.2) in the time of Septimius Severus (193–211) and Caracalla (211–217). A little further on, when dealing with the time of

Severus Alexander (222–235), Eusebius states that Hippolytus composed a treatise *On Easter,* in which he established a chronological method for determining the date of Easter that was based on the first year of the emperor's reign (222). Eusebius also gives a list of eight works of Hippolytus 6.22.

- *On the Hexaemeron*
- *On What Follows the Hexaemeron*
- *Against Marcion*
- *On the Song of Songs*
- *On Sections of Ezekiel*
- *On Easter*
- *Against All the Heresies*

Presumably he found the books, or perhaps only the list in the libraries of Jerusalem and Caesarea.

After Eusebius, there are two references to Hippolytus not as a writer but as a martyr. A Roman calendar, known as the *Chronograph of 354* says that in 235 Pontian, the Bishop of Rome, and Hippolytus, a presbyter, were deported to Sardinia. The *Depositio martyrum,* which is included in the same text and gives the dates of the martyrs' deaths and their places of burial, says that Hippolytus was buried on August 18 in the cemetery on the Via Tiburtina which even today bears his name. He would therefore have died in Sardinia, together with Pontian, and the two bodies would have been brought back to Rome and buried as martyrs. From more or less the same period, an epigram of Damasus, Bishop of Rome from 366 to 384, tells us that presbyter Hippolytus was a disciple of Novatian the schismatic (on Novatian, see below, ch. 18, sec. 9), but that during persecution he returned to the orthodox faith and, before dying, urged the community to take the Catholic side. The legend seeks to counter Novatian, a heretic who lived later than Hippolytus, with the testimony of a venerated martyr.

The identification of the writer and the martyr appears in two passages of Jerome (preface to the *Comm. Matt.,* and *Epist.* 36.16), who makes repeated mention of Hippolytus. In his book *Famous Men* (ch. 61) Jerome depends on Eusebius for Hippolytus's identity, but lists another twelve works:

- *On Exodus*
- *On Genesis*
- *On Zechariah*
- *On the Psalms*
- *On Isaiah*
- *On Daniel*
- *On the Apocalypse*
- *On Proverbs*
- *On Ecclesiastes*
- *On Saul and the Seeress*
- *On the Antichrist*
- *On the Resurrection*
- *Sermon in Praise of the Lord Savior*

Later authors mention still other titles. Theodoret of Cyrrhus lists nine titles and eighteen fragments. In the ninth century, Photius, Patriarch of Constantinople, gives some information on the *Treatise against Thirty-Two Heresies* (see below). He also says he has read the *Treatise on the Universe,* the *Commentary on Daniel,* and *On the Antichrist.* Finally, Ebedjesu, Nestorian metropolitan of Nisibis (d. 1318), speaks of the following works:

- *On Providence*
- *Chapters against Gaius*
- *Defense of the Apocalypse and of the Preaching of John*

At the beginning of the modern age, then, there existed a list of titles that grew ever longer through the centuries, accompanied by a few texts and rather dubious biographical notices. To the list was added a tradition about the martyr Hippolytus of Porto, who was simply a double of the martyr Hippolytus of Rome and came into existence due to the presence in Porto of a recently discovered church dedicated to him. Two discoveries, three centuries apart, were to change the terms of the question and to complicate what continues to be one of the most intricate riddles of early Christian literature.

The first discovery was the finding in Rome in 1551 of a statue of which the upper part was mutilated and which showed a figure sitting on a throne that carried inscriptions. Incised on two sides of it was a table for calculating the date of Easter beginning with 222. On the right rear column was a list of titles of works which one naturally supposes were composed by the author of the Easter table, which is included in the list. The first two lines of the list are lost except for the final letters. The other works are:

- *On the Psalms*
- *On the Ventriloquist*
- *In Defence of the Gospel according to John and the Apocalypse*
- *Apostolic Tradition about the Charisms*
- *(Books) of Chronicles*
- *Against the Greeks and against Plato,* or *Also about the Universe*
- *Exhortation to Severina*
- *Demonstration of the Dates of Easter,* or *What Is in the Table?* (i.e., the table incised on the statue)
- *Odes on All the Scriptures*
- *About God and the Resurrection of the Flesh*
- *About Good and the Source of Evil*

Since the Easter table corresponded to what Eusebius said about the table of Hippolytus, and since some of the titles matched those attributed by tradition to Hippolytus, the statue was identified as that of the martyr Hippolytus, and the table and the list of works were assigned to him.

Recently, however, M. Guarducci has shown that the statue was originally that of a woman. She also claims that the discovery did not take place near the catacomb of St. Hippolytus, as was maintained at the time, but in the Pantheon library, which had been organized by Julius Africanus. She asserts that the list was not of the works of a single author, but simply of those found closest to the statue in the library. This thesis seems open to criticism; V. Saxer would restore the list to Hippolytus. This is one of many unresolved issues about the statue.

The second discovery goes back to 1842. In a monastery of Mt. Athos a fourteenth-century manuscript was found, containing a refutation of all the heresies. The work goes under the name of Origen; it is in ten books, of which the first three and part of the fourth are missing. The first book was subsequently identified in other manuscripts of the works of Origen, and the whole appeared in print in 1851 under the name of Origen and with the title (see below, sec. 3a) of *Philosophoumena* or *Refutation (Elenchos) of All Heresies*. It was quickly shown that the work could not be by Origen, and shortly after that Hippolytus was proposed as the author, although no attempt was made to identify the work with the *Treatise against All the Heretics* that is mentioned by Eusebius, Jerome, and Photius. The point was made that the author refers to two of his earlier works: one is titled *On the Nature of the Universe* (10.32.4), which seems to correspond to one of the titles on the statue, to a treatise mentioned by Photius, and to the work of which a passage is preserved by John Damascene. The other is a work against heresies (proem. 1), which apparently should be identified with the *Treatise* summarized by Photius.

The almost universally accepted attribution to Hippolytus had important consequences for the biography of that author. Not only does he describe himself as a bishop (1. proem. 6; 9.12.21), but in book 9 he shows that he was involved in a doctrinal controversy in Rome. He reproaches Pope Callistus (217–222) for trinitarian modalism; modalism, stemming from a concern to safeguard the oneness of God, asserted that the Son is not an independent person but a "mode of being" of the Father. In return, Callistus accuses him of admitting two gods. He also attacks Callistus in the area of moral discipline, because the latter had allowed those who had sinned after baptism to receive forgiveness in the church, and had authorized the union of high-ranking women with men of more modest position. The author of the *Elenchos* refuses to acknowledge Callistus as bishop and establishes his own community, thus in practice setting himself up as an antipope. It was thought that this situation explained why the tradition knew Hippolytus as bishop of Rome even though his name was missing from the lists of popes, and why he was the only presbyter to be deported with the pope in 235 *(Calendar of 354)*. The fact that he was a martyr would have taken precedence over the fact that he had been a schismatic, and would have allowed him to be venerated as a saint.

Beginning in 1947, this consensus was challenged by P. Nautin, who proposed the following theses. The *Elenchos* displays important theological differences from the *Against Noetus*, which was passed down in a manuscript under the name of Hippolytus and probably represented the final section of the *Syntagma* of Hippolytus that Photius read. Despite its obvious dependence on the *Elenchos* (according to Nautin), the *Against Noetus* cannot be from the same author, whereas it is certainly from the author of the surviving exegetical works attributed to Hippolytus (*Commentary on Daniel, On the Antichrist, Blessings of Jacob and Moses*, and so on).

To the author of the *Elenchos*, on the other hand, belong two works which he himself mentions: *On the Nature of the Universe* (Photius and a fragment in John Damascene), and another, mentioned in connection with a biblical chronology (10.30.5), which allows us to identify it with a *Compendium of Times and Years from the Foundation of the World to the Present Day*, the text of which we have in translations and partly in the original Greek. These three works are found in the inscription on the statue (the 3d as *[Books] of Chronicles*) and point to an author who is interested in the secular sciences, unlike the writer of the exegetical writings handed down under the name of Hippolytus.

If the chronological table on the statue corresponds to the one that Eusebius attributes to Hippolytus, this is due to a secondary and erroneous attribution of the table to Hippolytus that was made before Eusebius's time, and was aided by the fact that Hippolytus too had composed a work *On Easter*. Finally, since in some manuscripts the work *On the Universe* is attributed to a Josepos *(Iōsēpos* or *Iōsipos)*, who according to Nautin cannot be the Jewish historian Flavius Josephus (as is commonly accepted), this must be the real name of the author of the *Elenchos* and the other works on the statue, namely, the Roman antipope. Hippolytus, the author of the exegetical works, could not have been a Roman and his works are to be dated toward the middle of the third century.

Nautin's thesis led to lively debates but not to a real consensus until it was taken up and modified, beginning in 1976, by a group of Italian scholars whose interests were archeological (especially M. Guarducci and P. Testini) and literary (especially V. Loi and M. Simonetti). We shall leave aside the discussion of details and the differences between the first stage of their proposals (1976, published in 1977) and the second (1989), and simply summarize here the results of the second stage, in which Simonetti, after Loi's death, did away with some obvious aporias in the division of works as hypothesized in 1971. The body of works in question is divided between two authors. The name "Josepos" is poorly attested as a possible name for one of the two, as Nautin wanted; it is probably a corruption of Flavius Josephus, to whom the work *On the Universe* was attributed by some.

On the one hand, then, we have the writer Hippolytus, to whom Eusebius, Jerome, and other sources refer. To him are attributed, among the surviving works:

- *David and Goliath*
- *On the Antichrist*
- *Blessings of Jacob and Moses*
- *Commentary on the Song of Songs*
- *Commentary on Daniel*
- *Against Noetus*

This author wrote at the end of the second century and the beginning of the third (the latter being the probable date of the *Against Noetus*) and lived in the East; he may have been bishop of a church in Asia Minor.

The other individual, the Roman schismatic, was active in the early decades of the third century and composed the *Elenchos,* the *On the Universe,* and the *Compendium of Times,* which is no longer to be called *Chronicles,* a practice born of the identification with the *Chronicles* listed on the statue. It is by chance that these works, unlike the first group, have come down either under another name or anonymously. As happened on other occasions in Christian antiquity, the uncertain identity of an author required, if the works were to be saved, that he be given another name. This individual may or may not have been named Hippolytus.

There remains the problem raised by the fact that the Easter calendar appears both in Rome (on the statue) and in Eusebius's list of works of the (eastern) Hippolytus. This difficulty may be met in either of two ways: by attributing it to the eastern Hippolytus and assuming that it was transcribed in Rome for the use of the community that met in the room where the statue was found; or by attributing it to the Roman author and accepting that when his works were put under the name of another, the name of the eastern Hippolytus was chosen for this work. Hippolytus of

Rome was doubtless the name used by the Roman and therefore familiar in his circle. Apart from the uncertainty about the work on Easter, the list given by Eusebius can be taken as reliable for the eastern Hippolytus, although Simonetti wavers somewhat on this point. In contrast, the list by Jerome already shows a confusion of the two writers; he attributes to Hippolytus of Rome a passage from the revision of the *Blessings of the Patriarchs,* a work of the eastern Hippolytus. Either way, the list on the statue is rendered useless by the hypothesis, accepted by Simonetti, that it has absolutely nothing to do with Hippolytus.

It is this last point in particular (apart, of course, from the name "Josepos") that distinguishes Simonetti's most recent suggestion from those of Nautin, although in comparison with the position taken in 1976, developed chiefly by V. Loi, the new suggestion represents to some extent a return to Nautin's theses. There is another important difference: according to Nautin, Hippolytus used the work of Josepos, and was therefore writing several years after 235; according to Simonetti, the *Against Noetus* is a source of the *Against Praxeas* of Tertullian, which was written around 213, and must therefore go back to the end of the second century or the beginning of the third. The affinities between the two authors of the Hippolytean corpus are therefore to be explained by the dependence of the Roman Hippolytus on the eastern Hippolytus.

The position that there were two writers of course requires completely separate biographies. Of the eastern Hippolytus we know only that he was a bishop. The Roman Hippolytus fits into the framework already sketched: a rigorist attitude, the clash with Callistus, the schism, the deportation and death in Sardinia. Nautin, of course, distinguishes his Josepos from Hippolytus, the Roman martyr. As recent scholarly contributions show, the debate has by no means died down between those who maintain a single author for the Hippolytean corpus, and those who claim two authors. It suffices to mention the articles on Hippolytus by C. Scholten in *RAC* 15 (1991), who opposes the distinction of authors and seems not to know of the Italian contributions made in 1989; and by V. Saxer in *DHGE* 24 (1993), who, contrary to what he said in the 1989 volume, seems to accept Simonetti's more recent suggestion.

In the past we have expressed reservations about the separation of authors, and we recognize that many problems remain unsolved. Among others, the rejection of the statue as evidence for Hippolytus seems necessary in the most recent formulation of the thesis. Furthermore, Simonetti is compelled to suspend judgment on writings other than those which were mentioned above and which led to not a few reservations about the 1976 thesis. Nevertheless, we now think it sensible to accept, as a hypothesis, the most recent suggestions advanced by Simonetti. The key difficulty is that of attributing the *Elenchos* to the author of the *Against Noetus* and the exegetical works. We shall therefore deal briefly first with the "Roman" set of works, then with the "eastern" set, and finally with the other texts.

BIBLIOGRAPHY

For guidance on the question, the reader can begin with: M. Richard, "Hippolyte de Rome (saint)," *DSp* 7,1 (1969): 531–71; defends a single Hippolytus.

P. Nautin, "Hippolytus," *EECh* 1 (2 vols.; trans A. Walford; ed. A. Di Berardino; Cambridge: Clarke, 1992), 383–85.

J. A. Cerrato, *Hippolytus between East and West: The Commentaries and the Prove-
    nance of the Corpus* (Oxford: Oxford University Press, 2002).
Two volumes published by Roman congresses are indispensable: *Ricerche su
    Ippolito* (SEAug 13; Rome: Augustinianum, 1977).
Nuove ricerche su Ippolito (SEAug 25; Rome: Augustinianum, 1989).

3. "Roman" Group

a. Refutation of All Heresies

As was indicated above, this work is composed of ten books. The first, which was
published before the others, perhaps for use as a manual of philosophy, has been
transmitted in four manuscripts as the work of Origen. The second, third, and beginning of the fourth books are lost. The remainder is preserved in Suppl. gr. 464 of the
Bibliothèque Nationale of Paris, from the fourteenth century. One sheaf of pages has
been lost from what has survived (chs. 4.27 and 4.28). The author's purpose, as stated
in the introduction, is to show that every Christian heresy derives from a Greek school
of philosophy; it is a claim that could appeal to the strong influence of Greek philosophy on gnostic teachings. To this end, a first part, comprising the first four books, explains the various Greek philosophical systems (first book), then the cults and
mysteries (lost books 2 and 3), and finally astrology and magic (book 4).

In the manuscripts the first and fourth books have the title *Philosophoumena*,
which the author mentions in 9.8.2; in the early editions this was often adopted as the
title of the entire work, although it ought to be reserved to the first part. Books 5
through 9 constitute the refutation of heresies proper: in the fifth, the Naassenes, the
Perati, the Sethians, and Justin the gnostic; in the sixth, the "Great Revelation"
(Megalē apophasis) attributed to Simon Magus, Valentinus and the Valentinians, and
Mark the Magician; and in the seventh, Basilides, Saturnilus, Menander, Marcion,
Prepo, Carpocrates, Cerinthus, the Ebionites, the two Theodotuses, the Melchisi-
dekians, the Nicolaites, Cerdo, Lucian, Apelles; in the eighth, the Docetists, Monoi-
mus, Tatian, Hermogenes, the Quartodecimans, the Montanists, the Encratites, the
Cainites, and the Ophites. The ninth book is devoted to heresies that arose in the
author's time: Noetus, Callistus, the Elkasites, and Jewish sects (Essenes, Pharisees,
Sadducees). The tenth takes the form of a twofold summary *(epitomē)* of the philosophical systems and of the heresies: the first is very short; the second is not limited to
recalling what had already been said, but to some extent produces further sources.

In the information on Greek philosophy, religion, astrology, and magic Hippolytus
does second-hand work, using preexisting compendia and the very gnostic sources he
intends to refute. For Christian heresies he uses existing heresiological works, among
them Irenaeus, but also original documents which he reproduces or to some extent
summarizes, thereby providing us with valuable testimonies. These include: the documentation on the Naassenes, the analysis of which is quite complicated (5.6–10); the
Book of Baruch by Justin the Gnostic (5.23–27); the *Great Revelation* of the Simonians
(6.9–18); an explanation of the Valentinian system that is very different from that
known to Irenaeus (6.29–36); a presentation of the system of Basilides that differs from
that given by Irenaeus (7.20–27); a source for the "Docetists" (8.8–10); and Monoimus,
who is apparently unknown to earlier writers (8.12–15).

Among contemporary heresies, the author includes that of his personal enemy, Callistus. He connects this with Noetus, claiming that when the disciples of Noetus went to Rome, they were encouraged by Bishops Zephyrinus (199–217) and Callistus (9.7.1–3; 9.11.1). He sketches a venomous picture of Callistus that is interesting, even in its one-sidedness, for the history of Roman Christianity during that period (9.11–12). Callistus was a slave of a Christian, Carpophorus; the latter entrusted Callistus with a large sum of money which he used to establish a bank, but the bank failed, and a great many Christians lost their money. When denounced to Carpophorus, Callistus was put to work turning a grindstone. On being subsequently freed, he caused confusion in the synagogue and was finally condemned by the prefect to the mines of Sardinia. When released, along with other Christians, through the intercession of Marcia, a Christian concubine of Emperor Commodus, Callistus returned to Rome in the time of Bishop Victor. When Victor was succeeded by Zephyrinus, Callistus became the latter's éminence grise.

Callistus himself succeeded Zephyrinus and developed a doctrine according to which the Father, who is inseparable from the Son, became incarnate with him and suffered with him—"patripassionism" or monarchianism. In moral matters he adopted the attitudes indicated above. The author fiercely condemns him as head of a sect, but he lets it be seen that Callistus, who was still alive when the work was being composed, which identifies the date, was regarded by many as the legitimate head of the Catholic church (9.12.25).

BIBLIOGRAPHY

Hippolytus, *Refutatio omnium haeresium* (ed. M. Marcovich; New York: de Gruyter, 1986).

———, *Philosophumena, or The Refutation of All Heresies* (trans. F. Legge; New York: Macmillan, 1921).

b. Compendium of Times and Years from the Foundation of the World to the Present Day

As indicated earlier, this work should be termed a *Chronicle* only if one identifies it with the *Books of Chronicles* mentioned on the statue. The first part (down to section 613) is preserved in Greek, in Greek codex 121 of Madrid; another fragment is found in P. Oxyrhynchus 6870. There are three Latin translations of the entire work (the *Excerpta Barbari* and two *Libri generationis*), one in Armenian, and one in Georgian. The work is essentially a chronology of the Bible. According to a calculation then popular among Christians, the total duration of the world was to be 6000 years, of which, according to the author, 5738 had already elapsed.

After a list of the early generations, from Adam to Noah (sec. 22–43), the basis of the presentation is provided by the *Diamerismos* or *Division* of the earth among the three sons of Noah (sec. 44–239, with geographical excursuses: 235, the twelve most famous mountains; 236–237, the most famous rivers; 238, the sources of the rivers of the earthly paradise). Then comes the *Stadiasmos,* or *Measurement in Stadia* of the distances along the Mediterranean between Alexandria and Spain, with information about ports and other matters useful for navigation (sec. 240–613). The author then moves on to the genealogy of the patriarchs beginning with Noah, and then to the genealogy of the judges and kings. Next come the dates of Easter, the kings of Persia, the Olympiads, and everything down to the thirteenth year of Severus Alexander (234–235). The work concludes with appendixes (sec. 718–778) that give lists of patriarchs, prophets, prophetesses, Jewish kings, kings of Samaria, high priests, Macedonian kings, and Roman emperors. The work testifies to an interest in "scientific" and historical questions that seem to fit better with the author of the *Elenchos* than with the exegetical works of Hippolytus. P. Nautin has noted the differences in chronological calculation from the *Commentary on Daniel* of Hippolytus.

BIBLIOGRAPHY

Edition

Hippolytus, *Die Chronik* (ed. R. Helm; GCS 46; 2d ed.; Berlin: Akademie-Verlag, 1955; repr., of ed. A. Bauer and R. Helm; GCS 36: Leipzig: Hinrichs, 1929).

c. On the Universe

This work is mentioned in the *Elenchos* (10.32) with the title *On the Nature of the Universe;* on the statue there is listed an *Against the Greeks and against Plato, or also on the Universe.* Photius summarizes this treatise in his *Lexicon* (codex 48), saying that in the manuscripts he had seen it attributed to Josepos. The same attribution is found in other testimonies about the work including the fragments published in 1965, and on this attribution Nautin bases his thesis that Josepos was the author of the works in the Roman group. Photius says, however, that he had read a marginal note attributing the work to Gaius, a Roman priest and author of the *Labyrinth* (another name of the *Elenchos*). Others attributed the work to Justin or Irenaeus.

On the Universe was composed of two books. Three of the fragments published by W. J. Malley in 1965, which attack the Greeks and Plato in particular, seem to have belonged in the introduction to book 1. Parts of the three fragments also exist in Armenian. According to Photius, the second book began with a demonstration of the greater age of Judaism as compared to Hellenism, a motif current in Jewish and Christian apologetics. A commentary on the story of creation follows; to this must belong a fragment on the creation of the firmament, preserved in *The Creation of the World* by John Philoponus (6th c.), and a passage on the creation of the human being, cited by Photius, which studies the relationship between the spirit and the components of the human body, namely, fire, earth, and air. All this was followed by discussions of demons, Hades, and the final judgment; a lengthy passage on eschatology was located here, containing a description of Hades, that has been transmitted in the *Sacra Parallela* of John Damascene. The same book must have contained the fourth fragment published by Malley, which has to do with the justice and judgment of God. It seems certain that the author was also the author of the *Elenchos*.

BIBLIOGRAPHY

W. J. Malley, "Four Unedited Fragments of the *De Universo* of the Pseudo-Joseph Found in the *Chronicon* of George Hamartolus (Coislin 305)," *JTS* 16 (1965): 13–25.

4. "Eastern" Group

a. Antichrist

In times of persecution people often asked whether the last times were at hand, which, according to the Jewish tradition inherited by Christianity, would immediately precede the coming of the Messiah. At that point, the activity of the devil on earth would reach its climax in the activity of one human being, the last and greatest enemy of God. He would persuade human beings to worship him and believers to apostatize, while killing those who resisted him. In Jewish apocalyptic writings this individual had taken on the traits of kings who were responsible for acts of special wickedness, in particular the profanation of the temple: Antiochus Epiphanes, Pompey, Caligula. For Christians, who had in mind the persecution of 64, it was Nero who best embodied these traits. Later, it was the Jewish revolutionary, Simon bar Kochba.

According to Christians the Messiah had already made his first appearance, so the eschatological adversary came to be described as an antichrist, that is, someone who would put on the same characteristics as Christ in order to lead the faithful astray. Inspired by this expectation with its wealth of tensions, Christians scrutinized the Scriptures in order to find in them the signs that would enable them to recognize the antichrist and the time of his coming. One Christian, Theophilus, asked Hippolytus for instruction on this subject, although the request may be a device of the author. Hippolytus met his wish with an exegesis of the relevant passages of the Bible, after an introduction in which he emphasized the divine inspiration of the prophecies discussed.

For the first time in the history of discussions of the antichrist, Hippolytus sketches, point by point, the opposition between the antichrist and Christ (ch. 6). He then dwells on the first point of correspondence, namely, the fact that both are called "lion" in the Scriptures: Christ in the blessings of Jacob (Gen 49:8–12), and the antichrist in the blessings of Moses (Deut 33:22), where he is described as the "lion of Dan." This origin in Dan, which was already addressed by Irenaeus, supposes a negative Jewish tradition about that tribe (ch. 14). The biblical texts on which the author especially focuses are: passages of Isaiah and Ezekiel on the arrogance of idolatrous kings; the prophecies in Daniel 2 and 7 on the four empires of world history, which are already favorites of the apocalyptic tradition; the prophecies in Revelation 17–18 on the condemnation of Babylon, which Hippolytus identifies with Rome (chs. 36–42). The reign of the antichrist is symbolized by the beast that rises out of the earth in Rev 13:11–18. After the Roman empire has been divided up by the subject peoples, the antichrist will make it one again and give it new vigor, while gaining the support of the Jews and persecuting Christians, until Christ returns and destroys him. Hippolytus refuses, however, to specify the name of the antichrist by interpreting the number 666 that signifies him in the Apocalypse (13:18); he does not want to foster eschatological excitement (ch. 50).

Hippolytus shows a good many contacts with the section on eschatology in the fifth book of Irenaeus, but he also has developments that go back to other traditions, a more intense anti-imperialist tendency, and interpretations of his own; perhaps he depends not directly on Irenaeus but on the latter's sources. The work precedes the *Commentary on Daniel,* which refers to it (4.7.1; 4.13.1; see 4.24.7); if the *Commentary* was written under the influence of the persecution of Septimius Severus in 202–203, the *Antichrist* can be dated to around 200. The work has survived in the original Greek (four manuscripts, plus indirect transmission) and in Old Slavic, Ethiopic, and Georgian translations, to which may be added Syriac and Armenian fragments; a Byzantine revision was made in the ninth century under the title *On the End of the World*.

BIBLIOGRAPHY

Ippolito, *L'anticristo. De antichristo* (ed. E. Norelli; Florence: Nardini, 1987); edition, translation, introduction, and commentary.

b. Commentary on Daniel

In Nautin's view, this commentary is dependent on the Easter table and chronological work of "Josepos," and was therefore composed after 235. However, references to recent persecutions of Christians suggest rather the persecution of Septimius Severus and, therefore, a date around 203–204. The work is preserved almost entirely in Greek in several manuscripts and in a complete Old Slavic translation, as well as in Syriac fragments; it is on these that the editions cited here are based. M. Richard gathered the scattered pages of an Athos manuscript that contained the four books but was difficult to read, and prepared a new edition which, we are told, will be published posthumously in *CCSG*.

This is the earliest Christian commentary that has come down to us; though we know that there were others, but on books of the New Testament (Heracleon on John, Melito on the Apocalypse). The first book, after a historical introduction intended to place the book of Daniel in the setting of the Babylonian exile (1.1–5), comments on Dan 1:1–19 and the story of Susanna (Dan 13).

The latter story is given a typological interpretation that takes its cue from Hippolytus's real world: Susanna is a figure of the church and her husband Joachim is a figure of Christ; the garden near her home is the gathering of the saints; Babylon is the world; and the two elders are the two peoples, the Jews and Gentiles, that attack the church, urged on by Satan (1.14–15). The author speaks in detail of the present situation of persecution and martyrdom (1.19–27). The details of the Susanna story are likewise allegorized: the "opportune day" on which Susanna enters the garden to bathe (Dan 13:15) is Easter, the bath is baptism, the two maids accompanying her are faith and love, the soap is the commandments of the Logos, the oil is the strength given by the Holy Spirit, and so on.

The second book comments on Daniel 2–3, with particular attention to the statue of Nebuchadnezzar, representing the four empires—Babylonian, Persian, Greek, and Roman—followed by ten "democracies" born of the dismemberment of the last empires (2.12.7: same teaching as in *Antichrist*), and to the three young men in the furnace. The latter story prompts a digression on the subject of martyrdom, answering the question: Why did God save the martyrs of that time but not those of today? (2.35–37). The third book deals with Daniel 4–6 and in particular the power of kings and the attitude of independence to be adopted toward earthly authorities. The fourth book (on Dan 7–12) is largely devoted to the vision of the four beasts, their correspondence to the four empires of the statue in Daniel 2, and the events at the end of the world. There are many contacts here with *Antichrist*, to which Hippolytus refers for a fuller treatment of the subject.

The express purpose of this fourth part is to dissuade readers from a distressing expectation of an imminent coming of the kingdom of God; the events predicted for the last times (he says) have not yet all taken place. Hippolytus mentions, as cautionary tales, stories of two recent occurrences in Syria and in Pontus. Two bishops who were convinced that Christ's return was imminent. One bishop persuaded his faithful to follow him into the wilderness; the other bishop persuaded his people to neglect their jobs and so ended up in need (4.16–20).

BIBLIOGRAPHY

Hippolyte, *Commentaire sur Daniel* (introd. G. Bardy; trans. M. Lefèvre; SC 14; Paris: Cerf, 1947); text, translation, introduction, and notes.

Critical Edition

Hippolytus, *Exegetische und homiletische Schriften* (trans. G. N. Bonwetsch; GCS 1; ed. G. N. Bonwetsch and H. Achelis; Leipzig: Hinrichs, 1897), 1–340.

c. Commentary on the Song of Songs

For this text we have a Georgian translation in a tenth-century manuscript made from an Armenian translation of the original Greek. The commentary covers 1:1 to 3:8, and perhaps represents everything the author wrote. There also exist a Greek fragment, an Armenian fragment, a few in Syriac and Old Slavic, and a summary Greek paraphrase. Noting a kind of emphasis and repetition that are not found in the other exegetical works, M. Richard agues that this was Hippolytus's first work of exegesis. The author works out an allegorical interpretation that translates into Christian terms the Jewish interpretation of the husband in the Song as God and the bride as Israel; here the bridegroom is Christ and the bride is the church.

The details are interpreted within this setting. For example, Song 1:3: "Your name is perfumed oil *poured*" means that as long as the Word was in the bosom of the Father, like perfume closed in a vessel, he gladdened no one, but when the Father sent forth his Spirit, the Word poured out joy upon all (2.5). This outpouring took several forms: in the creation of the human being by breathing upon him; upon the waters in order to cleanse them; among pagans, to gather them into the church; and upon Israel when unbelievers did not accept the Logos (2.8). "Who is this that comes up from the wilderness?" (Song 3:6) refers to the church that emerges from the midst of the pagans, who for a long time were a barren wilderness before God but became citizens in the kingdom of the saints (26.1). The commentary thus advances sentence by sentence. It is always addressed to a plural "you," and is homiletic in character.

BIBLIOGRAPHY

G. Garitte, *Traités d'Hippolyte sur David et Goliath, sur le Cantique des cantiques et sur l'Antichrist. Version georgienne* (2 vols.; CSCO 263–64; Louvain: Peeters, 1965).

P. Melloni, "Ippolito e il Cantico dei cantici," in *Ricerche su Ippolito* (SEAug 13; Rome: Augustinianum, 1977), 97–120.

d. Homily on David and Goliath

This work on 1 Kings 17 has been preserved in Georgian and in Armenian fragments from two catenas (see bibliography in sec. c above). Literal and typological exegeses are interwoven. For example, the anointing of Saul by Samuel leads the writer to the negative aspects of Saul's reign, whereas the anointing of David in Bethlehem is seen as rich in christological implications (4.1–3). Sometimes the typological interpretation, including moral exegesis, takes the upper hand. An example would be the interpretation of the war with the Philistines in ch. 7: always starting with the christological typology of the person of David, the victory of David over Goliath naturally prefigures the victory of Christ over the devil.

e. Blessings of Isaac, Jacob, and Moses

This is a treatise in two parts, or two treatises closely interconnected. The first part is a commentary on Genesis 37 (visions of Joseph), Genesis 27 (Isaac's blessing of Esau and Jacob: chs. 3–10), and, at greater length, Genesis 49 (Jacob's blessing of his twelve sons: chs. 11–28). The Greek text has reached us in a tenth-century manuscript in which it is erroneously attributed to Irenaeus. The work has also come down in an Armenian translation and in a Georgian translation made from the Armenian, both of which attribute the work to Hippolytus.

Of the biblical blessings on the twelve patriarchs, the blessing of Judah (Gen 49:8–12) had already been given a messianic interpretation in pre-Christian Judaism (for example, at Qumran: 4Q254 I, 1), and was then applied by Christians to Jesus (see Rev 5:5, Justin, Irenaeus, and others). The first work that developed an exegesis of all of Jacob's blessings, though not in the form of an exegetical commentary, was the *Testaments of the Twelve Patriarchs,* a text that was probably of Jewish origin but has come down to us with Christian interpolations. In that work we find, in the *Testament of Dan* 5.6, the idea of an eschatological opposition between the descendants of Dan and those of Levi and Judah, that is, the Messiah or Messiahs. This view was consistent with the idea, shared by Hippolytus in *Antichrist* and in the present treatise, that the antichrist would come from the tribe of Dan.

With these traditional ideas as his starting point, Hippolytus undertakes a systematic exegesis of all the blessings, an exegesis in which typology definitively wins out over a literal interpretation. Jacob in supplanting Esau becomes the type of Christians who come later but take precedence over the Jews. In general, Hippolytus refuses to refer what is said in the texts to events within the Old Testament, and instead gives an exclusively christological reading of them.

The structural analogy seen in the biblical texts leads Hippolytus to extend his interpretive effort to the blessings of Moses on the tribes of Israel (Deut. 33). Of this second treatise, which is logically connected with the first, only scattered Greek fragments remain. It survives in Armenian and Georgian translations, where it follows the first part.

The catenas have also preserved fragments of an interpretation of Genesis 49 under the name of Hippolytus. Jerome (*Epist.* 36, to Damasus) cites as coming from Hippolytus a lengthy passage on Genesis 27. These texts, while sharing the basic direction taken in the first of the two preceding treatises, also show important differences in details, so that it is difficult to assign them to the same author. Still, it has been shown that even greater difficulties arise when one attempts to assign each of the two works to one of the presumed authors of the Hippolytean corpus, as was proposed in 1976. There is no doubt that the treatises come from the eastern Hippolytus, given the close affinities with the exegesis of the same passages in *Antichrist*. M. Simonetti has suggested that the fragments come from a radical revision of the treatise on the blessings of Jacob, and this by a different author who possessed a more mature exegetical technique. Doubts remain, since there are points of contact between *Antichrist* and the fragments that are not shared by the treatises, but for the time being there is no better solution.

BIBLIOGRAPHY

Hippolytus, *Hippolyte de Rome sur les bénédictions d'Isaac, de Jacob et de Moïse* (trans. and ed. M. Brière, L. Mariès, and B.-C. Mercier; PO 27, 1–2; Paris: Firmin-Didot, 1954).

Ippolito, *Le benedizioni di Giacobbe* (trans. and ed. M. Simonetti; Rome: Città Nuova, 1982).

f. Against the Heresy of Noetus

This is a lengthy fragment preserved in Codex Vaticanus 1431 (12th c.) as a homily. The genre is debated. Some regard it as truly a homily (e.g., Butterworth). Nautin identifies it as the final section of the *Syntagma* of "Josepos," who, according to Photius, ended his work by refuting the heresy of Noetus. For still others, its length demands that it be treated as an independent work; among this group, some think it should be denied to both of the presumed authors and regarded as a late work. As indicated earlier, according to the tenth book of the *Elenchos,* Noetus was the founder of monarchianism in Rome. The refutation of the heresy of Noetus is followed by a "demonstration of the truth." At the beginning the author mentions that the heresy was maintained by "others," leaving it to be understood that it must have been preceded by others.

When P. Nautin launched his thesis about Hippolytus and "Josepos" in 1947, he based it to a great extent on the incompatibility between the *Elenchos* (which likewise refutes Noetus) and the *Against Noetus,* and on the affinity of the latter with the exegetical works. Although both works are based on a theology of the Logos, the *Elenchos* is concerned with the relation between Father and Son, but, as far as the Spirit is concerned, restricts itself to rejecting Callistus's teaching about the Spirit as a substratum common to Father and Son. The *Against Noetus,* by contrast, develops a trinitarian theology based on the idea of *oikonomia* and the division among the divine persons and their functions. M. Simonetti emphasizes that thus understood the *Elenchos* fits neatly into the binitarianism (concern only with the relations between Father and Son) that was dominant in Rome at the end of the second century and the beginning of the third, whereas the *Against Noetus* fits into the eastern theological world in which the doctrine of the Logos tended to expand into a trinitarian doctrine. Nautin has also called attention to the differences in heresiological method, spiritual formation, and style. Recent attempts to attribute the *Against Noetus* once again to the author of the *Elenchos* (J. Frickel) are not convincing.

BIBLIOGRAPHY

P. Nautin, *Hippolyte contre les hérésies; fragment: Étude et édition critique* (Paris: Cerf, 1949).

Hippolytus of Rome, *Contra Noetum* (ed. and trans. R. Butterworth; London: Heythrop College, 1977).

5. Fragmentary or Lost Works

We saw how, in the early church, the list of works attributed to Hippolytus grew from author to author. That trend was due either to a confusion of the eastern writer and the Roman martyr, or to the tendency of later writers to expand the list of works of the renowned exegete by attributing to him various works in that genre. We shall not list all of them, but refer the reader for accurate and complete information to *CPG* 1870–1924. We shall, however, mention the most important of them; for the debated *Apostolic Tradition* we refer to this volume (ch. 7, sec. 1b).

Eusebius mentions a work *On Easter* (*Hist. eccl.* 6.22.1), and the Hippolytus statue inscription lists a *Demonstration of the Dates of Easter, or What Is in the Table*, an obvious reference to the table incised on the same pedestal. There is a Greek ("extracted from the first book") and a Syriac fragment of a work of Hippolytus on Easter. According to Eusebius the work in question contained the table, so we need not hypothesize two different works. The interest in chronology seems to link the work rather with the Roman writer, and the statue confirms this, but this in turn raises the problem noted earlier of the presence of the title in Eusebius's list, which gives the works of the eastern Hippolytus. The table very quickly proved to be erroneous and was replaced by another from an unknown author in about 242–243.

We have repeatedly mentioned the *Syntagma against All Heresies*. Eusebius (*Hist. eccl.* 6.22.1), followed by Jerome, calls it *Against All Heresies*. Photius summarizes the work (*Lexicon*, codex 121). It refuted thirty-two heresies, from Dositheus to Noetus, and claimed to be a summary of lectures given on the subject by Irenaeus. Photius judges the language of the work positively. In the last century R. A. Lipsius showed that the work served as a source for the antiheretical works of Epiphanius, Filastrius of Brescia, and Pseudo-Tertullian; owing to the affinities among the three a list can be derived of thirty-one heresies, from Dositheus to Noetus. The work is attributed to Hippolytus by Eusebius and Photius; it seems to belong indeed to the eastern Hippolytus. If it is not from the author of the *Elenchos*, it cannot be identified with the earlier, summary refutation of all the heresies which the author of the *Elenchos* says he had once composed (*Elench.* 1. pref. 1).

Six fragments survive of a treatise *On the Resurrection* (same title in Jerome), dedicated to Empress Mammea and therefore written between 222 and 235. It must be identified with the work from which Theodoret cites two passages (on 1 Cor 15:20); he calls it *Letter to a Queen*. Another fragment, contained in a florilegium, has to do with the ark of the covenant. On the statue there is a title: *On God and the Resurrection of the Flesh*.

The statue lists, in three successive lines, a work *Apostolic Tradition about the Charisms;* it seems preferable to take this as a single work. Was it the same as the *Apostolic Tradition* that has been reconstructed, as a work of Hippolytus, from several canonical collections?

Only a few fragments, or even just titles, remain of many exegetical works attributed to Hippolytus; for details see, in addition to the *CPG*, the articles listed in the bibliography at the end of section 2. The reader may recall that the list on the statue contains a work *In Defense of the Gospel according to John and the Apocalypse*. Ebedjesu, Nestorian metropolitan of Nisibis (d. 1318), mentions as from Hippolytus some *Chapters against Gaius* and a *Defense of the Apocalypse and of the Preaching of John*. The two titles probably represent a single work, from which Dionysius bar Salibi (twelfth century) copied passages in his commentary on the Apocalypse, saying that he had gotten them from the *Chapters against Gaius*. These passages show material affinities with the *Antichrist* and therefore should be attributed to the eastern Hippolytus, but this creates problems because of the presence of the title on the statue. Gaius, a Roman priest at the end of the second century, in his attack on Marcionism, denied the Johannine authorship of the Fourth Gospel, because of the Paraclete, and of the Apocalypse, because of its millenarianism, attributing both to Cerinthus the gnostic. Hippolytus defends the authenticity of these biblical books and denies the supposed contradictions between the Apocalypse and Paul.

Chapter 14

ALEXANDRIA AND CLEMENT

1. Alexandria

Although the splendor of Alexandrian Hellenistic culture was in decline during the first centuries of Christianity, the city remained important. The Greek city had been artificially created in Egypt in 331 in order to strengthen the position of the conquerors, and had been wondrously enlarged and beautified by the Ptolemies, who made it their capital. It had welcomed a diverse population which reached a half million, including a Jewish colony, which was often in conflict with the Greek populace. The co-presence of eastern religions was the norm.

Since Alexandria served to control the vast and extremely important production of grain in Egypt, it was a major commercial center. During the Hellenistic period, it also became an important cultural center: poetry, philology, and the mathematical and natural sciences had developed in the setting of that extraordinary cultural institution, the Museum. This was founded by Ptolemy I Soter around 300 B.C. and achieved its greatest splendor under Ptolemy II Philadelphus (283–246). After a period of decline, it was given new life by Augustus. A particular focus of attention was philology, which took for its texts Homer and the tragic and comic poets; practitioners included Zenodotus, Alexander Aetolus, Lycophron, Aristophanes of Byzantium, and others. Philology meant textual criticism and the publication of texts, as well as exegesis (Aristarchus of Samothrace, 1st half of 2d c. B.C.). But the allegorical exegesis of Homer, which had been begun by grammarians and philosophers back in the sixth and fifth centuries in order to justify the anthropomorphism and immoral behavior of the Homeric gods, was now practiced not by the grammarians of Alexandria but by those of Pergamum. The philological work of Origen on the texts of the Bible (see the next chapter) cannot be explained apart from that tradition.

As early as the second century B.C., Aristobulus, a Jewish exegete of Alexandria, had applied the allegorical method of interpretation to the Jewish Scriptures; so, after him, did the anonymous author of the *Letter of Aristeas to Philocrates,* which is a defense of the Septuagint. But the decisive influence on the Christian theology of Alexandria was the work of Philo of Alexandria, a Jew (died ca. A.D. 40). He applied the Platonic distinction between the two levels of reality—the visible world and the intelligible world—to produce a wide-ranging allegorical interpretation of the Pentateuch. Here the laws and stories of the Bible became figures of spiritual and moral realities (strongly influenced by Stoicism, as was common at that time) but also of eschatological realities. Philo accepted the problems raised by Middle Platonism with a view to finding solutions by linking that philosophy to the Jewish religious tradition. As a result, he assigned a central role to the mediator of creation, the divine Logos, who is the locus of the divine ideas but also a savior and guide who makes possible the ascent to God. The influence of this set of ideas was decisive for Clement and Origen.

The origins of Christianity in Alexandria are obscure; the tradition connecting it with Mark (Eusebius, *Hist. eccl.* 2.15.1) is a later legend, and we have reliable historical sources beginning only from the end of the second century. It has been suggested that the obscurity is due to the silence kept by a subsequently consolidated "orthodoxy" about the early form of Alexandrian Christianity, which was gnostic (W. Bauer). This thesis is sharply criticized today. It is certain, however, and worth mentioning here, that in the second century Alexandria was one of the centers for the development of gnostic thought, especially by the disciples of Basilides and Valentinus. It appears not only from the texts recovered on papyri, among which "apocryphal" writings are no fewer in number than the "canonical," but also from the attitude of Clement, that even in the second half of the second century the city was characterized by many variants of Christianity. People there were open to the most diverse, more or less esoteric traditions, and simple Christians brushed shoulders with able speculative theologians, the latter doubtless belonging to the upper social classes. There was not yet a separation and mutual rejection between gnostics and other Christians.

It is in that setting that the question of the origin of the Didaskalion, the Christian school of Alexandria, must be raised. According to a late notice by Philip of Side in his *History,* which was written between 434 and 439, the first head of the school was the apologist Athenagoras, but the confused statement does not seem trustworthy. According to Eusebius (*Hist. eccl.* 5.10.1, 4), in the time of Emperor Commodus (180–192) the school of Alexandria, which had already existed for a long time, was headed by Pantaenus, who was succeeded by Clement (*Hist. eccl.* 6.6).

We know almost nothing of Pantaenus; according to Eusebius (*Hist. eccl.* 5.10), he converted from Stoicism, then went off to evangelize India. Arriving in India he found that he had been preceded by the apostle Bartholomew, who had left the gospel of Matthew there. This is evidently already the stuff of legend. More trustworthy is the testimony of Clement of Alexandria, who had Pantaenus as teacher (see below, sec. 2a). Apart from that we know nothing of Pantaenus, and he does not seem to have written anything; even the testimony of Clement says as much. Only two passages of his teaching survive. One is preserved by Clement (*Ecl.* 56.2), on the use of the present tense by the prophets. The other is found in Maximus the Confessor (frag. 48 of Clement, GCS 3.224): "God knows existing things not insofar as they are sensible but as they are found in his own will, since it is by will that God created them." Clement describes Pantaenus as a link in the chain of secret traditions inherited from the apostles. It is possible, therefore, that Pantaenus already maintained the idea, so dear to Clement, of esoteric tradition.

Returning to the question of what Eusebius describes as the catechetical school of Alexandria (*Hist. eccl.* 6.3.1, 3, 8; 6.15.1; 6.28.1; 7.32.30), it seems that the supposed school was a projection into the past of a state of affairs that began with Origen. There must previously have been catechumenal preparation on a modest scale, organized by the bishop, as well as private courses in philosophy and theology, given by a Pantaenus, Clement, and a young Origen, just as Justin gave them at Rome in the middle of the second century. Only after the persecution of 202–203, when catechists had been scattered, did Bishop Demetrius acknowledge the teaching of Origen by entrusting the catechetical school to him (see the next chapter). One reason for doing so was, of course, that he might exert better control. This was after all the age in which, in many places, episcopal authority got rid of "heretical" groups and closed ranks. In view of this, Méhat does not seem justified when he says that private teaching would not have been possible in a second-century community because of the strict control maintained by the bishop.

Alexandrian theology thus came to be dominated by the characteristics of the thinking of Clement and Origen, a thinking that developed through a confrontation with gnostic trends. This confrontation was marked by greater freedom on Clement's part, but with greater rigidity, and apparently with a mind less well informed, on Origen's part. As we shall see in greater detail in discussing Clement and Origen, this line of thought was characterized by a Platonism that distinguished two levels of reality; from this flowed a dualist anthropology in which only the *nous*, the higher part of the soul, bore the image of God and had the ability to (re-)acquire the divine likeness. The doctrine of God implied the distinction of three hypostases within the Trinity, and Christology was based on the Logos, the mediator of creation and human salvation.

In keeping with this cosmic and anthropological Platonism, levels of meaning in the Scriptures were distinguished, with the allegorical meaning regarded as more important than the literal meaning. The Greek philosophical tradition, as mediated also through the thinking of a Hellenized Judaism, was accepted and rethought as a framework for Christian theology. It was precisely this openness toward philosophy that caused Clement, and even more Origen, to be criticized by a party that was opposed to this outlook and was quite strong in the Alexandrian church. Nevertheless, even after the departure of Origen in 232–233, the school continued to follow his thinking, but purified now of elements that seemed untenable, chiefly the doctrine of the preexistence and fall of souls.

2. Clement

a. Life

Titus Flavius Clemens was born around 140–150 in Alexandria or, more probably, Athens (thus Epiphanius, *Pan.* 32.6). He was probably from a pagan family (Eusebius, *Praep. ev.* 2.3.64), and his writings suggest that he was initiated into the Eleusinian mysteries. He received a good training in philosophy. In listing his successive teachers (*Strom.* 1.11.2), Clement locates the first, an Ionian, in Greece; the second, from Coelesyria; the third, an Egyptian, in Magna Graecia; another in Assyria; one of Jewish origin in Palestine; and the last and best, in Egypt. Clement does not name this last, simply describing him as a "Siculian bee," but he is probably referring to Pantaenus, as Eusebius thought (*Hist. eccl.* 5.11.2). Eusebius adds that Clement often mentions Pantaenus in his *Hypotyposes* as having been his teacher; he is also named in the *Extracts from the Prophets* (56.2). Eusebius also says that Clement succeeded Pantaenus as head of the catechetical school of Alexandria, but, as noted, this is unlikely, and that Origen was one of Clement's pupils (*Hist. eccl.* 6.6).

We do not know for certain whether Clement was a priest. In any case, he does not seem to have been the official catechist of Alexandria; rather, he gave an extracurricular course. Eusebius's *Chronicle* dates Clement's *akmē* to 193 and his works to 203. In the persecution of Septimius Severus, 202–203, he was forced to leave Alexandria, although some have suggested the reason was conflict with the bishop. A letter of Bishop Alexander of Caesarea in Cappadocia, written around 205 according to some, or around 215 according to others, mentions a priest named Clement who was active in his church (Eusebius gives two passages from this letter in *Hist. eccl.* 6.11.5–6), but it is not certain that this is the same Clement. Another letter of the same Alexander to Origen in 215–216 (or in 231 according to Nautin) presupposes that Clement is dead. His death is also taken for granted in the *Calendars* of Julius Africanus, from 221. He writes that "Clement was known in Alexandria during the reign of Commodus," that is, between 180 and 192.

BIBLIOGRAPHY

General Works

G. Lazzati, *Introduzione all studio di Clemente Alessandrino* (Milan: Vita e Pensiero, 1939).
C. Mondésert, *Clément d'Alexandrie. Introduction à l'étude de sa pensée religieuse à partir de l'Écriture* (Paris: Aubier, 1944).
S. Lilla, *Clement of Alexandria: A Study in Christian Platonism and Gnosticism* (London: Oxford University Press, 1971).

Critical Editions

The complete works of Clement, with important indexes, can be found in:
Clement of Alexandria, *Protrepticus und Paedagogus* (vol. I in *Clemens Alexandrinus;* GCS 12; ed. O. Stählin; 3d ed. by U. Treu; Berlin: Akademie Verlag, 1972).
——, *Stromata Buch I–VI* (vol. II in *Clemens Alexandrinus;* GCS 15; ed. O. Stählin and L. Früchtel; 4th ed. by U. Treu; Berlin: Akademie Verlag, 1985).
——, *Stromata Buch VII und VIII, Excerpta ex Theodoto, Eclogae propheticae, Quis dives salvetur, Fragmente* (vol. III in *Clemens Alexandrinus;* GCS 17; ed. O. Stählin and L. Früchtel; 2d ed. by U. Treu; Berlin: Akademie Verlag, 1970).
——, *Register* (vol. IV in *Clemens Alexandrinus;* GCS 39; ed. O. Stählin; 2d ed. by U. Treu; Berlin: Akademie Verlag, 1980).
The most generally available and extensive English translation of Clement's works is found in volume 2 of *The Ante-Nicene Fathers* (ed. A. Roberts, J. Donaldson, and A. C. Coxe; repr., Peabody, Mass.: Hendrickson, 1995).

b. Exhortation to the Greeks

At the beginning of *Christ the Educator (Paedagogus)*, Clement outlines a program of education by the Logos in three stages. The Logos "exhorts" inasmuch as he concerns himself with *ēthē* or fundamental dispositions, to use a distinction made by Aristotle; he exhorts human beings to conversion. He continues his pedagogical activity by concerning himself with the other two components of the human being, passions and actions. He allays the former and properly directs the latter. Finally, he acts as teacher when he moves from moral formation to the kind of instruction that produces gnosis, or perfect knowledge (*Paed.* 1.1–3.3). It is clear that Clement intended to carry out the first part of this program in the *Exhortation to the Greeks (Protrepticus),* and the second in *Christ the Educator;* it is debated, however (see below, sec. 2d), whether and to what extent his other major work, the *Miscellanies,* is to be regarded as carrying out the third part.

Protreptic was a genre introduced by Aristotle in his now lost work of that name; Epicurus and especially the Stoics (Cleanthes, Chrysippus, Posidonius) composed analogous works. So too did Cicero, whose lost *Hortensius* exerted a decisive influence on the conversion of Augustine. While in these instances there was a question of urging readers to turn to philosophy, protreptic also became an element in academic practice, in the form of the lecture with which the leaders of schools began their course of studies, urging students to choose their particular discipline. In the field of medicine Galen composed a *Protreptic.* Clement thus takes his place in a tradition, elements of which are already found in the Christian apologists, in the form of an exhortation to embrace the new religion. The protreptic element is especially important in *Letter to Diognetus.* Indeed, Clement's *Exhortation* has many points in common with the apologists, and especially with Athenagoras, who has sometimes been thought to be the first teacher Clement had in Greece.

The work opens with a chapter in a lyrical key: the songs of pagan mythology, which spread error, are contrasted by Clement with the new song of the Logos, the bringer of light and truth. Human beings are deserting Helicon and Cythera and moving to the mountain of Zion, whence come the law and the Logos of God. If the mythic Orpheus tamed the wild beasts with his singing, the Logos has tamed the most savage of animals: human beings. After harmoniously ordering the world and humanity at creation, he now comes to save the human race, and because of this manifestation his song can be called new, although it has existed from the very beginning of things.

Ensuing chapters develop a critique of Greek religion: the second chapter attacks the sanctuaries and the mysteries the repugnant and obscene character of which Clement wants to expose. His detailed information on the Eleusinian mysteries suggests, as earlier noted, that he was an initiate; there are further detailed references in the *Miscellanies.* Clement also critiques astrology and the myths, in which he sees distorted insights into the human condition and destiny. Finally, he attacks the worship of demons, a popular theme in that age. For Clement, as for the Christian apologists, demons are the source of polytheism. The third chapter attacks the practice of human sacrifice and takes advantage of euhemerist ideas in interpreting the sanctuaries as having been originally the tombs of human beings. Extensive use is made of euhemerism in the fourth chapter, following a critique of the cult of images.

The fifth chapter reviews the opinions of the Greek philosophers on the divinity. The sixth attempts to show that the philosophers, especially Plato, were inspired by the Truth itself to say something true about God. The same is said of the Greek poets (ch. 7). From texts thus containing a glimmer of truth, Clement moves on (ch. 8) to the texts of those persons who convey a true knowledge of God, namely, the prophets. But in Clement's own day it is through his Logos that God calls (ch. 9), with the promise of freedom and salvation; to him all must hasten. Fear of abandoning the ways of the forefathers ought not make anyone hesitant, if the old ways are ways of error and marked by ignorance, folly, incontinence, injustice, and wickedness, and if the person is called to embrace virtues opposed to that heritage. One ought to embark on the search with trust in the goodness of God (ch. 10), for God has already shown his good will and his mercy throughout the history of the human race. The coming of the Logos is the culminating proof of God's beneficent attitude (ch. 11).

After this stream of eloquence, the work ends with a return to the lyrical tone (ch. 12) in an appeal to flee the sirens of pleasures and to board the ship of which the Logos is the steersman, to abandon the orgies of the mysteries and hasten to join the choir of the just, and to enter into a friendship with God, because, as the proverb has it, friends possess all in common and therefore whatever belongs to the God belongs to the believer as well. As a result, the believer is uniquely rich, wise, and noble, and thereby regains at last the likeness of God that was lost by sin.

The date of composition of the *Exhortation* is unknown, but since the beginning of *Christ the Educator* seems to allude to it, it must have been written earlier. A. Méhat has offered arguments for dating both of these works before the *Miscellanies* was begun, and suggests as a possible date the years 195–197.

The common ancestor of all the manuscripts of the *Exhortation* (and of *Christ the Educator*) is Paris gr. 451, which was made in 914 by Arta, Archbishop of Caesarea in Cappadocia. It also contained apologetic works, among them the writings of Athenagoras, two works wrongly attributed to Justin, and the first five books of the *Preparation for the Gospel* by Eusebius of Caesarea.

The work is thus a critique of pagan religion, which the Logos calls the reader to abandon. It is not a critique of the Greek tradition generally, since there, too, traces of divine revelation can be seen, even if in a fragmentary form. Here we have one of Clement's fundamental ideas, that of a twofold, parallel revelation in the preChristian period: incomplete in the pagan sages, more complete among the Jews, but in both cases the work of the divine Logos. It is therefore natural that possessors of Greek culture who want to live in conformity with the Logos (who is at the same Son of God and universal reason) should accept the call of the Logos and embrace faith in Christ.

Bibliography

Clément d'Alexandrie, *Le Protreptique* (ed. and trans. C. Mondésert; SC 2; 2d ed.; Paris: Cerf, 1949); Greek text, introduction, translation, and notes.

Clemente di Alessandria, *Il Protrettico* (ed. and trans. M. Galloni; Rome: Borla, 1991); Italian translation.

c. Christ the Educator

In Hellenistic society, a "pedagogue," as the etymology shows, was a slave whose duty was to lead, that is, accompany the young boy to school while protecting him from dangers but also teaching him to behave properly. Generally, the pedagogue's tasks included an overall attention to the child's good behavior, while instruction was the teacher's job. As we saw, Clement used this institution as a metaphor for the second stage of his program of formation. He did not shrink from assigning the pedagogue's function to the Logos, even though it was a lowly one in the society of the time and, as we shall see, not without its difficulties, even in the theological sphere. *Christ the Educator,* in three books, is addressed to a readership of baptized persons, who now need to be taught a way of life consistent with their Christian state, and this before moving on to a formation in "knowledge."

The first book is devoted to preliminary questions about the necessity and manner of the divine pedagogy and about the several parties involved. The first four chapters (1.1.1–1.11.2, according the numbering by books, sections, and subsections, which we follow here) set down general principles. The first explains the threefold function of the Logos, which we have already summed up in connection with the *Exhortation.* The second asserts that, since it is impossible for human beings not to sin, they need a Pedagogue who will heal their passions and will educate them. The third applies to the Pedagogue in a more particular way the traditional idea of the divine *philanthrōpia* or love for human beings. The fourth asserts that the Logos is by the same title the Pedagogue of both men and women. The remainder of the first book purposes to answer two questions: In the pedagogical relationship, who are the children and who is the pedagogue?

Chapters 5 and 6 answer the first question: we, the baptized, are the children. At this point Clement's main concern is to oppose the gnostics, who disparage the condition of "the child," assigning it to an inferior level, that of the "psychic," who needs law and morality, as compared with the state of the gnostic, who alone is "adult" and capable to reaching knowledge. For this reason Clement is careful to say that the "children" include *all* of the baptized. Thus he emphasizes passages of the Bible, and of the Gospels in particular, in which the disciples are called children, "not in order to signify the age of persons lacking in intelligence, as some have thought" (1.16.2), but, on the contrary, because those who make themselves childlike show that they have already advanced in the Christian life and acknowledge God alone as Father.

The gnostic interpretation contrasted the child, as an image of the imperfect believer, with the adult, as an image of the perfect believer. In the gnostic view, only the former needed the pedagogue, represented in Paul (Gal 3:23–25) by the law, which was meant to lead to Christ but lost its role once Christ had come. Oddly enough, Clement does not make use of the dialectical relationship of child–adult along dynamic lines in order to stress the formation that will lead from the former condition to the latter; it is likely that this approach would have come too close to the gnostic outlook. Instead, he makes the most of the condition of children who, after stripping off the old self and being regenerated, become like newborns, purified of corruption and vice (1.32.3–4).

Where Scripture contrasts the condition of the child with that of the adult, clearly emphasizing the limitations of the former (as Paul does in 1 Cor 14:20 or 13:12), Clement insists that the point of the opposition is not age. In his opinion, Paul contrasts the child, who is led by fear and is a symbol of the Jews under the old covenant, with the adult, who is led by reason, that is, by the Logos, and is a symbol of Christians under the new covenant (1.33.1–34.2). When Clement comments on a passage dear to the gnostics, such as 1 Cor 3:1–12, which contrasts milk, the food of infants, with the solid food of adults as symbols of elementary teaching as opposed to the spiritual knowledge reserved to the perfect, he takes great trouble to prove that "milk" signifies the simple, true, spiritual food that leads to perfection, while the "solid food" is God's self-revelation in the full light of the future world. Clement makes recourse, in a lengthy digression, to medical notions of the age to argue that his opponents are wrong in opposing milk to the solid food that is identified with the flesh and blood of Christ (see John 6:53), because milk is actually purified blood, and therefore the two are not different (1.33.1–52.1).

Admittedly, a passage such as Gal 3:23–25, which clearly restricts the pedagogue's role to the time preceding faith in Christ, cannot easily be harmonized with the idea of Christ as pedagogue. Clement understands the passage (in 1.31.1) as contrasting the law, accompanied by fear, with the Logos as pedagogue of free choice *(prairēsis)*; the law led the former people by means of fear, while the Logos leads the new people by means of love. Pedagogy is involved in both cases, because the law is "former grace" given by the Logos through Moses, but it has been succeeded by "eternal grace" that comes through Jesus (1.58.1–60.3). The extension of the idea of the pedagogue to the Christian age is clearly an innovation and, from Paul's point of view, even a contradiction.

Chapters 7–13 are given over to a description of the pedagogue: "the pedagogue, then, is of course the Logos, who leads the children, that is, us *(paidas . . . agōn)*, to salvation" (1.53.3). Pedagogy can take various forms: that of God "points out the right way of truth, leading to the goal of contemplation of God, and (provides) the model of holy actions in an everlasting perseverance" (1.54.1). But the pedagogical method sometimes calls for severity and chastisement. Once again, Clement must reject the viewpoint of the gnostics and Marcionites, who assert the incompatibility of divine goodness and retributive justice. This idea is extensively developed in the controversy with gnostics and Marcionites in the second and third centuries.

Clement makes use of Stoic categories when he argues that the good and the useful are one and the same; justice is useful and therefore justice is good (1.63.1–64.2). He also has recourse to the unanimous testimonies of Scripture about the co-existence of goodness and justice in God (1.71.1–74.4). Moreover God threatens chastisement, before chastising and rather than chastise, thereby stirring fear in order to impel people to avoid sin; this is good pedagogy. Then, when God does chastise, he does so not out of hatred or in revenge, but for the correction of the sinner. The remainder of the first book develops these ideas and applies them to the Logos. Moreover, Clement constantly plays on the several meanings of *logos* and in particular the relationship between the Word of God and human reason. The Logos/Son is the image of God; the human intellect *(nous)*, which is made in God's image, is assimilated by means of its understanding *(phronēsis)* to the Logos and thus becomes rational *(logikos; Protr.* 98.4). Thus a morality according to reason is necessarily a morality conformed to the Logos. The effort of human beings must be to make their souls like the Logos, who is the image of God (1.4.1–2).

In the final chapter of the first book, Clement starts with a historical principle: "Every action against the correct *logos* is a fault" (1.101.1) and concludes with the question: "If, then, disobedience to the *logos* produces a fault, how avoid the inference that obedience to the *logos,* or, in other words, what we call faith, will produce what is called duty *(kathēkon)*?" (1.101.1). *Logos* (reason) is here identical with the Logos (Son), and the faith of Christians is the same as adherence to the universal and divine reason of the Stoics. Here, as throughout his works, Clement carries out a plan (to which we shall return) of identifying the Christian system as *the* philosophical system.

While the first book sets down principles, the second and third contain a repertory of practical moral rules (*to biōpheles tēs paidagōgias*, 2.1.1) for all the circumstances of life. The rules are backed by citations from the Bible and also from the Greek writers. The author discusses eating, drinking, sleep, furnishings, participation in banquets, laughter, the need to avoid obscenities and mockery, the use of perfumes and garlands, and so on. The instructions go into minute detail, which is characteristic of the situation in which Clement is writing and of the attitude he has adopted. He evidently addresses a group of well-to-do Christians who have abundant and fine foods and beverages, luxurious furnishings, banquets at which the wine flows, stylish clothing, delicate perfumes, jewels and cosmetics, and servants. These are the same people for which *Salvation of the Rich* is intended, namely, a social class not too different from the one vividly described over a century earlier in *Trimalchio's Supper* by Petronius. But the rich here are Christians, and the problem arises for them, as for Clement, of how to live according to their faith.

Clement does not adopt the vehement rejection of spectacles, styles, and adornments that we see in Tertullian during those same decades. In Clement's view, the Christian faith is not opposed to the life of society but lives within it. Moreover, as we have seen, the rational morality that ought to regulate a society is identical to Christian morality. Consequently the Scriptures, but also the texts of Greek authors from which the teaching of the Logos shines forth, serve as the basis for a set of precepts. These precepts must determine, in instance after instance, what is in conformity with Christian principles and what is incompatible with them. Near the end of book 1, Clement remarks that the formation (*agōgē*) ensured by the Logos, which ennobles all the actions of life, is not excessively strained (*hypertonos*) but vigorous in the proper degree (*eutonos*, 1.99.2). These terms are from music, and point to the quest for an education inspired not by a rigor that is an end in itself, but by harmony.

Clement knows, of course, that he must make concessions to these aristocratic Christians, who have no intention of breaking away from the world that ensures their identity. Thus he offers a fine reminder not to mingle with people of irregular life. But he knows that if his readers are invited to a meal by nonbelievers, it will not be his place to forbid their attending it; therefore it is better that he set down rules for moderation in such circumstances (2.10). Likewise he insists that men and women should give forth the scent not of perfumes but of virtues; he tries to dissuade men from the use of perfumes by claiming that these will lead to a loss of virility, and then recommends that women choose perfumes that do not make men's heads swim. He asks, too, that the pleasure given by perfumes should in any case be matched by their usefulness, as with medicinal ointments (2.65.1–68.4).

But the choice made by Clement is not simply the choice of a lesser evil. Even though the principles he sets down tend toward asceticism, he explicitly dissociates himself from those who link Christian identity with a rejection of the things of the world. For example Clement expatiates on the dangers of wine; if drinking is intended to slake thirst, then water alone is necessary. Yet ultimately Paul does not forbid Timothy to drink wine (1 Tim 5:23), and Christ drank wine and blessed it; these facts, Clement remarks, are a specific argument against the encratites (2.33.1), the attack on whom occupies a good part of the third book of the *Miscellanies*.

In the third book of *Christ the Educator* precepts are interrupted by digressions, such as those in ch. 6 (Christians alone are rich, which adopts a Stoic theme about philosophers), ch. 7 (exhortation to frugality), and ch. 8 (usefulness of examples in teaching). The last two chapters, 11 and 12, give a summary of the best kind of life. In part this repeats what has already been said, and in part it completes it (for example, by taking up the subject of spectacles). The second of these two chapters may have been added in a second phase, as is suggested by a colophon in the manuscripts at the end of ch. 11. The work ends with a hymn to Christ the Savior.

Like the *Exhortation, Christ the Educator* has been preserved for us in Paris gr. 451 from the year 914, but the removal of a number of sheets has meant the loss of the text down to 1.96. For this first part, then, we are dependent on copies of that manuscript. The copies have also preserved the final hymn, which is lacking in the Paris manuscript.

Bibliography

Clément d'Alexandrie, *Le Pédagogue* (vol. I; ed. H.-I. Marrou; trans. M. Harl; SC 70; Paris: Cerf, 1970).

————, *Le Pédagogue* (vol. II; ed. H.-I. Marrou; trans C. Mondésert; SC 108; Paris: Cerf, 1965).

————, *Le Pedagogue* (vol. III; ed. H.-I. Marrou; trans. C. Mondésert and C. Matray; SC 158; Paris: Cerf, 1970).

M. G. Bianco, *Protrettico e Pedagogo di Clemente Allessandrino* (Turin: UTET, 1971).

d. Miscellanies

As we noted earlier, it seems that Clement intended to write a trilogy in which the *Exhortation* and *Christ the Educator* would be followed by a work titled *Teacher*. There is no work of his under that title, but we do have the *Miscellanies*. It is debated whether and to what extent the *Miscellanies* represents the planned third part, but the tendency today is to hold that they do not. Indeed, at the end of the sixth book Clement says that he has thus far concerned himself with the ethics of the "gnostic." For *theōria* or contemplative speculation, the subject proper to the Logos as teacher, he refers the reader to a further treatise on physics, which would begin with a study of the origin of the world (6.168.4). The next book is the last one actually composed; only rough drafts of the eighth remain. At the end of it he says that he has now ended the introductory exposition, having outlined what he has to say about ethics, and wants now to carry on the task he has undertaken (7.110.4).

In other words, Clement is saying that only at this point has he produced what he announced at the beginning of the work: the arguments preliminary to the knowledge revealed in contemplation presented allusively and in hints lest it be accessible to the profane reader. He adds that he will go forward with his treatise on physical theory, beginning with the origin of the world (1.15.2; see 1.18.1). More specifically, he has now finished his depiction of the moral personality of the gnostic, which he had already announced at the beginning of the fourth book (4.1.1–2) and again at the beginning of the sixth (6.1.1). The whole of the *Miscellanies* thus seems to be a discourse preliminary to the exposition of "gnosis" in the true and proper sense, intended to sketch the moral personality of the gnostic before passing on to contemplation, which will take for its starting point an exegesis of the biblical story of the creation of the world (4.3.3). In fact, the introduction to book 4 (4.1–3) outlines a plan of the present work, great parts of which are not taken up in the succeeding books, and states that the work, initially conceived of as a single book, has gradually grown larger. Moreover, the work is described as notes (see below) "to meet an urgent demand, since there is a great need of what must be said as an introduction to the truth" (4.3.1).

The entire work, then, is a prelude to a "truly gnostic physiology" which will move from a discussion of the origins of the world and ascend to a theological vision (4.3.1–2). Modifying an old thesis, A. Méhat has suggested that we see in the *Hypotyposes,* a systematic interpretation of the Bible of which only a few fragments remain (see below), the exposition that was to follow upon the *Miscellanies* and show the Logos acting as teacher.

The real and proper title of the work is *Stromata of Gnostic Notes according to the True Philosophy. Stromata,* meaning "hangings," is a name that, like others widespread in the Hellenistic and later the Byzantine world, befits a miscellany that brings together a variety of subjects drawn from a variety of sources. But Clement has been exonerated of the accusation, long leveled against him, that he is unable truly to compose a work, but continually goes off on byways, with the result that the *Miscellanies* lacks order and direction. The description of the work as "notes" *(hypomnēmata)* seems to signify the intention to bring together a variety of materials in order gradually to build up a unified work, one that does not follow the rules of rhetoric but is free to structure itself in complicated and often unanticipated ways that seem incoherent but are actually held together by a constant purpose: to sketch the "knowledge" that is identical to the true philosophy (see the title).

The *Miscellanies* have been transmitted in a single manuscript, Laurentiana 5.3 (11th c.); a second extant manuscript is a copy of the first. There are seven books, plus an eighth, which was probably edited after Clement's death and is not a continuation of the seventh book but rather a series of notes, comparable to the *Extracts from the Prophets* (see below). The character of the *Miscellanies* makes a summary in the proper sense impossible; we shall settle for an outline.

The manuscript of the first miscellany is missing its first page. The first extant page begins with a defense of putting into writing teachings handed down orally, against the objection that these teachings may thereby be put in the hands of the unworthy (1.1–10). The author describes the present work as notes meant to prevent him from forgetting the teachings of his own masters, with whom he cannot compare. He says that he will also gather together the views of the philosophers, because these contain seeds of truth, and he defends his procedure against the attacks of those who regard philosophy as the work of the devil (1.11–21).

Clement asserts that philosophy as wisdom differs from sophistry; he attacks the latter and defends the former as a preparation of the Greeks for the coming of Christ. In the light brought by Christ it can be seen that the Greeks and the barbarians shared in the truth in differing measures (1.22–58). The history of philosophy shows the extent to which the Greeks were dependent on the barbarians. Furthermore, if it was from Moses that they derived the truths contained in their thinking, this happened by divine providence, in order to prepare them to welcome the truth (1.59–100). Chronological calculations furnish proof that Moses and the Hebrew prophets preceded the Greek sages (1.101–47). The author therefore calls to mind the figure of Moses, prophet and legislator, general, statesman, and philosopher, from whom the Greeks drew inspiration in all these fields. Plato in particular depends on the philosophy of Moses.

The second miscellany introduces the theme of gnosis and faith; the latter is not an intellectual intuition that leaves proof aside, as the Basilideans claim, nor is it the mark of simple Christians as distinct from gnostics, as the Valentinians believe. Faith is voluntary adherence to the Logos and is the premise for knowledge, so that the two are not contradictory. Plato and other philosophers saw this, for, always following Moses, they described the wise person in a way that fits the person of faith (2.1–24). Faith is the first movement toward salvation and begets the virtues that lead to love and gnosis. The first of these virtues is fear, which is defended, along with law, against the gnostics (2.25–40). The virtues, which are interconnected, achieve their integration in love, and love becomes perfect in gnosis, which comes from three sources: contemplation, the practice of the commandments, and the formation of persons who are upright. True gnosis is mystical contemplation, which must never be separated from the practice of justice (2.41–55).

The author then takes up several questions regarding penance and the virtues characteristic of the gnostic, who lives in the image and likeness of God (2.56–102). The likeness of God is achieved through a gradual liberation from the passions; on this point the majority of the Greek philosophers agree with the Scriptures (2.103–36). This leads into the subject of chaste marriage (2.137–47).

The third *Miscellany* is wholly devoted to marriage and continence, with alternating attacks on libertine gnostics (followers of Basilides, Carpocrates, Epiphanes, the antitacts, and others) and encratites (Marcionites, Julius Cassian, and others). The correct view, according to the Scriptures, is to give preference to celibacy but at the same time to acknowledge the value of chaste marriage. The fourth miscellany, with a new introduction, continues the description of the true gnostic, who can take two forms. First is the martyr, who accepts separation from the world and persecution out of love of justice. The author here rebuts the gnostic tendency either to avoid martyrdom, as Heracleon does, or to regard it as a punishment for sins committed during a previous existence, as Basilides does. Second is the perfect person, who is characterized by a love that is not dictated by fear (4.89–172).

The fifth miscellany returns to faith and the compatibility of faith with gnosis. Faith in the way God expresses himself in the Scriptures comes first, but it gives rise to a search. This search, if carried out not for the sake of argument but for discovery, strengthens faith (5.1–18). But in order to speak of divine truths, all—barbarians, Greeks, and Jews—have used the genre of symbol *(tropos tēs epikrypseōs);* so too does the Christian tradition, as with Paul and Barnabas (5.19–64). How then are we to reach God? Through an analytic process of progressive abstraction from the qualities of things of the world. This process, however, can lead only to a negative knowledge of God (5.65–88). As for whatever true statements the philosophers have made about God, they stole them from biblical revelation (5.89–141).

The sixth miscellany begins by continuing, in a more polemical tone, the exposition of the "theft of the Greeks" from one another, from the biblical miracles, and from other peoples (6.1–38). Greeks and Christians acknowledge the same God, but the former do it imperfectly. Christian wisdom comes directly from the Logos. While Christians ought not scorn philosophy, neither ought they turn to Greek philosophy, but should rather acquire a share in gnosis (6.39–70). The author now comes at last to his portrait of the Christian gnostic. This is a person free of the passions and wholly united to God in love, so that he no longer has need even of the virtues, since the purpose of these is to help resist the passions. He makes the secular sciences his own, but uses them only as instruments for reaching truth; in this way he advances toward final glory (6.71–114). He alone is capable of the gnostic understanding of the Scriptures, which goes beyond the understanding that is based on simple faith and manifest to everyone; as an example, Clement gives a spiritual exegesis of the Decalogue (6:115–48). Greek philosophy, in contrast, has limited value, as shown even by its limited spread; quite different has been the spread of Christianity, despite persecutions (6.149–67).

The seventh miscellany seeks to show that only the gnostic worships God in a manner worthy of God. The most religious persons are the best beings on earth, just as the angels are in heaven. The Son, however, has the absolutely perfect nature, and this is now described (7.1–12). Clement then sketches in detail a religious and moral portrait of the gnostic and contrasts this with Greek superstition (7.13–88). If, despite everything, Greeks and Jews do not believe, it is because of the many Christian sects at war among themselves; the Greeks and Jews are unable to choose among them. The distinction can be made by means of the Scriptures, for the criteria are supplied by the Scriptures themselves, but the heretics read them in a one-sided and tendentious way. Moreover, the heretics do not hark back to the original tradition of the Lord's teaching but to later and erroneous traditions. Clement gives an example of correct interpretation of the Old Testament sacrificial law with its rules for clean and unclean animals. In his conclusion (see above) the author says that the discourse on ethics is complete, and announces a transition to "another beginning": this will mark the start of the properly gnostic discourse (7.89–111).

It is impossible to discuss the vast number of subjects treated in the *Miscellanies,* but a word must be said about the main subject: gnosis and the person of the gnostic. The modern debate on this subject is wide-ranging. The author certainly takes a polemical position, as is obvious from the mention of the "true" philosophy in the title, against gnostic groups that reject divine justice and assert, as at least some of them do, that salvation is obtained through nature, linking this to the knowledge *(gnōsis)* of the person's own divine origin and of secret traditions handed down from the apostles.

Clement agrees with them, however, on the connection between gnosis and esoteric tradition. His fundamental thesis is that the Logos is the sole source of knowledge of the Father (e.g., *Strom.* 1.97.2; 5.12.3; 7.2.2; 7.16.6). The Logos first communicated this knowledge, but only partially, to philosophers, and more completely to the prophets of the Old Testament. Then, having become incarnate, he entrusted it after his resurrection to some of his disciples: James, John, and Peter, who gave it to the other apostles, and these in turn to the seventy, among whom was Barnabas (thus frag. 13 of *Hyp.;* Clement values the letter circulating under Barnabas's name). The true tradition in doctrinal matters was passed on, beginning with Peter, James, John, and Paul, from teacher to teacher, down to Clement himself (*Strom.* 1.11.3), who at the beginning of his work asks himself whether he should put it in writing, thereby making it accessible to many. The same thoughts occur elsewhere in *Miscellanies* (1.13.2; 6.61.3; 6.68.2), and other works.

Time and again Clement repeats in the *Miscellanies* that gnosis or one of its equivalents—mystical discourse, holy teachings, true philosophy, and so on—is hidden and reserved to initiates. An identical structure can be seen in gnostic texts, as they claim a knowledge of the Father that has been revealed by the Son to some disciples and then passed by secret tradition. Clement himself says as much, as we have seen, in *Miscellanies* 7.106–8, and his claim that the gnostic tradition is erroneous and secondary depends on a polemical interpretation of relations between "orthodoxy" and "heresy" and does not set out a historically valid argument.

From this point of view, then, Clement's gnosis is in competition with the gnoses of his adversaries. Indeed, in his understanding of gnosis as a secret tradition Clement seems to have been influenced by the gnostics. His chosen approach is utterly different from that of Irenaeus, who opposes the public tradition of the great church to the secret tradition of the gnostics (*Haer.* 3.2–4). What Clement rejects, by contrast, is the connection between gnosis and certain categories of Christians: every believer can achieve gnosis, since faith begets the virtues that lead to gnosis (2.31.1–2), and faith and gnosis are closely connected (5.1). This holds true even though, according to the portrait drawn in *Miscellanies* 6 and 7, those who have attained gnosis stand very much apart from the simple faithful. Again, in 7.57.4 the author speaks of a twofold transition from paganism to faith and from faith to gnosis. Furthermore, gnosis may be sought, but ultimately it is a gift from God.

The content of gnosis appears to be extraordinarily complex, and the state of the gnostic seems to imply two phases: he is already a gnostic in the present life; he is continually advancing, and he will be the complete gnostic only in the end time. But even now his state anticipates eschatological perfection, implying the ascent of the soul to contemplation of God (4.116–117), the enjoyment of the intelligible world (e.g., 5.40.1; 7.13.1–2), and a foretaste of the future life with God (7.56.3–57.1). Gnosis is knowledge of God and of the Son, but religious knowledge, as we discussed earlier, finds expression in the hidden mode of symbol, not only in the Jewish-Christian tradition but in all forms of religious expression (*Strom.* 5). The gnostic must therefore grasp the hidden meaning of revelation, and this in the place where it is most perfect, the Bible.

Gnosis is therefore also an understanding of the spiritual sense of the prophetic Scriptures (2.54.1) and, in particular, of the gospel, which has revealed the meaning of the Old Testament (e.g., 4.134.3–135.1). The gnostic understands the Scriptures "according to the church's norm" (6.125.2–3), that is, according to the harmony between, on the one hand, the Law and the Prophets, and on the other, the revelation brought by Christ. The specification of this norm represents a restriction of boundaries as compared with the gnosis of the gnostic groups. Clement gives an allegorical interpretation of a passage in the Shepherd of Hermas, thus reading it on two levels: that of "letter by letter," which is proper to a faith that sticks to the seeming clarity of the text, and that "according to syllables," or the gnostic understanding, which is achieved as faith progresses (6.131.2–3). Two other aspects are to be emphasized: the connection between love and gnosis, in which the former is repeatedly singled out as the way to the latter (4.53.1; 7.68.1–2), and the intense mystical component of the gnostic, which is emphasized in the portrait in *Miscellanies* 6 and 7.

The gnostic is fully trained in all the disciplines, endowed with all the virtues; he has achieved freedom from the passions and has become like the Logos. In this way he has entered into contact with the divine. On the whole he represents a synthesis of the Hellenistic ideal of the wise man and the Christian ideal of the saint. This synthesis in turn represents Clement's deepest intention, which is not to dress Christianity in the clothes of something alien to it, but to bring together in unity the Greek, the Jewish, and the Christian experiences, and to understand Christian theology and ethics as the system of true philosophy in which the entire history of divine revelation through the Logos reaches its culmination. This requires the convergence of three elements (as S. Lilla has shown).

First, there is the philosophical tradition of Alexandrian Judaism and in particular of Philo, whose work Clement knew inside out, and who had already synthesized Platonism and Judaism. This synthesis gave Clement the identification of the Logos with the divine reason that becomes a separate hypostasis and locus of the divine ideas, the distinction between two levels of reality, and above all, the method of biblical interpretation based on that distinction, which opens the way for an allegorical interpretation that is meant to bring to light the divine mysteries hidden beneath the letter of the text. Second, there are the philosophical traditions, especially the Platonic school, a tradition in which Clement is located at the transition from Middle Platonism to Neoplatonism.

Third, there is gnosticism, which had already endeavored to interpret Christian revelation in the light of Platonism, while emphasizing certain aspects of that revelation: the unknowablility of God and the ways God is revealed through a divine intermediary. Clement tackles this problem of a Platonic interpretation of Christianity and, like the gnostics, seeks to solve it through the person of the gnostic, who is able to gain access to the divine mysteries through a spiritual understanding of the revelation contained in the Scriptures and through a personal assimilation to the divine Logos. In Clement, however, the gnostic is able to do this not by his nature but through a formation in which the interrelationship of faith and gnosis plays an essential part.

As Eusebius already pointed out (*Hist. eccl.* 6.6), the chronology given in the first miscellany lists events through the death of Commodus; this part of the work was composed, therefore, under Septimius Severus, between 192 and 211. This information, which holds only for the first book, is rather vague; we agree with Méhat in suggesting that the work was composed between 198 and 203.

BIBLIOGRAPHY

Complete edition in GCS (see the bibliography above, sec. 2a).

Edition with translation, introduction, and commentary under way in SC:

Clément d'Alexandrie, *Stromate I* (ed. C. Mondésert; trans. M. Caster; SC 30; Paris: Cerf, 1951).

———, *Stromate II* (ed. C. Mondésert; trans. P. T. Camelot; SC 38; Paris: Cerf, 1954).

———, *Stromate V* (ed. P. Voulet; trans. A. Le Boulluec; 2 vols.; SC 278, 279; Paris: Cerf, 1981).

———, *Stromate VI* (ed. and trans P. Descourtieux; SC 446; Paris: Cerf, 1999).

———, *Stromate VII* (ed. A. Le Boulluec; SC 428; Paris: Cerf, 1997).

———, *Stromate IV* (ed. A. Van Den Hoek; trans. C. Mondésert; SC 463; Paris: Cerf, 2001).

Clemente Alessandrino, *Stromati: Note di vera filosofia* (ed. G. Pini; Milan: Paoline, 1985); Italian translation, introduction, and notes.

Studies

W. Völker, *Der wahre Gnostiker nach Clemens Alexandrinus* (TU 57; Berlin: Akademie-Verlag/Leipzig: Hinrichs, 1952).

A. Méhat, *Étude sur les "Stromates" de Clément d'Alexandrie* (Paris: Seuil, 1966).

J. L. Kovacs, "Divine Pedagogy and the Gnostic Teacher according to Clement of Alexandria," *JECS* 9 (2001): 3–25.

e. Extracts from the Prophets

This work, like the *Miscellanies,* is preserved in P.Laur. V, 3, but the final two extracts are only in other codices. It is made up of brief annotations that in many cases take a citation from the Bible as their starting point. P. Nautin suggests that these are not notes but extracts from the *Hypotyposes,* but this is improbable in view of the thematic thread that links the various parts. The somewhat esoteric character and the literary form suggest that the work was not intended for the general reader but for use within the school of Clement. In this respect the work is close, perhaps even chronologically, to the *Miscellanies,* to which many verses are connected even thematically. For example, in no. 27 the question is asked, as it is at the beginning of *Miscellanies,* whether the oral tradition of the presbyters should be put in writing. The tradition of the presbyters is also mentioned in 11.1, and Pantaenus, teacher of Clement and heir to that tradition, in 56.2; other extracts, too, draw upon archaic exegetical traditions handed on by the presbyters.

Carlo Nardi distinguishes three sections: The first (1–26) focuses on baptismal themes, which are prefaced by reflections on the role of the waters in the creation story of Genesis. The second (27–50) deals with gnosis and the gnostic, who brings his baptismal faith to its completion, with thoughts on the twofold human destiny in the beyond, depending on fidelity, or lack of it, to the life of a Gnostic. The third (51–65) concentrates on the heavens, the angels, and the ascent of the gnostic soul to its heavenly destination.

BIBLIOGRAPHY

Clemente Alessandrino, *Estratti profetici. Eclogae propheticae* (ed. and trans. C. Nardi; Florence: Centro Internazionale del Libro, 1985).

P. Nautin, *Lettres et écrivains chrétiens des IIe et IIIe siècles* (Paris: Cerf, 1961).

f. Salvation of the Rich

This work, often called by its Latin title *Quis dives salvetur?* has come down in a twelfth-century manuscript in El Escorial and, in part, through indirect transmission. It takes the form of a homily on Mark 10:17–30, the incident of the rich young man, and was probably composed during the final period of the *Miscellanies.*

According to Clement, the exhortation of Jesus to sell one's possessions is not to be interpreted literally as a ridding oneself of possessions, which many had done before the coming of Christ, but as a rooting out of the desire for riches (11.2). "Spiritual" exegesis prevails here. Indeed, he suggests that the possession of riches is a good thing, as a means both of avoiding suffering and of helping the needy. One can obey the commands of Christ to give drink to the thirsty, food to the hungry, and so on, only if one has wealth (13.1–7). The rich who will have difficulty in entering the kingdom of heaven are those who make their lives depend on riches and are also rich in passions (19.3). Alms given to all the needy without distinction is an "extraordinarily fine exchange, a divine kind of trading" (32.1) because in it money is exchanged for incorruptibility.

This work has in mind the same public as *Christ the Educator:* aristocrats whom Clement wants to help live a Christian life without a complete change of lifestyle. This form of Christianity is becoming a mass phenomenon, adapting so as to penetrate all strata of society, and moving away from its original radicalism, which appealed to a very small minority. In pursuit of this goal, Clement pays the price of an obvious departure from the spirit of the gospel; he asks, what harm is done if, before becoming Christians, people have acquired wealth in an honest way so that they can live in comfort, or if they have been born into rich families? It is clearly unjust for God to condemn those born rich, because then he gives earthly comfort but takes away eternal comfort (26.3–4).

Bibliography

Clemente Alessandrino, *Quale ricco si salva? Il cristiano e l'economia* (ed. and trans. C. Nardi; Rome: Borla, 1991).

g. Excerpts from Theodotus

We discussed this work earlier (ch. 9, sec. 5) in dealing with the gnostics. It consists of passages copied from the work of Theodotus, a Valentinian, and other gnostics, which are then briefly commented on by Clement in such a way that it is not always easy to distinguish the comments from the gnostic texts. According to Sagnard, Clement is the author of chs. 4–5, in which he comments on the transfiguration of Jesus as a revelation reserved to a few disciples and compares it to the voice heard at the baptism of Jesus and made known to all who were to believe. Also from Clement are chs. 8–9, in which he comments on what is said about the Logos in the prologue of John's Gospel, and interpret "called" and "chosen" as degrees of faith. Chapters 10–15 are concerned with the heavenly nature of the Son, who is the Father's face, and with the corporeity of demons, angels, and souls. Chapter 17.2–20 discusses the Valentinian doctrine of the mingling of substances and the incarnation of the Logos. Finally, ch. 27 comments on the entrance of Christ, the High Priest, into the heavenly Holy of holies (see Heb 9:3–4) and the ascent of the soul, now separated from the body, as it attains gnosis and becomes itself the Logos. The theme here is the perfection of gnosis, which was, as we know, dear to Clement. Other remarks of Clement are scattered throughout the text.

The *Excerpts* demonstrate Clement's lively interest in a critical comparison with other writers who, like himself, reflect on the data of biblical and Christian tradition within the framework of a Hellenistic philosophical outlook and a "gnosis" that is connected with esoteric tradition.

BIBLIOGRAPHY

Clément d'Alexandrie, *Extraits de Théodote* (ed. and trans. F. Sagnard; SC 23; Paris: Cerf, 1948).

h. Letter to Theodore on the Secret Gospel of Mark

We dealt with this fragment in the chapter on the gospel tradition (ch. 2, sec. 10). Published in 1973 by M. Smith, it is of debated authenticity. As far as Clement is concerned, it is noteworthy for the assertion of the existence in the church of Alexandria of a "more spiritual" gospel of Mark, the reading of which was allowed only to those initiated into the "great mysteries," in other words, to gnostics. Of the texts known to us, this is the only passage in which Clement links the gnostic esoteric tradition with written works: both in the *Miscellanies* and in the *Extracts from the Prophets* he regards this as an oral tradition.

i. Fragments of Lost Works

Biblical commentaries attributed to Ecumenius (author of a commentary on the Apocalypse, ca. 600), Eusebius of Caesarea, the *Sacra Parallela* of John Damascene, and the *Spiritual Meadow* of John Moschus have all passed on to us fragments of the *Hypotyposes (Outlines)*. A lengthy fragment of several pages has reached us in a Latin translation of Cassiodorus, under the title of *Adumbrationes in epistulas canonicas*. The fragments are collected in vol. 3 of the edition (195–215). According to Eusebius (*Hist. eccl.* 6.13.2; 6.14.1), the *Hypotyposes* was a work in eight books that contained, in addition to traditions received by Clement, explanations of Scriptures from both Testaments, including controverted writings, among them the *Letter of Barnabas* and the *Apocalypse of Peter*.

There is certainly no suggestion of a systematic explanation of the Old and New Testaments: texts are cited from Book 4 on 1 and 2 Corinthians; from Book 5 on 1 Corinthians and Galatians and on the names of the seventy disciples; from Book 6 on the composition of the Gospels and of Mark in particular, but also on the healing of the leper in Matt 8:2–4 and parallels; from book 7 on the person of James and on 1 and 2 Timothy. There must have been brief notes on selected passages and questions. The Latin fragments, however, take the form of short remarks on the verses, mostly in order, of the Catholic Letters.

Clement appeals explicitly to the tradition of the presbyters (e.g., frag. 8 in the GCS edition, on the order in which the Gospels were written) or to tradition generally (frags. 12; 14). In addition, as we have seen, the secret tradition communicated by Jesus is the subject of one of the fragments (13). The tradition was certainly the source of information on individuals from the period of Christian origins, in particular Barnabas, Cephas (the man whom Paul attacked in Antioch was not the apostle Peter: frag. 4), James (13–14), the seventy disciples (4), and Mark (8–9). Clement described Luke as the translator into Greek of the letter that Paul wrote to the Hebrews in Hebrew (frag. 22).

Photius of Constantinople (*Lex.* 109) is very critical of some aspects of Clement's work, for in it Clement made wicked and fantastic statements: asserting the eternity of matter, bringing in the Platonic ideas, reducing the Son to the status of a creature, and telling stories about metempsychosis and worlds existing before Adam. Photius does not approve of Clement's exegesis of the formation of Eve, nor of his statements about relations between angels and women (see Gen 6:1) and about the incarnation of the Logos as only seeming to be real. Photius also cites a sentence to the effect that what was incarnated was not the Logos of God but a power of God, just as an emanation from his Logos, which had become intellect *(nous),* was spread abroad into the hearts of human beings. The Son is therefore called Logos by homonymy with the paternal Logos. The totality of these statements, which we have no way of controlling, give a picture of the *Hypotyposes* as a decidedly esoteric work containing very daring exegeses, especially as regards the beginnings of the world. Was this the sequel promised in the *Miscellanies?*

In the work *On Easter,* according to Eusebius (*Hist. eccl.* 6.13–9), Clement said he was compelled by friends to put in writing the traditions received from the ancient presbyters, and he reported, among other things, words of Melito and Irenaeus. Of this work some fragments survive which show close attention to the chronology of Easter and give an exegesis of the death of Jesus as Passover lamb (ed. in GCS 3, 216–18).

Fragments remain of an *Ecclesiastical Canon, or against Judaizers,* an *On Providence* (seemingly full of philosophical definitions), and an *Exhortation to Perseverance, or To the Newly Baptized,* as well as of some letters (GCS 3.218–224).

According to F. Overbeck, Clement gave birth to a true and proper Christian literature that took over the forms of the Greek literary tradition, after the "primitive literature" *(Urliteratur)* of the first two centuries had created out of its own resources the special forms needed for internal use. This judgment needs a great deal of revision, but it is true that Clement knows that he takes his place on the border between a Christianity that adopts secular literary forms and a Christianity wholly focused on its own oral tradition and concerned essentially with an intense labor on its own Scriptures and sacred traditions, still substantially using the tools of Judaism. Clement's own teacher, Pantaenus, was perhaps still within that tradition. Clement continually declares his debt to and respect for that tradition; yet while esotericism is an important element of his thought, it has its place within a program of gnosis that seeks to integrate and transcend a much larger cultural complex.

Clement exhibits striking intellectual openness that allows him to welcome, though certainly in a critical way, the cultural tradition of Hellenism, as well as the forces that were competing within Christianity, especially among the gnostics, to integrate Christian revelation into that tradition. As noted above, the very effective work already done by Philo in combining Greek philosophy and biblical revelation is an important point of reference for Clement, and this includes the hermeneutical tools Philo provided. Continuing the line taken by Justin and Athenagoras, but in a more systematic and penetrating way, Clement cannot bring himself to believe that the magnificent philosophy of the Greeks does not bear the mark of divine revelation. He therefore builds a system that combines Hellenism, Judaism, and Christianity in a history of progressive revelation, all originating in the one God.

The Logos, whom Clement finds in Greek philosophy, Hellenistic Judaism, and the Christian tradition, plays a key role in the accomplishment of this plan of unification. If this diversified tradition is to be traced back to its common denominator, it needs to be decoded; but this is true, according to Clement, of every religious discourse. The allegorical interpretation of the Scriptures, which he inherited from Philo and the gnostics, is therefore the privileged tool for appropriating revelation, and the gnostic is the person in whom divine revelation reaches its perfect form and finds its completion as it connects earthly existence with eschatological eternity.

At the same time, in Clement's mind the retrieval of the classical tradition does not mean the seizure of it, or of what seems useful in it, to the advantage of a Christian community that keeps its distance from its social setting. The retrieval requires rather that the bearers of that tradition, the ruling class of the Hellenistic world, should live their Greek "culture" (in the broadest sense of this term) in a Christian way. It can be said, then, that the apologetics of the *Exhortation* and the concessions made to that class of persons in *Christ the Educator* and *Salvation of the Rich* have their place in his overall plan.

These compromises appear to be heavy with consequences, as indeed they are; but they are also consistent with Clement's vision, in which the education of humanity by a progressive revelation is paralleled by the education of the individual in a course that leads him from enslavement to demonic divinities to the condition of a gnostic who is closely united with the Logos. The central place thus given to education takes concrete form in the instructional activity of Clement himself, to which his most complex texts, from the *Miscellanies* to the *Extracts from the Prophets,* seem to be connected. At first glance these works appear to lack any system, but their purpose is, like that of the other more "simple" works, and indeed even more so, to advance a carefully detailed plan. The progress of this plan probably brought with it an increasing tendency toward the mystical longing that shines through the final pages of the *Miscellanies* as well as the bold intellectual inventions that so scandalized Photius and, surely, many others.

Clement never wanted to isolate himself or be superior to simple believers; on the contrary, he always appealed to an ecclesial tradition toward which he showed a deep reverence. The gnostic as described by Clement remains at the service of brothers and sisters in the faith as they engage in their wearisome journey. Despite the problems involved in his project, and despite his lack of intellectual rigor as compared to Origen, Clement seems to be a theologian in the fullest sense of the word.

Chapter 15

ORIGEN

1. Life

We are quite well informed about the life of Origen. Eusebius of Caesarea describes it in the sixth book of his *Ecclesiastical History,* but does so in a perspective that is already hagiographical. He bases his narrative on Origen's correspondence, which was stored in the library at Caesarea. Meanwhile, after being imprisoned during the persecution of Maximinus Daia (307), Pamphilus, a presbyter who continued the school of Caesarea that Origen had founded, composed a *Defense of Origen* in five books, to which his pupil Eusebius added a sixth. Only the first has survived, but Photius, Patriarch of Constantinople, has passed on a summary of the others (*Lex.* 118). A pupil of Origen, traditionally identified as Gregory the Wonderworker (but see below, ch. 16, sec. 2), addressed to his teacher a speech of gratitude as he, Gregory, was leaving the school of Caesarea (228); this discourse has been preserved and contains valuable information about the routine of the school and its courses. P. Nautin has made a detailed critical study of the sources in a work that is now fundamental (see the bibliography), although some of his new suggestions are debated.

According to a somewhat vague statement of Eusebius, Origen's father was a Christian named Leonides. When Leonides died a victim of the persecution of Septimius Severus in 202, the son was not yet seventeen; Origen was therefore born in 185 in Alexandria. According to Eusebius, the father had insisted that the son study the secular disciplines and the Bible. After his father's death, a wealthy Christian women took Origen in and enabled him to continue his study of literature. As the eldest son, he undertook to teach literature to support the family after the father's possessions had been confiscated. The catechists had left the city for fear of persecution, so when Origen was approached by some pagans who wanted to learn about Christianity, he began his catechetical activity.

During a second wave of persecution set off by governor Aquila between 206 and 210, several of Origen's students perished. When Bishop Demetrius returned after Aquila's departure, he put Origen in charge of the catechetical school. Shortly afterward, Origen gave up the teaching of literature and sold his library. He began to live a strict ascetic life and went so far as to emasculate himself, because (according to Eusebius) of his excessively literal interpretation of Matt 19:12. We do not know whether this was the real motive for his action; many years later his commentary on that passage would sharply condemn such practices. Before or after his appointment as head of the catechetical school, Origen studied philosophy under Ammonius

Saccas, with Plotinus as a fellow student (according to a passage from Porphyry that is cited by Eusebius). In a letter Origen confirms that he studied philosophy but he does not give his teacher's name. Sometime around 215, during the reign of Pope Zephyrinus (199–217), he made a journey to Rome.

In the years that followed Origen met Ambrose, a wealthy Alexandrian with gnostic ideas, and converted him to orthodoxy. Ambrose made available to Origen stenographers and ample means of dictating and circulating his works; these resources were decisive for the composition of Origen's works and remained at his disposal even after he left Alexandria. The dates and circumstances of other journeys to "Arabia" (present-day Jordan) and Palestine are debated. During the second journey, undertaken perhaps because of tension between himself and Bishop Demetrius of Alexandria, Origen became a friend of Bishops Alexander of Jerusalem and Theoctistus of Caesarea, both of whom invited him to come and preach. This elicited a protest from Demetrius, who ordered Origen to return. In the fall of 231, Emperor Alexander Severus was in Antioch with his mother, Julia Mammaea, who was interested in Christianity. She had heard of Origen, and called him to her. He remained there probably until the spring of 232. He returned to Alexandria but left shortly afterward for Athens; his journey took him through Palestine and there, in Caesarea, Theoctistus ordained him a priest. Demetrius reacted harshly and turned to the bishop of Rome, accusing Origen of maintaining, among other things, a belief in the salvation of the devil.

This incident marked a fundamental break in Origen's life. He did not return again to Alexandria, primarily because when Demetrius died shortly afterwards, his successor Heraclas, proved no less harsh toward Origen, although he had once been a student of Origen and later his collaborator. Origen settled in Caesarea, and Ambrose sent stenographers that he might continue his *Commentary on John,* the sixth book of which he had begun before leaving Alexandria. He preached extensively (279 homilies have survived) but also worked on commentaries on the Scriptures and in the immense project of the *Hexapla,* having begun both of the latter enterprises in Alexandria. Bishops Alexander and Theoctistus took Origen with them to episcopal synods in order that he might act as judge in cases of bishops or clerics accused of heresy. He played the principal role in Bostra in the case of Bishop Beryllus and, probably also in Arabia, in that of Bishop Heraclides, to which we will return later.

Origen made other journeys, especially to Nicomedia, where Ambrose was staying, and to Athens. In 250, Emperor Decius ordered all citizens to sacrifice to the gods of the empire; during the extremely violent persecution that followed, Origen was arrested and tortured, but did not give in. He was still alive at the death of Decius in 251, as attested by some letters Eusebius had read, but he must have died shortly afterward as a result of the treatment he had endured, probably in 253 or 254. Photius says that according to the *Defense* of Pamphilus, Origen died at Caesarea, but he mentions another tradition accepted also by Jerome that Origen died and was buried in Tyre. He regards the latter tradition as more reliable on the basis of letters of Origen himself, provided, he writes, that these are not forgeries.

BIBLIOGRAPHY

On Origen generally: H. Crouzel, *Bibliographie critique d'Origène* (The Hague: Nijhoff/Steenbrugge: Abbaye St.-Pierre, 1971).

————, *Bibliographie critique d'Origène: Supplément I* (The Hague: Nijhoff/ Steenbrugge: Abbaye St.-Pierre, 1982).

P. Nautin, *Origène: Sa vie et son oeuvre* (Paris: Beauchesne, 1977).

J. W. Trigg, *Origen: The Bible and Philosophy in the Third-Century Church* (London: Beauchesne, 1983).

See also the acts of the international conferences titled *Origeniana* (various places of publication, 1975–).

2. Exegetical Works

The exegetical writings of Origen took three forms, which Jerome distinguishes in the preface to his translation of the homilies on Jeremiah and Ezekiel: (a) scholia (Latin *excerpta*): short explanations of individual difficult passages; (b) commentaries (Greek *tomoi;* Latin *volumina*): lengthy, continuous, and systematic commentaries on the various books of Scripture; and (c) homilies (Latin *homiliae* or *tractatus*): sermons on biblical texts. For convenience we shall review the works according to these categories. The references to Jerome, unless otherwise specified, are to Letter 33. For the reader's guidance we shall in each instance give a reference to the *Clavis patrum graecorum (CPG)*, vol. 1.

a. Scholia

On Genesis, Jerome mentions two books of "mixed homilies." This puzzling title may describe a collection that included both homilies and scholia; in fact, a fragment on Gen 5:26 is cited in an Athos manuscript (Lavra 184) as coming from the scholia of Origen on Genesis (*CPG* 1412).

On Exodus, Jerome mentions scholia, some bits of which seem to be preserved in the *Philocalia* (see below, sec. 4i) and in catenas, although some fragments from catenas on Exodus 12 have been shown to belong to the work on Easter (*CPG* 1413).

For Leviticus, too, Jerome speaks of scholia that are partly preserved in catenas (*CPG* 1415). Scholia on Numbers are attested by Rufinus in the preface to his translation of Origen's homilies on Numbers, where he says he has incorporated them into his translation. However, we are not sure of either the provenance or the authenticity of the fragments on this book that are preserved in catenas (*CPG* 1417). Nautin thinks he can derive a reference to scholia on Deuteronomy from passages in Origen's homilies on Luke (8:3). Jerome speaks of thirteen homilies on Luke, but only fragments of doubtful authenticity remain (*CPG* 1419).

Jerome mentions scholia on the entire Psalter and another series on Psalms 1–15, while Eusebius (*Hist. eccl.* 6.24.2) speaks of Psalms 1–25; this seems a more likely number. According to Nautin, the scholia on the entire Psalter (*CPG* 1427) are extracts from the complete commentary on the Psalms and were therefore composed at Caesarea, while the other scholia (*CPG* 1425) belong to the Alexandrian period. Fragments of both are found in the catenas. Fragments also remain of the scholia on Ecclesiastes (*CPG* 1431) and on Isaiah (*CPG* 1436), both of which are mentioned by Jerome.

Finally, Jerome also speaks of a book of scholia on some parts of the Gospel of John. Some items of dubious authenticity in the catenas may belong to that work; Origen seems to refer to it in a passage of his commentary on Matthew (see *CPG* 1453, note). The existence of scholia by Origen on the Apocalypse is doubtful (see *CPG* 1468).

b. Commentaries

Origen wrote a commentary on Genesis in thirteen books; Jerome lists fourteen books, but that is probably an error. Fragments survive in Pamphilus's *Defense*, in various works of Eusebius, in the *Philocalia*, and in catenas. Two fragments, of dubious authenticity, are preserved in papyri (*CPG* 1410).

Jerome mentions separate commentaries on thirty-nine Psalms, through Psalm 72, of which only the beginning is commented on. A separate book comments upon each Psalm except for Psalms 43 (two books), 44 (three books), 50 (two books), and 103 (to be corrected to 118 according to Nautin, two books). These seem to be parts of a vast but incomplete effort to comment on the entire Psalter, to be assigned to the period in Caesarea. Fragments remain of the preface and of individual psalms in the *Philocalia* and in catenas (*CPG* 1426).

On Proverbs, in addition to the seven homilies mentioned above, Jerome speaks of a commentary in three books, and a book of questions. Although it is not possible to be specific, to these three works belong two authentic fragments contained in Pamphilus's *Defense of Origen*, as well as other more doubtful ones found in catenas (*CPG* 1430). The *Philocalia* has preserved a fragment of Origen's commentary in two books on the Song of Songs "composed in his youth" (Jerome: *CPG* 1434); of another, later commentary in ten books there remain an abridged translation in four books by Rufinus and some Greek fragments (*CPG* 1433). A few fragments remain of a commentary on Isaiah in thirty books; according to Letter 33 of Jerome it ran to thirty-six books, but this is incorrect (*CPG* 1433). Fragments have also survived of five books on Lamentations (*CPG* 1439) and twenty-five books on Ezekiel (thus Eusebius; twenty-nine books according to Jerome; *CPG* 1440). A book on the name "Ephraim" in Hosea is attested. A fragment remains in the *Philocalia* of another commentary on Hosea, which Eusebius knew in a form that lacked beginning and end (*CPG* 1443). Of a commentary on Joel in one book a single papyrus fragment survives (*CPG* 1444). Nothing remains of the commentaries on Amos (six books), Jonah (one book), Micah (three books), Nahum (two books), Habakkuk (three books), Zephaniah (two books), Haggai (one book), the beginning of Zechariah (two books), and Malachi (three books).

Of the twenty-five books of the *Commentary on Matthew*, books 10 to 17 (on Matt 13:36–22:33) have survived in Greek, as have fragments in Eusebius, Pamphilus, the *Philocalia*, and in catenas. There is also a Latin translation of the section on Matt 16:13–27:63, probably by the Latin translator of the *Opus imperfectum in Matthaeum* (see vol. II of this history). The work is artificially divided into homilies. For the part that parallels the preserved Greek (down to 22:23), the work is usually published according to the division of the Greek, while the remainder is separated and goes under the title *Commentariorum series* (*CPG* 1450). Jerome mentions a commentary in fifteen books on Luke, but only fragments remain (*CPG* 1452), and it cannot be established with certainty whether they indeed come from that work; some come from other works of Origen. Of a *Commentary on John* in thirty-two books there remain, in Greek, nine books (1, 2, 6, 10, 13, 19, 20, 28, and 32, which ends with John 13:33). The fragments in the catenas are not trustworthy; some are certainly from other authors.

Jerome and Rufinus mention a commentary in fifteen books on Romans, of which there remains a Latin translation in ten books by Rufinus, who could not find all the books of the original, and who partly completed and partly abridged Origen's text. Greek fragments are preserved in the *Philocalia*, in one of the Tura papyri (on Rom 3:5–5:7), in works by Pamphilus and Basil of Caesarea, in an Athos manuscript, and in catenas (*CPG* 1457). A few fragments of the fifteen books on Galatians are preserved by Pamphilus (*CPG* 1459). Fragments of the three books on Ephesians come from Jerome's *Answer to Rufinus* and from catenas (*CPG* 1460). Very little remains of a book on the letter to the Philippians; only a few bits of information in manuscript Lavra 184 from Athos. Some fragments have been preserved of three books on Colossians (*CPG* 1461), of three on 1 Thessalonians, and one on 2 Thessalonians (*CPG* 1462–63). The same is true of a book on Titus (*CPG* 1464; see also the remarks below on the homilies) and a book on Philemon (*CPG* 1465). In his *Defense* Pamphilus cites four passages "from the books on the Letter to the Hebrews" (*CPG* 1467); these come perhaps from a commentary not attested elsewhere, or from the homilies (see above).

As for the chronology of the commentaries: relying on texts of Origen himself, Eusebius (*Hist. eccl.* 6.24.1–2) says that while in Alexandria Origen wrote the first five books of his *Commentary on John,* the first eight of the *Commentary on Genesis,* and the commentaries on Psalms 1–25 and Lamentations. In the preface to the sixth book of the *Commentary on John,* Origen explains to Ambrose that he had already begun writing this book in Alexandria, but now, after finding a little peace in Caesarea, he has started it again from the beginning, because he has not brought with him the work he had already done (6.8–12). P. Nautin believes he can date the commentaries on the twenty-five Psalms and on Lamentations to the years 222 to 225; the commentary on Genesis (books 1–7) to around 229, the period when he was writing *First Principles;* and books 1–4 of the *Commentary on John* to 231 and 232. The fifth book on John, he says, was composed during a stay in Antioch, the sixth sometime after he settled in Antioch, and the remainder during the rest of his life. The youthful commentary on the Song of Songs is obviously to be dated before all of these.

According to Eusebius (*Hist. eccl.* 6.32.1–2), during the reign of Gordian (238–244), Origen composed the commentaries on Isaiah and Ezekiel. On a journey to Athens he finished Ezekiel and wrote the first five books on the Song of Songs, ending this commentary in Caesarea. The commentaries on Matthew and the minor prophets belong to the period of Philip the Arab (244–249), according to Eusebius (*Hist. eccl.* 6.36.2). Having made a critical analysis of this data, P. Nautin suggests dating the Isaiah and Ezekiel commentaries at 244 to 245; those on the Song, the Minor Prophets, Psalms, Proverbs, and Ecclesiastes between 245 and 247; those on Luke and Matthew to 249.

It seems certain that Origen planned a systematic commentary on all of the Scriptures. As for the Octateuch, he was able to write a partial commentary on Genesis and only scholia on the remainder of Genesis and down to Numbers or possibly

Deuteronomy. Of the prophets he commented on Isaiah, Ezekiel, and the Minor Prophets. After finishing Ezekiel and while doing the Minor Prophets he tackled the wisdom books, beginning with the Song of Songs and then moving to Psalms and Proverbs. Except for the commentary on the Song, Nautin plausibly suggests that he followed the order of the Greek Bible (Psalms, Proverbs, Ecclesiastes, Song, Job), because he managed to write only scholia on Ecclesiastes and nothing on Job.

This grand project was a novelty in early Christianity. Before Origen we know only of commentaries on individual books. The *Hypotyposes* of Clement were short annotations and not full systematic commentaries. Origen's plan was probably connected to his method of teaching; as the *Address of Gratitude* attributed to Gregory the Wonderworker tells us, Origen would deal with theological subjects on the basis of passages of Scripture, perhaps in the framework of his systematic exegesis of the biblical books. To that extent, the commentaries give us a some access to Origen the instructor. However, in the commentaries Origen does not always take up the theological subjects suggested by the text; for example, in the *Commentary on John* 6.14 he states some problems concerning the soul, but he does not discuss them.

It is possible here to give only a faint idea of Origen's exegetical method. Its fundamental presupposition is the Platonic distinction between the true level of reality, which is intelligible, complete, and perfect, and a level that is sensible, transitory, and imperfect, an image of the first. This is matched by the idea that in the Scriptures there are two levels of meaning. The literal meaning is accessible to all but is in truth only a facade behind which is hidden a spiritual meaning; the literal is only a figure or image of divine realities (see the preface to *First Principles*). That the literal meaning of the Scriptures hides a deeper and true meaning was not, of course, original with Origen. As we saw in the preceding chapter, the Greek philosophers had recourse to allegory (*allēgoreō*, to say something else) to extract deeper truths from the texts of Homer and from the myths. In Alexandria, Philo had likewise taken Platonism as his basis and had developed an allegorical reading of the Pentateuch.

But Christianity also had an inherent tendency in this direction. Primitive Christians considered the Christ event to be the (1st) coming of the Messiah and, in consequence, looked upon themselves as the eschatological community. Not only were those biblical prophecies which explicitly looked to the future fulfilled in Christ and in his community, but also the whole of biblical revelation found its fullest meaning in them. This made possible, and even demanded, a reading that went beyond the immediate meaning of the texts and understood, on the basis of faith in Jesus Christ, how in those texts God had already shown that the whole of sacred history was to reach its completion in Christ. This explains how Paul could say that the rock from which the Hebrews drank in the wilderness was Christ, that the experiences of the Israelites in the wilderness as told in Exodus were "examples for us" who live in the fullness of time (1 Cor 10:1–11), or that the story of the two sons of Abraham in Genesis is "an allegory" (Gal 4:24). That is, it has a meaning different from its superficial meaning, in that it refers to two covenants and two Jerusalems, the earthly and the heavenly.

This last example shows how easily the minds of the early Christians could connect a "vertical" allegory (a reference to present but higher realities) analogous to that practiced by Philo, and a "horizontal" allegory (a reference to realities that were future when the text was written) according to which statements of the Bible prefigured the present history of Jesus and Christians. The Letter to the Hebrews is evidence of a considerable expansion in both directions. In this perspective, the immediate meaning of the text is downgraded to an imperfect image, while the allegorical meaning represents reality and fulfillment.

This understanding of the Scriptures runs through the whole of Christian exegesis prior to Origen, but Origen systematized it. To begin with, he raised the question of the criteria that established the need for an allegorical interpretation of the biblical text, and he found these criteria in characteristics of the text that prevent its being taken in its most obvious sense. Here Origen is influenced by the sensibility of the educated non-Jewish and non-Christian world, which was scandalized to find in the Jewish Bible a number of things, such as anthropomorphism and immorality, that were unworthy of a perfect God. Origen (*Princ.* 4.4) compiles a list of passages that would become impossible or irrational if taken in the literal sense, and he concludes that many incidents could not have really happened and that many precepts could not be carried out. Texts of this kind come not only from the Old Testament but also from the New; for example, why pluck out one's right eye on the grounds that it is an occasion of sin, when the right eye is not more guilty than the left? (Matt 5:29, discussed in *Comm. Matt.* 15.2).

Another influential factor was the conviction that nothing in the Scriptures was unimportant or useless for edification and instruction; yet this would be the case, for example, of many regulations in Leviticus, if taken literally. From such observations Origen infers the legitimacy and even the necessity of systematically searching the biblical texts for a deeper meaning. It must be admitted, however, that in justifying this principle Origen too often strains to find contradictions in the text (the *defectus litterae*).

The search for hidden meaning is further structured according to the line of thought being followed. The search connects three levels for reading the sacred texts with the current anthropology and its distinction of body, soul, and spirit. The result is a literal, a moral, and a spiritual reading. This last, however, can have different points of reference: the relations of the soul with God or Christ, Christ himself, the church, or the last times. Moreover, the fulfillment in its truest and fullest sense is not found in the first coming of Christ and in the church of the present age, for these, too, are images of the fulfillment that will occur only with the coming of Christ in glory. The law foreshadowed what would become a reality in the first coming of Christ, but this coming in turn foreshadowed what will be a reality in the second coming, in what the Apocalypse calls an "eternal gospel" (Rev 14:6), in contrast to the present gospel, which is temporary (*Princ.* 4.3.13).

Elsewhere, Origen formulates the relationship between the three readings on the basis of Hebrews 10:1, according to which the law had only a shadow of the good things to come, but not the true image of the realities. According to this pattern, Old Testament sacrifice is a shadow, which is followed at a higher level by the image, which is the sacrifice of Christ, while the reality consists of the heavenly good things that are linked to the intercession of the glorified Christ in the presence of the Father (*Hom. Ps.* 38.2.2). However, the New Testament is not simply an image of eschatological reality or of the eternal gospel; it is an image also of the spiritual reality that springs from the presence of salvation in the church; thus the cures worked by Jesus signify that he heals error and sin.

An example from the *Commentary on John* may serve as an illustration: the passage is John 2:14–17, the expulsion of the traders from the temple (*Comm. Jo.* 10.119–224). Origen remarks, to begin with, that Matthew, Mark, and Luke connect this incident with the triumphal entry of Jesus into Jerusalem before the passion, whereas John places these two episodes at different points in the life of Jesus. This discrepancy already bids us not to stick to the *historia,* the literal sense. Origen therefore moves on to a detailed search for the hidden meaning *(ta kekrymmena).*

Jerusalem, in its spiritual meaning, is the heavenly city, of which souls capable of ascending to spiritual realities are already citizens; but even these souls can be in a state of sin, so that here Jerusalem instead represents the church—another interpretation dear to Origen. In our passage, an explicit identification is made of the temple and the church: Jesus enters the city and the temple in order to save, for there are many who make the church a place of business. When Jesus overturns the tables with the money, he eliminates greed from souls; here, then, the temple represents the soul.

On the other hand, the driving out of the animals intended for sacrifice was a signal that soon there would be no more sacrifice according to Jewish usage. The animals driven out are then interpreted, type after type, as symbols of the evil inclinations of the soul. Origen dismisses an objection against such allegorical interpretation on the grounds that the animals in question are clean. He answers that it would have been impossible to bring unclean animals into the temple as sacrifices. For a moment, it seems that Origen is caught in a contradiction here, as he does not seem to allow the needed *defectus litterae,* but we see immediately that this is not the case: he goes on to say that the historical character of the event is questionable, since he does not see how Jesus could have carried out his action by himself (the disciples are not mentioned) without meeting resistance.

With this as his starting point, Origen studies the parallel account of the entry into Jerusalem in Matthew 21, and raises a series of difficulties against a literal interpretation: what interest could there be, after all, in reporting that Jesus was sitting on an ass and her colt? Furthermore, this detail does not really fulfill the prophecy cited by Matthew (Zech 9:10). Again: did the Son of God literally have need of an ass? Finally, there are other improbabilities, among them the ability of Jesus to single-handedly drive out the many sellers and buyers—which takes us back to the initial difficulty already found in John.

All this allows Origen to proceed to a detailed allegorical interpretation, of which it will be enough to cite one passage:

"Jesus is, then, the Word of God who enters the soul called Jerusalem, riding the ass which his disciples have released from its tether, that is, from the mere letter of the Old Testament, which is explained by the two disciples, who freed the ass, one of them by adapting the text to the healing of the soul and allegorizing the text for it, and the other by presenting to it the true future goods by means of what was in the shadow. He also rides the young colt, that is, the New Testament, for in both Testaments it is possible to discover the true word that purifies us and drives out all the rationalizations that buy and sell within us" (10.174–75).

There is no point in going through the lengthy continuation of the exegesis, which ends with a citation and refutation of Heracleon's exegesis of the passage. In general, the *Commentary on John* is perhaps Origen's exegetical masterpiece. The text that is the subject of the commentary and the point-by-point debate with one of the most complete products of gnostic exegesis, namely, the commentary of Heracleon, provide Origen with the opportunity to go deep into difficult and sensitive doctrinal issues, including, first of all, the preexistence of the Son and the Son's relationship with the Father.

This summary by way of example illustrates not only the use of the criterion of the *defectus litterae* in order to introduce the spiritual interpretation, but also a characteristic of spiritual interpretation, namely, that it is an open-ended search, a suggestion of numerous ways of exploiting the details of the text, an investigation along many lines, and far removed from any rigid and univocal allegorism. The dynamic character of Origen's exegesis in the commentaries and homilies is matched, as we shall point out, by a similar attitude in Origen's most systematic work, the *First Principles*. Still, Origen never claimed that his explanations exhausted the interpretation of the Scriptures; on the contrary, he sought to train his readers and hearers to engage in their personal searches, to "dig their own wells" as the patriarchs did, because in each person there is living water (John 4:11), which causes the mystical meaning to flow forth if it is not hindered by earth and rubble, that is, by laziness of the mind and by the sleep of the heart (*Hom. Gen.* 12.5).

c. Homilies

In Rufinus's Latin translation, which he says he has expanded for purposes of clarity, we have the sixteen homilies on Genesis (*CPG* 1411), the thirteen on Exodus (*CPG* 1414), the sixteen on Leviticus (*CPG* 1416), and the twenty-eight on Numbers (*CPG* 1418), all of which are mentioned by Jerome; but we do not have the thirteen on Deuteronomy, except for some doubtful fragments (*CPG* 1419). For the twenty-six homilies on Joshua (*CPG* 1420) and the nine on Judges (*CPG* 1421) we again have Rufinus's translation; in these, however, he says stays closer to the original than he does in his translation of the above-mentioned homilies. Jerome mentions at this point eight homilies on Easter, i.e., on Exodus 12 and other Old Testament passages on the subject. They were perhaps a collection of homilies and other works, which probably included the two treatises on Easter that were discovered at Tura (see below). Today are extant only two of the four homilies on 1 Samuel (1 Kgdms in the LXX), which are mentioned by Jerome and Cassiodorus: one on 1:2 in a translation by Rufinus, and one in the original Greek on 28:3–25, the incident of the witch of Endor who calls up the soul of Samuel (*CPG* 1423).

Jerome speaks of a total of one hundred twenty homilies on sixty-three Psalms, and lists the Psalms and the number of homilies on each. We omit these details. The following have survived: five on Psalm 36; two on Psalm 37; and two on Psalm 38, all in Rufinus's translation; plus a fragment of a homily on Psalm 82 (*CPG* 1428), which is cited by Eusebius (*Hist. eccl.* 6.38). The attribution to Origen of seventy-four homilies of Jerome on the Psalms (*CPG* 1429), as suggested by V. Peri in 1980, is debated.

Of the twenty-two homilies on Job, fragments are preserved in the catenas (*CPG* 1424) as well as in the remaining fragments of the *Tractatus in Iob* of Hilary of Poitiers. Some fragments, perhaps, remain in the catenas of the seven homilies on Proverbs (*CPG* 1430; see also above, sec. 2b, on the commentaries) and of the eight on Ecclesiastes (*CPG* 1431). Two homilies on the Song of Songs (*CPG* 1432) have been preserved in Jerome's translation. Also preserved in a translation by Jerome are nine of the thirty-two homilies on Isaiah (Jerome knew of only twenty-five), but the authenticity of one of these is debated (*CPG* 1437). Of the forty-five homilies on Jeremiah, twenty are preserved in Greek and fourteen in Jerome's translation; twelve of these match twelve of the Greek. There are also doubtful fragments in Greek (*CPG* 1438). Fourteen homilies on Ezekiel remain in Jerome's translation (*CPG* 1441).

For the New Testament, twenty-five homilies on Matthew are lost, but the thirty-nine on Luke survive in Jerome's translation (*CPG* 1451). Of the seventeen on Acts a single fragment from the fourth homily remains (*CPG* 1456). Catenas preserve some fragments of an unknown number of homilies on 1 Corinthians and of eleven on 2 Corinthians (*CPG* 1458). Nothing remains of the seven on Galatians, of the two on the Letters to the Thessalonians, and of the one on the Letter to Titus. The catena fragments on these letters may come from the homilies or from commentaries. Of the eighteen homilies on Hebrews there remain two fragments from Eusebius (*Hist. eccl.* 6.25.11–14); in one of these Origen challenges the attribution of the letter to Paul.

Finally, we note a number of fragments, mostly found on papyri, that come in good measure from homilies, and some fragments handed down in Armenian codices (for exact references see *CPG* 1503 and 1505 respectively).

Origen's homilies were all delivered during his stay in Caesarea, and when he was a presbyter. Not all of the latter group were delivered in that city; e.g., a homily on 1 Kingdoms [1 Samuel] was delivered in Aelia, that is, in Jerusalem. In addition, all those written down seem to belong to the last years of his life; Eusebius says (*Hist. eccl.* 6.36.1) that only after Origen reached the age of sixty (after the year 215) did he allow stenographers to write down his homilies. Indicators within the texts seem to confirm this claim.

Cross-references within the homilies make it possible to establish that the first homilies preached were those on the Psalms and on the other sapiential books, then those on the prophets, and finally those on the historical books. P. Nautin has reconstructed the order of liturgical assemblies and the cycle of readings at Caesarea, but it is not certain that this reconstruction holds for the time of Origen. A. Monaci Castagno suggests that Origen introduced the systematic explanation of the Scriptures in homilies addressed to catechumens, and that he began with the Psalms, not so much because he began to preach at that point in a triennial cycle of readings, but because the order—sapiential books, prophetic books, historical books—seemed to him more suited for the formation of his hearers. In any case, the homilies on the Old Testament were delivered at the meetings of catechumens that were held several times a week. The Eucharist seems to have been celebrated on Friday evenings (Wednesdays and Fridays were days of fasting) and, of course, on Sundays.

The New Testament texts were read during the eucharistic assemblies, which catechumens did not attend. A lector read the text, then the preacher delivered the homily, and common prayer followed. Both the texts commented on by Origen and the homilies themselves vary in length, so it is difficult to calculate the time spent, but it may have been an hour, on the average.

In his treatise on *First Principles* Origen clearly distinguishes among beginners, those making progress, and the perfect, and links these three classes respectively with the literal, moral, and allegorical interpretations of Scripture (*Princ.* 4.2.4). In his homilies Origen addresses the first class, but without denying them an allegorical interpretation. It is probably not an accident that in the homilies on Leviticus (5.5) he mentions the three interpretations—historical, moral, and mystical—but without connecting them with three different categories of readers. His problem, even in the homilies, is to lead a public, composed of the *simpliciores* (beginners), to the higher meaning, which escapes the majority, and which God has hidden in symbols to keep it from being debased by easy access (*Princ.* 4.2.7).

Origen is aware of the difficulties the beginners have with a literalist reading of such biblical books, such as Leviticus, with its legal and ritual regulations. He wants to lead them to the spiritual sense in order that they may have access to the real riches of the word of God. But he must do battle with criticism and derision not only from the *simpliciores* but also from teachers (e.g., *Hom. Lev.* 7.4). Origen must respond to these criticisms and reject a literal Jewish exegesis. We shall not go into the question of the extent to which Jewish exegesis was purely literal. At the same time he must also reject Marcionite and gnostic interpretations, which, as we can see from references in the homilies, had had some success among his faithful; Ambrose, for example, was formerly a gnostic. Sometimes Origen accuses all of these groups of being literalist; sometimes, with greater exactitude, he allows that the gnostics use allegorical exegesis, but to them he applies the standard of compliance with the apostolic rule of truth (*Hom. Ps.* 36.4.1). In his pastoral concern, however, Origen endeavors to turn the letter to advantage by finding in it pointers for moral behavior that will be useful to his hearers, as in the area of sexual ethics, or in warnings against recourse to magic and astrology.

BIBLIOGRAPHY

Given the complicated situation, especially for the fragments, the reader will always have to consult the *CPG* for editions (we have, by way of exception, given the pertinent references to that work). For some texts one must still use PG 11–17. For the *Philocalia*, see section 4i below.

Scholia

The fragments are of disparate origin and in various editions. See *CPG* at the numbers given.

Commentaries

On Matthew in GCS:
Origenes Werke (vol. 10; GCS 40; ed. E. Benz and E. Klostermann; Leipzig: Hinrich, 1935–1955).
———— (vol. 11; GCS 38; ed. E. Benz, E. Klostermann, and U. Treu; Berlin: Akademie-Verlag, 1976).
———— (vol 12, 1–2; GCS 41; 2d ed.; ed. E. Klostermann, L. Früchtel, and U. Treu; GCS 41, 2; Berlin: Akademie-Verlag, 1968).

On John in GCS:
Origenes Werke (vol. 4; GCS 10; ed. E. Preuschen; Leipzig: Hinrich, 1903).

In SC:
Song of Songs (SC 375, 376).

Matthew 10–11 (SC 161).
John (SC 120, 157, 22, 290, 385).

For the text of the commentary on Romans we must still go back to PG 14, to
which the fragments need to be added (see *CPG*).
Italian translation of the commentary on:
Song of Songs (trans. M. Simonetti; Rome: Città Nuova, 1976).
John (trans. E. Corsini; 2d ed.; Turin: UTET, 1979).
Romans (trans. F. Cocchini; 2 vols.; Casale Monferrato: Marietti, 1985–1986).

Homilies

The homilies have been published in the GCS edition of Origne, especially in
three volumes:
Origenes Werke (vol. 3; GCS 6; cd. E. Klostermann; Leipzig: Hinrich, 1901).
———— (vols. 6–8; GCS 29, 30, 33; ed. W. A. Baehrens; Leipzig: Hinrich, 1920,
1921, 1925).
———— (vol. 9; GCS 49; 2d. ed.; ed. M. Rauer; Leipzig: Hinrich, 1959).

The SC editions (usually using the GCS text), with French translation, introduc-
tion, and notes by various scholars, are very useful:
Genesis (SC 7).
Numbers (SC 29).
Song of Songs (SC 37).
Joshua (SC 71).
Luke (SC 87).
Jeremiah (SC 232, 238).
Leviticus (SC 286, 287).
1 and 2 Samuel (SC 328).
Ezekiel (SC 352).

Critical editions with introduction, Italian translation, and commentary on the
homilies:
The witch of Endor (ed. and trans. M. Simonetti; Florence: Nardini, 1989).
Psalms (ed. and trans. E. Prinzivalli; Florence: Nardini, 1991).

Italian translation of the homilies in CTePa on:
Genesis (CTePa 14, 262, 286, 303; ed. and trans. M. I. Danieli; Rome: Città
Nuova, 1978, 1992).
Exodus (CTePa 304; ed. and trans. M. I. Danieli; Rome: Città Nuova, 1981, 1991).
Leviticus (CTePa 305, 340; ed. and trans. M. I. Danieli; Rome: Città Nuova,
1985).
Numbers (CTePa 167, 350; ed. and trans. M. I. Danieli; Rome: Città Nuova,
2001).
Joshua (CTePa 108, 258, 369; ed. and trans. M. I. Danieli; Rome: Città Nuova,
1993).
Judges (CTePa 101; ed. and trans. M. I. Danieli; Rome: Città Nuova, 1992).

Song of Songs (CTePa 83, 357, 209; ed. and trans. M. I. Danieli; Rome: Città
Nuova, 1990).
Isaiah (CTePa 132, 224; ed. and trans. M. I. Danieli; Rome: Città Nuova, 1996).
Jeremiah (CTcPa 177; ed. and trans. M. I. Danieli; Rome: Città Nuova, 1995).
Ezekiel (CTePa 72, 165; ed. and trans. N. Antoniono; Rome: Città Nuova, 1997).

For the seventy-four homilies on the Psalms that are attributed to Origen by
V. Peri, see the translation, introduction, and notes by G. Coppa, *Se Hanta
quattro omelie sul libro dei Salmi* (Turin: Paoline, 1993).

Studies of Origen's Exegesis

H. de Lubac, *Histoire et esprit* (Paris: Aubier, 1950).
R. P. C. Hanson, *Allegory and Event: A Study of the Sources and Significance of
Origen's Interpretations in Scripture* (London: SCM, 1959).
For a first introduction: M. Simonetti, *Lettera e/o allegoria: Un contributo alla
storia dell'esegesi patristica* (Rome: Augustinianum, 1985) 73–98.
S. Leanza, "Origene," in *Da Gesù a Origene* (vol. 1 in *La Bibbia nell'antichità
cristiana;* ed. E. Norelli; Bologna: Dehoniane, 1993), 377–407.
Important for a critical study of the transmission of the Origen's exegetical works
is P. Nautin, *Origène: Sa vie et son oeuvre* (Paris: Beauchesne, 1977), 225–60
and passim.
H. Crouzel, *Origen* (trans. A. S. Worrall; San Francisco: Harper & Row, 1989).

On the Homilies

A. Monaci Castagno, *Origene predicatore e il suo pubblico* (Turin: Angeli, 1987).
M. Harl, *Origène et la fonction révélatrice du Verbe incarné* (Paris: Seuil, 1958).
N. de Lange, *Origen and the Jews* (Cambridge: Cambridge University Press,
1976).
G. Sgherri, *Chiesa e Sinagoga nelle opere di Origene* (Milan: Vita e Pensiero, 1982).

3. Hexapla

Origen used the Septuagint, the Greek translation of the Old Testament that was
adopted by the Christian churches, but he was well aware of the problems that text
raised. On the one hand, there were differences among the manuscripts of the Septuagint itself, raising the question of which variant was to be taken as the original. He was
not the only one to raise this question. Eusebius (*Hist. eccl.* 5.28.15–18) cites some
passages of a treatise against the followers of Artemon, written in Rome shortly after
217. The author of the treatise attacks those who dare to meddle with the Scriptures,
claiming that they have corrected it; the technical terms *diorthoō* and *katorthoō* show
their philological intention: to eliminate discrepancies. He cites some writers of these
publications, criticizing them for not keeping to the Scriptures as received from their
catechists, and for thinking themselves wiser than the Holy Spirit.

On the other hand, there was also the problem of differences between the Septuagint and the Greek translations in circulation among the Jews, who rebuked Christians for having adopted an inaccurate translation. The most disputed passage, but not the only one, was Isa 7:14, where the virginal conception and birth are found in the Septuagint but not in the Hebrew or in other Greek translations. In any case, Origen knew that compared to the Hebrew original the Septuagint displayed divergences that were not attributable to copyists' errors. He hypothesized that these stemmed from either a Hebrew original different from that known in his time, or deliberate choices by the translators.

As for the problems posed by the variants in the manuscripts of the Septuagint, he adopted the principle of giving precedence to those that match the Hebrew. However, he did not know Hebrew well enough to make his own independent check. He therefore created a working tool, namely an edition of the Old Testament in columns. The first column contained a transliteration of the Hebrew text into the Greek alphabet, and was subdivided into short lines of one or two words each. The other columns contained the translation of each set of words in the Greek versions that he had been able to collect. This enormous work was done by copyists, with Origen as supervisor, probably giving his attention above all to the Septuagint.

The original manuscript (or, more accurately, the manuscripts of the two editions; see below) of this monumental work was kept in the library of Caesarea, and was examined there by Eusebius. Eusebius and his teacher Pamphilus produced and corrected copies of the text of the Septuagint as established by Origen, who "corrected" the Septuagint with the help of his synopsis, as can still be seen from the colophons that have come down to us in later copies of the manuscripts of Eusebius and Pamphilus. It is not clear, however, whether Origen's recension of the Septuagint was one of the columns in the synopsis (see below).

At times, manuscripts of the Septuagint carried in the margins the variants in the other Greek translations, these being drawn from Origen's work. This is true of the exemplar of the Syriac version of the Syro-Hexapla, which Paul of Tella translated in 616–617 on the basis of Origen's recension, while retaining Origen's diacritical marks (see below) as well as the marginal variants and the colophons of the various books. Readings contained in the *Hexapla* are preserved not only by the manuscripts with their marginal variants but also by patristic citations and the catenas, that is, biblical commentaries made up of citations from the patristic writings, these being grouped together after each lemma or passage being commented on.

Four manuscripts have preserved fragments of the book of Psalms according to the original arrangement in columns (from the form of the synopsis that contained four translations); these probably came from a catena on the Psalms in which the copyist decided to incorporate at the end of each lemma the corresponding portion of Origen's text.

Finally, we have information on the *Hexapla* from Eusebius of Caesarea (*Hist. eccl.* 6.16), who had consulted it in the library of Caesarea; from Epiphanius of Salamis (*Pan.* 64.3.5); and from Jerome (*Comm. Tit.* 3.9; *Vir. ill.* 54). P. Nautin has shown that the only first-hand testimony is that of Eusebius, while the others depend on him. Epiphanius provides an independent source only to the extent that he used the lost *Defense of Origen* by Pamphilus and Eusebius.

Following the lead of Eusebius and the fragments, Nautin has shown that, despite Epiphanius's statement repeated by Jerome, Origen most probably did not have a first column with the text in Hebrew letters, followed by a transliteration, but had only the transliteration. We find Nautin convincing, but the debate continues.

Eusebius (*Hist. eccl.* 6.16.4) speaks of two forms of the synopsis. One of them, which he calls *Quadrupla (Tetrassa)*, contained, in addition to the Septuagint and the transliteration of the Hebrew, the translations by Aquila (done under Hadrian, 117–138), Symmachus (probably under Marcus Aurelius, 161–180), and Theodotion (ca. 30–50). The other form of the synopsis added "not only a fifth, but a sixth and a seventh." Since the use of the first four is documented in writings of Origen from the Alexandrian period and at the beginning of the stay in Caesarea, the *Quadrupla* (also called the *Tetrapla* in the sources) must have been compiled in Alexandria, or so Nautin asserts. According to others, the *Tetrapla* was an extract from the other form of the synopsis; there are even scholars who claim it never existed.

After leaving Alexandria, Origen got hold of other Greek translations while in Nicopolis near Actium and in Palestine, as he tells us in a passage preserved in some catenas on the Psalms and summarized by Eusebius. This passage speaks, however, only of a fifth and sixth translation, while alluding to some variants or notes for the fifth. Perhaps this led Eusebius to the idea of seven translations. Origen, then, produced a new edition with six translations plus the transliteration; we do not know whether he did this for the entire Old Testament or only for those books on which he had yet to comment. The title *Heptapla* and *Octapla* are attested, but they signify only this new edition. Such titles as *Tetraselides* are also used, from the word *selides,* "columns."

The Septuagint, which was Origen's base text, is found only in third place among the translations, being preceded by those of Aquila and Symmachus and followed by that of Theodotion. To explain this fact, which the ancients already found puzzling, it has been suggested that Origen got the idea for his synopsis from a Jewish synopsis that originally contained the text in Hebrew characters, a transliteration, and the very literal translation of Aquila. Its supposed purpose was to make possible the liturgical reading, the reading of the Hebrew being obligatory, and the understanding of the sacred texts among people who no longer knew Hebrew. Symmachus's column would then have been added by Symmachus himself, who may even have produced his translation precisely as part of the synopsis. We know that Origen came into possession of manuscripts belonging to Symmachus, and Nautin thinks that the Jewish synopsis was one of them.

Origen would then have had the texts recopied, but without the column in Hebrew characters and with the addition of columns containing the Septuagint and Theodotion. Later, in Caesarea, when he had acquired the other translations, he would have had the texts copied once again and thereby produced the *Hexapla.* As noted above, we do not know exactly which texts, but surely not the Pentateuch. With regard to the column containing the Septuagint, it is not clear whether this contained the recension made by Origen on the basis of a comparison with the other translations, or whether his recension was a separate work and the *Hexapla* contained only the current form of the Septuagint. The existing fragments point to the second alternative, since they have an ordinary Septuagint text and lack diacritical signs. Indeed, when Origen saw the Septuagint to be missing a portion of texts that was attested in the parallel translations, he introduced it into the Septuagint, being careful to mark it with an asterisk (*), while using an obelus (÷) to mark passages attested only by the Septuagint; in both cases he also indicated where the text in question ended. The asterisk and obelus were diacritical signs used by Greek philologists beginning in the third century A.D., but Origen changed their meaning.

In his *Commentary on Matthew* (15.14) Origen explains how, in comparing the translations, he was able to resolve the problem of variants in the manuscripts of the Septuagint: he did so by accepting the readings found in the other translations. He also reveals that he received criticisms for doing so. However, as Nautin has emphasized, Origen's purpose was not simply textual criticism of the Septuagint; his remarks also showed his awareness that the differences among the translations could go back to variants in the Hebrew exemplars, and that the purpose of a comparison of the translations was to allow him to get as close as possible to the original text of the Bible.

BIBLIOGRAPHY

F. Field, *Origenis Hexaplorum quae supersunt siue ueterum interpretum graecorum in totum Vetus Testamentum fragmenta* (2 vols.; Oxford, 1867–1875; repr., Hildesheim: Olms, 1964), has not yet been replaced but is no longer adequate because many fragments were discovered later on.

For editions of fragments see *CPG* I:174–77.

The ongoing Göttingen (Vandehoeck & Ruprecht) edition of the Septuagint gives the readings from the *Hexapla* and the *Syriac Hexapla* in the apparatus.

A fundamental critical re-examination of the subject is made by P. Nautin, *Origène: Sa vie et son oeuvre* (Paris: Beauchesne, 1977), 303–61.

See also G. Dorival, M. Harl, and O. Munnich, *Le Bible grecque des Septante: Du judaïsme hellénistique au christianisme ancien* (Paris: Cerf, 1988), 162–68.

4. Treatises

a. First Principles

This work, which was composed during the Alexandrian period (according to Eusebius, *Hist. eccl.* 6.24.3), probably around 229, is titled *Peri archōn*, thereby locating it within the Greek philosophical tradition. There phrase the designated, from early on, the search for the principles of being, the *archai*. Even though Origen acknowledges only one principle in the strict sense, namely, God, the title is justified because the treatises on "first principles" traditionally proceeded by discussing a series of fundamental subjects such as matter, the world, the human being, incorporeal beings, and freedom, and these are precisely the subjects of Origen's work.

The reference to a learned tradition is essential, for Origen is accepting the challenge implicit in the accusations that Christians are ignorant and superstitious people. In Alexandria, Philo had already rethought biblical revelation in the language of Platonic cosmology and anthropology. Later, among Christians and always under the influence of Platonism, Clement had confronted Greek culture and tried to define its relationship with Christianity as one of preparation for it. In his *First Principles,* however, Origen is not interested in taking a position in relation to the classical tradition, but rather in discussing the essential lines of a Christian theological system that could stand comparison, on the speculative level, with the philosophical tradition.

Before him, such an enterprise had been consciously attempted only by the gnostics and, in particular, by the school of Valentinus. Heavily influenced though they were by Platonism, the gnostics had turned Platonism "upside down" by describing the relationship between the sensible and divine world as the result of a deadly break, and therefore giving the sensible world a decidedly negative connotation and creating an opposition between the divinities of the two worlds. Some successors of Valentinus had gone on to rigidify the relationship between the two even further by developing a doctrine according to which the salvation of the individual is a priori conditioned by his or her nature. Origen explicitly opposes ditheism and the doctrine of natures and refutes the gnostics and Marcionites in a way that often oversimplifies their positions in the interests of a polemic geared to an uncompromising defense of free will.

Origen's vision of the world is likewise based on the distinction, originating in the Platonic tradition, between two levels of the universe: one, the divine world, which is higher and intelligible, the other, the human world, which is inferior and sensible. The second is an imperfect image, a shadow, of the first. In this picture of the world Platonism supplies only the basis of a sycretist vision that is extensively influenced by, for example, Stoicism. This perspective was quite widespread and is, for example, one of the presuppositions of the Letter to the Hebrews. Origen's great aim in the *First Principles* is to organize the data of Christian revelation in a systematic way within that setting. To this end, he is compelled to think out systematically, for the first time, a series of theological problems that had not yet received sufficient attention. The boldness of some of his solutions led to criticism of Origen even during his lifetime, while after his death it unleashed an opposition that resulted in 553 in the condemnation of theses more or less improperly attributed to him.

These controversies decisively affected the transmission of the *First Principles.* When in the course of the controversies Epiphanius tried to win over Jerome and Rufinus to the antiorigenist cause, he succeeded only with Jerome, whereas Rufinus in 398, after returning to Rome from the East, translated not only the first book of Pamphilus's *Defense of Origen* but also the treatise on *First Principles.* For the latter he wrote two prefaces, one each for books one and three, in which he explained that he had omitted seemingly unorthodox passages and had expanded others for purposes of explanation; he gave as his reason that heretics and adversaries had changed many points in Origen's works. Rufinus justified his procedure by recalling the analogous precedent of Jerome in his translation of the homilies. Jerome was irritated by the references to his about-face and by the irony that snaked through Rufinus's prefaces, and he responded, among other ways, by producing a literal translation of the *First Principles* that was intended to bring out the errors of Origen.

This translation is lost except for some passages which Jerome included in his Letter 124. Thus we know the *First Principles* in its entirety only through Rufinus's translation, which deliberately and systematically softened the points at which Origen was at odds with later orthodoxy. It is possible to check his translation, at least partially, by comparing it with Jerome's citations of his own translation in Letter 124 and with the twenty-four citations contained in and condemned in a letter of 543 from

Emperor Justinian to Menas, Patriarch of Constantinople, and also, above all, by comparing it with two lengthy passages in the *Philocalia,* namely, 3.1 and 4.1–3. The comparison shows a lengthy omission by Rufinus (in 4.3.7) but also omissions by the *Philocalia* regarding the preexistence of souls (in 3.1 and 4.2) in passages which Rufinus expressly says he has kept because he regards the subject as not yet dogmatically defined; some of the passages are also attested by Jerome. It is clear in many instances that Rufinus has made stylistic and explanatory additions; in other cases the reader is left uncertain. Excellent discussions of this question can be found in the works cited in the bibliography.

The structure of the *First Principles* cannot be automatically derived from the division into four books, which is certainly original although not mentioned by Eusebius. Of the outlines proposed, that of Simonetti is persuasive. A first fundamental break occurs between 2.3, on the origin and destiny of the created world, and 2.4, on the oneness of God. A second break occurs at the beginning of the third book, which begins the discussion of free will. The first two sections are thereby defined. In the first of these (1.1–2.3), a first part (1.1–6) shows an outline parallel to that in 2.4–11: both deal successively with God, rational creatures, and the end of the world. The part between these two (1.7–2.3) develops some themes already discussed in 1.5–6, and thus represents an appendix to the first part, intended to go more deeply into what has been said about rational creatures and about the destiny of the world in relation to those creatures. Let us look briefly at these first two sections.

In the preface (3) Origen sets down an important distinction: the apostles clearly defined some fundamental points of doctrine that might serve as a foundation for all believers, including those incapable of study, but they did not develop any rational proofs. The apostles also asserted the existence of other truths, but did not explain the origin and ways of expressing these, in order that believers worthy of receiving wisdom might exercise their minds on them. Origen goes on (4–10) to list both kinds of truths.

Defined teaching includes the doctrine of God as the Creator, who is just and good, the Father of Jesus, and author of the Law, the Prophets, and the Gospels; the doctrine of Christ as born of the Father before creatures, coworker in creation, truly incarnated, dead, and risen; the doctrine of the Holy Spirit as inspirer of the prophets and apostles. Not defined is whether the Spirit is begotten or not begotten, and whether or not he is a son of God. As for the soul, its final reward or punishment and its free will are defined; not defined are its origin and its relationship to the body. The existence but not the origin of the devil is defined; the creation and future destruction of the world are defined, but not what existed before creation and what will be afterwards. Also defined is the presence in the Scriptures of a meaning hidden behind the obvious meaning; in order to grasp that meaning the gift of the Holy Spirit is needed. Not defined are the meaning of the word "incorporeal," and whether God, Christ, the Spirit, and rational creatures are corporeal or incorporeal. Left to be defined are, finally, the exact nature of the angels and the stars.

What Origen plans therefore is truly a systematic dogmatics. In developing it he intends to take as his point of departure and justificatory criterion the data of the Scriptures. On that foundation he will develop rational arguments, but without forgetting those who reject such proofs, claiming that they wish to restrict themselves to the biblical data.

Origen then goes on to prove that, despite the biblical anthropomorphisms, God is incorporeal, a simple intellectual nature that cannot be known by any creature, including the angels and the human intellect. Although the latter is incorporeal, it is weakened by its contact with matter and can therefore excogitate an idea of God only through analogy (1.1). When it comes to Christ, Origen is interested primarily in his pre-existence and his divine nature, and to this end he analyzes the attributes given to Christ in the Scriptures: as the wisdom of God, he is always with the Father; he is begotten and not created; his generation is not in the form of an emanation (*probolē*, a term dear to the Valentinians in explaining the origin of the Son) because the substance of God cannot be divided; he is generated as the will is from the mind. But Origen tends to subordinationism, as indeed does the entire theology of the Logos, which expresses the mediating function of the Logos in terms of inferiority to the Father; thus the Son is the image of the goodness of God but he is not goodness in himself (1.2.13, a passage which is omitted by Rufinus and attested by Justinian and Jerome). In 1.3 Origen provides the first organized Christian treatise on the Holy Spirit: the Spirit is the only one who, along with the Son, knows the Father. It remains uncertain, partly because of Rufinus's interventions, whether Origen ultimately considers the Spirit to be created. Origen then emphasizes the Spirit's work of sanctification.

Part 1, ch. 4 introduces a basic theme: the creation and fall. Because God has always been good and did not change at any point, the objects of his goodness, that is, his acts of creation and creatures, have always existed. But how can creatures, if they are really such, have always existed? Origen suggests that creation has always existed in the form of ideas within the divine wisdom, which is the Son. In Origen's opinion, this allows us both to say that creatures are not coeternal with God and to avoid admitting a change in God, as though God began to create only at a certain moment.

The author then studies rational natures (1.5): the angels, the devil and his forces, and human souls. Now if we accept that the good angels are good by their nature and cannot sin, we must also accept that the wicked angels are wicked by the will of the Creator, which cannot be allowed. From this, as well as from a study of passages of Scripture, we must conclude that both the good and the wicked angels, and in general all rational creatures, have merited their condition. In 1.6, a key chapter, Origen accepts the consequences of that position, as he takes his start from biblical teaching on the end of the world, when everything will be subject to God. In this context (1.6.1) he proposes the theory of an apocatastasis, according to which God in his goodness will allow the salvation of all creatures.

But, on the basis of the principle widely accepted in Greek philosophy that the end corresponds to the beginning, we must suppose an initial state in which all creatures were in a condition of blessedness through participation in God. But because all were endowed with free will, some of them ignored that participation and succumbed to an inertia that dragged them downward; then the divine justice and providence assigned to all of them a condition in keeping with their behavior. Those who remained in their initial state, or even advanced in their participation in God, were assigned to the several orders of angels. Those who had fallen, but not irremediably, were subjected to the angels who would lead them to acquire again their original blessed condition; these are human beings. Those who sinned in a particularly unworthy way became the devil and his angels, but even for them a future return to goodness is not excluded, because this part of creation could not be allowed to be an exception to the final harmony. Finally Origen says that at the end of the world the form of temporal realities will pass away (1 Cor 7:31); material substance, however, will not be destroyed, but will be transformed.

As noted above, from 1.7 to 2.3 Origen goes more fully into some points of this discussion. Thus in 1.7 he describes the stars as rational beings who, on the basis of their behavior, have deserved to be subjected to the futility of creation (Rom 8:20), that is, to serve creation as luminaries until the final deliverance. In 1.8, even the tasks assigned to the angels depend on their merits. Origen then attacks those who allow a diversity of spiritual natures on which the individual's behavior and destiny depend (the Valentinians). He asserts once again that every nature, except that of God, Christ, and the Spirit, is capable of good and evil. This is true of angels, evil spirits, and human souls.

The first three chapters of book 2 deal with the material world, the variety of which corresponds to the variety of the initial movements and falls of spiritual beings. God has created harmony by organizing corporeal matter in a diversity of forms that embody those varied movements. Before and after material substance has served for solid bodies, it provided and will provide all rational beings with a support adapted to their condition of blessedness. Origen thus seems to admit an initial and final, lasting corporeity for rational creatures (2.2). In 2.3 he discusses the various possible destinies of corporeal matter: either the corruptible body will be transformed into an incorruptible body or it will be purified and thinned to the point of disappearing. In this second case, the possibility will remain of its being created anew, so that creatures may be able to sin again. However, Origen rejects the theory of an eternal return of all things, for this contradicts freedom. As for the destiny of the present universe, perhaps the part of it that is subject to corruption will disappear, while the realm of the fixed stars, where the blessed will dwell, will remain (2.3).

In 2.4, as noted earlier, the exposition begins again with God. Against the gnostics and Marcionites, Origen shows from the Scriptures that the God of the Old and New Testaments is one and the same God (2.4), that the just God and the good are one and the same (2.5). His arguments are traditional in second-century controversy. In 2.4 he speaks again of Christ, but this time from the viewpoint of the incarnation and in the content of the theory of the preexistence of souls. Unlike all the other souls that have descended into human bodies, the soul of Christ from the beginning of creation cleaved completely to the wisdom/Logos of God and let itself be wholly permeated by it, with the result that it was able to serve as an intermediary in the union of God with a body that took place in Jesus. Because the soul accepted the Son of God unreservedly into itself, it too, along with the flesh it assumed, is called Son of God. It was by its merits that the soul was given such a role, but its adherence to the Logos was so intense that what originally depended on free will ended by being transformed thereby into nature, just as the iron left in the fire becomes itself fire.

The second exposition on the Spirit (2.7) is, like that on God, more traditional than the first: the same Spirit inspired Moses, the prophets, and the apostles, while today it has made it possible for a large number of believers to gain a spiritual understanding of the Law and the Prophets. Speaking of the Paraclete, Origen expressly takes a position against the Montanists. In 2.8 he discusses the nature of the soul of animals, angels, and human beings: it is a spirit that has cooled from its original heat and thus is found in its present condition. In 2.9 Origen returns to the origin and destiny of souls, this time in controversy with the gnostic doctrine of the distinction of natures, a teaching he attributes, oddly enough, to Marcion; but perhaps he has in mind Marcion's disciples. While the gnostics consider the assignment of various conditions to creatures to be incompatible with the Creator's justice, Origen stresses the point that this assignment is the result of the free choices of these souls.

In 2.10 he discusses the end: he rebuts the gnostic rejection of the resurrection of bodies, but also those "among us" who believe in the resurrection of a body identical with the present body, an attack directed also against the millenarians. He then gives interpretations of the everlasting fire (the remorse that will torment sinners), the outer darkness (privation of the light of reason), and the other punishments mentioned in the Scriptures. He also reasserts the principle that this punishment serves to heal and cleanse souls. In 2.10 he deals in parallel fashion with the promises made to the saints: he again rejects the materialist understanding that characterizes the millenarians. In the heavenly Jerusalem the just will first be instructed on the true meaning of Israel and its institutions and on the true nature of created things. Then, as they leave the earthly paradise and pass through the heavens, they will acquire the knowledge of heavenly things, until at last they contemplate God in the measure granted to creatures.

A third part of the work consists of a quite limited treatment of moral questions (3.1–4) and, first of all, of free will (3.1). This fundamental theme of Greek philosophy, especially in relation to the Stoic claim of the inevitability of fate, was especially important to Origen, since in his controversy with the Valentinians he had made free will a foundation of his theological system. Against those who gave external influences the decisive role in human behavior, Origen insists that the possession of reason/logos implies responsibility for one's own choices, and he backs up this argument with Scripture. He then goes on (3.1.7–14) to give a lengthy exegesis of Exod 4:21 (and 7:3) where God says: "I will harden Pharaoh's heart," a text cited by the gnostics in support of their doctrine of salvation or damnation as controlled by nature. Origen rejects the logic of this doctrine and sets over against it the idea that God drew good from the (free) wicked behavior of Pharaoh.

The remainder of this lengthy chapter (3.1.15–24) examines other passages of Scripture that can create the same kind of difficulty and in particular the comparison of God to a potter who shapes the clay as he wishes, a comparison used later by Paul (Rom 9:18–21). In 3.2 Origen discusses the way in which the evil forces wage war on human beings. To begin with, he says that some temptations come not from those forces but from natural impulses. Moreover, God helps human beings in their struggle against these forces, and while he allows temptations, he also gives the strength to resist them, so that they do not detract from human responsibility.

In 3.2 Origen continues his discussion of the activity of the demonic forces. A subtle interpretation of 1 Cor 2:6 enables him to distinguish between the wisdom of this world and the wisdom of the rulers of this world. He sets a positive value on the former, that is, on the sciences: grammar, poetics, rhetoric, geometry, music, discipline; these enable human beings to know the world but not God or heavenly realities. For their part, the rulers of this world try to instruct human beings in their false philosophies and in their heresies. The end of the chapter is devoted to demoniacal possession. In 3.4 Origen discusses the special question of whether each human being has but a single soul, or both a fleshly soul and a spiritual soul. After studying the relevant passages of the Bible he leaves this question open.

The role of 3.5–6 is unclear. It takes up once more the subject of rational creatures, creation, and the end of the world, which has already been addressed twice in
earlier sections. Perhaps, as Simonetti suggests, the section represents a more precise
statement on these subjects in light of reactions elicited by the first two books, both
within and outside Origen's school.

Another well-defined unit is 4.1–3, which is devoted to Scripture and its interpretation. This subject is very important because in Origen's eyes the Scriptures are the
only way of reaching the knowledge of God that the human condition allows. In 4.1
Origen proves the inspired character of the Scriptures using traditional arguments,
especially the fulfillment of the prophecies in Christ; that the Scriptures are divine is
already evident because so many people have accepted them and braved hatred and
death to do so. In 4.2 he argues for an interpretation that goes beyond the letter, and
he sets down the criteria for such an interpretation; in 4.3 he makes a practical application of the methods by examining passages of Scripture that cannot possibly be
taken literally. We summarized these matters earlier in connection with the commentaries on Scripture. Note also that in 4.3.4 Origen says he does not intend to deprive
the letter of all value: many precepts are evidently to be taken literally, but this does
not exclude a deeper meaning. In short, all of Scripture has a spiritual meaning, but
not all of it has a literal meaning (4.3.5).

Finally, in 4.4 he summarizes some of the major themes of the work, but with a
series of clarifications: the incorporeity and eternity of the generation of the Son from
the Father; rejection of the idea that the entire divinity of the Son was contained by his
body; the Son's assumption of a real soul and not merely a body in the incarnation.
Further clarifications have to do with matter as the substratum of bodies and, finally,
with the immortality of the soul and the meaning of the statement that the human
being is in the image of God.

This all too schematic summary may give an idea of how bold Origen's plan was
in comparison with everything that had been done before. In conclusion, we wish to
emphasize two points. First, Origen intends to be faithful not only to the Scriptures
but to the church. His distinction between beginners, those advancing, and the perfect (*Princ.* 4.2.4) does not result in the elitism of the Christian gnostic that still to
some degree characterizes Clement, who is thereby rendered more explicitly open to
"unorthodox" influences, both external and internal to Christianity. Rather it is accompanied, as we saw in connection with the homilies, by a true pastoral solicitude
that does not accept criticism of the *simpliciores* and their teachers, but endeavors to
lift these people up, as far as possible, to that spiritual understanding which Origen regards as a specific mark of paradise (*Princ.* 2.10).

Second, Origen's intention, in systematic work as in exegetical, is to offer not a
closed, rigid system but an open-ended study, which he urges all to pursue on their
own. We have seen that beginning in the preface to *First Principles,* he distinguishes
between defined and undefined truths. Origen's purpose is to serve the church by promoting penetrating, systematic thought on the latter, but he never tires of repeating
that his is not the final word, and that readers can choose among several possibilities
(e.g., in *Princ.*: 1.6.4; 1.7.1; 2.3.7; 3.4.5). It was only subsequent hardenings of position, provoked in part by dislike and even bad faith, in the context of disagreements
that were in some cases tainted by ecclesiastical politics, that turned Origen into a
"heretic" on the basis of teachings that were rejected only after his time. By contrast,

in many areas he was the first courageously to tackle sensitive subjects, into which only the gnostic theologians had ventured previously in any depth.

BIBLIOGRAPHY

H. Crouzel and M. Simonetti, *Traité des principes* (5 vols.; SC 252, 253, 268, 269, 312; Paris: Cerf, 1978–1984); edition of Greek and Latin texts, introduction, and commentary.

M. Simonetti, *I principi di Origene* (Turin: UTET, 1968); translation with introduction and commentary.

J. R. Lyman, *Christology and Cosmology: Models of Divine Activity in Origen, Eusebius, and Athanasius* (Oxford/New York: Oxford University Press, 1993).

b. Against Celsus

The other major nonexegetical work of Origen is a polemical and apologetical work in eight books, composed toward the end of his life. According to Eusebius (*Hist. eccl.* 6.34; 6.36.1), Origen wrote it during the reign of Philip the Arab and after he had reached the age of 60, therefore between 245 and 249. This date is confirmed by internal markers, such as references to earlier writings and to a historical setting of peace in the church, although the threat of new persecutions does appear on the horizon, especially in connection with the rebellions against Philip that broke out in 248 (see, in particular, *Cels.* 3.15). The text of this apologetic work did not suffer, as did the *First Principles,* due to theological controversies and condemnations; the entire text has been preserved in Greek.

A problem has arisen, however, as a result of divergences between the direct and the indirect traditions. The second is represented, once again, by the *Philocalia,* which contains extracts that amount to about a seventh of the *Against Celsus.* The direct tradition is represented by 18 manuscripts of the entire work and by seven partial copies, all dependent, however, on one among them, Vatican Greek 386 from the thirteenth century. The direct tradition is also represented by a seventh-century papyrus, found at Tura in 1941, containing extracts from the first two books of the work. This latter witness, which gives at least partial access to a text six centuries older than the Vatican Codex, has made it possible to take a step forward in the controversy, ongoing since P. Koetschau's edition (1899), between scholars maintaining the superiority of the direct tradition and those favoring the *Philocalia,* for it has shown that neither of the two can claim an absolute priority.

The stimulus to the composition of the *Against Celsus* came from Ambrose, who, according to Origen's introduction, had asked him to refute the *True Discourse* (*Alēthēs logos*) which Celsus, a philosopher, had written around 177–180 as an attack on Christians. Origen says he does not know the reasons for his friend's request; nor has Neumann's hypothesis been accepted, that Celsus's work acquired a new topicality in the context of a revival of Roman religion in connection with preparations for celebrating the millennium of Rome (247–248). In fact, Celsus's work must not have elicited any strong response; there are no mentions of it independent of Origen. The work is lost and can be reconstructed solely from the *Against Celsus,* almost surely in its entirety, given the very detailed plan in pref. 6 of Origen's refutation, and despite the fact that Origen admits to some omissions.

Origen himself was uncertain of Celsus's identity; he had some information about Celsus the Epicurean who had lived under Hadrian and later (1.8), and he did not know whether his Celsus was the same as the author of books against magic (1.68). The obvious Platonic vein in the *True Discourse* made Origen cautious about any identification (4.54). The author of the books against magicians may have been the friend to whom the satirist Lucian of Samosata (ca. 120–180) dedicated his work *Alexander the False Prophet*, but there is nothing to prove that this friend was the author of the work refuted by Origen. Celsus's ideas seem to be those of an eclectic Middle Platonist. The title remains ambiguous: does he mean discourse, or treatise, that tells the truth? Or true teaching?

There have been several attempts to reconstruct the structure of the *True Discourse* with the help of Origen's refutation; we shall follow that given by M. Borret in the fifth volume of his edition (pp. 33–121), where he distinguishes a preface, three parts, and a conclusion.

The preface of the *True Discourse* (1.1–12 of Origen's work) pointed out the illegal situation of Christians and asked: Is their religion so reasonable as to merit their taking the risk they do? The first part (1.14–2.79) had to do with the origins of Christianity: a very ancient teaching, followed by peoples, cities, and wise men, was supposed to have come from Moses, who won a divine title by imposing on his uncultivated nation of shepherds this teaching in the form of a monotheism that was accompanied by worship of the angels, magic, and the Egyptian practice of circumcision. At this point, Celsus brought on the scene a Jew who criticized the claims of Jesus. Celsus evidently had access to Jewish sources because later anti-Christian Jewish polemics display elements of this criticism of Jesus having to do with his birth, the christological interpretation of the prophecies, and his ministry. Celsus's critique proceeded in the form of a dialogue between the Jew and Jewish Christians, who are rebuked for having apostatized from the religion of their forebears and for wrongly believing that Jesus is the Messiah and the Son of God.

The second part (3.1–5.65) undertook to disqualify Christianity as a religion. Celsus attributed to both Judaism and Christianity the mistake of expecting a savior, and he blamed both for an original sin of rebellion against religious and social order: the Jews originated by separating themselves from the Egyptian community and religion, and the Christians by separating from the community and religion of the Jews. Celsus then criticized the idea of a descent (future for Jews, past for Christians) of a Son of God to earth, for this contradicts the very nature of God by attributing a change to him. Celsus also, always from his viewpoint as a philosopher, mocked the claim of Jews and Christians to be the center of the universe. Nor did he accept the idea of the sending of an angel, and he criticized the angelology, eschatology, and sectarianism of Jews and Christians.

In a third part (6.1–8.71) Celsus compared traditional teachings with those of Jews and Christians in order show the inferiority of the latter on all points. Finally, he branded as sectarianism and intolerance the Christian rejection of altars and images and of the worship of demons and the emperor; these showed an irresponsible political outlook that weakened the authority and power of the state and exposed it to wicked and savage barbarians. In his conclusion (8.72–76) Celsus therefore exhorted

Christians to drop their universalism, to fight for the emperor, and to take part in the government of their native land in order to defend the laws and religion.

Two worlds were clashing in this encounter. Celsus spoke in the name of a philosophical tradition that appealed to reason in order to assert a harmonious universe, but not one for human beings, much less for this or that people or group. He spoke in the name of a primitive wisdom handed down from remotest antiquity; it was not the exclusive prerogative of a single people due to a supposed revelation. He spoke in the name of a religious tradition that claimed to be supported by reason and a sense of balance, and in the name of a political tradition meant to defend the achievements of order and civilization against rebellion and barbarism.

In Judaism and still more in Christianity Celsus saw the reversal of all these values: an origin already tainted by *stasis,* rebellion, and a break with an order and tradition which alone could link people to the primitive wisdom; ignorance, consistent with a lowly social condition; sectarianism, implying the claim to superior knowledge and, therefore, finally, fanaticism and intolerance. While he made fun of such attitudes, Celsus nevertheless ended his work on a positive note: an invitation to work together with the state for the protection of civil society. The end is thus linked in thought with the beginning and the question of the reasonableness of the motives of Christians to face death.

Celsus's objections to Christians were certainly widespread in the educated classes of the population. It has been easy for scholars to hypothesize that Celsus was responding to Justin, and that other Christian apologists were responding directly or indirectly to Celsus's work; this is a matter of ongoing discussion. As for Origen, he does not decline the challenge at any point. He does not simply reject Greek philosophy a priori; rather, beginning in his introduction (book 5), he acknowledges it as having a certain value, but he denies that this value finds expression in Celsus's book. He objects precisely to Celsus's assumption that Christians are an ignorant and simple people, and places himself instead on the same level as his partner in this dialogue by claiming for Christianity the *logos* which Celsus denied to it.

When Celsus urges the acceptance of teaching solely by following reason *(logos)* and a reasonable *(logikos)* leader, Origen answers that even if all human beings were able to devote themselves to philosophy, Christianity would still be the best way to follow, because it is based on a rigorous investigation *(exetasis)* of matters to be believed. But as things are, the best way to help the majority is the one given to the peoples by Jesus, for it allows those who do not reflect on their faith to improve their own lives nonetheless (1.9). In the same context, Celsus refers to Christian groups who reject thought in the name of faith (*"mē exetaze alla pisteuson,"* they say). We know that Clement and Origen must have met with hostility from such groups; all the more courageous, then, was Origen's decision to take up the debate at the philosophical level. Both Celsus and Origen moved with ease among the arguments developed by the various philosophical schools. For Origen, however, the foundation and ultimate norm is the divine revelation contained in the Scriptures.

Celsus allows that barbarians are capable of discovering some teachings, but he maintains that the Greeks are better at laying the foundations of such teachings, assessing their value, and adapting them for practical use. Origen answers that those who pass from philosophy to the gospel are able not only to judge the truth of Christian teachings but also to test their truth by putting them into practice and thereby accomplishing what seemed to be lacking in demonstrations of the Greek type (1.2). He also claims for divine revelation a special kind of demonstration, that of the Spirit and of power (1 Cor 2:4): of the Spirit in the fulfillment of the prophecies, and of power in miracles, "traces" of which remain in those who live according to the will of the Logos. These "traces" are the miracles still being worked among Christians (1.46; 2.8).

This twofold demonstration returns in a four-part form in 3.33: the divinity of Jesus is proved by the churches of those who have received his help, by the prophecies spoken about him, by the cures that take place in his name, and by the knowledge marked by wisdom and reason *(logos)* that is seen in those who endeavor to move beyond simple faith by delving into the Scriptures. So Origen appeals, on the one hand, to the practical demonstration given by the church's life in Christ and by the miracles worked in them, and, on the other, to the now traditional demonstration based on the christological prophecies and to his major theme: the allegorical reading of the Scriptures.

Celsus accepts the allegorization of the pagan myths but rejects that of the biblical texts. In his view biblical allegory cannot be allowed because the texts are nonsensical; it is imposed on more intelligent Christians by the shame they feel toward their sacred texts. He scoffs at the interpretations given in the *Dialogue of Jason and Papiscus,* which Origen for his part does not think ridiculous, although it is meant only for the simple (4.36–52). Origen counters by rejecting pagan allegory, which assigns a value to stories that are absurd, obscene, and corrupting (e.g., 4.48), and he points to characteristics of the biblical text that call for allegorization (e.g., 4.49–50; see above, sec. 2, on the exegetical works) and to allegorical interpretations within the Scriptures themselves, especially in Paul.

In all these lines of argument and in the work as a whole, the center of attention is always the person of Jesus, the divine Logos and Son of God, on whom the prophecies and the history of Israel are focused and whose presence supports the life of the churches and explains the miracles that take place in them. In this work, the rational demonstration of truth and the dignity of Christianity cannot be separated from the practical demonstration given by the life of the Christian communities. Christ is also the point of reference that links the Scriptures, and therefore all of history since the creation of the world, to the present and the future by his action in the church, and so creates a new continuity. He thereby renders meaningless the continuity which Celsus looks for in fidelity to the cultural and religious tradition of the ancient wise men and philosophers and in fidelity to the sociopolitical constitution of the empire. To the concern expressed by Celsus in the last part of his work about the danger of cultural and political disintegration caused by Christianity, Origen gives the now traditional answer that Christians indeed refuse to worship the emperor but they do not refuse to honor him as one given his place by God. Far from leaving him isolated and abandoned, such an attitude, if shared by all, would subject all the barbarians to laws and civilization by converting them to the Logos of God (8.68).

Bibliography

Origène, *Contra Celse* (ed. and trans. M. Borret; 5 vols.; SC 132, 136, 147, 150, 227; Paris: Cerf, 1967–1976); critical text, translation, extensive introduction, and indexes.

Origene, *Contro Celso* (trans. A. Colonna; Turin: UTET, 1971); Italian translation, introduction, and notes.

H. J. Blumenthal and R. A. Markus, eds., *Neoplatonism and Early Christian
Thought: Essays in Honour of A. H. Armstrong* (London: Variorum, 1981).

c. On Prayer

The treatise *On Prayer* was written in answer to a letter from Ambrose and
Tatiana, who may have been his sister (2.2). Origen cites a passage from this letter
(5.6) containing two questions: If God knows the future—and he must—is prayer not
useless? If God does not change what has been decreed, is prayer not useless? Internal
evidence allows the work to be dated to 234–235 (P. Nautin); it has been transmitted
by a Cambridge manuscript (14th c.), and in part by a Paris manuscript (15th c.).

After an introduction on the difficulty of the subject, which can be overcome
with the grace of God (1.2), the treatise can be divided into two sections, plus a short
appendix. The first part (chs. 3–17) begins with some points of vocabulary: it distinguishes, in the Greek Bible, between *euchē*, and *proseuchē*. The former sometimes
means "vow," a promise to give something in return if one receives a favor from God,
and sometimes has the general meaning of "prayer"; the latter has the same two
meanings. The text then answers objections to the usefulness of prayer; we have already referred to these.

Returning to the fundamental doctrine of free will (see *Princ.* 3), Origen remarks
that the decrees of God for the future of human beings, including the hearing of
their prayers, are only the consequences of their free choices, which God has as foreknowledge. Prayer remains necessary but it has meaning only if it is part of a pure life,
for this places human beings in the presence of God and requires a distancing from
passions and from the things of the present world. By means of this purity, the one
praying also participates in the prayer of the Logos of God, the intercessor with the
Father; nor is he the only one who prays together with those who pray worthily, for so
too do the angels and the souls of the deceased.

On the basis of 1 Tim 2:1, Origen distinguishes, and illustrates with examples
from the Bible, four kinds of prayer: entreaty *(deēsis)*, glorification *(proseuchē)*, confi-
dent petition *(enteuxis)*, and thanksgiving *(eucharistia)*. Characteristic of his subordinationist views is Origen's refusal to address *proseuche* to any begotten *(gennētos)*
being, even Christ; in the Our Father Jesus taught us to pray *(proseuchesthai)* not to
himself but to the Father. We must therefore not pray to Christ, even by associating
him with the Father, but rather pray together with Christ to the Father.

The second part of the treatise on prayer (chs. 18–30) is the first systematic commentary on the Our Father. Especially interesting in this context is the discussion of
the petition for *epiousios* bread (ch. 27); in order to explain this word, unknown elsewhere in Greek and, according to Origen, coined by the evangelists, he falls back on its
similarity to *periousios* and interprets *epiousios* bread as "that which is transformed
into one's substance." Since we must not think that Jesus is teaching us to ask for so
earthly and limited a thing as material bread, we must conclude that the petition has
to do with the heavenly bread, the Word of God, who, akin as he is to the substance of
the human being, brings the soul health, good habits, and strength, and communi-
cates immortality to the one who eats it. Chapters 31–33 are a kind of appendix on the

posture to be observed in prayer, the places of prayer, praying toward the East (where Christ, the true Light, arises), and on the parts of prayer.

Origen's treatise with its vibrant spirituality exerted a vast influence. He emphasizes the preliminary conditions for prayer: distancing from the passions, reconciliation with one's neighbor, recollection of soul in order to enter with purity into the world of the divine. He profoundly and constantly grounds his teaching in the Bible. The systematic character of a treatise moves from first principles to concrete instructions for actually praying, by way of a fine meditation, point by point, on the fundamental Christian prayer. All this and more explain the success of the treatise, beginning with the earliest monastic rules and reaching forward to the Christian spirituality of our day, in which it continues to be translated and read at various levels.

BIBLIOGRAPHY

Origenes Werke (vol. II; ed. and trans. P. Koetschau; GCS 3; Leipzig: Hinrichs, 1899), 297–403; critical edition.

Origene, *La preghiera* (ed. and trans. G. Dal Ton; Milan: Mondadore, 1984).

Origen, *Prayer; Exhortation to Martyrdom* (trans. J. J. O'Meara; ACW 19; Westminster, Md.: Newman, 1954).

d. Exhortation to Martyrdom

According to Eusebius (*Hist. eccl.* 6.2.6), during the persecution of Septimius Severus in 202, the youthful Origen wrote his imprisoned father a letter exhorting him to martyrdom and begging him not to change his mind out of concern for his family. Whatever the reliability of this claim, over thirty years later Origen did write an *Exhortation to Martyrdom* for his friend Ambrose, a deacon, and Protoctetus, a priest, both of whom had been arrested in 235 at the beginning of the persecution of Maximinus Thrax. *Exhortation to Martyrdom* is the title in three manuscripts; Pamphilus, Eusebius, and Jerome call it simply *On Martyrdom*.

The treatise begins by applying the words of Isaiah 28:9–11 (LXX) to the situation of the two addressees: "affliction upon affliction," but also "hope upon hope" if they persevere in their desire to reach God. As God ordered Abraham to leave his country, so God can order each person to leave this earth by confessing him and dying for the faith. If the person refuses, he falls into worse sins: idolatry and apostasy. There follows the exhortation proper to confess the faith and to carry the cross after Jesus for the sake of the great reward that is promised. Angels and men will be present to judge the behavior of the martyr; his acquaintances will perhaps mock and insult him, but he will be all the more blessed for having resisted amid evils. The example is then given of Eleazar and of the seven martyred brothers in 2 Maccabees.

Martyrdom is the cup of salvation of which the Psalm speaks (116:13); it is the baptism in blood that is necessary for the forgiveness of sins committed after baptism in water. It was not the crowds that Jesus exhorted to martyrdom, but his disciples, whom he calls friends: whoever confesses him, he will confess before the Father, but whoever denies him will be denied by the Son, and the Father as well. Origen also warns against supposing it a matter of indifference to offer sacrifice or to invoke the names of the gods on the grounds that these names are mere signs without connection to that which they designate. No: the odors from sacrifices nourish the demons. As for the names, even if the matter is quite murky, they must have some natural connection with the beings designated, as shown by the fact that in theurgy the demons are compelled to present themselves to the one who invokes their names. The treatise ends with concluding exhortations and the wish that the addressees may despise death, because with martyrdom imminent they already enjoy knowledge of the divine mysteries.

This work comes at an ideal point in Origen's life, halfway between the martyrdom of his father and his own martyrdom under Decius. It is part of a literary tradition of exhortations to martyrdom that begins, as far as we know, with Tertullian's work *To the Martyrs* (perhaps in 202) and continues with Cyprian's *To Fortunatus* (250 or 256) and his letters 6, 10, and 76. A great abundance of citations from the Bible, in good measure those already chosen by Origen, marks the *To Fortunatus,* which is little more than a collection of scriptural passages. Origen's work, which is not rhetorical like Tertullian's, is also of sociological interest for its effort to "construct," for a rich and influential man like Ambrose, who was probably also involved in public life, an understanding of his own martyrdom. Ambrose is to see that the loss of status in the eyes of his fellow citizens (see chs. 19, 36) will be offset by the glory deriving from a testimony, given in the presence of angels and men, that bases the true value of the person on his fidelity to God (ch. 18).

BIBLIOGRAPHY

Origenes Werke (vol. I; ed. and trans. P. Koetschau; GCS 2; Leipzig: Hinrichs, 1899), 3–47; critical edition.

Origene, *Esortazione al martirio* (ed. and trans. C. Noce; Rome: Pontifica Universitas Urbanianum, 1985); translation, introduction, and notes.

e. Dialogue with Heraclides

A papyrus codex (late 6th or early 7th c.) found at Tura in 1941, and now kept in Cairo, has given us the minutes of a discussion between Origen and Bishop Heraclides. We noted earlier that because of his competence as a theologian Origen was sometimes called on to question bishops whose orthodoxy was in doubt. This happened in the case of Beryllus of Bostra in Arabia, between 238 and 244, after a first meeting of bishops called to interrogate him had proved inconclusive (Eusebius, *Hist. eccl.* 6.33.2–3). Eusebius tells us that the records of the meeting with Beryllus existed in his time, but they have not come down to us. All the more interesting, then, is this single record now available for study.

The place and date of the interview are uncertain; it was conducted at the church of Heraclides, which was probably in Arabia, because the subjects of the discussion, notably the identity of soul and blood, are similar to subjects that, according to Eusebius (*Hist. eccl.* 6.37), Origen had to take up with "Arabs" on another occasion. Since that particular problem was being discussed between 244 and 249, the interrogation of Heraclides must have taken place during that period. P. Nautin suggests 239–244, but this hypothesis depends on another, rather weak one: that there was a disagreement between Origen and the bishops of Caesarea and Jerusalem after 244.

In a first stage, the bishops present at the interview had set forth their views as they challenged the faith of Heraclides; this stage was not recorded. Heraclides had then presented his own confession of faith, and with this the record begins. Questions by Origen and responses by the bishop follow, and there is an intervention by Maximus, perhaps one of the bishops present, whom Origen consults. Origen then invites those present to raise other questions; one of them, Dionysius, poses the problem of the identification of the soul with the blood, to which Origen gives an answer. Finally, some words of information addressed by Bishop Demetrius to Bishop Philip, who has just come in, lead to clarification by Origen on the immortality of the soul.

The error attributed to Heraclides seems to be that in order to safeguard the unity of God, he tends to play down the divinity of the Son. Origen says that he is not ready to yield to the opinion of those who "for the sake of an illusory monarchy" (p. 4) remove the Son from the Father and thus potentially do away with the Father himself, since if he has no son, he is not a father. Neither is he ready to accept the view that denies the divinity of Christ. He accepts the expression "two gods" in order to safeguard both the distinction of the Son from the Father and the divinity of the Son; and by way of a logical series of questions he brings Heraclides to accept that formula, although the bishop wants to clarify it by adding "the power *(dynamis)* is one" (p. 2).

Origen adds a further clarification regarding the *prosphora*, meaning, doubtless, the offering of the Mass: this, he says, must always be made to almighty God through Jesus Christ, for he, through his divinity, is the one who offers *(prosphorus)* to the Father. Since this clarification occurs in a context referring to disorders in the community, it is possible, as Scherer thinks, that the theological question arose out of a problem posed by liturgical practice.

To Maximus's question on the manner of the resurrection Origen replies by distinguishing in Christ the body that went down to death in the tomb, the soul that descended to the lower world, and the spirit that Jesus entrusted to his Father before dying. Body and soul are reunited in the resurrection, but in the ascension Jesus goes up to recover his spirit.

To the question of Dionysius, whether the soul is identical with the blood as Lev 17:11 would suggest, Origen answers by distinguishing the outward self, which is created out of earth (Gen 2:7), and the interior self, which is created in the image of God (1:26–27). The distinction between two creations, which had already been made in Philo, became dear to the gnostics; however, unlike the gnostics, Origen connects it with Paul's teaching on the interior self (Rom 7:22; 2 Cor 4:16). The members of the one creation are matched by an equal number of members of the other, and the soul exercises the same function in the interior self that the blood exercises in the outward self. As for the immortality of the soul: on the one hand, the soul can be said to be mortal insofar as it participates either in the death of sin, which makes a person alive for God (Rom 6:2), or in the death with regard to God, into which the sinner falls (Ezek 18:4); on the other hand, it is immortal according to the usual understanding of death as separation of soul from body.

While this text is of limited theological interest, it is nevertheless a valuable witness to Origen's concerns and method in a context in which so many theological questions were still poorly posed and caused difficulties for bishops. Thanks to his exceptional knowledge and profound meditation on the Scriptures, Origen managed to disentangle questions through patient and prudent combinations of texts and their exegesis. His results may not seem acceptable today, but that does not detract from the rigor with which he tackled the questions. Origen emerges from this stenographic report with an unmatched spontaneity as a man ready for dialogue and study in the service of the church.

BIBLIOGRAPHY

J. Scherer, *Entretien d'Origène avec Héraclide* (SC 67; Paris: Cerf, 1960).

Origen, *Treatise on the Passover; and, Dialogue of Origen with Heraclides and His Fellow Bishops on the Father, the Son, and the Soul* (trans. and annotated R. J. Daly; ACW 54; New York: Paulist, 1992).

f. Passover   *shows multiplicity of interpretations*

The manuscript containing the *Dialogue with Heraclides* has also yielded two previously unknown treatises on Passover, which are numbered 1 and 2 in the manuscript. As we saw earlier, in his list of Origen's works Eusebius mentions, after the writings on the book of Judges, eight homilies on Passover. This was probably a collection of eight different writings, two of which were discovered at Tura. The latter are not actually homilies, as can be seen from their formal characteristics, especially the fact that the biblical text is found not only at the beginning, as in homilies, but is divided into sections, which are commented on one by one, as in the exegetical works. Some fragments of the first treatise were already known from catenas and from Procopius of Gaza.

The first treatise begins by announcing an interpretation of Passover *kata lexin* "according to the letter"; it will be, in fact, an exegesis of Exod 12:1–11. This does not mean that Origen is renouncing allegorical exegesis, in which on the contrary he engages extensively. The words are intended either to refer to a detailed exegesis or in the sense that the literal interpretation is to serve as the basis. First, however, Origen clarifies the meaning of the word *Pascha*, rejecting the widespread tracing of the word to the Greek *paschō*, "suffer," in favor of the etymology accepted in the Jewish world, "passage" (from the root *psh*). That the word applies also to Christians is clear from 1 Cor 5:7–8, according to which Christ, our Passover, has been sacrificed. Therefore what was accomplished for the Hebrews at their coming out of Egypt is being accomplished today for believers in Christ.

At this point the detailed exegesis begins. In it, as usual, Origen takes advantage of the least details in the text in order to extract a spiritual meaning. For example, in the sentence "This month is for you the beginning of months, it is first for you among the months of the year" (Exod 12:2) he emphasizes the "for you," that is, for Moses and Aaron, who are figures of those who renounce the present world. "Beginning" and "first" both refer to Christ, who is "first" inasmuch as he is the firstborn of creation and "beginning" inasmuch as he is the divine Wisdom. As for the properly christological typology of the Passover, Origen allows that the Passover, as a saving event, is a type of Christ but not of his passion, because the immolation of the Passover lamb was the work of just persons, whereas the immolation of Christ was the work of transgressors of the law. Origen thus distances himself from the Quartodeciman tendency to exploit the themes of the passion, and instead points the way to the spiritual meaning: the Passover that is prefigured is the intelligible Passover that believers celebrate in and by their lives.

In the remainder of the treatise Origen proceeds along the same lines by applying the details of the normative Passover to the life of Christians. For example, if the lamb is chosen on the tenth day of the month but is not immolated until the fourteenth, five days later, it means that whose who are converted to Christ/the Lamb cannot eat him and depart from Egypt until Christ has first acted on their five senses, opening the eyes and ears of the heart, causing them to smell their own fragrance, to taste their own goodness, and to touch the Logos (1 John 1:1; pp. 17–19). An ecclesiological concern is visible in the exegesis of Exod 12:9, which is understood to mean that each person touches a specific part of the lamb. Origen connects this motif with that of the body of Christ (1 Cor 12:20–21), showing that participation in Christ is common to all but occurs in various ways according to individual persons. The treatise ends abruptly halfway through the exegesis of Exod 12:11. There are good reasons for thinking, with Sgherri, that the work has reached us in a mutilated form.

The second and shorter treatise is again an exegesis of a part of Exod 12:1–11, but also of other verses from the same chapter. The structure, however, is no longer the systematic kind based on the sequence of lemma and commentary. According to Nautin, this second treatise is a continuation of the first; according to others, on better grounds, it is an independent treatise. Indeed, it makes no reference of any kind to the first. It has its own introduction, which announces a spiritual interpretation, although this is not to be understood as contrary to the literal interpretation of the first treatise, which practiced chiefly a spiritual exegesis. Furthermore, while the first treatise rejected the typology of the immolation, the second adopts and develops it (pp. 42–44); and 1 Cor 5:7–8, central in the first treatise, is absent from the second.

While the first treatise interprets *pascha* as a *diabasis* (crossing over; passage), the second ignores this interpretation and concentrates instead on the idea of *hyperbasis*, the "passing beyond" of Christ, who ascends to heaven by stepping over the barriers set up by God as a result of Adam's disobedience (pp. 47–48) and the "passing beyond" of those who, by sharing in the paschal mystery, can be delivered from Egypt, that is, can activate a "conversion" from this world "that is passing away" (*peratikos*, in the obvious sense of transient) to the eternity of the Father (p. 45).

Stylistically, too, the second treatise differs greatly from the first: it is more arid, more scholastic, and sometimes obscure. Sgherri makes known his puzzlement with the authenticity of the work and gives reasons for it, but cannot decide against it. The question remains open. Nautin gives arguments for a date between the years 235 and 248, with a preference for ca. 245. If the two works are to be separated, the pointers are valid only for the first, while the second is left floating. Sgherri is of the opinion that this is a very late work, possibly composed after Origen's imprisonment during the persecution of Decius.

Bibliography

Origéne, *Sur la Pâque: Traité inédit* (ed. O. Guérard and P. Nautin; Paris: Beauchesne, 1979); first critical edition, with translation and extensive introductory study.

Origene, *Sulla Pasqua: Il papiro di Tura* (ed. and trans. G. Sgherri; Milan: Paoline, 1989); translation, introduction, and commentary.

Origen, *Treatise on the Passover;* and, *Dialogue of Origen with Heraclides and His Fellow Bishops on the Father, the Son, and the Soul* (trans. and annotated R. J. Daly; ACW 54; New York: Paulist, 1992).

g. Lost Treatises

Eusebius (*Hist. eccl.* 6.24.2) mentions two books titled *On the Resurrection.* Jerome lists "two books *On the Resurrection* and another two dialogues *On the Resurrection,*" and in another work speaks of four books on the resurrection (*Jo. Hier.* 25). According to Nautin, the "two . . . and another two" refer to distinct works, and Jerome's way of speaking of them indicates that the first two books were also in dialogue form. He suggests that the second two be identified with the dialogue with Heraclides and with the *De recta in Deum fide* of Adamantius, which was wrongly attributed to Origen. Of Origen's work four fragments have survived in Pamphilus's *Defense,* others in Methodius's *On the Resurrection,* and one in Theophilus of Alexandria (Jerome, *Epist.* 92.4). A reference to this work in *First Principles* (2.10.1) allows us to date it to the Alexandrian period, perhaps around 229. Origen accepted the resurrection of the body, but not of a body identical with that of the preceding life.

Of the treatise on natures there remains only a citation by Victor of Capua from the third book, on the wicked dispositions of Cain (Gen 4:7). This passage and its title show that the work must have been a polemic against the gnostic doctrine that salvation and damnation are due to natures.

Eusebius (*Hist. eccl.* 6.24.3) and Jerome speak of ten books of *Miscellanies (Stromata),* composed, according to Eusebius, in Alexandria. According to Jerome, who had read this work, Origen compared the Scriptures with texts of the philosophers and derived confirmation of Christian teachings from Plato, Aristotle, Numenius, and Cornutus (*Epist.* 70.4). A few fragments remain in the scholia of Codex Lavra 184, in catenas, and in Jerome. According to Nautin, it was from the *Miscellanies,* and not from the treatise on the resurrection, that Jerome took the reflections of Origen on the resurrection, which he reproduces in his *Against John of Jerusalem* 25–26.

h. Letters

Eusebius says that he found and collected in bundles over a hundred letters of Origen (*Hist. eccl.* 6.36.3). Jerome mentions one collection in nine books and another in two. For some letters we have only references in Eusebius and Jerome; among these are letters to Fabian, Bishop of Rome, and to other bishops about his own orthodoxy. In another letter, a passage of which Eusebius cites (*Hist. eccl.* 6.19.12–14), Origen defends himself against those who object to his interest in Greek culture. Here, in greater detail, are three other letters.

Rufinus of Aquileia (*Adult. libr. Orig.* 7) and Jerome (*Ruf.* 2.18) cite extensive passages from a letter to friends in Alexandria; here Origen protests against a bishop who claims to have been offended by him and who at the same time rebukes him for saying that the devil will be saved. Origen recalls the example of the reprimands given by the prophets to the leaders of the people, but asserts that, on the other hand, he wants to leave to God the task of rebuking those who are unwilling to accept the humble rebukes of their neighbor.

He then denies that he said the devil would be saved, and says that his teaching has been distorted, but this ought not be surprising since it has happened to him twice before. On one occasion, a heretic whom he had refuted in a public debate changed the minutes and then circulated them under Origen's name. On another occasion, a heretic who had not dared open his mouth against him in Ephesus composed and circulated in Antioch a completely false dialogue until Origen came to the city and unmasked the man. One of these dialogues, doubtless the first, is to be identified as Jerome suggests with a *Dialogue with Candidus,* a Valentinian, on two subjects: the generation of the Son, and the salvation of the devil. As for the bishop, Nautin has shown that the man in question must have been Heraclas, a former student and then fellow worker of Origen, who succeeded Demetrius in the see of Alexandria in 233.

The thirteenth chapter of the *Philocalia* contains a letter of Origen to someone named Gregory, who was studying law and philosophy. Origen exhorts him to take from Greek philosophy whatever can serve him as preparation for Christianity, and from the sciences those ideas useful for knowledge of the Scriptures; in this way he will follow the example of the Israelites, who took away with them from Egypt the utensils and precious cloths needed for making the furnishings of their worship. But other biblical examples warn of the dangers of going down into Egypt, for this can lead to idolatry; Origen therefore urges his addressee to devote himself to the Scriptures and prayer.

Eusebius (*Hist. eccl.* 6.30) identifies the addressee as Gregory the Wonderworker, a pupil of Origen in Palestine and author of the address of thanksgiving mentioned earlier. Nautin, however, rejects this identification, which had previously been generally accepted, because the references to the Bible seem to apply to a Palestinian who has come to study in Alexandria, and such a course of action is not attested for Gregory. In addition, Origen seems to exhort his addressee to take up the study of theology, and this does not fit in easily with the years of study that the author of the thanksgiving address has already spent with Origen. If the addressee is Gregory the Wonderworker, Origen could not have written to him before he came to study with Origen, because he did not know him at that time. Therefore doubts remain about the identity of the addressee.

A catena on the book of Daniel, found in two manuscripts of the tenth and eleventh centuries presently in the Vatican Library, and in others deriving from the earlier of those two, has preserved a letter of Julius Africanus (see ch. 16, sec. 2) to Origen, and Origen's reply.

In one of his discussions Origen had referred to the story of Susanna, one of the texts added to the Greek translation of Daniel, at the beginning or at the end depending on the version. This surprised his friend, who objected that the story was not authentic, as is demonstrated by several arguments: the manner of Daniel's prophesying, here by direct inspiration, but elsewhere by dreams and visions; the ridiculous way in which Daniel effects his refutation; plays on words which show that the story had not been translated from Hebrew; the historical improbabilities in depicting the conditions of life of the Jews in exile; the citation from Exod 23:7, for no prophet cites another; and the difference in style from the rest of the book.

In his answer, Origen challenges the principle which Africanus presupposes, that is, that we are to use only Scriptures found in the Hebrew. He cites, besides the additions in Greek Daniel, examples of additions and omissions in Job, Jeremiah, Genesis, and Exodus, and concludes that it is right to preserve the texts that Providence caused to be transmitted in other languages, instead of having to go and beg the Jews for "uncorrupted" texts. As for Origen himself, his work in biblical philology is meant to facilitate controversy with Jews and to keep them from mocking Christians as people ignorant of the authentic texts.

Turning then to the story of Susanna in particular, Origen maintains that the plays on words are possible in Hebrew as well, and that learned Jews whom he has consulted accept the story of Susanna and even know of midrashic traditions concerning it which identify the two elders as the false prophets Zedekiah and Ahab in Jer 29 (LXX 36):22–23. If the story is missing from the Hebrew Scriptures, it is because the Jewish scholars removed all passages containing accusations against elders, leaders, and judges, and especially those on the persecution of the prophets, some of which have been preserved in apocryphal works, as is the case with the martyrdom of Isaiah, and to which the New Testament often refers. Origen then takes up the other arguments of Africanus: like Jacob, Daniel could prophesy either as the result of dreams or by direct inspiration. The other arguments seem to him less serious: the judgment of Solomon (1 Kgs 3:16–28) is no less like comedy than the judgment of Daniel, plays on Greek words can skillfully render similar plays on words in a Hebrew original, other books of the Bible show that the way of life of exiled Jews as described in Daniel is not improbable, and one biblical writer frequently uses the expressions of another. Finally, Origen denies the difference in style, but without giving reasons.

Origen writes from Nicomedia (21) where he is staying for a short time with Ambrose and his family (24); the probable date is around 248. His opinion that the story of Susanna was originally part of the Hebrew book of Daniel is, of course, erroneous. His claim that the story was accepted by Jewish rabbis probably reflects a personal interpretation by the wise men whom he consulted and who in midrash fashion identified the two elders with the two false prophets in Jeremiah who were roasted to death by the king of Babylon because, according to the haggada that is also attested elsewhere, they had seduced the wives of other men. The idea of the suppression from the Scriptures of passages embarrassing to the Jews is pure hypothesis on Origen's part. It has its place in the broad debate over the integrity and trustworthiness of the Hebrew Bible and its Greek translations, already attested in Justin (*Dial.* 72.1–73.1), which claims that the Jews had removed some christological prophecies from the Scriptures. Nor are the considerations on possible plays on Hebrew words convincing.

Despite these several points, however, the correspondence with Julius Africanus shows on the part of both writers a high level of competence in biblical philology and an ability to discuss the text of the Scriptures that is superior to anything earlier Christians could have produced.

Bibliography

P. Nautin, *Origène: Sa vie et son oeuvre* (Paris: Beauchesne, 1977), 155–82.

H. Crouzel, *Grégoire le Thaumaturge: Remerciement à Origène, suivi de la lettre d'Origène à Grégoire* (SC 148; Paris: Cerf, 1969).

Origène, *Sur les Écritures: Philocalie, 1–20* (ed. and trans. M. Harl; SC 302; Paris: Cerf, 1983).

Origène, *La Lettre à Africanus sur l'histoire de Suzanne* (ed. and trans. N. de Lange; SC 302; Paris: Cerf, 1983).

i. Philocalia

Finally, we will briefly refer to a work already cited several times, the *Philocalia.* This is an anthology of texts of Origen, among which are inserted a passage from the Pseudo-Clementine *Recognitions* and one from Methodius of Olympus. The texts, arranged in twenty-seven chapters, were traditionally thought to have been chosen by Gregory Nazianzus and Basil of Caesarea, a view which M. Harl has challenged with solid arguments. The work is preceded by a letter of Gregory Nazianzus that accompanies it as a gift to a bishop; it seems prudent, nonetheless, to describe the editors simply as "philocalists," even though the work certainly has links with the world of the Cappadocians. The motive that produced the work, according to Harl, is not so much a defense of Origen or a defense of Christianity, as the need of a basic tool for using the Scriptures in the theological debates of the second half of the fourth century. The influence that Origen had on that scene as a philologist, controversialist, and pastor was undoubtedly the determining factor. In the present setting, these few points suffice.

Bibliography

Origen, *The Philocalia of Origen* (rev. and ed. J. A. Robinson; Cambridge: Cambridge University Press, 1893).

Origène, *Sur les Écritures: Philocalie 1–20* (ed. and trans. M. Harl; SC 148; Paris: Cerf, 1969); contains an important introduction on the origins of the *Philocalia* and on Origen's hermeneutics.

———, *Sur le libre arbitre: Philocalie 21–27* (ed. and trans. E. Junod; SC 226; Paris: Cerf, 1976).

Chapter 16

OTHER GREEK WRITERS OF THE THIRD CENTURY

The work of Origen, far greater in its extent, depth, and organization than anything earlier Christians had produced, was to signal the course of theological debate in coming centuries. Criticism of Origen's theology began, as we saw, even during his lifetime. After his death, opposition continued and increased, although during the period with which we are concerned here, it was still far removed from the violent tensions of the post-Nicene period. Opposition was less strong in Alexandria, where it took form especially in Peter, but sharper elsewhere, especially in Methodius. The first teachings of Origen on which the critics focused, largely due to misunderstanding, were the eternity of creation, the preexistence of souls, the conception of the risen body, and the final apocatastasis. Origen had been accused of maintaining the salvation of the devil as early as the time when he left Alexandria for Caesarea. Pamphilus's *Defense of Origen* was written in response to the first wave of objections leveled at Origen's work after his death.

The Arian crisis was completely in the line of the Origenist tradition, since it radicalized the subordinationist tendency present in Origen. The crisis made it urgent to define the relationship between Father and Son, especially in view of the reaction of westerners, who defended the oneness of God in forms that tended toward monarchianism. The urgency was all the greater inasmuch as the debate was for a long time conditioned by misunderstanding of the word *hypostasis,* which easterners used to distinguish between the divine "persons," whereas westerners understood it in the general sense of divine substance, and therefore saw the distinction of hypostases in God as likely to lead to ditheism.

BIBLIOGRAPHY

E. Prinzivalli, "Per un'indagine sull'esegesi del pensiero origeniano nel IV secolo," *ASE* 11 (1994), is concerned to a great extent with the writers discussed in the present chapter and gives an up-to-date bibliography.

See also ASE 3, 1 (1986), which is devoted to Origenism.

E. A. Clark, *The Origenist Controversy: The Cultural Construction of an Early Christian Debate* (Princeton: Princeton University Press, 1992).

1. Dionysius of Alexandria and Other Alexandrians

Our knowledge of the life and work of Dionysius comes chiefly from Eusebius, who cites extensively from his writings in *Ecclesiastical History* (books 5 and 7) and in *Preparation for the Gospel* (7.19; 14.23–27). Other information comes from Athanasius, Basil, and later sources that are not always reliable. Dionysius was born, probably in the last years of the second century, into a well-to-do pagan family of Alexandria; after converting to Christianity, he became a student under Origen. After Origen left Alexandria and after Bishop Demetrius died and was succeeded by Heraclas, a former student of Origen and joint leader with Origen of the school, Dionysius became the school's director (231–232). It was perhaps during this period that he wrote a treatise *On Nature*, addressed to his son Timothy. Fragments remain in the works of Eusebius (*Praep. ev.* 14.23–27) and John Damascene *(Sacra parallela)*. In this work Dionysius attacks the atomism of Democritus and Epicurus in the name of divine providence, using arguments from everyday life as well as from the constitution of the world and the human body. He shows a degree of philosophical training and refers to Homer, Hesiod, and Plato; he does not hesitate to connect "the wisest of the Greek philosophers, such as Plato, Pythagoras, the Stoics, and Heraclitus" with biblical and Christian teaching.

At the death of Heraclas around 247–248 Dionysius became bishop, while perhaps retaining responsibility for the school. When the persecution of Decius broke out shortly afterward, in October 249, Dionysius took refuge in the countryside with some friends. In a letter to Bishop Fabius of Antioch in 251 (see *Hist. eccl.* 6.41), he described the terrible trials that beset the Christians of Alexandria. In a letter to Germanus dated to 259 (*Hist. eccl.* 6.40) and in a festal letter to Domitius and Didymus (*Hist. eccl.* 7.11.20–25; erroneously assigned by Eusebius to the persecution of Valerian), he tells how after being arrested he managed to flee the city.

When the persecution ended with the death of Decius in 251, the problem arose of the *lapsi,* the Christians who had renounced the faith and were now asking to return to the church. In Rome, Novatian, a presbyter and supporter of a rigorist position, had himself elected antipope against Cornelius (see below, ch. 18, sec. 9). Dionysius wrote many letters in an attempt to end the schism; among them is one to Novatian, which Eusebius transcribes (*Hist. eccl.* 6.45), in which Dionysius says that it is better to suffer martyrdom in order to prevent a schism than in order to avoid sacrificing to idols, and he exhorts Novatian and his party to return to the church.

The Novatianist schism raised a further problem that had already arisen, decades earlier, in the case of the Montanists: if a schismatic wanted to come over to the church, could the baptism he had received among the "heretics" be accepted, with the person then receiving only the imposition of hands, as Stephen, Bishop of Rome (254–257), maintained, or was that baptism to be considered invalid, as maintained by Cyprian of Carthage and Firmilian of Caesarea? The disagreement was moving toward the point of breaking communion. Dionysius, who cared greatly about the unity of the church, endeavored in numerous writings to mediate between the two parties, as in letters to Stephen, to his successor Sixtus II (257–258; at least three letters), to Philemon, a Roman priest, and to Dionysius, a Roman priest who would shortly become pope. Passages from these letters are in Eusebius (*Hist. eccl.* 7.4–9), and fragments in Syriac and Armenian.

Eusebius (*Hist. eccl.* 7.24–25) has passed on extensive extracts from a work of Dionysius in two books, *On the Promises*. This was directed against Nepos, an Egyptian bishop and defender of millenarianism, who based his ideas on the Apocalypse of John and defended a literal interpretation of that book in a work, now lost, with the title *The Allegorist Refuted*. In his second book, Dionysius made a penetrating analysis of the Apocalypse; he refused to agree with those who attributed it to Cerinthus, as did Gaius in Rome (see above, ch. 13, sec. 5). He accepted that John was the real name of the author and that the author could have had a real revelation, and therefore he did not reject the book as such. But by a close comparison with the Gospels and the three Letters of John he showed the differences in approach, language, style, and content, and concluded that the author of the Apocalypse could not have been the author of the other writings. He suggested that the author of the Apocalypse was another John of Asia, perhaps one of the two whose tombs were pointed out in Ephesus. Dionysius's arguments are to a great extent still valid today.

In one of his letters to Sixtus II on baptism (*Hist. eccl.* 7.6), Dionysius had referred to a teaching that had recently emerged at Ptolemais in the Pentapolis and on which he had been called to give an opinion. By his account, that teaching contained errors about the Father, the Son, and the Holy Spirit. There must have been questions there not of Sabellianism in the strict sense, as Eusebius and Athanasius asserted, but of adversaries of the theology of the Logos as developed by Origen, who objected that he unduly separated the Father from the Son. In response to Dionysius's intervention (*Hist. eccl.* 7.26.1), the Libyans turned to Bishop Dionysius of Rome (259–268). The pope, who like all the westerners was exceedingly concerned to maintain the unity of God, answered them with an official letter, a good deal of which has been preserved by Athanasius of Alexandria (*Decr.* 26).

In that letter the pope condemned the Sabellians, who detracted from the divinity of the Son in order to safeguard the oneness of God, but he also condemned those (referring here to the Bishop of Alexandria) who broke up the divinity into three hypostases and even into three gods. At the same time the pope wrote a private letter to Dionysius, who answered with a now lost letter and a treatise in four books, *Refutation and Defense*, fragments of which have come to us through Athanasius, Eusebius, and John Damascene. Correcting some of his earlier incautious expressions, Dionysius confirmed his belief in the coeternity of the Son with the Father, but also insisted that the Trinity, a doctrine which could not be relinquished, indeed implied three hypostases, though not necessarily divided as his adversaries claimed. He therefore endeavored to find a formulation that would combine the indivisible divine monad with the Trinity; to this end he used the concepts of "extension" and "recapitulation." A recent attempt (L. Abramowski) to deny the authenticity of the documentation for this "controversy of the two Dionysiuses," a controversy that reveals the lack of understanding between the eastern and the western theologians, does not seem convincing (see Simonetti's study in the bibliography).

During the persecution of Valerian in 257, Dionysius was exiled to Cephro. He tells of this in his letter to Germanus, of which Eusebius gives sections (*Hist. eccl.* 6.40; 7.11.1–19). From there he kept in touch with his communities by means of letters and, in particular, the festal letters, which, as far as we know, he was the first to write.

These were letters in which the bishops of Alexandria made known the date of Easter and of the beginning of Lent and took up specific questions. In the festal letter of 262, which was addressed to Hermammone, Dionysius praised the government of Valerian's successor, Gallienus, who had recently rid himself of Macrianus the usurper. This was after Dionysius's return to Alexandria after the death of Valerian. Fragments of letters from his last years show the dejection caused him by the civil strife that was staining Alexandria with blood, and by the plague that devastated the city. He died in 264–265. He has also left a letter to Basilides, a bishop of the Pentapolis, which is preserved in the collections of ecclesiastical canons, and in which he compared and interpreted what is said in the Gospels about the resurrection of Jesus, for the purpose of determining when the pre-Easter fast should end. Other, exegetical fragments contained in catenas, among them some on the beginning of Ecclesiastes, are of doubtful authenticity.

Let us here recall Theognostus, successor to Dionysius as director of the school of Alexandria (between 260 and about 280), of whom we are informed by Photius. Theognostus wrote a work in seven books with the title *Hypotyposes,* in which he supposedly claimed that the Son was a created being but was placed at the head of all rational creatures. According to Photius, Theognostus remained faithful to the teaching and spirit of Origen. If we may judge by the fragments, Theognostus indeed emphasized the derivation of the substance *(ousia)* of the Son from that of the Father, and asserted that the Son was not created from nothing.

Theognostus's successor was Pierius, mentioned by Eusebius (*Hist. eccl.* 7.32.27) and Jerome (*Vir. ill.* 76). Jerome says that Pierius was known as Origen the Younger, and that after the persecution of Diocletian he spent the rest of his life in Rome. He died after 309. Jerome mentions a homily of his, *On the Prophet Hosea,* which was delivered at an Easter vigil; Photius (*Lex.* 119) gives the homily the name *On Easter and on the Prophet Hosea;* Philip of Side gives it the title *On the Beginning of Hosea.* Philip also mentions three other works: *On the Gospel of Luke* (also mentioned by Photius); *On the Mother of God;* and *On the Life of St. Pamphilus.* Some fragments of Pierius's writings have survived.

Some fragments also remain, some of them probably spurious, of many writings of Peter of Alexandria, bishop there from 300 to 311. In a treatise *On the Divinity* he insisted that Christ did not abandon his divinity when he became a man. In another work, *On the Lord's Coming,* he stressed the point that Christ was God by nature and a human being by nature. In a work *On the Soul* he rejected Origen's teaching on the preexistence of souls on the grounds that it was derived from Greek philosophy and alien to Christianity. Fourteen canons of Peter on penance have survived in a work also known as *Canonical Letter,* which derived from a festal letter of 306: the canons have to do with the penances to be imposed on the various categories of persons who apostatized during persecution. Peter is also a witness to the way in which criticisms of Origen became increasingly specific in the Alexandrian world.

BIBLIOGRAPHY

Dionysius of Alexandria, *The Letters and Other Remains of Dionysius of Alexandria* (ed. C. L. Feltoe; Cambridge: Cambridge University Press/New York: Macmillan, 1904); edition of the fragments.

Dionysius von Alexandrien, *Das erhaltene Werk* (ed. and trans. W. A. Bienert;
   Stuttgart; Hiersemann, 1972); translation of the fragments with introduction and notes.

Studies

W. A. Bienert, *Dionysius von Alexandrien: Zur Frage des Origenismus im vierten
   Jahrhundert* (New York: de Gruyter, 1978).
M. Simonetti, "Aspetti della cristologia del III secolo: Dionigi di Alessandria"
   (1989); repr., in *Studi sulla cristologia del II e III secolo* (Rome: Augustini-
   anum, 1993), 273–97; many studies in this last-named work are of primary
   importance for the questions raised in the present chapter.
T. Finan and V. Twomey, eds., *Scriptural Intrepretation in the Fathers: Letter and
   Spirit* (Blackrock, Co. Dobulin/Portland, Oreg.: Four Courts, 1995).

2. Gregory the Wonderworker and Other Writers of Palestine and Syria

The traditional reconstruction of Gregory's youthful years depends on his identification as the author of the *Address of Gratitude to Origen,* an identification based not
only on the attribution of the work to him in the manuscripts but also and above all
on Eusebius (*Hist. eccl.* 6.30), who says that among the most illustrious of Origen's
students in Caesarea, he himself knew "Theodore, who was the Gregory famous
among the bishops of our time, and his brother Athenodorus." But P. Nautin has
raised important objections to this identification and has concluded that Eusebius
knew the *Address* under the name of a Theodore who was a disciple of Origen for
eight years (*Orat. paneg.* 3), not for five as Eusebius claims. Eusebius arbitrarily identified this man with Gregory the Wonderworker, whom the adolescent Eusebius had
met, solely on the basis of the fact that both men had studied law. Gregory, then (according to Nautin), was never a student of Origen, and Origen's letter was addressed
to a different Gregory (see above, ch. 15, sec. 4h).

A balanced view that has recently been proposed by M. Simonetti values Nautin's
criticisms but leaves open the possibility that Eusebius really did know that Gregory
the Wonderworker studied under Origen. Simonetti therefore thinks that the attribution of the *Address* to Gregory the Wonderworker is possible, but with no greater degree of probability than the attribution of other debated writings: *Profession of Faith,
Dialogue with Gelian, To Philagrius on Consubstantiality,* and *To Theopompus on
Passibility and Impassibility in God* (on these, see below). In our view, Simonetti's position seems to be the better one. Others, like Crouzel, hold firmly that the *Address* is
by Gregory the Wonderworker and that Origen's letter was addressed to him. We regard this group of works as belonging to Gregory.

If we use the *Address* together with what Eusebius tells us to sketch out a biography of the young Gregory, the following outline emerges. Born in Pontus of a pagan
family around 210–213, and losing his father at the age of fourteen, he studied rhetoric, Latin, and Roman law with his brother Athenodorus. His original name, according to Eusebius, was Theodore, later changed to Gregory, "he who watches." Around

233, the two young men accompanied their sister to her husband in Caesarea, with the intention of then returning to Berytus (Beirut) to continue their study of law. But on hearing Origen, who had left Alexandria and recently reopened his school in Caesarea, they were captivated and remained with him for five years, according to Eusebius. During this period Gregory was baptized. After 238 Gregory left the Didaskaleion and on this occasion delivered the address of gratitude that tells us of his life and of the programs and methods of Origen's school.

For the remainder of Gregory's biography we are dependent on five, largely legendary lives that probably go back to oral tradition: one in Greek, one in Syriac, one in Armenian, and two in Latin. One of the latter is a chapter included by Rufinus of Aquileia among the additions he made in his translation of Eusebius's *Ecclesiastical History*. Between 240 and 250 Gregory was consecrated bishop of Neocaesarea: during his episcopate the persecution of Diocletian occurred, which he escaped by withdrawing into the mountains with many of the faithful, and a short but devastating invasion of the barbarian Goths and Borads into Pontus. Around 264 he and Athenodorus were said to have attended the synod of Antioch that was to pass judgment on Paul of Samosata, who had been accused of adoptionism. The majority of the bishops assembled there were former students of Origen.

This participation is attested by Eusebius (*Hist. eccl.* 7.28.1) on the basis of the synodal letter, which has a Theodore among the signers (*Hist. eccl.* 7.30). This fragile construction has also been criticized, rightly, by Nautin. Paul's defense of himself and the protection given him by Zenobia, Queen of Palmyra, prevented a decision. Paul was deposed only at a later (3d) synod, probably in 268, but Gregory does not appear among the signers. It is doubtful that he was already dead, since according to other sources he died under Aurelian, therefore between 270 and 275. In his native area Gregory remained famous chiefly as an apostle and worker of miracles (hence his nickname), which the lives hand on with obviously legendary expansions. If we accept Nautin's critique, we must conclude that the only sure information about Gregory is that he was bishop of Neocaesarea when Eusebius was a young man.

We begin with the writings attributable with certainty to Gregory. The *Canonical Letter* is a set of eleven canons (the 11th being a later addition), addressed by Gregory the Wonderworker to another bishop, having to do with the attitude to be adopted in the church toward problems raised by the invasion of the Goths and Borads: What attitude was to be taken toward women who had been violated and toward Christians who had taken advantage of the situation to enrich themselves by expropriating the possessions of their own brethren, or who had joined the barbarian invaders and participated in the killings? The norms to be followed are taken from the Bible. But in his determination to restore order, Gregory displays a balance and a leniency toward all who are ready to repent. Gregory has also left a *Metaphrasis of Ecclesiastes*, that is, a word-for-word transcription of that book into classical Greek.

We turn now to the debated works that were listed above.

The *Address of Gratitude to Origen* is a very careful rhetorical composition and must have been intended for a large and important readership. In an introduction (1–30) the author says that his lack of practice, his Latin studies, which have detracted from his ability to express himself in Greek, and the sublimity of the subject would all cause him to remain silent, but his gratitude to Origen compels him to speak. In a first part (31–92), after thanking God and his guardian angel for guiding him, he recalls the early part of his life and his meeting with Origen, who fired his soul with a love of philosophy. A second part (93–183) outlines Origen's program of instruction: after the study of a Socratic kind of dialectic, it moved on to the natural sciences, then to morality, and then to theology. The last-named study had two stages: first, the students read and commented on the Greek philosophers, excluding only the atheists; second, they advanced to the study of Scripture, in which Origen explained everything that was obscure in the sacred texts. A final part of the *Address* (184–207) expresses the author's sorrow at having to leave the school and asks Origen's prayers for his departing students.

The traditional view has been that the address bears witness to the deep impression made by Origen's teaching on his students and to the affection they had for him, but P. Nautin disagrees even on this point. Nautin seeks to show that the address had to do with teaching given by Origen personally to Theodore, for whom he would have been, during the period in question, a kind of tutor to whom the young man had been entrusted, against his will, by a relative. Whatever one may think of this theory, it is difficult to believe that in his "normal" teaching at Caesarea Origen reached the Scriptures only in a final stage.

A profession of faith is contained in Gregory of Nyssa's *Life of Gregory the Wonderworker;* its authenticity has likewise been recently called into question (by L. Abramowski). The profession consists of four articles, having to do respectively with the Father, the Son, the Spirit, and the Trinity; there is no reference to the incarnation. It is meant to remove the dangers of Origenist subordinationism by emphasizing the point that there is nothing created, nothing of a servant status, within the Trinity, nor anything introduced into the Trinity only at a certain point. The breadth of the last two articles cannot easily be fitted into the third century, since the points taken up in these two articles were still marginal at that time. In addition, Basil of Caesarea, who was well acquainted with the heritage of the Wonderworker, says nothing of this formula, even in circumstances in which it would have been useful to cite it. Gregory of Nazianzus quotes from the fourth article as from a recently composed profession of faith. While it is difficult to imagine Gregory of Nyssa forging anything, for it would have been quickly denounced, it is likely that at least the last two articles were formulated in the second half of the fourth century (M. Simonetti).

A dialogue between Gregory and someone named Theopompus, *On Passibility and Impassibility in God,* is preserved in Syriac under Gregory's name. Theopompus puts forward the opinions of someone called Isocrates, who, in the name of divine impassibility, refuses to accept the incarnation and the passion. Gregory defends these in the name of the freedom of God, who proves his own impassibility precisely by becoming passible and overcoming suffering and death. At the end, this God is identified with Jesus, which gives the work a modalist tone; this has led many scholars to doubt the authenticity of the work.

A work titled *To Philagrius on Consubstantiality* is attributed to Gregory the Wonderworker in a Syriac translation, but to Gregory Nazianzus or Gregory of Nyssa in the Greek manuscripts of their works, where it bears the title *To the Monk Evagrius on the Divinity.* The attribution to the Wonderworker is much debated, given the Sabellian approach of the work. A lost *Dialogue with Gelian,* composed by the Wonderworker, is cited by Basil of Caesarea (*Ep.* 210.5), whose adversary, Atarbius, used it in defense of his own Sabellian views, claiming that the Wonderworker said that there is but one hypostasis in God.

Henri Crouzel rejects the *Dialogue* as inauthentic, saying it is incompatible with Origen's distinction of hypostases in God, but M. Simonetti defends the authenticity of all of the last three treatises (Theopompus, Philagrius, Gelian) on the grounds that the works are apologetic in character and addressed to the pagan world, and Gregory would have been concerned to emphasize the oneness of God. In that case, the monarchian expressions in the works would not necessarily be incompatible with the Logos Christology of the *Address of Gratitude to Origen* (4.35–39). On the other hand, the assessment of the authenticity of Gregory's works on the basis of their correspondence to the teaching of Origen stands or falls on the identification of Gregory as a student of Origen; since this last point is itself in question, it cannot serve as the basis of argument.

A treatise *To Tatian on the Soul* seems to be spurious; two professions and some homilies are certainly such.

Pamphilus was an enthusiastic disciple of Origen. A biography in three books by Eusebius is lost, and we get our information from the same Eusebius's *Ecclesiastical History* (7.32.25), from his work on the *Martyrs of Palestine,* and from Photius (*Lex.* 118–19). Pamphilus was born in Berytus (Beirut) and studied theology at the school of Alexandria under Pierius (see above, sec. 1); there he acquired his enthusiasm for Origen. He then settled in Caesarea, where he was ordained a priest and opened a school with the intention of continuing the tradition of Origen, while devoting special care to the library which Origen had established there. It was from the latter that Eusebius (who called himself Eusebius Pamphili) secured the materials for his *Ecclesiastical History.* Pamphilus established a copyist's studio and himself copied many books; he saw to a classification of Origen's works that was followed by Eusebius, whose work was in turn used by Jerome. In 307 during the persecution of Maximinus Daia, Pamphilus was arrested. He remained in prison until he was beheaded on February 16, 310.

While in prison, using materials Eusebius brought to him, Pamphilus defended Origen against the attacks that were beginning to be made on him, by writing a defense of him in five books. A sixth was subsequently added by Eusebius. Only the first book has survived, in the Latin translation by Rufinus as well as some fragments in Syriac. In the introduction, Pamphilus responds to detractors who declared themselves scandalized by certain statements of Origen. He sets down a legitimate criterion for interpreting the Alexandrian's writings, insisting that the writer did not intend to answer questions in a definitive and dogmatic way but only to seek the meaning of the Scriptures to the best of his abilities, and, in so doing, to make it easier for his listeners and readers to enter into the Scriptures in a personal way. He then responds to objections against Origen on various dogmatic subjects; he answers questions, to a great extent, by citing Origen's own works. As a result, we owe to Pamphilus's work not only a knowledge of the criticism leveled at Origen during this period of controversy about him but also many fragments of his writings (see ch. 15).

Sextus Julius Africanus, born perhaps in Jerusalem around 160, was a civil servant under Septimius Severus and took part in that emperor's campaign against Edessa in 195. He set up a library for Severus Alexander in the Pantheon in Rome. In his *Chronicles* he told of having gone to Alexandria and the school of Heraclas, where he became a friend of Origen. He died at Nicopolis in Palestine around 210.

In Eusebius, *Dem. ev.* 8.2 and, above all, in George Syncellus, fragments remain of the *Chronicles (Chronographika)* of Africanus, in five books, which arranged in parallel columns the biblical history alongside Greek and Roman history down to 221. For Greece and the period before the first Olympiad he limited himself to a brief explanation of the myths, while remarking that even these postdated Moses. The work also included calculations of the seventy weeks of the prophecy in Daniel 9; Africanus regarded the weeks as completed at the coming of Christ. This work offers evidence of the entrance into the Christian world of an interest in a comprehensive vision of history in connection with a theological vision. By adopting a scheme attested by other authors such as Irenaeus and Hippolytus, Africanus calculated that the world would exist for 6000 years; the birth of Christ took place in 5500; the 6000 years were probably to be followed by the millennial reign of Christ. Eusebius, who was opposed to millenarianism, drew extensively on this work.

The *Kestoi* ("Embroideries") was an encyclopedic work in twenty-four books on very diverse subjects; it was dedicated to Severus Alexander. Only fragments remain to show how credulous Africanus was in regard to magic and superstitions.

We spoke earlier (ch. 15, sec. 4h) of a letter from Africanus to Origen in which he brought up arguments against the story of Susanna being an original part of the book of Daniel. A letter to Aristides, of which only fragments remain (Eusebius *Hist. eccl.* 1.7.2–16; and *Quaestiones in evangelia,* a catena on Luke), discussed the differences between the genealogies of Jesus in Matthew and in Luke and tried to reconcile them by appealing to the institution of the levirate: the genealogy in Luke, the author said, is a natural one; that of Matthew is legal.

These varied and learned interests of Julius Africanus drew the attention of Giacomo Leopardi, who devoted to that Christian writer a penetrating philological study, which is still unpublished.

Eusebius mentions the martyrdom of Lucian of Antioch at Nicomedia under Maximinus Daia on January 7, 312 (*Hist. eccl.* 9.6.3). Rufinus added to his Latin translation of the *Ecclesiastical History* the apology delivered by Lucian on that occasion; its authenticity is uncertain. Lucian has traditionally been regarded as the inaugurator of the Antiochene exegetical school with its literalist tendency, but in fact that school was begun by Diodorus of Tarsus (see vol. II of this history). Lucian was a teacher of Arius and of many of the latter's followers, who liked to call themselves "Collucianists." Lucian seems to have taught a strongly subordinationist Christology, thereby anticipating the Arian doctrine. On the other hand, the statement by Bishop Alexander of Alexandria in a letter written a decade after Lucian's death seems untrustworthy (the letter is in Theodoret, *Hist. eccl.* 1.4). According to the letter, Lucian was successor to Paul of Samosata; it may be that Lucian's subordinationism was intended to offset the monarchianism of Paul and, as a result, ended up devaluing the Son, but from an opposite point of view.

Lucian's critical work on the text of the Greek Bible was important; it was at the source of the "Antiochene text," from which in turn the "Byzantine" text derived.

BIBLIOGRAPHY

Gregory: The texts handed down in Greek and Latin can be read in PG 10; the treatise *To Philagrius* is in PG 46.

Gregory Thaumaturgus, *St. Gregory Thaumaturgus: Life and Works* (trans. M.
  Slusser; FC 98; Washington, D.C.: Catholic University of America Press,
  1998).
For the *Address*, see Grégoire le Thaumaturge, *Remerciement à Origène, suivi de la
  Lettre d'Origène à Grégoire* (ed. and trans. H. Crouzel; SC 148; Paris: Cerf,
  1969); with an extensive introduction.
P. Nautin, *Origène: Sa vie et son oeuvre* (Paris: Beauchesne, 1977), 81–86, 183–97.

Important

M. Simonetti, "Una nuova ipotesi su Gregorio il Taumaturgo," *RSLR* 24 (1988):
  17–41.
Text of the *Defense* by Pamphilus: PG 17:541–616.
H. Crouzel, "L'école d'Origène à Césarée," *BLE* 71 (1970): 15–27.
E. Junod, "L'auteur de l'Apologie pour Origène traduite par Rufin: Les té-
  moignages contradictoires de Rufin et de Jérôme à propos de Pamphile et
  d'Eusébe," in *Recherches et tradition: Mélanges patristiques offerts à Henri
  Crouzel* (ed. A. Dupleix; Paris: Beauchesne, 1992), 165–79.
Sextus Julius Africanus: PG 10:52–94.
———, *Les "Cestes" de Julius Africanus: Étude sur l'ensemble des fragments, avec
  édition, traduction et commentaire* (ed. and trans. J. R. Viellefond; Florence:
  Sansoni antiquariato/Paris: Didier, 1970).
G. Leopardi, *Sextus Julius Africanus,* manuscript being prepared for publication
  by C. Moreschini.

3. Methodius of Olympus and Adamantius

Little is known of the life of Methodius, of whom Eusebius says nothing. According to Jerome (*Vir. ill.* 83), Methodius was bishop first of Olympus in Lycia, then of
Tyre, and died a martyr at Chalcis in Greece at the end of the last persecution
(311–312). The same writer says that others dated Methodius's death to the persecutions of Decius or Valerius, but this possibility seems excluded by the fact that Jerome
cites a work of Methodius against Porphyry, which can only have been written after
270. But even the remainder of what Jerome says is doubtful; perhaps he confused the
writer with a martyr of the same name. Other sources assign various episcopal sees to
Methodius; the tendency today is to say that he was not a bishop. We must therefore
be content to regard him as a Christian teacher in Lycia toward the end of the third
century and the beginning of the fourth, if the tradition about his martyrdom in 312
is trustworthy.

The only work of Methodius that has come down to us in its entirety in Greek is
the *Symposium.* In addition to the version that has come down to us in direct transmission and partially in indirect transmission, there existed an interpolated recension, known to Photius, who regards it as a revision made by Arians. The work,
written in the form of a dialogue, evidently meant to transpose its model, the *Symposium* of Plato, into a Christian setting.

In an introduction and in a conclusion, Eubulius, a representative of the author himself, makes his appearance and asks Gregorion, a young girl, about the dialogues on chastity which took place one evening at supper among ten virgins. Gregorion repeats the account given by one of the virgins, Theopatra, who told her how they had been invited by Virtue, a daughter of Philosophy, into her garden, in order that each might give a discourse in praise of virginity. The author's intention is evidently to set up a contrast with the discourses on Eros which the guests are urged to give in the Platonic dialogue. The ten discourses of the virgins are followed by another given by Virtue and then by a hymn intoned by Thecla, which in twenty-four iambic-anapestic strophes sums up the main motifs of the work. We shall summarize here, by way of example, the first discourse, that of Marcella.

It begins with praise of the greatness of chastity, but then immediately explains that chastity consists not simply in avoiding bodily corruption but also in care of the soul. Just as salt in a sense paralyzes the flesh that is to be eaten so as to prevent its being putrefied, so spiritual meditation on the Scriptures paralyzes bodily desires and eliminates every possible focus of putrefaction. But the plant of virginity was not sent immediately to the first generations of human beings, and Marcella sketches a history of the way to virginity: from the age when men married their own sisters without any objection being raised (providence permitting this because human beings were few), through marriage with non-relatives, avoidance of adultery, and continence, to virginity, which by scorning the flesh leads the person to incorruptibility. The process regarding continence is illustrated by citations from the Bible: from Abraham to the prophets and especially to the sapiential books. As for virginity, it was precisely in order to teach the way to this that the Word was sent into the world; the new way of life that he inaugurated is illustrated by the outstanding place given to virgins in the Apocalypse.

Following Marcella, in a second discourse Theophila acknowledges the excellence of the gift of chastity, but for her part takes up the defense of continence and also of fatherhood and motherhood as a choice for those to whom virginity is not granted. In each discourse, more so even in those that follow than in the first two, the argument is based on a literal and allegorical exegesis of passages of Scripture. The allegory is heavily influenced by Origen's methods, but is accompanied by a warning against doing away completely with the literal exegesis. That is what happens in one case, the first chapters of Genesis, where Origen, following in the footsteps of Philo, had resolutely chosen an allegorical exegesis. The *Symposium's* second discourse, that of Theophila, interprets Gen 1:28 literally as a command to beget children, but follows up with an allegorical interpretation of Gen 2:21: the sleep of Adam during which Eve is produced is a symbol of the stupefaction caused by the sexual relations, during which another being is formed by the sperm issuing from his bones and his flesh.

This is an allegory of a special type, being physiological rather than psychological, as in the interpretation of Philo and Origen. But Methodius is also able to give the same passage an interpretation in keeping with Origen's allegorism; in 3.70–73, relying on the Adam-Christ typology of Paul and modifying the Eve-Mary typology developed by Justin and Irenaeus, he makes the sleep of Adam a symbol of the death of Christ, from which emerged the new Eve, the church. Methodius is naturally inclined to go in for allegorical exegesis especially in dealing with the ritual legislation of the Pentateuch (e.g., 120–124 on Num 6:1–4). Still, we must note, with H. Musurillo, that the *Symposium* is not only an exhortation to chastity but also a handbook of Christian doctrine and an introduction to the allegorical methods of the Asiatic writers. In it can be seen the practical and ethical concerns of Methodius's theological thought.

Other treatises of Methodius have reached us in their entirety only in a Slavic translation; they were translated and preserved because Methodius was confused with the saint of the same name who evangelized the Slavs. But the treatise *On Free Will* has also reached us in large measure in Greek, partly (1–7.5) in direct transmission in P. Laurentiana, and partly in indirect transmission; 5–12 appear in Eusebius (*Praep. ev.* 7.22), other fragments in Photius and John Damascene. Eznik of Kolb also cites passages in an Armenian translation in his *Against the Sects.* The work is a dialogue between an orthodox Christian and a Valentinian, in which Methodius assigns the origin of evil to the free human will and denies that evil is either an independent reality or a quality necessarily inherent in a real being. Evil does not come from nature *(physis)* but from habit (*chrēsis;* ch. 15). In his resolute defense of free will Methodius agrees with Origen. He distances himself from Origen, however, by refusing to accept the preexistence of rational souls and an endless succession of worlds.

The dialogue *Aglaophon, or on the Resurrection,* in three books, has reached us in Greek and Syriac fragments and in an Old Slavic translation, the second and third books of which are abridged. Aglaophon denies the resurrection of the material body, relying on philosophical and physiological arguments and on biblical texts, including Origen's exegesis of Gen 3:21, according to which the garments of skins that God makes for Adam and Eve after their sin are their material bodies, thus showing that they were created without these bodies. Proclus then cites the teaching of Origen against the resurrection of the material body (1.19–26). Methodius then engages in a lengthy discussion of Origen's teaching that connects the body with sin, and he rejects it.

The treatise *On Life and Rational Activity,* an exhortation to be content with the gifts God has given us, is preserved only in a Slavic translation. The same is true of three works devoted to an allegorical interpretation of biblical texts: *On Foods* (on dietary regulations and on the ashes of the red heifers in Num 19), *On Leprosy* (on Lev 13), and *On the Leech* (on Prov 30:15–16 and Ps 18:2). Of the treatise *Xenon* or *Of Created Things* only some Greek fragments transmitted by Photius remain. In these Methodius harshly attacks, among other things, Origen's allegorical exegesis of the biblical story of creation (ch. 12), with which Methodius himself had agreed in the *Symposium.* Some wish to see in this a confirmation of Jerome's statement (*Ruf.* 1.11) that Methodius gradually deepened his opposition to Origen, but reservations about Origen's allegorism are already to be found in the *Symposium.* Lost are the *Books against Porphyry*—the authenticity of the fragments attributed to this work is doubtful—and other exegetical writings mentioned by Jerome (*Vir. ill.* 83).

On the whole, Methodius is a witness to the anti-Origenist attacks made during the first generations after the Alexandrian's death. He does not always penetrate very deeply into Origen's teachings, as in the controversy over the resurrection, but he does present them correctly and without distortion, in contrast to future attacks. His challenges have to do with particular points, especially the teaching on creation and the resurrection, whereas on other points, such as the defense of free will, he agrees with Origen and is greatly influenced by him in his exegetical methods.

We now refer to the dialogue *On Orthodox Faith in God,* the work of a contempo-rary of Methodius, which comes to us in the original Greek and in a translation by Rufinus. The work is a dialogue in five books: a defender of the orthodox faith first re-futes Megetius and Mark, two Marcionites, then Marinus, a follower of Bardesanes, and finally two Valentinians. Since the orthodox defender is named Adamantius, the work was attributed to Origen, who was nicknamed Adamantius. It was because of this attri-bution that Rufinus translated it. But the author seems rather to be an anti-Origenist; he uses the treatises of Methodius on free will and on the resurrection. In Rufinus's translation, the persecutions seem to be a present reality; in the Greek, however, the corresponding passages refer to the Constantinian era, while the theological language used of the Trinity likewise seems to fit into the fourth century. The pagan judge, Eutropius, finally gives the victory to Adamantius and converts to orthodox Christian-ity. The work, though modest from a literary standpoint, is important for our knowl-edge of the Marcionites, Bardesanites, and Valentinians of the fourth century.

BIBLIOGRAPHY

Editions of Methodius

Methodius of Olympus, *Methodius* (ed. and trans. G. N. Bonwetsch; GCS 27; Leipzig: Hinrichs, 1917).
Méthode d'Olympe, *Le banquet* (ed. and trans. H. Musurillo and V.-H. Debidour; SC 95; Paris: Cerf, 1963).

Studies

V. Buchheit, *Studien zu Methodios von Olympos* (TU 69; Berlin: Akademie-Verlag, 1958).
E. Prinzivalli, *L'esegese biblica di Metodio di Olimpo* (Rome: Augustinianum, 1985).
L. G. Patterson, *Methodius of Olympus: Divine Sovereignty, Human Freedom, and Life in Christ* (Washington, D.C.: Catholic University of America Press, 1997).

Editions of Adimantius

W. H. van de Sande Bakhuizen, *Der Dialog des Adimantius: PERI TÊS THEON ORTHES PISTEOS* (GCS 4; Leipzig: Hinrichs, 1901).
V. Buchheit, *Tyranni Rufini librorum Adimantii Origenis aduersus haereticos interpretatio* (Munich: Fink, 1966); Latin.

Chapter 17

THE FIRST CHRISTIAN LITERATURE
OF THE WEST

The first Christian literary forms did not make their appearance in the West until more than a century after they had appeared in the East. And if we look for the rise of "literature" in a strict sense, there is a period of 150 years between the Pauline letters and the first "original" work, that is, not a translation, in the Latin language. These first Latin works are *Against Dice Players,* which von Harnack and others attribute to Pope Victor (189–198), or the first works of Tertullian (ca. 197). Various explanations have been offered for this phenomenon, but in literature it is not possible to reach the same certainty—or probability—as in the interpretation of historical or economic facts.

It cannot be said with certainty that Christianity reached Rome at a later date than it did the cities of the East. It may be, however, that its spread among the wealthier classes, who had the money for a higher education and the cultivation of literature, was slower in the West than in the East. Similarly, the average level of education was lower in the western world than in the eastern, where the literary tradition, going back as it did to the ages of classical Greece and the Hellenistic kingdoms, was certainly older than in the West. Perhaps, too—to repeat what was commonly said by critics in the last century—the greater readiness and greater interest of the Greek world in artistic creativity made the western world, by contrast, seem tardy. This is confirmed by the fact that the first Christian writings in Latin appeared in Rome, but were almost all of a practical nature.

Another trait immediately marked Christian Latin literature, namely, a notable sequence of periods connected with geographical areas. The third century A.D. is the period in which the Roman Province of Africa played a dominant role in Christian cultural life. This is simply the natural reflection, in the Christian sphere, of an evolution in Latin pagan culture, which in the second century had been essentially African: Tertullian, Minucius, and Cyprian are the genuine counterparts, in the area of Christian culture and literature, of Fronto and Apuleius. The fourth century saw an increasing spread of Christian culture in the West, with Italy and Gaul being the first areas affected: the more important personages of the fourth century came from Italy and Gaul. Even Augustine, the greatest Christian thinker of the West, received a good part of his educational formation in Italy. The strong penetration of Christianity into Gaul in the fourth century, combined with the relative conservatism of ancient culture as supported by the Romano-barbarian kingdoms of the age, gave primacy to

Gaul during the fifth century, when barbarian invasions led to the political and cultural fragmentation of the empire.

Africa, crushed under the violent and persecutorial control of the Vandals, fell to a second level, while a position of importance belonged no longer to Italy as a whole but chiefly to Rome, where the lay and "statal" structure of papal power, together with the pope's growing political and religious authority, called for an efficient organization of education. This was ensured, at least at a certain level, by the papal chancellery, the power of which was directed toward the defense of orthodoxy; in the fifth century the Roman see began to consider this defense to be its special duty. As a result, while the breakup of ancient classical civilization increased radically in the sixth century and then reached the point of no return in the decadence that attacked the Mediterranean world in the precarolingian era, Rome continued to exercise a primacy in the cultural area. This primacy belonged almost exclusively to the papal see. Even laymen such as Boethius and Cassiodorus, the former having had an exclusively philosophical education and the latter an exclusively rhetorical training, had to reckon with the papacy. The decadence of Africa continued, that of Gaul began, and Christian culture at the end of the sixth century, where our work stops, was cultivated and promoted chiefly in Visigothic Spain.

1. Christian Latin and Translations of the Bible

In order to emphasize the importance which the Bible has in Christian life as the text that contains the revelation of God in written form and therefore as a sacred text, we are often reminded that Muslims call Christians and Jews "peoples of the book." But while the importance of the Bible at the spiritual level is something accepted by all of Christianity, it was utterly decisive for Latin Christianity, which was based on a translation of the sacred book. When Greek-speaking Jewish Christians and other ethnic Christians of the eastern Mediterranean came to Christianity, most could learn this new teaching without difficulty in the language they already spoke. The same cannot be said of the Western world where the language most commonly used was Latin. After a period of about two centuries, varying from place to place, during which Christians continued to read the biblical text in Greek, the need arose to put the contents of the new religion into the language of everyday use.

Initially, the Scriptures consisted solely of the Law and the Prophets, that is, the Hebrew canon, but in the west they were not read in Hebrew or even in the current Greek translation of Alexandria. The early Latin translation of the sacred books agrees with the text preserved by a tradition that originated in Syria (although in Greek) and in the fourth century was to establish itself in Antioch. Alongside the Old Testament there circulated collections of extracts, to which modern scholarship has given the name *testimonia*. These were mainly messianic in character, and their content had been revised and adapted to a new theological and apologetic context, chiefly for use against the Jews. These prophecies, together with the more important Psalms, must have been among the first texts to be translated into Latin.

The Latin translations of the Bible thus derived from a freer and more popular non-Alexandrian tradition of the Greek text. Christians, who were not sensitive to the noble traditions of ancient culture, caused these works no longer to be circulated in the form of the scroll *(volumen),* but in the more convenient and more popular form of the codex, which had hitherto been reserved for technical works and practical use, but was already widespread in the West. As Gribomont observes, devout Jews, who paid the sacred scroll no less honor than they did the language in which the sacred text was written, inevitably perceived this revolution as almost a sacrilege, an act no less reprehensible than the abandonment of the temple and the sabbath.

There is a fact that proves the fundamental importance of the Bible in early Christian civilization, so much so that the history of the one can shed light on the history of the other. That fact is that the final persecution by the Roman authorities, the root-and-branch persecution by Emperor Diocletian between 303 and 313, was aimed specifically at the seizure and destruction of the sacred texts, no less than at the arrest of Christians. On that occasion, Christians coined the term *traditores* (from Latin *tradere,* "to hand over, deliver up") for those who gave these texts to the pagans. The police demanded from bishops and priests any complete or partial copies of the Bible in their possession, and kept scrupulous records of the number handed over and of their possessors. Others, however, refused to hand them over. Also to be noted here is that the books handed over usually belonged to the local church and not to private individuals. The pagan authorities were well aware of how important the Bible was to Christians: without it there was no instruction and therefore no conversion to the new religion.

In the literature of the church of Rome, Greek remained in use until the third century by such western writers as Clement, Hermas, and Hippolytus in Rome and Irenaeus in Lyons; it continued in liturgical use even into the fourth century. But while the liturgy is by nature strongly conservative, and while literature, for its part, continued to feed without difficulty at the sources of Greek culture, the Christian people soon felt the need to read the texts in the language which they spoke. This is confirmed by the concrete testimony of Christian funerary inscriptions, for the use of Greek in these prevailed in Rome throughout the third century, while inscriptions in Latin became increasingly frequent in the Province of Africa and in Mauritania.

Scholars have asked which circles first felt the need to translate the sacred text into Latin. One hypothesis attributes the origin of the New Testament in Latin to Marcion the heretic (see above, ch. 9, sec. 3); but his translation was in a heretical form, later replaced by the "regular" version, which the orthodox church produced in opposition to it. Alternately, Tatian, the author of the *Diatessaron,* a harmony of the four Gospels (see above, ch. 10, sec. 4) is credited. But no hypothesis has been clearly confirmed, and there is a tendency today to think that the first versions known to us were produced by the orthodox churches that used them.

2. African Bible and European Bible

Just as the use of the Latin language in worship, liturgy, and sacred rites spread first in the Christian communities of Africa, so too the first translation of the Bible appeared in Africa. We shall see also that the first Christian Latin writers came from the African world. This first translation can be reconstructed, at least approximately, from extensive citations of it by third-century African writers and from the biblical text as found in some often fragmentary manuscripts, some of them very old, which preserved earlier versions. But when it comes to literary testimonies, we need to use caution, since Tertullian probably did not have an already complete Bible in front of him, and therefore at times made his own translation of the Greek original. Two generations later, however, a Bible translated substantially in its entirety already existed, so that Cyprian could make regular use of it and even have the *testimonia* in Latin. That text continued in use through the fourth century and was stubbornly defended by the Donatists, who, in their schismatic isolation, remained obstinately attached to the past, and first and foremost to Cyprian, the local saint of Africa, and to their now ancient Bible.

The term "European Bible" is used in a similar way when speaking of the sacred text that circulated in Latin-speaking regions of Europe. We must not think, however, that this Bible had a different origin from that of the African Bible. Indeed, according to some scholars, the European Bible was an African Bible that had been imported and then modified locally on the basis of diverging oral redactions. For the European version of the Bible the same general considerations hold. The first written texts—less numerous during the third century than the African—give us the material for accessing those versions. These texts include the second-century Latin translation of *1 Clement,* and then the works of Novatian, who was active in Rome around the middle of the third century. After the third century we find the church of Rome using a fluent Latin in its correspondence, although biblical citations are rare in it, as indeed they are in Latin writers through the fourth century down to the time of Lucifer of Cagliari.

Beginning in around 360, writers of Latin provide us with abundant evidence of the state of the biblical text that they were using. That text can therefore be studied, but with the reservation that some of these writers, who used Greek texts, may have correspondingly altered the biblical citations they intended to include in their works; one such writer was Ambrose. The initial Latin text of the Bible, which was characterized by a strong literalism, was then slowly normalized, in the sense that the writers using it sought to produce a good Latin, insofar as they were permitted by the social and cultural environment in which the work was to be circulated. They also sought to harmonize their Latin text with the text of the Alexandrian Greek recension of the Bible, which was the most correct and authoritative of all the recensions, as noted above.

One thing should be kept in mind here: when we speak, for simplicity's sake, of an "African Bible" and a "European Bible," we are not dealing with a homogeneous body of texts, one in Africa and another in Europe; accuracy would require that we speak in the plural of "Bibles" or of *Veteres Latinae,* "ancient Latin versions."

3. Characteristics of the Latin Translations of the Bible

These translations, produced as they were (at least initially) in an environment of humble and largely uneducated people and intended for the lowest strata of society, must have made extensive use of the *sermo cotidianus,* that is, everyday language. This is attested by, among others, Arnobius and Lactantius, who report pagan criticisms of the low artistic level of these translations, but at the same time justify their lack of rhetorical development by the need for simplicity that befitted the proclamation of the true religion. Because of the inadequate literary care that they show, the translations mark a break with the tradition of literary purism and rhetorical elaboration that characterized ancient literature as well as the period itself, that is, the imperial age during which these translations were circulated, for that age was strong on rhetorical education. Even translations of non-Christian Greek texts into Latin were at that time of a literary quality, and had been from the beginnings of Latin culture. The translations of the Bible, on the contrary, were marked by a strict literalism that sprang from a reverence for the sacred text containing the word of God, which demanded scrupulous respect.

But in making these remarks we must exercise caution and not think that we are dealing with a "popular language" or a pure and simple "language in ordinary use." The literalism of these translations of the Bible is not the literalism of uneducated people, but rather stems from the intention of being accurately faithful to the original. The same norm had been employed in the Septuagint, which is frequently an imitation of the Hebrew text in Hellenistic Greek; thus the Seventy introduced into their Greek version phrases and idioms unknown to non-Jewish writers. The persuasion that translators must be extremely faithful in dealing with the sacred text is visible even in an expert translator such as Jerome, who says that "in the translation of the sacred text even the order of the words constitutes a mystery" (*Epist.* 57.5). It is thought that this conservative and respectful attitude was typical of the Roman mentality, for it also marked pagan religion, whose ancient chants were still being repeated by priests in the imperial age, despite the fact that their content was by then unknown to both cantor and listener. A reverential fear prevented any change in the inherited text.

Another tendency visible in these Latin translations of the Bible is the refusal to use terminology from the pagan religions in explaining Christian doctrine. The translations were anonymous and, it seems, quite numerous, scattered around in most places where the presence of a Christian community called for them. Each community jealously clung to its translation and was reluctant, for example, to accept Jerome's revision; Augustine found Jerome's work on the sacred text to be mostly useless and a source of misunderstanding for the faithful. There is a well known statement of Augustine: "Those who have translated the Scriptures from Hebrew into Greek can be counted on the fingers of one hand, whereas those who have translated them from Greek into Latin are without number, because anyone taking up a Greek manuscript and thinking he knew even but a little of both languages, immediately set about translating."

The Latin translations of the Bible have in every age exerted a strong influence on the literary language of Christians. The transformation that Christianity brought about in society showed itself also in a transformation of the Latin language, which in the works of Christians proves to have taken a special shape.

The specific traits of Christian literary works have been emphasized by the "Nijmegen school," which, indeed, coined the very term "Christian Latin" in order to highlight this specific linguistic novelty. But the Nijmegen school went too far when it defined Christian Latin in so precise a way. The objection was raised that Christians who used, among themselves, the special terminology of the new religion for the acts of worship, the rites, and the new ideas that distinguished Christian from pagan were still people of their age and society, and therefore could not have expressed themselves differently than the pagan world around them. For this reason, other scholars who investigated the linguistic development from Latin to the Romance languages tended to include the language of Christians within this overall development. The Nijmegen school, on the contrary, sought to identify the linguistic peculiarities of Christian speakers, that is, the "special language" or "group language" of the Christian community, which wanted consciously to differentiate itself from the larger pagan community around it. But these peculiarities are logically to be seen more in vocabulary than in syntax, which must have remained substantially the same as that of non-Christians.

Even if it is not possible to speak of a "Christian language" in a rigid and unqualified sense, it is certain that at the literary level a specifically Christian language did take shape, that is, a language influenced by the Christian book par excellence, the Bible. This language marked all of Christian literature without exception. There was no writer who did not feel to some extent the influence of the language of the Bible, and there is no Christian work that did not recall the Bible in some respect, even, and above all, on the literary plane. By the end of early Christianity this language would achieve canonical status and constitute a kind of purism, so effective that even Jerome in his critical study of earlier versions would not dare to get rid of certain expressions and translations, even when erroneous, which had taken root and become traditional.

"Christian Latin," the Latin of Christian writers, appears to have been marked throughout its existence by a rejection of conservatism and purism; by the introduction of popular forms, and in this respect it may have influenced the language of the early translations of the Bible; by the use of words from liturgical language and ecclesiastical language, the language of institutions and of the church's life; and by the acceptance of Grecisms and Hebraisms. While syntactical structures, as noted above, remained substantially the same as those of non-Christian writers, the presence of Semitisms stands out. We cite here only the most familiar: the use of the genitive that serves as an adjective *(odor suavitatis, terra promissionis);* the elative or intensifying genitive *(saecula saeculorum, vanitas vanitatum);* the use of *in* with the ablative to denote instrumentality *(percussit in virga)* or with the accusative functioning as a predicate *(accepit in uxorem).*

The influence of Grecisms, by contrast, was usually exerted through the language of the Septuagint: the genitive after verbs indicating superiority or perception; the expressions *credere in, fidere in, sperare in* with the accusative; the more frequent use, already found sporadically in pagan writers, of the indirect question with *si* and the replacement of objective statements using the infinitive by the form *dico quia, dico quod,* and similar turns of phrase. Prepositions are often doubled *(desub, desuper);* adjectives replace nouns in the genitive case *(apostolica traditio, oratio dominica, spiritus propheticus);* and paratactic constructions predominate, with the frequent use of the conjunction *et* between one sentence and the next.

Turning to vocabulary, instances of Hebraisms and Grecisms are even clearer and widely known. Some Hebrew words entered irremovably into Latin and then into the Romance languages *(Sabaoth, cherubim, Satanas, hosanna, alleluia, amen);* a larger number of words came rather from Greek, due to the original bilingualism of the Christian communities. These Grecisms were used for realities of the church's life:

ecclesia, apostolus, baptisma, eucharistia, pascha, or for typically Christian concepts and ideas: *abyssus, blasphemia, scandalum, zizania.*

Finally, there were the lexical calques used to put ideas and conceptions proper to the new religion into Latin by having recourse to new words, or old words with a new meaning, that were made up from the preexisting Latin linguistic base: *iustificare, resurrectio, revelatio, salvare, salvator, sanctificare, beatificare,* and many others, in coining which the translator conformed to the general requirements of his own language. It is known, for example, that beginning in the second century A.D., multiple new coinages appear in Latin as a whole; that is to say the same usage is attested in Christian as well as in pagan writers. Finally, vocabulary was renewed inasmuch as various words in common use in the language of the classics or, in any case, of non-Christians, acquired new meaning derived from the new Christian reality: it is obvious that *dominus,* "lord," like its Greek antecedent *kyrios,* meant one thing in pagan life and culture and another in Christian life and culture, where there was a direct influence of the Hebrew *adonai.*

4. The Bible as a Christian Literary Text

We spoke earlier of literary criticisms that pagans voiced against the Bible. When judged by the rhetorical standards that marked the education of readers and writers, the Bible seemed to resist any attempt to fit it into traditional Roman culture, and was therefore unworthy of consideration. This condemnation, based on literary requirements, accompanied the pagan's contempt for Christians, who at least during the first century were usually of lowly origins, and were for the most part uneducated. The literary sphere confirmed pagans in their condemnation of the new religion, which seemed in the eyes of intellectuals educated in philosophy and in certain principles of classical civilization to be a form of popular superstition. Such was the judgment of such literary men and philosophers as Tacitus, Pliny the Younger, and Marcus Aurelius.

As we noted earlier, the responses of Christian writers to these criticisms stuck to one constant idea: the value of the Bible resides not in its words but in its contents, not on its surface but in its depths; it is meant not to give pleasure but to help. This topos, however, gradually came to be supplemented by considerations of a literary kind that tended to give the sacred text its own nobility. As Christianity gradually entered the culture, Christian men of letters came to realize, not without reason, that the Bible too had its artistic value, but it could not and should not be identified or judged by the standards of contemporary rhetorical traditions. Nevertheless, during the first three or four centuries, Christian writers did not manage to find a norm of judgment that would grasp the special worth of the sacred text, namely, its novelty; they still did not defend the Bible by remarking that pagans were unable to appreciate its artistic values precisely because these were new. Instead, they tried to find in the Bible elements that could be matched to standards by which secular texts were usually judged.

It must be noted, though, that the attitude of Christian men of letters was more nuanced in this area than is usually thought. For example, the topos of the intentional simplicity of Scripture, in contrast to the empty rhetorical ornamentation of secular literature, is completely lacking in Tertullian. Some (Fredouille, for example) have inferred from this that Tertullian's attitude toward the literary aspect of the Bible must have been the typical one of a pagan rhetor, which he had indeed been until his conversion at about the age of thirty-five. Once he became a Christian, the argument goes, he would have preferred to remain silent, because he essentially accepted the pagan condemnation of the literary character of sacred text. On the other hand, we find, even in Tertullian, isolated thoughts on some Pauline Epistles: the apostle writes "elegantly," Tertullian sometimes says, or he emphasizes the "violent" style of 1 Corinthians (see below, ch. 18, sec. 2e). It is certain that Tertullian does not use citations from the Bible when he writes his apologetical works, which are intended for pagan readers, and he acknowledges that "people by and large do not give their assent to our books, since the only ones who approach these are the ones who have already become Christians" (*Test.* 1.4).

This is not Cyprian's practice when he writes *To Demetrian,* thereby incurring the reproach of Lactantius. The latter writes in *Divine Institutes* (5.1.26–27) that it is inappropriate to include citations from the Bible in apologetical works addressed to pagans, and that pagans make fun of Cyprian precisely for having told "fairy tales for little old ladies" in his works. Others have thought, however, that Cyprian was convinced that the Scriptures possessed a well defined literary dignity of their own and were a model of style. He says several times that Paul's style is "strong and sublime"; in his vocabulary the word "strong," when applied to a style, is often contrasted with "eloquent," although it cannot be disproved that this is a contrast between the vigorous content of Christian teaching and the vacuously eloquent style of pagan literature. Elsewhere he stresses the point that Scripture is characterized by a brevity, a focus on essentials, which has the ability to strengthen souls in the practice of virtue and in facing martyrdom. In this judgment Cyprian is only confirming the necessity, shown in practice in his own works (see below, ch. 18, sec. 6g), of setting a clear and balanced eloquence of a Ciceronian kind over against the rhetorical traditions of African baroque.

The problem of biblical style was to be taken up with greater maturity in both theory and practice by such writers as Jerome and Augustine. The former aims at giving his revision of the Scriptures a new literary character, distinct from his own personal style, which is the flowery rhetorical style of fourth century writers. Augustine, for his part, seeks to use the same rhetorical categories employed by pagans to bring out the characteristics of the sacred text. But Christian culture still had a long road to travel before it could reach this kind of literary awareness.

5. First Christian Latin Texts

As in the case of the Bible, the first documents of Christian Latin consisted of translations from the Greek. These texts, which were very simple as far as their doctrinal content and undoubtedly even more elementary as to their literary form, would have been documents of a culture that was still Jewish Christian, rather than simply Christian; thus Daniélou, although his reconstruction seems heavily weighted in favor of his thesis. According to this scholar, Latin-speaking Jews must have existed from the very earliest period, so that there must have been a Jewish Latin before there was a Christian Latin.

Let us now mention some examples of an early Christian literature. *The Two Ways (De duabus viis)* is a little work that derives its material from the *Didache* and from the *Letter of Barnabas,* although it is not a translation of either of these two works. There is also a very early translation (see above, ch. 5, sec. 1) of *1 Clement,* that is only slightly later than the original (second century). A Latin translation turned the Shepherd of Hermas into a text fairly well known even in Africa; it is well known to Tertullian and the author of the *Passion of Perpetua and Felicity,* who was a contemporary of Tertullian (see below, ch. 18, secs. 2i and 3). This translation, too, came only a very little while after the composition of the original, because the Shepherd is cited as a recent edifying though not canonical work by the *Muratorian Fragment* (or *Canon*); this last is an anonymous text which Muratori discovered in the Ambrosian Library of Milan and which gives a list of canonical books for the Christians of the Roman community. It was drawn up during the episcopate of Pius, around the middle of the second century. The Latin translation must have been made, therefore, after the composition of the Shepherd of Hermas (that is, after about 130) and before the *Muratorian Canon.*

The Latin Shepherd has come down to us in two redactions: a more recent, the so-called "Palatine," which is written in a correct language, and another, much older version, which has been said to show the same characteristics as the early translations of the Bible, such as a heightened literalism and a vocabulary inspired by popular speech. The *Letter of Barnabas* was translated into Latin and proved useful to the new religion by giving a theoretical justification for distancing itself from the Jewish tradition.

The *Muratorian Canon* is of interest both for the history of the biblical canon, because it seeks to eliminate apocryphal writings, and for our knowledge of the Roman environment in which it was composed. We learn that there were the "Alogi," who were under the leadership of presbyter Gaius and probably linked to the monarchian heresy, and who were so named because they rejected the revelation of the Logos, that is, the gospel and Apocalypse of John. The *Canon* condemns such a dogmatic position. The *Canon* is also important for the history of the New Testament, because it is the first evidence of the official recognition in the West of the four Gospels, and of the idea that the Gospel of John concludes the line of Gospels, and that no other gospels are accepted as authentic. It is also important for the authenticity of the Pauline letters: it tells us that the major Pauline letters are seven in number and were sent to seven Christian churches, two each to the Corinthians and the Thessalonians, and that the letters to Titus and Timothy have to do with ecclesiastical order and discipline. The Acts of the Apostles are treated as acts of all the apostles, in contrast to the acts of single apostles, that is, the apocryphal acts. The *Muratorian Canon* also recalls Paul's journey to Spain and Peter's martyrdom, which are not in the Acts of the Apostles but in *1 Clement.*

According to some, the rise and spread of heresies, which led the church of Rome to set down its own canon of authentic writings, resulted in the composition of a catalogue of heresies, which has been transmitted among the writings of Tertullian but is not his work. Some scholars assert that this catalogue came into existence in Roman circles at the end of the second century; others attributed it to Victor of Pettau, a martyr under Diocletian (see below, ch. 19, sec. 3). The work in question is *Against All the Heresies (Adversus omnes haereses)*, which makes extensive use of another catalogue of heresies, the *Syntagma* of Hippolytus.

According to some, this early Latin Christian literature, which arose over the second century, also includes a work transmitted among those of Cyprian, *Against Dice Players (Adversus aleatores)*, a condemnation of games of chance, which implied idolatrous practices. According to von Harnack, this work, written by a bishop who enjoyed special standing and addressed it to his colleagues, was composed by Victor, Bishop of Rome from 189 to 198. This hypothesis, which initially met with some favor, now seems improbable; we shall refer to it again later (ch. 18, sec. 7).

According to Daniélou, some other works preserved among the writings of Cyprian, but certainly not his, belong to this period and are very much characterized by Jewish Christian motifs. The works include: *Against the Jews (Adversus Iudaeos)*, *Mount Sinai and Mount Zion (De montibus Sina et Sion)*, and *The Computation of Easter (De pascha computus);* a work apart is the *Sermon on the Hundredfold, Sixtyfold, and Thirtyfold Reward (De centesima, sexagesima, tricesima;* see below, ch. 18, sec. 7). The Jewish Christian traits supposedly marking these rather early works, which however became parts of later collections, include: interpretations of the biblical texts resembling those of the rabbis but remaining isolated; scriptural citations that are special in form and content and occur only in these works; words and sayings of Christ that are not found in the Gospels *(agrapha);* and a very primitive theology that does not assign the Son a role and a reality distinct from that of the Father.

6. First Christian Latin Poetry

We spoke earlier (see above, ch. 12) of the first Christian poetic forms in Greek. What is attested for the first decade of the second century in the East will, quite logically, also be found in the Latin world: the Pauline exhortation to praise God in hymns and spiritual songs inevitably held for every Christian community. It is not enough to stress the antiquity of this poetry; we must also take into account the importance for Christianity of the praise of God expressed in song, especially in the liturgical assembly. Hymnology is therefore an essential element in Christian spirituality, and music and songs have always been used in the voicing of this spirituality. While we do not have any written second-century evidences of Christian poetry in Latin, which would probably have been in the form of hymns, as in the Greek world, Tertullian attests to its existence at the end of that century and the beginning of the next.

Tertullian several times writes (e.g., *Apol.* 39.18; *An.* 9.4; *Or.* 27) of songs sung by the Christian community, and even of songs sung by husband and wife in their home (*Ux.* 2.8.8) or by solitary Christians (*Exh. cast.* 10.2). The subject matter of these songs would have been the New Testament hymns to which we referred earlier, and then surely the Psalms, the Christian poetry par excellence, which would play such a large part in the formation of the Christian style—we need think only of the *Confessions* of Augustine. Finally, there were also extemporaneous compositions.

Despite all of these examples, it was characteristic of Christian literature that poetry in the true and proper sense appeared quite late, essentially with the dawning of the Constantinian era and the strong impetus given to literary forms by the new conditions and the changed historical situation with the triumph over paganism. Many attempts have been made to explain this strange delay, which is all the more striking when we consider that the first pagan literary forms in both Greek and Latin were poetry. But Christianity originated in an environment very different from that in which Greek and Latin literary culture arose. Christianity spread throughout a world that was already strongly acculturated, and the formation of the Christian religion's own literature was a conquest, not an inheritance.

Some have suggested that poetry was the most literary and rhetorical form of the culture of that time, and therefore the most difficult for new men of letters (the Christians) to access. But other literary forms, of prose, were also experiencing intense rhetorical development. Another suggestion is more probable: the situation in which Christianity found itself as a persecuted religion suggested or even made it necessary that Christians devote themselves to literary forms that had a greater impact on real life, such as apologetical works, works of controversy, and letter writing. There was a more urgent need for theological literature, given the necessity of establishing an orthodoxy and a canon of religious texts, than of poetic compositions, which seemed more disinterested in character. Another suggested explanation is that poetry seemed to Christians to convey the essence of pagan culture, and was therefore avoided, and the condemnation of the poets as liars and excogitators of immoral myths helped keep alive a Christian aversion to poetry. However, anti-pagan Christian polemicists attacked with equal violence both poetry and prose, because their concern was with the content, not the forms, of pagan literary works.

BIBLIOGRAPHY

The *Vetus Latina* is being edited by the Abbey of Beuron and published by Herder of Freiburg. For the parts still lacking two works are indispensable:

Itala: Das Neue Testament in altlateinscher Überlieferung (ed. A. Jülicher; 2d ed.; 4 vols.; New York: de Gruyter, 1970–).

Bibliorum Sacrorum Latinae versiones antiquae seu Vetus Italica (ed. P. Sabatier; 3 vols.; Rheims: 1743–1749; photographic repr., Turnhout, Belgium: Brepolis, 1976).

J.-C. Fredouille, "Les lettres chrétiens face à la Bible," in *Le monde latin antique et la Bible* (ed. J. Fontaine and C. Pietri; BiToTe 2; Paris: Beauchesne, 1985), 25–42.

J. Gribomont, "Les plus anciens traductions latines," in *Le monde latin antique et la Bible* (ed. J. Fontaine and C. Pietri; BiToTe 2; Paris: Beauchesne, 1985), 43–65.

P. Petitmengin, "Les plus anciens manuscrits de la Bible latine," in *Le monde latin antique et la Bible* (ed. J. Fontaine and C. Pietri; BiToTe 2; Paris: Beauchesne, 1985), 89–127.

R. Braun, "L'influence de la Bible sur la langue latine," in *Le monde latin antique et la Bible* (ed. J. Fontaine and C. Pietri; BiToTe 2; Paris: Beauchesne, 1985), 129–42.

V. Saxer, "Bible et Liturgie," in *Le monde latin antique et la Bible* (ed. J. Fontaine and C. Pietri; BiToTe 2; Paris: Beauchesne, 1985), 339–69.

J. Schrijnen, *I caratteri del latino cristiano antico* (IT and app. C. Mohrmann; ed. S. Boscherini; Bologna: Patron, 1977).

C. Mohrmann, *Études sur le latin des Chrétiens* I–IV (Rome: Storia e Letteratura, 1961–1977).

P. Prigent, *Les Testimonia dans le Christianisme primtif* (Paris: Gabalda, 1961).

J. Daniélou, *The Theology of Jewish Christianity* (trans. J. A. Baker; London: Darton, Longman & Todd/Chicago: Regnery, 1964).

————, *Le origini del cristianesimo latino* (Bologna: Dehoniane, 1991).

E. Gallicet, "Cipriano e la Bibbia" in *Forma Futuri: Studi in onore del Cardinal Michele Pellegrino* (Turin: Bottega d'Erasmo, 1975), 43–52.

J. Fontaine, *Naissance de la poésie dans l'occident chrétien: Esquisse d'une histoire de la poésie chrétienne du IIIe au VIe siècle* (Paris: Études Augustiniennes, 1981).

R. Palla, "Aspetti e momenti della poesia cristiana latina del quarto secolo" in *La poesia: Origine e sviluppo delle forme poetiche nella letteratura occidentale* (ed. G. Arrighetti; Pisa: ETS, 1991), 97–116.

J. Den Boeft and A. Hilhorst, eds., *Early Christian Poetry: A Collection of Essays* (VCSup 22; New York: Brill, 1993).

P. I. Kaufman, *Church, Book, and Bishop: Conflict and Authority in Early Latin Christianity* (Boulder, Colo.: Westview, 1996).

S. E. Porter, *Handbook of Classical Rhetoric in the Hellenistic Period, 330 B.C.– A.D. 400* (Leiden: Brill, 1997).

J. Vanderspoel, "Claudian, Christ, and the Cult of the Saints," *CQ* 36, 1 (1986): 244–55.

Chapter 18

THE CHRISTIAN LITERATURE OF AFRICA

The short works we briefly discussed in the preceding chapter—the *Muratorian Canon* and *Against Dice Players*—give at least a glimpse of the Christian world of Rome with its religious and ethical concerns and its animating desire to establish the church's "authority" over the settling of a "canon" of writings. This was a new idea, alien to the Roman religions. New also was the conviction that the sacred text possessed an authority deriving from God, and that therefore its authenticity had to be ensured. The documents that allow us to acquire a first idea of the African Christian world are dated a few decades later than the Roman documents.

It has been thought that Christianity was spread in Africa by missionaries from Rome at a very early period, perhaps even by the end of the first century. The African community, as attested by a long and stubborn tradition attested by Tertullian, always felt itself linked to Rome more than to any other see, and kept its eyes fixed on the capital. Even when it would have to contend with Rome during the third century, Carthage saw the Roman see as its only partner in dialogue.

In some ways, this situation is readily explained by the close relations that existed between Carthage, the most important city of the West after the capital itself, and Rome. There had been a heavy Roman colonization of Africa ever since the republican period. Moreover, in the second century Africa was the most intensely acculturated province in the western part of the empire; Fronto and Apuleius were proof of this, and Tertullian, perhaps the most important Christian writer of the time, was able to hear the brilliant lectures of Apuleius, the famous orator of Madaura. In its spread through Africa, as elsewhere, Christianity had to address an upper social class that was concerned with culture; it is likely that at least some Christian converts were educated men. Rhetoric pervades the works of all the African writers of the third century, who had trained in it before their conversion, and afterwards retained it as an essential *forma mentis*.

In our opinion, then, to fully understand the phenomenon of Christian literature we must emphasize the intense Romanization of the province of Africa in the imperial age, a Romanization that affected all levels of life and not just the literary sphere. We need only advert to the evidence that archeology has supplied as it has uncovered the manner of life of the inhabitants of the region. The northern coast of Africa from Leptis Magna in Libya to Mauritania, and from the second to the fourth centuries supplies clear evidence of the Roman lifestyle as manifested in the building of country houses, baths, basilicas, and amphitheaters. We find less convincing the view of those who maintain that Christianity in Africa came from the East, without Roman mediation, and that the idea of a derivation of the church of Carthage from the church of Rome is a construct of Tertullian and does not fit the facts.

In any case, the local Punic tradition does not seem to have been dominant, although it is attested. There is little evidence for a radical antagonism between Punic civilization and Roman civilization as the source of the differences that emerged among Christian writers of the third century, as though the attacks of Tertullian and Cyprian on pagan Rome were due to their African origin. Moreover, the attacks show inconsistencies and were not radical. The rejection of paganism as a religion and an ideology was certainly unqualified and entailed the condemnation also of the pagan way of life. No Christian ever challenged this condemnation, at least in theory. But this did not mean that African Christianity condemned the *entire* pagan world. Furthermore, it is not valid to extend to the entire African church rebellious statements that come for the most part from Tertullian and only at well-defined moments, or to maintain that the entire attitude of African Christianity was reducible to this spirit of rebellion. Tertullian's relationship to the secular world was always ambiguous; this ambiguity was inevitable, inasmuch as Christians had to live in a world that was not really their own.

It has also been noted that African Christianity regarded martyrdom as the supreme value, unlike contemporary Alexandrian Christianity, which saw gnosis as the means of reaching perfection. But this attitude has been improperly interpreted as due essentially to racial factors. In this view, African Christianity, in calling for martyrdom, would resemble the local cult of Saturn, which at one time, under Punic control, called for human sacrifices. Indeed, martyrdom had a fundamental value for Christianity in the Greek world, beginning with Ignatius of Antioch, and it occurred no less often in the East than in the West. Meanwhile, the great importance given to gnosis was typical of certain individuals and certain circles and not of the overall manner in which people conceived the Christian faith.

Carthage could vie for importance with the other cities of the empire, such as Rome and Alexandria. It was not only a commercial center but also a cultural center of the first rank and was visited by Apuleius, a man of letters. It is probable that Fronto, who around 160 wrote a book against Christians, also went to the capital of the province. As a cosmopolitan city, Carthage had a sizable Jewish community with its own cemetery. Tertullian—and surely other Christians as well—knows Jewish customs, although Tertullian's knowledge remained superficial and he was unfamiliar with the development of Jewish thought in his own day. As in every age, relations between Jews and Christians were sometimes good, sometimes bad; on occasion Tertullian accused the Jews of promoting persecution, but we know that this was mainly a commonplace. He also wrote a work against Jews in which he made his own the accusations that had been repeated for at least a century.

There were also easterners in Carthage, and there were many inscriptions in Greek in honor of Serapis. As in the rest of the Latin West, Greek was the language spoken by educated people. Tertullian, probably responding to social reality, wrote some of his works in Greek, which he knew rather well. Christianity was known to pagans in Carthage and in Africa and, although it was subjected to sporadic persecutions and occasional acts of violence, it lived in the open, as we know from Tertullian's *Apology*. Christians, moreover, had their own cemetery which was hidden away, and pagans occasionally vandalized it with the approval of the Roman governor. There was surely at least one church, perhaps part of a private home, and there were other meeting places.

BIBLIOGRAPHY

P. Monceaux, *Histoire littéraire de l'Afrique chrétienne depuis les origines jusquä l'invasion arabe* (vol. I; Paris: Leroux, 1901–1923).

E. Buonaiuti, *Il cristianesimo nell'Africa romana* (Bari: Laterza, 1928).

W. H. C. Frend, *Martyrdom and Persecution in the Early Church* (Oxford: Blackwell, 1965).

T. D. Barnes, *Tertullian: A Historical and Literary Study* (3d ed.; Oxford: Oxford University Press, 1984).

P. Siniscalco, *Il cammino di Cristo nell'impero romano* (Bari: Laterza, 1987).

E. Dal Covolo, *I Severi e il Cristianesimo* (Rome: Las, 1989).

R. D. Sider, *Ancient Rhetoric and the Art of Tertullian* (London: Oxford University Press, 1971).

For English translations consult volumes 7, 11, 15, 18 of *The Ante-Nicene Fathers* (ed. A. Roberts, J. Donaldson, and A. C. Coxe; repr., Grand Rapids, Mich: Eerdmans, 1996–2001).

1. Acts of the Scillitan Martyrs

Whether it came from Rome or from the Greek world, Christianity was already present in Africa by about 170–180. The former date is approximately that of the *Metamorphoses* of Apuleius. According to many scholars, in one passage of his novel (9.14) this pagan intellectual, who accepted Platonism and practiced the worship of the Egyptian goddess Isis, described a dissolute woman, to whom he attributed the defects and crimes of which the common people usually accused Christians.

A more accurate and much more important witness to African Christianity is the *Acts of the Scillitan Martyrs,* a concise account of a trial that ended with a death sentence for some Christians. As we are likewise told by Tertullian, Vigellius Saturninus, Proconsul of Africa, was probably the first persecutor of Christians in that region; on July 17, 180, he passed sentence on some citizens of Scilli or Scillium, a city of that province. The condemned were surely of humble origin and, if we may judge by their names (Speratus, Nartzalus, Cittinus, Donata, Secunda, and Vestia), even of the Punic population. The content of the discussion at the trial is highly interesting, for it shows with great clarity some of the typical Christian motifs, such as alienation from this earthly world and the refusal of any compromise with paganism, especially the worship of the emperor. After a short introduction that tells about the trial, the *Acts* tell us of the debate between the most imposing person among the martyrs and the proconsul. The proconsul offers the Christians an imperial pardon if they repent, but the Christians do not even consider the offer, saying only that they have always behaved in a blameless way. They are thus condemned solely for being Christians.

With these *Acts,* the literature of Acts and Passions began in the West. Strictly speaking, however, the *Acts of the Scillitan Martyrs* are only a report of a trial and therefore simply a document similar to many others, which we imagine were gradually stylized in situations of that kind. What is new is the intention of the redactor of the *Acts,* so that we speak here of a new literary genre: the account is meant to keep alive in the community of the faithful an admiration for and the memory of those who have died for the faith. In addition, the account is implicitly an exhortation, addressed to the entire community, to emulate these martyrs. We shall speak later of the spirituality that focused on martyrdom (see below, sec. 10).

BIBLIOGRAPHY

The Acts of the Christian Martyrs (ed. H. Musurillo; Oxford: Oxford University Press, 1972).

G. Lanata, *Gli atti dei martiri come documenti processuali* (Milan: Giuffrè, 1973).

Atti e Passioni dei Martiri (ed. A. A. R. Bastiaensen; trans. G. Chiarini et al.; Milan: Fondazione Valla-Mondadori, 1987); collective volume.

Atti dei Martiri Scillitani (ed. and trans. F. Ruggiero; Rome: Accademia Nazionale dei Lincei, 1991).

2. Tertullian

A few years after the condemnation of the Scillitan martyrs, and a few kilometers from their obscure village, the capital of the province saw the beginning of the literary career of the first great African writer, one of the greatest (even counting the pagans) in the Latin language, pagans included. His greatness rests not only on his artistry but also on the contribution he made to the thought of western Christianity.

The life of Quintus Septimius Florens Tertullianus is a mystery. We know nothing certain about his life and death, except for his birth in Carthage. His works offer only a few indications of a chronological kind; to these we should add information from Jerome, who dedicates ch. 53 of his *Famous Men* to Tertullian, along with part of ch. 24, which completes what Augustine says in *Heresies* (86). Jerome seems to have used some works of Tertullian that are now lost, such as the work *On Ecstasy (De extasi)* in seven books, and some vague oral traditions. He supposedly received information from someone named Paul, who lived in Concordia and told him a story about Cyprian: whenever Cyprian wanted to read a work of Tertullian—and this was a daily occurrence—he used to say to his secretary: "Hand me the teacher." Jerome is also the only one to speak (*Epist.* 22.22; *Jov.* 1.13) of a work Tertullian supposedly composed before his conversion, on the subject of the difficulties that trouble the life of the married wise man *(To a Philosopher Friend [Ad amicum philosophum])*. He must therefore have been a mature man before his conversion in 197, and his birth can be dated to around 160.

BIBLIOGRAPHY

On the early, lost works of Tertullian: P. Frassinetti, "Gli scritti matrimoniali di Seneca e Tertulliano," Rend. Istit. Lomb. Scienze e Letter 87 (1955): 151–.

C. Tibiletti, "Un opuscolo perduto di Tertulliano: 'Ad amicum philosophum,'" Atti Accad. d. Scienze di Torino 95 (1960–1961): 122–66.

There was a lawyer named Tertullian whose works are known from extracts in the *Digest* and *Codex* of Justinian, and it has been thought that the Christian writer and the lawyer were the same person. This hypothesis must be rejected, for it is based substantially on the captious and pettifogging attitude of the Carthaginian writer, an attitude which may have been the result of his rhetorical training. This is not to say, however, that Tertullian did not have some knowledge of Roman law, if for no other reason than because of the consequences of that law for the juridical status of Christians and for the persecutions carried out against them.

Jerome always speaks of Tertullian as a priest, but this information has been rejected by some scholars. One of his statements (*Exh. cast.* 7.3) seems to contradict the idea: "Are not we lay persons also priests?" But this has also been interpreted as meaning: "Is it not the case that, *even if we were laypersons,* we would still be priests?" Another statement in *The Soul* (9.4) refers to an incident during a Sunday service at which Tertullian addressed the faithful, who were then dismissed. Jerome ends by saying that Tertullian "lived to a great age," which leads us to place his death in around A.D. 230. The last facts about his life seems to be those reported by Augustine (*Haer.* 86), who tells us that Tertullian supposedly founded his own church of "Tertullianists," after distancing himself from that of the Montanists, to which he previously belonged. This conventicle of Tertullianists survived, though ever decreasing in number, to Augustine's time; Augustine then brought its last survivors back to orthodoxy.

The other dates of Tertullian's life are those related to his works. The group consisting of *To the Heathen* and the *Apology* belong at the beginning of his activity as a Christian writer; specific references to the wars between Septimius Severus and his rivals for the throne place the two works in 197. An equally precise indicator in the first book *Against Marcion* takes us with certainty to 207–208. References to the persecution of 212 are found in *To Scapula* and, with lesser probability, in *The Crown* and in *Flight in Persecution.* The work on *Monogamy* must be later, for in it (3.8) Tertullian makes a chronological calculation on the basis of the dating of 1 Corinthians, which leads us to date the work to about 217. *Modesty* seems to be the final work. It has been suggested in the past that this work refers to events during the pontificate of Callistus or during the episcopate of Bishop Agrippinus of Carthage (around 220); both interpretations, however, have less a following today. We must note, finally, that according to some the work on *The Pallium* signaled Tertullian's abandonment of Montanism and his founding of the sect of Tertullianists; if so, this short work must be his last, and therefore dated after 220.

a. First Apologetic Works

It is worth noting that the works Tertullian wrote before his conversion have been lost, although Jerome knew them. At the very beginning of Tertullian's literary activity stands a group of works devoted to the defense of Christianity (*To the Heathen* and *Apology* [*Ad nationes* and *Apologeticus*]). There is one on the anti-Christian persecution that ultimately calls for and gives the stimulus to apologetics; we refer to the exhortation *To the Martyrs (Ad martyras).* The *Apology* is to be dated to 197 and, more precisely, to the fall of that year, because it refers to the recent campaign of Septimius Severus against the Parthians (37.4). The other work, *To the Heathen,* was composed a few months earlier, because it refers (1.17.4) to the victory of the same Septimius Severus over Claudius Albinus at Lyons in February of that year.

The two works are quite similar in content and details. It has been thought that this similarity can be explained by seeing in the one a real attack on pagans, and in the other, the *Apology*, a defense of Christians. However, the two attitudes, of attack and defense, are present in both works and are already to be found in the Greek apologetic tradition on which the Latin writer depends. If a distinction is needed, it is preferable to say that the two works display, as is typical of Greek apologetics, two different types of defense: one addressed to the educated public, the other to the magistrates of Carthage. The most likely explanation is that *To the Heathen* is an incomplete work in the form of a sketch, which is repeated and filled out a few months later in the *Apology*.

It should also be noted that the *Apology* has reached us in two redactions. One of them is contained in the manuscript tradition that we now have, the so-called "vulgate redaction." The other can be reconstructed from readings taken from a now lost manuscript, which had been kept at one time in the Fulda library, and placed by humanist Francesco Modius in the margin of Barraeus's fifteenth century edition: the "Fulda redaction." In addition, Modius drew from the same Fulda manuscript the continuous text of ch. 19 in a form which is not the same as in the vulgate text or in the Fulda redaction, and which is known as the "Fulda fragment." The most likely explanation is that all these redactions resulted from successive versions of the work by the author himself, who published last the version that has been handed down as the "vulgate redaction."

So, then, the work addressed to the pagans would stand at the beginning of the laborious editorial process that ended with the publication of the vulgate redaction of the *Apology*. It is in the course of that development that the letter of exhortation *To the Martyrs* has its place; it was written during the same period of wars and violence that convulsed the Roman empire and to which the *Apology* likewise bears witness. The *Apology* is the most remarkable work of this literary genre in Latin, and one of the most important composed by Tertullian, who had the skill to use traditional elements from Greek apologetics to create something entirely new.

As can be seen from the works of Justin, Tatian, and Athenagoras, it was traditional to base the defense of Christianity on the antiquity of Jewish antecedents, the purity of the new religion, the rigorous moral code that distinguished its followers, and their loyalty to the authorities of the state, especially the emperor. It was also traditional to reproach the pagans for their dissolute lives, the immoral principles that governed their conduct, and their rebelliousness and disloyalty to established authority. It was typical of Greek apologetics to present the pagan reader, for whom the work was intended, with a quick summary of Christian teaching, which made use of philosophical ideas, mostly Stoic, and would be easily understood by educated people. The purpose of this summary was to show that Christianity, while not properly a philosophy, was nevertheless the completion and crown of all that was most admirable in pagan philosophy.

In contrast, Tertullian's impetuous personality emerges most clearly when he proves, beyond possibility of refutation, the absurdity of the legal procedure applied by provincial governors in their persecution of Christians. He speaks of their following the rescript of Trajan, which prohibited the official searching out of Christians by the pagan authorities, but called for their condemnation when they were denounced and convicted for being Christians. Thus the latter would be guilty only of being Christians and not of any violation whatsoever of the law. This attack comes at the beginning of the *Apology* and serves to lead the reader into an apologetical treatise skillfully constructed according to the rules of rhetoric. In this respect the work differs from those of the Greeks, which were for the most part verbose and disorganized.

Fundamental for Tertullian, and substantially missing in Greek apologetics, is a reconsideration of political realities from a new and Christian point of view. Into this reflection the author introduces all the ambiguities and uncertainties of his own religious faith, as he wavers between an open and loyal acknowledgment of the validity of the state as an institution and a no less clear denial of its intrinsic goodness. As an institution that in certain respects is approved by God, the empire is a good thing and serves to "hold back" the final catastrophe that awaits the human race. On the other hand, the state is always the work of human beings, and furthermore, of human beings enslaved to idolatry, so that there can be no agreement between Christ and Belial. This wavering between recognition and denial of the empire is one of the most interesting of the political ideas of the Carthaginian writer, for in this thinking he retains the original Christian tradition, which as early as the New Testament writings implied these two contrasting attitudes. Note, however, that Tertullian's denial of the empire never reaches the point of insubordination; he emphasizes the necessity of obedience even during times of persecution.

There is another demand made of the state which Tertullian voices in the *Apology* and will reemphasize fifteen years later in 212 in a letter addressed to Scapula, governor of the province, but obviously intended for publication. During Scapula's proconsulate, anti-Christian violence was given a new impulse, and it appears that the proconsul's personal attitude played a part therein. Addressing Scapula, Tertullian skillfully alternates threats and advice. He lists all the instances of violent and brutal death that have felled persecutors of Christians, thus anticipating the "death of persecutors" motif that Lactantius will systematically develop a century later. He stresses the favor which the new religion has enjoyed in the past among "good" emperors (a motif already found in the *Apology*) and now enjoys in the imperial palace. This difference of attitude toward Christians was typical of an age in which, as is clear with Scapula's persecution, violence could be ordered by the governor of a province without the emperor even being aware of it.

More interesting still is the fact that Tertullian expresses clearly and decisively the insuppressible need of every human being for freedom of worship. Strictly speaking, Tertullian had no reason to state this principle, since the Roman empire had always traveled the road of religious toleration and accepted the practice of any and every religion, provided it was not contrary to law. But this principle had not been observed for 150 years in the case of Christianity, hence the demand that Christians too be able to enjoy civil freedom to worship the God in whom they believe.

As noted above, with the *Apology* can be linked the letter of exhortation *To the Martyrs*, in which Tertullian uses the literary genre of "protreptic" in a new situation: martyrdom. The writer also uses many traditional ideas and many arguments derived from the quite masculine philosophy of the Stoics when he exhorts Christians to endure torture and death. There is a motif that serves as a link between the *Apology* and another work, *The Soul's Testimony (De testimonio animae)*. In this work the writer applies a doctrine of Stoic origin to Christianity: he maintains that when the human soul is stripped of the errors instilled in it by false teachings, when it is free of prejudices coming from outside, and when it is able to express itself freely and to voice what Stoics called the "innate idea" of God, it will bear witness to the existence of the only true God, who is almighty, good, and just. Therefore this universally valid testimony of the soul is also a defense of the true religion.

When Tertullian's apologetics is considered in the much broader setting of Christian apologetics, both Greek and Latin, it is very rich in motifs and ideas that go beyond the simple defense of Christianity. It provides an insight into the writer from the first moments of his activity in the service of the new religion, which he had embraced only a short time before. It can be said of Tertullian that polemics was his basic mindset. This does not mean that his polemics came down to simple litigiousness or quibbling; this happened only rarely. Rather, it was a tool and vehicle for new and personal ideas.

The attitude is a constant one in Tertullian, and we find it everywhere, even in works composed after the apologetic writings. He was an impatient and dissatisfied person, seldom acquiescent, unable to adapt himself, often intolerant, as he himself was forced to admit. Even when he acknowledges he was mistaken, he does so with a sense of resentment against the one who caught his mistake. Thus he found in polemics the most comfortable way to express himself and make known his ideas. His series of antiheretical works had for their purpose not only to rebut the doctrinal deviations at which they were aimed, but also to serve as the best instrument for presenting Tertullian's own teaching. Even treatises which, according to their titles are explicitly dogmatic and not polemical and were intended for discussion of a particular point of Christian doctrine, are written essentially against someone. Similarly, in works on ethics that are devoted to the study of practical problems and Christian discipline, Tertullian skillfully maintains a position different from that of other Christians, and is therefore compelled, once again, to engage in polemics.

BIBLIOGRAPHY

C. Becker, *Tertullians Apologeticum: Werden und Leistung* (Munich: Kösel, 1954).
On the juridical problem, see the broader question of the persecutions, on which the bibliography is immense. We shall cite only some more recent works that are more readily accessible to Italian readers:
M. Sordi, *Roma e i cristiani* (Bologna: Cappelli, 1970).
R. Klein, *Tertullian und das römische Reich* (Heidelberg: Winter, 1968).
P. Siniscalco, *Il cammino di Cristo nell'impero romano* (Bari: Laterza, 1987).
E. Peretto, *La sfida aperta* . . . (Rome: Borla, 1998).

b. Antiheretical Polemics

"Prescription" *(praescriptio)* was in use before Tertullian began his attacks on heresies and constituted the juridical basis for those attacks. By appealing to this concept, drawn from Roman judiciary practice, Tertullian sought to bar heretics in principle from any use of the Scriptures, on the grounds that legitimate ownership of them belonged to the orthodox church alone. In Roman trials *praescriptio* was a formula that served to shorten the proceedings by predetermining the judgment in favor either of the accuser or of the accused. There were several kinds of *praescriptio;* the formula on which Tertullian primarily depends is that of the *longi temporis praescriptio,* according to which possession of the Scriptures over a long period of time legitimated the possession. This was precisely a prerogative of the "catholic" (i.e., universal) church, in which the teaching of Christ had been entrusted to the apostles and, by transmission from them, to the various churches they founded. The heretical churches came into existence after the orthodox churches, and consequently, their teaching, whenever distorted, amounted to forgery.

The treatise *Prescription against Heretics (De praescriptione haereticorum)* serves Tertullian as a vehicle for this antecedent barring of heretics, but it is of greater interest in that it explains the fundamental concept of early Christianity, that is, *traditio,* "tradition" here being understood as the "passing on" of the deposit of faith from generation to generation, from the Mother church to churches founded by her. That is how Tertullian describes, in broad lines, the spread of Christianity from the apostles down to the churches of his own time. His conviction was that all the Christian sees, whether founded directly or indirectly by the apostles, enjoy equal dignity and autonomy; Carthage, all the same, felt closest to Rome. In this work Tertullian also provides information about the practice of Christian catechesis, part of which was already a baptismal "symbol" that can be regarded as an early type of "creed."

The use of *praescriptio* would not by itself have convinced anyone, least of all heretics, who boasted that they relied on a secret tradition. It was therefore necessary to oppose them on their own ground, as had already been done by Justin and Irenaeus, authorities to whom Tertullian appeals. His set of antiheretical works is a remarkable product of Christian controversy in the western world and is matched only by those of Augustine. As noted earlier, however, their importance was not due solely to their polemical and destructive element but also to their formulation of the dogma of the Trinity, which was built up laboriously through the dismantling of heretical constructs of it.

We leave aside the work *Against the Valentinians (Adversus Valentinianos)*, written perhaps about 210, for it contains no substantially new ideas, but simply mocks the heretics and refutes them with arguments often drawn verbatim from the *Against Heresies* of Irenaeus.

The same cannot be said, however, of the work *Against Hermogenes (Adversus Hermogenem)* from about 205. It is quite interesting, despite the fact that the teaching of this heretic had found very little echo. Hermogenes was inspired by contemporary Platonism and taught that God had created the world out of matter that is coeternal with God. Hermogenes therefore rejected the exclusively Christian concept of *creatio ex nihilo.* In the *Against Hermogenes* Tertullian develops for the first time a theology of the Logos as coeternal with God. In doing so he develops more fully some hints in the Greek apologists and also uses some ideas from Stoicism and Platonism, e.g., the distinction between the "uttered word" and the "word within the human mind" (that is, thought).

Stoicism, to a greater extent even than Platonism, undergirds a later work (ca. 215) that is important for the history of Latin theology, namely, the *Against Praxeas (Adversus Praxean).* Tertullian wrote it because he had encountered a new and no less dangerous heresy, which we may call "modalism," simplifying here, for brevity's sake, later developments and restructurings. This heresy, which originated in Asia Minor and spread mainly in that region, was hostile to any theology of the Logos. It was especially insidious because it brought to light the discomfort caused by the Christian doctrine that there are three divine "persons." A proof of this is that modalism continued in existence, with some adaptations to new situations, down to the fourth century in both the East and the West. Many thought they could avoid conflict by thinking of the Son and the Spirit as simply "modes" or ways in which the one divine nature, which belongs to the Father alone, manifested itself. This accounts for the modern name "modalism" for a heresy that the ancients traced back to a no better known person named Sabellius.

In arguing with the modalists Tertullian clarifies his own teaching on the Trinity, and does so with remarkably acute reasoning and an extensive use of scriptural testimonies. In this teaching he stresses the real and individual existence of the divine Persons within the one nature. He uses the term *substantia,* rarely found hitherto even in Latin philosophy, to mean the divine substance, and while not yet using the term "person," he speaks of the "Three" who constitute the divine substance. We must bear in mind that in Tertullian, and for almost two centuries after him, the doctrine of the Holy Spirit was still being formulated in an imperfect and summary way; a theological grasp of the reality of the third Person would have to wait for Ambrose and above all Augustine. In the Greek world, though it was more advanced than the Latin in dealing with theological problems, the development was no different. The doctrine of the Trinity as worked out by Tertullian was seen again in Novatian and Lactantius and remained the customary form of it at least until Hilary of Poitiers in the middle of the fourth century.

No less important is another of Tertullian's antiheretical works and the longest of all his writings, the *Against Marcion (Adversus Marcionem)* in five books. He wrote three successive versions of it between 205 and about 213, each version longer than the preceding. In it he tackles the very dangerous heresy of Marcion. Opposing the heretic's *Antitheses,* he shows in the first book that the supreme god of Marcion did not exist, and in the second that the God of the Old Testament and of Christians was not the inferior god of Marcion. The third book refutes Marcionite Christology, which claimed that the Christ who came was not to be identified with the Messiah of the Jews, for whom they were still waiting. The fourth book is devoted to refuting the heretic's interpretation of the gospel of Luke, the only one the Marcionites regarded as authentic; Tertullian shows that the teaching on Christ in that Gospel was not opposed to the teaching of the Old Testament. The fifth book, finally, seeks to refute the falsifications, deletions, and textual changes that Marcion made in the Pauline letters in order to make them fit his own teaching.

The *Against Marcion* makes especially wearisome reading because of its length, but it is a wide-ranging work. In addition to containing an effective refutation of that particular heresy, it undertakes a successful retrieval of the Old Testament, which was customarily rejected by all the heretics as being the revelation of an inferior god and therefore imperfect and open to criticism. In achieving his purpose Tertullian did not fall back on allegorical interpretation, as was customary in early Christianity; on the contrary, he reinterpreted the Jewish religion by basing his exegesis on the ideas of correspondence and development between the Old Testament and the New. The Marcionites had rejected the Old Testament by emphasizing for polemical purposes its anthropomorphisms and the absurdities that follow from a literal interpretation, which Marcion, like the Jews, regarded as the only one possible.

Tertullian accepts the same exegetical premises (which he found congenial) and demonstrates the central importance of the Old Testament for Christians by emphasizing, solely by means of a strict objective comparison, the correspondences between the New Testament and the Old, between Pauline teaching and that of the ancient Scriptures. He says: "As the fruit comes from the seed, while being other than the seed, so the New Testament proceeds from the Old, being other but not divergent." And he sums up his conception of the relationship in one of his rhetorically effective sentences: "O Christ, you are ancient even when you teach new doctrines!"

Against Apelles, a disciple of Marcion, Tertullian wrote a work now lost: *Against the Followers of Apelles (Adversus Apelleiacos)*.

Associated with the third book of the *Against Marcion* is a work that has come down to us in a fragmentary and sketchy state; only the first part of this work *Against the Jews (Adversus Iudaeos)* seems to be authentic. Tertullian had stressed that by refusing to recognize in the Christ who came the one whom the Jews thought of as the Messiah and whom they still awaited, the Marcionites placed themselves on essentially the same level as the Jews. In the authentic part of the *Against the Jews* we find the traditional themes of anti-Jewish polemics, ubiquitous themes in early Christian works: the messianic interpretation of the best-known prophecies, and the conviction that the correct interpretation of the Scriptures was now barred to the Jews, because of the hardness of their hearts as manifested in their disobedience to the law of God and their refusal to accept the gift of the Spirit.

In Tertullian's work, which, as noted earlier, comes to us in a sketchy form, all these motifs, which are not fully developed, derive from Justin's *Dialogue with Trypho*. Tertullian wrote this work not in order to convince Jews but to persuade pagans to be converted to Christianity and not to Judaism. He considers Judaism to be a faith which is true in its principles, but which has become fossilized and has been surpassed by Christianity. It is a faith that no longer deserves attention, because it has been abandoned by the Spirit of God.

BIBLIOGRAPHY

A. d'Alès, *La théologie de Tertullien* (Paris: Beauchesne, 1905).

A. Orbe, *En los albores de la exegesis Iohannea (Joh. 1, 3)* (Rome: Gregorian University, 1955).

―――, *Estudios Valentinianos* (Rome: Gregorian University, 1958).

M. Simon, *Verus Israel: Études sur les relations entre chrétiens et juifs dans l'Empire Romain* (2d. ed.; Paris: De Boccard, 1964).

J.-C. Fredouille, *Tertullian et la conversion de la culture antique* (Paris: Études Augustiniennes, 1972); cited here on the problem of antiheretical polemics.

J. Moingt, *Théologie trinitaire de Tertullien* (4 vols.; Paris: Aubier, 1966–1969).

R. Braun, *Deus Christianorum: Recherches sur le vocabulaire doctrinal de Tertullien* (2d ed.; Paris: Études Augustiniennes, 1977).

G. L. Prestige, *God in Patristic Thought* (2d ed.; London: SPCK, 1952).

J. N. D. Kelly, *Early Christian Doctrine* (2d ed.; New York: Harper & Row, 1960).

E. A. Isichei, *Political Thinking and Social Experience: Some Christian Interpreta-tions of the Roman Empire from Tertullian to Salvian* (University of Canter-bury Publications 6; Christchurch, New Zealand: University of Canterbury Press, 1964).

T. P. O'Malley, *Tertullian and the Bible: Language, Imagery, Exegesis* (LTP 21; Nijmegen/Utrecht: Dekker & Van de Vegt, 1967).

D. A. Rankin, *Tertullian and the Church* (Cambridge/New York: Cambridge University Press, 1995).

c. Other Doctrinal Contributions

In addition to these explicitly antiheretical works there are others written during the same period of intense activity (205–ca. 215) and linked to the former, inasmuch as they deal with problems of fundamental importance for Christianity, even if they are more openly dogmatic. The purpose of the treatise *The Flesh of Christ (De carne Christi)* is to show the reality and concrete character of the incarnation of Christ, in opposition to the belief almost universally held by heretics, that human flesh is con-temptible and a source of sin. Some currents of pagan thought shared a similar encratite persuasion. According to the heretics, then, Christ assumed only a sem-blance of flesh, or in the Valentinian hypothesis, a flesh of a different kind, a spiritual or psychic flesh comparable to the human soul. But Tertullian objects: If Christ did not have true flesh he could not have saved human beings.

The defense of human flesh is taken up again in an extensive work that is one of Tertullian's most important writings: *The Resurrection of the Flesh (De resurrectione carnis)*. In it the writer investigates the anthropological problem in its entirety. The Athenians long ago had laughed at the doctrine of the resurrection when Paul wished to speak of it in his address on the Areopagus (see Acts 17:32), and the attitude of the gnostics on this point did not differ from that of the pagans. This treatise of Tertullian, the first work by a western Christian writer on the dogma of the resurrec-tion, is especially important. Starting with the teaching of Irenaeus, Tertullian main-tains that human beings, made in the image of God (that is, of Christ), have from God not only a soul but flesh as well. When Christ came to earth as a human being, he too was clothed in flesh; the flesh is therefore not only a work of God but can also be un-derstood as a pledge of the salvation for which human beings are destined.

This approach of Irenaeus and Tertullian, an approach concretely embedded in soteriology, would be abandoned in later speculative thought, which, under the influ-ence of Platonic anthropology, preferred to see the human image of God as residing primarily in the person's spiritual component. In his doctrine of the "image," Tertullian successfully gives a more profound justification of the dignity of human flesh, for he does not limit himself simply to asserting that it is God's work.

In a treatise of an unusual character Tertullian investigates the nature of *The Soul (De anima)*. The certainty of the soul's immortality is essential for Christians, and Tertullian does not dwell on it, precisely because he takes it for granted. He does, how-ever, think it necessary to go into the subject because his concern is with the problem of the soul's nature. Having already written a now lost work *The Origin of the Soul Against Hermogenes (De censu animae adversus Hermogenem)* in a controversy with that heretic, he now intends to explain the nature of the soul and must deal once again with a new problem. He relies therefore on a broad range of information, drawing not only on philosophy but also on pagan medical literature.

In the process he attacks gnostic and Platonic teachings because in his view the soul is not alien to the body with which it is connected. Consequently, in keeping with the Stoicism that serves as his basis, Tertullian maintains that the human soul is material. Indeed, even God is material, since everything that exists must have a "body," even if this be *sui generis* (*Prax* 7.8). Since the soul is corporeal and closely bound up with the body, it takes its origin from the souls of the begetters (traducianism), just as the body of the newborn is the product of the bodies of the parents. In this way Tertullian is able to confirm his teaching on the resurrection of the dead: as in this life, so in the next, soul and flesh make up a single indissoluble whole.

Turning to the question of the soul's destiny, Tertullian offers some quick thoughts based on an interpretation of Matt 5:26 ("and you shall not come out from the prison until you have paid the last penny of your debt"). These words are to be understood as a first sketchy idea of the doctrine of purgatory. But the hints are uncertain and somewhat contradictory, since elsewhere in the same work (ch. 55) Tertullian says that souls, even those of the just, will remain in the lower world until the universal judgment; only the souls of the martyrs are given immediate access to heaven (see *Res.* 43.4). This teaching was apparently also maintained in a now lost work *Paradise (De paradiso)*.

Bibliography

H. Finé, *Die Terminologie der Jenseitsvorstellungen bei Tertullian* (Bonn: Hanstein, 1958).

S. Otto, *Natura und Dispositio: Untersuchungen zum Naturbegriff and zur Denkform Tertullians* (Munich: Hüber, 1960).

W. Bender, *Die Lehre über den Heiligen Geist bei Tertullian* (Munich: Hüber, 1961).

R. Cantalamessa, *La cristologia di Tertulliano* (Fribourg: Edizioni Universitarie, 1962).

d. Ethics and Rigorism

Tertullian carried on his teaching activity not only in the major antiheretical and doctrinal treatises that we have been discussing but also in a rich series of short works on moral subjects that emphasize the most important moments of Christian life. These works are of interest both because they enable us to glimpse the real life of the Carthaginian church at that time and because they contain stimulating ideas. Some of them, the most important, we shall cite when we discuss Tertullian's Montanist teachings. Here we shall simply point out some of the ethical treatises, most of them short, that belong to the period when the writer had not yet cut himself off from the Catholic church. In these works we see a different side of the man, who was sometimes a violent polemicist, but was also sensitive to human needs, to the psychology of Christians, and to the needs of sinners.

Among the first of these works is *Baptism (De baptismo)*, written around 198–200. This treatise takes as its point of departure a statement by a heretic of the

Cainite sect, that an immersion in water cannot purify the soul. Tertullian's response is one of great beauty as he extols the attractions of water, its usefulness (water was precious in parched Africa), and the life it contains. He describes the rite of baptism and recalls the biblical passages in which it is prefigured. Baptism is necessary for salvation, but it is not appropriate to bestow it on infants, since they are unable to understand its importance.

Contemporaneous with *Baptism* is *Prayer (De oratione)*, which is addressed to catechumens and explains the Christian prayer par excellence; this little work is the earliest exegesis of the Our Father. The author extends his inquiry, however, and provides the faithful with some precepts for the best way to pray; these are of great interest for our knowledge of Christian practice.

From the same period comes the treatise on *The Shows (De spectaculis)*, in which the writer takes some learned, antiquarian information from Suetonius in order to explain the special characteristics of the various shows. These had been instituted by the Romans and then had spread through the various cities founded or colonized by the Romans. They were therefore popular in the city of Carthage, which, as noted earlier, was quite close in spirit to Rome. Christians were not always aware that after their conversion they ought to abandon their enthusiasm for these shows, which were often immoral (e.g., the gladiatorial games) or lacking in cultural value (e.g., the shows put on by actors). This was all the more true since these games were often placed under the protection of a pagan god, and should therefore be regarded as a manifestation of idolatry, so that to attend was interpreted as an act of worship of idols.

The same basic problem and the same situation are the subject of the treatise *Idolatry (De idololatria)*, the date of which is uncertain. According to some scholars it can be dated to the same period, that is, to the years immediately following Tertullian's conversion. According to others, who base their view primarily on the harsh rigorism of the work, it belongs to the Montanist period. Tertullian sees the sin of idolatry as pervading the whole life of pagan society, including business, teaching, and the trades. Christians are obliged to avoid every occasion of idolatry and must therefore inevitably cut themselves off from the community life of the pagan city.

Tertullian turns to exhortations of a practical kind in *The Apparel of Women (De cultu feminarum)*. It may be that two different works were combined to form a single work in two books: the first titled *Womanly Dress*, the second *The Apparel of Women*, which provided the final title. The subject is rather obvious: a condemnation of feminine ambition and luxury. Nevertheless, the work does not make disagreeable reading.

Also notable are *Patience (De patientia)* and *Repentance (De paenitentia)*. The first gives a Christian cast to Stoic motifs: patience is the strength to endure adversity. For the Stoics this was the virtue proper to the wise. The second work gives us knowledge of penitential practice at a very early period of Christianity. There are two repentances: the first happens upon being converted and is necessary in order to obtain forgiveness of sins committed during one's life as a pagan. The baptism that follows this repentance is the real "washing": this is the meaning of the word "baptism" in both Greek and Latin. The second repentance occurs within the Christian community and is effective only once. Tertullian considers forgiveness of the most serious sins to be possible; at the end of his life, after he has accepted Montanism, he rejects this possibility.

BIBLIOGRAPHY

R. Cantalamessa, ed., *Etica sessuale e matrimonio nel cristianesimo delle origini* (Milan: Vita e Pensiero, 1976).

H. Crouzel, *L'Église primitive face au divorce, du Ier au Ve siècle* (Paris: Beauchesne, 1971).

P. A. Gramaglia, *La condizione femminilie nelle prime communità cristiane* (Rome: Borla, 1984).

————, *Il matrimonio nel cristianesimo preniceno* (Rome: Borla, 1988).

C. Mazzucco, *"E fui fatta maschio": La donna nel Cristianesimo primitivo* (Florence: Le Lettere, 1989).

H. Pétré, *Caritas: Étude sur le vocabulaire latin de la charité chrétienne* (SSL 22; Louvain: Spicilegium Sacrum Lovaniense, 1948).

C. Rambaux, *Tertullien face aux morales des trois premiers siècles* (Paris: Les Belles Lettres, 1979).

V. Saxer, *Mort, martyrs, reliques en Afrique chrétienne aux premiers siècles . . .* (Paris: Beauchesne, 1980).

C. Tibiletti, *Verginità e matrimonio in antichi scrittori cristiani* (2d ed.; Rome: Herder, 1983).

e. Tertullian and Montanism

Early historians of the church and of heresy called Montanism "the Phrygian heresy," because Montanus, who inspired this movement of enthusiasts and ascetics, was a native of Phrygia. In its initial phase it seems to have produced a revival of the eschatological expectation of Christ's Parousia and a more lively interest in some forms of encratism. It has been thought that Montanism reached Africa only in the early years of the third century, because there is no trace of it in the *Acts of the Scillitan Martyrs,* but this is evidently an argument from silence.

The first testimonies to Tertullian's acceptance of Montanism are from 207–208, the time of the writing of book 1 of the *Against Marcion.* Here (1.29.4) he speaks of the "spiritual teaching" provided by the Paraclete regarding a fundamental point of discipline, namely, the intrinsic value of marriage. At that time, according to Tertullian, the Paraclete advised against marriage, although he did not condemn and reject it as the Marcionites did. Another important reference to Montanism is found at a later point in *Against Marcion:* discussing the millennium and its inauguration by the descent of the heavenly Jerusalem to earth, Tertullian cites some eschatological prophecies (Ezek 48:30–35; Rev 21:2) and "the message of the new prophecy, which is preserved as part of our faith" (2.24.4). There had supposedly been a vision, a few years before, of the heavenly Jerusalem descending to earth; this was in the time of the expedition of Septimius Severus against the Parthians around 198.

From that point on, Tertullian remained faithful to what he called the "New Prophecy" and defended it in lost works such as *Ecstasy (De exstasi)* in seven books; the last of these books was a debate with Apollonius, an anti-Montanist who lived at the end of the second century. It is uncertain whether another now lost work, *The Hope of the Faithful (De spe fidelium),* was written during the Montanist period or preceded it. In that work, as Tertullian himself tells us, he stressed the need for an allegorical interpretation of the future restoration of the kingdom of Judah, which the Jews took literally, defending the doctrine of the millennium.

Tertullian had had a lively expectation of the Parousia ever since the time when he wrote his *Apology*. Thanks to Montanism, he was now sure that the final years of the world were at hand. It seems, then, that a revived eschatological expectation, a greater disciplinary severity, and the certainty of a more vital and strengthening presence of the Paraclete were the reasons why Tertullian accepted the New Prophecy. Later Montanism would be likened to the Modalist heresy of Noetus, but that was in a period after Tertullian; such a distortion of the "rule of faith" would surely have seemed unacceptable to him, especially since his defense of the "rule of faith" became increasingly inflexible even while his Montanist convictions hardened. Among the latter were a defense of glossolalia and of individual inspiration, which usually occurred during ecstasy. His treatise on the soul, which was contemporaneous with the first books of the work against Marcion, gives us an idea of the eucharistic assemblies of the Carthaginian Montanists; one participant in these meetings was a sister in the faith who had once had a vision during an ecstasy.

In the Montanist works a heavy emphasis is placed on asceticism, especially in the areas of fasting and marital practice. The condemnation of second marriages, which was a form of rigorism widespread in early Christianity and which Tertullian advised in his exhortation *To His Wife (Ad uxorem)*, becomes in the Montanist works an unqualified prohibition. There it is combined with what is essentially a depreciation of marriage as an institution. Here Montanism and Tertullian adopted the encratite positions that were typical especially of the Christian East and known to us from, for example, remarks of Clement of Alexandria, but that were consistently condemned by the church.

This progressively less humane rigorism found expression in the very skillful and irritable use of sophisms, put forth as a way to make up for the weaknesses in the interpretation of the scriptural passages which Tertullian thought should support his views. We refer here to two works that have the same subject matter as *To His Wife*, namely, the *Exhortation to Chastity* (*De exhortatione castitatis*, in which *castitas*, for Tertullian, means "encratism") from about 207–211, and *Monogamy (De monogamia)* from about 215. In the latter work the writer, who seeks to justify his prohibition of second marriages stemming from his deeply held eschatological expectation, gives an arbitrary interpretation of 1 Corinthians 7 and a description of the apostle which, as Fontaine has justifiably remarked, fits Tertullian himself more than Paul. Tertullian writes: "The entire first Letter to the Corinthians is written not with ink but with bile, for it is full of indignation, rebukes, threats, and resentment."

In what was probably his final work, *Modesty (De pudicitia,* ca. 220), Tertullian turns back to an earlier question and in his response emphasizes the encratite elements. He takes as his point of departure the normative statement of a bishop—an *edictum*, he calls it, using a pagan term in a fitting but polemical way. Unfortunately, no one has yet been able to identify the bishop. Those who suggested Callistus of Rome were inspired by the desire to see an opposition between Rome and Carthage. Others have suggested Agrippinus, bishop of Carthage at that period. In any case, the *edictum* granted the church's forgiveness to those who were guilty of the capital sin of adultery but had done penance. Tertullian drops the more tolerant attitude he had adopted in his *Repentance,* the preceding work of the Catholic period, and maintains that the earthly church does not have the authority to grant forgiveness of capital sins (adultery, murder, and apostasy). *Modesty* is of special interest not only because it gives us Tertullian's views on penance but also because it provides the writer with the opportunity to develop his views on ecclesiology, to which we shall turn in a moment.

It is possible that in his increasing rigorism Tertullian allowed himself to be swayed by a tendency in his own character, which became increasingly intolerant and harsh. One notes that the encratism of his Montanist works was already substantially present in his earlier works as well. The writer is well aware that these rigorist attitudes were a novelty in the Christian ethical tradition, but he justifies them by referring to the teaching of the Paraclete. Important in this context is a passage (ch. 1) from his *The Veiling of Virgins (De virginibus velandis):* "The rule of faith is indeed unqualifiedly one; it alone is immutable and irreformable. . . . But while this rule of faith remains firm, everything having to do with discipline and Christian life is open to the novelty of reform, since until the end of time the grace of God is at work to improve us."

Also significant is that while the Montanist texts usually speak of the doctrine of the Spirit, Tertullian prefers to speak of the doctrine of the Paraclete, thus emphasizing, by using the word for the third person of the Trinity, the ethical aspect of Montanism, which regarded the Spirit as "the consoler" and "the teacher." This spiritual teaching took the form of a hardening of discipline in all areas: the practice of fasting *(On Fasting, against the Psychics [De jejunio adversus psychicos])*, and the obligation to face persecution, which is enjoined in *The Crown (De corona)* and in *Flight in Persecution (De fuga in persecutione)*, whereas in his non-Montanist writings Tertullian had allowed that one might avoid the test. Therefore, too, in contrast to the Valentinians, who did not consider martyrdom to be required by God, there is an obligation to face martyrdom, as in *Antidote for the Scorpion's Sting (Scorpiace)*. The scorpion's poison was a symbol of heretical teaching. This work was probably composed during the persecution by Scapula (211–212).

Even though he had adopted under Montanism some ideas that were contrary to those of the Carthaginian church to which he belonged, and even though he showed dissent not only stubbornly and immoderately but violently, Tertullian chose a limited field in which to follow the New Prophecy, that of ethics and Christian practice. Since, as we noted above, the rule of faith was in his eyes inviolable, it was precisely in the works of his Montanist period that Tertullian was best able to develop his theological method, which would remain normative in the West for almost two centuries. We refer here not only to his works on Trinitarian theology but also to those mentioned above in which he discussed the dogma of the resurrection or posed the problem of the incarnation of Christ (and therefore of the human person and the divine person).

Despite these orthodox doctrinal contributions, Tertullian came to a real separation from those whom he scornfully described as *psychici,* that is, using Pauline terminology, those who remained on the lowest level of Christian life, did not grasp spiritual realities, and were therefore limited to a very simple form of Christianity. When Tertullian writes as a Montanist, he always sets himself over against a community of people far larger than his own. There would thus have been a schism in Carthage, but certainly not one involving a large number of people. One indication of this, and not simply an argument from silence, may be seen in the fact that Cyprian, while privately calling Tertullian "the teacher" and quite often making use of his works on morality, never mentions Tertullian explicitly. Still, that schism, like the later schism of the "Tertullianists," was not a very serious one, since we do not hear it mentioned again.

BIBLIOGRAPHY

Many of the works cited in the preceding bibliography deal also with the problem of Tertullian's Montanism.

P. de Labriolle, *La crise montaniste* (Paris: Leroux, 1913).

V. Morel, "Le développement de la 'disciplina' sous l'action du Saint-Esprit chez Tertullien," *RHE* 35 (1939): 243–65.

F. Blanchetière, "Le montanisme originel," *RevScRel* 52–53 (1978–1979): 118–34, 1–22.

f. Ecclesiology

Montanism played a fundamental role in the final form of Tertullian's ecclesiology, but we must keep in mind that in this area, as in others, his acceptance of Montanism only caused a development along certain lines and did not completely change it, since the basic lines of his thinking about the church were already present in his early works. In *Modesty* Tertullian does indeed explicitly disparage the material nature of the hierarchy when contrasted with the spiritual value of the church, opposing the "church of the Spirit" to the "church as a number of bishops," but in his early exhortation to the martyrs he already speaks of *mater ecclesia*. He imagines the church as a human, visible reality when he says in the *Apology* that Christians form a *corpus* based on the "awareness of professing the same religion and having a single discipline and their own covenant of hope" (39.1). Scholars have observed that this statement of Tertullian reflects the Pauline triad of faith, charity, and hope (1 Thess 1:3; 5:8; 1 Cor 13:13) but inserted into the concrete idea that Christians form "a body." It is not the case, however, that Tertullian is using the likewise Pauline concept of the "body of Christ," since he is here describing to pagans what the Christian community is.

Thus the two ideas of "the church as mother" and the "body of Christianity" are present from the outset in Tertullian's thinking about the church. They show up again in one of his last and certainly Montanist works, *The Veiling of Virgins:* "For us and for them [the psychics] there is a single faith, a single God, the same Christ, the same hope, the same sacrament of baptism; to put it briefly, we constitute a single church. Therefore everything belonging to our members is ours; otherwise you divide the one body." In the church the Spirit is present who comes from the Lord and the common Father: "The church exists in one or two Christians, and the church is Christ. Therefore if you humble yourself before your brethren, you are touching Christ, you are pleading with Christ. And when the brethren shed tears at your repentance, it is Christ who is suffering, it is Christ who is pleading with the Father" (*Paen.* 10.4–6).

The idea that "one or two Christians constitute the church" recurs in a sentence in the *Exhortation to Chastity:* "Where three Christians are present, the church is there, even if they be laypersons" (7.3). The church is the body of God: "Where the Three, the Father, the Son, and the Holy Spirit, are, there too is the church, which is the body of the Three" (*Bapt.* 6.2). This sentence corresponds in substance to what we read in his final and thoroughly Montanist work, *Modesty:* "The church is, properly speaking and first of all, the Spirit, in whom is the Trinity, the Father, the Son, and the Holy Spirit, all possessing the one divine nature" (21.16).

We may conclude, then, that the idea of a "spiritual church" did not come to Tertullian from Montanism, but was already present in his "Catholic" works. In the latter, this spiritual conception is balanced by a much more concrete and "historical" idea of the church, which came from the apostolic "tradition": Christian reality (i.e., faith, doctrine, discipline, and practice) derives from the teaching of the apostles, who received it from God. Beginning with the apostles, this teaching spread "through tradition" to each Christian church. During his Montanist period, however, Tertullian emphasized the spiritual aspect of the church, identifying the latter not with the assembly of real, existing Christians but with the assembly of the spirituals, that is, the perfect. The church as such cannot sin. In this conception of the church there is already present in germ the fundamental idea of Donatism.

BIBLIOGRAPHY

K. Adam, *Der Kirchenbegriff Tertullians* (Paderborn: Schöningh, 1907).

C. Munier, "L'autorité de l'Église et l'autorité de l'Esprit d'après Tertullien," *RevScRel* 58 (1984): 77–90.

R. Braun, "Tertullien et le montanisme: Église institutionnelle et Église spirituelle," *RSLR* 21 (1985): 245–57.

g. The Pallium

We turn last to *The Pallium,* which many scholars consider to be Tertullian's final work (instead of *Modesty*). It is a short treatise, written in an affected and cryptic style; E. Norden considered it the most difficult work written in Latin. The subject seems so commonplace that one logically supposes it to have a deeper meaning: the writer had ceased to wear the toga of a Roman citizen and had instead donned the *pallium,* a short cloak usually worn by Cynic philosophers. With it Tertullian adopted an attitude and here he seeks to justify his choice, but in an ironic way. The change itself did not require any justification, but it signified something else, and this something else becomes only the starting point for the work, the meaning of which, however, is still unclear.

Some have thought that in *The Pallium* Tertullian wished to announce publicly either his conversion to Christianity, or the transition to the extreme position he took in founding the sect of the Tertullianists, or, in any case, his self-imposed exclusion from the common life, the undifferentiated ways of behavior practiced by both pagans and Christians. A chronological reference in the work, which might have been written under three reigning emperors, does not help because it applies equally well to 193, 203, or 218. Another hypothesis is that the writer wanted to make known his new anti-Roman attitude. The objection has been raised, against both hypotheses, that wearing the pallium instead of the toga was such a normal choice that no one would have gathered a programmatic, much less a polemical meaning from it. It has therefore been suggested that what *The Pallium* makes known is not a protest but irony directed at himself: Tertullian is saying to everyone that he who has always been a subject of controversy has adapted himself to living like everyone else. No interpretation has thus far been convincing.

Since there is no satisfactory explanation of the work's meaning, it remains for us to consider it mainly as a work of art and to admire the extraordinary linguistic skill, the flowery, baroque style, and the passion for contrivances that flow from a deliberately hermetic and affected inventiveness. The work of Tertullian can well compete with the sophistic compositions of the age, those which Roman citizens of Africa and perhaps Tertullian himself as a young man had heard in the flowery and persuasive speech of Apuleius when he delivered his addresses; important passages of these are collected in the anthology *Florida*.

BIBLIOGRAPHY

J.-C. Fredouille, *Tertullien et la conversion de la culture antique* (Paris: Études Augustiniennes, 1972).

A. V. Nazzaro, *Il de pallio di Tertulliano* (Naples: Edizioni Intercontinentalia, 1972).

h. Philosophy and Pagan Culture

"Who is more learned than Tertullian?" asked Jerome (*Epist.* 70.5), who saw "the entire wisdom of the world" in his writings. Tertullian was a Roman citizen of second-century society with its varied and heterogeneous interests, its concern to revive a past, both Latin and Greek, that was the culmination of a lengthy civilizing process in the ancient world and gave rise to the rhetorico-literary culture known as the "Second Sophistic." Like his countryman Apuleius, Tertullian had a good command of both languages, even writing some of his works in Greek (e.g., *The Veiling of Virgins*, *The Shows*, and *Baptism*). He showed no interest in Punic, the local language spoken by the people, an interest which, on the contrary, is quite alive in Augustine, some centuries later.

After becoming a Christian, Tertullian was to take advantage of the primarily rhetorical education he had acquired during his earlier training, and use it in his battles against the pagans and heresies. The church had from the outset developed two attitudes toward secular culture: on the one hand, an attitude of severance, opposition, and rejection; and on the other, an attitude of readiness to accept whatever might prove helpful or might be at least partially true. The first outlook is to be seen in Col 2:8: "See to it that no one takes you captive through philosophy and empty deceit, according to human tradition, according to the elemental spirits of the universe, and not according to Christ." The other outlook was that of Justin and many other important individuals, especially in the Greek world, who did not view Christianity as representing a break with human wisdom but, on the contrary, a more advanced position, a definitive progress. According to this view, the best part of human wisdom, which has its origin in God, helps constitute the new culture, in about the same way that the Old Testament tradition helps constitute it, even though the end result is of far greater value.

But the attitude of refusal and rejection is also to be found among the Greeks, as in Tatian and Theophilus. In the West the attitude of hostility begins with Tertullian and then becomes a commonplace. Tertullian's criticism of philosophy is more important and substantial, for he sees in philosophy the presence of an unacceptable curiosity. In this accusation he sums up, for practical purposes, the radical opposition between science and religion, the human and the divine. Curiosity links philosophers and heretics; it proposes to the mind questions that are essentially useless, since questions that are realistic and profound have already been raised and solved by Christianity. In such an approach, however, the condemnation of curiosity is in danger of turning into a condemnation of knowledge and rationality. Tertullian takes this step as well, although scholars have often stressed the supposed irrationalism of the man without an accurate assessment of the data and while simply repeating the trite and obvious *credo quia absurdum.* In any case, it is more likely that in adopting this provocative and extreme attitude (which, moreover, he never expressed in those exact terms), Tertullian wanted only to say that faith involves a reality that is beyond our comprehension, and therefore our need is to believe rather than to reason in regard to it.

But even Tertullian could not deny the evidence that at times philosophy has reached some truth, if only partial, and that there can be an agreement between the teaching of the gospel and the reasoning of the philosophers. For example, he admits (*Nat.* 1.10.41) that some philosophers have demolished polytheism thanks to an inspired grasp of the truth. Repeating an argument already found in Jewish apologetics, Philo, and Justin, he emphasizes the anteriority of the Bible in relation to Greek culture and repeats the accusation that the truths put forward by the pagan philosophers were simply "stolen" from biblical teaching (see *Apol.* 47.2). Another explanation he offers is that a demon may have taught the pagans a partial truth. Alongside his depreciation of philosophy, then, Tertullian introduces a different explanation that is substantially positive: some truths are the "common ideas" of which the Stoics speak and may therefore have been suggested to the philosophers in the exercise of their minds and by the very structure of thought, both of which are common to all human beings and are a gift from God. However, philosophy is useless to Christians since in the gospel they find the truth explained better and more fully.

Finally, perhaps the most important reason why Tertullian was distrustful of philosophy is that he saw in it an ally of polytheism and heresy. Despite the fact that some philosophers attacked and derided polytheism, Tertullian knows that philosophy does not provide a well-grounded refutation of it. He knows that the Stoics developed an allegorical interpretation of traditional religion, seeing in it the material form of their philosophical truths (Zeus is the heavens, Hera the air, and so on). Furthermore, he is aware of the henotheism of his age, that is, under the influence of Platonism many educated persons among the pagans believe that there is a supreme God. He also knows that the existence of this God does not eliminate the existence of lesser gods, whom Christians call idols or demons. Further, according to Tertullian, it is philosophy that has provided the gnostics with all the intellectual help and tools for organizing their bold and absurd constructions. Valentinus had been a Platonist; Plato is the "patriarch of heretics"; Hermogenes had derived his heresy from pagan philosophy. This conviction, though not regarded as valid by modern critics, was common to early heresiologists and was shared by Irenaeus of Lyons, who, in Tertullian's view, was an authority on the subject.

Despite all this, Tertullian makes use of doctrines taken from pagan philosophy: the critique of polytheism, the proof of the existence of demons, faith in the survival of the soul, reward or condemnation in the next world. In the *Apology* he refers to the Stoic concept of the Logos as maker of the universe in order to persuade his pagan readers to accept the Christian doctrine of the Word who creates everything. Thus his opposition to philosophy, though almost absolute in theory, was toned down in practice.

In using philosophy to work out Christian doctrines, Tertullian adheres primarily to Stoicism. He resolutely asserts that God is corporeal—although with a body that is *sui generis*—as well as rational and that he is not an unknowable God as maintained in Platonism but is reachable by considering the beauty and harmonious order of nature and by trusting in the soul's innate teaching that God exists. The idea of God as a spirit, as Scripture teaches, fits nicely with such a conception of God, because according to Tertullian "spirit" does not mean something immaterial, as Christians inspired by Platonism thought, but rather a body more subtle than others but still material. The same is to be said of the soul.

The influence of Stoicism is also to be seen in other teachings. It is probably from Stoicism that Tertullian takes the term *substantia*, which will become fundamental in western theology, as meaning primarily the material substrate that exists in every individual being. In studying the Christian datum that God is one, Tertullian makes a strict distinction between *unio* and *unitas: unio* means singleness or oneness in number; *unitas* signifies rather a single whole in which the parts are distinct but not separate. On the other hand, there is little echo of Platonism in the work of Tertullian, and he often speaks with a certain distrust of it.

Philosophy forms only the background of Tertullian's thinking, which moves wholly within the circle of Christianity and seeks exclusively to clarify traditional doctrines. It would be a mistake to portray Tertullian as one who develops a Stoic kind of theology, for we must not forget the influence of the Old Testament tradition, taken over completely and at times literally, on the formation of his religious thought. God is conceived in personal terms and is not the abstract "divinity" of the philosophers. His "wrath" is to be understood as something concrete. The creation of the world was really from nothing. All these doctrines were unacceptable to Greek philosophy and to the gnostics who were Tertullian's contemporaries.

BIBLIOGRAPHY

J.-C. Fredouille, *Tertullien et la conversion de la culture antique* (Paris: Études Augustiniennes, 1972).

R. D. Sider, *Ancient Rhetoric and the Art of Tertullian* (Oxford: Oxford University Press, 1971).

H. A. Wolfson, *The Philosophy of the Church Fathers* (3d ed.; Cambridge, Mass.: Harvard University Press, 1970).

R. Braun, *Deus Christianorum: Recherches sur le vocabulaire doctrinal de Tertullien* (2d ed.; Paris: Études Augustiniennes, 1977).

———, "Tertullien et la philosophie païenne: Essai de mise au point," *BAGB* (1971): 231–51.

T. D. Barnes, *Tertullian: A Historical and Literary Study* (3d ed.; Oxford: Oxford University Press, 1984).

J. Daniélou, *Les origines du christianisme latin* (Paris: Cerf, 1978); ET: *The Origins of Latin Christianity* (ed. J. A. Baker; trans. D. Smith and J. A. Baker; London: Darton, Longman & Todd/Philadelphia: Westminster, 1977).

i. Tertullian's Biblical Exegesis

Tertullian, like all Christian writers, takes it for granted that the Scriptures in their entirety are divinely inspired. Thanks to their common origin in inspiration, all the biblical books are in agreement among themselves; however, this agreement must be accurately determined through the study of the Scriptures. For Tertullian, then, there is no difference between the Old and the New Testaments as far as their authority is concerned. Nevertheless, in controversy with the Jews, Tertullian maintains that the precepts of old law have been rendered obsolete by the new Christian life. This conviction is emphasized during his Montanist period when he stresses that the old norms, including those of the early Christian period, have changed, but only to become stricter; yet this change is not in opposition the rule of faith.

Also important is the assertion of a complete identity between the two testaments, a point he emphasizes especially in the controversy with Marcion: if a separation between the two is admitted, it is to be admitted only "in the direction of a reform, an amplification, an improvement. Just as the fruit comes from the seed, while being other than the seed, so the New Testament comes from the old, being other but not divergent" (see above, sec. 2b). The New Testament, then, completes the Old.

The biblical canon seems to have been settled in Tertullian's time, although he never cites four of the books eventually accepted (Ruth, Haggai, Esther, and Tobit). The Letter to the Hebrews, which he considers to be the work of Barnabas, is on a lesser level of authority than the other texts. Of the noncanonical books he cites the *Book of Enoch* and regards it as authoritative; he was probably also familiar with the fourth book of Ezra. Initially, the Shepherd of Hermas, which was widely circulated, as we noted above (ch. 17, sec. 5), was listed by Tertullian among books whose authority was to be respected; later, however, when he wrote *Modesty*, he condemned the Shepherd as being too lax. He also rejected the *Acts of Paul* as inauthentic.

The problem of Tertullian's biblical text is very much debated, and even today no conclusion has been reached. In the eighteenth century it was believed that Tertullian used an already existing Latin translation of the Bible. It is not possible, however, to exclude the hypothesis that only some of the biblical books circulated in a Latin translation among the Christian communities of Africa—obviously the ones better known and more widely circulated—and that Tertullian made use of these, while making his own translations of other passages. This hypothesis would seem to be confirmed by the fact that sometimes the writer adds brief reflections on the meaning of a passage, probably because he translated it as he was writing.

Tertullian is the first Christian writer of the Latin world to have left criteria, albeit somewhat disorganized, to be followed in interpreting the sacred text. Probably antiheretical polemics was fundamentally responsible for his raising the question of the interpretation of Scripture, for these controversies necessitated a clarification of the exegetical norms for interpreting the texts being debated. At the beginning of such controversies Tertullian maintains that ultimately the church alone has the authority to decide how the Scriptures are to be interpreted, for it alone possesses the rule of faith. But this unrestricted norm remains essentially a dead letter, since it is useless in a debate with heretics. Also unusable is the analogous criterion of "prescription," which we described earlier.

When Tertullian became a Montanist, he added to the rule of faith as the norm for correct interpretation a further norm: the teaching of the Paraclete. Even then, however, he does not excuse himself from tackling the exegesis of a text according to criteria inherent in the text. Above all, he remarks that interpretation by heretics is vitiated from the outset either by arbitrariness so that the words lose their precise meaning and are replaced by a forced interpretation (it is typical of them "to torture even the simplest expressions"), or by the antecedent claim that they are drawing on a secret tradition, so that they alone can reach the truth. Tertullian is well aware that while the Marcionites held stubbornly to the literal meaning of the texts, the gnostics, and the Valentinians in particular, interpreted everything allegorically. He objects: if everything is allegory, what happens to the reality on which the allegory is based? For this reason, we ought not look for symbols everywhere; there must also be concrete realities. For Tertullian, the concreteness of what the Scriptures say is an undeniable principle; only the interpretation can be spiritual.

He has a similar objection against the Jews: they have lost the possibility of understanding the Scriptures ever since they refused to receive the Spirit of God. They hope only for earthly things and so have lost the things of heaven.

It was therefore necessary to establish some rules for interpretation. Tertullian adopts the norm typical of pagan exegesis, namely, that the part must be interpreted in light of the whole (*secundum plura intellegi pauciora; Prax.* 20). Consequently, it is necessary to start with what is certain in order to draw acceptable conclusions regarding uncertain passages, rather than to launch out on a series of conclusions that are uncertain. A sound exegetical criterion that he urges is not to engage in exegesis of each individual detail of a passage. The parable of the Good Shepherd, for example, is to be interpreted as a whole; we ought not ask why the sheep are one hundred in number. The exegesis of the parable of the lost coin should not set out to explain why the coins were ten in number or what is meant by the broom that the woman uses in her search for the coin.

As far as the character of Tertullian's own exegesis is concerned, it has been remarked that he generally leans toward literalism. Yet he does not reject allegory a priori, because it is needed for the interpretation of some texts that would otherwise seem absurd. Allegory is particularly important for passages whose content is prophetic. In adopting this outlook Tertullian follows the exegesis of the previous century, in particular that of Justin. He is therefore familiar with the meaning and use of the terms from ancient exegesis: not only "allegory" but "type," "symbol," and "figure." In addition, he has a good knowledge of the traditional interpretations, both messianic and christological, that Christian exegesis had put into circulation during the first two centuries. He also makes use of critical tools foreign to the Christian exegetical tradition, and has recourse to forms of interpretation from pagan rhetoric, e.g., the contrast between what the author writes and what he intends; the difference between what Paul ordered to be written down and his specific intention—which, however, he did manage to convey.

BIBLIOGRAPHY

G. Zimmermann, *Die hermeneutischen Prinzipien Tertullians* (Würzburg: Triltsch, 1937).

O. Kuss, "Zur Hermeneutik Tertullians," in *Neutestamentliche Aufsätze. Festschrift J. Schmidt* (Regensburg: Pustet, 1963), 138–60.

J. H. Waszink, "Tertullian's Principles and Methods of Exegesis," in *Early Christian Literature. . . . Mélanges R. M. Grant* (Paris: Beauchesne, 1979), 17–31.

T. P. O'Malley, *Tertullian and the Bible* (Utrecht: Dekkers Van de Vegt, 1967).

M. Simonetti, *Lettera e/o Allegoria* (Rome: Augustinianum, 1985).

C. Moreschini, "La letteratura cristiana di fronte al testo sacro. I. Tertulliano," in E. Norelli, ed., *La Bibbia nell'antichità cristiana* I (Bologna: Dehoniane, 1993), 335–59, especially 335–53.

j. The Art of Tertullian

Lactantius, an admirer of Cicero and a man who lived in a quite different cultural and spiritual world, found Tertullian's style to be "wearisome, inadequately worked on, and quite obscure" (*Inst.* 5.1.23). Jerome, who read Tertullian attentively, says of his style: "rich in aphorisms but wearisome in their expression" (*Epist.* 58.10). The style of Tertullian, who was probably the greatest Christian writer in the Latin language, has found a perceptive and acute critic in Jacques Fontaine, who admires the subtle and mannered style which at its extreme becomes a real hermeticism of form:

> Overburdened, rough, violent, and explosive, it is the expression of the same baroque spirit found in the sculpture and decorative arts of the age of the Severi. This oratorical style . . . is close to that of Apuleius in its affected and emotive vocabulary, its use of familiar language, its preference for short, broken, or prolonged sentences, its curt statements, and its distant echoes of Sallust's "irregularity" *(inconcinnitas)* and Tacitus's dissymetries.

Tertullian's mastery can be seen in his control of the language, which is used to create a continuous tension and leads to unexpected turns of phrase. Even in his most serious works, even in those in which he gives vent to his rigorism, the writer allows himself to enjoy rhetorical games and paradoxes and improvisations, in which he engages in irony, satire, and carefully placed witty remarks. These traits are accentuated in his later works, prompted by the violent attacks on the psychics.

This strong rhetorical tension is a manner of expression typical of a personality whose fundamental characteristic, and one that long ago impressed Christian writers after Tertullian, was "a penetrating and impetuous intelligence" (Jerome, *Vir. ill.* 53). This assessment of the Carthaginian writer was widespread. Generally people admired his literary talent but criticized his teaching; they read him extensively but did not speak of him openly. Jerome writes: "I think that we ought sometimes to read Origen for our further instruction, as we ought also to read Tertullian and Novatian, Arnobius and Apollinaris . . . choosing what is good in them and avoiding what is bad, as Paul the apostle says: 'Examine everything, and retain whatever is good'" (*Epist.* 62.2).

A central problem in Tertullian's work is its language, which is rendered more difficult by the fact that he was essentially the first Christian Latin writer. The few texts cited in the preceding chapter were not works of literary art, and were not intended for a public of educated readers. It has been remarked that despite his "novelty," which is due to his desire to break away from the cultural climate in which he lived, his observance of the syntactical norms of the time is substantially in accord with the other writers of his age, including pagans. This is evidence of the great extent to which, as noted above, Tertullian was, for all his polemical outlook, a man who had his place in a well defined culture and had received a pagan education. In any case, a Christian could only to a certain extent set his own new and unusual standards.

What elicits wonder is Tertullian's vocabulary, in which we see an almost unrestrained freedom, an unmatched capacity for creativity. Eighteenth century critics, having in mind that he was essentially the first Christian Latin writer, thought that he had "created" Christian Latin. This was to confuse the lexical aspect with the literary aspect; the use of these numerous neologisms was limited to Tertullian, so it was clearly the product of a personal style and not of a language common to Christians.

Later, around 1930–1940, the Dutch Nijmegen school, of which we spoke earlier, took into account the advances made in linguistics and stylistics in the first decades of the century and tried to establish the terms specific to Tertullian's language and those, on the other hand, that could be effectively shown to have been produced under the influence of the language of the Bible. That school believed it could isolate a "Christian language" that would also have been that of Tertullian. The problem is one of both language and style. The Carthaginian writer surely used the technical terms of the Christian religion while exercising in an extreme form his artistic freedom within that specific language. Still, his linguistic freedom could not have been completely arbitrary; some neologisms took shape in the framework of the Latin language of his time—for it was impossible for Tertullian to speak or write a different language—and the "novelty" of his style had a historical and cultural setting. It is certain that after Tertullian this innovative violence in the area of vocabulary was no longer to be seen; this is perhaps a sign that no writer wanted—or was able—to follow his example.

BIBLIOGRAPHY

Complete Editions

CSEL 20 (ed. A. Reifferscheid and G. Wissowa, 1890).
CSEL 47 (ed. A. Kroymann, 1906).
CSEL 69 (ed. H. Hoppe, 1939).
CSEL 70 (ed. A. Kroymann, 1942).
CSEL 76 (ed. A. Kroymann, V. Bulhart, and P. Borleffs, 1957).
CCSL 1–2 (1954).
G. Claesson, *Index Tertullianus* (Paris: Études Augustiniennes, 1974–1975); an indispensable reference work.

Editions of Individual Works

Tertullian, *Apologeticum* (ed. P. Frassinetti; CSLP; Turin: Paraviae, 1965).
———, *De baptismo* (ed. B. Luiselli; CSLP; Turin: Paraviae, 1968).
———, *Adversus Marcionem* (ed. C. Moreschini; Milan: Cisalpino, 1971).

Editions of Individual Works with Text, Introduction, Translation, and Commentary

Tertullian, *Ad martyres* (ed. and trans. A. Quacquarelli; Rome: Desclée, 1963).

————, *Ad Nationes I* (ed. and trans. A. Schneider; Neuchâtel: Institute Suisse de Rome, 1968).

————, *Ad Scapulam* (ed. and trans. A. Quacquarelli; Rome: Desclée, 1957).

————, *Adversus Iudaeos* (ed. H. Tränkle; Wiesbaden: Steiner, 1964).

————, *Adversus Marcionem* (ed. and trans. E. Evans; 2 vols.; Oxford: Clarendon, 1972).

————, *Adversus Praxean* (ed. and trans. G. Scarpat, CP; Turin: Società Editrice Internazionale, 1985).

————, *Adversus Valentinianos* (trans. A. Marastoni; Padua: Gregoriana, 1971).

————, *Apologia del cristianesimo* (ed. C. Moreschini; trans. L. Rusca; Milan: Rizzoli, 1984).

————, *Apologetico* (trans. A. Resta Barrile; Milan: Mondadori, 1994).

————, *Apologétique* (ed. and trans. J.-P. Waltzing with A. Severyns; Paris: Les Belles Lettres, 1931).

————, *De anima* (ed. J. H. Waszink; Amsterdam: Meulenhoff, 1947).

————, *De corona* (ed. and trans. F. Ruggiero; Milan: Mondadori, 1992).

————, *De corona* (ed. and trans. J. Fontaine; Paris: Presses Universitaires de France, 1966).

————, *De idololatria* (ed. and trans. P. G. van der Nat, J. H. Waszink, and J. C. M. van Winden; New York: Brill, 1987).

————, *De monogamia* (ed. and trans. R. Uglione, CP; Turin: Società Editrice Internazionale, 1993).

————, *De pallio* (ed. and trans. S. Costanza; Naples: Libreria Scientifica Editrice, 1968).

————, *De spectaculis* (ed. and trans. E. Castorina; Florence: La Nuova Italia, 1961).

————, *De testimonio animae* (ed. C. Tibiletti; Florence: Nardini, 1985).

————, *La carne di Cristo* (ed. and trans. C. Micaelli; Milan: Rizzoli, 1984).

————, *L'eleganza delle donne* (trans. S. Isetta; Florence: Nardini, 1986).

————, *On Baptism* (ed. and trans. E. Evans; London: SPCK, 1964).

————, *On Prayer* (ed. and trans. E. Evans; London: SPCK, 1953).

————, *On the Incarnation* (ed. and trans. E. Evans; London: SPCK, 1956).

————, *On the Resurrection* (ed. and trans. E. Evans; London: SPCK, 1960).

————, *Scorpiace* (ed. G. Azzali Bernardelli et al.; trans. P. S. Zanetti; Florence: Nardini, 1990).

————, *Tertullian's Treatise against Praxeas* (ed. and trans. E. Evans; London: SPCK, 1948).

In the Sources chrétiennes collection, the project of rendering all of Tertullian into French will continue.

Tertullian, *À son épouse* (SC 273; ed. and trans. C. Munier; Paris: Cerf, 1980).

————, *Contre les Valentiniens* (SC 280–81; ed. and trans. J.-C. Fredouille; Paris: Cerf, 1980).

————, *Contre Marcion* (SC 365, 368, 399; ed. and trans. R. Braun; Paris: Cerf, 1990, 1991, 1994).

————, *De la patience* (SC 210; ed. and trans. J.-C. Fredouille; Paris: Cerf, 1984).

————, *Exhortation à la chastété* (SC 319; ed. and trans. C. Moreschini; Paris: Cerf, 1985).

————, *La chair du Christ* (SC 216–17; ed. and trans. J.-P. Mahé; Paris: Cerf, 1975).

————, *La pénitence* (SC 316; ed. and trans. C. Munier; Paris: Cerf, 1984).

————, *La pudicité* (SC 394–95; ed. C. Micaelli and C. Munier; trans. C. Munier; Paris: Cerf, 1993).

————, *La toilette des femmes* (SC 173; ed. and trans. M. Turcan; Paris: Cerf, 1971).

————, *Le mariage unique* (SC 243; ed. and trans. P. Mattei; Paris: Cerf, 1988).

————, *Les spectacles* (SC 332; ed. and trans. M. Turcan; Paris: Cerf, 1986).

————, *Traité du baptême* (SC 35; ed. R. F. Refoulé; trans. R. F. Refoulé and M. Drouzy; Paris: Cerf, 1952).

Translation of Individual Works, with Notes, in English

Tertullian, *Treatises on Marriage and Remarriage* (ed. and trans. W. P. Le Saint; ACW 13; Westminster, Md.: Newman, 1951).

————, *The Treatise against Hermogenes* (ed. and trans. J. H. Waszink; ACW 24; Westminster, Md.: Newman, 1956).

————, *Treatises on Penance and on Purity* (ed. and trans. W. P. Le Saint; ACW 28; Westminster, Md.: Newman, 1959).

Critical Works

P. Monceaux, *Histoire littéraire de l'Afrique chrétienne depuis les origines jusquä l'invasion arabe* (vol. I; Paris: Leroux, 1901).

C. Guignebert, *Tertullien: Étude sur ses sentiments à l'égard de l'Empire et de la société civile* (Paris: Leroux, 1901).

T. D. Barnes, *Tertullian: A Historical and Literary Study* (3d ed.; Oxford: Oxford University Press, 1984).

J.-C. Fredouille, *Tertullien et la conversion de la culture antique* (Paris: Études Augustiniennes, 1972).

R. Braun, *Approches de Tertullien* (Paris: Études Augustiniennes, 1992); a collection of earlier essays.

J. Fontaine, *Aspects et problèmes de la prose de l'art latine au IIIᵉ siècle* (Turin: Bottega d'Erasmo, 1968).

H. Hoppe, *Sintassi e stile di Tertulliano* (IT; Brescia: Paideia, 1985).

E. Löfstedt, *Zur Sprache Tertullians* (Lund: Gleerup, 1920).

G. Thörnell, *Studia Tertulliana* (4 vols; Uppsala: Akademiska Boktryckeriet, 1918–1926).

G. L. Bray, "The Relationship between Holiness and Chastity in Tertullian," StPatr 16 (1985), 132–35.

W. E. Helleman, "Tertulian on Athens and Jerusalem," in *Hellenization Revisited* (Lanham, Md.: Univerisity Press, 1994).

Note, finally, that works on Tertullian have been gathered and critically evaluated
in R. Braun, J.-C. Fredouille, and P. Pettitmengin, "Chronica Tertullianea,"
REA (1976–).

3. *Passion of Perpetua and Felicity*

This *Passion,* which is undoubtedly the most beautiful of the Christian *passiones*
and the one richest in spiritual motifs, tells of the arrest, imprisonment, and martyrdom of several catechumens, including Revocatus, Felicity, Saturninus, and Secun-
dulus. Among them were some slaves, and Vibia Perpetua, a woman of noble birth.
To their number was added Satyrus, who had been their instructor in the Christian
faith and was unwilling to abandon them in prison; he was therefore martyred with
the others.

The structure of this *passio* is unusual. It is made up of two different but inter-
secting entities: a narrative part, which consists of two documents, namely, reports
of Perpetua's trial and of her life in prison; and a description of the visions had
by Perpetua and Satyrus. Both documents are written in the first person and are
probably reports by the martyr Perpetua; these documents are set in a narrative
framework that is different in style, written by the editor of the work. The historical
information in the work guarantees its antiquity. It is set in the year of birth of Geta,
Septimius Severus's second child; the year in which the Christians were condemned at
Carthage must have been 203. The *Passion* was translated into Greek. There are also
some *Acts* from a later date, which are clearly derived from the *Passion.* In a passage of
The Soul (55.4) Tertullian refers to the work but confuses the vision of Satyrus with
that of Perpetua.

According to some scholars, the editor of the *Passion* was Tertullian. According to
others, that hypothesis is plausible if we take account simply of the doctrinal contents,
but there is nothing characteristic of Tertullian in the *Passion* that is not also generi-
cally Montanist; the special linguistic characteristics of the work do not seem to be
those of Tertullian. The most that might be said is that the *Passion* was written in a
Montanist atmosphere very close to that of Tertullian. Reasons for identifying the
work as of Montanist origin include the following: the martyrs it describes have visions and revelations, and they manifest in their behavior the work of the Spirit, a
point stressed by the anonymous editor at the beginning and end of the documents.
In addition, one passage speaks of a conflict between Bishop Optatus and Aspasius, a
presbyter and teacher. All this would link the work to the characteristic traits of
Montanism that we find amplified and deepened in the work of Tertullian.

Corsini has justifiably rejected this interpretation of the work. He notes, first of
all, that the content of the visions is not Montanist. Moreover, the purpose of the editor is explicit: to gather and make known "new [that is, contemporary] examples" of
faith, which are not less valuable than those of ancient times. There is no question,
then, of a "new discipline." The editor indeed remarks that these examples of faith are
due to the constant presence of the Holy Spirit in the church, but this conviction was
certainly not of Montanist origin; it was shared, for example, by the ecclesiology of
Cyprian. Furthermore, the writer emphasizes not so much the presence of the Spirit

as the multiplicity of his "operations," which is a typically Pauline idea. The opposition between the martyrs and the ecclesiastical hierarchy was something that occurred quite often in Tertullian's time, because it was thought that martyrs too had authority to grant peace (reconciliation). The conflict would be resolved by Cyprian in a restrictive way: martyrdom has no value if it occurs outside the church.

It may be said in conclusion that the *Passion* is an attempt to systematize, in a theoretical way, a fundamental aspect of Christian experience, namely, martyrdom. Indeed, martyrdom is the highest manifestation of Christian perfection. In this sense, the author can be set alongside Tertullian, but not him alone, for Clement of Alexandria and Hermas likewise praise martyrdom in a reaction to gnosticism (see above, sec. 2e, re. Tertullian's *Scorpiace*). Martyrdom is seen against a very vivid eschatological background, which is intensified by a penetrating reading of the Apocalypse, as in Tertullian and contemporary Montanism, but this does not mean that the *Passion* is a Montanist work.

The visions of Perpetua and Satyrus have a definite catechetical purpose as they seek to present the Christian interpretation of the world, and their content is typical of African Christianity and certainly not of Montanism. Indeed, ever since the age of Pauline Christianity, visions have had the purpose of teaching and instructing the community. Along with dreams, which are at a lower intellectual level, visions are a detailed way of learning the nature of reality, not only earthly, but also and especially celestial and eschatological. The text is therefore to be addressed to the entire assembly of the faithful, to whom it was to be read; it was at precisely such an assembly that Tertullian read it.

Such visions are very important for understanding the mindset of African Christianity at that time, but it is not possible to discuss them here in detail, with their heavily symbolic language. They have the character of revelations: here it is Christ who in the garb of the Good Shepherd encourages those girding themselves for martyrdom; there it is the Christ who lives in the church. The vision of the other world in which Perpetua's brother Dinocrates appears to her is especially complex. The condition of such a person who had died as an infant stirred discussion in the time of Augustine, in relation to the problem of original sin and the punishment of infants. The vision here does not make clear whether or not Dinocrates had been baptized. It has been suggested that he was set in a place that was not of the *refrigerium*, of eternal peace, but was a kind of "purgatory." The *Passion* has even been regarded as a one of the first witnesses to the doctrine of purgatory, parallel to those we see in Tertullian.

Dinocrates is saved thanks to the baptism of Perpetua, in keeping with the very ancient Christian idea, present in Corinth and already known to Paul, of baptism "on behalf of the dead." Such a practice existed, therefore, in Africa as well.

By dying and being buried with Christ, Perpetua works the salvation of her brother.

The *Passion of Perpetua and Felicity* enjoyed a great deal of celebrity. The two martyrs were included in the calendar of the saints as early as the fourth century, and the account of their suffering was read in the churches in Augustine's time and was looked upon almost as a canonical writing. Some of Augustine's correspondents took their cue from the *Passion* in asking for answers to some questions about infant baptism. Augustine himself delivered homilies for the feast of the two saints.

BIBLIOGRAPHY

Text

H. Musurillo, *The Acts of the Christian Martyrs* (Oxford: Clarendon, 1972).
A. A. R. Bastiaensen et al., *Atti e Passioni dei martiri* (Milan: Fondazione Valla-Mondadori, 1987).
R. Braun, "Tertullien est-il le rédacteur de la *Passio Perpetuae?*" *REL* 33 (1955): 79–.
E. Corsini, "Proposte per una lettura della *Passio Perpetuae*," in *Forma Futuri: Studi in onore del Cardinale M. Pellegrino* (Turin: Bottega d'Erasmo, 1975), 481–541.
J. E. Salisbury, *Perpetua's Passion: The Death and Memory of a Young Roman Woman* (New York: Routledge, 1997).

4. Spread of Christianity in Africa

In several works against pagans (e.g., the *Apology* and the letter *To Scapula*) Tertullian challenges his enemies with the claim that Christianity has spread everywhere and in every stratum of society, and he names various well known individuals, even at court, who have embraced the new religion. The claims have a clearly propagandist purpose, but they must have been based on a core of truth. Vibia Perpetua, for example, whose *Passion* we have just described, belonged to a noble family, and the account contains the interesting detail that when her father learned of the sin committed by his daughter in embracing an illicit religion, he harshly mistreated her; thus she is an example of religious conflict within families. Tertullian tells of the existence of Christianity in at least four cities in addition to Carthage: Thysdrus, Hadrumetum, Lambesi, and Uthina. There were also Christian communities in Mauritania. Christian inscriptions from this early period, many of them in Punic, are largely lacking.

Councils preceding Cyprian's episcopate can offer some idea of Christianity's spread. According to Augustine (*C. litt. Petil.* 13.22), the council held under Agrippinus, on the problem of the rebaptism of heretics, was attended by about seventy bishops. When Cyprian refers to that same council (*Ep.* 71.4; 73.3), he says that "many thousands of heretics" were converted. Shortly after 236 another council was held in Carthage in which, as Cyprian notes, ninety bishops took part (*Ep.* 59.10). Their sees were for the most part in Proconsular Africa, with the greatest concentration along the Mediterranean coast, but the interior region around Carthage was also represented. Cyprian himself tells the name of his immediate predecessor: Donatus (*Ep.* 59.10). The most important city after Carthage was Cirta.

Pagan witnesses such as the historian Herodian tell of the size and importance of Carthage during the rebellion of the Gordians (7.6.1ff.). The wealth and civilization of Africa are also attested by the architecture and splendid mosaics discovered in Roman villas and now preserved in the Bardo Museum in Tunis and in other Tunisian cities. During his episcopate Cyprian collected a hundred thousand sesterces for the ransoming of some Christians who had been carried off during Berber raids

(*Ep.* 62.4). On the other hand, Cyprian's account of African Christianity during the persecution of Decius describes a throng of Christians who are neither fervent in their faith nor detached from the world, but live in a peaceful coexistence with the pagans. However, his characterization may be exaggerated, given the bishop's critical attitude toward his faithful).

The situation seems to have been calm until the time of Scapula's persecution in 212, although Cyprian speaks of some Christians who had in past times suffered because of their faith. The *Octavius* of Minucius Felix likewise refers to persecutions of Christians (see 9.5; 28; 37). But the surprise Christians got in 250 when the authorities demanded that they sacrifice to the gods shows that they had grown accustomed to peace. This lengthy peace had been disturbed, not so much for religious reasons as for political ones, for a short time during the rebellion of the Gordians against Emperor Maximinus Thrax (238). By this time the spread of Christianity was no longer limited to the lower classes but had reached higher classes, more so than in the time of Tertullian. In the East, Origen maintained that Christians had been well received in intellectual circles (see *Cels.* 3.9 and 30); Origen himself is an example of a learned Christian who was known and esteemed even by pagans. The same applies to scholars such as Julius Africanus, who had dealings with Emperors Elagabalus and Alexander Severus, and was even given a public assignment by the latter: to restore a library in Rome.

During the reign of the Severi, then, and of their immediate successors down to Diocletian there were fifty years of relative peace, meaning few episodes of anti-Christian violence, despite the fact that Eusebius of Caesarea records two persecutions during those years: those of Septimius Severus and of Maximinus Thrax. However, these measures did not last long and, in keeping with the juridical ambiguity implicit in the rescript of Trajan, did not target Christians in a systematic way but rather repeated the anti-Christian measures of the preceding century. There had been outbursts of persecution and violence even in Tertullian's time, but it is clear that by and large a *modus vivendi* existed between the Christian communities and the pagan world around them. All people were affected by the devastating crises that struck the empire in the third century: plague, famines, inflation, and barbarian invasions. These afflicted all the provinces of the empire, making no distinction between Christians and pagans.

BIBLIOGRAPHY

P. Monceaux, *Histoire littéraire de l'Afrique chrétienne depuis les origines jusquä l'invasion arabe* (vols. I–II; Paris: Leroux, 1901–1902).

W. H. C. Frend, *Persecution and Martyrdom in the Early Church* (Oxford: Blackwell, 1965).

V. Saxer, *Vie liturgique et quotidienne à Carthage vers le milieu du IIIe siècle: Le témoignage de Saint Cyprien et de ses contemporains d'Afrique* (Vatican City: Libreria Editrice Vaticana, 1969).

E. R. Dodds, *Pagan and Christian in an Age of Anxiety* (New York: Norton, 1965).

S. Mazzarino, *L'impero romano* (Rome-Bari: Laterza, 1973).

M. Mazza, *Lotte sociali e restaurazione autoritaria nel III secolo d. C.* (2d ed.; Rome-Bari: Laterza, 1973).

5. Minucius Felix

An example of these opposing attitudes—polemics and, at the same time, an effort to reach a solution to difficulties—is given in the *Octavius* of Minucius Felix, a little work that shows no great depth but is pleasant reading and is marked by a noteworthy stylistic refinement. It offers a picture of pagan and Christian culture and the relations between them in the African world of the time. Some scholars, however, place the life and activity of Minucius not in Africa but in Rome; Jerome even says (*Epist.* 70.5) that Minucius was a Roman lawyer. But although the *Octavius* is set near Rome, it shows a strong knowledge of the African milieu. Caecilius, one of the speakers in the dialogue, calls Fronto, the pagan orator, "our [fellow] citizen of Cirta." Caecilius is a pagan, and Fronto had written a work against Christians in the preceding century; we may infer from these words that Caecilius is from the same city. A Caecilius Natalis is named in six inscriptions from Cirta. A Minucius Felix is named in an inscription of Tebessa and in another of Carthage. An Octavius Januarius is named in an inscription from Bougie.

In a question long debated, we agree with those critics who consider the *Octavius* to be of later date than the *Apology* of Tertullian. Close similarities of content have been observed in some passages of the two works and, since there is uncertainty regarding the biography of Minucius, the question has been asked which of the two served as model for the other. At the present time, the hypothesis that Minucius depended on Tertullian is the one most favored; it is difficult to think that someone with a personality like Tertullian's would have so closely followed a writer like Minucius. This view seems to be confirmed by the fact that Jerome, who in his *Famous Men* gives a chronological list of Christian writers, has Tertullian (53), Minucius (58), and Cyprian (67) in that order. We know the title of Minucius's apologetical work not from the manuscripts but from information given by early scholars: Lactantius (*Inst.* 5.1.22; see 1.11.55) and Jerome (*Vir ill.* 58; *Epist.* 70.5). Independently of the question of the priority between the two writers, we should note that both the *Octavius* and the *Apology* of Tertullian are used by Cyprian in the work *That Idols Are not Gods,* the authenticity of which used to be challenged but is now accepted. In other works, too, Cyprian seems to echo Minucius on more than one occasion.

BIBLIOGRAPHY

B. Axelson, *Das Prioritätsproblem Tertullian—Minucius Felix* (Lund: Gleerup, 1941).

J. Beaujeu, "Introduction" in Minucius Felix, *Octavius* (2d ed.; Paris: Les Belles Lettres, 1974).

In introducing his work Minucius says that in years past he had practiced law in Rome and that his conversion came in his mature years. In the work he girds himself to write, he intends to remember his friend Octavius and report the dialogue in which the latter persuaded their mutual friend, Caecilius Natalis, from Cirta in Numidia, to join the new religion after having been a stern enemy of Christianity. The three friends have gone to Ostia while the Roman courts are on holiday, and the dialogue takes place on the beach there. After some witty remarks, Caecilius, a worshiper of the Egyptian god Serapis, suggests beginning a dialogue on religion with Octavius; Minucius will serve as arbiter.

In summary, Caecilius repeats the usual accusations against Christians. Accusations circulating among the ignorant common people include: immorality, cruelty, Thyestian meals, and worship of an ass's head. Educated people cite the absurdity of the religion and teachings, the ignorance and the pig-headed and rebellious behavior of Christians, and the absence of any "philosophical" outlook in the Christian vision of the world and in the Christian manner of life. In defending paganism and accusing Christians, Caecilius uses teachings from Cicero, Seneca, and Varro. References to the philosophy of Plato are also represented, but these come second-hand from more recent writers. Caecilius shows himself to be a defender of skepticism and denier of divine providence, and in order to support his ideas, makes extensive use of the third book of Cicero's *The Nature of the Gods*. This is quite interesting, for since the pagan takes this approach in his attack, there is no place for the traditional accusation of atheism against Christians; if anything, it is Caecilius himself who would seem to be an atheist.

The attitude of skepticism is something new in the attacks made on Christianity by educated people. It is also to be seen in Celsus, the second-century pagan intellectual, who for this reason has wrongly been described by some as an Epicurean, and Origen aims at refuting criticism of that kind. As a result, in his reply Octavius does not insist on ridiculing pagan polytheism, as he could have done, since Caecilius did not support it. Along with this radical skepticism, Caecilius, like Cicero, suggests traveling the only way considered valid by civilized and educated people, by the pagans in an era when the ancient Roman tradition was acquiring an ever increasing value, as though it were a form of religion, in the attempt to respond to the calamities of that age. This way implied an acceptance of the very ancient cultic and religious traditions of Rome, traditions that had built the empire. Such acceptance might not have been based on conviction, but it was loyal and beyond discussion, being justified by obedience to the laws of the state.

In replying to Caecilius's charges, Octavius begins by dismantling the opposition between the supposed wisdom of philosophy and the ignorance of Christians: wisdom ought to be within the reach of all, regardless of the social position of the inquirer. Christians ought not to be accused of ignorance simply because of their humble state. For this reason, pagan accusations against Christians will be refuted by an analogous use of the traditional arguments inherited from the whole of earlier apologetics. Given this background, it is a matter of opposing the truth of the Christian religion to the skepticism of pagans. To a great extent this truth is, in Octavius's mind, not to be distinguished from pagan culture, that is, from what is noble in it. So while Caecilius uses the arguments of pagan skepticism to stress the absence of any divine providence, Octavius makes similar good use of pagan philosophy (Stoicism) to call attention to the wonders of the universe that God has created (chs. 17–18). The writer deliberately avoids any specifically Christian dogma; Tertullian had already had recourse to certain forms of Stoic universalism, e.g., for the doctrine of God as known *naturaliter* by the soul. Such recourse had been customary among the apologists of the second century, and Origen would do the same in *Against Celsus*.

The narrow horizons of Minucius's Christianity have often been criticized since very early times; Lactantius, for example, emphasizes the inadequacy of Minucius's teaching from the viewpoint of faith (see *Inst.* 5.1.21), and not without reason. Minucius makes his defense of Christianity without ever naming Jesus Christ, to whom allusion is made once by Caecilius (9.4) and once by Octavius (29.2–3). There is no reference to specifically Christian dogma, and Christianity in its entirety is essentially reduced to monotheism. Sacred Scripture is never cited. There is an allusion only to the dogma of the final resurrection (ch. 38).

All this can be explained if we take into account that the work is intended for pagan readers, for whom a detailed explanation of Christian dogma would have been irksome. More specifically, the writer has to convince pagans of the value of the Christian "philosophy"; these same educated pagans at that time practiced "monotheism" in the form usually described as "henotheism," the recognition of a single supreme god, with other gods subordinated to him. We should in all likelihood not agree that Minucius was only imperfectly Christian, as Arnobius was at a later date; Arnobius's inadequate knowledge of Christianity is attested by ancient sources, whereas there is no such evidence for Minucius. Perhaps the latter's apology was *sui generis.* Or perhaps it was not an apology at all; not without reason Fontaine thinks the *Octavius* to be an exhortation to Christianity.

A central problem in the work is the attitude of these provincials, Caecilius and Octavius, to the power of Rome, which ultimately was the power of the state to which they both belonged, be they Christian or non-Christian. Caecilius repeats the cliché of pagan propaganda that Rome's great successes had been due to its religious spirit and its meticulous worship of the gods (6.2). Octavius rejects all that very vigorously, and his attacks on Rome are perhaps even stronger than those of Tertullian (see chs. 25–28). Tertullian had indeed ironically rejected the supposed piety of the pagans and the ancient Romans (*Apol.* 25), and their illusory notion that the gods had given them power as a reward for their religiousness. But Tertullian had never gone so far as to say as explicitly and clearly as Minucius that the Roman empire was the fruit of violence and pillage.

It seems, then, that the outline of Minucius's personality is not as sharp and his traits are not as marked as those of Tertullian and Cyprian. When set between these two, Minucius seems crushed and confined, but he does not for this reason deserve the essentially negative evaluation he has received beginning in the nineteenth century, after having enjoyed a high reputation in the seventeenth and eighteenth centuries. He has his own individuality and his own role in the history of Christian culture. It is enough to understand his intention, which was to write not an apologetical work—and then be blamed for not having the power of a Tertullian— but an exhortation to the Christian religion, which seemed to many educated people to be a form of philosophy. So too his art has an individuality of its own, despite the fact that it has often erroneously been regarded as a document in the history of Ciceronianism and nothing more. His prose, which prefers unobtrusiveness and elegant descriptions, is often mannered at points where Minucius has an opportunity to display his refinement, but this does not signify a lack of talent. His talk resembles that of Cicero's dialogues, and he presents his personages and scenes in a flowery and harmonious style.

BIBLIOGRAPHY

Editions

Minucius Felix, *Octavius* (ed. C. F. Halm; CSEL 2; Vindobonea: Gerold, 1867).
———— (trans. J. Beaujeu; 2d ed.; Paris: Les Belles Lettres, 1974).
———— (ed. and trans. M. Pellegrino; 2d ed.; CSLP 81; Turin: Paraviae, 1963).
———— (ed. and trans. B. Kytzler; Munich: Kösel, 1965).

Commentaries

Minucius Felix, *Octavio* (ed. and trans. M. Pellegrino; Turin: Società Editrice Internazionale, 1967).
———— (ed. and trans. G. W. Clarke; ACW 39; New York: Newman, 1974).

Translations

Minucius Felix, *Octavio* (trans. Rusca; Milan: Rizzoli, 1957).
———— (trans. Buonaiuti-Paratore; Bari: Laterza, 1971).

6. Cyprian, Bishop of Carthage

In Thascius Caecilius Cyprianus we meet a man of letters who was also bishop of Carthage, the most important city of Africa, the same city in which the great Tertullian had lived and done his polemical writing. Unlike Tertullian, however, Cyprian was a man who carried weighty responsibilities in governing his church during an especially difficult period for Christianity. He was an authoritarian leader, convinced that it was for him alone to make certain decisions and doubtless displaying in the process a resolute personality that was, in some respects, no less passionate than Tertullian's. His government of the Carthage community is attested by his correspondence, the first collection of Christian letters. These works are important for a reconstruction of the events of the time and a knowledge of how the hierarchy was strengthened within the church and how certain values such as martyrdom were determined within and outside it. This was also the reason why Cyprian's works were widely circulated both in late antiquity and in the Middle Ages. They set down, in an authoritatively formulated and defended way, the juridical principles on the basis of which the church became the center of the lives of Christians, even if these Christians were martyrs.

The difficulties Cyprian had to face during his episcopate are indirectly confirmed by the *Life of Cyprian*, a biography that has come down to us anonymously in all the earliest manuscripts but was later attributed to Pontius, a deacon who, according to Jerome (*Vir. ill.* 68), accompanied the bishop into exile and wrote the *Life* immediately after the martyrdom. The *Life* is motivated by the need to defend Cyprian against accusations leveled at him; we shall speak of these further on.

Cyprian's life before his conversion is almost completely unknown. Even Augustine, who lived in Africa and celebrated the martyrdom in the church built at the place of Cyprian's suffering (*Serm.* 310), admitted that he did not know when Cyprian was born. In view of the fact that he was already a bishop in the time of Decius's persecution, his birth has to be dated to around 200–210. Jerome and Pontius tell us that Cyprian had won renown for himself as an orator before his conversion.

The question arises whether he had a personal acquaintance with Tertullian, whom he calls "the teacher" par excellence, as already noted (see above, sec. 2). Jerome says (*Epist.* 84.2) that "Blessed Cyprian followed Tertullian and regarded him as his real teacher, as his works show." In any case, activity as an orator implied a careful literary training, and this kind of educational formation is quite evident in Cyprian, even though his writings (which, like Tertullian's, date from after his conversion) contain not a single citation of secular writers. Cyprian often takes an attitude different from that of Tertullian, but unlike Tertullian he does not say that he is not interested in theological problems. He came perhaps from a wealthy family and was on his way to a career as a civil servant; it is certain that he owned property in Carthage and that he had to some extent a bureaucratic mentality.

Cyprian tells us of the spiritual crisis that led to his conversion in his first work, *To Donatus,* which was written shortly after his baptism, around 245. For this reason the work can be regarded to some extent as an anticipation of Augustine's *Confessions.* The picture of Cyprian's world recalls that given in the *Octavius* of Minucius Felix; Cyprian sketches a dark picture of the moral corruption and the decadence of his age. It is clear, though not explicitly stated, that this perception of decadence, combined with a confused sense of being close to the end of time, led to the writer's conversion. In any case, having been converted, Cyprian has fled the disorder of the world and reached the harbor of salvation. Though full of Christian ideas and terms, the work is addressed to his former pagan companions and is therefore written in a highly developed rhetorical style.

Cyprian tells us that an elderly presbyter, Caecilius or Caecilian, helped him in his conversion. The future bishop then won great renown for selling many of his possessions and giving generous gifts to the poor. He soon became a presbyter and was then elected bishop by the people of Carthage (248–249; see *Ep.* 59.6). His election met with strong resistance, perhaps among other reasons because the new bishop's ascent in the church had been so rapid. Pontius tells us that five bishops opposed his election (*Vit. Cypr.* 5.6), and in a letter written from exile Cyprian laments that the wickedness of some presbyters delayed his return to his see at Easter of 251, when the persecution of Decius had been over for some time. Among these presbyters were probably Felicissimus and Novatus, who subsequently rebelled against their bishop about decisions made regarding the *lapsi.*

a. Before the Persecution

It was probably in 248–249 that Cyprian made a collection of biblical passages, the *Testimonia,* relating to central problems of Christian teaching. The treatise, *To Quirinus: Testimonies against the Jews (Ad Quirinum testimonia adversus Iudaeos),* is in three books and was requested by a friend who wanted a compendium of the church's teaching on Judaism and on the relationship and opposition between Judaism and Christianity. The collection is of shapeless material, *testimonia* pure and simple, texts already commonly used in the second century in anti-Jewish polemics (see above, ch. 17, sec. 1), and its purpose is the traditional one. From the same period comes another treatise, likewise a compilation, which contains material taken chiefly from Tertullian and Minucius Felix, and which has for its purpose, as did the material from those two writers, to combat pagan religion; its title is *That Idols Are not Gods (Quod idola dii non sint)*. For a long time this treatise was considered not to be from Cyprian. It is indeed attributed to him by Jerome and Augustine, but it is not found in the manuscripts of his works. Pontius the biographer and an early catalogue of Cyprian's works, compiled in 359, do not list it.

Another little work from these first years of Cyprian's episcopate is *The Dress of Virgins (De habitu virginum)*, which takes up a particular problem of Christian ethics, namely, the behavior of women who had chosen a life dedicated to virginity. Cyprian takes as his model a work on a similar subject by his teacher, Tertullian; he stresses, however, the need for modesty and simplicity of dress and takes a resolute position on the excesses attending the practice of *virgines subintroductae*, that is, of those women who shared their lives with men, while observing virginity in agreement with them. This was a problem to which the bishop returned later in some letters.

b. Persecution of Decius in Africa

Such was the situation of the church of Carthage in the first years of Cyprian's episcopate; essentially they were not much different from those we can imagine in so many Christian communities of that period. Everything changed, suddenly and violently, as a result of what is usually called the Decian persecution, for this led to other serious problems concerning the order and hierarchy of the church.

Gaius Messius Traianus Decius was a senator, a provincial of Italian origin though born in Illyria. In September of 249 he was chosen emperor by the troops that had been sent into Moesia to combat barbarian invaders. When he met up with the existing emperor, Philip the Arab, who was known for his sympathy toward Christianity, Decius defeated and killed him near Verona. Whether Decius was hostile to Christianity due to his pagan traditionalism, as was typical of senators, or whether he wanted to test in a concrete way the loyalty of the citizens of the empire, he issued an order at the end of 249 that all citizens should make a solemn act of submission to him personally, in the form of a *supplicatio*, that is, a prayer to the gods for the safety of the emperor and his family. Indeed there was need of such an assurance, because the fifteen years preceding Decius's accession to the throne had been among the most turbulent years of the empire; in the previous ten years the populations of Africa had chosen four emperors.

Decius had no reason to be especially concerned about Christians. Thirty years earlier, the God of the Christians had come to an agreement with the esoteric religion of Elagabalus and had been given a place among the divinities to which a subject of the empire could pay worship. Alexander Severus too, had permitted Christians to profess their own faith (see *Writers of Imperial History*, Elagabalus 3, Alexander Severus 21). In the course of two generations many accommodations had been made between Christian discipline and the demands of the world. Many magistrates, aristocrats, officials, and soldiers were Christians. Christians and pagans had become accustomed to live side by side in everyday life, whether with tolerance or mutual indifference or even antipathy.

We have a good knowledge of the successive events caused by Decius's persecution in Africa because we find echoes of them in some short works of Cyprian and especially in his correspondence. While the facts are abundantly known, the interpretation of them is a complex and ticklish matter. They involve questions of the juridical order, such as according to what norms did the presumed persecution take place? There are also questions of disciplinary order, such as what was the attitude of North African Christians at this juncture? In addition, the chronology of events is uncertain, since Cyprian's letters have not come down to us in chronological order. It is certain, however, that we must not accept an irenic and optimistic vision of a Christian community united behind its bishop in defense of the faith and ready to face the hardest trials.

The procedure followed by the Roman authorities in dealing with Christians was this: by a certain date every citizen had to take part in the ceremony of the *vota publica*. The local authority entered the appearance of each in a register and issued a card *(libellus)* attesting to his or her participation in the sacrifice. Those who did not present themselves by the set date because they were unwilling to participate in the *vota* could fraudulently obtain the *libellus,* often for money. If the refusal to offer sacrifice was overt, the proconsul would sentence the person to exile for a set period or, in cases of serious obstinacy, to "deportation," which was usually accompanied by the complete or partial confiscation of property. Those who were not captured would be condemned by default. When captured, the rebels were kept in prison to await sentence. If we go by what Cyprian tells us, most Christians yielded in the very first days of the test; very few failed to present themselves for the public ceremony.

Here, we bear in mind a distinction, established essentially on this occasion, between "martyr" and "confessor." A martyr is one who professes the Christian faith by sacrificing his own life—although Cyprian himself sometimes calls even such individuals "confessors." A "confessor" is one who professes the Christian faith before the authorities and for doing so suffers a punishment, sometimes severe, such as torture and harsh imprisonment, sometimes more tolerable, such as exile and confiscation of property. After this punishment, a confessor would often be released and could return to the Christian community, sometimes to be haloed with a well deserved glory, sometimes to be ruined by pride. A confessor could then become a disturbing element in the community, if he adopted an insubordinate attitude toward the ecclesiastical hierarchy. We shall see from Cyprian's experience that this disturbance occurred on a massive scale.

The emperor's decision to summon everyone to the celebration of the *vota publica,* with the anti-Christian intention behind it, was implemented in Africa with a ceremony on January 3, 250; this date marked the beginning of the persecution. The bishop's actions in this situation were summed up by Cyprian (*Ep.* 20.2.1): he did not fail to instruct the clergy or to encourage confessors and those who were exiled or to exhort the entire community of the faithful to obtain the mercy of God. Subsequently, Cyprian continued, torture was used, and he all the more exhorted confessors and martyrs to have faith. Torture was used not to extort confessions from prisoners, since they had already professed their faith, but to inflict punishment; sometimes, of course, the condemned person might die as a result of the torture. But it also happened that some confessors after being tortured, others after being held in prison for some months, were released; still others, while in prison, were able to send letters to the brethren. An exchange of letters between the confessors of Rome and the confessors of Carthage has been preserved. Others, finally, were not imprisoned but "detained," that is, subjected to a preventive detention lest they flee, and enjoyed some freedom, to the point where Cyprian (*Ep.* 5) had to warn them to behave cautiously, that is, not to engage in acts of insubordination and not to demonstrate their faith in an arrogant way.

The question remains why the authorities did not carry their persecution of confessors to the extreme. Some scholars have suggested that the intention of the pagan authorities was to identify those who were rebellious toward their bishop and to let them go free for the undeclared but obvious purpose of creating division within the community. Or, as others remark, "the whole plan relied on the presumption that a Christian once brought to renouncing the church was lost to it once for all. In reality, however, those forced to sacrifice at once streamed back to their old communities" (Campenhausen, 40). This return was not without its difficulties, since the more rigorous and austere members of the community were inclined to reject the guilty even if they were repentant. It took the political genius and inflexible authority of Cyprian to resolve the problem, in his time and for the future.

c. Problem of the Lapsi

In Carthage, after being elected bishop against the strong opposition of some presbyters, as indicated above, Cyprian immediately found himself in difficulties. A few months later, specifically before Easter of 250, the confessors were confined and began the *lapsi* controversy, which was so dangerous for the African community, and which was settled only thanks to the political ability and firmness of Cyprian. The opposition was definitively surmounted only later on, however, and then thanks to the credit Cyprian had gained through his martyrdom.

The bishop's position was certainly very awkward, and his enemies did not fail to call attention to its peculiarity. During the persecution he had left Carthage in order to avoid capture. His biographer, Pontius, makes the point that in his absence Cyprian was able untiringly to help his community, and Cyprian tells us that he was easily available to anyone. It is likely, however, that not all (the confessors, in particular) were convinced of this, especially since we have no evidence that he had been sought out by the authorities, although he was condemned in his absence and his property was confiscated. In theory, there was nothing blameworthy about his behavior, and that same behavior had been accepted by the church in times past. It was considered permissible "to take flight during persecution," even though, as we saw, such conduct was criticized by Tertullian.

Cyprian was embarrassed by the criticism and probably also by the fact that his personal situation seemed perhaps too comfortable in comparison with that of the confessors. He several times says (see, e.g., *Ep.* 20) that, although he had saved himself by flight, he lost all his possessions and ran the risk of being denounced by anyone and that, though absent, he did not fail to send his exhortations and advice to those facing the test. It was certainly not easy for him to assert episcopal authority over a throng of martyrs and confessors.

In addition, criticism had reached him from the clergy of Rome, whose bishop, Fabian, had died at the beginning of the persecution; the Roman priests had sent a letter to the clergy of Carthage (*Ep.* 8) mocking the bishop's flight. Cyprian replied to them (*Ep.* 9) in a clear but polemical way: while he extolled the martyrdom of Fabian, he asked himself whether the letter from Rome was really authentic, so strange did it seem to him, and he sent it back for a more careful examination. Furthermore, responding indirectly to the criticism against him, he pointed out that the death of the bishop of Rome had left the flock without a leader. In addition, even in Alexandria Bishop Dionysius had avoided capture by fleeing and in a letter to Bishop Germanus had rejected accusations on this account and justified his action (see Eusebius, *Hist. eccl.* 6.40 and 7.11).

As early as March of 250 the question arose of readmitting to communion those who had committed the sin of apostasy. Preserved among Cyprian's letters is one (*Ep.* 22) from Lucian, a confessor, who writes to Celerinus, another confessor, that he has had a vision in which Paul the apostle has urged him to grant communion to repentant sinners. In making the affair known to the clergy of Rome (*Ep.* 27) Cyprian assigns responsibility for it to Lucian alone, but *Epistle* 23 tells us that the decision was a unanimous one of all the confessors. But here precisely was the danger: the confessors, though praiseworthy in certain respects, could be manipulated by those who would profit by isolating or excluding Cyprian from the community, especially since he was so resolute in stressing the authority of the hierarchy over all Christians, the *auctoritas sacerdotalis* that came directly from Christ.

The pagan magistrates had adopted a two-faced attitude toward the confessors: sometimes harsh, with the use of torture and prison, and sometimes accommodating. The reason was that after a short period, once the confessors had "confessed" and survived, they would be restored to freedom. But even during the period in custody and prison, and even more afterwards, these confessors had adopted a rebellious attitude. To begin with, they had granted forgiveness to all the *lapsi,* who were in turn divided into the *sacrificati,* those who had actually offered a sacrifice to the gods, and the *libellatici,* those who had somehow acquired the certificate or *libellus* saying they had sacrificed. As a result, the confessors and the *stantes* (those who had been unshaken in bearing witness to their faith) would gain the admiration and support of the majority of the faithful, precisely because they were ready to grant peace.

The rebellion against the bishop, which acquired new strength from those who in the past had opposed his appointment, was led primarily by Novatus, a presbyter, who appointed a deacon, Felicissimus, who in turn not only granted peace indiscriminately to the *lapsi* but also accused Cyprian. Initially the bishop sternly resisted the rebellious confessors, partly because their praiseworthy steadfastness before the pagan authorities was not matched by an equally praiseworthy moral integrity (see *Ep.* 13). At that time he made an energetic reply to Novatus and Felicissimus (see *Ep.* 43). Later, at the end of the same year (251), he was compelled to adopt a more moderate attitude toward the *lapsi,* as he admits in *Epistle* 55, in which he justifies both his initial severity and his subsequent softening. But every decision in the matter, he says, would have to be made by a council, which would be held in Carthage on his return to his see.

Toward the middle of 251 the persecution died out, partly due to the death of Decius, who fell in battle against the Goths. Cyprian was able to return to Carthage, where he wrote *The Lapsed (De lapsis),* a work in which he sums up his earlier position, justifies it, and inaugurates his way of acting in the future.

Right at the beginning, the writer turns to those who had hoped he would be unable to return, and he has special praise for the confessors who had not rebelled. A few remarks are addressed to those martyrs who bore witness in prison and then were set free; they are the objects of repeated sarcasm, because they arrogated to themselves the right to decide anything having to do with Christian discipline, and Cyprian denies them any such authority in this lapidary sentence: "it is the gospel that makes martyrs, not martyrs that make the gospel." The duty of the confessors is simply to return to their proper place. Cyprian's attention then turns to those who had obtained a certificate saying they had sacrificed, and to those *lapsi* to whom the confessors had granted forgiveness. He dwells mainly on the latter, with an emphasis on their weakness of spirit and feeble discipline.

This little work, which is one of Cyprian's most beautiful, is also one of his most passionate and polemical, and displays all the bitterness of a man who has been kept apart from his subjects and has seen himself passed over because of the insubordination of a few. The work is also important for its portrayal of Christian practice, for, along with the many letters that are similar in content, it sketches the essential lines of penance while excluding in a balanced way every concession to either rigorism or laxity and asserting the full authority of the church in the administration of penance. Neither the confessors nor the martyrs have the right to remit sins, as had been commonly thought during preceding decades. Attestations of such a penitential practice are to be found even in Tertullian.

d. The Church according to Cyprian

In the last six years of his life after returning to Carthage, Cyprian organized his diocese and outlined his conception of the episcopal office, a subject on which few had spoken before him. He did this in a series of letters to the local clergy and to the clergy of Rome. His formulation, based on standards of a juridical kind, quickly became normative, even outside of Africa. Evidence of this is the fact that as early as the fourth century the idea of *auctoritas*, till then used exclusively in the civil sphere, was taken up, with all its implications, by the church as well, and that the body of Cyprian's letters, in which his conception of episcopal authority is set down in detail, was circulated over a very wide area and was continually read even in the Middle Ages. This period also saw the schism of Felicissimus and Novatus, the first of whom indulged in excessive laxity toward the *lapsi*, while the second was guilty of rigorism. Cyprian lumps them together, using all the language typical of political polemics: rash, seditious, sacrilegious, and so on (see, e.g., *Ep.* 41; 43; 52; 59). It would be a mistake to think of this language as simply rhetorical commonplaces.

In order to present his conception of the church in an organized way, Cyprian wrote *The Unity of the Catholic Church (De catholicae ecclesiae unitate)*. According to some scholars, this work was composed on the occasion of the council held in Carthage immediately after his return. According to others, the problem of church unity presented itself to Cyprian only some years later, at the time of the Novatian schism. They argue that the very word *catholica* as applied to the church was foreign to Cyprian and that he must have gotten it from its use by the Roman community and only when he became involved in the dispute between Cornelius and Novatian.

This little work is an attack on the sowers of discord within the church. On the basis of Matt 16:18, it emphasizes the oneness of the church's authority on earth as granted to it by Christ. Even though all the apostles were given the same authority, the *primatus* was certainly bestowed on Peter alone. But this primacy does not signify a personal authority of Peter over all the other disciples; it means rather that by the Lord's express command Peter is the foundation of the church's unity. Even though bishops are many, the church they serve is one in its origin, and all the bishops have received the authority of Peter. It follows that the sacraments and salvation are valid and effective only within the church. Baptism conferred outside the church is null and void; Cyprian will return to this point a few years later in opposition to Rome. Martyrdom likewise has no value outside the church. The rebellious confessors are once again rebuked by the bishop. Cyprian thus formulates his conception of "priestly authority" and of "ecclesiastical discipline," applying to the church juridical concepts hitherto used by the Roman state.

Chapter 4 of this work has reached us in two forms: in one Cyprian comes out in favor of the primacy of Rome (the so-called *Primatus Textus*), while in the other he says nothing about this subject (the *Textus Receptus*). According to Bévenot, the second text is a reworking of the primacy text by Cyprian himself at the time of the dispute with Pope Stephen (see below, sec. 6e). According to others, the first redaction is not authentic but contains a later interpolation that was meant to support the primacy of Rome and was introduced in the time of Pope Pelagius II (6th c.).

This authority comes directly from God, whose steward on earth the bishop is (*Ep.* 59.2.2). In order to organize this authority and to proclaim it publicly, Cyprian convoked an annual council in Carthage for six successive years. After each council, synodal letters were sent to inform all Christians of decisions on disciplinary matters. These councils formulated teachings, surely inspired by Cyprian, that were similar to Roman political doctrines and that used terms from the language of empire: Cyprian is the "priest of God" and "governs the church"; he possesses an *auctoritas* and a *potestas sacerdotalis* that transcends and is directly opposed to any human power. Prerogatives usually belonging to the emperor really belong to God, especially the prerogatives of *maiestas* and *voluntas*. God governs the people through the priest, who, when he judges, exercises a function received from God (see *Ep.* 59–65). The governing bishop has at his side a priestly college (*Ep.* 55), whose unanimity manifests and makes concrete the unity of the Catholic church (*Ep.* 48.3–4). African Christianity (and following its advice, Roman Christianity as well), was being organized as an association conceived in a juridical manner.

Another short work of Cyprian, *The Lord's Prayer (De dominica oratione)*, dates from this period, probably from 252. It is a very simple and clear explanation of the Our Father; in writing it Cyprian used Tertullian's work, *Prayer*, and made an unobtrusive use of allegory. Around 253 he wrote a work on *Mortality (De mortalitate)*, in which he exhorted his community to endure with courage the plague that at that time was ravaging the empire and that, like other misfortunes, had long ago been foretold by Christ as one of the signs of the last times. The just, Cyprian says, should place their hope solely in the promises of the next world and should not complain that God is striking pagans and the faithful without distinction; they ought not complain if the plague deprives men and women of the glory of martyrdom, for that glory is God's gift alone. Similarly, in his book on *Works and Almsgiving (De opere et eleemosynis)*

Cyprian teaches that if perfection cannot be attained through martyrdom, it is always possible to make oneself worthy of God through almsgiving, which is perhaps less heroic but no less efficacious.

The work *Mortality* is permeated by an anxious sense of the nearness of the end, which is advanced by the continuous aging of the world. This motif had already been present in such pagan writers as Lucretius and Seneca. It then became more common in Christian writers, on whom apocalyptic themes exerted an especially strong influence. Now, says Cyprian, we must not believe that the disasters that indiscriminately afflict pagans and Christians have been willed by the gods of Rome because they are offended by the spread of Christian "atheism." This was a longstanding charge that would continue until the time of the barbarian invasions and Augustine's *City of God*. Cyprian refutes the charge in *To Demetrian (Ad Demetrianum)*, an otherwise unidentified pagan enemy of Christians.

Among those rebelling against Cyprian's authority was Novatus, who just at this time allied himself with Novatian, an influential presbyter of Rome, even though the latter held views opposed to those of Novatus. Initially, Novatian had sided with Cyprian on the question of the *lapsi*, but later, because he failed to win election as bishop of Rome, where Cornelius had been chosen, he became an open rebel. The rapprochement between Cyprian and Cornelius had led to a break between Cyprian and Novatian. Indeed, even the Roman confessors who were released from prison in the spring of 251 realized that it was not suitable to elect as bishop such a dangerously extremist confessor as Novatian.

Once Cyprian's authority was consolidated, he was able to relax his original rigorist attitude to the *lapsi* (see *Ep.* 55.6.1), just as Bishop Cornelius was doing in Rome. Far from having a reputation as a rigorist, Cornelius had actually sacrificed (see *Ep.* 55.1–2) and, if he had not been warned by Cyprian, would have recognized the community of Felicissimus and Novatus. A short time after Novatian rebelled, the authorities banished Cornelius from Rome to Centumcellae, where he died in 253. His successor, Lucius, was likewise banished; shortly afterwards, however, he was restored to his see (autumn 253). Lucius did not have any other troubles, but he died a short time later (March 254) and was succeeded by Stephen, a bishop who seemed to have a more conciliatory attitude toward the imperial authorities. He also adopted a conciliatory attitude toward his faithful, so much so that Cyprian accused him of having maintained communion with some Spanish bishops who maintained their positions despite being notorious apostates.

BIBLIOGRAPHY

M. Bévenot, "*Primatus Petro datur:* St. Cyprian and the Papacy," *JTS* 5 (1954): 19–35.

H. Koch, *Cathedra Petri* (Berlin: Töpelmann, 1930).

U. Wickert, *Sacramentum Unitatis* (New York: de Gruyter, 1971).

P. A. Gramaglia, "Cipriano e il primato romano," *RSLR* 27 (1992): 185–213.

P. B. Hinchliff, *Cyprian of Carthage and the Unity of the Christian Church* (London: Chapman, 1974).

G. S. M. Walker, *The Churchmanship of St. Cyprian* (Richmond: John Knox, 1969).

e. Controversy over Second Baptisms

The friendship between Rome and Carthage that had begun with Cyprian and Cornelius deteriorated during the pontificate of Stephen due to the question of second baptisms. To tell the truth, this problem did not seem very pressing in such troubled times, and the conflict must have been displeasing to many Christians. It is noteworthy that Cyprian's biographer does not speak of it—surely on purpose, not out of ignorance. Life in the empire, and therefore the life of Christians, was troubled by much more serious problems, such as the barbarian invasions, the war with the Persians, famine, and plague. Still, the problem was to settle the validity or invalidity of baptism administered by heretics to pagans who had converted to Christianity and then decided to leave the heretical church. Put briefly, the problem was whether the sacramental act had its value *ex opere operato* (by virtue of the action performed), regardless of who performed it or whether the value derived from the person performing the act. The church of Rome held that baptisms administered by heretics were valid because Christ's name was part of the creed (see *Ep.* 73.16). Cyprian, however, maintained that such baptisms had no validity and therefore had to be repeated.

If we may go by the account of Eusebius (*Hist. eccl.* 7.5.3–5; 7.7.5), the practice of the Africans had been approved at earlier councils (ca. 230) at Iconium and Synnada (Asia Minor) and at Carthage under Agrippinus. Eusebius's account is supported by Firmilian, Bishop of Caesarea in Cappadocia, who sent Cyprian a letter that is preserved in a Latin translation—probably made by Cyprian himself—as *Epistle* 75 in Cyprian's correspondence. Cyprian held that baptism is one and indivisible and that to accept baptisms by heretics meant bringing heresy into the church. The sacrament is effective only if the one administering it possesses the Holy Spirit, and since no one outside the church possesses the Spirit, baptisms administered outside the church lack validity, even if the same creed is used (*Ep.* 69 and 70).

Stephen, in contrast, held a radically liberal view that did away with any distinction between those baptized in an orthodox rite and those baptized in a heretical rite. In 255 he sought to impose his view, arguing from the apostolic tradition possessed by the church of Rome, and acting as Bishop Victor had done sixty years earlier in connection with the opposition to the eastern churches on the date of Easter, when he condemned the practice of celebrating that feast on the date established by the Jewish calendar. Cyprian replied that each church should be free to follow its own traditions (*Ep.* 73). It should not have been difficult to reach an agreement, seeing that a few years after this dispute the Christian church everywhere accepted the Roman interpretation. On this matter Cyprian managed to gather all the bishops not only of the province of Africa but also the neighboring provinces for a council at Carthage in the spring of 256. He secured their agreement and then sent Stephen a tough but courteous letter (*Ep.* 72) informing him of the council's decision. Stephen met the resistance of the African bishops with what was essentially an excommunication, and accused Cyprian of being "a false Christian, a false apostle, an impostor" (*Ep.* 75.25.1).

In addition to the dispute over second baptisms, a conflict arose between Cyprian and Stephen over who had jurisdiction over the sees of Legio, Asturica, Emerita (in Spain), and Arles (in Gaul). Meanwhile, after some upheaval, Valerian, another senator (and therefore a strong traditionalist), ascended the imperial throne in 253.

Probably from this period come two sermons that Cyprian wrote without any precise reference to the current situation. One praises *The Advantage of Patience* (*De bono patientiae*, beginning of 256), in which he again uses Tertullian. The other condemns *Jealousy and Envy* (*De zelo et livore*, summer of 256).

f. Cyprian's Martyrdom

The controversy over rebaptism lasted for several months, until the persecution of Valerian came along to end it. The problem was then set aside for fifty years, when with the help of the state and Emperor Constantine the church of Rome imposed its interpretation of baptism and quashed the opposition of the Donatists.

On August 30, 257, Cyprian was banished by the emperor to Curubis but was able there to continue peaceful contacts with all of his faithful. Another opponent of Stephen, Dionysius of Alexandria, had been exiled to Cephro, while at the same time Stephen, who had died a martyr on August 8, 257, had been succeeded by Pope Sixtus.

Proconsul Aspasius Paternus had summoned Cyprian and told him of receiving a letter from Emperors Valerian and Gallienus saying that those who did not practice the religion of the Romans must nevertheless "recognize the validity of Roman ceremonials." Cyprian was thus faced with the dilemma that Christians had always faced: was it, or was it not, permitted to take part in pagan ceremonies, while of course not believing in idols? That was essentially the problem of apostasy, since the imperial authorities required only a formal, external assent to religious ceremonies that had a purely civil significance. Cyprian's answer was the one we read in the acts of the martyrs (e.g., the Scillitan martyrs) from the very beginning: Christians worship no one but the true God, and they pray to him for the well being of everyone, even the emperor. The proconsul also asked Cyprian for the names of the presbyters, but he refused to give them. The proconsul's judgment was not expressed in harsh language: because of his answer, Cyprian would have to go into exile; under threat of punishment, Christians were not to assemble anywhere, even in cemeteries.

Cyprian's exile lasted until the beginning of summer of the next year, when he returned to Carthage to resume leadership of his church, seemingly without running into difficulties from the imperial authorities. The few letters he sent to his community during this period of exile seem to be marked by a burning, anxious expectation of trial and martyrdom, although we need not foresee its approach. An example is *Epistle* 79, which was sent to nine fellow bishops and some presbyters and deacons who had been sent to hard labor in the mines of Sigus in southwest Numidia. In the letter the writer imagines seeing his companions in exile as future martyrs, condemned as they were to a life of suffering in the *metalla*. Also permeated by the idea of martyrdom is Cyprian's last work, *To Fortunatus* (*Ad Fortunatum*), which consists of a collection of biblical passages that require Christians to face the supreme test.

More problematic is the interpretation of *Epistle* 80, which was sent around mid-August of 258, when Cyprian had already returned to Carthage. It is addressed to his colleague Successus, bishop of Abbir Germaniciana. From it we learn that Cyprian, convinced that the supreme test was near, was increasing the spiritual tension of the entire Carthaginian community so that its members might be ready to face martyrdom. The bishop had sent some messengers to Rome to bring him accurate information on the situation and the imminent persecution, since the talk of it by the people of Carthage was based mainly on hearsay.

On returning, the messengers reported that Bishop Sixtus had been executed in a cemetery on August 6, along with four deacons; that Valerian had sent the Roman senate a rescript in accordance with which bishops, presbyters, and deacons were to be executed; that Christian senators and other Christians of the highest levels, including even knights, were to be stripped of property and rank; that these persons were to be given a death sentence if they persevered in their faith, and their matrons were to be stripped of possessions and sent into exile. Along with this rescript to the senate, Valerian, then at Antioch, sent a copy of his letter regarding provincials; this letter could arrive at any moment even in Carthage. Finally, in Rome the persecution was in full swing, following the norms set down by the emperor. In short, what is commonly called "the persecution of Valerian" had begun.

This information is regarded by critic Saumagne as absurd and untrustworthy. Apart from other objective difficulties that emerge from a careful and unprejudiced examination of what Cyprian says, the procedure established by Valerian, with all its cruelty, would have been contrary to any legal rule, because it would not have taken into account any of the rights of citizens. Furthermore, the condemnation to death of all the persons listed by Cyprian would have meant the setting up of an absurd terrorist regime of which there is no other trace. In addition to the execution of Sixtus and his four deacons at Rome, the supposed persecution of Valerian was, Saumagne says, limited to the condemnation to death of Cyprian, Quadratus, and the *massa candida* of Utica. This expression refers to the crowd of Christians who were killed at Utica on August 10 of that year, as a result of a popular uprising of the kind that occurred frequently in the second and third centuries. They were a *massa candida,* as Prudentius calls them (*Perist.* 13.76ff.), because their corpses were thrown into a common grave filled with quicklime.

Beyond these few instances, we do not hear anything of a persecution of Valerian, at least in Africa. When Augustine preaches a sermon (no. 311) in honor of Quadratus and mentions that persecution, the only others he names are Cyprian and the *massa candida.* We must also keep in mind that during those decades the Roman authorities in Africa often had to deal with rebellions and especially with raids by people from the interior, which made citizen uprisings seem even more dangerous. For this reason, Proconsul Galerius Maximus, after departing in great haste from Carthage, set up an *extra ordinem* process and condemned to death as the person responsible Quadratus, bishop of Hippo-Diarrhytus (modern Byzerta), on whom the clergy of Utica were dependent. It is likely that the inquiry was extended from Quadratus to Cyprian. The proconsul stayed in Utica for about three weeks in order to settle matters and send a detailed report to Rome. He would then receive from Rome instructions to proceed according to legal norms.

Meanwhile, Cyprian wrote his final letter (*Ep.* 82). Believing a general persecution to be imminent in light of the news he has received from Rome and then sent to Quadratus, he anticipates a direct threat to himself and exhorts all Christians to becalm. On September 14, 258, the proconsul summoned Cyprian into his presence; Cyprian had not expected such a summons and came a day late. The interrogation began; Galerius Maximus ordered Cyprian, in the name of the *sacratissimi imperatores,* to sacrifice to the gods. Cyprian refused and was condemned to death according to the procedure with which we are already familiar from the time of Hadrian's rescript.

The condemnation to death occurred in a setting that excluded any political harassment: a large crowd heard the sentence and followed Cyprian to the place of torture, and the soldiers did not hold them back. A watch was kept over the martyr's body during the day, and in the night the procession began that brought Cyprian's mortal remains to the cemetery of Procurator Macrobius Candidus, close to the cisterns of Carthage. Everything took place with maximum "publicity," something that would have been unthinkable in an ongoing persecution.

g. Cyprian the Writer

Critics have usually described Cyprian's style by contrasting it with Tertullian's: the latter's style is rough, fragmented, and strained, while Cyprian's is balanced and abounds in turns of phrase. The education of the two men, though they were from the same city and probably went to the same school, had different results. Cyprian avoids any preciosity and any impassioned language, his sentences are cadenced and bear the mark of Cicero. The evaluation of Cyprian by Lactantius, a Ciceronian, might be a judgment on an orator of the classical age: "He had a ready, abundant, pleasing, and clear mind; clarity is the essence of his style, so that you could not say whether he was more flowery in his expression, more successful in his exposition, or more effective in persuading" (*Inst.* 5.1.24–25). Tertullian could hardly have been a stylistic model for a nature so balanced as Cyprian's and for a writer so clear as he was. On the other hand, the style of Cyprian, as Fontaine remarks, is the first of the truly "converted" Latin styles; it is the ornate and at the same time clear and cadenced style of a servant of the Christian church, that is, of a bishop. In Cyprian we already see the limpid harmony and classical intonation that characterize the Latin liturgy.

BIBLIOGRAPHY

Editions

Cyprian, Bishop of Carthage, *S. Thasci Caecili Cypriani opera omnia* (CSEL 3, 1–2; ed. and trans. G. Hartel; Vindobonae: Geroldi, 1868–1871).

———, *Sancti Cypriani episcope opera* (CCSL 3–3D; ed. R. Weber et al.; Turnhout: Brepols, 1972–).

Partial Editions with Introduction and Translation

Cyprian, Bishop of Carthage, *Correspondance* (ed. and trans. L. Bayard; 2d ed.; Paris: Les Belles Lettres, 1961–1962).

———, *L'oraison dominicale* (ed. and trans. M. Réveillaud; Paris: Presses Universitaires de France, 1964); with introduction, translation, and commentary.

———, *De lapsis; and, De ecclesiae catholicae unitate* (trans. M. Bévenot; Oxford: Oxford University Press, 1971).

———, *Ad Demetrianum* (ed. and trans. E. Gallicet; CP 4; Turin: Società Editrice Internazionale, 1976).

———, *A Donat et La vertu de patience* (ed. and trans. J. Molager; SC 291; Paris: Cerf, 1982).

Translations with Introduction and Commentary

Cyprian, Bishop of Carthage, *Opere* (trans. G. Toso; CdR 36; Turin: UTET, 1980).

———, *The Letters of St. Cyprian of Carthage* (ed. and trans. G. W. Clarke; 4 vols.; ACW 43–44, 46–47; New York: Newman, 1984–1989).

———, *Opuscoli* (ed. and trans. S. Colombo; Turn: Società Editrice Internazionale, 1935).

Studies

A. d'Alès, *La théologie de saint Cyprien* (Paris: Beauchesne, 1922).

M. Pellegrino, *Studi su l'antica apologetica* (Rome: Edizioni de Storia e Letteratura, 1947).

J.-P. Brisson, *Autonomisme et Christianisme dans l'Afrique Romain de Septime Sevère à l'invasion vandale* (Paris: de Boccard, 1950).

H. von Campenhausen, *The Fathers of the Latin Church* (trans. M. Hoffman; Stanford: Stanford University Press, 1964).

S. Deléani, *"Christum sequi": Étude d'un thème dans l'oeuvre de St. Cyprien* (Paris: Études Augustiniennes, 1974).

L. Duquenne, *Chronologie des Lettres de Saint Cyprien* (Brussels: Société des Bollandistes, 1972).

M. M. Sage, *Cyprian* (Cambridge: Cambridge University Press, 1975).

C. Saumagne, *Saint Cyprien, évêque de Carthage, "pape" d'Afrique, 248–258* (Paris: Éditions du CNRS, 1975).

U. Wickert, *Sacramentum unitatis: Ein Beitrag zum Verständnis der Kirche bei Cyprian* (New York: de Gruyter, 1971).

A. A. R. Bastiaensen, *Le cérémonial épistolaire des chrétiens latins* (Nijmegen: Dekkers and Van de Vegt, 1964).

H. von Soden, *Die Cyprianische Briefsammlung: Geschichte ihrer Entstehung und Überlieferung* (Leipzig: Hinrichs, 1904).

———, *Das lateinische Neue Testament in Afrika zur Zeit Cyprians* (Leipzig: Hinrichs, 1909).

Beginning in 1986, the *REA* expanded what had been its "Chronica Tertullianea" into a "Chronica Tertullianea et Cyprianea," edited by R. Braun, S. Deléani, F. Dobeau, J.-C. Fredouille, and P. Petitmengin.

M. A. Fahey, *Cyprian and the Bible: A Study in Third-Century Exegesis* (Tübingen: Mohr, 1971).

M. Bévenot, *The Tradition of Manuscripts: A Study in the Transmission of St. Cyprian's Treatises* (Oxford: Clarendon, 1961).

h. Life of Cyprian

The *Life of Cyprian* was written by Pontius, one of that bishop's deacons, for the clearly apologetic purpose defending Cyprian against those who criticized him for having avoided the persecution of Decius and who, in contrast, admired the martyrs of that period. Following the usual method Pontius begins not with the first years of the bishop's life, about which we unfortunately know very little, but with his conversion to Christianity. Information on later events is derived primarily from the bishop's works. For this reason, the *Life* is regarded as summary and defective from the historian's viewpoint. On the other hand, the *Acts of the Martyrdom of Cyprian,* which have a narrative power of their own are trustworthy. Pontius's biography is heavily governed by rhetoric; it has a prologue that is full of commonplaces and uses other traditional elements. Some details, however, have attracted the narrator's interest, such as the dream of Cyprian, in which Pontius sees a clear warning from God, and the description of the condemnation and martyrdom.

BIBLIOGRAPHY

Editions

M. Ponzio, *Vita e martirio di San Cipriano* (ed. and trans. M. Pellegrino; Alba: Paoline, 1955).

The collective work *Atti e Passioni dei martiri* (ed. A. A. R. Bastiaensen et al.; trans. G. Chiarini et al.; Milan: Fondazione Valla-Mondadori, 1987).

H. Delehaye, *Les passions des martyrs et les genres littéraires* (Brussels: Bureaux de la Société des Bollandistes, 1921).

P. Franchi de'Cavalieri, *Note agiografiche* (Rome: Vaticana, 1912).

7. Pseudo-Cyprianic Works

Some inauthentic works have come down to us among the writings of the bishop of Carthage. However, many of these have to do, in one way or another, with events in the life of Cyprian, and some provide interesting information on Christian life in the third century. In the eyes of their authors, the attribution of these works to Cyprian guaranteed their orthodoxy and therefore their survival in later centuries. If some of them were written by Novatian, then the attribution to Cyprian was deliberately made, after Novatian's death, by one of his followers. It must be kept in mind, however, that the placement of the works in the African world is not certain for any of them.

Against Dice Players (Adversus aleatores) is a short work to which reference was made earlier (see ch. 17, sec. 5); according to some scholars, it was written by a bishop who made use of Cyprian's works; this would exclude von Harnack's thesis.

Praise of Martyrdom (De laude martyrii) is a highly rhetorical celebration of martyrdom, written in an affected and precious style. It belongs more to secular literature than literature dealing with Scripture. An attribution to Novatian has been suggested but is not convincing.

Against the Jews (Adversus Iudaeos) is a homily exhorting Jews to convert and acknowledge Christ. This too has been attributed to Novatian, but doubts remain.

Mount Sinai and Mount Zion (De montibus Sina et Sion) is a treatise composed in Africa between 210 and 240 in a popularizing language. It is easy to see that the two mountains in question symbolize the Old and New Testaments. The argument is rather confused, uses bold allegories, and contains many ancient doctrines, which according to Daniélou were Jewish Christian.

To Bishop Vigilius on the Jewish Rejection of Belief (Ad Vigilium episcopum de judaica incredulitate). This seems to be a preface, or dedicatory letter, to the Latin translation, made in the third century by someone named Celsus, of the dialogue of Ariston of Pella against Jews (see ch. 10, sec. 3).

Shows (De spectaculis) takes up the subject of Tertullian's little work of the same name, which is also extensively used. There are also echoes of Cyprian's *To Donatus*. This work has also been attributed by some to Novatian.

The Advantage of Modesty (De bono pudicitiae). The style suggests that it is by the author of *Shows.* The highest degree of modesty is virginity, the next highest is continence (i.e., widowhood), and the third highest is marriage. Once again, scholars have suggested Novatian as the author.

On the other hand, the rigorism of Novatian is the object of violent attack in several other works, which follow.

To Novatian (Ad Novatianum). It seems, however, that the author of this little work, which is certainly excessively acrimonious, is on the side not of Cyprian and his balanced outlook but rather of Felicissimus and his laxism. An attempt has been made to trace this work, too, back to the Roman world (e.g., to Sixtus II), but its true place seems more probably to be in the African world.

The controversy on second baptisms seems to be the setting for another little work: *Rebaptism (De rebaptismate),* which was written, probably by a bishop and in an acrimonious spirit, against Cyprian and in defense of Stephen. One would therefore logically think of an Italian author, but against this is the absence of any reference to Rome and to Peter. Perhaps it is to be identified with a work to which Cyprian refers in *Epistles* 73.4–5 and 74 and which had been circulated in opposition to him. It would thus be earlier than the council of Carthage on September 1, 256, which established the position of the African bishops. The short polemical essay essentially makes one argument: that Cyprian and his followers are going against Christian tradition. Baptism in water derives its efficacy solely from the name of Christ and independently of the dignity and merits of the minister. Baptism by a heretic or a schismatic is therefore valid.

The Calculation of Easter (De pascha computus) was written in the fifth year of Emperor Gordian, that is, before Easter of 243, and explains the way of reckoning the date of this feast. The author seems to have been an African.

Bachelorhood in Clerical Life (De singularitate clericorum) is an exhortation to churchmen not to live with *virgines subintroductae;* this was the problem already faced by Cyprian in *The Dress of Virgins.* According to some, this work is to be identified with the *Book for Confessors and Virgins (Liber ad confessores et virgines)* by Macrobius, a Donatist bishop living in Rome in 363–375; at the least it comes from Donatist circles.

Exhortation to Repentance (Exhortatio de paenitentia) is similar in structure to the Cyprianic collections of *testimonia*, for example, those written for Quirinus and Fortunatus. It assembles biblical passages that show the possibility of repentance, and would therefore have been composed in opposition to the views of Novatian. But the composition would seems rather late (end of the 4th c. or beginning of the 5th).

Another rather late work (2d half of the 7th c.) is probably of Irish origin: *The Twelve Evils of the World (De duodecim abusivis saeculi),* that is, the most serious evils afflicting life in the present world.

There are works explicitly attributed to Cyprian, such as letters (probably compilations made in Donatist circles), prayers of exorcism, a work titled *To Fortunatus on the Two Martyrdoms (De duplici martyrio ad Fortunatum;* probably a compilation from the pen of Erasmus of Rotterdam, and finally, and much more interesting, some poems, which we shall discuss later, with the Christian poetry of the fourth and fifth centuries.

Also worthy of mention is the *Sermon on the Hundredfold, Sixtyfold, and Thirtyfold Reward (Sermo de centesima, sexagesima, tricesima),* a homily on Matt 13:3 that sets down a scale of perfection that would become famous. The martyr represents the seed that yields the greatest fruit. The "struggler" *(agonista)* is the man or woman who masters their own flesh to the point of becoming a eunuch for the kingdom of heaven, thereby obtaining a sixtyfold reward. The upright person, the baptized and married Christian who remains chaste, receives a thirtyfold reward. This symbolism was repeated and adapted to a variety of situations in subsequent centuries: the martyr was replaced by the person who practices a total continence; the "struggler" was the person who preserves complete continence even in marriage; the upright man was one who remained a widower and refused a second marriage. According to some critics, this work extensively imitates Cyprian's *The Dress of Virgins;* according to others, it is older than Cyprian's work, possibly from the second century. Even if it dates from the third century, it reflects the influence not so much of Cyprian as of encratite views. Daniélou traces it back to the more extensive ascetical literature of Jewish Christianity.

BIBLIOGRAPHY

Editions

Cyprian, *S. Thasci Caecili Cypriani opera omnia* (CSEL 3, 3; ed. and trans. G. Hartel; Vindobonae: Geroldi, 1871).

A. von Harnack, *Der pseudocyprianische Traktat "De aleatoribus," die älteste lateinische christliche Schrift, ein Werk des römischen Bischofs Viktor* (vol. I; Leipzig: Hinrichs, 1888).

————, *Der pseudocyprianische Traktat "De singularitate clericorum" ein Werk des donatistischen Bischofs Macrobius in Rom* (Leipzig: Hinrichs, 1903).

R. Cacitti, in *Etica sessuale e matrimonio nel cristianesimo delle origini* (ed. R. Cantalamessa; Milan: Vita e Pensiero, 1976).

P. F. Beatrice, "Martirio ed ascesi nel sermone pseudo-cipriano *De centesima, sexagesima, tricesima,*" in *Paradoxos Politeia: Studi patristici in onore di G. Lazzati* (ed. R. Cantalamessa and L. F. Pizzolato; Milan: Vita e Pensiero, 1979), 3–24.

P. Sellew, "The Hundredfold Reward for Martyrs and Ascetics: Ps.-Cyprian, De Centesima, Sexagesia, Tricesima," StPatr 36 (Berlin: Akademie-Verlag, 2001), 94–98.

On some of these works see J. Daniélou, *The Origins of Latin Christianity* (ed. J. A. Baker; trans. D. Smith and J. A. Baker; London: Darton, Longman & Todd/Philadelphia: Westminster, 1977).

M. Marin, "Problemi di ecdotica ciprianea: Per un'edizione critica dello pseudo-ciprianeo *De aleatoribus,*" VC 20 (1983): 141–239.

8. Commodian

It seemed that the same African environment that witnessed the strong personality of Cyprian and the conflicts he experienced, also produced an obscure poet, Commodian, who remained almost unknown until the middle of the last century, but seems increasingly worthy of attention.

The only reference to Commodian by ancient writers is in the *Famous Men* of Gennadius of Marseilles, a church historian from the end of the fifth century. Gennadius says that Commodian was converted during his studies in secular literature; after his conversion, he wanted to do something in thanksgiving to Christ, the author of his salvation, and wrote a work against the pagans "in a middle style resembling verse" *(mediocri sermone quasi versu)*. But since he was not sufficiently knowledgeable about Christian doctrine, his work was better in its polemics than in its teaching. "For this reason, when discussing the promises of God against the pagans, he gave them a rather trite and rough meaning, so to speak, astonishing the pagans and making us despair, and this on the basis of Tertullian, Lactantius, and Papias." Perhaps it was for this doctrinal inadequacy that the *Decretum Gelasianum,* an "index of prohibited books" attributed to Pope Gelasius 1 (492–496), condemned Commodian's work.

But while Gennadius's statement is true in some respects, it also raises difficulties, because it dates Commodian after Lactantius, while the most common view is that he lived in the third century. On the basis of Gennadius, Courcelle places him in fifth-century Gaul. One of Commodian's works, *The Instructions (Instructiones)* is composed of two books and divided into chapters; its content could be inferred from an acrostic based on the first letters of each verse. The final composition of the second book has the title *Nomen gasei;* when the initial letters are read from bottom to top, they yield the words, *Commodianus mendicus Christi.* This *gaseus* is meant to give Commodian's name. Among the various hypotheses about the meaning of *gaseus* the most likely is that it is a corruption of a Hebrew word for "poet." "Beggar of Christ" is to be taken in a spiritual sense.

Commodian would thus have been a native of the East, a point confirmed by some of his information about eastern pagan cults, but would have lived in Africa; in Salvatore's hypothesis, he resided in the Africa of Cyprian's time. In *The Instructions (Instructiones)* he repeats the positions taken in principle by the bishop of Carthage; the question of the *lapsi,* the place of the martyrs and confessors in the church, and the condemnation of the schism of Novatus and Felicissimus are all echoed in Commodian's verses. Similarly, Commodian's *Apologetical Poem (Carmen apologeticum)* seems to use the first two books of Cyprian's *To Quirinus: Testimonies against the Jews* even to the extent of paraphrasing them. Commodian's work also bears the title *Poem about Two Peoples (Carmen de duobus populis)* because it is directed against the pagans and the Jews. The writer seems more knowledgeable even than Cyprian about Jewish literature, while he exhorts pagans not to yield to Jewish proselytizing. This was the actual purpose of almost all anti-Jewish works since the time of Justin.

The work is also directed against pagans and, more specifically, against the senatorial class, which was the class of Roman society most stubbornly pagan and anti-Christian. The poem ends with an apocalyptic vision of the end of the world, and of the millennium that would follow. The poet, like so many others of his time, was a convinced millenarian, following the example of Tertullian, if not of Cyprian, restricting ourselves to the African world. This point is brought out and censured by Gennadius. Many details of this apocalyptic vision, and others forecasting the end, are inspired by events in the period 250–260, such as the invasion of the Goths, the Decian persecution, the death of that emperor and of the senators who were his friends, the ensuing persecution of Valerian, and the invasion by the king of Persia. The poem ends with a description of the elect who come from unknown regions of the East to defeat the antichrist.

If Commodian was indeed originally from the East but lived in Africa in Cyprian's time, then he provides in his *Apologetical Poem* an interesting picture of the life of African Christians, more so than do the treatises of Cyprian, which are the work of so acculturated a mind. Alongside the authoritative and balanced bishop of Carthage, who organized his church after the manner of a Roman magistrate and firmly set forth the orthodox teachings of the faith, we have this obscure poet, who had little education, as is evident from his "bad" Latin and his still worse verses, who came from among the people, had little awareness of the needs of the empire, and was indifferent to all attempts to create a peace between Christians and pagans. We are far removed from Minucius Felix, and we once again see the variety and liveliness of African Christianity.

The subject of *The Instructions* is the same as that of the *Apologetical Poem*. The first book of *The Instructions* contains a vehement critique of idols and of the pagans who worship them, written in a condemnatory tone that recalls the Old Testament prophets. The second book, which is addressed to the Christian communities, aims to "instruct" them in the orthodox faith and correct behavior, while placing emphasis on the ideal of the *militia Christi*, which draws upon Pauline ideas; it is widespread in the works of Tertullian and Cyprian. In this work, too, can be seen many interesting aspects of the life of the author's Christian community. It ends with a strong attack on the Jews, which leads into a prophecy of the fast-approaching millennium.

Commodian write his two poems in dactylic hexameters, but if this easterner had little expertise in the Latin language, he had even less in metrics. There is not a single correct verse in his compositions, a sign that he had only a vague idea of the prosody and quantities of a language foreign to him. However, he does have a clear idea of the role of accent so that his verses seem quite rhythmic. In all speakers of Latin this accent was already a tonic accent. In Commodian the stress accent replaces the musical accent that was proper to classical Latin poetry. It cannot be said, then, that Christian Latin poetry began with Commodian—to see the difference, read the poetry of the fourth century. But Commodian's effort was nevertheless effective, as he spread his wings, to use Fontaine's description, with the seriousness of an Old Testament "oracle." The French critic claims that Commodian, who came from Syria, succeeded in combining the qualities of Semitic sentences with those of popular Latin verse, completely bypassing the mediation of the Greeks, which had always been an essential factor in Roman culture.

BIBLIOGRAPHY

Editions

Commodianus, *Commodiani Carmina* (ed. B. Dombart; CSEL 15; Vindobonae: Geroldi, 1987).

———— (ed. and trans. J. Martin; CCSL 128; Turnhout: Brepols, 1960).

————, *Carme apologetico* (ed. and trans. A. Salvatore; CP 5; Turin: Società Editrice Internazionale, 1977).

J. Fontaine, *Naissance de la poésie dans l'occident chrétien* (Paris: Etudes Augustiniennes, 1981); with introduction, translation, and commentary.

Because of its linguistic peculiarities Commodian's work is held in high esteem by students of the development of Latin into the Romance languages; interested readers should consult their works (Löfstedt, Väänänen, Battisti, etc.).

For English translations of Commodian's work, consult volume 4 of *The Ante-Nicene Fathers* (ed. A. Roberts, J. Donaldson, and A. C. Coxe; repr., Peabody, Mass.: Hendrickson, 1995).

9. Novatian

We met this presbyter earlier in connection with the friendly or conflicted relations between the church of Carthage and the church of Rome during the years of Cyprian's episcopate. Of Novatian himself we know little; as a result of his condemnation, the information we have comes solely from his adversaries. He must have been born around 200, but there is little likelihood that he came from Phrygia, as late sources claim. He had training in rhetoric and a good education. He was not ignorant of Stoicism, although it should not be assumed that he had a real doctrinal grasp of that philosophy. The same was true of other contemporary authors, e.g., Tertullian; in the Latin culture of the imperial age a superficial knowledge of Stoicism was widespread. After being converted to Christianity in his middle years, Novatian was appointed a presbyter by Pope Fabian. It is likely that before that point (ca. 235–240) he composed his most important work, *The Trinity (De trinitate)*. During the episcopate of Cornelius, Novatian acquired a certain renown and following in the Roman community, even though Cornelius claimed, surely for polemical reasons, that Novatian had behaved basely during the persecution.

During the summer of 250, when Fabian was some months dead and his successor had not yet been elected, Novatian wrote to Cyprian guaranteeing the latter his support. He let Cyprian know that the position he had taken on granting reconciliation only to those among the repentant *lapsi* who were on the point of death had been approved by the Roman clergy and by the confessors whom he, Novatian, had contacted. Novatian conceived of the church as an "assembly of the saints" *(coetus sanctorum)*, but shortly afterwards Cyprian rejected that idea, remarking that there was a place in the church not only for saints but also for the imperfect. Even in Rome, as in Carthage, there had been efforts to readmit the *lapsi* without any prior guarantee. A little later, Novatian sent an even harsher letter approving the ecclesiastical consecration by Cyprian of some of his right-hand men and confirming his support of the relatively stern position of the bishop of Carthage. Just at that time Novatian's views were becoming increasingly influential in the church of Rome; he sent letters to Sicily as well. His position was clear: those who had denied Christ could look forward to repentance but not to forgiveness, which was reserved to God alone.

But as the problem of the *lapsi* became increasingly acute in Rome, Novatian's influence decreased. In the spring of 251 the Roman community did not elect Novatian the rigorist, but first Lucius, then Cornelius, both less prominent personalities who nevertheless fared better than Novatian because of their more tolerant attitude. Adding to Novatian's resentment was the support unexpectedly given to him by Novatus, who had rebelled against Cyprian and had come to Rome at this time in search of help. Even though their positions were diametrically opposed—one was a rigorist, the other a laxist—they reached an unexpected agreement on strict views. Novatian then rebelled against Cornelius; he looked for support outside of Italy and found three bishops who consecrated him bishop of Rome.

Both Cornelius and Novatian then sought support from Cyprian, who found himself in a difficult position and initially acted cautiously, waiting until Cornelius came out openly against the schism of Felicissimus (see *Ep.* 44) before deciding against Novatian (*Ep.* 48). Novatian then sent messengers to Fabius of Antioch, Dionysius of Alexandria, Helenus of Tarsus, and Theoctistus of Caesarea (see Eusebius, *Hist. eccl.* 6.46). Dionysius had looked for a mediating position but then, in the name of church unity, had come down on Cornelius's side. Even though he was defeated, the rigorist views of the Roman presbyter won a noteworthy degree of acceptance even in the East. After having found the middle ground between opposing tendencies, Cyprian and Cornelius each gained the upper hand in their own communities.

We have no information about the subsequent years of Novatian's life; according to later testimonies, he died during the persecution of Valerian in 257. On April 1, 1932 a funerary inscription was found in a catacomb on the Via Tiburtina near the basilica of St. Lawrence: "Gaudentius, deacon, placed this in honor of the most blessed martyr Novatian." This suggests an identification with the schismatic we have been discussing.

The Trinity

Despite its title, the first such in Latin literature, this work is not a real discussion of the Trinity. Among other things, the term *Trinitas* is never used in the text of the work. Rather, in keeping with the tendencies and the problems of the times, the work is primarily a defense of the "rule of faith" against heresies. In controversy with the Marcionites, Novatian maintains that the Father is the creator of the universe and that there is only one God. He then explains the teaching of the faith about the person of the Son. Here he rebuts docetism, adoptionism, Sabellianism, and Marcion; the Son is the son of the creator of the universe. Finally, Novatian asserts that it is not possible to speak of two gods, because the Father and the Son constitute the one divine nature.

His speculation on the Spirit is limited and inadequate, and even represents a regression in relation to the thinking of Tertullian, who was stimulated during the last years of his life by his acceptance of Montanism. Novatian does not attempt to define the nature and origin of the Spirit, but is content to describe the Spirit's activity. In this matter, he depends not so much on Tertullian as on the *Against the Heresy of Noetus* of Hippolytus of Rome. Novatian distances himself from Tertullian on other points as well. For example, he emphasizes the immateriality of God, whereas for Tertullian the Spirit, who constitutes the divine substance, is corporeal. For Novatian the ineffableness of God plays a much greater role. The difference between the immanent Logos and the expressed Logos is less emphasized by Novatian. The idea, originating in apologetics, that the generation of the Logos from the Father occurs in view of the creation of the world is also less clear. According to Loi, in certain respects Novatian anticipates Origen's conception of the eternal generation of the Son.

On the other hand, Novatian's theological language is that of Tertullian and, in other respects, new: he takes over from Tertullian some technical terms such as *dispositio, substantia,* and *persona,* and adds others not found in Tertullian's works.

Some, contradicted by Jerome, even denied that *The Trinity* was Novatian's work and attributed it to Cyprian. The very title shows the dependence of Novatian on Tertullian, for the latter seems to have coined the term *trinitas* in his *Against Praxeas.* Jerome realized this dependence when, with some exaggeration, he described *The Trinity* as "an epitome, if I may so put it, of the work of Tertullian" (*Vir. ill.* 70). *The Trinity* was transmitted as a work of Tertullian and was called such in the Middle Ages and in the first editions printed in the sixteenth century. It was Jacques de Pamèle who restored the work to Novatian in 1579, on the basis of Jerome's remarks.

We have already spoken briefly, in connection with Pseudo-Cyprianic writings (see above, sec. 7), of some short works that are attributable to Novation; although less important than *The Trinity,* they help us gain an idea of his interest in ethics.

Novatian is a vigorous writer who loves disagreements and debates, out of which he is able to produce a rigorous demonstration. Sometimes, however, he also makes use of stylistic embellishments that suggest he is preening himself on his dialectical gifts and on his brilliant powers of expression and poetic affectations. His rhetorical training enables him to write, especially in his letters, bravura passages that far remove him from the balance and spacious flow of Cyprian's language.

BIBLIOGRAPHY

Editions

Novatianus, *De Trinitate* (ed. H. Weyer; Düsseldorf: Patmos, 1962).
——, *Opera* (ed. G. F. Diercks; CCSL 4; Turnhout: Brepols, 1972); also includes *De cibis iudaicis, De bono pudicitia, Ad Novatianum, De spectaculis,* and *Adversus Iudaeos,* which were mentioned in connection with the Pseudo-Cyprianic works, and *Epistles* 30, 31, and 36 from the correspondence of Cyprian.
——, *La Trinità* (ed. and trans. V. Loi; CP 2; Turin: Società Editrice Internazionale, 1975); introduction, critical text, translation, and commentary.

Studies

A. D'Alès, *Novatien: Étude sur la théologie romaine au milieu du III*ᵉ *siècle* (Paris: Beauchesne, 1925).
H. J. Vogt, *Coetus Sanctorum: Der Kirchenbegriff des Novatian und die Geschichte seiner Sonderkirche* (Bonn: Hanstein, 1968).
R. J. DeSimone, *The Treatise of Novatian, the Roman Presbyter, on the Trinity: A Study of the Text and the Doctrine* (SEAug 4; Rome: Institutm Patristicum Augustinianum, 1970).

10. Rise of Hagiography

The intellectual and cultural vitality of Christianity was spreading rapidly in the third century, despite all the threats of persecution and all the internal crises. This is confirmed by the continued mastery of existing literary forms. Thus the period of Cyprian saw the beginning of a literary genre that would become especially exuberant throughout the Middle Ages: the genre known as hagiography. The *Life of Cyprian,* of which we spoke earlier, is one of the first examples. It is necessary, however, to distinguish between later hagiography, which consists of biographies in the true and proper sense, "lives of the saints," and early hagiography, which begins with "historical" documents such as the *Acts* and *Passions of the Martyrs.* These documents, as their titles indicate, are intended to remind the communities of the faithful of the passion and death of their martyrs. Considered, then, from the viewpoint of their literary genre, they are an imperfect kind of hagiography. Important examples of these early documents are the *Acts of the Scillitan Martyrs* and the *Passion of Perpetua and Felicity.*

Later, in its more developed and mature form, hagiography would have a rather obvious connection with pagan biography, as indeed did all the other Christian literary forms, because they were practiced by individuals who shared teachers, schools, and texts with the pagans. On the one hand, the discourses of the main personalities, the structure of the story, and so on, can be regarded as traditional elements of hagiographical literature. On the other hand, Christian writers, especially in the first three centuries, depended extensively on the Bible, as they looked to the Old Testament for the models of life and the spiritual motifs to which the protagonist of the hagiographical narrative had then to conform. For this reason, caution is needed when it comes to searching for typical elements of pagan biography in Christian hagiography.

A distinction is usually made between the *Acts of the Martyrs* and the *Passions of the Martyrs.* The *Acts* take the form of the official minutes of a trial, which someone in attendance has taken down, whereas the *Passions* are reports of eyewitnesses. The spirituality of martyrdom that pervades the earliest documents is essentially the same as that found in contemporary literary productions, such as the works devoted to martyrdom by Tertullian *(To the Martyrs; Scorpiace)* and Cyprian (some letters; *To Fortunatus: Exhortation to Martyrdom).* Still visible to some extent in this spirituality is the Jewish tradition that reached its high point in the interpretation of the death of the persecuted prophet. In Tertullian's eyes the great prophets are the models of the Christian martyr.

But the strongest factor in this spirituality is the typically Christian conviction regarding the "imitation of Christ," meaning that the martyr reproduces in himself the suffering of Christ and that Christ is present in him. This idea is clearly attested in the *Letter of the Martyrs of Lyons* and in the *Passion of Perpetua and Felicity.* In the latter, Blandina and Felicity know that while their suffering as human beings is theirs alone, their suffering as martyrs will be that of Christ present in them, and that they will no longer feel this suffering. Also basic for Christians is the idea of "bearing witness" to Christ. While was the original meaning of the word "martyr," derived from Greek, was "one who bears witness," the word came to mean "one who dies for Christ." As Christ gave his life for human beings, so human beings give their life for Christ (see

Matt 10:32–33). It was this spirituality that caused the Greek word *pathos* and the Latin word *passio* ("passion"), which in everyday language meant simply "suffering," to take on the deeper meaning of "martyrdom."

Another typical Christian characteristic of hagiography is its commemorative spirit, the desire to remind the faithful, wherever they may be, of the martyr's glorious death. To this commemorative intention was joined another, that of exhorting Christians to face martyrdom. For this reason, the *Acts* and the *Passions* were often read during the liturgy, especially in Christian Africa. Written under the emotional impact of the events, the documents were striking in their simplicity and immediacy and were capable of stirring the enthusiasm and admiration of the faithful.

Later hagiographical texts, composed in the age when the church was victorious over paganism, are infected with an inflamed triumphalism and often seem repetitious and removed from all realism; they abound in commonplaces and the artificialities peculiar to devotional literature. In this kind of work, the martyr is generally anonymous, that is, his name is recorded but nothing of his earlier life, family, native place, or education. He often belongs to a group in which class differences, such as those between masters and slaves, do not exist. The hagiography of the earliest period focuses on the martyr, while later on, after the Peace of Constantine, hagiography focuses on monasticism. Typical of this second and different literary genre is the *Life of Antony,* which spread widely from the East into the West. Even the biographies of bishops, which are also abundant beginning in the fourth century, almost always have a connection with monasticism—for example, those of Ambrose and Augustine. But we shall discuss this in a later chapter.

Bibliography

Texts

H. Musurillo, *The Acts of Christian Martyrs* (Oxford: Oxford University Press, 1972).

Atti e passioni dei martiri (ed. A. A. R. Bastiaensen; trans. G. Chiarini et al.; Milan: Fondazione Valla-Mondadori, 1987); collective work.

For the spirituality of the *Passions* literature, see C. Leonardi, "Agiografia," in *Il Medioevo latino* (vol. 1 of *Lo spazio letterario del Medioevo;* Rome: Salerno, 1993), 426–62; with a discussion of earlier bibliography.

Chapter 19

THE AGE OF THE TETRARCHS
AND OF CONSTANTINE

1. Religious Syncretism

Although divided internally by the watershed of the great anti-Christian persecution of 303–313, the result of which was completely contrary to what the pagan emperor intended, the period from the reign of Diocletian to the death of Constantine (282–337) gives the impression of being essentially one in both pagan and Christian culture, the reigns of the two men being two sides of the same reality. This period saw the culmination of the pagan-Christian syncretism that had already manifested itself during the third century under some emperors who were more or less favorable to Christianity, e.g., the Severi and Philip the Arab. When the period ended, however, the situation was entirely different: paganism was in trouble, while the Arian controversy, the first doctrinal conflict to involve the entire church, introduced into Christianity the ancient principle followed in the Roman empire, that religion is first and foremost a concern of the state. Eusebius of Caesarea was the most representative intellectual of this period, and he inaugurated the new way in which the church conceived of its relation to the state.

When we speak of "religious syncretism," we run the danger of being vague, using a term that remains undefined. On the pagan side, syncretism manifested itself in the form of henotheism, that is, faith in a single god, but a god who was not the Christian God and who allowed for the existence of other, inferior gods, namely, the gods of the various religions of the empire. Some gods and divinities were proclaimed not only by philosophers and educated people but by new sources that deserve more attention than can be given to them here. These were the religious oracles that were the mouthpieces of communities of intellectuals who gathered at the great pagan sanctuaries or, in any case, of writers who made use of the oracular literature as a way of spreading their own ideas.

Alongside the philosophies, which looked for their origin to classical Greece, the most important being was Neoplatonism, there was a general culture, sometimes deeper, other times more superficial, that maintained in a vague way common religious, ethical, and ascetical ideas. As a result, Neoplatonism at times agreed with Christianity, but at other times emphasized the otherness of Christianity and its alienation from the Greco-Latin tradition, and combated it as best it could. An example is Porphyry, who wrote a famous work *Against the Christians,* but at the same time taught some doctrines that were adopted by such Christian intellectuals as Marius Victorinus, Ambrose, and Augustine. He was thus emblematic of the importance and influence of pagan culture on Christianity. Christian culture in turn was itself sometimes influenced by the pagan vagueness and lack of precision in conceiving the being of God; as a consequence, its thinking resembled that of the pagans, resulting in a substantial retrogression in theology as compared with the speculation of Tertullian or even of Novatian.

The personal religion of Constantine, though much praised by Christians, was initially marked by this syncretism. Even at the time of the edict of Milan (313) in which Constantine and Licinius granted religious peace, and on the triumphal arch that Constantine erected in Rome in 315, he spoke of a "divinity" which was not so much the God of Christians as the supreme being of pagan intellectuals. The idea of *divinitas* did not offend any religion and could satisfy all of them; for this reason it had undoubted advantages in an empire that had always claimed the prerogative of overseeing religion on the grounds that it was an important structure of society. The passage of Constantine from such a henotheism to Christianity took place in stages and reached its end, for practical purposes, at the council of Nicea (325), which condemned Arianism. Then Constantine was baptized at the point of death—the usual practice at that time—and this by the philo-Arian bishop, Eusebius of Nicomedia.

Constantine developed what is usually called the "theology of victory," that is, the common view, endorsed by the literary men of his court—or at least close to his court, such as Lactantius and Eusebius—that his definitive victory over Maxentius at the Milvian Bridge was due to the favor and protection of the "divinity," a favor which he, Constantine, had earned. On the triumphal arch that he erected in Rome in 315, he placed an inscription saying that he had acted "under an impulse from the divinity" *(instinctu divinitatis)*.

This conception of what had happened would be openly set down by Lactantius in his pamphlet *The Deaths of the Persecutors (De morte persecutorum)*. It can even be said that we find in Lactantius a similar revolution that brings him close to the ideology of Constantine. This writer sets forth the emperor's official ideology; he had been appointed tutor to the emperor's son and was therefore a courtier at the imperial residence in Trier, where his role was not much different from that of the official panegyrists, whose works are preserved in the collection of *Panegyrici Latini*. The idea set forth in Lactantius's final work is the same as that of the court bishop, Eusebius of Caesarea, in the last three books (written after 312) of *Ecclesiastical History*. The description of the battle at the Milvian Bridge, which Lactantius vividly describes, shows Constantine's army praying to God with a single voice. Lactantius also tells us of the future emperor's famous dream or vision.

To these collections of official propaganda we may perhaps add, if it is judged authentic, the *Address to the Assembly of Holy Men (Oratio ad sanctorum coetum)*, written by Constantine or, more accurately, his chancellery and sent to the body of bishops gathered at the Council of Antioch during Holy Week of 325. This text is transmitted among the works of Eusebius.

In general, Constantine had the skill to create among Christians a climate of opinion that was favorable to him, so much so that they always applauded and agreed with him, while ignoring his acts of cruelty, which were no different than those of a pagan despot. By contrast, the pagans more or less explicitly criticized this revolutionary emperor who had broken with ancient Roman tradition; Julian the Apostate was un-yielding in his criticism of Constantine. Also, Constantine had the same absolutist con-ception of imperial power that had characterized his predecessors. In substance he made his own the theocratic ideology of Diocletian. Like Diocletian, and even more so, Constantine maintained his right to intervene in the administration of the church, which for its part had called him "the equal of the apostles" or "the thirteenth apostle." Constantine's mother was declared a saint. The emperor convoked and presided over the Council of Nicea, which had for its purpose to settle the question posed by the spread of Arius's teaching; after all, Arianism was a source of disturbance and disorder in the church, and therefore indirectly in the state.

The European culture of the last three centuries has accustomed us to thinking of civic life and religious life as two distinct areas, but that was not the thinking of the Roman state ever since the republican age. The identification of the two spheres of life, regarded as obvious by imperial civilization, continued to be undoubted in the Roman-Christian empire of the fourth and fifth centuries and into the Byzantine era. This was naturally a source of serious disturbance in the life of the church, in which the emperors intervened by full right and without any scruple: they participated in doctrinal discussions, convoked councils, and inspired or perhaps imposed specific solutions to theological problems. Factions hostile to the reigning emperor were not better treated or more tolerated than Christians of earlier centuries had been by the pagans.

It has been suggested that imperial protection guaranteed Christians greater free-dom of speech and therefore favored the rise of a typically Christian culture. This was only partially the case. There is evidence that a good deal of acculturation occurred even in the preceding centuries; Tertullian, Novatian, and Cyprian were writers of no less culture and literary skill than the pagans of their time, a sign that access to educa-tion was not closed to Christians. When they describe the society in which they were living, these writers make it clear that, provided there were no actual persecutions going on, Christians were not denied a normal life. But the "peace" of Constantine did not give rise to a Christian culture. Schooling was still based on classical rhetoric and on the traditional disciplines and their content. The rhetors of the fourth century, even if they had become Christians, continued to teach Cicero and Virgil to pagan and Christian students alike. The Christian rule of Constantine had not changed the culture by transforming it from pagan to Christian. It did, however, give a new impe-tus to Christianity by broadening its horizons, and this impulse, which originated at the court, produced a phenomenon of great importance: Christian poetry.

The person of Constantine was central in the history of Christianity; he was looked upon as the greatest emperor who ever practiced, defended, and spread the or-thodox faith. The influence and importance that the tradition assigned to him lasted at least until the end of the Renaissance. For this reason, we also must speak briefly of other aspects, beyond the literary, that set him apart.

We have already remarked that pagans detested the emperor, even though the first panegyrists, his contemporaries, celebrated him as it was their duty to do. But the pagan panegyrists had to make a virtue of necessity, so they spoke of him either as a descendant of Claudius the Goth, one of the most respected pagan emperors of the third century, or as the ideal heir of the tetrarchic system. These views were obviously an invention of his contemporaries and could not stand up to the test of facts. The fourth-century historian, Eutropius, rebuked Constantine for acts of cruelty, for the worsening of his administration as time passed (i.e., it gradually multiplied provisions favorable to Christianity), the uselessness of many of his laws, and the severity of some of these; here again we understand what the pagan historian has in mind.

It is certain that in his attitude toward these two contrasting yet coexisting realities, the pagan and the Christian, Constantine moved from a primitive theism, probably learned from his father, Constans Chlorus, who did not apply in his territory the persecution decreed by the tetrarchs, to an increasingly emphasized Christianity. This initial theism, which was shared by many pagan intellectuals of the age, enabled him to remain for several years at the pagan court of Diocletian. Burckhard accuses Constantine of ideological duplicity, inasmuch as the emperor used either pagan or Christian religion, depending on which was politically advantageous to him. Burckhard also asserts that the emperor found in Eusebius of Caesarea the most contemptible of flatterers. An example of Constantine's supposed attitude would be that before the battle of the Milvian Bridge with the pagan Maxentius in October of 312, he ordered his soldiers to paint the *signum* (later interpreted by Christians as the *signum crucis*) on their shields.

It will never be possible to determine at what point Constantine converted to Christianity. It is certain that after the Milvian Bridge battle and after the Edict of Milan in 313 Constantine's legislation became increasingly favorable to Christians. Much emphasis has been laid on the story that he refused to take part in the solemn procession up to the Campidoglio during the *ludi saeculares* of 315, thereby stirring the resentment of pagans, and that he supposedly preferred to reside in cities other than Rome, the headquarters of the pagan senate; after 326 he never went to Rome again. But these are incidents that allow for other interpretations. For example, residence not in Rome but in Nicomedia or Trier was already the practice of Diocletian, due to administrative necessity. In the opinion of many scholars, even the foundation of Constantinople, which was planned in 324 after the victory over Licinius, begun in 328, and completed in 330, did not necessarily mean that Constantine wanted to establish an exclusively Christian city over against Rome. So, too, it is not possible to speak of Constantine having a really anti-pagan policy. The most that can be said is that the measures he took favored Christianity, thereby implicitly doing harm to paganism.

On the other hand, Constantine's policy of building churches throughout the empire, from Phoenicia to Numidia, from Rome to Jerusalem, seems to have been openly Christian. In addition, the great Roman basilicas were endowed by the emperor with wealth chiefly in the form of vast estates to support them; this is the case with the large basilicas "within the walls of Rome" and the basilicas "outside the walls." Note that it was precisely during this period that the word *basilica,* which in Latin meant "an assembly hall, a hall for meetings and conferences," acquired the meaning of "church." In the first group were the basilica of the Holy Cross of Jerusalem and the basilica of St. John Lateran, which was begun on November 11, 312, fifteen days after the battle of the Milvian Bridge and after the barracks of the troops supporting Maxentius had been razed. Among those outside the walls, which were the tombs and basilicas of the martyrs, were those of St. Peter, St. Agnes, St. Lawrence, and Sts. Marcellinus and Peter.

Thus was born the reputation of Constantine as chief defender of the church and its benefactor through the so-called "donation" to it of Rome and the West. The "donation" was a forgery that originated among hagiographers in the eighth century and was exposed by the "new" critical approach of Valla. Dante, who like the many rigoristic thinkers of his age challenged the church's right to possess earthly goods, nevertheless justified Constantine and his donation.

BIBLIOGRAPHY

The literature on Constantine is, of course, vast. We shall mention in particular various authors in G. Bonamente and F. Fusco, eds., *Costantino il Grande: dall'antichità all'umanesimo* (2 vols.; Colloquio sul cristianesimo nel mondo antico, Macerata, December 18–20, 1990; Macerata: Università degli studi di Macerata, 1993).

S. Calderone, "Letteratura costantiniana e 'conversione' di Costantino."

R. Krautheimer, "The Ecclesiastical Building Policy of Constantine."

M. Mazza, "Costantino nella storiografia ecclesiastica."

M. Sargenti, "Costantino nella storia del diritto."

L. Banfi, "Costantino in Dante."

R. Fubini, "Contestazioni quattrocentesche della donazione di Costantino: Nicolò Cusano, Lorenzo Valla."

In Addition

S. Calderone, *Costantino e il cattolicesimo* (Florence: Sansoni, 1962).

A. Alföldi, *The Conversion of Constantine and Pagan Rome* (trans. H. Mattingly; Oxford: Clarendon, 1969).

A. Momigliano, ed., *The Conflict between Paganism and Christianity in the Fourth Century: Essays* (Oxford: Clarendon, 1963).

L. Di Giovanni, *Costantino e il mondo pagano* (4th ed.; Naples: D'Auria, 1989).

T. D. Barnes, *The New Empire of Diocletian and Constantine* (Cambridge, Mass.: Harvard University Press, 1982).

M. Grant, *Constantine the Great: The Man and His Times* (New York: Macmillan International, 1994).

A. H. M. Jones, *Constantine and the Conversion of Europe* (New York: Collier, 1962).

H. A. Pohlsander, *The Emperor Constantine* (London/New York: Routledge, 1996).

2. Arnobius

No less emblematic of his age than Lactantius was Arnobius; a violent critic of paganism, but as far as his Christian faith was concerned, he was at bottom an orator and pagan philosopher. Jerome tells us something of the man's life in *Famous Men* (ch. 79): "In the time of Emperor Diocletian, Arnobius of Sicca, a city in Africa, was a very brilliant teacher of rhetoric and wrote some books against the pagans that one can find everywhere." Further on (ch. 80) and in *Epist.* 70.5, Jerome adds that Lactantius had been a student of Arnobius. This is probable, even though Lactantius never mentions

Arnobius's name. Since Lactantius was summoned to teach at Nicomedia toward the end of the third century (see below, sec. 4), Arnobius must have been born before 250.

Elsewhere, in his *Chronicle,* Jerome gives some further, very interesting information about Arnobius, but the date he gives, 326–327, is mistaken; it is at best the date of Arnobius's death. Jerome writes: "Arnobius used to teach the art of public speaking to the young in Sicca. When still a pagan, he was moved by some dreams to believe, but the bishop did not allow him to profess the faith which he had always fought against. He then composed some fine books in criticism of his previous religion and finally, after giving a guarantee (if we may so put it) of his devotion, he won the right to join the new religion." It is on these various bits of information that we construct the entire biography of Arnobius, whose name some take to be of Greek origin.

That there was a bishop of Sicca Veneria (today El Kef in Tunisia) is attested by the presence of a bishop from that place at the Council of Carthage under Cyprian in 256. An unjustified hypercritical attitude that has only a superficial understanding of religion in antiquity has cast doubt on the idea that Arnobius's conversion was inspired by dreams—as if late antiquity were not an age in which the gods manifested themselves in dreams. On the other hand, Arnobius's skill in the art of rhetoric seems to be confirmed by the work he wrote after his conversion. If the purpose of the work was to prove the sincerity of the author's faith, it must have been more than convincing; Arnobius speaks in it as a man moved by repentance for his past error (see 1.39). It was logical for the bishop not to have been entirely convinced of Arnobius's conversion, since the latter had been an enemy of Christianity. In addition, even in the work meant to prove the sincerity of his faith, Arnobius's Christianity seems quite deficient, indicative of a conversion that had not been thought through.

The work *Against the Pagans (Adversus nationes)* was written under Diocletian. More precisely, since reference is made (4.36) to some specific measures such as the destruction of churches and the sacred books, it was written during the persecution, between 304 and 310. The first three books may have been written earlier, and it seems that books 1 and 2 may go back to 297–300. Like all the defenses of Christianity, the *Against the Pagans* is both a defense and a polemical work.

The first book intends to defend Christians against unjust accusations of pagans who maintain that the evils afflicting the world are caused by the atheism of Christians. Arnobius answers that God does not take revenge because God is not subject to human passions. Christians worship a supreme God to whom even the pagan gods are subject, if they exist—and if they do, they must be regarded as demons. The second book deals chiefly with the person of Christ and the scandal of the incarnation.

The book is especially interesting, however, because it takes on a markedly philosophical cast, presenting as Christian various teachings derived from paganism. One example is the corruptibility of the soul as such, which is made immortal as a reward for its merits in this life. Another is the lowliness of the soul's substance, which some philosophers contemporary with Arnobius consider to be of divine origin, whereas its condition is intermediate between God and matter. The conviction that the human soul is mortal involved Arnobius in a controversy with some philosophers whom he vaguely describes as "new [that is, recent] men" *(viri novi)*. These were probably followers of Porphyry, the Platonist who a few years before had written a famous work *Against Christians* and was the most important figure in the pagan thought of that period. It is also possible that they were followers of hermetism or, even more probably, not of a particular sect but of the general pagan culture of Arnobius's time, in which all these philosophical and religious trends played their part.

In challenging the doctrine that the soul descends from heaven and is endowed with a natural excellence, Arnobius makes use of ideas that go back to Epicureanism and had been made part of Latin culture by Lucretius. Thus we have the unusual phenomenon—an indication of Arnobius's imperfect Christianity—of a Christian writer making use of Epicureanism, which was detested. As a result, some modern scholars have regarded Arnobius himself as an Epicurean.

After two books of an essentially theoretical kind, Arnobius moves on to a fierce and detailed controversy with the pagan world and in particular with idolatrous religions. It would take too much space to set forth in detail the content of these five books, in which the writer, with a harshness justified by the long hostility against Christianity, and more bitter than that of Tertullian, examines from every angle, and insults from every point of view, the pagan rites and cults, both those of the official religion and those of the mystery religions. He mocks both the best known myths of the Greco-Roman pantheon and the more lowly and ridiculous ones of the local cults and of archaic Rome. He asserts that the myths are wicked and immoral, their anthropomorphism is disgusting, and the attempts at allegorical interpretation and religious syncretism, to which the best educated pagans have recourse, are arbitrary and inconsistent. Pagan religion is devastated by this lengthy series of attacks and insults, which are based on detailed descriptions that deliberately include many obscene and revolting particulars. The writer uses not so much argument as ridicule, and is not satisfied with half-measures.

At times this enormous mass of material seems to be piled up in a confused way; perhaps Jerome was aware of this when he said (*Epist.* 58.10) "Arnobius is uneven and profuse and confused because he did not know how to structure his work," that is, because he did not properly distinguish among the arguments he was using. Since such *divisio* was an essential part of rhetoric, the inability to "divide" the material he was expounding would have been a serious fault in one who had taught rhetoric. Writing as he was a work of controversy, Arnobius was more intent on acquiring a vast amount of information about the object of his criticism than he was on improving his knowledge of the religion he had recently embraced. For this reason, there is little in the *Adversus nationes* that can be called truly Christian.

Arnobius acquired his knowledge of pagan religion from the works of Varro. He seems to have made room, in addition, for Cornelius Labeo, an obscure philosopher and scholar of the imperial age. For the Greek world his main source seems to have been Clement of Alexandria. Leaving aside the question of a *divisio* that is not handled by the rules of the art, Arnobius's work was shaped by the rhetoric he had taught for many years, and it included the most important authors read in the schools; he used a great deal of material taken from manuals, especially in the area of Greek culture. Among the Latin writers a dominant place is given to Lucretius, something unusual in the culture of the imperial age, pagan no less than Christian. Lucretius would have supplied him with his information on Epicureanism, which was so much in harmony with his own convictions and so useful in combating the spiritualism of the Platonists. Arnobius regarded this spiritualism as a sign of human pride pure and simple, and emblematic of contemporary paganism.

We can get a fairly clear idea of Arnobius's pagan culture, but when it comes to his Christian culture the matter is much more complex. The general observation about apologists applies to him no less than to others: in addressing pagans, Christian writers cannot give an extended explanation of their own faith. No wonder, then, that Arnobius does not say much about Christianity, just as the works of Minucius Felix, Lactantius, and to some extent even those of Tertullian, are deliberately deficient in this area.

But this limitation seems to be far greater in Arnobius, for it can be said that nothing of the essentials of Christianity can be found in his work, and furthermore, that there are real doctrinal errors. His teachings have been linked to gnostic influences, although it has not been possible to identify their origin exactly. It was probably the syncretistic culture of the age that so deeply distorted his Christianity. The intense pessimism that characterizes his work is utterly non-Christian; it was influenced, as noted above, by certain strains of Lucretian teaching, and it mocked the optimistic belief in providence of the Stoics and Platonists. Indeed, early Christianity was closer to the latter than to the Epicureans. For all these reasons, Arnobius's writings were not widely read, and he was condemned in the *Decretum Gelasianum* at the end of the fifth century.

For good or for ill, Arnobius's work seems to be the most important product of the rhetoric that pervaded imperial Latin literature. As a master of this art, he applied it to his work and used all the figures and devices with which it supplied him. One characteristic of the *Against the Pagans* is its wealth of vocabulary, but this was the result of the assiduous study of literary texts and an intense search, prompted by a stylistic mannerism, for rare words. Never do we find the customary and the simple in his diction; in giving vent to his love of the satirical and the controversial, Arnobius maintains a steady tone and sometimes reaches the point of a paradoxical tension through repetition, anaphora, and the repetitive beat of ideas and sarcastic remarks. As a result, the discussion advances slowly, because the writer gives himself unrestrainedly to the description of details. Still he is never boring or dull, because for all his refined rhetoric he never loses sight of his adversaries; he addresses them even when the discourse threatens to become abstract, and brings variety into his discussion by means of hypothetical objections and answers.

As Fontaine observes, Arnobius appropriates the ancient biblical satire directed at idols, and does so with visionary realism in the footsteps of Persius and Juvenal. His gift for satire is perhaps superior even to that of Tertullian. His style is especially interesting for another peculiarity: the rhythm of his sentences. These are structured in ways that are not always faithful to the prosodic succession of syllables typical of classical antiquity, but already look ahead to the system at work in the medieval *cursus*, which would be based on accent.

Bibliography

Editions

Arnobius of Sicca, *Arnobii Adversus nationes libri VII* (ed. A. Reifferscheid; CSEL 4; Vindobonae: Geroldi, 1875).
——— (ed. C. Marchesi; CSLP 62; Turin: Paraviae, 1934; 1958).
———, *Contre les gentes* (ed. and trans. H. Le Bonniec; Paris: Les Belles Lettres, 1982).

Translations

Arnobius of Sicca, *The Case Against the Pagans* (ed. and trans. G. McCracken;
ACW 7–8; Westminster, Md.: Newman, 1949).
———— (ed. R. Laurenti; Turin: Società Editrice Internazionale, 1972).

Studies

P. Monceaux, *Histoire littéraire de l'Afrique chrétienne depuis les origines jusquä
l'invasion arabe* (vol. 3; Paris: Leroux, 1905).
S. Colombo, "Arnobio Afro e i suoi sette libri *Adversus Nationes*," *Didaskaleion* 9
(1930): 1–124.
F. Gabarrou, *Arnobe: Son oeuvre* (Paris: Champion, 1921).
E. Rapisarda, *Clemente fonte di Arnobio* (Turin: Società Editrice Internazionale,
1939).
————, *Arnobio* (Catania: Crisafulli, 1946).
H. Hagendahl, *Latin Fathers and the Classics* (SGLG 6; Göteborg: Wettergren &
Kerber, 1958).
M. B. Simmons, *Arnobius of Sicca: Religious Conflict and Competition in the Age of
Diocletian* (New York: Oxford University Press, 1995).

On Particular Issues

A.-J. Festugière, "La doctrine des *viri novi* sur l'origine et les sorts des âmes,"
in *Mémorial Lagrange* (1940): 97–132; Festugière, *Hermétisme et Mystique
païenne* (Paris: Aubier et Montaigne, 1967), 261–312.
P. Courcelle, "Les sages de Porphyre et les *viri novi* d'Arnobe," *REL* 31 (1953):
247–71.
M. Mazza, "Studi arnobiani I: La dottrina dei *viri novi* nel secondo libro
dell'*Adversus Nationes* di Arnobio," *Helikon* 3 (1963): 111–69.
F. Scheidweiler, "Arnobius und der Marcionitismus," *ZNW* 45 (1955): 42–67.
E. F. Micka, *The Problem of Divine Anger in Arnobius and Lactantius* (Washing-
ton, D.C.: Catholic University of America Press, 1943).
R. Laurenti, "Il platonismo di Arnobio," *Studi Filosofici* 4 (1981 [1983]): 3–54.
————, "Spunti di teologia arnobiana," *Orpheus* 6 (1985): 270–303.

Language and Style

H. Hagendahl, *La prose métrique d'Arnobe: Contributions à la connaissance de la
prose littéraire de l'Empire* (Göteborg: Wettergren & Kerber, 1936).

3. Victorinus of Pettau and Reticius of Autun

At the opposite end of the empire and specifically in Pettau, an obscure locality
on the Drava and on the frontier of Noricum (present-day Austria), lived Bishop
Victorinus, of whose life we know nothing except that he died a martyr during the
persecution of Diocletian (probably in 304). His work, which has reached us in frag-

mentary form, enjoyed little esteem in antiquity, whether because of his plain style and poor Latin vocabulary or because of the inconsistency of his exegesis. He was exclusively an exegete and is remembered as the first Latin author to write a treatise on the interpretation of the Old Testament. Despite these deficiencies, which were emphasized especially by a demanding writer such as Jerome, Victorinus enjoyed a brief renown in the fourth century until he was overshadowed by the more penetrating exegesis of such personalities as Hilary, Ambrose, and Jerome.

Victorinus wrote commentaries on nine books of the Bible, which seem to have been chosen with the idea of studying the most famous of the historical (Genesis, Exodus, Leviticus) and prophetic (Isaiah, Ezekiel, Obadiah, Ecclesiastes, Song of Songs) books, and the Apocalypse. He also authored a commentary on Matthew. His exegesis was completely under the influence of Origen, who at that time was the most famous student of the sacred text; thus his fame had spread from Alexandria to distant Noricum. The method Victorinus followed seems to have been to compose "scholia" after the manner of Origen. The interpretation is primarily allegorical, with a marked interest in arithmology. Despite his spiritualist exegesis, Victorinus supposedly professed millennialism in its crudest form, and for this he was much criticized.

His best known work, which was perhaps already being used by Lactantius (*Inst.* 4.20), is the *Commentary on the Apocalypse*, the original version of which was not published until 1916. It was previously known in a redaction by Jerome in about 400, in which that great man of letters had improved the language, modernized the biblical citations, corrected certain doctrines, and in particular eliminated the millennialism. This revision by Jerome was in its turn corrected and expanded, especially in its citations of the Apocalypse, by Beatus of Liébana, a Spanish priest, in 784. These two revisions were then reworked during the Middle Ages.

There has also come down to us a short fragment titled *The Creation of the World (De fabrica mundi)* that seems to be part of an exegetical treatise on Genesis. The fragment deals chiefly with the symbolic value of the numbers four and seven, and thereby confirms the millennialist convictions of the author.

Victorinus is sometimes regarded as the author of a work that has reached us in its entirety, although it has little historical value: *Against All the Heresies (Contra omnes haereses)*. This is a catalogue, rather than a refutation, of heresies down to that of Praxeas. The work has been transmitted among the works of Tertullian. According to others, however, this list is much older and dates from the time of Pope Zephyrinus (end of 2d, beginning of 3d c.; see above, ch. 17, sec. 5).

Another rather obscure exegete was Reticius, Bishop of Autun in the time of Constantine. He wrote a *Commentary on the Song of Songs (Commentarii in Cantica Canticorum)*, well known to Jerome for its eloquence but also for some doctrinal errors. Reticius also wrote a work *Against Novatian (Adversus Novatianum)*.

Bibliography

Editions

Victorinus, *Victorini episcopi Petavionensis opera* (ed. J. Haussleiter; CSEL 49; Vindobonae: Temsky, 1916).

Studies

M. Dulaey, "Jérôme 'éditeur' du Commentaire sur l'Apocalypse de Victorin de Poetovio," *REA* 37 (1991): 199–236.

S. A. Cooper, *Metaphysics and Morals in Marius Victoriunus' Commentary on the Letter to the Ephesians: A Contribution to the History of Neoplatonism and Christianity* (AmUst.P 155; New York: Lang, 1995).

4. Lactantius

As noted above, a bond of teacher and student joined Arnobius to Lactantius, who was likewise an apologist but took a far different approach and had a wider range of views. Lactantius marks the end of the age of apologetics in the West, but his apologetics are already much different from those of Tertullian, thus reflecting the changing times. We have seen that apologetics was no longer a matter of defense and controversy but could also be, exhortatory, as in Minucius Felix. Now, for Lactantius, it becomes a tool of controversy with pagans and therefore, while more learned, also less specifically Christian. The ability to debate and teach, to broaden the scope of one's research, and to explore problems without aprioristic exclusions, but rather with the outlook of a Christian who lives in this world and peacefully awaits the end time, was not valued in the later centuries of early Christianity. Jerome writes sourly: "Would that he had been able to teach our doctrines with the same ease with which he could tear down those of others!" (*Epist.* 58.10).

Lactantius was born of a pagan family in Africa around 250, and was converted as an adult. He moved to Nicomedia in Bithynia, the residence of Emperor Diocletian, who between 290 and 300 appointed him to teach rhetoric there, as he had already done in Africa. He supposedly wrote a *Symposium* (see Jerome, *Vir. ill.* 80) while still living in Africa, and later a *Travel Diary (Hodoeporicon)* in verse, in which he described his journey to Nicomedia. Both works have been lost. In Nicomedia, which was in a Greek-speaking area, he had few students, perhaps only members of the court. When the persecution of Diocletian broke out, Lactantius saw with his own eyes the destruction of houses of Christian worship in Nicomedia and heard the fierce accusations by pagan intellectuals. He had to abandon his profession and was reduced to extreme poverty.

During those years Lactantius was probably already acquainted with Constantine, who was at that court in 306. Yet he does not seem to have left Bithynia during the persecution, during which he wrote almost all his works. In about 314–315, having thereby acquired a certain reputation as a Christian man of letters, Lactantius was summoned by Constantine to be tutor of his son Crispus, who was living in Trier. Lactantius seems to have remained in Trier until his death, which occurred around 325.

BIBLIOGRAPHY

E. D. Digeser, *The Making of a Christian Empire: Lactantius and Rome* (Ithaca, N.Y.: Cornell University Press, 2000).

a. Workmanship of God

This, the *De opificio Dei,* is the first work of Lactantius that has come down to us. It was composed, as the author himself tells us, during the persecution of Diocletian, around 304. In some ways it represents a preparation for his most important work, the *Divine Institutes.* Lactantius's thesis is that the entire reality of the world and the structure and perfection of the human body, all created by God, prove the existence of a perfect, providential, and rational God. The approach was not new, for it was one of the commonplaces used by the Stoics in asserting the same thesis. Lactantius's work, as it stands, could very well have been written by a Stoic in controversy with the Epicureans, especially since, while the persecution was raging, the author carefully avoided any open declaration of Christianity. In this work Lactantius already shows himself a convinced follower of the Ciceronian style.

The author has not been a convert long and is still at home chiefly in the culture in which he had hitherto been teaching. Thus this work does not contain any citation of the Bible; at most one may discern some echoes of Christian writers who preceded him. On the other hand, he says that his intention is to take up and expand upon the brief references to the problem in the fourth book of Cicero's *Republic.* Cicero's *The Nature of the Gods* has provided Lactantius with a great deal of material. Like Arnobius before him, he makes use of the learning of Varro. Finally, the very structure of the work is based on the divisions of rhetoric, and has a polemical part and a didactic part. It is more difficult to say why Lactantius composed this work, which has its place primarily in the pagan philosophical tradition. It does, however, refer to the persecution and is addressed to a readership of Christians, with the intention of convincing them, on the basis of human reality, of the existence of divine providence. The work seems therefore to have had a protreptic or at least a didactic purpose, during a period of anguish for its readers.

BIBLIOGRAPHY

M. Perrin, *L'homme antique et chrétien* (Paris: Beauchesne, 1981).

b. Divine Institutes

A short time later came Lactantius's principal work, on which his fame rests. The *Divine Institutes (Divinarum Institutionum)* mirrored the tormented period of the persecution by Diocletian and Galerius. When the author reached the end of the work the persecution was not yet over; it was written therefore after 304 and before the Edict of Milan in 313.

The usual duality of apologetics—defense of Christianity and, at the same time, an explanation of the new religion—is broadened in this wide-ranging, meditative and systematic work. The title shows that the writer wants to teach the Christian religion according to the rules of *institutio,* that is, of the teaching of law. The title also suggests that Lactantius wants to answer the *Institutio oratoria* of Quintilian with a Christian *institutio* that is as vast and complex as that of the master of pagan rhetoric. The author means to demonstrate, once and for all, the value of the Christian religion as a religion of salvation; he means to respond not to the accusations of the masses but to those formulated by magistrates and pagan intellectuals, to the effect that Christianity is a wicked and harmful religion. Lactantius insists that, on the contrary, Christianity is a religion of revelation in the same way, and to a greater degree, as Hermetism and the theosophy of oracles.

In this treatise, which unfolds "the education of God" as imparted to human beings, Lactantius leads the reader step by step from error to truth. The work is addressed to a public of pagan intellectuals, and this goal can justify to some extent the fact that Lactantius teaches little of Christian doctrine. He says that to use Christian doctrine as a means of defending that doctrine against pagan charges would be a contradiction, and he criticizes Cyprian for having taken that tack. The writer therefore restricts himself to essentials, and the sacred texts he cites are probably taken from the same collections of *testimonia* that Cyprian had used, for it has been observed that there is no biblical citation in Lactantius that is not already found in Cyprian. Recently, however, some scholars have thought to see in Lactantius a broader knowledge of Scripture, although it is contaminated by elements from noncanonical texts.

In any case, in order to explain the main events of Christian history, Lactantius is forced to fall back on typological and allegorical forms of interpretation. Nor can it be denied that he has some knowledge of texts with a messianic meaning and of the spiritual interpretations that were offered of Jewish practices, although he dwells on those that were probably best known to pagans, such as circumcision and dietary prohibitions. In addition, like the other apologists, he has recourse to all the typical motifs of anti-idolatry polemics, and he embraces the conviction, already put forward by the Greek apologists, that the Hebrew Scriptures from which Christianity drew its origin are older than all the boasted wisdom of the Greeks, and that the Greeks drew upon those Scriptures. This persuasion leads Lactantius to an attention to chronology and to the reliability of historical evidence that is typically his, and unknown to other Christian writings.

In conclusion, the work attempts a systematic *summa* of the new religion as seen through the eyes of a man of letters. The *summa* therefore includes literature as well: Lactantius is the first consciously to formulate the need of creating a Christian culture. So strong is this tendency that he looks in an exclusively literary way at the works of the writers who preceded him: Tertullian, Cyprian, and Minucius.

The *Divine Institutes,* though polemical in character, are devoted to a global reappraisal of the pagan past, in order to condemn it, yes, but also to salvage it where the author believes it to have borne its best fruits. As such, the work is an intelligent effort to mediate between Christianity and paganism, and a work of harmonious synthesis that would bear its fruit in the Renaissance when the rediscovery of the classical world would have to take account of the Christian religion. Lactantius became a model for the synthesis or syntheses attempted by the Renaissance. This writer's interpretation of Virgil, as a poet who did not end up very far from the truth, is typical of the Christianity of his age and also a symbol of that synthesis.

The first two books give a detailed refutation of polytheism. The controversy with paganism is developed on a scientific level that requires rational discussion and the use of historical testimonies and the authorities of the past. The writer's aim is to show that pagan polytheism is an absurdity and the unacceptable end of a process in which the original monotheism was debased, although some traces of it are preserved in some of the thinkers and theologians (meaning "those who have spoken about

God") of the past. Among these are some of the poets, Hermes Trismegistus, the Sibyls, and a few others. Polytheism is thus refuted on the lines of criticism customary in Christian apologetics: polytheism entails anthropomorphism, immorality, and absurdity, and represents simply the divinization of those very early human beings who acquired merits through the blessings they brought to humanity. This position (euhemerism) is already present in Greek philosophy. The development of polytheism was the work of demons, who in turn emerged from one of the two spirits whom God created and who became corrupt and turned into God's adversary *(antitheus)*. The human task is to continue the struggle against evil, which God chooses not to eradicate from the earth.

The third book refutes pagan philosophy which after false religion is the second source of all error. This philosophy has shown itself unable to satisfy the thirst for wisdom and happiness that is innate in human beings. The mutual opposition of the various systems proves the emptiness of philosophy, says Lactantius, taking over a topos common to all pagan philosophy and more specifically to skepticism. The Christian polemicists liked to use pagan culture's own weapons against it. The fourth book is devoted to the teaching of true wisdom and true religion, which have been given to humanity by Christ, the Son of God, who descended to earth as the end of the world was drawing near, to teach justice to humanity.

The fifth book is devoted to explaining what is the true justice that Christ has brought to humanity. This justice existed at humanity's beginnings but was then corrupted by the spread of idolatry, as in the final analysis Cicero has shown in *The Republic*, and as we see from the behavior of Virgil's Aeneas, who is wrongly regarded as *pius*, that is, "religious." True justice consists of acknowledging the essential equality of all human beings as children of God. The exercise of this justice is true worship of God and consists of adoring God *(religio)* and loving human beings (sixth book). Finally, the seventh book is devoted to a description of the blessed life of human beings in the final days of the race, when the millennium, the reign of Christ on earth, shall be established. The world shall reach its goal when the just are transformed into angels and the wicked are sent off to eternal punishment. Lactantius thus makes known to his pagan readers the teaching derived from the Apocalypse of John and from Christian millenarian traditions.

Given its purpose and considering the cultural formation of the author, the work is one of the most learned produced by Latin Christianity. Its range is all-encompassing, and global; it aims to refute the entire reality of paganism, except for the little bit of truth that can be rescued from it, and to do this systematically, and not simply by means of an attack suitable to a particular moment as preceding apologists had done. Thus the entire cultural wealth available to a high-level rhetor of late antiquity is present in *The Divine Institutes:* the classical authors of the Latin school, especially Cicero and Virgil; Lucretius and, even better, the satirical poets; Seneca, often cited; Roman history, known through manuals and compendia; and Greek culture, within which a large role is reserved for Plato.

Much more interesting are the cultural influences from Lactantius's own time that appear in the work: oracles that circulated in the Greek world, the *Sibylline Oracles,* hermetic texts, and, in short, everything that was characteristic of late antiquity and seemed to Lactantius to have greater validity than the traditional culture. Indeed, according to Lactantius, it is from these "theological," religious, and philosophical writings that truth emerges, more than from the arid speculations of the philosophers, for these texts contain teaching that comes from a revelation, even if imperfect.

It is characteristic of the *Divine Institutes* that some manuscripts contain additions lacking in the others. Some of the additions are addresses to Emperor Constantine, lengthy apostrophes of an encomiastic kind, or simple mentions of his name. Others have been described as "dualistic additions": these give voice to a moderate dualism, already essentially implicit in the author's teaching, openly maintaining the thesis that God has willed and created evil. An addition of the same kind appears also in *The Workmanship of God*. According to some scholars, these additions are not from Lactantius but were interpolated by a rhetor of his time; others maintain that the additions were original to the work and were later removed. But it is difficult to see why people should have been scandalized by Lactantius's addresses to Constantine; therefore some scholars have concluded that while the dualistic additions are spurious, those addressed to Constantine were in the original.

The most likely explanation is that both the dedication of the work to Constantine and the "dualistic additions" are from Lactantius and were introduced during a subsequent revision of the work, a revision not completed. The first version would therefore have been finished before 311, and the second would have been begun at the court of Constantine.

A few years later, Lactantius composed an *Epitome of the Divine Institutes (Epitome divinarum institutionum)*, consisting not only of summaries of some parts but also of a new, abridged version of the main work, for in addition to omissions and changes there are expansions and modifications. For example, the proof of God's existence as the only God seems better organized, there is a deeper reflection on the problem of the origin of evil, and new references are given to the philosophical literature. But this work was not widely circulated and was rediscovered only at the beginning of the eighteenth century.

c. Wrath of God

In the *Divine Institutes* (2.17.5) Lactantius already referred to a theological subject which he intended to discuss later on, namely the "wrath of God," and to this he did in fact devote a separate treatise. The writer's purpose in this work is to refute the Epicureans, who maintained that God took no interest in human affairs, and the Stoics, who allowed God only the attribute of kindness. Since religion consists chiefly of the fear of God—a statement deriving from the Roman conception of religion, in which fear played an irreplaceable role—it follows that God gets angry, for otherwise there would be no room for fear. This anger is, of course, always a just anger because it is provoked by human misdeeds and plays a part in their punishment. The *Wrath of God (De ira Dei)* is one of the most carefully written of Lactantius's works. The date of composition is uncertain; it is evidently later than the *Divine Institutes*, and according to some scholars it dates from the last years of the writer's life.

d. Deaths of the Persecutors

Lactantius's last work, probably written at Constantine's court in Trier, seems to have been the one on the *Deaths of the Persecutors (De morte persecutorum)*, unless it is earlier than the work on the *Wrath of God*. Some recent scholars are inclined to date the work to the period when Lactantius was still in Bithynia.

The writer's purpose is to show how all the persecutors of the true religion have been punished by God with a terrible, but well-deserved death. He first refers briefly to emperors whom the Christian tradition had already written down as persecutors, some of them condemned even by pagans, namely, Nero, Domitian, Decius, Valerian, and Aurelian. He then dwells on contemporary events and specifically the persecution that he must have seen with his own eyes in Nicomedia. He identifies those responsible as being chiefly Diocletian, Maximinus Daia, and Galerius. He describes their wretched ends, the destruction of their power, and the vanity of their plans, which were quashed by the Edict of Milan that rendered justice to Christians.

This writing is more a pamphlet than a historical work, and because of the fierce hatred it shows toward the enemies of Christians, it is hard to reconcile with the humane and balanced attitude Lactantius shows in his other works. For this reason, the work was for a long time regarded as spurious, but this judgment was surely mistaken, for the little work simply repeats numerous motifs of anti-pagan journalism by both Jews and Christians and their interpretation of history. In fact, in the *Divine Institutes* (5.23) Lactantius already spoke of God's wrath toward persecutors. Furthermore, Jerome knew that Lactantius had written a work on "persecution." The *Deaths of Persecutors* should be read without fixing attention solely on the enthusiasm that the triumph of Christianity has stirred in the author.

As more perceptive scholars have pointed out, a sincere acceptance of the values of Roman culture is always present in Lactantius; thus even the *Deaths of Persecutors* displays an effort to achieve a Christian renewal of what is best in the Roman world. Persecutors, in the author's view, have violated not only the rights of Christians but also the true values of the Roman spirit. Lactantius shows that this is his assumption when he places a strong emphasis on recovering the traditions of ancient Rome; he paints an ideal picture of a new Roman-Christian culture based on Constantine. By contrast, the predecessors of this new emperor, and not only the tetrarchs, had distinguished themselves chiefly by their ferocity and barbarism; the nadir of that inhumanity had been reached in Maximinus Daia.

This work, which was widely circulated in the Middle Ages, contributed to the legend of the victory of Constantine by including in its conclusion a description of the emperor's victory over Maxentius at the Milvian Bridge. Of course, in 312 Constantine was already a Christian in Lactantius's eyes, while Maxentius, who did not persecute Christians, was represented as an enemy of Rome.

BIBLIOGRAPHY

F. Amarelli, "Il *De mortibus persecutorum* nei suoi rapporti con l'ideologia coeva," *SDHI* 36 (1970): 207–64.

A. Søby Christensen, *Lactantius the Historian: An Analysis of the* De mortibus persecutorum (Copenhagen: Museum Tusculanum, 1980).

F. Corsaro, "Le *mos maiorum* dans la vision éthique et politique du *De mortibus persecutorum*," in *Lactance et son temps* (ed. J. Fontaine and M. Perrin; Paris: Beauchesne, 1979), 25–49; collective work.

Lactantius, *Lactantius: Divine Institutes* (trans. A. Bowen and P. Garnsey; Translated Texts for Historians 40; Liverpool: Liverpool University Press, 2003).

e. Other Works and Style

Lactantius supposedly wrote other works that have been lost. In addition to the *Travel Diary* and the *Symposium*, of which we spoke earlier, there was a *Grammarian (Grammaticus)*, apparently on some aspect of grammar, and two books *To Asclepius*, a writer mentioned in *The Divine Institutes* (7.4.17) as author of *The Providence of the Supreme God*, which was dedicated to Lactantius.

Because of his style, Lactantius has been described as a "Christian Cicero" by Pico della Mirandola, Rudoph Agricola, and Erasmus—but the fifteenth-century humanists also had harsh criticisms for Lactantius's "doctrinal errors." Lactantius's style can be called a revision of Cicero's, but a revision that was intelligently done, as was that of Minucius. After Quintilian and Pliny the Younger, Christian writers proved to be the best conscious imitators of Cicero. The Ciceronianism of Lactantius is a more independent accomplishment than the nickname given him might suggest; his prose is influenced, for example, by the trends to be seen in the contemporary *cursus*.

BIBLIOGRAPHY

Editions

Lactantius, *L. Caeli Firmiani Lactanti opera omnia* (ed. S. Brandt and G. Laubmann; CSEL 19, 27, 1–2; Vindobonae: Tempsky, 1890, 1893, 1897).
In the Sources chrétiennes:
Lactantius, *L'ouvrage du Dieu créateur* (SC 213–14; ed. M. Perrin; Paris: Cerf, 1974).
———, *Institutions divines: Livre I* (SC 326; ed. P. Monat; Paris, Cerf, 1986).
———, *Institutions divines: Livre II* (SC 337; ed. P. Monat; Paris, Cerf, 1987).
———, *Institutions divines: Livre IV* (SC 377; ed. P. Monat; Paris, Cerf, 1992).
———, *Institutions divines: Livre V* (SC 204–5; ed. P. Monat; 2 vols.; Paris, Cerf, 1973).
———, *La colère de Dieu* (SC 289; ed. C. Ingremeau; Paris: Cerf, 1982).

Critical Studies

H. Hagendahl, *Latin Fathers and the Classics* (SGLG; Göteborg, 1958).
R. M. Ogilvie, *The Library of Lactantius* (Oxford: Oxford University Press, 1978).
A. Goulon, "Les citations des poètes latins dans l'oeuvre de Lactance," in *Lactance et son temps* (ed. J. Fontaine and M. Perrin; Paris: Beauchesne, 1929), 107–56.
E. Heck, "Laktanz und die Klassiker," *Phil* 132 (1988): 160–79.
P. Monat, "Lactance et Cicéron," *REL* 53 (1975): 248–67.
A. Wlosok, "*Cumaeum Carmen* (Verg. Ecl. 4, 4)," in *Forma Futuri: Studi in onore del Cardinale M. Pellegrino* (Turin: Bottega d'Erasmo, 1975), 693–711.
P. Courcelle, *Lecteurs païens et lecteurs chrétiens de l'Énéide* (Paris: Études Augustiniennes, 1984).
A. Wlosok, *Laktanz und die philosophische Gnosis* (Heidelberg: Winter, 1960).

O. Gigon, "Lactanz und die Philosophie," in *Kerygma und Logos: Festschrift C. Andresen* (Göttingen: Vandenhoeck & Ruprecht, 1979), 196–213.

M. Perrin, "Le Platon de Lactance," in *Lactance et son temps* (ed. J. Fontaine and M. Perrin; Paris: Beauchesne, 1929), 203–34.

S. Pricoco, "Per una storia dell'oracolo nella tarda antichità," *Aug* 29 (1989): 351–74.

V. Loi, *Lattanzio nella storia del linguagio et del pensiero teologico pre-niceno* (Zurich: Pas-Verlag, 1970).

P. Monat, *Lactance et la Bible* (Paris: Études Augustiniennes, 1982).

B. Studer, "La sotériologie de Lactance," in *Lactance et son temps* (ed. J. Fontaine and M. Perrin; Paris: Beauchesne, 1929), 253–71.

5. The Correspondence of Seneca with St. Paul

Seneca's renown among Christians appeared quite early. Tertullian speaks of him as a writer who is "often one of ours." Lactantius opines that "Seneca could have been a true devotee of God if someone had shown God to him" (*Inst.* 6.24). It is not surprising, then, that during the Constantinian period one product of the typical religious syncretism of that age was this apocryphal correspondence. The letters were known as early as Jerome (*Vir. ill.* 12), who was thereby confirmed in his persuasion that there had been a real affinity between Seneca and Christianity, so much so that he included Seneca among the "famous men" of the Christian religion. This correspondence, consisting of eight letters from Seneca and six from Paul, is not especially interesting and contains nothing more than an exchange of polite greetings. Even though it makes rather disappointing reading, it enjoyed a certain fame subsequently.

A comparable forgery of the Constantinian age is the *Letter of Annas to Seneca*, recently discovered by B. Bischoff and preserved in fragmentary form. According to its author, the letter was written by Annas, the high priest from 62 to 68, and sent to the brethren as an exhortation to avoid idolatrous worship. But given this purpose, why would it have been sent to Seneca, as the title claims? The author must have been a Jew.

BIBLIOGRAPHY

Editions

L. Bocciolini Palagi, *Il carteggio apocrifo di Seneca e san Paolo* (Florence: Olschki, 1978).

J. N. Sevenster, *Paul and Seneca* (Leiden: Brill, 1961).

6. Acts of the Martyrs

The period under consideration saw a new flowering of literature on martyrdom connected, of course, with the great persecution of 303–313. There had been some instances of martyrdom during the preceding years, but these years were remembered as years of relative "peace" for the church; Valerian, who had unleashed the persecution to which Cyprian fell victim, was himself conquered and taken prisoner by the Persians in 260.

The region in which this literature most flourished was, once again, Africa, and it is notable that this literary genre, which was so deeply rooted there, continued to be employed from 316 on when the empire, now Christian, began to persecute the Donatist schismatics. The passions of Donatist martyrs then written were no different from those of the Christian martyrs of earlier decades: the Donatists regarded themselves as the true church of Christ, accused the orthodox of colluding with the empire, and leveled the charge of atheism against both.

The flowering of literature on martyrdom during the fourth century raises the problem, which will become more acute for later hagiographical literature, of the revisions to which the original texts were subjected with the passage of time, and even of the invention of the incident (martyrdom or passion) that would supply the justification for a local cult. This century gave a strong impetus to the cult of the saints, and it is certain that this enthusiastic growth of popular veneration led to many forgeries. But writings which during the period of positivism seemed to be forgeries pure and simple are now more likely to be interpreted by other standards. We may view these works as manifestations of the different ways in which a Christian community approached the reading of a martyr's "passion"—initially liturgical, then didactic and encomiastic. This literature celebrating the martyrdom of a saint became the basis of later Christian "calendars." The modern urge to determine the historical facts, which certainly ought to be ferreted out as the basis of every "passion" story, should not lead us to regard simply as a deliberate falsification anything added to the original nucleus.

BIBLIOGRAPHY

The hagiographical literature that became ever more extensive beginning in the Constantinian era is of interest to us solely as literature; in a deeper study of this literature account must be taken of hagiography as an independent discipline. In the present context we shall simply refer the reader to the essential aids: the *Analecta Bollandiana* and the *Subsidia Hagiographica*.

Texts

H. Musurillo, ed., *The Acts of Christian Martyrs* (Oxford: Oxford University Press, 2000).

A. A. R. Bastiaensen, ed., *Atti e passioni dei martiri* (trans. G. Chiarini; Milan: Mondadori, 1987).

On the Literature of Martyrdom

G. Lazzati, *Gli sviluppi sulla letteratura dei martiri nei primi quattro secoli* (Turin: Società Editrice Internazionale, 1956).

G. Lanata, *Gli atti dei martiri come documenti processuali* (Milan: Giuffrè, 1973).

P. Brown, *The Cult of the Saints: Its Rise and Function in Latin Christianity* (Chicago: University of Chicago Press, 1981).

Among the many *Acts of the Martyrs* connected with the trials of Christians in Africa, two stand out: the *Passion of St. Maximilian (Passio sancto Maximiliani)* and the *Passion of St. Marcellus (Passio sancti Marcelli)*, which celebrate the martyrdoms of two soldiers who were punished for being conscientious objectors. This problem, which rises from the depths of Christian ethics, is already brought out in all its tragic character in the similar episode recorded by Tertullian in *The Crown*. These two *Passions* are told with a vigor that might be described as tragic. More picturesque and filled with pathos are the *Passion of Sts. Maxima, Donatilla, and Secunda (Passio sanctarum Maximae, Donatillae et Secundae)* and the *Passion of St. Crispina (Passio sanctae Crispinae)*.

BIBLIOGRAPHY

P. Siniscalco. *Massimiliano, un obiettore di coscienza nel tardo impero: Studi sulla Passio s. Maximiliani* (Turin: Paravia, 1974).

7. Firmicus Maternus

Strictly speaking, Firmicus Maternus does not belong to the age of Constantine, for he wrote his Christian work, *The Error of the Pagan Religions (De errore profanarum religionum)*, between 343 and 350, under Constantius I and Constans, the successors of Constantine. The writer urges the emperors to forbid, once and for all, the pagan worship which he pillories for its absurdities and immorality in a final example of a literary genre—apologetic—that was henceforth outdated. But in its content this work fits into the age of Constantine, and the writer's cultural formation is typical of the syncretism of that age. Indeed, before his conversion to Christianity, Firmicus wrote a work that typifies the paganism of the age: the *Books of Astrology (Matheseos libri)*, in which he explains the rules of astrology and celebrates the emperor Constantine, who is still alive. Firmicus moves easily from henotheism to Christian monotheism.

A native of Sicily, Firmicus seems to have practiced law in Rome and to have become the friend of some influential individuals, among them the prefect of the city and members of the senatorial aristocracy. In his Christian work he devotes himself to a traditional treatise that is both apologetic and polemical. However, the subject is limited to the pagan religions and in particular the mystery religions, which were still active in his time. The more properly apologetical part, the defense of Christianity against accusations from pagans, is omitted because it no longer meets a real need.

In order to refute the errors of pagan cults (the Latin *profanus* means that these cults are alien to the true religion), Firmicus has recourse to all the traditional themes of the Christian critique, but emphasizes the absurd and immoral aspects of the cults, as Arnobius had already done. Polytheism is nothing but the worship of false gods who were given an existence through the deification of primordial elements or of certain individuals, or as the products of sheer invention by evil men. Pagan symbols and rites are counterfeits of Christian rites; to each symbol of the mystery religions the writer opposes the truth of Christ, the only Savior.

Firmicus adopts a new attitude in keeping with the changed political situation; by about 350 Christianity was no longer on the defensive but was the most widespread religion in the empire and enjoyed imperial support. Firmicus therefore openly urges the rulers to abolish pagan forms of worship by law and if necessary by force, as actually happened during these years by some imperial orders. He thus initiated among Christians the same intolerance from which Christians themselves had previously suffered. And yet, composed as it was in a period in which the intra-Christian quarrels caused by Arianism were already raging, Firmicus's work seems backward. A comparison with Athanasius, who likewise wrote a work *Against the Pagans* during the same years, shows even better how backward Firmicus was.

Firmicus's work lacks new and personal ideas and important cultural attitudes. It remained completely unknown in subsequent centuries; even Jerome never mentions it. Still, the author deserves some consideration as a writer who possessed a solid rhetorical training, although the rhetoric is very artificial. Like the writings of the first Christian apologists, his work takes the form of an address delivered in the presence of the emperors.

BIBLIOGRAPHY

Editions

Firmicus Maternus, *De errore profanarum religionum* (ed. C. Halm; CSEL 2; Vindovonae: Geroldi, 1867).
———— (ed. and trans. A. Pastorino; Florence: La Nuova Italia, 1956); with an introduction, translation, and commentary.
———— (ed. and trans. R. Turcan; Paris: Les Belles Lettres, 1982).
————, *Firmicus Maternus: The Error of the Pagan Religions* (ed. and trans. C. A. Forbes; ACW 37; New York: Newman, 1970).

8. The Rise of Christian Poetry

The new cultural climate of the age of Constantine also saw the rise of a truly Christian poetry. Attention has already been called to the late emergence of this genre as compared to literary genres in prose (see above, ch. 17, sec. 6). By speaking of a late emergence, we mean that the earlier poetry of Commodian should be regarded as an effort in a different genre. Precisely for that reason his poetry possessed an originality of its own, since it was not linked to the learned tradition to which the poetry of the Constantinian age and the poetry that followed upon it in the course of the fourth century were consciously connected. The Christian poetry that saw the light in this new period was intended as concomitant with, and equal in dignity to, the pagan poetry of the time. In other words, Christian poetry showed a fitting literary elaboration and used the same means and rhetorical devices that were typical of non-Christian poetry. Juvencus, the most representative poet of the age, was very conscious of this deliberately sought novelty, for in addition to his capacity for producing good literature, he formulated in a clear way the ideals and purposes of Christian poets.

On the one hand, these poets sought to separate themselves from pagan poets, as we just noted, but on the other, they had a place within the broader literary world of the years of Constantine's reign, which saw a noteworthy variety of poetic genres, although not the presence of great writers. Christian poetry too was varied, ranging from the *Travel Diary* of Lactantius (see above, sec. 4) to paraphrases of the Bible, hymnic poetry, and poetic hagiography. It is fitting, therefore, to consider this poetry and that which succeeded it—the great flowering at the end of the fourth century and the beginning of the fifth—in the broader context in which pagan forms and Christian forms are joined by use of the same literary genres. The technical tools also remained the same and can be traced back to the classical age; one example would be *aemulatio,* variation within imitation of the poets taken as models: Virgil first and foremost, and then Horace, Lucan, Statius, and Seneca.

The emperor, or at least his chancellery, paid careful attention to the literary forms that praised and spread his political and religious ideals; Lactantius and, even more, Eusebius are proof of this. He also let it be known that the imitation of certain, henceforth authoritative models such as Virgil must be a firm point of reference. In short, the classicism of the period derived its inspiration from the court, for which not only pagan poets wrote but Christian poets as well, now that all obstacles had been removed in their relations with the no-longer-pagan imperial authority. Thus Juvencus and Lactantius address Constantine, and this change in atmosphere and addressee truly mark the rise of a literary poetry after the hymnody of the early Christian communities and the aggressive writing of Commodian, a foreigner in Africa who addressed at the same time the faithful and the enemies of the new religion.

a. Psalmus Responsorius

An anonymous hymn was discovered in 1865 in a papyrus written in Egypt during the fourth century. The work may predate the age of Constantine, in which case it would be one of the first embodiments of a Christian poetry. But even if it belongs to the age of Constantine, it is of no less historical importance, because unlike other contemporary poetry it is an example of a non-classicizing poetry. It is an abecedary composition that has come down to us incomplete: there are only twelve strophes instead of twenty-four, plus a strophe that serves as a refrain. It sings the praises of God and probably played a role in the liturgy, being sung alternately by a soloist and a chorus. A later example of the same genre will be the *Psalmus contra partem Donati* which Augustine wrote against the Donatists. Both are in rhythmic prose rather than in the meters of classical poetry. To the extent that the earlier *Psalmus responsorius* is a hymn, it anticipates by a century the similar, but learned, compositions of Hilary and Marius Victorinus.

BIBLIOGRAPHY

Edition

Himne a la Verge Maria, "Psalmus responsorius": Papir llatí del segle ir (ed. and trans. R. Roca Puig; Acad. de Buenas Letras 30; Barcelona: Asociación de Bibliofilos de Barcelona, 1965).

Study

E. Peretti, *Mar* 22 (1967): 255–65.

b. Lactantius as Poet (Phoenix)

The manuscript tradition attributes to Lactantius the *Phoenix (De ave phoenice)*, a short poem in elegiac distichs. Its authenticity has been challenged in modern times, but solely on the grounds that the Christian content is not as openly displayed as the critics think it should have been. The poem gives an allegorical interpretation of the myth of the phoenix, a bird that dies and then rises from its own ashes, symbolizing the resurrection of Christ and the rest of humanity. Some features, however, are specifically Christian, such as the exaltation of virginity and the idea of death as a passage to true life. On the other hand, this very myth had been regarded from the earliest times as symbolizing the resurrection (Clement of Rome, *1 Clem.* 25–26; Tertullian, *Res.* 13; Commodian, *Carm. apol.* 139ff.). It is, however, characteristic of Lactantius generally that he chooses crypto-Christian subjects, the true significance of which only a careful reader was in a position to discover, whereas a pagan reader could appreciate the polished and elegant evocation of a myth that had always lent itself to a spiritual interpretation.

BIBLIOGRAPHY

Editions

Lactantius, *L. Caeli Firmiani Lactanti opera omnia* (ed. S. Brandt and G. Laubmann; CSEL 27, 1; Vindobonae: Temsky, 1893).

E. Rapisarda, *Il Carme de ave phoenice di Lattanzio* (2d ed.; Catania: Centro di Studi di Letteratura Cristiana Antica Università Catania, 1952).

Studies

M. Walla, *Der Vogel Phoenix in der antiken Literatur und der Dichtung des Laktanz* (Vienna: Notring, 1969).

J. Fontaine, *Naissance de la poésie dans l'Occident chrétien: Esquise d'une histoire de la poésie chrétienne du IIIe au VIe siècle* (Paris: Études Augustiniennes, 1981).

c. Praises of the Lord

Constantine is directly addressed at the end of the anonymous short poem titled *Praises of the Lord and a Description of the Miracle that Occurred in the Territory of the Aedui (Laudes Domini cum miraculo quod accidit in Aeduico)*. The miracle took place in the land of the Aedui in Gaul as follows: a young man, already dead, greeted his mother, who was present at his deathbed. On this account the poet extols Christ as creator of the world and liberator of humanity and wishes victory to Constantine and his house. It is assumed that this poem (148 hexameters) was written by a rhetor from the famous school of rhetoric that was flourishing in Autun; it is a good imitation of Virgil and other classical poets.

BIBLIOGRAPHY

Editions

P. Van der Weijden, *Laudes Domini: Tekst, vertaling en commentaar* (Amsterdam: Paris, 1967).

J. Fontaine, *Naissance de la poésie dans l'occident chrétien* (Paris: Études Augustiniennes, 1981).

9. Juvencus

Another poet who addresses Constantine is a Spanish priest of noble birth named Gaius Vettius Aquilinus Juvencus, born perhaps in Illiberis, near present-day Granada. In 329–330, according to Jerome, Juvencus wrote four *Books of the Gospels* (*Evangeliorum libri*). The work is especially interesting, if not for its content then for its literary form, which this poet seems to have invented: a paraphrase in verse of the sacred text. This invention was popular in late antiquity in both the Latin and the Greek worlds.

We must not be deceived by the term "paraphrase," for it is not to be understood as an unimportant transformation of a text by way of a rhetorical exercise. Paraphrase as understood here had been tried as early as the time of Quintilian and called for three different versions of the same theme, the second and third involving increasing difficulty: first, a summary of a particular text; second, the introduction of ornamentations into it; and third, a real rewriting of it. In the final analysis, there was not much difference between the paraphrases of later antiquity and Latin adaptations of works of Greek literature.

Because the prejudiced Romantics of the past condemned the entire art of late antiquity as lacking "originality" and "poetic invention," Juvencus was regarded as a mediocre poet. In contrast, the new approach to the art of the imperial age typical of modern criticism, has discovered that paraphrase has a literary dignity of its own. The paraphrase practiced by Juvencus is a rewriting of the four Gospels in hexameters. The work is in four books, not in the sense that each book corresponds to a Gospel, but simply in the sense that as the Gospels are four, so the paraphrase is in four books. The Gospel of Matthew serves as the base text of the narrative, while the other three Gospels provide insertions. Thus Luke is used for the early events of Christ's life, and John for some pericopes at the end.

An introduction and a conclusion, in which the author speaks of himself, distinguish the paraphrase from traditional epic poetry. Juvencus's paraphrase eliminates repetitions and summarizes the narrative sections while amplifying mainly the discourses of Jesus. The work is a kind of *Diatessaron* in Latin; some scholars even think that Juvencus followed the *Diatessaron* of Tatian. The work is also of interest because it uses a rather old Latin translation of the Gospels; the author is faithful to this, often citing it verbatim and preserving many Grecisms, even some that are very difficult. The *Books of the Gospels* is a worthy literary production and one that deliberately seeks an elevated style, this being considered suitable to a "discourse about God." The meter is more correct than is usually the case in the poetry of that age; the poet has studied the classics (Virgil, Ovid, Horace, Lucretius, and Lucan) and imitates them with some skill. Juvencus seeks a linguistic purism and eliminates the technical terms of Christian parlance, replacing them with words from Latin epic vocabulary. It is appropriate to speak of "classicism," although the term does not entirely capture Juvencus's work.

As a man of letters, Juvencus is important because he is quite conscious of introducing a new literary genre, namely, Christian poetry. As I. Gualandri has remarked: "In his introduction Juvencus defines his position and clearly enunciates some themes that were to have a long life down to the Middle Ages. He refers to Homer and Virgil, the princes of epic writing, in order to show that his place is in an acknowledged tradition, but also in order to set himself apart by emphasizing everything that is opposed to that tradition: pagan poetry is based on fiction, Christian poetry on truth; the fame flowing from a literary work allows the pagan poet to survive in men's memory for many centuries, but the sacred subject of Christian verse becomes for its author a source of merit that will help him to eternal salvation."

In his desire to set himself apart, and with his eyes on a new form of poetry, Juvencus tones down everything in his gospel model that reminds the reader of things Jewish (place names and patronymics), gives the biblical story a Roman setting, and writes with the intention of edifying. Edification was alien to epic in the strict sense of this term, but in the Roman world it could be seen at work from the time of Lucretius: epic did not necessarily have to tell only the military exploits of its heroes; their spiritual deeds, too, could be the subject. By taking this approach, Juvencus meets the ideals of the Constantinian era and achieves what Lactantius had accomplished in *The Divine Institutes,* namely, the christianization of the culture and the fusion of a new content with the most elevated literary style.

BIBLIOGRAPHY

Edition

Juvencus, *Gai Vetti Aquilini Iuvenci Evangeliorum libri quattuor* (ed. J. Huemer; CSEL 24; Vindobonae: Temsky, 1891).

Studies

D. Kartschoke, *Bibeldichtung* (Munich: Finck, 1975).
R. Herzog, *Die Bibelepik der lateinischen Spätantike* (Munich: Finck, 1975).
J. Fontaine, *Naissance de la poësie* (Paris: Études Augustiniennes, 1981).
S. Costanza, "Da Giovenco a Sedulio," *CClCr* 6 (1985): 254–86.
A. Hilhorst, "The Cleansing of the Temple (John 2:13–25) in Juvencus and Nonnus," in *Early Christian Poetry* (ed. J. den Boeft and A. Hilhorst; Leiden: Brill, 1993), 61–76.

Literary production fell off in the twenty years after Lactantius, until the spread of the Arian controversy to the West stimulated debate and a renewal of Christian thought. In terms of chronology, Firmicus Maternus might be taken as the most authoritative representative of the years 330–350 but by his formation and in his interests he belongs to the preceding period, and it is there that we have discussed him. Perhaps the twenty-year silence is due to the fact that all the representative Latin writers of the Constantinian period were, like their predecessors, natives of Africa; with the exception of Novatian, there are few traces of a non-African western Christianity. As a result, once the day of Africa's great literature had passed, due either to the exhaustion of inspiration or to the difficult situations caused by the Donatist schism, and once the interest in poetry fueled by Constantinian ideology had died out, the Latin West continued to be what it had been earlier outside of Africa, that is, essentially unpretentious in its thought and its literature. On the other hand, contemporary pagan literary production likewise did not stand out either for its originality or for the excellence of its results. In summary, we have the impression that there was a degree of laziness in Latin Christianity before the Arian storm swept in to shake the West.

10. Eusebius of Caesarea: Philology, History, and Apologetics for a Triumphant Christianity (by Lorenzo Perrone)

a. A Leading Figure of His Time

At the beginning of the fourth century after the birth of Christ, a century rich in creative individuals capable of developing Christian literature in the most varied areas, the many-sided figure of Eusebius of Caesarea (ca. 265–ca. 340) stands out. He dominated the scene, and not only the literary stage, during the years between the great persecution by Diocletian (303–313) and the struggles that followed upon the Council of Nicea (325) and within the empire ruled by Constantine, a leader now openly favorable to the church. A Palestinian bishop, Eusebius is emblematic of this crucial period, which was a watershed between the early stage of Christianity and its subsequent history down to the modern period. He is admittedly emblematic in only a partial way, as will appear more clearly when he is compared with Athanasius of Alexandria, the other major leading personage of the post-Nicene church, who was active until the last quarter of the century. The historical importance of Eusebius consists in his having founded ecclesiastical historiography, thereby providing the model, normative for a very long time, of a new literary genre, and in having made himself the theological spokesman of Constantine's vision in the area of the increasingly complex relations between empire and church.

b. In the Tradition of Origen: The School of Pamphilus

Eusebius's vocation as philologist and scholar constitutes the man's greatest continuity with the tradition of Origen; he was indeed directly linked to that tradition thanks to his personal history and formation. The link was ensured by a personage who was representative of Origenism in the third and fourth centuries. This was the presbyter Pamphilus, who was first a student of Pierius in Alexandria and then heir in Caesarea to the example of Origen, whose library he tended and expanded (Eusebius, *Hist. eccl.* 6.32.3).

Following Origen's example and combining ascetical fervor and study in his own life (*Mart. Pal.* 11.2), Pamphilus, too, gathered a group of disciples and fellow workers from various backgrounds, the most outstanding of whom was Eusebius (*Hist. eccl.* 7.32.25). These men were engaged in a revision of the biblical text, a task already begun by Origen in his *Hexapla*. This philological work on the sacred book was not their exclusive concern; both the master and some disciples showed philosophical interests (*Mart. Pal.* 5.2; 7.5; 11.19). But it seems to have been their primary activity, confirming a shift in contemporary tendencies in Origenist circles, which were clearly in the ascendant after the deposition of Paul of Samosata, bishop of Antioch (268–269). Their dominance, however, did not mean that there were no disagreements and disputes, as the case of Methodius of Olympus shows. Eusebius in his turn was to give this development an even more sustained impetus and thus create the conditions for the birth of the Antiochene school.

In the atmosphere of zealous study, Eusebius's intimate association with Pamphilus, whom he regarded as his "master" (*Mart. Pal.* 11), to the point of linking his own name with him after the manner of freedmen, advanced the career of this future bishop of Caesarea by means of works that show characteristic philological sensitivities, as well as apologetical concerns relevant to and in keeping with the Constantinian revolution. The association with Pamphilus was sealed with the sign of Origen during the imprisonment of Pamphilus, who fell victim to measures being taken against Christians. For in the time before his martyrdom, the master was able, with the disciple's help, to write a large part of a *Defense of Origen*, which Eusebius completed after the martyr's death in 310. To speak in broader terms, the Alexandrian tradition left its imprint on the whole of Eusebius's literary production, making him the closest and most complete Christian version of the Hellenistic scholar. He owed this position to learning that embraced philology, history, geography, rhetoric, and philosophy.

c. Biography and Literary Production

Eusebius's activity as a writer reflects the several periods of his life, even if it is not possible to establish a detailed chronology of his works. To begin with, we owe to his association with Pamphilus and the library at Caesarea the impulses for those writings that show Eusebius to be a biblical philologist: the tables of concordances among the Gospels in the *Letter to Carpian*, or the researches in the geography of Palestine contained in the *Onomasticon*. But this association also, above all, shows him as the archivist of early Christianity, especially for his *Chronicle* and, later, the *Ecclesiastical History*.

This first phase yielded abruptly to the period of persecutions, but without any real break in the continuity of Eusebius's intellectual habits and routines as a writer. Although he was not directly affected by the persecution but escaped its most serious consequences because of his withdrawal to Egypt, later, in the lost *Life of Pamphilus* and especially in *The Martyrs of Palestine* and the supplements to *Ecclesiastical History* (books 8–10), he became a witness to and propagandist for the deaths of the martyrs as pledges of the future triumph of the church.

The renewal of peace for the church saw Eusebius's ascent to the episcopal see of Caesarea, from which he played an intimate role in ecclesiastical politics for about thirty years without any discernible lessening of his literary diligence.

Eusebius developed intellectual plans that were closely related to the ideology of the Christian empire with an exceptional timeliness that was due, moreover, to the apologetical perspective that directed his historiographical undertaking from the outset and was explained more fully in the *Preparation for the Gospel* and the *Demonstration of the Gospel*. He extolled the first—and in his eyes providential—interpreter of this ideology when he gave the official address for the thirtieth anniversary of Constantine's reign (335) and when he celebrated the emperor after his death (337) in his *Life of Constantine*. His intimacy with the emperor repaid Eusebius amid the difficulties he experienced at the outbreak of the Arian crisis, due to the fact that initially he had openly supported the Alexandrian presbyter, although without fully sharing his ideas. As a result, he was called upon to attest to his own orthodoxy at the Council of Nicea. He did so by introducing the creed of the church of Caesarea. Subsequently he gave that church an account of his action in a letter that showed a certain confusion in regard to the *homoousios* dogma, the "of one substance" of the Nicene Creed.

Nevertheless, the period after the Council saw this Palestinian bishop growing in prestige and authority, and he was even considered as a successor to the episcopal throne of Antioch after the deposition of Eustathius (327). He also neutralized the other more important representative of the stricter Nicene line, in the person of Athanasius. After 335 he devoted the last years of his life to controversy with Marcellus of Ancyra, whose ideas he combated in the *Against Marcellus* and *Ecclesiastical Theology*.

d. Language and Style: Compilation and Reuse of Materials

Eusebius claims originality not only for his *Ecclesiastical History*, in which he describes himself, with justified pride, as the real inaugurator of the discipline (1.2.3 and 5), but also for other works, on the grounds that he provided an exact Christian counterpart to the several types of writing and literary genres of paganism for example, his *Praise of Constantine* and *Life of Constantine* are counterparts of the pagan panegyric. A similar claim sometimes advanced by Eusebius in relation to earlier Christian literature (*Praep. ev.* 1.3.5) can be applied to *Questions on the Gospels,* as this work is the first Christian example known to us of a genre destined for special success in late patristic and medieval literature. The genre was not applied solely in the area of exegesis, although that application predominated.

The literary innovations credited to Eusebius would not, however, seem adequately supported by a corresponding result in the structure and form of the writings. The ancients already passed a negative or at least reserved judgment in that area, alleging a heaviness of the style, which they generally regarded as wearisome and lacking in elegance (Photius, *Lex.* 13). Like the majority of the Fathers, Eusebius was in principle more concerned with content than with form, although this does not mean that his literary results were always untidy or displeasing.

In short his principal defects are mainly those of a compiler, who constructs many of his own writings by assembling and harmonizing a variety of materials. With perceptible qualitative and quantitative differences, this is the basic approach taken in his two major works: the *Ecclesiastical History* and the *Preparation for the Gospel*. In addition, he reuses materials in different works or reworks his writings in different versions to meet new needs. One of many possible examples is in the *Life of Constantine* as compared with the *Ecclesiastical History.* Rewriting is thus a characteristic element of Eusebius's literary activity, but it is precisely this recurring practice that enables us to check not only the impact of current needs or the didactico-pedagogical inclinations of the author, but also his capacity for *variatio,* the art of innovating while repeating. This applies both to stylistic and rhetorical expressions and to vocabulary, and not only in those genres, such as panegyric, which most lent themselves to rhetorical elaboration. As can be seen from the *Against Hierocles,* among other works, Eusebius does not overlook the rhetorical devices taught by the Second Sophistic.

Given these several aspects of Eusebius's writing, we must suppose that the public to which he addressed his works consisted for the most part of educated readers who could share with him literary and philosophical interests over a fairly wide range. It could not have been otherwise if we consider the prodigious learning Eusebius displays in both areas. This being the case, readers of his works were not limited to the Christian world but came also from within pagan and even Jewish circles, or at least from groups that were less certain of the religion to which they belonged and therefore more open to the Christian faith. This claim is supported by the *Ecclesiastical History,* but applies even more to explicitly apologetical works such as the *Against Hierocles.* In this work Eusebius refrains from using the Bible and seems to identify still more closely with the cultural world of the time, in order to use it and move beyond it.

e. Our Presentation of the Works

The difficulty of establishing with any accuracy the chronology of Eusebius's works, except in a few instances, makes it advisable to discuss them under thematic headings, to which, on the whole, the related literary genres correspond. Some works in the list of Eusebius's writings have been lost entirely or in part. We no longer have such works on the martyrs as the "collection of early acts of the martyrs" (*Hist. eccl.* 4.15.47) or such biographical works as the three books of the *Life of Pamphilus* (*Hist. eccl.* 6.32.3; *Mart. Pal.* 11.3). Nor do we any longer have large parts of apologetical works. Especially regrettable among the latter is the loss of about ten books of the *Demonstration of the Gospel* and the loss of the *Against Porphyry* (Jerome, *Vir. ill.* 81). Among the dogmatic works a no less serious loss is that of five books of the *Defense of Origen.* Among works on biblical subjects a sizable part of the *Onomasticon* has not come down to us, nor has the original version of the *Questions on the Gospels.* The quick success of Eusebius's historical works, which were soon translated and imitated in Latin and other languages, has made it possible to salvage at least part of the *Chronicle* in Jerome's revision and in an Armenian translation.

Then, too, Eusebius's authority as a writer extended to other fields. This can be seen, for example, in the influence of the *Commentary on the Psalms* on such Latin authors as Hilary of Poitiers and Eusebius of Vercelli, and on an adversary such as Athanasius.

f. Works of Historical Interest

Eusebius's literary diligence was to manifest itself quite early in the realm of history, which was especially congenial to him, so much so that he wrote works of varying degrees of innovativeness in three different genres of history: the *Chronicle*, the *Ecclesiastical History*, and finally the *Life of Constantine*. The relationship between the *Chronicle* and the *Ecclesiastical History* was one of continuity in both form and ideas, as the author makes clear when he describes the former as an "epitome" of the latter (*Hist. eccl.* 1.1.6). By writing the *Chronicle*, the first edition of which goes back to the years around 303 or possibly even to the preceding decade, Eusebius was creating the proximate conditions for the composition of the *Ecclesiastical History*. Not only does the latter get its chronological framework from the *Chronicle*, while giving it a structural importance at least in the first seven books, but both texts reflect, in different ways and with varying effectiveness, the apologetical urgencies that are to a large extent common to both.

In compiling the *Chronicle* Eusebius took up a longstanding concern that is attested from the beginnings of the apologetical literature and that was behind the first manifestations of an interest in history among Christian writers. That concern was to respond to pagan accusations of "novelty" by giving a structured form to the "argument from antiquity," that is, the argument that the Jewish Christian tradition could boast of an origin more remote than that of the religious and philosophical patrimony of the classical world, which, being more recent, was indebted to the former in its best expressions.

An approach of this kind required a synoptic comparison between the stages of sacred history in the Old and New Testaments and the stages in the history of other peoples (see *Praep. ev.* 10.9.1–11). In meeting this need Eusebius had based his work on the *Chronological Tables (Chronikoi kanones)*, although these constituted only the second part of the work, while the first reviewed the history of the various ancient peoples down to and including the Romans. This synchronic approach, supplemented by a series of points of information on essential matters, produced something new as compared with the essentially Alexandrian model of chronography, to which Eusebius also referred and which had been given its most important preceding embodiment in the Christian world in the *Chronography* of Sextus Julius Africanus. The difference from this third-century author also showed in other aspects of Eusebius's method: in addition to basing his work on a wider array of sources, Eusebius dropped the millenarian idea that the history of the world would last six thousand years, a conception that still encumbered the work of his predecessor. Eusebius also began his own chronology not with the creation of the world but with Abraham.

Eusebius thus made clear in advance his qualifications as a scrupulous historian who was careful to report past events on the basis of reliable testimonies and was therefore concerned to let these speak by way of extended citations. It is precisely these factors that give the *Ecclesiastical History* a place of unparalleled importance in the whole range of patristic literature but also in relation to the canons of classical historiography. It must also be said, however, that Eusebius's merits in the area of documentation elicit reservations, since he is suspected of bias and even manipulation. A correct assessment of these merits requires one to take into account the apologetic perspective of even the *Ecclesiastical History*, since it inevitably directs the selection of texts and their use in support of particular theses. In any case, thanks to the abundance of the sources cited by Eusebius, the *Ecclesiastical History* is an irreplaceable text for our knowledge of the first three centuries of Christianity.

The writing of the *Ecclesiastical History* seems to have followed closely upon that of the *Chronicle*, at the end of the third and the beginning of the fourth century. But the composition of the *History* was more complex and troubled, due to the fact that the final part of the work (books 8–10), added at a second stage and connected with current events, showed the influence of several changes of situation between the end of the persecutions (313) and the sole rule of Constantine (324). The introduction summarizes the original plan of the work, which is thought to have included only the first seven books (1.1.1–2).

In the opening words of the introduction Eusebius says that a chief theme will be a description of the "lines of succession *[diadochai]* to the apostles." He thus introduces a word that was important in theological language beginning with the antignostic debate of the second century but was also applied by philosophers to the genealogy of teachers within each school. It is likely that Eusebius had both usages in mind, his intention being to trace the historical shape of the early church both in its hierarchic and institutional forms and in its theological and doctrinal manifestations. The latter, too, are seen as in substantial continuity, but without being regarded as the exclusive prerogative of the bishops. The author's interest in the martyrs adds the "charismatic" aspect to the institutional and doctrinal "lines of succession," thereby bolstering his vision of a church triumphant over all obstacles and adversities thanks to the power brought into action by the teaching of the gospel.

In keeping with this program, the *Ecclesiastical History* proceeds by following the coordinated chronologies of the principal episcopal sees: the apostolic churches of Rome, Alexandria, Jerusalem, and Antioch. These in turn are correlated with the imperial dynasties, which provide the basic chronological grid. Space is also given to mainly prosopographical information and literary history. The last-named aspect is clearly seen in the many notices Eusebius gives of contemporary writers in the periods he describes; he gives a short sketch of an author's life or, more often, a list of his works. An example of this approach, though one that is much lengthier and more important, is book 6, which is devoted almost entirely to a biography of Origen and a detailed review of his writings. Part of this concern for literary history is Eusebius's interest in the history of the canon (3.3.3), which is signposted by references to the number of biblical books gradually received by each author. While Eusebius thus provides the first literary history of Christianity, at the same time he provides a summary sketch of early heresies, as well as persecutions, the effects of which are called to mind by relating some of the most important Acts of the martyrs.

The epochal changes of which Eusebius had personal experience led him to add three books to the *Ecclesiastical History*. These describe the ups and downs of the great persecution and the restoration of peace to the church down to the final triumph of Constantine. The difference between these books and the preceding shows in a series of motifs. First, there is a reduction in the broad range of matters previously connected with the "lines of succession," which reach only to the next-to-last decade of the third century. At the same time, there is a focus on the martyrologico-political aspect of the history. Second, there are differences in approach and style, since on the one hand the author abandons the archivistic-documentary approach and reduces the citation of other texts, and on the other hand he intervenes in the first person and shows off his rhetorical skills.

The variants in the two families of the manuscript tradition probably reflect two or even three editions of the work. The eighth book in particular must have undergone several revisions, since it contained initially only an abridged version of *The Martyrs of Palestine*, but was later revised to give a picture less restricted to that region. Further changes were occasioned by, among other things, the fall of Licinius, which compelled Eusebius to alter passages in which he had mentioned this rival of Constantine.

This historian's merits are confirmed by *The Martyrs of Palestine*, the most detailed account that has come down to us of the impact of the last persecution at the local level. The fullest recension, perhaps dating from 311 and transmitted integrally in Syriac, has a greater abundance of biographical detail, especially for those martyrs whom Eusebius had known personally as members of Pamphilus's circle. The work as a whole is written in a rather unadorned style, but the solemn introduction to the martyrdom of Pamphilus displays an effort at formality. This tendency toward formality is more evident, however, in the long recension. But the inclination to the panegyrical that shows here and there is controlled by the author's overreaching commitment to be a faithful chronicler and to rely on direct testimonies. As proof of his critical awareness, Eusebius shows himself quite reluctant to emphasize the miraculous or extraordinary aspects of events (9.13). On the other hand, his knowledge of the martyrological literature certainly influenced his typology of martyrs.

The works on Constantine likewise deserve to be numbered among those of historical interest, even if the encomiastic intention that governs them finds expression in panegyric. This literary genre as applied to the emperor cannot be judged a mere exercise in celebrative oratory. Rather, allowing for the laws proper to the genre and the limitations inherent in these laws, it reflects a historical vision of the role of the sovereign according to the politico-religious ideology of the time. For this very reason, it is a valuable contribution to the history of ideas and mentalities. This claim applies chiefly to the *Praise of Constantine;* it is somewhat less applicable to the *Life* because of the biographical story and the documentary apparatus, which introduce noteworthy variants as compared with the model that inspired the work.

The *Praise of Constantine* transmits two different addresses, which were brought together in 335, but the title applies, strictly speaking, only to the first (chs. 1–10), the official address for the thirtieth anniversary of Constantine's reign. The second (chs. 11–18), which is more fittingly called *The Tomb of Christ*, is a short treatise presented to Constantine at the solemn dedication of the Basilica of the Anastasis in Jerusalem. In the *Praise of Constantine*, we have the retrieval in a Christian key of the sacral conception of royal power, which had been developed in Hellenism and then taken over by the Roman imperial world. To the Logos with his universal kingship over creation there corresponds in the order of the inhabited world the person of the sovereign, the living incarnation of the virtues. In his earthly governance he imitates his "archetype," the wise action of heaven's government of the world (5.4). Once again, Eusebius praises the "monarchy" in the providentialist perspective that sees a harmony between the coming of Christianity and the unification of the Mediterranean world under the scepter of Rome (3.6), while at the same time confirming the uniqueness of Constantine and his evangelizing mission in the history of humanity.

In confirmation of the exceptional nature of the contents of the discourse, Eusebius stresses the difference between his encomium and the many examples in pagan literature, both because he is unwilling to subordinate his work to esthetic norms and because he is dealing with far more important matters. Specifically, he is setting out the emperor's actions in conformity with God, rather than recalling inferior and secondary aspects of his reign. Despite these statements of principle, Eusebius does choose to venture onto the formal plane by using elaborate language that is not lacking in rhetorical embellishments and echoes of the classics.

In the address on *The Tomb of Christ*, Eusebius makes more frequent and direct recourse to Scripture. The language is plain and generally without constructions shaped by rhetoric. Spurred on by the need to defend Constantine against pagan criticisms of the monumental edifices he had built in the holy places of Palestine, Eusebius's text turns into a brief, essentially apologetical treatise that sums up the "theology" and the "economy" of the Logos. According to the terms set down in the *Ecclesiastical History* (1.1.7ff.), the theology and economy of the Logos have to do with his divine status and his revelatory action. The work also contains echoes of the controverted question of the relationship between the Son and the Father. This effective compendium of Christology summarizes the first three books of Eusebius's *Divine Manifestation*, confirming once again the unity of his vision.

The various ideas connected with the person of the emperor in the earlier works are systematically organized in the four books of the *Life of Constantine*, which is conceived as a concrete embodiment of the ideal construction set down in the *Praise of Constantine*. The work has been the subject of debate, and some critics have denied Eusebius's authorship. Doubts arise especially from a comparison with the *Ecclesiastical History*, in which, for example, we find no mention of the famous vision of the cross before the battle of the Milvian Bridge. But many difficulties can be resolved if the reader considers the way that Eusebius readapts his own material. In this work, being the last by the bishop of Caesarea, it is likely that death prevented a final editing.

This work again confirms the author's intention of distancing himself from the literary genres of paganism, since not only is the purpose of celebrating the emperor interwoven with the biographical purpose, but both aim at introducing a Christian content (1.10–11). The novelty of Eusebius's work is emphasized at the level of form by a characteristic peculiar to him as historian and apologist: his recourse to the citation of sources. The use of the state archives, which supplemented the libraries consulted in the writing of the *Ecclesiastical History*, is accompanied by first person testimony, which, when necessary, does not remain silent about confidences received from Constantine in private.

The biographical plot of the work is marked by a carefully orchestrated narrative crescendo in the author's portrait of Constantine. He traces the course of the emperor's life from his first steps, taken in the shadow of his father Constantius Chlorus, to the campaign against Maxentius. The campaign story gives the author an opportunity to explain the motives behind Constantine's choice of religion, by showing the original nucleus of the connection between the confession of the true God and the emperor's politico-military success. After control of the West has been won, the unexpected difficulty caused by the Donatist conflict sheds light on a new role of the emperor as "common bishop," zealous for the peace of the church and magnanimous toward the fomenters of disorder who lurk among churchmen, as is proved by the Arian controversies in particular (1.44–45; see also 4.24). Constantine's humaneness and the benevolent protection he gives the churches lead to a conflict with Licinius and help ultimately to create an image of the emperor as "a lover of God" and "a new Moses." The recognition of Constantine's uniqueness reaches its climax when he receives baptism before his death: it is a consistent seal upon a life based, in Eusebius's eyes, on a confession of the true God.

The thorough sharing of ideas by the panegyrist and his hero is also to be seen in the *Oration . . . to the Assembly of the Saints,* which has come down in the manuscripts under Constantine's name, as an appendix to the *Life.* Its focus is on apologetical themes dear to Eusebius, such as the denunciation of the error of polytheism and the demonstration of the truth of the Christian message. Among other things, this oration, which can be dated to the period between 313 and 325 and was written originally in Latin, gives a christological interpretation of Virgil's fourth *Eclogue,* just as Lactantius did in the *Divine Institutes* during these same years in the Latin world.

g. Apologetic Works

The priority of apologetics in the thinking and work of Eusebius finds expression in an even lengthier series of writings. At the center of these, as a kind of real *summa,* stand the imposing *Preparation for the Gospel* and *Demonstration of the Gospel.* The immense range of his work in this genre makes Eusebius the major exponent of the theological and literary tradition which, since the first half of the second century, had been justifying Christianity to the pagan and, to a lesser extent, Jewish worlds. He is obviously indebted to the writers who preceded him, but he also has his own merits. He has the ability to synthesize the motifs adopted by his predecessors with his eye always on a global vision. In support of that objective, he employs his novel method of proof, which is supported by an unparalleled scientific and documentary commitment.

In this set of writings, the *Against Hierocles* has a place apart, a position also shown by the fact that Eusebius does not reuse it elsewhere; the work was presumably written toward the end of the persecutions and in controversy with one of their main instigators. In a work of Hierocles, *The Lover of Truth (Philalēthēs),* this high-ranking imperial official not only repeated the usual themes in pagan criticism of Christianity, but dwelt in particular on a comparison between Jesus and Apollonius of Tyana, and asserted the superiority of the miracles performed by the first-century philosopher-thaumaturge. Hierocles relied on the *Life of Apollonius,* which was written by Philostratus at the beginning of the third century and was full of legendary incidents.

It is on this *Life* that Eusebius's criticism focuses, his purpose being to show that Philostratus's narrative is improbable and gives a false impression of the historical Apollonius. Eusebius also refers back to Origen's refutation in *Against Celsus.* By dismantling what is in his view a false image of Apollonius as a magician and charlatan, who on the contrary deserved respect as a philosopher and ascetic, Eusebius displays an attitude in which he adopts the demands of reasonableness found in pagan culture. This leads him to condemn the inconsistencies in the story, to reappraise them and attribute them to the action of demonic forces, and to reject belief in fate as intrinsically contradictory to any supposed magical activity. In thus renewing a central motif in the thinking of Origen, Eusebius works out a first defense of free will (450–448) which he will place on a broader base in the *Preparation for the Gospel.*

Behind Hierocles can already be glimpsed the figure of Porphyry, the most renowned and energetic representative of pagan polemics in the time of Eusebius.
Around 270 he wrote an *Against Christians* in fifteen books, which elicited many refutations from the Fathers of the fourth and fifth centuries. Among the earliest of these
Fathers, after Methodius of Olympus, was Eusebius in his lost work *Against Porphyry,*
which was chronologically close to the *Against Hierocles.* His reply, in twenty-five
books, must have dealt with the Neoplatonic philosopher's challenges to the biblical
books, and more particularly to the contradictions in the Gospel genealogies of Jesus
and in the stories of the resurrection. It is therefore possible that traces of that work
have entered the *Questions on the Gospels,* although the latter does not seem to reflect
a very polemical setting.

Likewise from the period before his episcopate and between the *Chronicle* and the
Ecclesiastical History is the *Basic General Introduction* in ten books, of which only
books 6–9 remain. The latter are known as *Extracts from the Prophets,* being a selection, with commentary, of Old Testament messianic prophecies. A systematic inven-
tory is made of such prophecies in the historical (*Ecl. proph.* 1) and the poetic and
prophetic books (2–3), with special attention to Isaiah (4). As the overall title with its
didactic implication suggests, this was a first introduction to the gospel, intended to
strengthen the faith of the newly baptized, and perhaps connected with Eusebius's
work of teaching the Bible. In any case, it was a prelude to the apologist's more important effort, which is to be seen in the comprehensive plan of the *Preparation for the
Gospel* and the *Demonstration of the Gospel.*

In view of the great size of this double work, the execution of the plan must have
taken a fairly long time—for example, the years between the end of the persecutions
and the war of Constantine against Licinius (314–321; or according to another hypothesis, 312–322). The two titles signal the distinct but interconnected parts of a
work which Eusebius thought of as forming a unity: the *Preparation for the Gospel,* in
fifteen books, refutes pagan polytheism and proves the superiority of Judaism insofar
as it was a preparation for the gospel. The *Demonstration of the Gospel,* in twenty
books, of which the first ten and part of the fifteenth have survived, explains the reasons for a faith founded on the teaching of Christ as he replied to the Jews.

The necessity of once again demonstrating the validity of the faith had been
made clear in the distress caused by the persecutions, as is shown by the apologetical
writings composed in their wake, from Arnobius and Lactantius to the *Against the Pagans* of Athanasius. The need for a new reply became even more urgent after the effective attack of Porphyry, who had given a new intellectual depth to anti-Christian
polemics. Thus it became necessary to refute the subtle arguments of this philosopher
who had endeavored to restore legitimacy to the traditional religion, now widely challenged, by rethinking it in the categories of Neoplatonism. The followers of Christ
were usually rebuked for a twofold betrayal: not only had they abandoned the beliefs
of their fathers and joined a "barbaric" religion, but they had changed the faith of the
Jews and thereby committed a second kind of infidelity. In replying to these two accusations, Eusebius uses them to give structure to the extensive material of his treatise,
which he says is addressed first to those who do not know Christianity (*Praep. ev.*
1.1.1) or who have only a superficial knowledge of it despite having accepted it.

In the *Preparation,* then, Eusebius first explains that Christians have abandoned
pagan religion after due consideration (books 1–6), because that religion is a form of

idolatrous worship and inspired by demons, whether in its traditional mythological forms or in philosophical reinterpretations of it, such as that of Porphyry, or in the widespread practice of using oracles. The refutation of paganism is followed by a justification of the appeal to the Jewish tradition by Christians, since they are the heirs of Abraham (books 7–10). The first "friends of God," such as Abraham and the other patriarchs, were spokesmen for an authentic and reasonable worship of the true God and a life consistent with that worship. The superiority of Judaism over paganism is then argued at length on the grounds that Moses preceded Plato, who simply plagiarized from the prophets (books 10–15). Finally, in the *Demonstration* Eusebius completes the basis for a consistent choice of Christianity by turning to Judaism and asserting the legitimacy of the gospel over against it by a structured repetition of the traditional argument from prophecy.

Within this basic approach, the bishop of Caesarea draws on all the resources of his great learning and directs his main effort not to developing his own theses but to gathering documentation in support of them. He does this in keeping with the demand for "scientific" proof which he regarded as the most suitable way of attaining the simultaneously apologetical and didactic objective of his work (*Praep. ev.* 1.5.14). The critique of paganism is worked out from within paganism itself by using its own sources. These may be the works of partial allies or companions on the journey, as is the case with all those, beginning with Plato, who distanced themselves from the traditional religion, even though not yet reaching the full truth of Christianity. Or they may be the works of convinced defenders of paganism, even though these sources may have been recast in philosophical language, as in the work of Porphyry. In this last case, Eusebius is concerned to bring out weaknesses in argument or points of contradiction and set these over against the perspectives adopted by the first group.

Thanks to this quest of "objectivity," we owe to Eusebius the preservation of many classical texts, some of them attested only in his work. In addition, the overall result of this strategic use of documentation is a revisitation of the whole of pagan culture, which is examined in its various areas of learning—religio-mythological, historico-literary, and philosophical—in order to bring out their inadequacy but also their points of contact with Christianity.

Eusebius was able to take advantage of the labors he had engaged in for his own apologetical *summa* by summarizing it, in part, in the *Divine Manifestation*. This work, dated after 324, focuses once again on the motif of the manifestation of the Logos in creation and in history, a motif that is the central element in his historico-theological vision. The indebtedness to the *Preparation* and the *Demonstration* emerges at various points in the first three books. There are also references to the *Ecclesiastical History*. The fourth book deals with the miracles of Jesus and with the New Testament preaching that confirms his divinity, while the fifth book, which is again based on the *Demonstration*, rejects the charge of sorcery against Christ and of imposture against the apostles. The aim of the bishop of Caesarea seems to be to reach a larger public, both pagan and neophyte, who may have been discouraged by the great size and imposing documentation of the major apology. The *Divine Manifestation* itself was rewritten, too, and its contents simplified, the first three books were extensively revised in *The Tomb of Christ*, in order to make their teaching more accessible to Constantine.

h. Dogmatic Writings

Eusebius shows himself to be a less fruitful and original writer in the area of dogma, where he intervened solely for polemical reasons having to do with the need to safeguard the theological heritage of Origen. At the beginning of his literary activity, Eusebius joined Pamphilus in composing a *Defense of Origen* in six books, the last of which he wrote after his teacher's martyrdom. Of this work we know only the first book, which has been preserved in Rufinus's translation. The work eloquently attests to the bitterness generated by the controversy over the great Alexandrian in the third and fourth centuries. Enthusiastic admiration, even to the point of regarding Origen as a new apostle, was matched by drastic condemnation from those who saw him as a promoter of heretical teaching, as Methodius of Olympus put it in his denunciation, to which the *Defense* was probably a reply. The accusation was repeated in the post-Nicene period by Marcellus of Ancyra.

In view of these attitudes, Eusebius and Pamphilus endeavored, by way of introduction, to shed light on the characteristic traits of Origen's theology as an investigation based on Scripture, but without any claim to definitive solutions in areas in which the Scriptures did not decide, and conforming to the contents of the apostolic preaching. There followed a list of specific charges against the Alexandrian's Christology, anthropology, and eschatology, as well as against his use of allegory as allegedly emptying the historical element in biblical revelation.

Motives of fidelity to Origen were also among the proximate causes of Eusebius's opposition to Marcellus of Ancyra, who, together with Athanasius, had attacked the more visible proponents of "Semiarianism." Those theologians, with Eusebius, favored a line of thinking that differed from the radicalism of Arius with its clear distinction between the natures of the Father and the Son. They were, however, responsive to Origen's theology of the three trinitarian hypostases, while retaining the connected encumbrance of subordinationism, which weighed more or less heavily depending on individual cases. After the deposition of Eustathius and Athanasius, Marcellus, the last spokesman for Asiatic monarchianism, was condemned in 336 at a synod in Constantinople.

Eusebius then felt the need to support his own party in two works against the bishop of Ancyra: the *Against Marcellus* and the *Ecclesiastical Theology*. The first work, in two books, takes the form of a refutation of Marcellus's theses, which are set forth in a wealth of extracts from one of his works, together with remarks by Eusebius on the agreement among the extracts. In the first book, he takes pleasure in bringing out his adversary's lack of skill in dealing with the Bible. He criticizes Marcellus's methods of interpretation as inadequate in relation to the divinely inspired character of the sacred text, and he rejects his criticism of Origen. In the second book, the bishop of Caesarea documents Marcellus's errors in Trinitarian theology and in Christology, emphasizing first his denial of the hypostasis of the Logos and then the provisional nature of the economy of the incarnation and the end of the reign of Christ.

Eusebius takes a more positive approach in the three books of the *Ecclesiastical Theology*. With numerous repetitions caused by the needs of controversy, he develops his own christological teaching in reply to Marcellus. As the title indicates, the intention of the bishop of Caesarea is not to expound personal ideas but to explain the teaching he regards as conformed to the tradition of the church. This teaching is de-

rived from representative "Fathers." The errors of Marcellus likewise have a genealogy, but a negative one, in the heresies of Sabellius and Paul of Samosata. Indeed, the
Christology of Eusebius, which represents the final stage in the theology of the Logos
as developed by the apologists and the Alexandrian Fathers, seems to be supported by
a cosmological vision to a greater extent than was the case with Origen. The Logos is a
"hypostasis" or "substance" distinct from that of the Father and inferior to him, and
serves as an intermediary between God and creatures. In the incarnate Logos, then,
there is no human soul, since its function is performed by the Logos.

i. Works on Biblical Subjects

In this field, too, Eusebius had a noteworthy impact due to some peculiarities and
a breadth of interests, although we are able to gain only a partial impression of these
because many works have not come down to us or have been transmitted in an incomplete form. The bishop of Caesarea's approach to the Scriptures had its roots in
the experience he gained from Pamphilus, who trained him to analyze the sacred text
philologically after the manner of Origen but with attention also to the practice of the
Alexandrian grammarians. In addition, Eusebius continued the work of the *scriptorium* of Caesarea, and Constantine asked him to provide fifty copies of the Bible for
use in the new churches of Constantinople (*Vit. Const.* 4.36).

A lesser fruit of Eusebius's work as a biblical scholar, but one fated for great success
down to present-day editions of the New Testament, is the *Gospel Canons,* the workings
of which he explains in his *Letter to Carpian.* These canons were inspired by Ammonius
of Alexandria (mid-3d c.), who had set the text of Matthew beside the parallel passages
of the other evangelists. Eusebius eliminated the drawback of having a continuous text
only of the first evangelist by dividing the gospel text into small, successively numbered
sections, and on the basis of these constructing ten tables, which accurately show the
agreements—or lack of agreement—among the four Gospels.

The most outstanding fruit of Eusebius's learned philological zeal as applied to
the Bible is the *Onomasticon,* which is the surviving section of an extensive encyclopedia of biblical geography and topography; here again his model was similar works of
Alexandrian philology. The complete original work had four parts: (a) a translation
into Greek of the names of peoples in the Old Testament; (b) a description of ancient
Israel with an indication of the territories occupied by the twelve tribes; (c) a description of Jerusalem and the temple; (d) an alphabetical list of place names in Scripture,
the *Onomasticon* in the narrow sense. Only this last part has come down to us in
Jerome's revision of it (*The Location and Names of Hebrew Places—De situ et nomini-
bus locorum hebraicorum*). The *Onomasticon* was composed at the request of Paulinus
of Tyre (d. 331). Inasmuch as the work could serve as a "travel guide" for use by
pilgrims, it is probably connected with a new situation that arose as a result of the imperial promotion of the sacred places, and the growth of pilgrimages to Palestine.

To a great extent, Eusebius's learned approach here also marks his biblical commentaries, which pay special attention to the letter of the text and to historical data. In
this context, while not overlooking the bishop of Caesarea's link with the tradition of
Origen, we note a certain caution with regard to allegorical interpretation. However,
his method varies from work to work in view of their differing purposes. Thus the *Extracts from the Prophets* rarely go beyond the literal sense. Allegory plays a larger part

in the *Demonstration of the Gospel*, but literal exegesis usually predominates. The same is true of the *Against Marcellus* and *Ecclesiastical Theology*. The pursuit of an exegesis of the literal kind is also clear in the two major commentaries, which take up again, in fuller detail, two biblical books already discussed in the *Extracts from the Prophets*, but with a greater interest in Christology: the *Commentary on the Psalms* and the *Commentary on Isaiah*.

Of the first of these two, which was rather extensive and soon became widespread in the Latin world through translations by Hilary of Poitiers and Eusebius of Vercelli, only about a third of the original has come down to us (Ps 51–95:3). The remainder of the work can be partially reconstructed thanks to catenas, in which, however, many spurious texts are to be found. The mention of the basilica of the Anastasis shows that the work must have been completed around 335, or at least that the definitive edition goes back to that time.

The *Commentary on Isaiah*, which according to Jerome was in ten or fifteen books, was likewise known initially through catenas, but then was found almost complete in a codex of the Laurentian Library in Florence. The commentary, which can be dated to after 324, betrays its dependence on Origen, whose example also greatly conditions the philological approach, since Eusebius interprets the prophet on the basis of the Septuagint text in the Hexapla. However, the following of Origen's allegorical model is limited by a hermeneutical statement that there are prophecies to be interpreted only literally, with the result that the second level of meaning is no longer to be found everywhere in the Scriptures, as Origen claimed. Developing the apologetical aspect dear to him, Eusebius makes an extended application of the messianic passages in Isaiah to the coming of Christianity and to the present situation of the church, which was now triumphant over its enemies.

Eusebius's historical and apologetical interests caused him to give a privileged place to exegesis of the Old Testament, but he also had an opportunity to satisfy these interests in the New Testament in an original work, the *Questions on the Gospels*. Composed as a parallel to the *Demonstration of the Gospel*, this work has been transmitted in a faithful epitome as well as in numerous fragments in Greek and Syriac catenas. The original had two parts: the first, in two books, dealt with problems of the gospel infancy accounts and especially the genealogies; the second, of unspecified length, dealt with the difficulties raised by the accounts of the resurrection.

Eusebius's *Quaestiones* are important inasmuch as they are the first Christian example of the genre. They also have formal characteristics quite different from those of a predecessor, the *Questions on Genesis and Exodus* of Philo. They are more closely related to the classical grammatical and rhetorical tradition as established by Aristotle for dealing with the difficulties of Homeric criticism and as currently practiced in Alexandrian philology. In addition, Eusebius differs from Philo in his exegetical method, since he has relatively little recourse to allegorical interpretation. The use of the biblical *quaestio* or aporia, which was common beginning in the fourth century, tended to reflect a body of current problems, as could already be seen in the discussions of Celsus, Origen, or Sextus Julius Africanus on the genealogies of Christ, or even in Eusebius's lost work *The Polygamy of the Patriarchs* (*Dem. ev.* 1.9.20). In the case of Eusebius, however, it showed his skill in identifying problematic passages and the subtlety of the solutions he proposed.

BIBLIOGRAPHY

Texts

Eusebius (*CPG* 3465–3507).
———— (PG 12, 19–24).
————, *Life of Constantine* (GCS 1,1).
————, *Ecclesiastical History* (GCS 2).
————, *The Martyrs of Palestine* (GCS 2).
————, *Onomasticon* (GCS 3,1).
————, *Divine Manifestation* (GCS 3,1).
————, *Against Marcellus* (GCS 4).
————, *Ecclesiastical Theology* (GCS 4).
————, *Chronicle* (GCS 5).
————, *Demonstration of the Gospel* (GCS 6).
————, *Preparation for the Gospel* (GCS 8).
————, *Commentary on Isaiah* (GCS 9).
————, *Ecclesiastical History* (SC 31, 41, 55, 73).
————, *Preparation for the Gospel* (SC 206, 215, 228, 262, 266, 292, 307, 338, 369).
————, *Against Hierocles* (SC 333).
————, *Storia ecclesiastica* and *I martiri della Palestina* (ed. and trans. G. Del Ton; Rome: Desclée, 1964).
————, *Kirchengeschichte* (ed. and trans. by H. Kraft; Munich-Darmstadt: Kösel, 1967).
————, *Storia ecclesiastica* (ed. M. Ceva; Milan: Rusconi, 1979).
————, *Preparation for the Gospel* (trans. E. H. Gifford; Grand Rapids, Mich.: Baker, 1981).
————, *Sulla vita di Costantino* (ed. and trans. L. Tartaglia; Naples: D'Auria, 1984).
H. A. Drake, *In Praise of Constantine: A Historical Study and New Translation of Eusebius' Tricennial Orations* (Berkeley, Calif.: University of California Press, 1976).

Studies: Eusebius and His Age

T. D. Barnes, *Constantine and Eusebius* (Cambridge, Mass.: Harvard University Press, 1981).
H. Berkhof, *Die Theologie des Eusebius von Cäsarea* (Amsterdam: Uitgevers maatschappij Holland, 1939).
R. Farina, *L'impero e l'imperatore cristiano in Eusebio di Caesarea: La prima teologia politica del cristianesimo* (Zurich: Pas, 1966).
C. Luibhéid, *Eusebius of Caesarea and the Arian Crisis* (Dublin: Dublin Irish Academy, 1978).
J. Moreau, "Eusebius von Caesarea," *RAC* 6 (1966):1052–88.
E. Schwartz, "Eusebios," *PW* 6 (1907): 1370–1439.
J. Sirinelli, *Les vues historiques d'Eusèbe de Césarée durant la période prénicéenne* (Dakar: Université, 1961).

D. S. Wallace-Hadrill, *Eusebius of Caesarea* (London: Mowbray, 1960).

A. Weber, *ARCHÊ: Ein Beitrag zur Christologie des Eusebios von Cäsarea* (Rome: Neue Stadt, 1963).

F. Winkelmann, *Euseb von Kaisareia: Der Vater der Kirchengeschichte* (Berlin: Union, 1991).

Studies: Literary Activity

L. Allevi, "Eusebio di Cesarea e la storiografia ecclesiastica," SC 68 (1940): 550–64.

H. W. Attridge and G. Hata, eds., *Eusebius, Christianity and Judaism* (Detroit: Wayne State University Press, 1992); numerous studies of Eusebius as apologist and exegete.

T. D. Barnes, "The Composition of Eusebius' *Onomasticon*," *JTS* 26 (1975): 412–15.

M. R. Cataudella, "Sul problema del *Vita Constantini* attribuita a Eusebio di Caesarea," *MSLCA* 13 (1963): 41–59.

———, "La persona di Licinio e l'authenticità della *Vita Constantini*," *AT* 48 (1970): 46–83, 229–50.

G. F. Chesnut, *The First Christian Histories: Eusebius, Socrates, Sozomen, Theodoret, and Evagrius* (Paris: Beauchesne, 1977).

C. Curti, *Commentarii in Psalmos* (vol. 1 in *Eusebiana;* Catania: Centro di Studi sull'Antico Cristianesimo, 1987).

E. Dal Covolo, "La filosofia tripartita nella *Praeparatio evangelica* di Eusebio di Cesarea," *RSLR* 24 (1988): 515–23.

G. Del Ton, "Contenuto, struttura, scopi della *Storia ecclesiastica* di Eusebio di Cesarea," *Div* 6 (1962): 320–39.

M. Gödecke, *Geschichte als Mythos: Eusebs "Kirchengeschichte"* (New York: Lang, 1987).

R. M. Grant, *Eusebius as Church Historian* (Oxford: Clarendon, 1980).

H. Grégoire, "L'authenticité et l'historicité de la *Vita Constantini* attribuée à Eusèbe," *BAB* 39 (1953): 462–79.

P. Henry, *Recherches sur la "Préparation évangélique" et l'édition perdue des oeuvres de Plotin* (Paris: Leroux, 1935).

M. J. Hollerich, "Myth and History in Eusebius's *De Vita Constantini: Vit. Const. 1.12* in Its Contemporary Setting," *HTR* 82 (1989): 421–45.

M. Kertsch, "Traditionelle Rhetorik und Philosophie in Eusebius' *Antirrhetikos gegen Hierokles*," *VC* 34 (1980): 145–71.

R. Laqueur, *Eusebius als Historiker seiner Zeit* (Berlin: de Gruyter, 1929).

J.-R. Laurin, *Orientations maîtresses des apologistes chretiens de 270 à 361* (Rome: Apud Aedes Universitatis Gregorianae, 1954).

G. Lazzati, "Note su Eusebio epitomatore di Atti dei Martiri," in *Studi in onore di Aristide Calderini e Roberto Paribeni* (vol. 1; Milan: Ceschina, 1956), 377–84.

A. Louth, "The Date of Eusebius' *Historia ecclesiastica*," *JTS* 41 (1990): 111–23.

R. L. P. Milburn, *Early Christian Interpretations of History* (London: Black, 1954).

A. A. Mosshammer, *The Chronicle of Eusebius and Greek Chronographic Tradition* (Lewisburg, N.J./London: Bucknell University Press, 1979).

F. Overbeck, *Über die Anfänge der Kirchengeschichtsschreibung* (Basel: Reinhardt, 1892).

E. des Places, *Eusèbe de Césarée commentateur: Platonisme et Écriture Sainte* (Paris: Beauchesne, 1982).

L. Perrone, "Le *Quaestiones evangelicae* di Eusebio di Cesarea: Alle origini di un genere letterario," *ASE* 7 (1990): 417–35.

M. Simonetti, "Esegesi e ideologia nel Commento a Isaia di Eusebio," *RSLR* 19 (1983): 3– .

———, "Eusebio e Origene: Per una storia dell'origenismo," *Aug* 26 (1986): 323–34.

M. Tetz, "Christenvolk und Abrahamsverheissung: Zum 'kirchengeschichtlichen' Programm des Eusebius von Caesarea," *JACErg.B* 9 (1982): 30–46.

F. Winkelmann, *Die Textbezeugung der Vita Constantini des Eusebius von Cäsarea* (Berlin: Akademie Verlag, 1962).

GENERAL BIBLIOGRAPHY

This list contains only some standard or recent works, without any claim to completeness; further bibliography will be found in these works.

Bibliographical Lists

L'année philologique bibliographie critique et analytique de l'antiquité Gréco-latine. Paris, 1924/1926–.

ATLA Bibliography Series. Lanham, Md., 1974–.

Bibliographia patristica: Internationale patristische Bibliographie. Berlin, 1956–.

Bibliographia patristica: Supplementum. Berlin/New York, 1980–.

Bulletin de littérature ecclésiastiqu. Toulouse, 1899– (previously: *Bulletin théologique, scientifique et littéraire de l'Institut catholique de Toulouse*).

Bulletin signalétique: 527, Histoire et sciences religieuses. Paris, 1979–1990 (theology was previously included in the *Philosophie* section).

Elenchus of Biblical Bibliography. Rome, 1985– (previously: Elenchus bibliographicus biblicus of Biblica).

Gnomon: Kritische Zeitschrift für die gesamte klassische Altertumswissenschaft. Munich, 1925–.

Langevin, P.-E. *Bibliographie biblique. Biblical Bibliography. Biblische Bibliographie. Bibliografia biblica. Bibliografia bíblica.* Quebec, 1972–.

New Testament Abstracts. Weston, Mass.; Cambridge, Mass., 1956– .

Religion Index. Chicago: 1. *Periodicals*, 1977/1978– (previously: *Index to Religious Periodical Literature*, 1949/1952–1975/1976); 2. *Multi-author Works*, 1970/1975–.

Revue bénédictine: Supplément. Maredsous, 1921–.

Revue d'histoire ecclésiastique: Bibliographie. Louvain, 1900– .

Science of Religion. Amsterdam, 1980– (previously: International Bibliography of the History of Religions. Leiden, 1952–).

Zeitschrifteneinhaltsdienst Theologie. Tübingen, 1975– (reprints the tables of contents of the periodicals received by the library).

Work Tools

Aland, K., ed. *Vollständige Konkordanz zum griechischen Neuen Testament.* 2 vols. in 3. Berlin/New York: de Gruyter, 1978–1983.

Allenbach, J. et al., eds. *Biblia Patristica: Index des citations et allusions bibliques dans la littérature patristique.* 7 vols. Paris: Editions du Centre national de la recherche scientifique, 1975.

Bauer, W. *A Greek-English Lexicon of the New Testament and Other Early Christian Literature.* 4th ed. Edited by W. F. Arndt and F. W. Gingrich. Chicago: Chicago University Press, 1967.

Baur, C. *Initia Patrum Graecorum.* 2 vols. Vatican: Biblioteca Apostolica Vaticana, 1955.

Bibliotheca hagiographica Latina antiquae et mediae aetatis. 2 vols. Brussels: Société des Bollandistes, 1898–1901.

Blass, F., and A. Debrunner. *Grammatik des neutestamentlichen Griechisch.* 16th ed. Revised by F. Rehkopf. Göttingen: Vandenhoeck & Ruprecht, 1984.

CETEDOC Library of Christian Latin Texts. Turnhout: n.p., 1991– (CD-ROM concordance of Christian Latin texts).

Dekkers, E. *Clavis patrum latinorum.* 2d ed. Steenbrugis: Abbatia Sancti Petri, 1961.

Fros, H., ed. *Bibliotheca hagiographica Latina antiquae et mediae aetatis: Novum supplementum.* Brussels: Société des Bollandistes, 1986.

Geerard, M. *Clavis patrum graecorum.* 5 vols. Turnhout: Brepols, 1974–1987.

Goodspeed, E. J. *Index patristicus, sive, clavis patrum apostolicorum operum.* Leipzig: Hinrichs, 1907. Repr. 1960.

Halkin, F. *Bibliotheca hagiographica Graeca.* 3d ed. 3 vols. Brussels: Société des Bollandistes, 1969.

———. *Novum auctarium bibliotheca hagiographica Graeca.* Brussels: Société des Bollandistes, 1984.

Kittel, G., and G. Friedrich, eds. *Theological Dictionary of the New Testament.* Translated by G. Bromiley. Grand Rapids, Mich.: Eerdmans, 1985.

Kraft, H. *Clavis patrum apostolicorum: Catalogum vocum in libris partum qui dicuntur apostolici non raro occurrentium.* Munich: Kösel, 1963.

Lampe, G. W. H., ed. *A Patristic Greek Lexicon.* Oxford: Clarendon, 1961.

Moulton, J. H., and G. Milligan. *The Vocabulary of the Greek Testament.* Peabody, Mass.: Hendrickson, 1997.

Vattasso, M. *Initia partum aliorumque scriptorium ecclesiasticorum latinorum ex Mignei Patrologia et ex compluribus aliis libris conlegit ac litterarum ordine disposuit Marcus Vattasso.* 2 vols. Rome: Typis Vaticanis, 1968.

Reference Works

The Anchor Bible Dictionary. 6 vols. New York: Doubleday, 1992.

Dictionary of the Apostolic Church. 2 vols. New York: Scribner's Sons, 1916–1918.

Dictionnaire d'archéologie chrétienne et de liturgie. Paris: Letouzey et Ané, 1924–1953.

Dictionnaire d'histoire et de géographie ecclésiastiques. Paris: Letouzey et Ané, 1912–.

Dictionnaire de la Bible: Supplément. Paris: Letouzey et Ané, 1928–.

Dictionnaire de spiritualité ascétique et mystique, doctrine et histoire. Paris: Beauchesne, 1937–.

Dictionnaire de théologie catholique. Paris: Letouzey et Ané, 1903–1972.

Encyclopedia of the Early Church. 2 vols. New York: Oxford University Press, 1992.

Klauser, T. *Reallexikon für Antike und Christentum.* Edited by F. J. Dölger and H. Lietzmann. Stuttgart: Hiersemann, 1950–.

Lexikon für Theologie und Kirche. 3d ed. Freiburg: Herder, 1993–2001.

Oxford Dictionary of the Christian Church. 3d ed. New York: Oxford University Press, 1997.

Pauly, A. F. *Paulys Realencylopädie der classichen Altertumswissenschaft.* 49 vols. Edited by G. Wissowa. Munich: Druckenmüller, 1980 (the fundamental reference work for Greek and Roman antiquity, including Christianity).

Realencyclopädie für protestantische Theologie und Kirche. 3d ed. Leipzig: Hinrichs, 1896–1913.

Die Religion in Geschichte und Gegenwart. 3d ed. Tübingen: Mohr, 1956–1965.

Theologische Realenzyklopädie. Berlin/New York: de Gruyter, 1976–.

Handbooks of Patrology

Altaner, B., and A. Stuiber. *Patrologie: Leben, Schriften und Lehre der Kirchenväter.* 10th ed. Freiburg: Herder, 1993.

Bosio, G., E. Dal Covolo, and M. Maritano. *Introduzione ai padri della chiesa.* 3 vols. Turin: Società Editrice Internazionale, 1990–1993 (with an anthology).

Dattrino, L. *Patrologia: Introduzione.* Casale Monferrato: Piemme, 1991.

Mannucci, U., and A. Casamassa. *Istituzioni di patrologia.* 6th ed. 2 vols. Rome: Ferrari, 1948–1950.

Peters, G., *Lire les pères de l'église: Cours de patrologie.* 2d ed. 3 vols. Paris: Desclée De Brouwer, 1988.

Quasten, J. *Patrology.* 3 vols. Westminster, Md.: Newman, 1950–1960. 4th vol. edited by A. de Berardino. *Patrology IV: The Golden Age of Latin Patristic Literature from the Council of Nicea to the Council of Chalcedon.* Translated by P. Solari. Westminster, Md.: Newman, 1992.

Histories of Early Christian Literature

Amatucci, A. G. *Storia della letteratura latina cristiana.* 2d ed. Turin: Società Editrice Internazionale, 1955.

Aufstieg und Niedergang der römischen Welt. Berlin/New York: de Gruyter, 1974.

Aune, D. E. *The New Testament in Its Literary Environment.* Philadelphia: Westminster, 1987.

Bardenhewer, O. *Geschichte der altkirchlichen Literatur.* 2d ed. 5 vols. Freiburg/St. Louis, Mo.: Herder, 1912–1932 (these dates include the most recent editions of individual volumes).

Beck, H. G. *Kirche und theologische Literatur im Byzantinischen Reich.* 2d ed. Munich: Beck, 1977.

Campenhausen, H. von. *The Fathers of the Church: A Combined Edition of The Fathers of the Greek Church and The Fathers of the Latin Church.* Translated by M. Hoffman. Peabody, Mass.: Hendrickson, 1998.

D'Elia, S. *Letteratura latina cristiana.* Rome: Jouvence, 1999.

Dibelius, M. *Geschichte der urchristlichen Literatur: Neudruck der Erstausgabe von 1926 unter Berücksichtigung der Änderungen der englischen Übersetzung von 1936.*3d ed. Edited by F. Hahn. Munich: Kaiser, 1990.

Dihle, A. *Die griechische und lateinische Literatur der Kaiserzeit: Von Augustus bis Justinian.* Munich: Beck, 1989.

Fontaine, J. *La letteratura latina cristiana: Profilo storico.* Bologna: Mulino, 1973.

Haase, W., and H. Temporini. Aufstieg und Niedergang der römischen Welt: Principat. Berlin/New York: de Gruyter, 1974 (vols. 25–27 of this section are devoted to pre-Constantinian Christian literature).

Harnack, A. von. *Geschichte der altchristlichen Literatur bis Eusebius.* 2d ed. 2 vols. in 4. Leipzig: Hinrichs, 1958 (remains fundamental).

Herzog, R., and P. L. Schmidt, eds. *Handbuch der lateinischen Literatur der Antike.* Munich: Beck, 1989– (a French translation is also being published: Turnhout, 1993–).

Koester, H. *Introduction to the New Testament.* 2d ed. 2 vols. New York: de Gruyter, 1995–2000.

Labriolle, P. de. *Histoire de la littérature latine chrétienne.* 3d ed. 2 vols. Revised and augmented by G. Bardy. Paris: Les Belles Lettres, 1947.

Monceaux, P. *Histoire littéraire de l'Afrique chrétienne depuis les origines jusqu'à l'invasion arabe.* 7 vols. Paris: n.p., 1901–1923.

Moricca, U. *Storia della letteratura latina cristiana.* 3 vols. in 5. Turin: Società Editrice Internazionale, 1925–1934.

Pellegrino, M. *Letteratura greca cristiana.* 3d ed. Rome: Studium, 1983.

———. *Letteratura latina cristiana.* 4th ed. Rome: Studium, 1999.

Puech, A. *Histoire de la littérature grecque chrétienne depuis les origines jusqu'à la fin du IVe siècle.* 3 vols. Paris: Les Belles Lettres, 1928–1930.

Salvatorelli, L. *Storia della letteratura latina cristiana, dalle origine alla metà del VI secolo.* Milan: Vallardi, 1946.

Schmidt, W. and O. Stählin. *Geschichte der griechischen Literatur.* 2 vols. Munich: Beck, 1929. Based on *Wilhelm von Christ's Geschichte der griechischen Litteratur.* Munich: Beck, 1912–1924 (NB: O. Stählin, pp. 1105–492, on Christian literature).

Simonetti, M. *Letteratura cristiana antica greca e latina.* Le Letterature del mondo 49. Milan: Accademia, 1969.

Strecker, G. *History of New Testament Literature.* Translated by C. Katter and H.-J. Mollenhauer. Harrisburg, Pa.: Trinity Press International, 1997.

Vielhauer, P. *Geschichte der urchristlichen Literatur: Einleitung in das Neue Testament, die Apokryphen und die Apostolischen Väter.* 2d ed. Berlin/New York: de Gruyter, 1978.

Important Collections of Texts

Original Texts (With or Without a Translation)

Biblioteca patristica. Florence, 1984 (critical edition, Italian translation, introduction, and commentary).

Bibliothēkē hellēnōn paterōn kai ekklēsiastikōn syngrapheōn. Athens, 1955– (Greek texts).

Collection des Universités de France. Paris, 1920– (classical texts, but contains a number of critical editions, with French translations, of Christian authors).

Corona patrum. Turin, 1975– (critical edition, Italian translation, and commentary; previously: Corona patrum Salesiana).

Corpus Christianorum: Initia patrum Latinorum. 2 vols. Turnhout, 1971–1979 (very important collection).

Corpus Christianorum: Instrumenta lexicologica Latina. Turnhout, 1982– (very important collection).

Corpus Christianorum: Series Apocryphorum. Turnhout, 1983– (critical edition, translation into modern languages, and commentary; very important collection).

Corpus Christianorum: Series Graeca. Turnhout, 1977– (only a critical edition of texts; very important collection).

Corpus Christianorum: Series Latina. Turnhout, 1954– (only a critical edition of texts; very important collection).

Corpus scriptorum ecclesiasticorum Latinorum. Vienna, 1866 (very important; some of its editions have been taken over into the Corpus Christianorum).

Fontes christiani. Freiburg, 1990– (critical edition, German translation, introduction, and notes).

Die griechischen christlichen Schriftsteller der ersten drei Jahrhunderte. Berlin, 1897– (critical edition of the original texts; collection is of primary importance).

Hamann, A., ed. Patrologiae cursus completes: Series Latina, Supplementum. 5 vols. Paris, 1958–1974 (texts not included in the main series, edited according to more modern standards).

Kleine Texte für (theologische und philosophische) Vorlesungen und Übungen. Bonn, 1902 (short texts in careful critical editions).

Krüger, G., ed. Sammlung ausgewählter kirchen- und dogmengeschichtlichen Quellen. Tübingen, 1891–.

Loeb Classical Library. Cambridge, Mass., 1912– (two series, Greek and Latin, including many Christian writers; original text and English translation).

Migne, J.-P., ed. Patrologiae cursus completes: Series Graeca. 167 vols. Paris, 1857–1866. T. Hopner. Indexes. 2 vols. Paris, 1928–1938 (basic collection of all the texts known at the time, in the best editions of the 16th through 18th centuries, whose introductions and notes are also reproduced; accompanied by a Latin translation; texts abound in typographical errors and are not up to modern critical standards; indispensable for the large number of texts not yet reedited).

———. Patrologiae cursus completes: Series Latina. 221 vols., including indexes. Paris, 1841–1864 (basic collection of all the texts known at the time, in the best editions of the 16th through 18th centuries, whose introductions and notes are

also reproduced; texts abound in typographical errors and are not up to modern
critical standards; indispensable for the large number of texts not yet reedited).
Oxford Early Christian Texts. Oxford, 1971– (critical edition, English translation).
Patristische Texte und Studien. Berlin, 1963– (numerous critical editions, with or
without translation and commentary).
Schwarz, E., ed. *Acta conciliorum oecumenicorum.* Berlin, 1914– (major critical edition).
———. *Acta conciliorum oecumenicorum: Second Series.* Berlin, 1984 (major critical
edition).
Society of Biblical Literature (SBL) Texts and Translations. Missoula, Mont., 1972–
(texts, English translation; several parallel series).
Sources chrétiennes. Paris, 1941– (critical edition, French translation, and notes; a
sometimes thorough commentary; very important collection).
Studies and Documents. London, 1934–.
Texte und Untersuchungen zur Geschichte der altchristichen Literatur. Berlin, 1882–
(in several successive series; fundamental collection originally intended to ac-
commodate preparatory editions and studies for the GCS; includes many important editions of early Christian texts).
Textes et documents pour l'étude historique du christianisme. Paris, 1904–1912 (20
volumes appeared with text and French translation).
Texts and Studies: Contributions to Biblical and Patristic Literature. Cambridge,
1891–.

Translations Only

Ancient Christian Writers. Westminster, Md., 1946– (English translations).
Bibliothek der Kirchenväter. Kempten, 1869–1938 (German translations).
Collana di testi patristici. Rome, 1976– (Italian translations).
Collection Les pères dans la foi. Paris, 1977– (French translations).
Erbetta, M., ed. *Gli apocrifi del Nuovo Testamento.* 3 vols. in 4. Turin, Marietti,
1966–1981 (Italian translation; the most extensive collection of early Christian
apocrypha).
Letture cristiane del primo millennio. Milan, 1987– (previously: Letture cristiane
delle origini. Rome, 1979–; Italian translations with introductions and notes).
Library of Early Christianity. Philadelphia, 1986– (English translations).
Moralid, L., ed. *Apocrifi del Nuovo Testamento.* 2d ed. 3 vols. Casale Monferrato, 1994
(Italian translation).
Roberts, A. and J. Donaldson, eds. Ante-Nicene Fathers. 10 vols. Peabody, Mass., 1994
(English translations).
Schaff, P., ed. Nicene and Post-Nicene Fathers. First Series. 14 vols. Peabody, Mass.,
1994 (English translations).
———. Nicene and Post-Nicene Fathers. Second Series. 14 vols. Peabody, Mass., 1994
(English translations).
Schneemelcher, W., ed. *New Testament Apocrypha.* 2 vols. Translated by R. McL. Wil-
son. Louisville, Ky., 1991–1992.

INDEX OF ANCIENT SOURCES